# RIGHT TO A FAIR TRIAL

# RIGHT TO A FAIR TRIAL

## A Practical Guide to the Article 6 Case-Law of the European Court of Human Rights

Päivi Hirvelä
Satu Heikkilä

INTERSENTIA
Cambridge – Antwerp – Chicago

Intersentia Ltd
8 Wellington Mews
Wellington Street | Cambridge
CB1 1HW | United Kingdom
Tel: +44 1223 736 170
Email: mail@intersentia.co.uk
www.intersentia.com | www.intersentia.co.uk

*Distribution for the UK and*
*Rest of the World (incl. Eastern Europe)*
NBN International
1 Deltic Avenue, Rooksley
Milton Keynes MK13 8LD
United Kingdom
Tel: +44 1752 202 301 | Fax: +44 1752 202 331
Email: orders@nbninternational.com

*Distribution for Europe*
Lefebvre Sarrut Belgium NV
Hoogstraat 139/6
1000 Brussels
Belgium
Tel: +32 (0)800 39 067
Email: mail@intersentia.be

*Distribution for the USA and Canada*
Independent Publishers Group
Order Department
814 North Franklin Street
Chicago, IL 60610
USA
Tel: +1 800 888 4741 (toll free) | Fax: +1 312 337 5985
Email: orders@ipgbook.com

Right to a Fair Trial. A Practical Guide to the Article 6 Case-Law of the European Court of Human Rights


Artwork on cover: clivewa / shutterstock

ISBN 978-1-83970-094-1
D/2021/7849/47
NUR 828

British Library Cataloguing in Publication Data. A catalogue record for this book is available from the British Library.

# ACKNOWLEDGEMENTS

The European Court of Human Rights delivers a large number of judgments annually, adding to its already extensive case-law. As a result, it may sometimes be difficult for people outside of the Court system to know which cases are the most significant and break new ground for fair trial issues. This book seeks to address this issue by focusing on the most important cases from the Court as concerns Article 6 of the European Convention on Human Rights. The cases are selected, *inter alia*, following the Court's Jurisconsult's opinion of their jurisprudential interest. In addition, the book includes a number of other cases that either raise issues of general interest, establish new principles, or develop or clarify the Court's existing case-law.

Our aim has been to write a book which is easy to use and which provides a comprehensive and up-to-date documentation of the case-law of the Court on Article 6 matters. We have tried to write the case summaries in such a way that the readers' attention is drawn to the essential points, allowing them to focus on the jurisprudential significance of a particular case. The most relevant legal principle has been explained in the text while the footnotes contain a reference to the Court's judgment or decision and its exact paragraph. We have also tried to use a structure comprising a large number of titles for greater navigational capacity and to provide readers with an extensive index in order to facilitate the navigation of the text, allowing them to quickly locate the relevant case-law for any practical need. We hope and believe that our book constitutes a useful resource for practitioners, academics and students in the field of human rights. The Court's case-law has been analysed up until the end of 2020.

We have worked on this book for several years and are happy to finally see it in printed form. First of all, we would like to thank Ann-Christin Maak-Scherpe and Intersentia for accepting to publish our book and for effectively pursuing this project. During the writing process and especially during production, we have received excellent comments and assistance from Ahmed Hegazi, who has read through our manuscript and proposed several improvements to the text. Our warmest thanks to Ahmed for all his work. We would like to also thank all other persons at Intersentia with whom we have had the pleasure to work with. We are also grateful to Geneviéve Woods at the library of the European Court of Human Rights for the excellent service she provided to us under the very exceptional circumstances caused by the pandemic. We would also like to give our warmest thanks to Richard Savage, who conducted the language review of the early version of the book. It was a great pleasure to work with you. Naturally, all mistakes in the book and all interpretations provided by us are purely our own.

This publication is dedicated to our loved ones, our parents and siblings and to Sara, Matu, Isla and Aava.

Päivi Hirvelä and Satu Heikkilä
Helsinki and Strasbourg
December 2020

# CONTENTS

# LIST OF CASES

## GRAND CHAMBER JUDGMENTS AND DECISIONS

## CHAMBER AND COMMITTEE JUDGMENTS

## DECISIONS

## COMMISSION'S REPORTS AND DECISIONS

## RULINGS OF THE COURT OF JUSTICE OF THE EUROPEAN UNION

# CHAPTER 1
# INTRODUCTION

**Article 6: Right to a fair trial**

1. *In the determination of his civil rights and obligations or of any criminal charge against him, everyone is entitled to a fair and public hearing within a reasonable time by an independent and impartial tribunal established by law. Judgment shall be pronounced publicly but the press and public may be excluded from all or part of the trial in the interests of morals, public order or national security in a democratic society, where the interests of juveniles or the protection of the private life of the parties so require, or to the extent strictly necessary in the opinion of the court in special circumstances where publicity would prejudice the interests of justice.*
2. *Everyone charged with a criminal offence shall be presumed innocent until proved guilty according to law.*
3. *Everyone charged with a criminal offence has the following minimum rights:*
   - *a) to be informed promptly, in a language which he understands and in detail, of the nature and cause of the accusation against him;*
   - *b) to have adequate time and facilities for the preparation of his defence;*
   - *c) to defend himself in person or through legal assistance of his own choosing or, if he has not sufficient means to pay for legal assistance, to be given it free when the interests of justice so require;*
   - *d) to examine or have examined witnesses against him and to obtain the attendance and examination of witnesses on his behalf under the same conditions as witnesses against him;*
   - *e) to have the free assistance of an interpreter if he cannot understand or speak the language used in court.*

Article 6 of the European Convention on Human Rights ("the Convention") guarantees everyone a right to a fair trial. Article 6 does not guarantee a right to a perfect or ideal trial but a right to a fair or due process. The primary concern of the European Court of Human Rights ("the Court") under Article 6 §1 is to evaluate the overall fairness of the proceedings. When making this assessment, the Court will look at the proceedings as a whole, having regard to the rights of defence but also to the interests of the public and the victims, to the obligation that the crime is properly prosecuted and, where necessary, to the rights of witnesses. It is also worth remembering that the admissibility and assessment of evidence is a matter for regulation by national law and national courts, and that the Court's only concern is to examine whether the proceedings have been conducted fairly.[1]

Article 6 is applicable when determining an individual's civil rights and obligations or the existence of any criminal charge against him. The provision guarantees certain procedural rights but it does not create any new material rights. Article 6 thus gives certain procedural guarantees[2] in relation to existing rights but it does not apply if the domestic legal order does not provide any material right.[3] The right to a fair trial is to be interpreted widely.

The fair trial guarantees are so important that their restrictive interpretation would not be in compliance with the aim and meaning of the provision.[4] The Court's supervisory function relates in particular to the overall assessment of the fairness of the proceedings, in which a single procedural mistake is not so relevant if the proceedings as a whole are not thereby rendered unfair.[5]

Article 6 §1 applies to all types of judicial proceedings: civil, administrative and criminal. Requirements of a fair hearing are often stricter in the sphere of criminal law than under the civil limb of Article 6.[6] Articles 6 §2 and 6 §3 apply only to criminal proceedings. Nevertheless, in certain circumstances the guarantees of criminal proceedings have been expanded, in accordance with the effectiveness principle, to apply also to civil proceedings.[7] On the other hand, the criminal-head guarantees will not necessarily apply with their full stringency in all criminal cases, in particular in those cases that do not belong to the traditional categories of criminal law, such as proceedings concerning

---

1 See, among others, *Ibrahim and Others v. the United Kingdom* [GC], App. nos. 50541/08+, §§250–252, 13.9.2016; *Taxquet v. Belgium* [GC], App. no. 926/05, §84, 16.11.2010; *Al-Khawaja and Tahery v. the United Kingdom* [GC], App. nos. 26766/05+, §118, 15.12.2011; *Gäfgen v. Germany* [GC], App. no. 22978/05, §175, 1.6.2010; and *Doorson v. the Netherlands*, App. no. 20524/92, §70, 26.3.1996.

2 *Z. and Others v. the United Kingdom* [GC], App. no. 29392/95, §89, 10.10.2001; *Roche v. the United Kingdom* [GC], App. no. 32555/96, §117, 19.10.2005; *Editions Périscope v. France*, App. no. 11760/85, §35, 26.3.1992; and *Zander v. Sweden*, App. no. 14282/88, §22, 25.11.1993.

3 On this ground, for example, the case *Nylund v. Finland* (dec.), App. no. 27110/95, 29.6.1999 was declared inadmissible as the applicant father had requested confirmation of his alleged biological paternity. The Court found that a right to have mere biological paternity examined by scientific methods was not a right recognised in Finnish law; nor was there any right guaranteed in the Finnish Paternity Act to request the annulment of the husband's paternity and the establishment of the applicant's own.

4 *Delcourt v. Belgium*, App. no. 2689/65, §25, 17.1.1970.

5 *Ibrahim and Others v. the United Kingdom* [GC], App. nos. 50541/08+, §§250-252, 13.9.2016; and *Taxquet v. Belgium* [GC], App. no. 926/05, §84, 16.11.2010.

6 *Moreira Ferreira v. Portugal (No. 2)* [GC], App. no. 19867/12, §67, 11.7.2017; and *Carmel Saliba v. Malta*, App. no. 24221/13, §67, 29.11.2016.

7 See, for example, the classic case of *Airey v. Ireland*, App. no. 6289/73, §§79–80, 9.10.1979, in which the right to legal aid in certain civil matters was construed as a right of access to a court under Article 6 even if a right to free legal aid is guaranteed under the Convention only in criminal matters.

tax surcharges,[8] minor road traffic offences,[9] or an administrative fine for having provided premises for prostitution.[10] Article 6 has been very generally drafted and its wording does not provide any extensive understanding of what a fair trial can mean in different contexts. The wording of the article provides only a basis upon which the real content is expanded by the Court's case-law.

The core areas of the right to a fair trial concern judicial proceedings before a court or a tribunal. In addition, some of its parts may also apply to some stages before and after the judicial proceedings. In criminal matters, the fair trial guarantees also apply to relevant parts of the pretrial investigation and the consideration of charges.[11] The effects of Article 6 do not end immediately after a pronouncement of a judgment or its finality but extend until the execution of the judgment.[12]

## 1.1. GENERAL OBLIGATIONS OF A STATE

According to Article 1 of the Convention, a Contracting State shall secure for everyone within its jurisdiction the rights and freedoms defined in the Convention. It is thus the obligation of a State to guarantee a fair trial. The Court has not accepted a lack of economic or other resources to be an excuse for procedural errors or repetitive violations. A State is expected to organise its legal system in such a way that the rights guaranteed under Article 6 can be secured.[13]

A State may not interfere with the functioning of the judiciary by giving orders about procedure or the outcome of a case pending before a court or a tribunal and it must respect the democratic principle of separation of powers and the independence and impartiality of the courts.[14] As concerns the administration of justice, a State is thus responsible for the general organisation of the judiciary and its proper functioning.

---

8 *Jussila v. Finland* [GC], App. no. 73053/01, §43, 23.11.2006.

9 *Marčan v. Croatia*, App. no. 40820/12, §37, 10.7.2014.

10 *Sancaklı v. Turkey*, App. no. 1385/07, §§43–52, 15.5.2018.

11 See, for example, *Salduz v. Turkey* [GC], App. no. 36391/02, §50, 27.11.2008.

12 See, among others, *Burdov v. Russia*, App. no. 59498/00, §34, 7.5.2002; *Hornsby v. Greece*, App. no. 18357/91, §40, 19.3.1997; and *Konovalov v. Russia*, App. no. 63501/00, §36, 23.3.2006.

13 *Guincho v. Portugal*, App. no. 8990/80, §41, 10.7.1984; and *Burdov v. Russia*, App. no. 59498/00, §35, 7.5.2002.

14 *Stran Greek Refineries and Stratis Andreadis v. Greece*, App. no. 13427/87, §§46–49, 9.12.1994; *Van de Hurk v. the Netherlands*, App. no. 16034/90, §54, 19.4.1994; and *Pabla Ky v. Finland*, App. no. 47221/99, §§29 and 34, 22.6.2004. In the latter case a Justice of the Appeal Court was also at the same time a Member of Parliament. The Court did not find, however, that he had participated in enacting the provision in question or that he had in any other way intervened in his position as a Member of Parliament in the disputed issue.

## 1.2. WHO MUST GUARANTEE A FAIR TRIAL?

For each individual case, a judge must take care to ensure that, in the proceedings conducted by him or her, the fair trial requirements are respected.[15] In this respect each judge is a human rights judge.

In addition, public authorities other than judges, such as public prosecutors and the police, are responsible for making sure fair trial guarantees are respected. Pretrial investigative authorities and prosecutors must ensure that criminal investigations are adequate and effective, that the presumption of innocence and the dignity of the parties are respected, that the safety of witnesses and vulnerable victims is protected,[16] that the gathering of evidence is appropriately done, and that legal procedures are applied that do not jeopardise the fairness of the trial.[17] Administrative judicial authorities must for their part guarantee that the proceedings they are responsible for are legal and appropriate. This obligation is particularly accentuated in situations where the fundamental rights of an individual are at stake, such as when issuing child care orders, or deciding on expropriation of property and certain administrative permissions.

The obligation to guarantee a fair trial does not only concern those who, in their official duty, hold public authority. An applicant's counsel and lawyers are also responsible for the realisation of a fair trial: they function as "watchdogs" in securing a fair trial.[18] In addition, the legal assistance they provide must be appropriate and of sufficient quality and, by being so, must contribute to the realisation and effectiveness of the fair trial guarantees.

---

15 For example, in the cases *V. v. the United Kingdom* [GC], App. no. 24888/94, §§87–90, 16.12.1999; and *T. v. the United Kingdom* [GC], App. no. 24724/94, §§85–89, 16.12.1999 the question at stake was whether the proceedings concerning two 11-year-old applicants was fair when they had been charged with a widely publicised murder in a public hearing. Most of the trial had been conducted in accordance with the procedural norms designed for adults. The Court found it to be essential that a child charged with an offence was dealt with in a manner which took full account of his age, level of maturity and intellectual and emotional capacities. It was also important to take measures which promoted a child's capacity to understand the trial and to participate in it. Similarly, if a young child was being accused of a grave crime which had attracted extensive media and public interest, it would have been necessary to conduct the hearing in such a way as to reduce, as far as possible, his or her feelings of intimidation and inhibition.

16 *Al-Khawaja and Tahery v. the United Kingdom* [GC], App. nos. 26766/05+, §118, 15.12.2011. In this case the position of the victim of the crime was taken into account as a part of a holistic evaluation under Article 6 and the fair trial criteria. The rights of victims of a crime are normally, however, examined under Article 8, not under Article 6 of the Convention.

17 It is especially relevant to guarantee the accused the rights under Article 6 §3 in the pretrial phase, and therefore the authorities responsible for this phase have an important duty. This emphasised duty is clearly visible, for example, in the context of an investigation into child abuse cases and concerning the right of the suspect to put questions to the child.

18 Normally the term "watchdog" has been used in freedom of expression cases to illustrate the role of the press as a controller of the functioning of a democratic society. In the case *Animal Defenders International v. the United Kingdom* [GC], App. no. 48876/08, §103,

## 1.3. AUTONOMOUS INTERPRETATION OF CONCEPTS

The fair trial guarantees provided by the Convention apply only to such proceedings which concern determination of "civil rights and obligations" or of "a criminal charge". The Court's case-law on these concepts and their content is wide and constantly evolving. These concepts are interpreted in accordance with the principle of autonomous interpretation, according to which the concepts have their own, autonomous meaning which is not necessarily the same as in domestic legal systems.[19] There is no general and overall definition of these concepts in the Court's case-law, but their scope of application has been developed in the light of separate, individual cases.[20]

The content given to the concepts of "civil rights and obligations" and "a criminal charge" in Article 6 of the Convention may deviate from the content given to these concepts in domestic law. For example, in Finland the national concept of criminal charge has traditionally been less wide than the meaning given to a criminal charge in the Court's case-law. The concept of criminal charge, as expressed in Article 6 of the Convention, also covers some proceedings under administrative law in which the imposed sanction has been equated with a criminal punishment. Therefore, administrative law proceedings may also be equated to some extent with criminal proceedings.[21] Nor are these two concepts of "civil rights and obligations" and "criminal charge" necessarily mutually exclusive: if Article 6 §1 is applicable under its civil head, the Court may assess whether the same article is also applicable under its criminal head.[22]

Over the years, the scope of application of Article 6 of the Convention has gradually widened. The content of "civil rights and obligations" and "a criminal charge" will now be examined in more detail.

---

22.4.2013 it was used also in respect of non-governmental organisations. In the case *Ensslin, Baader and Raspe v. the Federal Republic of Germany* (dec.), App. nos. 7572/76+, 8.7.1978 the Court referred to this term within the context of Article 6 by considering a legal counsel as a controller of the fair trial guarantees.

19 *Ringeisen v. Austria*, App. no. 2614/65, §94, 16.7.1971; *König v. Germany*, App. no. 6232/73, §88, 28.6.1978; *Georgiadis v. Greece*, App. no. 21522/93, §34, 29.5.1997; *Bochan v. Ukraine (No. 2)* [GC], App. no. 22251/08, §43, 5.2.2015; and *Naït-Liman v. Switzerland* [GC], App. no. 51357/07, §106, 15.3.2018.

20 *Benthem v. the Netherlands*, App. no. 8848/80, §35, 23.10.1985.

21 For example, in the case *Jussila v. Finland* [GC], App. no. 73053/01, §38, 23.11.2006 the Court found that tax surcharges could be interpreted as a deterrent and as punitive sanctions regardless of their minor nature, and that they therefore fell within the criminal limb of Article 6, requiring to a certain extent that the guarantees for criminal proceedings were also followed. Similarly, in the case *Ruotsalainen v. Finland*, App. no. 13079/03, §47, 16.6.2009, the imposition of a three-fold fuel fee in administrative proceedings for tax evasion on fuel was considered as a criminal punishment. The act was thus a crime and Article 4 of Protocol No. 7 was thus applicable. See for more details Chapter 3, section 3.2.2.3.

22 *Ramos Nunes de Carvalho e Sá v. Portugal* [GC], App. nos. 55391/13+, §121, 6.11.2018. See also Stefan Kieber, "The jurisprudence of the European Court of Human Rights in 2018", *European Yearbook on Human Rights 2019*, pp. 189–220, at pp. 198–200.

# CHAPTER 2

# CIVIL RIGHTS AND OBLIGATIONS

**Article 6: Right to a fair trial**

1. *In the determination of his civil rights and obligations ...*

The concept of civil rights and obligations under Article 6 of the Convention has the following dimensions: (1) the right or obligation must have a basis in domestic law; (2) it must be of civil nature; and (3) there must be a real dispute, which (4) must concern directly the applicant's rights and obligations. All the above conditions must be fulfilled in order for Article 6 §1 to be applicable. Each of these dimensions is examined below in more detail.

## 2.1. WHAT ARE "CIVIL RIGHTS AND OBLIGATIONS"?

### 2.1.1. RIGHT HAVING A BASIS IN DOMESTIC LAW

The rights and obligations mentioned in Article 6 of the Convention refer to the rights and obligations guaranteed by domestic law.[23] There must therefore be a legal basis for the right claimed by the applicant or for the obligation imposed on him or her in domestic law.[24] The starting-point is thus the provisions of the relevant domestic law and their interpretation by the domestic courts.[25] It is not for the Court to question the interpretation of the domestic law by the national courts, unless there are strong reasons to depart from their conclusions and to find that there was arguably a right recognised by domestic law.[26]

Article 6 does not create any rights in the sense that it creates any new material rights which do not exist in domestic law or, as far as the

---

23 *H. v. Belgium*, App. no. 8950/80, §40, 30.11.1987.

24 *Fayed v. the United Kingdom*, App. no. 17101/90, §65, 21.9.1994; *Károly Nagy v. Hungary* [GC], App. no. 56665/09, §§60–61, 14.9.2017; *Roche v. the United Kingdom* [GC], App. no. 32555/96, §199, 19.10.2005; and *Boulois v. Luxembourg* [GC], App. no. 37575/04, §91, 3.4.2012.

25 *Al-Dulimi and Montana Management Inc. v. Switzerland* [GC], App. no. 5809/08, §97, 21.6.2016; and *Regner v. the Czech Republic* [GC], App. no. 35289/11, §100, 19.9.2017.

26 *Naït-Liman v. Switzerland* [GC], App. no. 51357/07, §116, 15.3.2018; and *Károly Nagy v. Hungary* [GC], App. no. 56665/09, §§60 and 62, 14.9.2017.

EU Member States are concerned, in binding EU law.[27] Therefore Article 6 was not applicable, for example, to a situation in which domestic law did not afford any right for a man to have his biological paternity confirmed when the child in question was born in wedlock to a mother married to another man.[28] Article 6 is, however, applicable to disputes of a "genuine and serious nature" which concern the actual existence of a right, as well as the scope or manner in which it is exercised.[29]

Article 6 of the Convention may be applicable if there are *procedural* obstacles to access to a court in respect of a right guaranteed by domestic law[30] but not when these obstacles are *material*.[31] The existence of a right and the nature of possible material or procedural restrictions must be assessed from the point of view of domestic law and interpreted in the same manner that they were domestically.[32] The Court has, for example, found that restricted civil liability for damage caused by army personnel was a material restriction which thus fell outside of the scope of application of Article 6.[33]

Normally it is also necessary that the applicant's claim to a right is arguable and could as such lead to the outcome he or she is claiming.[34] It is, however, not necessary that the applicant would win his or her case on the presented grounds.[35] The right need exist only when the proceedings are started: it is thus no longer relevant if the domestic law is amended during the proceedings.[36] If the applicant does not have an arguable case under domestic law, Article 6

27 *Neves e Silva v. Portugal*, App. no. 11213/84, §37, 27.4.1989; *Pudas v. Sweden*, App. no. 10426/83, §34, 27.10.1987; and *Gustafsson v. Sweden*, App. no. 15573/89, §66, 25.4.1996. See also *Gutfreund v. France*, App. no. 45681/99, §39, 12.6.2003 in which the Court referred both to domestic law as well as to the Convention, insinuating that Article 6 would apply whenever the dispute concerned a right guaranteed by the Convention irrespective of whether the said right was also recognised by domestic law or not.

28 *Nylund v. Finland* (dec.), App. no. 27110/95, 29.6.1999.

29 *Benthem v. the Netherlands*, App. no. 8848/80, §32, 23.10.1985.

30 *Al-Adsani v. the United Kingdom* [GC], App. no. 35763/97, §§46–47, 21.11.2001; and *Fogarty v. the United Kingdom* [GC], App. no. 37112/97, §25, 21.11.2001.

31 *Roche v. the United Kingdom* [GC], App. no. 32555/96, §119, 19.10.2005; and *Lupeni Greek Catholic Parish and Others v. Romania* [GC], App. no. 76943/11, §100, 29.11.2016.

32 *Masson and Van Zon v. the Netherlands*, App. nos. 15346/89+, §49, 28.9.1995; and *Roche v. the United Kingdom* [GC], App. no. 32555/96, §120, 19.10.2005.

33 *Roche v. the United Kingdom* [GC], App. no. 32555/96, §124, 19.10.2005. See also *Hotter v. Austria* (dec.), App. no. 18206/06, 7.10.2010; and *Andronikashvili v. Georgia* (dec.), App. no. 9297/08, 22.6.2010.

34 *Boulois v. Luxembourg* [GC], App. no. 37575/04, §§90 and 104, 3.4.2012. The case concerned a "right" to leave from prison. The Court found that domestic law did not guarantee such a right, nor was it guaranteed by the Convention. Article 6 did not therefore apply. See also Arman Zrvandyan, *Casebook on European Fair Trial Standards in Administrative Justice*, Council of Europe Publishing, Strasbourg 2016, p. 25.

35 *Neves e Silva v. Portugal*, App. no. 11213/84, §37, 27.4.1989; and *Le Calvez v. France*, App. no. 25554/94, §56, 29.7.1998.

36 *Reid v. the United Kingdom* (dec.), App. no. 33221/96, 26.6.2001.

is not applicable.[37] In this manner, Article 6 acts as a check to ensure that the proceedings concerning domestic rights and obligations are fair.

### 2.1.2. DISCRETIONARY DECISIONS

Discretionary decisions do not, as a rule, fall within the scope of application of Article 6.[38] According to the established case-law of the Court, disputes concerning, for example, a civil servant's recruitment, fall outside of the scope of Article 6.[39] For instance, in the case *Ahtinen v. Finland*, the Court found that the applicant, who was a priest, had no "right" under domestic law to claim a post in a certain parish and the Cathedral Chapter could unilaterally, within its margin of appreciation, decide to remove him and place him in the post of priest in another parish.[40] Nor was Article 6 applicable to proceedings in which priests of the Czechoslovak Hussits Church challenged the termination, by the authorities of their church, of their clerical service.[41]

Nevertheless, Article 6 is applicable in general when the dispute concerns the continuation of an employment relationship or the conditions under which it is exercised. Normally in domestic legal systems labour law confers on employees in the private sector the right to bring legal proceedings to challenge their dismissal or unilateral changes to their employment contract. The same applies generally also to public-sector employees, save in cases where the exception provided for in *Vilho Eskelinen and Others v. Finland* applies.[42]

When national law does not confer on an individual any substantive right, it may nevertheless confer a right to a procedure by which the individual's claim can be examined in order to know whether the decision was arbitrary or *ultra vires* or whether there were procedural irregularities.[43] The Court found, for

---

37 *Papoulakos v. Greece* (dec.), App. no. 24960/94, 11.1.1995.

38 *Boulois v. Luxembourg* [GC], App. no. 37575/04, §93, 3.4.2012.

39 See, for example, *Neigel v. France*, App. no. 18725/91, §43, 17.3.1997. Compare and contrast with the newer case-law, such as *Tsanova-Gecheva v. Bulgaria*, App. no. 43800/12, §§84–85, 15.9.2015, *Majski v. Croatia (No. 2)*, App. no. 16924/08, §50, 19.7.2011; and *Fiume v. Italy*, App. no. 20774/05, §35, 30.6.2009.

40 *Ahtinen v. Finland*, App. no. 48907/99, §43, 23.9.2008.

41 *Duda and Dudová v. the Czech Republic* (dec.), App. no. 40224/98, 30.1.2001. In this case, the Court concurred with the domestic court's findings that the judicial determination of issues such as the continuation of a priest's service within a church would be contrary to the principles of autonomy and independence of churches guaranteed by, *inter alia*, the Czech Charter of Fundamental Rights and Freedoms.

42 *Regner v. the Czech Republic* [GC], App. no. 35289/11, §117, 19.9.2017. See also Robert Spano, "'Arbitrary or manifestly unreasonable': the arbitrariness exception to the fourth instance doctrine under Article 6 of the European Convention on Human Rights", in Koen Lemmens, Stephan Parmentier, Louise Reyntjens (Eds.), *Human Rights with a Human Touch – Liber Amicorum Paul Lemmens*, Intersentia, Cambridge/Antwerp/Chicago 2019, pp. 523–537, at pp. 533–534.

43 *Van Marle and Others v. the Netherlands*, App. nos. 8543/79+, §35, 26.6.1986; and *Regner v. the Czech Republic* [GC], App. no. 35289/11, §105, 19.9.2017.

example, in the case *Penttinen v. Finland* that even though the applicant, who had applied for several posts, had no right under domestic law to be appointed to any of these posts, he still had a right to apply for these posts and to challenge in a court the fact that he had not been chosen. He thus had, under domestic law, a right within the meaning of Article 6 of the Convention to apply for posts and to challenge the outcome of the selection procedure in court proceedings but no right to be chosen for any post.[44] Such a right may rise also in the context of calls for contract tender.[45]

If the margin of appreciation of the domestic authorities is limited, Article 6 may be applicable to this limited margin of appreciation.[46] In such situations applicants have the right to have a decision made about the exercise of this margin of appreciation in court proceedings which fulfil the procedural criteria guaranteed by Article 6 of the Convention.[47]

## 2.2. WHAT DOES "CIVIL" MEAN?

One of the most problematic issues when applying the Convention, is the application of Article 6 §1 to cases other than criminal ones. According to Article 6 §1, it is applicable when a person's "civil rights and obligations" are determined. In the French-language version these are referred as "*droits et obligations de caractère civil*". So, what are these civil rights and obligations?

### 2.2.1. MATTERS FALLING WITHIN THE SCOPE OF CIVIL LAW

In the Court's early case-law it was considered that, since the Convention used the term "civil rights" ("*les droits de caractère civil*"), the drafters of the Convention had meant to draw a line between civil law and public law in such

---

44 *Penttinen v. Finland* (dec.), App. no. 9125/07, 5.1.2010. See also *Lombardi Vallauri v. Italy*, App. no. 39128/05, §62, 20.10.2009; *Fiume v. Italy*, App. no. 20774/05, §§35–36, 30.6.2009; and *Josephides v. Cyprus*, App. no. 33761/02, §§52–55, 6.12.2007.

45 *Mirovni Inštitut v. Slovenia*, App. no. 32303/13, §§28–30, 13.3.2018.

46 *Pudas v. Sweden*, App. no. 10426/83, §34, 27.10.1987; *Allan Jacobsson v. Sweden (No. 1)*, App. no. 10842/84, §69, 25.10.1989; and *Miessen v. Belgium*, App. no. 31517/12, §48, 18.10.2016. See also Karen Reid, *A Practitioner's Guide to the European Convention on Human Rights*, Sweet & Maxwell/Thomson Reuters, London 2019, p. 129.

47 For drawing a line between the two, see for example *Masson and Van Zon v. the Netherlands*, App. nos. 15346/89+, §§50–52, 28.9.1995 (no right); *Anne-Marie Andersson v. Sweden*, App. no. 20022/92, §36, 27.8.1997 (no right); *Le Calvez v. France*, App. no. 25554/94, §58, 29.7.1998 (right); *Bozhilov v. Bulgaria* (dec.), App. no. 41978/98, 22.11.2001 (no right); and *Massa v. Italy*, App. no. 14399/88, §26, 24.8.1993 (right). The question of whether Article 6 applies if the applicant has, instead of a right, only a legitimate expectation was still left open in the case *Mennitto v. Italy* [GC], App. no. 33804/96, §27, 5.10.2000.

a manner that civil rights specifically referred to civil law rights.[48] According to this interpretation, rights and obligations between private individuals clearly fall within the scope of Article 6 while rights and obligations between private individuals and the State do not necessarily do so. This division was not, however, very clear. On one hand, the Court may have excluded certain decisions from the scope of Article 6 for the reason that a line was to be drawn between civil law and public law. On the other hand, however, it may have been for the reason that the drafters of the Convention wanted to exclude certain matters from the scope of Article 6.[49]

The Convention does not therefore guarantee a fair trial in respect of all rights and obligations guaranteed by domestic law. Many of the lacunae created by the wording of Article 6 have, however, been filled through the Court's case-law. Even if the Court still sometimes draws a line between civil law and public law,[50] the trend in the newer case-law is more and more to include rights and obligations guaranteed in domestic law in the scope of Article 6 of the Convention.

### 2.2.2. AUTONOMOUS INTERPRETATION

Right from the start, the Court has given to both the concepts of "criminal charge" and "civil rights and obligations" their own independent meaning that is not bound by domestic concepts and that does not always even assume that Article 6 is applicable.[51] Therefore, Article 6 may be applicable to some cases falling within the scope of public law but not necessarily to some cases which domestically fall within the civil law domain.[52] Currently, it can be generally said that almost all material rights which a person can claim under domestic law fall within the scope of Article 6 of the Convention.

Although the Court has given an autonomous interpretation to the concept of civil rights, it has not given to it any abstract definition which would go beyond the boundaries of civil law and public law.[53] Instead, the Court has created

48 *Ringeisen v. Austria*, App. no. 2614/65, §94, 16.7.1971; and *König v. Germany*, App. no. 6232/73, §95, 28.6.1978.

49 For example, in the case *Neumeister v. Austria*, App. no. 1936/63, §22, 27.6.1968 the Court found that Article 6 did not apply to a request to be released from pretrial detention.

50 See, for example, *Ferrazzini v. Italy* [GC], App. no. 44759/98, §29, 12.7.2001.

51 *König v. Germany*, App. no. 6232/73, §88, 28.6.1978; and *Kennedy v. the United Kingdom*, App. no. 26839/05, §179, 18.5.2010.

52 See, for example, the cases *Feldbrugge v. the Netherlands*, App. no. 8562/79, §§28 and 40, 29.5.1986; and *Deumeland v. Germany*, App. no. 9384/81, §§62 and 74, 29.5.1986.

53 In the case *Benthem v. the Netherlands*, App. no. 8848/80, §35, 23.10.1985, the Court refused to give such a definition.

certain guidelines in concrete cases which are helpful for defining the civil law character of a certain matter. These are: (1) the nature of the right or obligation in question; (2) a general pan-European consensus about the nature of the right or obligation; (3) classification of the right or obligation in the domestic legal system; and (4) the aim and the scope of the Convention.

#### *2.2.2.1. Nature of the Right or Obligation*

The Court considers the nature of the right or obligation to be paramount.[54] Therefore, there is no domain of law that governs the matter domestically (civil law or administrative law) and no authority with responsibility (general court or tribunal, administrative court or other authority) that has greater importance than any other.[55]

As such, legal relationships between private individuals fall within the scope of domestic civil law and within the competencies of civil courts. Much more complicated are the relationships between private individuals and the State, because in these cases the nature of the right or obligation in question becomes relevant. In such cases the Court must assess whether the State is acting within the core areas of its sovereign powers or outside of them. A State is acting within its core areas when, for example, it decides on expulsion from the country or expropriation of land. It acts outside of its sovereign powers when, for example, it buys furniture for State offices. From the point of view of the applicability of Article 6, it is therefore the nature of the right or obligation in question which is relevant.[56]

#### *2.2.2.2. Pan-European Consensus*

When defining the nature of the right or obligation, it is also relevant whether from the legal systems of the Contracting States a common pan-European consensus can be found as far as the classification of the right or obligation is concerned. This way of thinking originates from the cases *Feldbrugge v. the Netherlands* and *Deumeland v. Germany*, in which the Court found that, in respect of a certain social benefit, there was no pan-European consensus as to whether the right in question was to be regarded as falling within the scope of

---

54 *König v. Germany*, App. no. 6232/73, §90, 28.6.1978. Most cases concern only rights since the majority of the cases examined by the Court are lodged by plaintiffs. In the case *Schouten and Meldrum v. the Netherlands*, App. nos. 19005/91+, §51, 9.12.1994, the Court found that the method of assessment was similar in respect of the obligations.

55 *Ringeisen v. Austria*, App. no. 2614/65, §94, 16.7.1971.

56 *König v. Germany*, App. no. 6232/73, §90, 28.6.1978.

private law or public law. The choice between private law and public law was thus made on the basis of the nature of the right in question.[57]

The Court has also left open the question of whether Article 6 §1 of the Convention applies to leave-to-appeal proceedings in which a supreme court decides whether or not to admit an appeal on points of law in a civil case for examination. It noted that there was an apparent discrepancy in its case-law regarding the applicability of Article 6 §1 to such proceedings.[58] However, in a subsequent case, *Hansen v. Norway*, the Court expressed that Article 6 §1 "seems to be" applicable also to leave-to-appeal proceedings, depending on the special features of the proceedings involved.[59]

#### 2.2.2.3. *Classification in Domestic Law*

Although the domestic classification between private law and public law is not, from the Court's point of view, decisive, relevance must still be given to what kind of content the right or obligation has applied to in the domestic law. For example, in the case *König v. Germany* the Court examined the content of domestic law when assessing whether the right to practise as a medical professional was a private law or public law right.[60] For this reason it is possible that a certain right or obligation may in certain countries fall within the scope of Article 6 and in others not, irrespective of the autonomous interpretation of the concept of civil rights and obligations.

#### 2.2.2.4. *Aim and Scope of the Convention*

The Court has also given relevance to the supposed aim and scope of the Convention. Accordingly, the exceptions to the applicability of Article 6 have been interpreted strictly. For example, in the case *Vilho Eskelinen and Others v. Finland* this method was relevant when the Court found that certain employment law matters relating to public-sector collective agreements fell within the scope of Article 6.[61]

---

57 *Feldbrugge v. the Netherlands*, App. no. 8562/79, §29, 29.5.1986; and *Deumeland v. Germany*, App. no. 9384/81, §63, 29.5.1986.

58 *Valchev and Others v. Bulgaria* (dec.), App. nos. 47450/11+, §73, 21.1.2014.

59 *Hansen v. Norway*, App. no. 15319/09, §55, 2.10.2014. See also James Welch (Ed.), "Case and comment: selected decisions from the European Court of Human Rights from September and October 2014 – Appeals, *Hansen v. Norway* (Application No. 15319/09)", *European Human Rights Law Review*, Issue 1, 2015, pp. 98–101.

60 *König v. Germany*, App. no. 6232/73, §89, 28.6.1978. See also *Perez v. France* [GC], App. no. 47287/99, §57, 12.2.2004.

61 *Vilho Eskelinen and Others v. Finland* [GC], App. no. 63235/00, §49, 19.4.2007. See also Sejal Parmar, "*Vilho Eskelinen v. Finland*: The Further Extension of ECHR Article 6 to Disputes Concerning Civil Servants", *European Human Rights Law Review*, Issue 4, 2007, pp. 441–449, at p. 444.

### 2.2.3. CASE-LAW ON THE LINE BETWEEN CIVIL LAW AND PUBLIC LAW

#### *2.2.3.1. Relations between Private Individuals*

It is clear that the legal relationships concerning rights and obligations between private individuals, *inter se*, fall within the scope of civil rights. Therefore, the rights and obligations relating to contract law,[62] law of torts,[63] family law,[64] law of succession,[65] employment law,[66] commercial law,[67] insurance law[68] and law of personal and real property[69] are civil, and fall within the scope of Article 6.

#### *2.2.3.2. Relations between a State and Private Individuals*

The situation is less clear in cases which involve the relationship between private individuals and the State. The Court has found in its case-law that what is relevant in these cases is the nature of the right or obligation in question. If such a right or obligation is to be regarded as a civil one, it must be decided by a court or a tribunal. If it concerns an administrative decision, there must be the possibility to appeal to a court or a tribunal. The most common situations will be examined next in more detail.

##### 2.2.3.2.1. Pecuniary Rights

When determining the nature of the relations between private individuals and a State, it is often relevant whether the rights and obligations are of a pecuniary nature or whether they have pecuniary consequences for the applicant.[70] If this

---

62 See, for example, *Ringeisen v. Austria*, App. no. 2614/65, 16.7.1971.

63 See, for example, *Golder v. the United Kingdom*, App. no. 4451/70, §27, 21.2.1975 (compensation in a defamation case); and *Axen v. the Federal Republic of Germany*, App. no. 8273/78, 8.12.1983 (traffic accident).

64 See, for example, *Airey v. Ireland*, App. no. 6289/73, §21, 9.10.1979 (separation); as well as *Mizzi v. Malta*, App. no. 26111/02, §76, 12.1.2006; and *Rasmussen v. Denmark*, App. no. 8777/79, 28.11.1984 (disavowal of paternity).

65 See, for example, *C.D. v. France*, App. no. 42405/98, 7.1.2003 (succession).

66 See, for example, *Buchholz v. Germany*, App. no. 7759/77, §46, 6.5.1981 (dismissal); and *Regner v. the Czech Republic* [GC], App. no. 35289/11, §121, 19.9.2017.

67 See, for example, *Edificaciones March Gallego S.A. v. Spain*, App. no. 28028/95, 19.2.1998.

68 *Feldbrugge v. the Netherlands*, App. no. 8562/79, §40, 29.5.1986; and *Deumeland v. Germany*, App. no. 9384/81, §74, 29.5.1986.

69 See, for example, *Bramelid and Malmström v. Sweden* (dec.), App. nos. 8588/79+, 12.10.1982 (share valuation); and *Pretto and Others v. Italy*, App. no. 7984/77, §23, 8.12.1983 (sale of land).

70 *Editions Périscope v. France*, App. no. 11760/85, §37, 26.3.1992 (State liability for damages); and *Stran Greek Refineries and Stratis Andreadis v. Greece*, App. no. 13427/87, §40, 9.12.1994 (compensation for breach of contract).

is the case, the matter normally falls within the scope of Article 6,[71] unless the State is acting within the core areas of its public authority prerogatives, such as taxation.[72] As far as taxation is concerned, it is not sufficient to show that the dispute is of a pecuniary nature, as this element alone is not sufficient to attract the applicability of Article 6 in taxation matters.[73]

##### 2.2.3.2.1.1. Right to Property

The right to property is clearly a right of a pecuniary nature. Therefore, in cases in which a State action is directly decisive for real or personal property rights, the matter is civil and falls within the scope of Article 6. The fair trial principles have thus been applied to, for example, expropriation of land[74] and to the regulation of the use of private land. With regard to the latter, cases have concerned planning or building permission[75] and other use of land, among other things.[76] With regard to personal property, Article 6 has been applied to situations in which a State has restricted a person's capacity to administer property[77] or in which a State has otherwise decided on the fate of personal property rights.[78] If the State's

---

71 For example, the obligation of a French public accountant to repay public monies which had been lost as a result of his negligence fell within the scope of Article 6, because, despite the public law dimension of the case, it had a pecuniary impact on the accountant. See *Martinie v. France* (dec.), App. no. 58675/00, §29, 13.1.2004.

72 *Ferrazzini v. Italy* [GC], App. no. 44759/98, §29, 12.7.2001.

73 *Ferrazzini v. Italy* [GC], App. no. 44759/98, §25, 12.7.2001. See also David Harris, Michael O'Boyle, Ed Bates, Carla Buckley, *Law of the European Convention on Human Rights*, 4th edition, Oxford University Press, Oxford 2018, p. 387.

74 *Sporrong and Lönnroth v. Sweden*, App. nos. 7151/75+, §79, 23.9.1982; and *Aldo and Jean-Baptiste Zanatta v. France*, App. no. 38042/97, §25, 28.3.2000. See also *Raimondo v. Italy*, App. no. 12954/87, §43, 22.2.1994 (confiscation); and *Poiss v. Austria*, App. no. 9816/82, §48, 23.4.1987 (land consolidation).

75 See, for example, *McGonnell v. the United Kingdom*, App. no. 28488/95, §41, 8.2.2000; *Chapman v. the United Kingdom* [GC], App. no. 27238/95, §124, 18.1.2001; *Haider v. Austria* (dec.), App. no. 63413/00, 29.1.2004; and *Gillow v. the United Kingdom*, App. no. 9063/80, §68, 24.11.1986.

76 See, for example, *Zander v. Sweden*, App. no. 14282/88, §27, 25.11.1993 (water extraction); *Ludescher v. Austria*, App. no. 35019/97, §16, 20.12.2001 (obligation to plant forest); *Posti and Rahko v. Finland*, App. no. 27824/95, §52, 24.9.2002 (fishing rights); and *Oerlemans v. the Netherlands*, App. no. 12565/86, §48, 27.11.1991 (nature conservation).

77 See *Winterwerp v. the Netherlands*, App. no. 6301/73, §73, 24.10.1979, which concerned a mentally disabled person.

78 See, for example, *Vasilescu v. Romania*, App. no. 27053/95, §39, 22.5.1998 (seizure of gold coins); *Ruiz-Mateos v. Spain*, App. no. 12952/87, §32, 23.6.1993 (restitution of shares); *Tinnelly & Sons Ltd and Others and McElduff and Others v. the United Kingdom*, App. nos. 20390/92+, §61, 10.7.1998 (public contracts); *Pafitis and Others v. Greece*, App. no. 20323/92, §87, 26.2.1998 (shareholder's voting rights); *Capital Bank AD v. Bulgaria*, App. no. 49429/99, §86, 24.11.2005 (bankruptcy); *Credit and Industrial Bank v. the Czech Republic*, App. no. 29010/95, §64, 21.10.2003 (compulsory administration of a bank); *British-American Tobacco Company Ltd v. the Netherlands*, App. no. 19589/92, §67, 20.11.1995 (patent rights); and *Procola v. Luxembourg*, App. no. 14570/89, §39, 28.9.1995 (milk levy).

decision concerning real or personal property has been taken in administrative proceedings, there must be the possibility to challenge it before a court or a tribunal that complies with the Article 6 requirements.

#### 2.2.3.2.1.2. Right to Practise a Profession or to Engage in a Commercial Activity

The right to engage in a commercial activity, which is also a right of a pecuniary nature, is also a civil right. Therefore, State decisions withdrawing a commercial licence or other authorisation to engage in a commercial activity are governed by Article 6.[79] The same also applies to the right to practise a liberal profession.[80] If the withdrawal of a licence to engage in commercial activity is a criminal sanction, it is sufficient that the criminal proceedings have complied with the Article 6 requirements.[81]

Article 6 is applicable both to the granting and to the withdrawal of a licence, other authorisation or right to practise a liberal profession. In the case *König v. Germany*, the Court specifically emphasised that the case concerned a right to continue to practise medicine and to operate a medical clinic. Therefore, it was not a question of granting a new licence but the legitimate expectation of the licence-holder to have his licence continued.[82] In the case *Benthem v. the Netherlands* and in some newer cases, the Court has also applied Article 6 to the granting of new licences in situations in which the granting of a licence or permission has not been at the State's discretion.[83] Article 6 is, however, applicable only if a person has an arguable legal right to something.

79 See, for example, *Tre Traktörer AB v. Sweden*, App. no. 10873/84, §43, 7.7.1989 (licence to sell alcohol); *Kingsley v. the United Kingdom* [GC], App. no. 35605/97, §32, 28.5.2002 (gaming licences); *Pudas v. Sweden*, App. no. 10426/83, §38, 27.10.1987 (transport licence); *König v. Germany*, App. no. 6232/73, §95, 28.6.1978 (right to continue to practise medicine in a private medical clinic); *Benthem v. the Netherlands*, App. no. 8848/80, §36, 23.10.1985 (licence to sell liquid petroleum gas); as well as *Hornsby v. Greece*, App. no. 18357/91, §40, 19.3.1997; and *Ingrid Jordebo Foundation of Christian Schools and Ingrid Jordebo v. Sweden* (dec.), App. no. 11533/85, 6.3.1987 (permission to run a private school).

80 *König v. Germany*, App. no. 6232/73, §93, 28.6.1978 (medicine); *G.S. v. Austria*, App. no. 26297/95, §27, 21.12.1999 (pharmacy); *H. v. Belgium*, App. no. 8950/80, §§47–48, 30.11.1987 (practising law); *Thlimmenos v. Greece* [GC], App. no. 34369/97, §58, 6.4.2000 (accountancy); and *Guchez v. Belgium* (dec.), App. no. 10027/82, 5.12.1984 (architecture).

81 *X. v. Belgium* (dec.), App. no. 8901/80, 16.10.1981.

82 *König v. Germany*, App. no. 6232/73, §91, 28.6.1978.

83 *Benthem v. the Netherlands*, App. no. 8848/80, §36, 23.10.1985; and P. van Dijk, "The Benthem case and its aftermath in the Netherlands", *Netherlands International Law Review*, vol. 34, no. 1, 1987, pp. 5–24. See also *Allan Jacobsson v. Sweden (No. 1)*, App. no. 10842/84, §73, 25.10.1989 (building permit); *Nowicky v. Austria*, App. no. 34983/02, §38, 24.2.2005 (licence to sell medicines); *Kraska v. Switzerland*, App. no. 13942/88, §24, 19.4.1993 (right to practise medicine); and *De Moor v. Belgium*, App. no. 16997/90, §43, 23.6.1994 (right to practise law).

In the case *Mirovni Inštitut v. Slovenia*, the Court held that participation in a call for tenders organised by the Ministry of Education, Science and Sport for the purpose of awarding grants for scientific research projects was a "civil right" and created for the applicant institute a procedural right to the lawful and correct adjudication of the tenders, including a right to an oral hearing.[84]

#### 2.2.3.2.1.3. Right to Compensation for Illegal State Action

In the Court's case-law the right to compensation for injury resulting from illegal State acts has also been recognised as being civil, on the basis of its pecuniary nature. Therefore, for example in the case *X. v. France*, the Court held that Article 6 applied to a claim for damages initiated before an administrative court in a situation in which the applicant had contracted HIV from a blood transfusion because of the negligence of the authorities.[85] Although the case concerned a matter of public law, its outcome was nevertheless decisive for private rights and obligations. A similar approach was adopted in the case *Editions Périscope v. France*.[86] In both cases the Court gave a very general meaning to a pecuniary interest and held that such an interest was of a private law character.

The Court has also held in other types of situations that claims for compensation for illegal State acts were considered civil rights. Such claims have concerned, for example, compensation for ill-treatment by the police,[87] unlawful detention,[88] unreasonable length of judicial proceedings,[89] breach of contract,[90] seizure of property,[91] and various other compensation claims.[92]

Statutory rights to receive compensation from the State for wrongful conviction or unjustified detention in connection with criminal proceedings

---

84 *Mirovni Inštitut v. Slovenia*, App. no. 32303/13, §§29–30, 13.3.2018.

85 *X. v. France*, App. no. 18020/91, §30, 31.3.1992. See also *H. v. France*, App. no. 10073/82, §47, 24.10.1989; and *Z. and Others v. the United Kingdom* [GC], App. no. 29392/95, §89, 10.5.2001.

86 *Editions Périscope v. France*, App. no. 11760/85, §40, 26.3.1992.

87 See, for example, *Assenov and Others v. Bulgaria*, App. no. 24760/94, §110, 28.10.1998 (assault); *Balogh v. Hungary*, App. no. 47940/99, §72, 20.7.2004 (assault); *Baraona v. Portugal*, App. no. 10092/82, §44, 8.7.1987 (illegal arrest); *Veeber v. Estonia (No. 1)*, App. no. 37571/97, §69, 7.11.2002 (illegal search and seizure); *Aït-Mouhoub v. France*, App. no. 22924/93, §44, 28.10.1998 (police theft and other illegalities); and *Kaukonen v. Finland* (dec.), App. no. 24738/94, 8.12.1997 (malicious prosecution).

88 *Aerts v. Belgium*, App. no. 25357/94, §59, 30.7.1998; and *Göç v. Turkey* [GC], App. no. 36590/97, §41, 11.7.2002.

89 *Pelli v. Italy* (dec.), App. no. 19537/02, 13.11.2003, which concerned the domestic remedy for excessively lengthy proceedings, known as the Pinto law.

90 *Stran Greek Refineries and Stratis Andreadis v. Greece*, App. no. 13427/87, §40, 9.12.1994.

91 *Air Canada v. the United Kingdom*, App. no. 18465/91, §56, 5.5.1995.

92 See, for example, *Beaumartin v. France*, App. no. 15287/89, §28, 24.11.1994 (claim for compensation under a treaty); *Neves e Silva v. Portugal*, App. no. 11213/84, §37, 27.4.1989 (compensation claim relating to official malpractice); and *Société Anonyme Sotiris and Nikos Koutras Attee v. Greece* (dec.), App. no. 39442/98, 9.12.1999 (refusal of State subsidy).

also fall within the scope of Article 6 as civil rights.[93] In such cases it is also required that the applicant has the right to receive compensation on the basis of domestic law and that such a right is not discretionary.[94] Compensation for unjustified detention has been claimed, for example, in cases of discontinuation of the proceedings,[95] acquittal of an accused[96] or the quashing of a conviction on appeal.[97] Such cases do not normally involve any Article 5 violations (right to liberty and security): instead, the right to compensation is based on the national legislation and on the fact that the detainee was not finally convicted.[98]

Lastly, schemes created to compensate for damage caused by criminal offences fall within the scope of Article 6 due to their pecuniary nature, even if they do not involve any illegal acts by a State. In these cases, it is also required that there is a legal right to compensation and that the compensation is not an *ex gratia* payment.[99] For example, discretionary State compensation for victims of natural disasters falls outside of the scope of Article 6 of the Convention.[100]

#### 2.2.3.2.1.4. Right to Social Security and Social Assistance

The greatest development in widening the scope of Article 6 has taken place in the field of social security and social assistance. In its early case-law, the Court adopted a "balancing approach" in which the private law aspects of a certain right were weighed against its public law aspects. If the former outweighed the latter, Article 6 applied to the case.[101]

---

93 *Humen v. Poland* [GC], App. no. 26614/95, §57, 15.10.1999.

94 *Masson and Van Zon v. the Netherlands*, App. nos. 15346/89+, §52, 28.9.1995, in which this right was missing.

95 See, for example, *Göç v. Turkey* [GC], App. no. 36590/97, §41, 11.7.2002. See also Eva Brems, "Conflicting human rights: an exploration in the context of the right to fair trial in the European Convention for the Protection of Human Rights and Fundamental Freedoms", *Human Rights Quarterly*, vol. 27, no. 1, 2005, pp. 294–326, at pp. 307–309.

96 See, for example, *Werner v. Austria*, App. no. 21835/93, §35, 24.11.1997; and *Lamanna v. Austria*, App. no. 28923/95, §29, 10.7.2001.

97 See, for example, *Humen v. Poland* [GC], App. no. 26614/95, §57, 15.10.1999; and *Hałka and Others v. Poland*, App. no. 71891/01, §18, 2.7.2002.

98 Article 5 has its own *lex specialis* provisions for situations in which the legality of a person's detention is examined; see Articles 5 §3 and 5 §4 for the fair trial guarantees and Article 5 §5 for compensation. Article 6 does not apply to these situations.

99 *Rolf Gustafson v. Sweden*, App. no. 23196/94, §40, 1.7.1997, which concerned a legal right to compensation; and *August v. the United Kingdom* (dec.), App. no. 36505/02, 21.1.2003, which concerned an *ex gratia* payment.

100 *Nordh v. Sweden* (dec.), App. no. 14225/88, 3.12.1990.

101 See, for example, the cases *Feldbrugge v. the Netherlands*, App. no. 8562/79, §§28 and 40, 29.5.1986, which concerned an employment sickness benefit; and *Deumeland v. Germany*, App. no. 9384/81, §§62 and 74, 29.5.1986, which concerned an industrial injuries benefit.

In the current case-law this model is no longer applied. The general rule nowadays is that Article 6 applies to all social security and social assistance matters.[102] In addition, the Court has stressed that these rights are of a pecuniary nature.[103] Thus, Article 6 has been applied to cases concerning invalidity and disability pensions,[104] a widower's pension,[105] maternity benefits,[106] disability allowances,[107] and to compensation paid for forced labour in war time.[108] These days, these types of matters fall routinely within the scope of application of Article 6 without the respondent States even trying to challenge its applicability.[109] If such an objection is raised, however, the Court normally finds such a right to be a civil one due to its pecuniary nature.[110]

The right to social security or to social assistance does not need to be linked to a contract of employment[111] or depend upon contributory payments to pension funds.[112] It is, however, required that the persons applying for the benefit have a legal right to it on the basis of domestic law, since discretionary benefits or assistance fall outside of the scope of Article 6.[113] This has nothing to do with the civil or non-civil nature of a certain benefit or assistance but is rather related to the fact that Article 6 only applies to dispute-related rights which have a basis in domestic law.[114]

#### 2.2.3.2.2. Non-Pecuniary Rights

Rights other than pecuniary rights and obligations may also be governed by Article 6 owing to their private law character. One such non-pecuniary right is the right to respect for family life. Therefore, for example, decisions by State

---

102 The distinction between social security and social assistance is not wholly clear. Social assistance is normally paid according to the different individual needs of each person while social security payments are normally payments of the same amount made to all qualifying persons.

103 *Schuler-Zgraggen v. Switzerland*, App. no. 14518/89, §46, 24.6.1993. See also Karen Reid, *A Practitioner's Guide to the European Convention on Human Rights*, Sweet & Maxwell/Thomson Reuters, London 2019, p. 130.

104 *Schuler-Zgraggen v. Switzerland*, App. no. 14518/89, §46, 24.6.1993; and *McGinley and Egan v. the United Kingdom*, App. nos. 21825/93+, §84, 9.6.1998.

105 *Pauger v. Austria*, App. no. 16717/90, §48, 28.5.1997.

106 *Grof v. Austria* (dec.), App. no. 25046/94, 14.4.1998.

107 *Salesi v. Italy*, App. no. 13023/87, §19, 26.2.1993.

108 *Woś v. Poland* (dec.), App. no. 22860/02, §93, 1.3.2005.

109 See, for example, *Duclos v. France*, App. no. 20940/92, §53, 17.12.1996.

110 See, for example, *Süßmann v. Germany*, App. no. 20024/92, §42, 16.9.1996.

111 See, for example, *Giancarlo Lombardo v. Italy*, App. no. 12490/86, §16, 26.11.1992, which concerned pensions in the public sector.

112 See, for example, *Salesi v. Italy*, App. no. 13023/87, §19, 26.2.1993.

113 *Salesi v. Italy*, App. no. 13023/87, §19, 26.2.1993; and *Mennitto v. Italy* [GC], App. no. 33804/96, §28, 5.10.2000.

114 See section 2.1.1. above.

authorities to take children into public care[115] or to restrict a prisoner's right to contact his family[116] fall within the scope of application of Article 6 of the Convention. Also, certain preventive measures imposed on individuals perceived to be dangerous – such as night-time curfews or restrictions on leaving the district where one lives, on attending public meetings or on using mobile phones or radio communication devices – fall within the sphere of personal rights and are therefore civil in nature within the meaning of Article 6.[117]

Other non-pecuniary rights which qualify as civil rights are, for example, the right to life,[118] physical integrity,[119] liberty[120] and private life,[121] right to a healthy environment,[122] right to have paternity established,[123] right of access to administrative documents,[124] right to reputation,[125] freedom of expression and assembly,[126] and freedom of association.[127] However, the right to report matters stated in open court is not a "civil" right within the meaning of the Convention.[128]

In the case *Selmani and Others v. "the former Yugoslav Republic of Macedonia"*, which concerned the freedom of expression of journalists, the Court held that the applicants' freedom of expression was a "civil right" for the purposes of Article 6 §1 of the Convention, because, according to domestic law, the accredited journalists had a right to report from the Parliament and this reporting from the parliamentary gallery was necessary for the applicants as accredited journalists to exercise their profession and to inform the public about its work.[129] Similarly, the

115 *Olsson v. Sweden (No. 1)*, App. no. 10465/83, §§88–91, 24.3.1988; and *Eriksson v. Sweden*, App. no. 11373/85, §73, 2.6.1989. See also *Keegan v. Ireland*, App. no. 16969/90, §57, 26.5.1994, which concerned adoption.

116 *Ganci v. Italy*, App. no. 41576/98, §25, 30.10.2003.

117 *De Tommaso v. Italy* [GC], App. no. 43395/09, §§154–155, 23.2.2017.

118 *Athanassoglou and Others v. Switzerland* [GC], App. no. 27644/95, §44, 6.4.2000.

119 *Athanassoglou and Others v. Switzerland* [GC], App. no. 27644/95, §44, 6.4.2000; and *Okyay and Others v. Turkey*, App. no. 36220/97, §67, 12.7.2005.

120 *Laidin v. France (No. 2)*, App. no. 39282/98, §76, 7.1.2003; *Aerts v. Belgium*, App. no. 25357/94, §59, 30.7.1998; and *Reinprecht v. Austria*, App. no. 67175/01, §§49–50, 15.11.2005.

121 *Mustafa v. France*, App. no. 63056/00, §14, 17.6.2003 (choice of surname).

122 *Taşkın and Others v. Turkey*, App. no. 46117/99, 10.11.2004.

123 *Alaverdyan v. Armenia* (dec.), App. no. 4523/04, §33, 24.8.2010.

124 *Loiseau v. France* (dec.), App. no. 46809/99, 18.11.2003.

125 *Tolstoy Miloslavsky v. the United Kingdom*, App. no. 18139/91, §58, 13.7.1995; *Werner v. Poland*, App. no. 26760/95, §33, 15.11.2001; and *Fayed v. the United Kingdom*, App. no. 17101/90, §58, 21.9.1994.

126 *Reisz v. Germany* (dec.), App. no. 32013/96, 20.10.1997; *Kenedi v. Hungary*, App. no. 31475/05, §33, 26.5.2009; *Selmani and Others v. "the former Yugoslav Republic of Macedonia"*, App. no. 67259/14, §47, 9.2.2017; and *Shapovalov v. Ukraine*, App. no. 45835/05, §49, 31.7.2012.

127 *AB Kurt Kellermann v. Sweden* (dec.), App. no. 41579/98, 1.7.2003; and *APEH Üldözötteinek Szövetsége and Others v. Hungary*, App. no. 32367/96, §36, 5.10.2000.

128 *Mackay and BBC Scotland v. the United Kingdom*, App. no. 10734/05, §§20–22, 7.12.2010.

129 *Selmani and Others v. "the former Yugoslav Republic of Macedonia"*, App. no. 67259/14, §27, 9.2.2017.

right to be a member of an association is a civil right.[130] Even if under domestic legislation the question of freedom of association belongs to the field of public law, legal proceedings concerning the lawful existence of an association concern that association's civil rights.[131] Moreover, the right to continue higher education studies or primary education is also a civil right.[132]

Although most of these rights are human rights guaranteed in the Convention, the Court does not normally mention this connection in its judgments.[133] Nor does the Court normally give any reasons as to why it considers that a certain right is a civil right. It may not even address the matter but act on the basis that that right is a civil one.[134] Often the Court only refers to the equation between civil rights and obligations and private law rights and obligations established in its early jurisprudence.[135] There are also other examples. In the case *O'Reilly v. Ireland*, the Court weighed up the private and public law aspects of the matter and came to the conclusion that the private law elements were predominant.[136]

#### 2.2.3.2.3. Public Law Rights and Obligations

Whereas the rights and obligations of a private law character fall within the scope of Article 6 as civil rights and obligations, public law rights and obligations do not. There is only a limited number of such rights and obligations and, due to the wide interpretation adopted in the Court's case-law, their number is declining. When assessing the public law character of a right, the Court uses two different principles. First, it uses a restrictive interpretation of what rights and obligations fall outside of the scope of application of Article 6.[137] Second, the Court regards the Convention as a living instrument that must be interpreted dynamically.[138] Notwithstanding the application of these principles, some rights and obligations relate to matters that form such a hard core of public authority prerogatives that, despite their pecuniary nature, these rights remain excluded from the scope of Article 6.[139]

---

130 *Sakellaropoulos v. Greece* (dec.), App. no. 38110/08, 6.1.2011; and *Lovrić v. Croatia*, App. no. 38458/15, §§55–56, 4.4.2017.

131 *APEH Üldözötteinek Szövetsége and Others v. Hungary*, App. no. 32367/96, §§34–35, 5.10.2000.

132 *Emine Araç v. Turkey*, App. no. 9907/02, §§18–25, 23.9.2008; and *Oršuš and Others v. Croatia* [GC], App. no. 15766/03, §104, 16.3.2010.

133 Such connection has only been made in respect of pecuniary rights and property rights, see *Procola v. Luxembourg*, App. no. 14570/89, §39, 28.9.1995.

134 See, for example, the cases *Olsson v. Sweden (No. 1)*, App. no. 10465/83, §§88–91, 24.3.1988; *Eriksson v. Sweden*, App. no. 11373/85, §73, 2.6.1989; and *Keegan v. Ireland*, App. no. 16969/90, §57, 26.5.1994.

135 *APEH Üldözötteinek Szövetsége and Others v. Hungary*, App. no. 32367/96, §34, 5.10.2000.

136 *O'Reilly and Others v. Ireland* (dec.), App. no. 54725/00, 4.9.2003.

137 *Vilho Eskelinen and Others v. Finland* [GC], App. no. 63235/00, §49, 19.4.2007.

138 *Ferrazzini v. Italy* [GC], App. no. 44759/98, §26, 12.7.2001.

139 *Ibid*, §29.

#### 2.2.3.2.3.1. Obligation to Pay Tax

The Court found in its Grand Chamber judgment in the case *Ferrazzini v. Italy* that the obligation to pay taxes to the State was not a civil obligation because of its public law nature. Although the obligation was a pecuniary one, the public nature of the relationship between a taxpayer and tax authorities remained predominant.[140] The same applies also to customs duties.[141] However, if, in a taxation case, tax surcharges have been imposed, this fact turns them into criminal cases which are examined under the criminal limb of Article 6.[142]

#### 2.2.3.2.3.2. Political Rights and Obligations

Political rights and obligations do not fall within the scope of Article 6 due to their public law character, even if they also have pecuniary aspects. Therefore, for example, the right to stand for election to a national parliament does not fall within the scope of Article 6.[143] Other types of disputes relating to elections also fall outside the scope of Article 6.[144] Generally speaking, the right to engage in political activities is not a civil right or related to a criminal charge, so that, for example, a right to vote,[145] electoral sanctions,[146] or a dissolution of a political party[147] do not fall within the scope of Article 6. Also, disputes which relate to the election of an officer of a non-governmental organisation,[148] or of an employees' council representative,[149] to the right to a pension as a former Member of Parliament,[150] or to a membership of and exclusion from a political party or association[151] remain, on the same grounds, outside the scope

---

140 *Ferrazzini v. Italy* [GC], App. no. 44759/98, §29, 12.7.2001. See also David Harris, Michael O'Boyle, Ed Bates, Carla Buckley, *Law of the European Convention on Human Rights*, 4th edition, Oxford University Press, Oxford 2018, p. 387.

141 *Emesa Sugar NV v. the Netherlands* (dec.), App. no. 62023/00, 13.1.2005.

142 *Jussila v. Finland* [GC], App. no. 73053/01, §38, 23.11.2006.

143 *Pierre-Bloch v. France*, App. no. 24194/94, §51, 21.10.1997; *Tapie v. France* (dec.), App. no. 32258/96, 13.1.1997; *Asensio Serqueda v. Spain* (dec.), App. no. 23151/94, 9.5.1994; and *Guliyev v. Azerbaidjan* (dec.), App. no. 35584/02, 27.5.2004.

144 See, for example, *Priorello v. Italy* (dec.), App. no. 11068/84, 6.5.1985, which concerned local elections.

145 *Hirst v. the United Kingdom* (dec.), App. no. 74025/01, 8.7.2003, which concerned a prisoner's right to vote.

146 *Pierre-Bloch v. France*, App. no. 24194/94, §§53–60, 21.10.1997.

147 *Yazar and Others v. Turkey*, App. nos. 22723/93+, §67, 9.4.2002; *Reisz v. Germany* (dec.), App. no. 32013/96, 20.10.1997; and *Refah Partisi (The Welfare Party) and Others v. Turkey* [GC], App. nos. 41340/98+, 13.2.2003.

148 *Fedotov v. Russia* (dec.), App. no. 5140/02, 23.11.2004.

149 *Novotny v. the Czech Republic* (dec.), App. no. 36542/97, 1.7.1998.

150 *Papon v. France* (dec.), App. no. 344/04, 11.10.2005.

151 *Lovrić v. Croatia*, App. no. 38458/15, §55, 4.4.2017.

of Article 6. Instead, they can be examined under Article 3 of Protocol No. 1 as a right to free elections and/or under Article 13 as a right to an effective remedy.[152]

The Court has also confirmed that matters relating to conduct in political office, in particular the duty not to place oneself in a conflict of interests, are political rather than civil.[153] However, lustration proceedings – that is, proceedings used by post-Communist countries in which people holding high positions in society and who previously collaborated with the former regime or secret service must denounce their previous activities and consequently be dismissed from their functions for a definite period of time – could come within the criminal head of Article 6 where those proceedings have criminal connotations.[154]

#### 2.2.3.2.3.3. Entry, Stay and Removal of Aliens and Right to Passport

Disputes which concern entry, stay or removal of aliens are also of a public law character and fall outside the scope of Article 6, both its civil and criminal heads. In the case *Maaouia v. France*, the Court found that this type of matter did not concern the determination of an applicant's civil rights and obligations, although a removal decision could have major repercussions for the applicant's private and family life or for his prospects of employment.[155] Article 6 does not therefore apply to asylum cases.[156] The same is true also for extradition cases,[157] for European arrest warrant proceedings,[158] for an action in damages by an asylum-seeker on account of the refusal to grant asylum,[159] and for an inclusion of an alien in the Schengen Information System.[160] However, if a prison sentence has been replaced on appeal/review by deportation and exclusion from national territory, it may be treated as a penalty on the same basis as the one imposed at the time of the initial conviction.[161]

---

152 *Mugemangango v. Belgium* [GC], App. no. 310/15, §122, 10.7.2020. In this case the examination of a complaint calling for a recount of ballot papers had not been impartial, since it had been examined by members of parliament whose election was called into question by the applicant. The safeguards afforded to the applicant during the procedure had been insufficient and the procedure itself partial.

153 *Cătăniciu v. Romania* (dec.), App. no. 22717/17, §35, 6.12.2018.

154 *Matyjek v. Poland* (dec.), App. no. 38184/03, 30.5.2006. Compare and contrast with *Sidabras and Diautas v. Lithuania* (dec.), App. no. 55480/00, 1.7.2003; and *Polyakh and Others v. Ukraine*, App. nos. 58812/15+, §§56–59, 17.10.2019.

155 *Maaouia v. France* [GC], App. no. 39652/98, §38, 5.10.2000; and *Mamatkulov and Askarov v. Turkey* [GC], App. nos. 46827/99+, §82, 4.2.2005. See also David Harris, Michael O'Boyle, Ed Bates, Carla Buckley, *Law of the European Convention on Human Rights*, 4th edition, Oxford University Press, Oxford 2018, pp. 388–389.

156 See, for example, *V.P. v. the United Kingdom* (dec.), App. no. 13162/87, 9.11.1987; and *Taheri Kandomabadi v. the Netherlands* (dec.), App. no. 6276/03, 29.6.2004.

157 *Mamatkulov and Askarov v. Turkey* [GC], App. nos. 46827/99+, §82, 4.2.2005; and *Peñafiel Salgado v. Spain* (dec.), App. no. 65964/01, 16.4.2002.

158 *Monedero Angora v. Spain* (dec.), App. no. 41138/05, 7.10.2008.

159 *Panjeheighalehei v. Denmark* (dec.), App. no. 11230/07, 13.10.2009.

160 *Dalea v. France* (dec.), App. no. 964/07, 2.2.2010.

161 *Gurguchiani v. Spain*, App. no. 16012/06, §§40 and 47–48, 15.12.2009.

The right to hold a passport and the right to nationality are not civil rights either for the purposes of Article 6.[162] Nor do visa practices engage a civil right within the meaning of Article 6 §1 of the Convention. They do not become "civil" merely because their execution is sought before the courts and they give rise to a judicial decision.[163] However, a foreigner's right to apply for a work permit may come under Article 6, both for the employer and the employee, even if, under domestic law, the employee has no *locus standi* to apply for it, provided that what is involved is simply a procedural bar that does not affect the substance of the right.[164]

In addition, the right to freedom of movement under EU law is a public law right which falls outside the scope of Article 6.[165] The expulsion of a State's own citizens would most likely also not be covered by Article 6. Article 6 can be applicable only in the most exceptional circumstances, in which there is sufficient evidence to suspect that the person to be deported would be at risk of being subjected to a flagrant denial of justice in the country to which he or she is to be removed. Such would be the situation, for example, when evidence obtained by torture is to be used against the applicant.[166]

#### 2.2.3.2.3.4. Employment in the Public Sector

Rights and obligations arising out of employment in the public sector are also excluded to some extent from the scope of Article 6, although this exception is nowadays more limited than before. The Court reconsidered its earlier case-law in 2007 in the case *Vilho Eskelinen and Others v. Finland* and introduced a new two-part test which starts from the presumption that Article 6 *does* apply to employment in the public sector. In order to refute the presumption, the State must show that the domestic law expressly excludes access to a court for the post or category of staff in question. If this is the case, Article 6 nonetheless still applies unless the exclusion under national law is justified on objective grounds. These grounds must relate to the nature of the dispute between the State and the public servant. The State must therefore be able to show that the said dispute is related to the exercise of State powers or that there is a special loyalty bond between the State and the public servant. The State therefore does not, in principle, have any justification for excluding from the scope of Article 6 any ordinary labour disputes, such as those relating to salaries, allowances or similar entitlements,

---

162 *Šoć v. Croatia* (dec.), App. no. 47863/99, 29.6.2000; *Karassev and family v. Finland*, App. no. 31414/96, Commission decision, 14.4.1998; *Peltonen v. Finland*, App. no. 19583/92, Commission decision, 20.2.1995; and *Sergey Smirnov v. Russia* (dec.), App. no. 14085/04, 6.7.2006.

163 *M.N. and Others v. Belgium* [GC] (dec.), App. no. 3599/18, §§137–139, 5.5.2020.

164 *Jurisic and Collegium Mehrerau v. Austria*, App. no. 62539/00, §§54–62, 27.7.2006.

165 *Adams and Benn v. the United Kingdom* (dec.), App. no. 28979/95, 13.1.1997.

166 *Othman (Abu Qatada) v. the United Kingdom*, App. no. 8139/09, §§258–261 and 267, 17.1.2012; and *Al Nashiri v. Poland*, App. no. 28761/11, §§569–571, 24.7.2014.

on the ground that there would be a special loyalty bond between the State and the public servant.[167] For example, in the case *Denisov v. Ukraine*, the Court held that although the dismissal of the president of an administrative court did not concern a civil law dispute, it was a public law dispute with the characteristics of an "ordinary labour dispute" involving members of a public service, including judges. The civil limb of Article 6 was thus applicable.[168]

In the case *Vilho Eskelinen and Others*, the Court did not even have to go that far, as Article 6 was applicable already on the ground that the applicant had had access to domestic courts. Similarly, on the same grounds, Article 6 was applicable even to active army officers and their claims before a military court.[169] The principles established in the *Vilho Eskelinen* case have subsequently been applied in many cases: Article 6 has been applicable, for example, to an employee of an embassy,[170] a head accountant,[171] a police officer,[172] an army officer and a regular soldier,[173] a prosecutor,[174] a State-employed bailiff,[175] to proceedings regarding the right to obtain the post of parliamentary assistant,[176] to disciplinary proceedings against a judge or a termination of their post,[177] and to proceedings relating to the promotion of a customs officer.[178]

The Court had already held in the *Pellegrin* case that pension disputes concerning a public official fell within the scope of Article 6 irrespective of whether he exercised public authority or not.[179] This principle has been

167 *Vilho Eskelinen and Others v. Finland* [GC], App. no. 63235/00, §62, 19.4.2007. See also Sejal Parmar, "*Vilho Eskelinen v. Finland*: The Further Extension of ECHR Article 6 to Disputes Concerning Civil Servants", *European Human Rights Law Review*, Issue 4, 2007, pp. 441–449; and José Luís Da Cruz Vilaça, *EU Law and Integration - Twenty Years of Judicial Application of EU Law*, Hart Publishing, Oxford and Portland, Or. 2014, pp. 197–202. See also *Baka v. Hungary* [GC], App. no. 20261/12, §103, 23.6.2016; and *Regner v. the Czech Republic* [GC], App. no. 35289/11, §107, 19.9.2017.

168 *Denisov v. Ukraine* [GC], App. no. 76639/11, §§53–57, 25.9.2018.

169 *Pridatchenko and Others v. Russia*, App. nos. 2191/03+, §§47–48, 21.6.2007.

170 *Cudak v. Lithuania* [GC], App. no. 15869/02, §§44–47, 23.3.2010. See also Dragoljub Popović, "Access to Justice in the Recent Grand Chamber Judgments of the European Court of Human Rights", in Sonia Morano-Foadi, Lucy Vickers (Eds.), *Fundamental Rights in the EU - A Matter for Two Courts*, Hart Publishing, Oxford and Portland, Or. 2015, pp. 201–217, at pp. 213–216.

171 *Sabeh El Leil v. France* [GC], App. no. 34869/05, §39, 29.6.2011.

172 *Šikić v. Croatia*, App. no. 9143/08, §§17–20, 15.7.2010.

173 *Vasilchenko v. Russia*, App. no. 34784/02, §§34–36, 23.9.2010; and *R.S. v. Germany* (dec.), App. no. 19600/15, §34, 28.3.2017.

174 *Zalli v. Albania* (dec.), App. no. 52531/07, 8.2.2011.

175 *Bayer v. Germany*, App. no. 8453/04, §38, 16.7.2009.

176 *Savino and Others v. Italy*, App. nos. 17214/05+, §§75–78, 28.4.2009.

177 *Olujić v. Croatia*, App. no. 22330/05, §§35–43, 5.2.2009; *Baka v. Hungary* [GC], App. no. 20261/12, §103, 23.6.2016; *Kamenos v. Cyprus*, App. no. 147/07, §73, 31.10.2017; *Denisov v. Ukraine* [GC], App. no. 76639/11, §§53–57, 25.9.2018; and *Ramos Nunes de Carvalho e Sá v. Portugal* [GC], App. nos. 55391/13+, §120, 6.11.2018.

178 *Fiume v. Italy*, App. no. 20774/05, §§33–37, 30.6.2009.

179 *Pellegrin v. France* [GC], App. no. 28541/95, §67, 8.12.1999.

confirmed in the Court's subsequent case-law, *inter alia*, on the ground that pension issues concern pecuniary rights.[180]

Lustration proceedings, as discussed in section 2.2.3.2.3.2. above, may fall, depending on the specific circumstances of each case, either under the civil or criminal limb of Article 6.[181]

#### 2.2.3.2.3.5. Other Public Law Rights and Obligations

Obligations which are a part of normal civic duties in a democratic society are not regarded as civil and thus fall outside the scope of Article 6.[182] Therefore, the obligation to pay fines[183] or to give evidence in court proceedings[184] are civic duties falling outside the scope of Article 6, as are the rights to nationality,[185] liability for military or non-military service,[186] certain matters relating to the administration of justice,[187] education,[188] medical treatment,[189] public housing[190] and award of administrative contracts.[191]

---

180 *Tričković v. Slovenia*, App. no. 39914/98, §40, 12.6.2001 (military pension); *Silveri v. Italy*, App. no. 44353/98, 17.10.2000 (police pension); and *Vasilopoulou v. Greece* (dec.), App. no. 47541/99, 22.3.2001 (judicial pension). See also *R. v. Belgium*, App. no. 33919/96, §44, 27.2.2001, in which the Court held that the applicant's pension claim against the State could not be regarded as civil as he had been called in for military service as a reserve officer in which context he had been injured.

181 *Ivanovski v. "the former Yugoslav Republic of Macedonia"*, App. no. 29908/11, §§117–121, 21.1.2016. See also Kevin Aquilina, "The Independence of the Judiciary in Strasbourg Judicial Disciplinary Case Law – Judges as Applicants and National Judicial Councils as Factotums of Respondent States", in Paulo Pinto de Albuquerque, Krzysztof Wojtyczek (Eds.), *Judicial Power in a Globalized World – Liber Amicorum Vincent de Gaetano*, Springer, Cham 2019, pp. 1–32. See also *Karajanov v. "the former Yugoslav Republic of Macedonia"*, App. no. 2229/15, §64, 6.4.2017.

182 *Schouten and Meldrum v. the Netherlands*, App. nos. 19005/91+, §50, 9.12.1994.

183 *Schouten and Meldrum v. the Netherlands*, App. nos. 19005/91+, §50, 9.12.1994.

184 *British Broadcasting Corporation v. the United Kingdom* (dec.), App. no. 25798/94, 18.1.1996; and *Van Vondel v. the Netherlands* (dec.), App. no. 38258/03, 23.3.2006.

185 *S. v. Switzerland* (dec.), App. no. 13325/87, 7.8.1988 (nationality); *Peltonen v. Finland*, App. no. 19583/92, Commission decision 20.2.1995 (passport); and *X. v. the United Kingdom* (dec.), App. no. 8208/78, 7.12.1978 (peerage).

186 *Nicolussi v. Austria* (dec.), App. no. 11734/85, 8.5.1987 (non-military service); and *Zelisse v. the Netherlands* (dec.), App. no. 12915/87, 13.4.1989 (exemption from military service).

187 *Schreiber and Boetsch v. France* (dec.), App. no. 58751/00, 11.12.2003 (challenge to a judge); *X. v. the Federal Republic of Germany* (dec.), App. no. 3925/69, 2.1.1970 (right to legal aid); *B. v. the United Kingdom* (dec.), App. no. 10615/83, 3.7.1984 (lawyer's costs); *Atkinson, Crook and The Independent v. the United Kingdom* (dec.), App. no. 13366/87, 3.12.1990; and *Loersch and Nouvelle Association du Courrier v. Switzerland* (dec.), App. nos. 23868/94+, 24.2.1995 (right to court reporting).

188 *Simpson v. the United Kingdom* (dec.), App. no. 14688/89, 4.12.1989 (elementary education).

189 *L. v. Sweden*, App. no. 10801/84, §87, Report of the Commission, 3.10.1988.

190 *Woonbron Volkshuisvestingsgroep and Others v. the Netherlands* (dec.), App. no. 47122/99, 18.6.2002.

191 *I.T.C. Ltd v. Malta* (dec.), App. no. 2629/06, 11.12.2007 (public procurement).

### 2.2.3.2.4. Rights Connected to Criminal Proceedings and Imprisonment

The Convention does not contain any right to have third parties charged or convicted.[192] Nor does Article 6 §1 require that there be a national court with competence to invalidate or override the law in force.[193] Article 6 §1 of the Convention applies normally to compensation claims which are connected to criminal proceedings,[194] except when such claims are raised purely in revenge or for punishment purposes.[195] In order for such a situation to fall within the scope of Article 6 of the Convention, such a right must be inherently connected to the victim's right to bring a civil action under domestic law, even if it would only concern symbolic compensation or a civil right, such as right to reputation.[196] Article 6 thus applies to a civil action brought by the victim from the moment he or she, by bringing the action, joins the criminal proceedings, unless he or she has clearly waived the right to compensation, and applies as long as the criminal proceedings are decisive for the civil right to compensation being asserted.[197]

According to the wording of Article 6 itself, the criminal head of Article 6 applies only to the person who faces a criminal charge, and would therefore not apply to, for example, proceedings brought by private prosecution. In such cases Article 6 does not apply under its civil head either, since proceedings brought by one person to challenge a decision not to prosecute another do not themselves seek to determine "civil rights and obligations".[198]

Several rights connected to criminal proceedings are also covered by the civil head of Article 6. It covers, *inter alia*, the right to a good reputation;[199] the right of access to administrative documents or to evidence in the investigation file;[200] disputes regarding the non-inclusion of a conviction in a criminal record;[201] an appeal against an entry in a police file affecting the right to reputation, the right to protection of property or the possibility of finding employment and hence

---

192 *Perez v. France* [GC], App. no. 47287/99, §70, 12.2.2004; and *Mustafa Tunç and Fecire Tunç v. Turkey* [GC], App. no. 24014/05, §218, 14.4.2015.

193 *James and Others v. the United Kingdom*, App. no. 8793/79, §81, 21.2.1986.

194 *Perez v. France* [GC], App. no. 47287/99, §§70–71, 12.2.2004.

195 *Sigalas v. Greece*, App. no. 19754/02, §29, 22.9.2005; and *Mihova v. Italy* (dec.), App. no. 25000/07, 30.3.2010.

196 *Perez v. France* [GC], App. no. 47287/99, §70, 12.2.2004. As concerns symbolic compensation, see *Gorou v. Greece (No. 2)* [GC], App. no. 12686/03, §§24–26, 20.3.2009.

197 *Perez v. France* [GC], App. no. 47287/99, §70, 12.2.2004; *Nicolae Virgiliu Tănase v. Romania* [GC], App. no. 41720/13, §207, 25.6.2019; and *Alexandrescu and Others v. Romania*, App. nos. 56842/08+, §22, 24.11.2015.

198 *Mustafa Tunç and Fecire Tunç v. Turkey* [GC], App. no. 24014/05, §218, 14.4.2015.

199 *Helmers v. Sweden*, App. no. 11826/85, §29, 29.10.1991.

200 *Loiseau v. France* (dec.), App. no. 22093/93, 6.4.1995; and *Savitskyy v. Ukraine*, App. no. 38773/05, §§143–145, 26.7.2012.

201 *Alexandre v. Portugal*, App. no. 33197/09, §§54–55, 20.11.2012.

earning a living;[202] and proceedings concerning the application of non-custodial preventive measures.[203]

The civil head of Article 6 applies also to some restrictions on detainees' rights, and to the possible repercussions of those restrictions, since they are deemed to fall within the scope of "civil rights".[204] The Court has held that Article 6 applies to prisoners' detention arrangements, such as restrictions inherent to a placement in a high-security unit or in a high-security cell,[205] to disciplinary proceedings resulting in restrictions on family visits to prison,[206] or to other types of restrictions on prisoners' rights.[207] Article 6 has also been applied to special supervision measures in the context of a compulsory residence order which entails restrictions on an individual's freedom of movement. In the case *De Tommaso v. Italy* the Court held that some restrictions – such as the prohibition on going out at night, leaving the district of residence, attending public meetings or using mobile phones or radio communication devices – fell within the sphere of personal rights and were therefore "civil" in nature.[208]

## 2.3. "DISPUTE" CONCERNING CIVIL RIGHTS AND OBLIGATIONS

For Article 6 to apply, there must be a dispute at the national level between either private individuals or between a private individual and the State, and the outcome of this dispute must directly determine the civil rights and obligations of the applicant. The Court has generally interpreted this requirement in a way which does not create unnecessary obstacles to the application of Article 6.[209]

202 *Pocius v. Lithuania*, App. no. 35601/04, §§38–46, 6.7.2010; and *Užukauskas v. Lithuania*, App. no. 16965/04, §§32–40, 6.7.2010.

203 *De Tommaso v. Italy* [GC], App. no. 43395/09, §151, 23.2.2017.

204 *De Tommaso v. Italy* [GC], App. no. 43395/09, §§147–150, 23.2.2017.

205 *Enea v. Italy* [GC], App. no. 74912/01, §§97–107, 17.9.2009; and *Stegarescu and Bahrin v. Portugal*, App. no. 46194/06, §§35–39, 6.4.2010. See also Dragoljub Popović, "Access to Justice in the Recent Grand Chamber Judgments of the European Court of Human Rights", in Sonia Morano-Foadi, Lucy Vickers (Eds.), *Fundamental Rights in the EU – A Matter for Two Courts*, Hart Publishing, Oxford and Portland, Or. 2015, pp. 201–217, at pp. 211–213.

206 *Gülmez v. Turkey*, App. no. 16330/02, §30, 20.5.2008.

207 *Ganci v. Italy*, App. no. 41576/98, §25, 30.10.2003.

208 *De Tommaso v. Italy* [GC], App. no. 43395/09, §§151–155, 23.2.2017. See also Sofia Galani (Ed.), "Case and comment: selected decisions from the European Court of Human Rights from January and February 2017 – Special supervision measures, *De Tommaso v. Italy* (Application No. 43395/09)", *European Human Rights Law Review*, Issue 3, 2017, pp. 332–335; and Stefan Kieber, "The jurisprudence of the European Court of Human Rights in 2017", *European Yearbook on Human Rights 2018*, pp. 229–265, at p. 237.

209 *Oerlemans v. the Netherlands*, App. no. 12565/86, §46, 27.11.1991. In the case *Moreira de Azevedo v. Portugal*, App. no. 11296/84, §66, 23.10.1990, the Court even questioned the existence of this requirement, on the ground that the English version of the Convention does not mention this requirement at all.

The existence of a dispute should not be construed too technically and it should be given a substantive rather than a formal meaning.[210] Article 6 of the Convention does not, however, apply to unilateral petitions or declarations, or to non-contentious civil cases in which there is no counterpart or in which the right in question has not been contested.[211]

A dispute may concern a question of law or of fact.[212] It does not have to concern only the actual existence of a right but it can also concern its scope of application and the manner in which it is exercised in respect of the applicant.[213] The dispute must, however, be genuine and of a serious nature.[214] This requirement clearly excludes from the scope of Article 6 hypothetical cases such as, for example, complaints that pending law reforms would, if enacted, violate the applicant's rights,[215] as well as cases which the applicant has not pursued seriously at the domestic level, for example by not presenting evidence.[216]

For a dispute to be genuine and serious, it must have something at stake for the applicant. For example, in the case *Kienast v. Austria*, the Court held that such an interest was missing when two small plots of land owned by the applicant were united to form one plot without affecting his ownership, the use of the land or any other right.[217] For a dispute to be regarded as genuine and serious, however, the applicant does not need to claim damages; a request for declaratory judgment is also sufficient.[218]

A dispute must also be such that it lends itself to judicial resolution. In the case *van Marle v. the Netherlands*, the majority of the Grand Chamber held that Article 6 did not apply as the dispute was about the applicants' competence as accountants. The Court held that evaluating knowledge and experience for carrying on a profession under a particular title was akin to a school or university

210 *Le Compte, Van Leuven and De Meyere v. Belgium*, App. nos. 6878/75+, §45, 23.6.1981; and *Gorou v. Greece (No. 2)* [GC], App. no. 12686/03, §§27 and 29, 20.3.2009.

211 *Alaverdyan v. Armenia* (dec.), App. no. 4523/04, §§34–35, 24.8.2010.

212 *Albert and Le Compte v. Belgium*, App. nos. 7299/75+, §27, 10.2.1983.

213 *Le Compte, Van Leuven and De Meyere v. Belgium*, App. nos. 6878/75+, §49, 23.6.1981; *Benthem v. the Netherlands*, App. no. 8848/80, §32, 23.10.1985; and *Cipolletta v. Italy*, App. no. 38259/09, §31, 11.1.2018. For example in the case *Naït-Liman v. Switzerland* [GC], App. no. 51357/07, §107, 15.3.2018, the Court found that there was a dispute since it related to the extra-territorial application over a right.

214 *Boulois v. Luxembourg* [GC], App. no. 37575/04, §90, 3.4.2012; *Benthem v. the Netherlands*, App. no. 8848/80, §32, 23.10.1985; and *Sporrong and Lönnroth v. Sweden*, App. nos. 7151/75+, §81, 23.9.1982.

215 Nevertheless, complaints which concern negative effects created by the existing legislation vis-à-vis applicants fall within the scope of Article 6. See *Posti and Rahko v. Finland*, App. no. 27824/95, §55, 24.9.2002.

216 *Kaukonen v. Finland* (dec.), App. no. 24738/94, 8.12.1997. See also *Kiryanov v. Russia* (dec.), App. no. 42212/02, 9.12.2004.

217 *Kienast v. Austria*, App. no. 23379/94, §43, 23.1.2003.

218 *Helmers v. Sweden*, App. no. 11826/85, §29, 29.10.1991.

examination and was so far removed from the exercise of the normal judicial function that Article 6 did not cover resultant disagreements.[219]

The Court has found in a number of cases that where proceedings relate solely to issues of observance of admissibility criteria, there is no "dispute" over "civil" rights and obligations.[220] In such cases a dismissal of the action is a foreseeable consequence in respect of which the applicants have no prospects to have the situation complained of reversed. However, the situation is different where the domestic courts are called upon for the first time to determine the legal issue raised.[221] A domestic court can also be found to lack jurisdiction after a detailed examination of the applicable law.[222]

## 2.4. "DETERMINATION" OF CIVIL RIGHTS AND OBLIGATIONS

It is not only necessary that there is a dispute about something but this dispute must also be directly decisive for the applicant's civil rights and obligations.[223] This requirement is clearly fulfilled in cases in which the determination of the applicant's rights and obligations is the primary purpose of the decision-making process. Article 6 applies thus, for example, when ordinary courts decide on liability for damages between private individuals,[224] when administrative courts decide on negligence by State hospitals, or when the restoration of a person's legal capacity is at stake.[225]

Article 6 also applies to those judicial proceedings which do not have the determination of civil rights and obligations as their primary purpose but which nonetheless are decisive for applicants. For example in the case *Ringeisen v. Austria*, the Court held that administrative proceedings in which the applicant

---

219 *Van Marle and Others v. the Netherlands*, App. nos. 8543/79+, §36, 26.6.1986. See also Jochen A. Frowein, "The transformation of constitutional law through the European Convention on Human Rights", in *Dialogue between judges, European Court of Human Rights/Council of Europe*, Strasbourg 2007, pp. 71–90, at p. 81; and Karen Reid, *A Practitioner's Guide to the European Convention on Human Rights*, Sweet & Maxwell/Thomson Reuters, London 2019, p. 127. See also *Le Bihan v. France* (dec.), App. no. 63054/00, 1.6.2004; *Nowicky v. Austria*, App. no. 34983/02, §35, 24.2.2005; and *Kervoëlen v. France*, App. no. 35585/97, §30, 27.3.2001.

220 *Nicholas v. Cyprus* (dec.), App. no. 37371/97, 14.3.2000; *Neshev v. Bulgaria* (dec.), App. no. 40897/98, 13.3.2003; *Astikos Oikodomikos Synetairismos Nea Konstantinoupolis v. Greece* (dec.), App. no. 37806/02, 20.1.2005; *Stavroulakis v. Greece* (dec.), App. no. 22326/10, 28.1.2014; and *Arvanitakis and Others v. Greece* (dec.), App. no. 21898/10, 26.8.2014.

221 *Markovic and Others v. Italy* [GC], App. no. 1398/03, §§100–101, 14.12.2006.

222 *Károly Nagy v. Hungary* [GC], App. no. 56665/09, §§60, 72 and 75, 14.9.2017.

223 *Ringeisen v. Austria*, App. no. 2614/65, §94, 16.7.1971; and *Le Compte, Van Leuven and De Meyere v. Belgium*, App. nos. 6878/75+, §47, 23.6.1981.

224 See, for example, *Guincho v. Portugal*, App. no. 8990/80, 10.7.1984.

225 See, for example, *H. v. France*, App. no. 10073/82, §47, 24.10.1989; and *Stanev v. Bulgaria* [GC], App. no. 36760/06, §233, 17.1.2012.

sought approval from the authorities to buy land was, despite its administrative character, decisive for his civil rights.[226] But such a connection must be direct, since a tenuous connection or remote consequences for the applicant's civil rights and obligations do not suffice.[227] For example, in liberal professions a disciplinary action may be decisive for a person's civil right to exercise his or her profession, since there may be a direct connection between these two issues.[228] In contrast, an appointment of a person to a public post has only a distant connection to his colleagues' own right to be appointed themselves.[229]

In the case *Athanassoglou and Others v. Switzerland*, the Court held that the applicants' civil rights were not directly determined in the proceedings which concerned the renewal of a licence for a nuclear power station. Article 6 did not apply, as the applicants living nearby could not produce evidence showing that the station's operation exposed them to a specific and imminent danger of an infringement of their civil rights.[230] However, in another case, proceedings concerning permission to build a dam had a direct impact on the lifestyle and property of the members of the applicant association, as well as on the public interest of environmental protection, since the building of the dam would certainly have flooded their land and property.[231]

---

226 *Ringeisen v. Austria*, App. no. 2614/65, §94, 16.7.1971. See also Dragoljub Popović, "Access to Justice in the Recent Grand Chamber Judgments of the European Court of Human Rights", in Sonia Morano-Foadi, Lucy Vickers (Eds.), *Fundamental Rights in the EU – A Matter for Two Courts*, Hart Publishing, Oxford and Portland, Or. 2015, pp. 201–217, at pp. 202–203.

227 *Le Compte, Van Leuven and De Meyere v. Belgium*, App. nos. 6878/75+, §47, 23.6.1981; and *Benthem v. the Netherlands*, App. no. 8848/80, §32, 23.10.1985.

228 See, for example, *Le Compte, Van Leuven and De Meyere v. Belgium*, App. nos. 6878/75+, §47, 23.6.1981. If the disciplinary proceedings concern a lesser sanction than a withdrawal of the right to practise (for example imposing of fines or a non-public warning), such proceedings are not directly decisive for the applicant's right to continue to exercise his profession. However, the proceedings are decisive when the case concerns the right itself to exercise a profession. See, for example, the case *A. v. Finland* (dec.), App. no. 44998/98, 8.1.2004, in which a non-public warning given to the applicant in the disciplinary proceedings was not as such decisive for his right to be a member of the Bar Association, but as it was not excluded at the beginning of the disciplinary proceedings that he would be expelled from the Bar, this right was at stake and Article 6 applied. See also *W.R. v. Austria*, App. no. 26602/95, §30, 21.12.1999.

229 *Revel and Mora v. France* (dec.), App. no. 171/03, 15.11.2005.

230 *Athanassoglou and Others v. Switzerland* [GC], App. no. 27644/95, §55, 6.4.2000. See also Loukis Loucaides, "Environmental protection through the jurisprudence of the European Convention on Human Rights", *British Yearbook of International Law*, vol. 75, 2004, pp. 249–267, at p. 252. See also *Balmer-Schafroth and Others v. Switzerland*, App. no. 22110/93, §40, 26.8.1997; and *F.X. Martin v. Ireland* (dec.), App. no. 8569/79, 8.5.1985 (*actio popularis* application).

231 *Gorraiz Lizarraga and Others v. Spain*, App. no. 62543/00, §47, 27.4.2004. For other similar cases relating to environmental protection, see also *Taşkın and Others v. Turkey*, App. no. 46117/99, §133, 10.11.2004 (permit to operate a gold mine); *Zander v. Sweden*, App. no. 14282/88, §§24–25, 25.11.1993 (environmental permit); *L'Erablière A.S.B.L. v. Belgium*, App. no. 49230/07, §§28–30, 24.2.2009 (planning permit); *Sdružení Jihočeské Matky v. the Czech Republic* (dec.), App. no. 19101/03, 10.7.2006 (nuclear power station); *Zapletal v. the Czech Republic* (dec.), App. no. 12720/06, 30.11.2010 (noise pollution from a factory); and *Ivan Atanasov v. Bulgaria*, App. no. 12853/03, §§90–95, 2.12.2010 (plant for treatment of mining waste).

Article 6 also applies when a decision has financial consequences for the applicant even if it would not be directly decisive for his or her civil rights and obligations. For example, the proceedings for obtaining a permit for a new runway were directly decisive for the applicants' rights, since awarding such a permit would undoubtedly have diminished the value of the land they owned.[232]

In contrast, in deportation matters Article 6 cannot become applicable even if the alien to be removed claims that the removal decision is decisive for his or her civil rights, such as an employment contract, for example. The connection in such a case is too tenuous.[233] The situation is similar in respect of the obligation to do military service and its possible consequences for the person's civil rights.[234] On the other hand, if the applicant has accepted a job for which the authorities find him to be unsuitable, such a connection exists.[235]

Article 6 of the Convention does not apply either if, for example, in an official enquiry the applicant's civil right to reputation is violated. Because in such a situation the case may only be at an investigative stage, none of the applicant's civil rights and obligations has yet been judicially determined.[236]

Civil rights and obligations can also be determined in criminal proceedings. Article 6 applies when the victim of a crime presents his or her claim for compensation or otherwise pursues his or her civil rights. By contrast, Article 6 does not apply if the victim's purpose is not to pursue his or her own case but to have the perpetrator convicted or to bring an *actio popularis* type of action.[237] Nor is Article 6 applicable if the only aim of the victim's defamation action is to have the perpetrator convicted.[238]

## 2.5. ADMINISTRATIVE DECISIONS

Despite the fact that administrative decisions have been rendered by administrative authorities, they fall within the scope of Article 6 if they are directly decisive for a person's civil rights and obligations. In such cases, it is not necessary that the administrative organs themselves fulfil the Article 6 criteria

---

232 *SARL du Parc d'activités de Blotzheim v. France*, App. no. 72377/01, §19, 11.7.2006. Compare with *Krafft and Rougeot v. France* (dec.), App. no. 11543/85, 5.3.1990.

233 *Saleem v. the United Kingdom* (dec.), App. no. 38294/97, 4.3.1998; and *Maaouia v. France* [GC], App. no. 39652/98, §38, 5.10.2000.

234 *Zelisse v. the Netherlands* (dec.), App. no. 12915/87, 13.4.1989.

235 *X. v. the United Kingdom* (dec.), App. no. 28530/95, 19.1.1998.

236 *Fayed v. the United Kingdom*, App. no. 17101/90, §61, 21.9.1994. See also *Kervoëlen v. France*, App. no. 35585/97, §30, 27.3.2001.

237 *Perez v. France* [GC], App. no. 47287/99, §70, 12.2.2004.

238 *Rékási v. Hungary* (dec.), App. no. 31506/96, 25.11.1996.

set for the courts and tribunals but it is sufficient that there is the possibility to challenge such decisions before a court or a tribunal fulfilling these criteria.[239] Normally it is required that such a court or tribunal has the full jurisdiction to examine all questions of fact and law in the case.[240]

### 2.5.1. POLICY DECISIONS

In some cases, it is sufficient that there is the possibility to challenge discretionary administrative decisions only on legal grounds while the expediency considerations of such decisions are left for the deciding organ, even if such a decision would be decisive for a person's civil rights and obligations. For these types of cases it is typical that the decision making requires wide professional and technical knowledge or exercise of administrative discretion in order to achieve wider political aims.[241] Decisions typical of this include, for example, decisions to expropriate land for building roads or for the purposes of public housing. Article 6 does not in such cases require the possibility to challenge the merits,[242] if the manner on which the initial administrative decision was adopted sufficiently complies with the Article 6 requirements.[243] In other words, if the administrative decision making has been far from quasi-judicial, Article 6 requires that the applicant must be able to challenge such a decision before a court or tribunal on questions of both fact and law.[244] If the court or tribunal in question is able to give a ruling on the applicant's complaints, the Article 6

239 *Le Compte, Van Leuven and De Meyere v. Belgium*, App. nos. 6878/75+, §51, 23.6.1981.

240 *Albert and Le Compte v. Belgium*, App. nos. 7299/75+, §37, 10.2.1983, in which the Court found that there was no appellate organ in that case which would have fulfilled the criteria for a court or a tribunal. See also *Terra Woningen B.V. v. the Netherlands*, App. no. 20641/92, §§53–55, 17.12.1996; *Koskinas v. Greece*, App. no. 47760/99, §30, 20.6.2002; *Chevrol v. France*, App. no. 49636/99, §77, 13.2.2003; *Crişan v. Romania*, App. no. 42930/98, §29, 27.5.2003; *Veeber v. Estonia (No. 1)*, App. no. 37571/97, §71, 7.11.2002; *Kilián v. the Czech Republic*, App. no. 48309/99, §31, 7.12.2004; *Capital Bank AD v. Bulgaria*, App. no. 49429/99, §98, 24.11.2005; *Linnekogel v. Switzerland*, App. no. 43874/98, §40, 1.3.2005; *Schmautzer v. Austria*, App. no. 15523/89, §35, 23.10.1995; and *Tsfayo v. the United Kingdom*, App. no. 60860/00, §48, 14.11.2006. See also Chapter 4, section 4.5.1. below.

241 *Kingsley v. the United Kingdom* [GC], App. no. 35605/97, §32, 28.5.2002; and *Tsfayo v. the United Kingdom*, App. no. 60860/00, §46, 14.11.2006.

242 *Zumtobel v. Austria*, App. no. 12235/86, §32, 21.9.1993. See also *ISKCON and 8 Others v. the United Kingdom* (dec.), App. no. 20490/92, 8.3.1994.

243 *Bryan v. the United Kingdom*, App. no. 19178/91, §47, 22.11.1995; *Chapman v. the United Kingdom* [GC], App. no. 27238/95, §124, 18.1.2001; *Potocka and Others v. Poland*, App. no. 33776/96, §58, 4.10.2001; *Holding and Barnes Plc v. the United Kingdom* (dec.), App. no. 2352/02, 12.3.2002; and *A.P.B. Ltd, A.P.P. and E.A.B. v. the United Kingdom* (dec.), App. no. 30552/96, 15.1.1998.

244 See, for example, *Tsfayo v. the United Kingdom*, App. no. 60860/00, §48, 14.11.2006.

requirements are fulfilled even if that court does not have the competence in respect of the complaints of another applicant.[245]

In such cases, the court or tribunal must also have the competence to remedy the situation if the applicant wins his or her case. For example, in the case *Kingsley v. the United Kingdom*, the Court found a violation of Article 6 in respect of access to a court when the reviewing court was not competent to quash the decision rendered by a biased administrative organ.[246] Full jurisdiction required that the reviewing court was not only able to consider the complaint but also had the ability to quash the impugned decision and to remit the case for a new decision.[247]

### 2.5.2. ASSESSMENT OF THE PROPORTIONALITY OF ADMINISTRATIVE DECISIONS

The Court has not yet taken a stand on the issue of whether a court or tribunal reviewing an administrative decision must be competent to also rule upon on the proportionality of that decision. The Court has found in the context of Article 13 that an effective remedy must be one which gives the individual the opportunity to challenge the proportionality of the decision.[248] This question has not yet been decided under Article 6 in respect of civil rights and obligations.[249]

## 2.6. WHICH STAGES OF PROCEEDINGS FALL WITHIN THE SCOPE OF "CIVIL RIGHTS AND OBLIGATIONS"?

### 2.6.1. APPLICABILITY FROM THE START OF JUDICIAL PROCEEDINGS

Article 6 of the Convention normally begins to apply when the court proceedings are instituted.[250] This has most relevance when assessing the reasonable time of

---

245 *Oerlemans v. the Netherlands*, App. no. 12565/86, §56, 27.11.1991; *Zumtobel v. Austria*, App. no. 12235/86, §32, 21.9.1993; *X. v. the United Kingdom* (dec.), App. no. 28530/95, 19.1.1998; *Ortenberg v. Austria*, App. no. 12884/87, §34, 25.11.1994; *Wickramsinghe v. the United Kingdom* (dec.), App. no. 31503/96, 9.12.1997; and *Crabtree v. the United Kingdom* (dec.), App. no. 32788/96, 9.4.1997.

246 *Kingsley v. the United Kingdom* [GC], App. no. 35605/97, §32, 28.5.2002. See also Ian Leigh, "Bias, necessity and the Convention", *Public Law*, Autumn 2002, pp. 407–414.

247 *Albert and Le Compte v. Belgium*, App. nos. 7299/75+, §36, 10.2.1983.

248 *Smith and Grady v. the United Kingdom*, App. nos. 33985/96+, §137, 27.9.1999.

249 Such an allegation was made, however, in the case *Air Canada v. the United Kingdom*, App. no. 18465/91, §57, 5.5.1995.

250 See, for example, *Guincho v. Portugal*, App. no. 8990/80, §29, 10.7.1984.

the proceedings involving determination of civil rights and obligations.[251] It may be relevant also in other contexts, such as when assessing from which point of time onwards the applicant has a right to counsel.

Article 6 may begin to run even before the institution of the court proceedings.[252] This was the case, for example, when the applicants were required to seek rectification in administrative proceedings before they could lodge an appeal before a court,[253] or when the applicants were expected to object to a draft plan for land consolidation prior to a tribunal hearing.[254] In the first situation, the Court found it was only fair to require that this had happened expeditiously, as the applicant had to exhaust that remedy. In the second situation, the Court found that the dispute arose when the objections to the draft plan were officially lodged and not later, when the applicant had instituted tribunal proceedings. Article 6 does not apply, however, to private negotiations aimed at solving a dispute before it is referred to arbitration.[255] By contrast, Article 6 is applicable to arbitration proceedings.[256]

### 2.6.2. ACCESSORY PROCEEDINGS AND INTERIM DECISIONS

Article 6 of the Convention applies not only to the proceedings in which liability is determined but also to any separate court proceedings in which the amount of damages is assessed,[257] or costs are allocated,[258] since these proceedings are a continuation of the substantive litigation.

Article 6 does not normally apply to interlocutory decisions given by the domestic courts. These include, *inter alia*, challenges to the composition of the court.[259] The Court left it open in the case *H. v. France* whether a pretrial

251 See also Chapter 4, section 4.4.3. below.

252 *Golder v. the United Kingdom*, App. no. 4451/70, §32, 21.2.1975.

253 *König v. Germany*, App. no. 6232/73, §98, 28.6.1978; and *Schouten and Meldrum v. the Netherlands*, App. nos. 19005/91+, §62, 9.12.1994.

254 *Erkner and Hofauer v. Austria*, App. no. 9616/81, §64, 23.4.1987; and *Wiesinger v. Austria*, App. no. 11796/85, §51, 30.10.1991.

255 *Lithgow and Others v. the United Kingdom*, App. nos. 9006/80+, §199, 8.7.1986.

256 *Mutu and Pechstein v. Switzerland*, App. nos. 40575/10+, §§56–59, 2.10.2018.

257 *Silva Pontes v. Portugal*, App. no. 14940/89, §33, 23.3.1994; and *Torri v. Italy*, App. no. 26433/95, §19, 1.7.1997.

258 *Robins v. the United Kingdom*, App. no. 22410/93, §30, 23.9.1997; and *Ziegler v. Switzerland*, App. no. 33499/96, §25, 21.2.2002. Proceedings for the award of costs in which the applicant had withdrawn her claim were held not to fall within Article 6, see *Alsterlund v. Sweden* (dec.), App. no. 12446/86, 5.5.1988.

259 *Schreiber and Boetsch v. France* (dec.), App. no. 58751/00, 11.12.2003.

application for legal aid in respect of litigation concerning a civil right and obligation was to be included in the reasonable time guarantee.[260]

### 2.6.3. ORDINARY AND EXTRAORDINARY APPEAL PROCEEDINGS

Article 6 of the Convention does not guarantee a general right to appeal.[261] If the domestic legal system provides the applicant with the possibility to appeal, Article 6 applies also to appeal and judicial review proceedings.[262] The applicant does not have a right to a certain form of an appeal or manner of treatment.[263] As concerns leave-to-appeal proceedings, the applicability of Article 6 has been somewhat uncertain. However, since the judgment in the case *Hansen v. Norway*, the prevailing approach seems to be that Article 6 §1 is applicable to such proceedings.[264] The reasonable time guarantee applies until the time for an appeal or application for judicial review by the parties expires and the judgment becomes final.[265] Article 6 is also applicable to a third-party appeal which has a direct impact on the applicants' civil rights and obligations,[266] and to costs proceedings conducted separately from the substantive "civil" proceedings.[267]

Constitutional disputes may also come within the ambit of Article 6 if the constitutional proceedings have a decisive bearing on the outcome of the dispute in the ordinary courts.[268] In the case *Paksas v. Lithuania* the Court nevertheless held that this did not apply where the disputes related to a presidential decree granting citizenship to an individual as an exceptional measure, or to the determination of whether the President had breached his constitutional oath.[269] It is irrelevant whether the proceedings before a constitutional court concern a

---

260 *H. v. France*, App. no. 10073/82, §49, 24.10.1989. See also *Gutfreund v. France*, App. no. 45681/99, §§38–44, 12.6.2003.

261 A right to appeal is guaranteed only in criminal matters if the Contracting State has ratified Article 2 of Protocol No. 7 to the Convention.

262 *König v. Germany*, App. no. 6232/73, §98, 28.6.1978; and *Delcourt v. Belgium*, App. no. 2689/65, §25, 17.1.1970.

263 *Monnell and Morris v. the United Kingdom*, App. nos. 9562/81+, §56, 2.3.1987.

264 *Hansen v. Norway*, App. no. 15319/09, §55, 2.10.2014. See also *Monnell and Morris v. the United Kingdom*, App. nos. 9562/81+, §54, 2.3.1987; *Martinie v. France* [GC], App. no. 58675/00, §§11 and 53–55, 12.4.2006; and *Pasquini v. San Marino*, App. no. 50956/16, §89, 2.5.2019.

265 *Pugliese v. Italy (No. 2)*, App. no. 11671/85, §16, 24.5.1991; and *Lorenzi, Bernardini and Gritti v. Italy*, App. no. 13301/87, §13, 27.2.1992. In the case *Pretto and Others v. Italy*, App. no. 7984/77, §30, 8.12.1983, the Court held that the reasonable time guarantee ran until the Court of Cassation's judgment was deposited with the court registry, whereupon it became final.

266 *Kakamoukas and Others v. Greece* [GC], App. no. 38311/02, §32, 15.2.2008.

267 *Robins v. the United Kingdom*, App. no. 22410/93, §29, 23.9.1997.

268 *Ruiz-Mateos v. Spain*, App. no. 12952/87, §37, 23.6.1993.

269 *Paksas v. Lithuania* [GC], App. no. 34932/04, §§65–66, 6.1.2011.

referral of a question for a preliminary ruling or a constitutional appeal against judicial decisions, since Article 6 is in principle applicable to both situations.[270] Article 6 §1 can also apply to an interim measure issued by a constitutional court if the conditions indicated in the case *Micallef v. Malta* are fulfilled.[271]

Article 6 does not apply to extraordinary appeals.[272] This is also true when the extraordinary remedies are relied upon after the finding of a violation by the Court.[273] However, Article 6 applies to the new, reopened proceedings after the reopening request has been accepted.[274] Article 6 may apply exceptionally to extraordinary proceedings also when no other civil law remedy exists.[275]

Such an exceptional situation arose in the case *Bochan v. Ukraine*, in which the Court in 2007 found a violation of Article 6 §1 of the Convention on the ground that the decisions of the domestic courts had failed to respect the fair trial guarantees of impartiality, legal certainty and the requirement of sufficient reasons. Relying on the Court's judgment, the applicant sought reopening by lodging an extraordinary appeal before the Ukrainian Supreme Court. However, the court dismissed the appeal, finding that the domestic decisions had been correct and well-founded. The Court considered, in the light of the specific features of the case, that Article 6 §1 applied to the Supreme Court proceedings, and found that that court had grossly and arbitrarily misinterpreted the Court's findings, thus finding a violation of Article 6.[276]

On the other hand, in the Grand Chamber case *Moreira Ferreira v. Portugal (No. 2)*, the Court found no violation even though the Supreme Court had refused to reopen the applicant's criminal case after the Court had found a violation of Article 6. The Court found that the domestic court's reasoning for rejecting the reopening was adequate and in accordance with the Court's case-law. Although the Court had in its initial judgment considered that reopening

---

270 *Voggenreiter v. Germany*, App. no. 47169/99, §§31–33 and 36, 8.1.2004.

271 *Kübler v. Germany*, App. no. 32715/06, §§47–48, 13.1.2011. See also section 2.6.5. below.

272 *Bochan v. Ukraine (No. 2)* [GC], App. no. 22251/08, §44, 5.2.2015; *Moreira Ferreira v. Portugal (No. 2)* [GC], App. no. 19867/12, §§60–67, 11.7.2017; *Sablon v. Belgium*, App. no. 36445/97, §86, 10.4.2001; *Rudan v. Croatia* (dec.), App. no. 45943/99, 13.9.2001; and *Huhtamäki v. Finland*, App. no. 54468/09, §31, 6.3.2012.

273 *Verein gegen Tierfabriken Schweiz (VgT) v. Switzerland (No. 2)*, App. no. 32772/02, §24, 4.10.2007; and *Bochan v. Ukraine (No. 2)* [GC], App. no. 22251/08, §45, 5.2.2015.

274 *Bochan v. Ukraine (No. 2)* [GC], App. no. 22251/08, §§46–50 and 65, 5.2.2015; and *Kaisti v. Finland* (dec.), App. no. 70313/01, 14.9.2004.

275 *Kiiskinen and Kovalainen v. Finland* (dec.), App. no. 26323/95, 1.6.1999; *Nikula v. Finland* (dec.), App. no. 31611/96, 30.11.2000; and *Melis v. Greece*, App. no. 30604/07, §§19–20, 22.7.2010.

276 *Bochan v. Ukraine (No. 2)* [GC], App. no. 22251/08, §§50 and 63–65, 5.2.2015 (violation). See also Pere Pastor Vilanova, "Third parties involved in international litigation proceedings: what are the challenges for the ECHR?", in Paulo Pinto de Albuquerque, Krzysztof Wojtyczek (Eds.), *Judicial Power in a Globalized World – Liber Amicorum Vincent de Gaetano*, Springer, Cham 2019, pp. 377–393, at p. 389.

the case could in principle be a proper way of compensating the applicant for the violation, this was only one option for executing the Court's judgment. Contrary to the *Bochan* case, the ruling by the Supreme Court had not been arbitrary nor had it misinterpreted the Court's judgment.[277]

It can also be necessary to allow reopening in exceptional cases concerning more serious violations under Articles 2 and 3 of the Convention. Such was the case in *Jeronovičs v. Latvia*, in which the Court, having accepted a unilateral declaration by the respondent and struck the case from the list of cases, held that the applicant should be able to request reopening in order to have his case concerning violence by the authorities examined. If the case had not been examined and the applicant had only been compensated by payment of just satisfaction, it would have meant that the State authorities would go unpunished for the most serious violations of the Convention.[278]

### 2.6.4. EXECUTION

Article 6 applies also to the execution of judgments. The Court found in the case *Hornsby v. Greece* that this was particularly relevant in respect of the length of the proceedings, since the requirement of reasonable length also concerned the execution stage.[279] Cases examined by the Court have concerned, for example, the execution of compensation awards[280] or judgments on public housing.[281] In the case *Okyay and Others v. Turkey*, the issue at stake was a failure to close

---

277 *Moreira Ferreira v. Portugal (No. 2)* [GC], App. no. 19867/12, §§85–97, 11.7.2017. The Court reiterated in this case that it did not have jurisdiction to order the reopening of proceedings (§§48–49). See also Sofia Galani (Ed.), "Case and comment: selected decisions from the European Court of Human Rights from July and August 2017 – Article 6 and remedial practice, *Moreira Ferreira v. Portugal (No. 2)* (Application No. 19867/12)", *European Human Rights Law Review*, Issue 6, 2017, pp. 615–617; and Robert Spano, "'Arbitrary or manifestly unreasonable': the arbitrariness exception to the fourth instance doctrine under Article 6 of the European Convention on Human Rights", in Koen Lemmens, Stephan Parmentier, Louise Reyntjens (Eds.), *Human Rights with a Human Touch – Liber Amicorum Paul Lemmens*, Intersentia, Cambridge/Antwerp/Chicago 2019, pp. 523–537, at pp. 535–537.

278 *Jeronovičs v. Latvia* [GC], App. no. 44898/10, §§104 and 116–123, 5.7.2016. See also Sofia Galani (Ed.), "Case and comment: selected decisions from the European Court of Human Rights from July and August 2016 – State's unilateral declarations, *Jeronovičs v. Latvia* (Application No. 44898/10)", *European Human Rights Law Review*, Issue 6, 2016, pp. 687–690.

279 *Hornsby v. Greece*, App. no. 18357/91, §40, 19.3.1997. This case concerned only final judgments, meaning that any appeal possibilities must have been exhausted first. See also Matti Pellonpää, "The European Court of Human rights and the European Union", in Lucius Caflisch, Johan Callewaert, Roderick Liddell, Paul Mahoney, Mark Villiger (Eds.), *Liber Amicorum Luzius Wildhaber: Human Rights, Strasbourg Views/Droits de L'homme, Regards de Strasbourg*, N.P. Engel, Kehl/Strasbourg/Arlington, Va. 2007, pp. 347–370, at p. 368. See also *Ouzounis and Others v. Greece*, App. no. 49144/99, §21, 18.4.2002; and *Romańczyk v. France*, App. no. 7618/05, §53, 18.11.2010.

280 *Burdov v. Russia*, App. no. 59498/00, §35, 7.5.2002.

281 *Teteriny v. Russia*, App. no. 11931/03, §§42–43, 30.6.2005.

down a polluting power station, which was clearly also illegal domestically.[282] In the case *Ekholm v. Finland*, the Court found a violation owing to the non-execution of administrative decisions concerning noise emissions because the local municipal board had failed to execute, for almost 10 years, the decisions of the administrative courts. The decision had been executed only when the application lodged with the Court was communicated to the government.[283] Article 6 has also been applied when the release of an accused person held in pretrial detention was delayed after his acquittal.[284] However, regardless of whether Article 6 is applicable to the initial proceedings, an enforcement title determining civil rights does not necessarily have to result from proceedings to which Article 6 is applicable.[285]

According to the principles adopted in the *Hornsby* case, if the State has lost its case the execution of judgments must take place automatically. The State is also responsible for private parties executing the judgments rendered against them. The State must therefore ensure that, for example, the awarded compensation is paid,[286] the custody of an adopted child is transferred,[287] tenants are evicted[288] and that buildings built without a permit are demolished.[289] The State must also guarantee that court bailiffs are assisted by the police if needed.[290] The State may even be ordered to ensure that the local Bar Association offers an attorney opportunities to exercise his profession as stipulated by the judgment.[291] The Court does not require the existence of any specific type of execution procedure but only needs to ensure that such a procedure is adequate and effective.[292]

The case *Avotiņš v. Latvia* concerned the application of the Brussels I Regulation under the EU law. The Court held that it was compatible with Article 6 §1 to enforce in Latvia a foreign civil judgment rendered by a Cypriot

---

282 *Okyay and Others v. Turkey*, App. no. 36220/97, §73, 12.7.2005. See also David Harris, Michael O'Boyle, Ed Bates, Carla Buckley, *Law of the European Convention on Human Rights*, 4th edition, Oxford University Press, Oxford 2018, pp. 397–398.

283 *Ekholm v. Finland*, App. no. 68050/01, §§72–75, 24.7.2007.

284 *Assanidze v. Georgia* [GC], App. no. 71503/01, §183, 8.4.2004. See also Francis G. Jacobs, Robin C.A. White, Clare Owey, *The European Convention on Human Rights*, Oxford University Press, Oxford 2017, p. 290.

285 *Buj v. Croatia*, App. no. 24661/02, §19, 1.6.2006.

286 *Satka and Others v. Greece*, App. no. 55828/00, §57, 27.3.2003.

287 *Pini and Others v. Romania*, App. no. 78028/01, §183, 22.6.2004.

288 *Immobiliare Saffi v. Italy* [GC], App. no. 22774/93, §66, 28.7.1999; and *Popov v. Moldova*, App. no. 74153/01, §54, 18.1.2005.

289 *Antonetto v. Italy*, App. no. 15918/89, §29, 20.7.2000; and *Kyrtatos v. Greece*, App. no. 41666/98, §31, 22.5.2003.

290 *Immobiliare Saffi v. Italy* [GC], App. no. 22774/93, §70, 28.7.1999. See also Arman Zrvandyan, *Casebook on European Fair Trial Standards in Administrative Justice*, Council of Europe Publishing, Strasbourg 2016, pp. 124–125.

291 *Turczanik v. Poland*, App. no. 38064/97, §51, 5.7.2005.

292 *Fociac v. Romania*, App. no. 2577/02, §69, 3.2.2005.

court even though the applicant had not been summonsed properly by the latter court. The applicant had had the opportunity to seek the reopening of his case in Cyprus, an opportunity he had failed to take.[293]

The Court has found that referring to a lack of money[294] or other resources[295] is not an acceptable reason not to execute judgments. Sometimes certain specific circumstances may justify delays in the execution of judgments if they do not deprive the applicant of the right protected by Article 6.[296] Such a situation was at stake, for example, in the case *Casa di Cura Valle Fiorita S.r.l. v. Italy*, in which squatters had occupied a building and had been evicted but the eviction order was not enforced for many years for social reasons because of fears about public disorder. The Court held that even though such reasons could justify delays in execution, they could not justify the fact that the eviction order was not enforced at all.[297] Similarly, the conduct of the parties may justify certain delays.[298] The State has, however, the burden of proof to show there is an acceptable reason for any delays.[299] The State's obligation to proceed to a rapid execution becomes greater the poorer the applicant's situation.[300] In the case *Jasiūnienė v. Lithuania*, the Court found the non-execution of a judgment to be a grave violation of Article 6 because it had deprived the right protected by the Convention of all useful effect.[301]

### 2.6.5. INTERIM MEASURES

Although Article 6 applies to execution, it does not normally apply to interim measures issued by a court, such as requests to stay proceedings.[302] The reason

---

293 *Avotiņš v. Latvia* [GC], App. no. 17502/07, §§120–127, 23.5.2016. See also *Saccoccia v. Austria* (dec.), App. no. 69917/01, 5.7.2007.

294 *Tchokontio Happi v. France*, App. no. 65829/12, §§50–52, 9.4.2015; and *Burdov v. Russia*, App. no. 59498/00, §35, 7.5.2002. The failure to execute a judgment debt may also be a breach of the right to property under Article 1 of Protocol No. 1 to the Convention. For the obligation to pay enforcement costs, see *Apostol v. Georgia*, App. no. 40765/02, §§62–63, 28.11.2006.

295 For example, for public housing, see *Shpakovskiy v. Russia*, App. no. 41307/02, §29, 7.7.2005.

296 *Burdov v. Russia*, App. no. 59498/00, §35, 7.5.2002. See also Arman Zrvandyan, *Casebook on European Fair Trial Standards in Administrative Justice*, Council of Europe Publishing, Strasbourg 2016, pp. 125–126.

297 *Casa di Cura Valle Fiorita S.r.l. v. Italy*, App. no. 67944/13, §§53–54, 13.12.2018.

298 *Jasiūnienė v. Lithuania*, App. no. 41510/98, §29, 6.3.2003.

299 *Dubenko v. Ukraine*, App. no. 74221/01, §46, 11.1.2005.

300 Compare, for example, with *Dubenko v. Ukraine*, App. no. 74221/01, §45, 11.1.2005, in which the applicant needed money to avoid bankruptcy; and *Shmalko v. Ukraine*, App. no. 60750/00, §44, 20.7.2004, which concerned the payment for medication.

301 *Jasiūnienė v. Lithuania*, App. no. 41510/98, §§30–31, 6.3.2003.

302 *Lamprecht v. Austria* (dec.), App. no. 71888/01, 25.3.2004 (preservation of evidence); and *Hagman v. Finland* (dec.), App. no. 41765/98, 14.1.2003 (stay of forced sale). Article 6 applies, however, where an interim order for relief effectively determines the merits, see *Markass Car Hire Ltd v. Cyprus* (dec.), App. no. 51591/99, 23.10.2001.

for this is that civil rights and obligations are determined within the meaning of Article 6 of the Convention only when the case is considered on its merits. Although this is an acceptable interpretation, it does not necessarily take into account the fact that interim measures may have relevance to the outcome of the case. Therefore, the Court found in 2009, in its Grand Chamber judgment in the case *Micallef v. Malta*, that Article 6 applied exceptionally to interim measures if both the interim measure and the merits of the case determined to a significant extent civil rights and obligations and when the violations caused by interim measures were no longer rectifiable at the later stage of the proceedings. The application of an interim measure required, however, that the following conditions were fulfilled: both the interim measure and the merits had to determine civil rights or obligations; and these rights or obligations were effectively determined through such an interim measure. How long the interim measure was in force was not relevant.[303] In such a situation it may be acceptable for the procedure to not comply with all of the requirements of Article 6.[304]

In a subsequent case, the Court held that Article 6 applied to an interim measure that had the same object as the main proceedings, concerned the same right that was at stake in the main proceedings, and was immediately executable.[305] In the case *Kuczera v. Poland*, the fair trial guarantees would have applied to interim measures, had the case been admissible.[306] In the case *Mercieca v. Malta*, the interim measure determined the same rights as the merits and Article 6 was thus applicable. There was a separate remedy that gave protection against any damage that might not have been redressed when appealing only on the merits.[307] The Court has also held in a disciplinary matter that an interim measure prohibiting an attorney from acting as legal counsel during the duration of the investigation into a criminal matter is civil, both as regards the merits (disciplinary matter) and the interim measure, and that the civil limb of Article 6 applies. Therefore, the applicant's right to an oral hearing had been violated when the disciplinary board rejected the request for an oral hearing when deciding on the interim measure.[308]

---

303 *Micallef v. Malta* [GC], App. no. 17056/06, §§83–85, 15.10.2009. See also Karen Reid, *A Practitioner's Guide to the European Convention on Human Rights*, Sweet & Maxwell/Thomson Reuters, London 2019, p. 126. See also *Central Mediterranean Development Corporation Limited v. Malta (No. 2)*, App. no. 35829/03, §§21–23, 24.10.2006.

304 *Micallef v. Malta* [GC], App. no. 17056/06, §86, 15.10.2009. See also Dragoljub Popović, "Access to Justice in the Recent Grand Chamber Judgments of the European Court of Human Rights", in Sonia Morano-Foadi, Lucy Vickers (Eds.), *Fundamental Rights in the EU – A Matter for Two Courts*, Hart Publishing, Oxford and Portland, Or. 2015, pp. 201–217, at pp. 206–208.

305 *RTBF v. Belgium*, App. no. 50084/06, §§64–65, 29.3.2011.

306 *Kuczera v. Poland*, App. no. 275/02, §50, 14.9.2010. In that case the Court used a formulation "even assuming that Article 6 is applicable". The case was declared inadmissible as it had been lodged too late.

307 *Mercieca and Others v. Malta*, App. no. 21974/07, §§50–51, 14.6.2011.

308 *Blum v. Austria*, App. no. 33060/10, §§61–74, 5.4.2016.

# CHAPTER 3
# CRIMINAL CHARGE

**Article 6: Right to a fair trial**

1. *In the determination ... of any criminal charge against him ...*

## 3.1. AUTONOMOUS INTERPRETATION

Article 6 of the Convention is also applicable when the case concerns a "criminal charge" against an individual. As in the context of other key concepts of the Convention, the concept of criminal charge has also been given its own autonomous interpretation, the content of which is independent of the content given to this concept in the domestic law of Contracting States.[309] The autonomous interpretation by the Court aims at unifying the national case-laws and the procedural norms in different Contracting States. The autonomous interpretation of Article 6 also brings certain procedures, which at the domestic level are regarded as administrative, within the scope of criminal procedural guarantees of Article 6.

A criminal charge consists of two separate concepts, namely "criminal" and "charge", both of which have to coexist for the criminal limb of Article 6 to apply. Both of these elements will be examined separately.

## 3.2. THREE CRITERIA OF AN OFFENCE (THE *ENGEL* CRITERIA)

The autonomous interpretation of the concept of "criminal" was developed in the case *Engel and Others v. the Netherlands*, in which the Court created a test to clarify the concept of an offence. The test is composed of three different criteria which can either alone or together qualify an act as an offence.

309 *Blokhin v. Russia* [GC], App. no. 47152/06, §179, 23.3.2016; and *Adolf v. Austria*, App. no. 8269/78, §30, 26.3.1982.

These criteria are: classification of the act in the legal system of the respondent State; the nature of the offence; and the degree of severity of penalty that the person concerned risks incurring.[310] The first criterion, if met, is decisive in itself. In situations in which the act has not been classified as an offence in domestic law, the two other criteria become relevant. The criteria are both alternative and cumulative. Therefore, an act can be defined as an offence solely on the basis of its nature or on the basis of the penalties. Even if none of the criteria are fulfilled as such, an act can qualify as an offence and fall within the scope of the criminal limb of Article 6 on the basis of the cumulative effect of all three criteria.[311]

### 3.2.1. CLASSIFICATION IN DOMESTIC LAW

The first part of the *Engel* test concerns the classification of the act in the legal system of the respondent State. If in domestic law an act is classified an as offence, it is automatically also an offence for the purposes of Article 6 of the Convention. Therefore, if an act already qualifies as an offence in domestic law, the proceedings must fulfil the general Article 6 §1 fair trial requirements and the specific requirements in Article 6 §3 concerning criminal proceedings.

### 3.2.2. NATURE AND PURPOSE OF THE ACT

If the act does not fulfil the first criterion, the analysis must be continued to the second criterion concerning the nature and purpose of the act. In order to qualify as an offence, the nature of the provision concerning the act must, first of all, be such that it aims to deter, punish or prevent reoffending. The main purpose of the provision must not be compensatory or concern monetary liability.[312] In addition, the legal rule in question must be directed towards all citizens and not just towards a given group possessing a special status.[313] It may, however, be restricted to relate to wider, specific categories of people, such as taxpayers,

---

310 *Engel and Others v. the Netherlands*, App. nos. 5100/71+, §82, 8.6.1976. See also David Harris, Michael O'Boyle, Ed Bates, Carla Buckley, *Law of the European Convention on Human Rights*, 4th edition, Oxford University Press, Oxford 2018, pp. 377–378.

311 *Ezeh and Connors v. the United Kingdom*, App. nos. 39665/98+, §86, 9.10.2003; and *Bendenoun v. France*, App. no. 12547/86, §47, 24.2.1994.

312 *Janosevic v. Sweden*, App. no. 34619/9, §68, 23.7.2002; and *Porter v. the United Kingdom* (dec.), App. no. 1514/02, 8.4.2003. In the latter case the aim was regarded as compensatory.

313 *Lauko v. Slovakia*, App. no. 26138/95, §58, 2.9.1998. The provision was directed towards all citizens, not just a given, restricted group.

drivers or road users.[314] The fact that the act in question concerns a minor act or negligence does not deprive it of its criminal nature.[315]

### 3.2.2.1. *Disciplinary Proceedings*

According to the Court's case-law, it is acceptable to separate criminal proceedings from disciplinary proceedings since the criminal limb of Article 6 and its procedural guarantees do not normally apply to the latter. However, disciplinary sanctions which have consequences for a person's right to practise a profession fall within the civil limb of Article 6 and the same guarantees apply to them as in civil proceedings in general.[316]

The Court has in its case-law examined many cases which, according to domestic law have not been criminal but disciplinary, or have concerned the breach of certain rules, but which nevertheless have been regarded as criminal in accordance with the *Engel* criteria as a result of their nature or sanctions. It is not easy to draw any clear and conclusive line of interpretation in this matter, as in many cases the analysis of the nature of the act and its sanctions has concerned the specific facts or merits of the case. Nonetheless, the nature of the act and its sanctions must fulfil certain general characteristics before Article 6 becomes applicable under its criminal limb to such proceedings.

In the context of disciplinary sanctions, decisive relevance has been given to whether the proceedings concern only a certain specific group of people who hold a special position in society – such as army personnel, police officers or prisoners – or whether they concern the wider population's disrespect for the norms of society. Only the latter's misdemeanours are in general defined as offences and fall within the scope of Article 6.[317] For example, in the case *Ezeh and Connors v. the United Kingdom*, the applicants were convicted of violent threat and assault following prison disciplinary proceedings and given a disciplinary sanction prolonging their time in custody by several days. Although such punishment would normally only concern prisoners whose conduct fell outside the criminal limb of Article 6, the same acts were punishable as offences under the generally applicable criminal law outside of prison. This fact, together with the fact that the applicants' actual time in custody was extended, led to

---

314 *Bendenoun v. France*, App. no. 12547/86, §46, 24.2.1994.

315 *Ezeh and Connors v. the United Kingdom*, App. nos. 39665/98+, §104, 9.10.2003; and *Lauko v. Slovakia*, App. no. 26138/95, §57, 2.9.1998.

316 *Müller-Hartburg v. Austria*, App. no. 47195/06, §42, 19.2.2013; *König v. Germany*, App. no. 6232/73, §§87–95, 28.6.1978; *W.R. v. Austria*, App. no. 26602/95, §§25–31, 21.12.1999; *Goriany v. Austria*, App. no. 31356/04, §21, 10.12.2009; and *Blum v. Austria*, App. no. 33060/10, §§59–60, 5.4.2016.

317 *Engel and Others v. the Netherlands*, App. nos. 5100/71+, §§28, 30 and 103–107, 8.6.1976.

the conclusion that the acts were regarded as criminal within the meaning of Article 6.[318] On the other hand, decisions which clearly concern order within prisons, such as transferring a prisoner to a special ward[319] or deciding on prison leave,[320] are not matters falling within the scope of the criminal limb of Article 6. However, recently, the Court has often considered that the *civil* limb of Article 6 can be applicable to matters concerning the maintenance of order or discipline in prisons.[321] As regards disciplinary proceedings before sport federation tribunals, the Court has held that the criminal limb of Article 6 does not apply.[322]

Besides those cases concerning certain specific groups, the "nature and purpose of the act" criterion has also considered the applicability of the provision more generally to the wider public. In the case *Weber v. Switzerland*, a sanction was imposed on the applicant in disciplinary proceedings for having disclosed confidential information relating to a criminal investigation. Although the proceedings were not regarded as criminal under Swiss criminal law, the Court found them to be criminal because such proceedings also applied, in addition to judges and other lawyers, to other persons and therefore concerned the wider public.[323] The proceedings were also regarded as criminal in the case *Demicoli v. Malta*, in which a journalist was punished for having disclosed in his article confidential parliamentary information. The ground for this was that the publication took place outside Parliament and the sanctions were not only limited to persons working in Parliament but applied to everybody.[324]

By contrast, a sanction imposed on an attorney for disorderly conduct before a court was not considered to be criminal in the case *Ravnsborg v. Sweden*. In this

---

318 *Ezeh and Connors v. the United Kingdom*, App. nos. 39665/98+, §104, 9.10.2003. See also Francis G. Jacobs, Robin C.A. White, Clare Owey, *The European Convention on Human Rights*, Oxford University Press, Oxford 2017, p. 276. Conversely, in the case *Štitić v. Croatia*, App. no. 29660/03, §56, 8.11.2007, the imposition of seven days' solitary confinement did not fall within the scope of Article 6, as it did not in any way extend the applicant's prison term.

319 *Enea v. Italy* [GC], App. no. 74912/01, §98, 17.9.2009.

320 *Boulois v. Luxembourg* [GC], App. no. 37575/04, §85, 3.4.2012. In this case, the Court found that the civil limb of Article 6 did not apply to prison leave either. There was no legal basis for such a right in domestic law, or in the Convention. See also Arman Zrvandyan, *Casebook on European Fair Trial Standards in Administrative Justice*, Council of Europe Publishing, Strasbourg 2016, p. 25.

321 In the case *Enea v. Italy* [GC], App. no. 74912/01, §98, 17.9.2009, the transfer of a prisoner to a special ward was considered a civil right by the Court and the civil limb of Article 6 §1 thus applied. See also *Musumeci v. Italy*, App. no. 33695/96, §36, 11.1.2005; *Gülmez v. Turkey*, App. no. 16330/02, §§27–31, 20.5.2008; and *Stegarescu and Bahrin v. Portugal*, App. no. 46194/06, §§35–39, 6.4.2010.

322 *Ali Rıza and Others v. Turkey*, App. nos. 30226/10+, §154, 28.1.2020.

323 *Weber v. Switzerland*, App. no. 11034/84, §33, 22.5.1990. See also Karen Reid, *A Practitioner's Guide to the European Convention on Human Rights*, Sweet & Maxwell/Thomson Reuters, London 2019, p. 116.

324 *Demicoli v. Malta*, App. no. 13057/87, §§33–34, 27.8.1991.

case, the Court found the situation to be different from the *Weber* and *Demicoli* cases because measures ordered by courts under such rules were more akin to the exercise of disciplinary powers than to the imposition of a punishment for committing a criminal offence.[325] Also in the Grand Chamber case *Ramos Nunes de Carvalho e Sá v. Portugal*, the Court considered that a matter relating to a judge's disciplinary sanction, which concerned the issue of whether there was a lack of an oral hearing, fell within the civil limb of Article 6. The Court held, as a result, that the applicant had not been heard in an adequate manner as required by Article 6, taking into account the severity of the accusations against him and the limited nature of the legal safeguards available in the disciplinary proceedings.[326]

Similarly, in its most recent Grand Chamber judgment in *Gestur Jónsson and Ragnar Halldór Hall v. Iceland*, the Court considered that the proceedings concerning the applicant lawyers convicted *in absentia* of contempt of court and of delaying the proceedings did not involve the determination of a "criminal charge" within the autonomous meaning of Article 6. It found that the first and the second *Engel* criteria were not met. As to the third *Engel* criterion and in contrast to previous contempt-of-court cases in which Article 6 was found to apply, the misconduct for which the applicants had been held liable could not have been sanctioned by imprisonment, nor could the fines imposed be converted into a deprivation of liberty in the event of non-payment. Nor had the fines been entered on the applicants' criminal record. The amount of the fines imposed, 6,200 euros, and the absence of an upper statutory limit on their amount, did not suffice for the Court to deem the severity and nature of the sanction as "criminal" within the autonomous sense of Article 6 of the Convention.[327]

Disciplinary sanctions applying to some liberal professions do not generally fall within the criminal limb of Article 6 despite the fact that the sanctions may be severe, such as significant economic consequences, the withholding

---

325 *Ravnsborg v. Sweden*, App. no. 14220/88, §34, 23.3.1994. Although the fine was convertible into a term of imprisonment, it was not sufficiently important to warrant classifying the situation as criminal. See also *Putz v. Austria*, App. no. 18892/91, §§33–37, 22.2.1996. Compare and contrast with *Mariusz Lewandowski v. Poland*, App. no. 66484/09, §§29–31, 3.7.2012; and *Kyprianou v. Cyprus* [GC], App. no. 73797/01, §§61–64, 15.12.2005.

326 *Ramos Nunes de Carvalho e Sá v. Portugal* [GC], App. nos. 55391/13+, §214, 6.11.2018. See also Eléonore Aubry,"Disciplinary proceedings – *Ramos Nunes de Carvalho E SÁ v. Portugal* (Application Nos. 57728/13, 55391/13)", *European Human Rights Law Review*, Issue 2, 2019, pp. 221–224; and Stefan Kieber, "The jurisprudence of the European Court of Human Rights in 2018", *European Yearbook on Human Rights 2019*, pp. 189–220, at pp. 198–200.

327 *Gestur Jónsson and Ragnar Halldór Hall v. Iceland* [GC], App. nos. 68273/14+, §§84–98, 22.12.2020.

of rights, or dismissal. Such proceedings include, for example, disciplinary proceedings for improper conduct by attorneys,[328] medical doctors,[329] priests[330] or holders of a taxi licence.[331] Such sanctions may be more properly examined under civil rights and obligations and thus fall within the civil limb of Article 6. However, the sanction of five days' imprisonment imposed on an attorney for contempt of court fell within the criminal limb of Article 6.[332] On the other hand, the striking off of an attorney from the register of lawyers kept by a Bar Association and the imposition of a fine for fraud did not render the disciplinary proceedings against the applicant criminal, nor had they any effect on the *ne bis in idem* rule.[333] In the case *Albert and Le Compte v. Belgium*, the Court held that it was not necessary to decide whether or not disciplinary proceedings fell within the criminal limb of Article 6, since the right to continue to practise constituted a private right and thus a civil right within the meaning of Article 6.[334]

---

328 *Brown v. the United Kingdom* (dec.), App. no. 38644/97, 24.11.998. In this case an attorney was given a disciplinary sanction for his connections to criminal activities. Improper conduct by an attorney was also at stake in the case *Ravnsborg v. Sweden*, App. no. 14220/88, §34, 23.3.1994. In the case *Klein v. Austria* (dec.), App. no. 57028/00, 4.5.2006, the attorney had lost his licence as he was subject to bankruptcy proceedings. As far as his loss of pension was concerned, the case was not criminal. Nor in the case *Müller-Hartburg v. Austria*, App. no. 47195/06, §§40–49, 19.2.2013, were the disciplinary proceedings regarded as criminal in nature, although the attorney lost his living because of the striking off from the register of lawyers kept by the Vienna Bar Association. In the case *Blum v. Austria*, App. no. 33060/10, §§59–60, 5.4.2016, the Court held that an interim measure prohibiting the applicant from acting as a legal counsel fell within the civil limb of Article 6, both in terms of the merits (disciplinary sanction) and the interim measure.

329 The case *Wickramsinghe v. the United Kingdom* (dec.), App. no. 31503/96, 9.12.1997, concerned disciplinary sanctions imposed on a medical doctor. The situation was also the same in the case *Haarvig v. Norway* (dec.), App. no. 11187/05, 11.12.2007.

330 The case *Tyler v. the United Kingdom* (dec.), App. no. 21283/93, 5.4.1994, concerned a priest in the Church of England who was dismissed for adultery as a result of a decision taken by the judicial organs of the Church. A dismissal was also considered to be disciplinary in the cases *Kulpakko v. Finland* (dec.), App. no. 25761/94, 15.5.1996; and *Ahtinen v. Finland*, App. no. 48907/99, §§41–43, 23.9.2008. The latter case concerned the transfer of the applicant to another parish and the fact that he could not challenge this decision taken by the Church administration before the general courts. The Court held that, on the basis of domestic law or the Court's case-law, there were no grounds to consider that the applicant had a right under Article 6. Article 6 did not therefore apply.

331 *Manasson v. Sweden* (dec.), App. no. 41265/98, 8.4.2003.

332 *Kyprianou v. Cyprus* [GC], App. no. 73797/01, §61, 15.12.2005. See also Giovanni Bonello, "More common law than common sense – how the European Court of Human Rights saves the United Kingdom from itself", *Human Rights Law Journal* (HRLJ), vol. 34, nos. 7–12, 31 December 2014, pp. 239–245, at pp. 241–242.

333 *Müller-Hartburg v. Austria*, App. no. 47195/06, §§40–49 and 65–67, 19.2.2013.

334 *Albert and Le Compte v. Belgium*, App. nos. 7299/75+, §30, 10.2.1983. See also David Harris, Michael O'Boyle, Ed Bates, Carla Buckley, *Law of the European Convention on Human Rights*, 4th edition, Oxford University Press, Oxford 2018, p. 394.

Similarly, disciplinary proceedings concerning civil servants may fall within the civil limb of Article 6.[335] They do not normally fall within the criminal limb of Article 6 even if the proceedings lead to the civil servant's dismissal or to other severe consequences, such as restricting pension rights or suspension from office.[336]

#### *3.2.2.2. Misdemeanours and Petty Offences*

Certain proceedings concerning misdemeanours and petty offences may, according to the Court's case-law, be regarded as criminal even though they have not been classified as criminal in the domestic legal system. In the case *Öztürk v. Germany*, careless driving was classified in the domestic system as a "regulatory offence" but not a criminal offence. Despite the minor nature of the offence, the Court considered it to be criminal for the purposes of Article 6 of the Convention. It was relevant that the proceedings fulfilled all the criteria established in the Court's case-law: they were directed towards all citizens in their capacity as road users, they prescribed conduct of a certain kind, and made the resultant requirement subject to a sanction that was punitive. It was also relevant that misconduct of the kind committed by the applicant continued to be classified as part of criminal law in the vast majority of the Contracting States.[337] Similarly, the accumulation or docking of points on a licence for traffic offences

---

335 In the case *G. v. Finland*, App. no. 33173/05, §34, 27.1.2009, the dismissal of a judge was examined under the civil limb of Article 6 in accordance with the principles established in the case *Vilho Eskelinen and Others v. Finland* [GC], App. no. 63235/00, 19.4.2007. Article 6 of the Convention applied to ordinary labour disputes involving civil servants. For Article 6 not to be applicable, the State needed to show that the civil servant in question did not have access to a court according to domestic law and that such lack of access was justified. In that case it was clear that the applicants had had access to a court and Article 6 §1 was thus applicable. The Court found a violation in the case due to the excessive length of the proceedings.

336 *Linde Falero v. Spain* (dec.), App. no. 51535/99, 22.6.2000. In the case *X. v. the United Kingdom* (dec.), App. no. 8496/79, 8.10.1980, the applicant was a police officer who had been given a disciplinary sanction. The case *Kremzow v. Austria* (dec.), App. no. 16417/90, 7.11.1990, concerned a retired judge who had committed a homicide and who thereafter in the disciplinary proceedings lost his pension rights. Dismissal from the military was not a criminal sanction within the meaning of Article 6, see *Tepeli and Others v. Turkey* (dec.), App. no. 31876/96, 11.9.2001; *Moullet v. France* (dec.), App. no. 44485/98, 26.3.2002; *Trubić v. Croatia* (dec.), App. no. 44887/10, §26, 2.10.2012; and *Suküt v. Turkey* (dec.), App. no. 59773/00, 11.9.2007. Nor was it a criminal sanction to dismiss a bailiff as a result of disciplinary proceedings, see *Bayer v. Germany*, App. no. 8453/04, §37, 16.7.2009; or a judge, see the case *Oleksandr Volkov v. Ukraine*, App. no. 21722/11, §§94–95, 9.1.2013; and *Kamenos v. Cyprus*, App. no. 147/07, §§51–53, 31.10.2017.

337 *Öztürk v. Germany*, App. no. 8544/79, §53, 21.2.1984. See also David Harris, Michael O'Boyle, Ed Bates, Carla Buckley, *Law of the European Convention on Human Rights*, 4th edition, Oxford University Press, Oxford 2018, p. 378; and Francis G. Jacobs, Robin C.A. White, Clare Owey, *The European Convention on Human Rights*, Oxford University Press, Oxford 2017, p. 277.

may bring the matter within the criminal limb of Article 6 if being given or penalised a certain number of points leads to the withdrawal of a driving licence or a limited-time ban from driving.[338]

Some economic sanctions imposed for violating administrative rules or ordinances have also been regarded as criminal within the meaning of Article 6 if their aim has been punitive or deterrent. Such sanctions are, for example, those imposed for violation of trade or business rules or competition law,[339] restrictions imposed on the organisation of public demonstrations and the sanctions levied for their violation,[340] as well as violations of customs rules whose aim is to prevent money laundering and terrorism and for which fines can be imposed.[341] In contrast, an administrative fine imposed for failure to respect planning regulations,[342] the withdrawal of the right to sell alcohol[343] or the withdrawal of a driving licence or a driving ban without establishment of guilt[344] are not considered criminal and therefore fall outside the criminal limb of Article 6.

### 3.2.2.3. *Applicability to the Wider Public*

It is also of relevance that the legal rule in question is directed towards all citizens and not towards a given group possessing a special status. This issue has been examined by the Court, for example, in the context of taxation cases. In particular, the Court has found in its case-law that imposing tax surcharges in taxation proceedings brings the matter under the criminal limb of Article 6.[345] In the Grand Chamber case *Jussila v. Finland*, the tax surcharges were examined

338 *Malige v. France*, App. no. 27812/95, §§38–39, 23.9.1998.

339 In the case *Deweer v. Belgium*, App. no. 6903/75, §§45–46, 27.2.1989, the Court examined the background of the applicable law in question, which was enacted to prevent black market trade after the War, as well as the nature of the imposed sanction. The criminal limb of Article 6 was applicable to the case. The situation was similar in the case *Garyfallou ABBE v. Greece*, App. no. 18996/91, §34, 24.9.1997, in which the severity of the imposed sanction was decisive. However, in the case *OOO Neste St. Petersburg and Others v. Russia* (dec.), App. nos. 69042/01+, 3.6.2004, the *Engel* criteria were not fulfilled. The competition law norm was enacted to prevent a creation of a monopoly and its applicability was restricted only to certain activities. Nor was the sanction such that it would have led to the application of Article 6.

340 *Belilos v. Switzerland*, App. no. 10328/83, §62, 29.4.1988; and *Ziliberberg v. Moldova*, App. no. 61821/00, §§32–36, 1.2.2005.

341 *Saquetti Iglesias v. Spain*, App. no. 50514/13, §§29–30, 30.6.2020.

342 *Inocencio v. Portugal* (dec.), App. no. 43862/98, 11.1.2001.

343 *Tre Traktörer AB v. Sweden*, App. no. 10873/84, §46, 7.7.1989. A withdrawal of a permit to sell alcohol was not a punishment directed towards the permit holder but depended on the suitability of the person to sell alcohol.

344 *Escoubet v. Belgium* [GC], App. no. 26780/95, §§31–39, 28.10.1999. Compare with *Malige v. France*, App. no. 27812/95, §§39–40, 23.9.1998.

345 *Janosevic v. Sweden*, App. no. 34619/97, §71, 23.7.2002. See also Arman Zrvandyan, *Casebook on European Fair Trial Standards in Administrative Justice*, Council of Europe Publishing, Strasbourg 2016, pp. 22–23.

in accordance with the *Engel* criteria. The Court found first that in domestic law the tax surcharges were not classified as criminal but as part of the fiscal regime. This was, however, not decisive. The second criterion, the nature of the offence, was more important. The Court observed that tax surcharges were imposed by general legal provisions applying to all taxpayers generally. The tax surcharges were not intended to provide pecuniary compensation for damage but to act as a punishment to deter reoffending. This was enough to establish the criminal nature of the offence, and the minor nature of the penalty could not remove the matter from the scope of Article 6.[346] Prior to the *Jussila* case, the Court's case-law was somewhat inconsistent, since sometimes minor tax surcharges did not necessarily lead to the application of Article 6 although tax surcharges otherwise fulfilled the *Engel* criteria.[347]

Similarly, in the case *Ruotsalainen v. Finland*, the deterrent and punitive purpose of the sanction and its applicability to the wider public rendered the proceedings criminal. The applicant had been ordered in administrative law proceedings to pay three times the fuel fee for having used more leniently taxed fuel than diesel in the tank of his vehicle, without having paid the due additional tax. The relevant provision was directed towards all citizens rather than towards a group possessing a special status. Moreover, the sanction of paying the fuel fee at three times the normal rate established its character as not only a compensatory measure but also as a deterrent and punitive measure. The Court considered that this suitably established the criminal nature of the offence.[348]

### 3.2.3. NATURE AND SEVERITY OF THE PUNISHMENT

The third *Engel* criterion concerns the nature and severity of the punishment. Attention is drawn to the general nature and severity of the punishment available, not to the punishment actually suffered by the applicant. In the case *Engel v. the Netherlands*, the Court held that the imposition of serious punishments involving deprivation of liberty was to be considered as criminal irrespective

---

346 *Jussila v. Finland* [GC], App. no. 73053/01, §§35–39, 23.11.2006. See also Paul Mahoney, "Flogging a dead horse: the appropriate human rights policy for judicial treatment of competition fines", in David Edward, Jackelyn Maclennan, Assimakis Komninos (Eds.), *Ian S. Forrester – A Scot without Borders, Liber Amicorum, Vol. 1*, Concurrences Review, New York 2015, pp. 225–240, at pp. 234–235.

347 *Morel v. France* (dec.), App. no. 54559/00, 3.6.2003. As the case did not pass the admissibility stage, it cannot be given as much significance as the cases which have been examined on the merits.

348 *Ruotsalainen v. Finland*, App. no. 13079/03, §46, 16.6.2009. The case concerned double jeopardy under Article 4 of Protocol No. 7 to the Convention. As the definition of "criminal" is the same throughout the Convention, the *Engel* criteria applicable under Article 6 §1 of the Convention were applicable also in this case.

of its duration, manner or execution. The purpose of imprisonment was always to act as a deterrent. However, concerning Mr Engel, the Court found that his deprivation of liberty lasting for two days was of too short a duration to fall within the scope of criminal law and he had already served it.[349] Nevertheless, even a minor fine which can be converted into a prison term upon non-payment generally falls within the criminal limb of Article 6.[350] The same is true also for significant monetary payments, such as tax surcharges or fuel fees and duties which cannot be converted into a prison term.[351] Lesser fines which are imposed as the only sanction and which cannot be lead to prison time upon failure to pay or show up on criminal records may also bring a case under the criminal limb of Article 6, in particular if the second criterion, namely the nature of the act, is also fulfilled.[352]

## 3.3. AUTONOMOUS MEANING OF A CHARGE

The second requirement in order for the criminal limb of Article 6 to apply is that a person is charged. As in the context of the definition of criminal, a charge also has an autonomous meaning under Article 6.[353] A person is subject to a "charge" when, *inter alia*, a preliminary investigation has been opened in his or her case and, although not necessarily under arrest, the applicant has officially learned of the investigation or has begun to be affected by it.[354]

A person is charged within the meaning of the Convention when he or she has been arrested,[355] detained,[356] or questioned about his or her suspected involvement in acts constituting a criminal offence, irrespective of the fact

349 *Engel and Others v. the Netherlands*, App. nos. 5100/71+, §85, 8.6.1976. From the reasoning, it can be deduced, however, that a more severe punishment could have brought the disciplinary sanction under the criminal limb of Article 6.

350 *Weber v. Switzerland*, App. no. 11034/84, §34, 22.5.1990. In that case, the applicant was given a fine of 500 francs, which in certain circumstances could be converted into a prison term. See also *Luchaninova v. Ukraine*, App. no. 16347/02, §§39–40, 9.6.2011, in which the applicant had been convicted of petty theft. According to domestic law, it was punishable by a fine or corrective work. As the legal provision in question was of a general character and had a deterrent and punitive purpose, the Court considered that the proceedings at issue were criminal for the purposes of the Convention.

351 *Ruotsalainen v. Finland*, App. no. 13079/03, §46, 16.6.2009; and *Janosevic v. Sweden*, App. no. 34619/97, §69, 23.7.2002.

352 *Lauko v. Slovakia*, App. no. 26138/95, §58, 2.9.1998.

353 *Deweer v. Belgium*, App. no. 6903/75, §42, 27.2.1980.

354 *Eckle v. Germany*, App. no. 8130/78, §73, 15.7.1982; *Kangasluoma v. Finland*, App. no. 48339/99, §26, 20.1.2004; *Ibrahim and Others v. the United Kingdom* [GC], App. nos. 50541/08+, §249, 13.9.2016; and *Simeonovi v. Bulgaria* [GC], App. no. 21980/04, §110, 12.5.2017.

355 *Heaney and McGuinness v. Ireland*, App. no. 34720/97, §§41–43, 21.12.2000; and *Brusco v. France*, App. no. 1466/07, §§47–50, 14.10.2010.

356 *Wemhoff v. Germany*, App. no. 2122/64, §19, 27.6.1968.

whether he or she is formally treated as a witness.[357] Similarly, a person is charged when he or she has been informed about the pressing of formal charges[358] or when a pretrial investigation against him or her is started and he or she has been informed about it.[359] A person is also charged when he or she is asked to provide the authorities with information or clarification about the suspected crime or, for example, when his or her bank account is frozen, when a seizure, a search of a domicile[360] or an enforcement inquiry[361] is conducted, when a business is closed down by the authorities on the basis of criminal suspicions[362] or when a public prosecutor demands the immunity of a parliamentarian be lifted.[363]

In the case *Deweer v. Belgium*, the Court held that charges were not to be construed as having too formal a content, but that the actual circumstances and the concrete effect of the measures on the applicant's situation had to be taken into account. In that case the fact that a letter had been sent to the applicant by the public prosecutor, advising him of the closure of his business establishment and soliciting him to pay a sum of money as a settlement for avoiding prosecution, amounted to a "criminal charge" which triggered the applicability of Article 6 of the Convention.[364]

## 3.4. WHICH STAGES OF PROCEDURE FALL WITHIN THE SCOPE OF CRIMINAL CHARGE?

### 3.4.1. BEGINNING AND END OF A CRIMINAL CHARGE

The Court has in its case-law taken a stand on what constitutes the beginning of a criminal charge, in particular when assessing the starting point of the criminal

357 *Aleksandr Zaichenko v. Russia*, App. no. 39660/02, §§41–43, 18.2.2010; *Yankov and Others v. Bulgaria*, App. no. 4570/05, §23, 23.9.2010; *Schmid-Laffer v. Switzerland*, App. no. 41269/08, §§30–31, 16.6.2015; *Stirmanov v. Russia*, App. no. 31816/08, §39, 29.1.2019; and *Kalēja v. Latvia*, App. no. 22059/08, §§36–41, 5.10.2017. However, if a person is questioned in the context of a border control and there is no reasonable suspicion that an offence has been committed, there is no criminal charge involved, see *Beghal v. the United Kingdom*, App. no. 4755/16, §121, 28.2.2019.

358 *Pedersen and Baadsgaard v. Denmark* [GC], App. no. 49017/99, §44, 17.12.2004; and *Pélissier and Sassi v. France* [GC], App. no. 25444/94, §66, 25.3.1999.

359 *Kangasluoma v. Finland*, App. no. 48339/99, §26, 20.1.2004.

360 *Funke v. France*, App. no. 10828/84, §44, 25.2.1993; and *T.K. and S.E. v. Finland* (dec.), App. no. 38581/97, 16.3.2004. In the latter case, Article 6 §1 started to apply following a seizure. The Court did not find a violation in respect of the excessive length of the proceedings, even if the proceedings had lasted for more than five years, as the case concerned very extensive economic crimes.

361 *Elomaa v. Finland* (dec.), App. no. 37670/04, 16.3.2010.

362 *Deweer v. Belgium*, App. no. 6903/75, §§9 and 46, 27.2.1980.

363 *Frau v. Italy*, App. no. 12147/86, §14, 19.2.1991.

364 *Deweer v. Belgium*, App. no. 6903/75, §§41–47, 27.2.1980. See also *Blaj v. Romania*, App. no. 36259/04, §§73–74, 8.4.2014.

proceedings in order to assess the reasonable time requirement.[365] A criminal charge starts from the moment when a person is charged. This moment is when a person is arrested,[366] detained,[367] informed about the charges[368] or about the start of a pretrial investigation,[369] or when a person is subject to a seizure, search of domicile[370] or an enforcement inquiry.[371] In tax surcharge cases, the starting moment is when the applicant has been informed about the tax surcharges, for example in the context of a tax inspection report.[372]

A person is being charged until the charges have been finally decided.[373] Article 6 of the Convention does not as such guarantee a right to appeal against the first instance judgment[374] but if the domestic system provides for such a possibility, the fair trial guarantees apply also at the appeal stages.[375] Article 6 ceases to apply when the examination of charges is no longer continued. That is, for example, when the public prosecutor decides not to bring charges, the case is settled or it lapses due to the lack of liability of the accused or some other reason, or when charges are dismissed.[376] If the criminal proceedings have ended in the accused's acquittal, the possible lack of fair trial guarantees no longer has any relevance, and such proceedings can only be complained about as far as the length of the proceedings is concerned.

### 3.4.2. TO WHAT IS A CRIMINAL CHARGE NOT APPLICABLE?

As already stated above, the concept of a criminal charge covers all the stages of the proceedings which fall within the scope of the autonomous interpretation of

---

365 *Corigliano v. Italy*, App. no. 8304/78, §34, 10.12.1982.

366 *Heaney and McGuinness v. Ireland*, App. no. 34720/97, §§41–43, 21.12.2000.

367 *Wemhoff v. Germany*, App. no. 2122/64, §19, 27.6.1968.

368 *Pedersen and Baadsgaard v. Denmark* [GC], App. no. 49017/99, §44, 17.12.2004.

369 *Kangasluoma v. Finland*, App. no. 48339/99, §26, 20.1.2004.

370 *Funke v. France*, App. no. 10828/84, §44, 25.2.1993; and *T.K. and S.E. v. Finland* (dec.), App. no. 38581/97, 16.3.2004. In the latter case Article 6 §1 started to apply from the seizure. The Court did not, however, find a violation in respect of excessive length of the proceedings, even though the proceedings had lasted for more than five years, as the case concerned a very extensive economic crime.

371 *Elomaa v. Finland* (dec.), App. no. 37670/04, 16.3.2010.

372 *Kesko Oyj v. Finland* (dec.), App. no. 65611/09, §21, 25.9.2012.

373 *Eckle v. Germany*, App. no. 8130/78, §77, 15.7.1982.

374 However, a right to appeal is guaranteed in criminal matters if the Contracting State has ratified Article 2 of Protocol No. 7 to the Convention.

375 *Eckle v. Germany*, App. no. 8130/78, §76, 15.7.1982; *Slezevicius v. Lithuania*, App. no. 55479/00, §27, 13.11.2001; and *Antoine v. the United Kingdom* (dec.), App. no. 62960/00, 13.5.2003.

376 *Zuckerstätter and Reschenhofer v. Austria* (dec.), App. no. 76718/01, 2.9.2004; *Khlyustov v. Russia*, App. no. 28975/05, §103, 11.7.2013; and *Batmaz v. Turkey*, App. no. 714/08, §36, 18.2.2014.

a criminal charge, as interpreted by the Court, including the pre-trial stage of the proceedings.[377] The Article 6 guarantees apply also to appeals on points of law and to constitutional proceedings where such proceedings are a further stage of the relevant criminal proceedings and their results may be decisive for the convicted persons.[378] Similarly, supervisory review proceedings resulting in the amendment of a final judgment also fall under the criminal head of Article 6.[379]

On the other hand, a criminal charge does not cover any additional proceedings before or after criminal proceedings, such as the granting of legal aid,[380] pretrial detention (to which Article 5 applies),[381] subjecting a person to police surveillance in order to prevent crime,[382] committal for trial,[383] the reopening of proceedings[384] or a warning given by the police.[385] Proceedings concerning the execution of sentences – such as proceedings for the application of an amnesty,[386] parole proceedings,[387] transfer proceedings under the Convention on the Transfer of Sentenced Persons,[388] or *exequatur* proceedings relating to the enforcement of a forfeiture order made by a foreign court[389] – do not fall within the ambit of the criminal head of Article 6.

Nor do the proceedings on entry, stay or expulsion of an alien concern a criminal charge.[390] Similarly, proceedings concerning the extradition of a person to another State in order to stand trial[391] and proceedings relating to

377 *Dvorski v. Croatia* [GC], App. no. 25703/11, §76, 20.10.2015; and *Vera Fernández-Huidobro v. Spain*, App. no. 74181/01, §§108–114, 6.1.2010.

378 *Meftah and Others v. France* [GC], App. nos. 32911/96+, §40, 26.7.2002; *Gast and Popp v. Germany*, App. no. 29357/95, §§65–66, 25.2.2000; and *Caldas Ramírez de Arrellano v. Spain* (dec.), App. no. 68874/01, 28.1.2003.

379 *Vanyan v. Russia*, App. no. 53203/99, §58, 15.12.2005.

380 *Gutfreund v. France*, App. no. 45681/99, §§36–37, 12.6.2003.

381 *Van Thui v. the Netherlands* (dec.), App. no. 20510/02, 9.12.2004.

382 *Guzzardi v. Italy*, App. no. 7367/76, §108, 6.11.1980.

383 *Mosbeux v. Belgium* (dec.), App. no. 17083/90, 8.4.1991.

384 *Fisher v. Austria* (dec.), App. no. 27569/02, 6.5.2003; *Withey v. the United Kingdom* (dec.), App. no. 59493/00, 26.8.2003; *Kullaa v. Finland* (dec.), App. no. 42621/98, 10.12.2002; and *Moreira Ferreira v. Portugal (No. 2)* [GC], App. no. 19867/12, §§60–61, 11.7.2017. If the request for reopening has been granted, the new proceedings can be regarded as concerning the determination of a criminal charge, see *Löffler v. Austria*, App. no. 30546/96, §§18–19, 3.10.2000; and *Öcalan v. Turkey* (dec.), App. no. 5980/07, 6.7.2010 (which concerned a request for the reopening of criminal proceedings following the Court's finding of a violation).

385 *R. v. the United Kingdom* (dec.), App. no. 33506/05, 4.1.2007; *Raimondo v. Italy*, App. no. 12954/87, §43, 22.2.1994; and *De Tommaso v. Italy* [GC], App. no. 43395/09, §143, 23.2.2017.

386 *Montcornet de Caumont v. France* (dec.), App. no. 59290/00, 13.5.2003.

387 *A. v. Austria*, App. no. 16266/90, Commission decision, 7.5.1990.

388 *Szabó v. Sweden* (dec.), App. no. 28578/03, 27.6.2006. Compare and contrast with *Buijen v. Germany*, App. no. 27804/05, §§40–45, 1.4.2010.

389 *Saccoccia v. Austria* (dec.), App. no. 69917/01, 5.7.2007.

390 *Mamatkulov and Askarov v. Turkey* [GC], App. nos. 46827/99+, §82, 4.2.2005; and *Maaouia v. France* [GC], App. no. 39652/98, §40, 5.10.2000.

391 *Peñafiel Salgado v. Spain* (dec.), App. no. 65964/01, 16.4.2002.

the European arrest warrant[392] do not fall within the scope of a criminal charge. Only in specific situations, in which there is sufficient evidence that the expelled or extradited person would be subjected to a flagrant denial of justice in the receiving country, may an issue be exceptionally raised under Article 6.[393]

The Court found in *Phillips v. the United Kingdom* that Article 6 §1 is undoubtedly applicable to confiscation proceedings. However, the applicability to confiscation proceedings of the principle of presumption of innocence guaranteed in Article 6 §2 is not clear cut. If the confiscation relates to the benefits of a crime for which the applicant has already been convicted, the presumption of innocence does not extend to confiscation proceedings since the applicant's guilt has already been determined. The issuing of a confiscation order following a criminal conviction does not involve a new charge and therefore does not engage Article 6 §2 of the Convention. Article 6 §2 protection ceases with the applicant's conviction and the confiscation proceedings themselves do not create any new criminal charge.[394] On the other hand, forfeiture measures adversely affecting the property rights of third parties in the absence of any threat of criminal proceedings against them do not amount to the "determination of a criminal charge" but fall instead under the civil head of Article 6.[395]

It should also be remembered that Article 6 does not guarantee the right not to be criminally prosecuted.[396] Nor does it guarantee an absolute right to

---

392 *Monedero Angora v. Spain* (dec.), App. no. 41138/05, 7.10.2008.

393 *Mamatkulov and Askarov v. Turkey* [GC], App. nos. 46827/99+, §91, 4.2.2005. The concept of "a flagrant denial of justice" was first defined in the case *Soering v. the United Kingdom* [GC], App. no. 14038/88, §113, 7.7.1989, and has been subsequently confirmed by the Court in a number of cases (see, *inter alia*, *Al-Saadoon and Mufdhi v. the United Kingdom*, App. no. 61498/08, §149, 2.3.2010). In the case *Othman (Abu Qatada) v. the United Kingdom*, App. no. 8139/09, §§258 and 267, 17.1.2012, the Court held that there is a flagrant denial of justice if the trial is clearly incompatible with the basic principles of Article 6. This may include, for example: a conviction *in absentia* with no possibility of subsequently obtaining a fresh determination of the merits of the charge; a trial which is summary in nature and conducted with a total disregard for the rights of the defence; detention without any access to an independent and impartial tribunal in order to have the legality of the detention reviewed; deliberate and systematic refusal of access to a lawyer, especially for an individual detained in a foreign country; or admission of torture evidence. In the *Othman (Abu Qatada)* case, the Court held that the applicant's removal to Jordan was contrary to Article 6 as it was likely that torture evidence would be used against him as his co-defendants had been tortured into providing the case against him.

394 *Phillips v. the United Kingdom*, App. no. 41087/98, §39, 5.7.2001. See also Miklos Hollan, "Confiscation of the proceeds from crime and the principle of presumption of innocence", in Kimmo Nuotio (Ed.), *Festschrift in Honour of Raimo Lahti*, University of Helsinki/Faculty of Law, Helsinki 2007, pp. 363–372. For more details, see Chapter 4, section 4.2.7.1. below.

395 *Air Canada v. the United Kingdom*, App. no. 18465/91, §54, 5.5.1995 (seizure of an aircraft); and *AGOSI v. the United Kingdom*, App. no. 9118/80, §§65–66, 24.10.1986 (forfeiture of gold coins). See also *Silickienė v. Lithuania*, App. no. 20496/02, §§45–46, 10.4.2012.

396 *International Bank for Commerce and Development AD and Others v. Bulgaria*, App. no. 7031/05, §129, 2.6.2016.

obtain a judgment in respect of criminal accusations against an applicant, in particular when there is no fundamental irreversible detrimental effect on the parties.[397] Similarly, a posthumous criminal conviction of a dead applicant violates the Article 6 principles because, by its very nature, it is incompatible with the principle of the equality of arms and all the guarantees of a fair trial.[398]

The criminal limb of Article 6 does not apply to ordinary tax proceedings but it applies if tax surcharges have been imposed, even if the amount of the tax surcharge is low.[399] Article 6 under its criminal head has been held to apply to customs law,[400] to penalties imposed in budgetary and financial matters,[401] and to cases concerning economic, financial and competition law issues.[402] On the other hand, the criminal limb of Article 6 does not apply to private criminal prosecution. The right to have third parties prosecuted or sentenced for a criminal offence cannot be asserted independently in practice unless it is indissociable from the victim's exercise of a right to bring civil proceedings in domestic law, even if only to secure symbolic reparation or to protect a civil right such as the right to "good reputation".[403]

---

397 *Kart v. Turkey* [GC], App. no. 8917/05, §113, 3.12.2009.

398 *Magnitskiy and Others v. Russia*, App. nos. 32631/09+, §281, 27.8.2019. See also Klara Đurkin, "Abuse of whistle-blowers – *Magnitskiy v. Russia* (Application Nos. 32631/09 and 53799/12)", *European Human Rights Law Review*, Issue 6, 2019, pp. 669–671. See also the case *Grădinar v. Moldova*, App. no. 7170/02, §§90–104, 8.4.2008, which concerned proceedings after the death of an accused, conducted upon the request of his wife with an intention to obtain confirmation that her husband had not committed the offence. The Court examined this case under the civil limb of Article 6.

399 *Jussila v. Finland* [GC], App. no. 73053/01, §38, 23.11.2006; *Steininger v. Austria*, App. no. 21539/07, §§34–37, 17.4.2012; and *Chap Ltd v. Armenia*, App. no. 15485/09, §36, 4.5.2017.

400 *Salabiaku v. France*, App. no. 10519/83, 7.10.1988.

401 *Guisset v. France*, App. no. 33933/96, 26.9.2000.

402 *Lilly France S.A. v. France* (dec.), App. no. 53892/00, 3.12.2002; *Dubus S.A. v. France*, App. no. 5242/04, 11.6.2009; *A. Menarini Diagnostics S.R.L. v. Italy*, App. no. 43509/08, 27.9.2011; *Produkcija Plus Storitveno podjetje d.o.o. v. Slovenia*, App. no. 47072/15, §§45–46, 23.10.2018; and *Grande Stevens and Others v. Italy*, App. nos. 18640/10+, §§94–101, 4.3.2014. See also Ian S. Forrester, "Due process in competition cases: is *Menarini* the last word?", in *Liber Amicorum Dean Spielmann – Mélanges en L'honneur de/Essays in Honour of Dean Spielmann*, Wolf Legal Publishers, Oisterwijk 2015, pp. 187–198.

403 *Perez v. France* [GC], App. no. 47287/99, §70, 12.2.2004; and *Arlewin v. Sweden*, App. no. 22302/10, §§51–52, 1.3.2016.

# CHAPTER 4
# RIGHTS GUARANTEED BY ARTICLE 6 §1

**Article 6: Right to a fair trial**

1. *In the determination of his civil rights and obligations or of any criminal charge against him, everyone is entitled to a fair and public hearing within a reasonable time by an independent and impartial tribunal established by law. Judgment shall be pronounced publicly but the press and public may be excluded from all or part of the trial in the interests of morals, public order or national security in a democratic society, where the interests of juveniles or the protection of the private life of the parties so require, or to the extent strictly necessary in the opinion of the court in special circumstances where publicity would prejudice the interests of justice.*

If there is a determination of a person's civil rights and obligations or a criminal charge against him, a person has a right to a fair trial complying with the requirements of Article 6 of the Convention. The Court's primary concern under Article 6 §1 is to assess the overall fairness of the proceedings. In making this evaluation, the Court will look at the proceedings as a whole, having regard to the rights of the defence, the interests of the public and the victims and, where necessary, to the rights of witnesses, while ensuring that the right to have the crime properly prosecuted is upheld.[404]

The wording of Article 6 requires first of all that there is a right to a public trial within a reasonable time in an independent and impartial court or tribunal and that the judgment is pronounced publicly. The criminal proceedings must satisfy the additional requirements of presumption of innocence and the special guarantees established in Article 6 §3.

The right to a fair trial does not only contain the rights expressly mentioned in Article 6 but also those rights which cannot be directly inferred by its wording but which have been added to its scope by the case-law of the Court. Such rights are, for example, the right of access to a court, the right to be heard, the protection of an individual from incriminating him- or herself, equality of arms and the right to have a reasoned judgment or decision.

---

404 *Taxquet v. Belgium* [GC], App. no. 926/05, §84, 16.11.2010; *Al-Khawaja and Tahery v. the United Kingdom* [GC], App. nos. 26766/05+, §118, 15.12.2011; *Gäfgen v. Germany* [GC], App. no. 22978/05, §175, 1.6.2010; and *Doorson v. the Netherlands*, App. no. 20524/92, §70, 26.3.1996.

However, in the context of Article 6 §1 it must be remembered that it does not guarantee a right to perfect or ideal proceedings but to a fair or due process. The Court's supervisory function relates specifically to the overall assessment of the fairness of the proceedings, in which a single procedural mistake is not so relevant if the proceedings as a whole are not rendered unfair. In its examination, the Court pays attention to the rights of the parties, the public, the defendant and victim in criminal proceedings, and, if need be, to the rights of witnesses. However, the admissibility and assessment of evidence, and the application of domestic law are tasks for the domestic courts. In this respect, the Court's role is to evaluate the fairness of the proceedings as a whole.[405]

It is also possible to waive one's right to a fair trial. Such a waiver must, however, be unambiguous; there must be minimum safeguards vis-à-vis the consequences of such a waiver; and the waiver must not be contrary to important public interests.[406] This right to waiver will be examined in more detail below in the context of each of the rights guaranteed by Article 6 §1.

## 4.1. ACCESS TO A COURT

One of the most creative interpretations of the Court's case-law occurred in the case *Golder v. the United Kingdom*, in which the Court guaranteed the applicant a right of access to a court.[407] According to this judgment, Article 6 §1 not only concerns a fair trial after the proceedings have been initiated but also access to a court in the first place. Although the Convention is silent on this, such a right was deduced from the wording of Article 6.

Access to a court is a significant part of the concept of rule of law, which forms the common heritage of all Council of Europe Member States. To not guarantee access to a court under Article 6 would have contradicted the legal principles accepted worldwide and allowed States to block access to a court

---

405 See, for example, *Taxquet v. Belgium* [GC], App. no. 926/05, §84, 16.11.2010; *Al-Khawaja and Tahery v. the United Kingdom* [GC], App. nos. 26766/05+, §118, 15.12.2011; *Gäfgen v. Germany* [GC], App. no. 22978/05, §175, 1.6.2010; and *Doorson v. the Netherlands*, App. no. 20524/92, §70, 26.3.1996.

406 See, for example, *Navalnyy and Ofitserov v. Russia*, App. nos. 46632/13+, §100, 23.2.2016; *Scoppola v. Italy (No. 2)* [GC], App. no. 10249/03, §135, 17.9.2009; and *Natsvlishvili and Togonidze v. Georgia*, App. no. 9043/05, §§90–91, 29.4.2014.

407 *Golder v. the United Kingdom*, App. no. 4451/70, 21.2.1975. In this case, a convicted prisoner was prevented from contacting his counsel to bring a civil action against an employee of the prison. See also Dragoljub Popović, "Access to Justice in the Recent Grand Chamber Judgments of the European Court of Human Rights", in Sonia Morano-Foadi, Lucy Vickers (Eds.), *Fundamental Rights in the EU – A Matter for Two Courts*, Hart Publishing, Oxford and Portland, Or. 2015, pp. 201–217, at pp. 209–210; and David Harris, Michael O'Boyle, Ed Bates, Carla Buckley, *Law of the European Convention on Human Rights*, 4th edition, Oxford University Press, Oxford 2018, pp. 399-400.

without violating the Convention.[408] The Court's interpretation in the *Golder* case offers a solid basis for the right of access to a court.

Nevertheless, the right of access to a court is not absolute. It may be subject to limitations, but these must not restrict or reduce the access left to the individual in such a way or to such an extent that the very essence of the right is impaired.[409] A limitation will not be compatible with Article 6 §1 if it does not pursue a legitimate aim and if there is not a reasonable relationship of proportionality between the means employed and the aim sought to be achieved.[410]

The right of access to a court has most relevance in the context of civil rights and obligations. Civil rights and obligations may concern civil actions between private parties as well as actions against State or administrative decisions.[411] For example, in the case *Posti and Rahko v. Finland*, the Court found that there should have been an opportunity to appeal to a court against a general ministerial decree as the decree concerned the civil rights and obligations of certain individuals.[412] In the case *Baka v. Hungary*, the Court held that there was a violation of the applicant's right of access to a court competent to examine the premature termination of his mandate as President of the Supreme Court, because the curtailment of his tenure by reducing the judicial retirement age was

408 Ibid., §§34–36. See also *Zubac v. Croatia* [GC], App. no. 40160/12, §§76–79, 5.4.2018.

409 *Philis v. Greece (No. 1)*, App. nos. 12750/87+, §59, 27.8.1991; *De Geouffre de la Pradelle v. France*, App. no. 12964/87, §28, 16.12.1992; *Stanev v. Bulgaria* [GC], App. no. 36760/06, §229, 17.1.2012; *Baka v. Hungary* [GC], App. no. 20261/12, §120, 23.6.2016; and *Naït-Liman v. Switzerland* [GC], App. no. 51357/07, §113, 15.3.2018.

410 *Lupeni Greek Catholic Parish and Others v. Romania* [GC], App. no. 76943/11, §89, 29.11.2016; and *Naït-Liman v. Switzerland* [GC], App. no. 51357/07, §115, 15.3.2018. See also Sofia Galani (Ed.), "Case and comment: selected decisions from the European Court of Human Rights from November and December 2016 – Access to a court and religious minorities, *Lupeni Greek Catholic Parish v. Romania* (Application No. 76943/11)", *European Human Rights Law Review*, Issue 2, 2017, pp. 204–206.

411 See, for example, *Sporrong and Lönnroth v. Sweden*, App. nos. 7151/75+, §§84–87, 23.9.1982, which concerned the lack of opportunity to appeal in an expropriation matter; *Keegan v. Ireland*, App. no. 16969/90, §§58–60, 26.5.1994, which concerned the lack of opportunity to appeal in an adoption matter; and *Linnekogel v. Switzerland*, App. no. 43874/98, §§31–40, 1.3.2005, which concerned the lack of opportunity to appeal in an administrative matter.

412 *Posti and Rahko v. Finland*, App. no. 27824/95, §65, 24.9.2002. See also Satu Heikkilä, *From Final Judgment to Final Resolution – Effectiveness of the Execution of Judgments of the European Court of Human Rights in Finland*, Wolf Legal Publishers, Tilburg 2019, p. 412; and Dragoljub Popović, *European Human Rights Law – A Manual: An Introduction to the Strasbourg Court and its Jurisprudence*, Eleven International Publishing, The Hague 2013, p. 185. By contrast, in the case *Alatulkkila and Others v. Finland*, App. no. 33538/96, §52, 28.7.2005 the Court did not find a violation in a similar situation because the applicants had had a chance to challenge the sizes of their fishing quotas (which were based on an international agreement) through extraordinary appeal proceedings in the Supreme Administrative Court, which had examined the legality of the fishing restrictions. See also *Stark and Others v. Finland* (striking out), App. no. 39559/02, 9.10.2007. See also Karen Reid, *A Practitioner's Guide to the European Convention on Human Rights*, Sweet & Maxwell/Thomson Reuters, London 2019, pp. 154–155.

imposed by law. The Court applied to the case the principles established in the *Vilho Eskelinen and Others* case, finding that they did not apply and, therefore, that there should have been access to a court.[413]

The Court also found a violation of Article 6 due to a lack of access to a court in the case *Miryana Petrova v. Bulgaria*, when the applicant could not get the grounds of her dismissal examined by a court. The applicant worked at the National Security Service and had access to State secrets. After a psychological evaluation, she was no longer considered fit to fulfil the criteria for the security clearance required by the job, and she was dismissed. The domestic court refused to examine the ground of dismissal, namely the refusal of security clearance. The Court held that although legitimate national security considerations could justify limitations on the rights enshrined in Article 6 §1 of the Convention, they should not have the effect of preventing a judicial determination of the merits of an applicant's complaints. The applicant had therefore been denied access to a court in violation of Article 6.[414]

Similarly, in the case *Regner v. the Czech Republic*, the Court held that even though the content of the confidential security clearance had not been disclosed to the applicant – a discharged employee of the Ministry of Defence – or to his counsel, this did not constitute a violation of Article 6. The case fell within the civil limb of Article 6. The Court recognised that the applicant had had access to a court and that the trial had been, as a whole, fair. It was sufficient that the courts had had unlimited access to all the classified documents and that they could have ordered disclosure of those documents they considered did not warrant classification. Moreover, the jurisdiction of the courts examining the dispute had encompassed assessment of all the facts of the case and had not been limited to an examination of the contents of the security clearance. The restrictions on the applicant's rights had thus been offset in such a manner that the fair balance between the parties was not affected.[415]

However, not all labour law disputes are protected by Article 6. There was no incompatible restriction of access to a court when the complaint of a person who had applied for a post in an international organisation but had not been chosen was dismissed by the domestic court, since the organisation in question had offered the applicant an opportunity to undergo arbitration proceedings which he, however, had not agreed to use.[416] The case *Lovric v. Croatia* involved the

---

413 *Baka v. Hungary* [GC], App. no. 20261/12, §§103, 105, 109–110, 114 and 117–122, 23.6.2016. See also Sandor Szemesi, "Introductory note to *Baka v. Hungary* (Eur. Ct. H.R.): [June 23, 2016]", *International legal materials*, vol. 56, no. 2, 2017, pp. 273–274; Mart Susi, "The Baka case: the unbearable price of individual justice", *Hungarian Yearbook of International Law and European Law, 2014*, pp. 121–130; and Gábor Kártyás, "The labour lawyer's reading of the Baka case", *Hungarian Yearbook of International Law and European Law, 2014*, pp. 131–138.

414 *Miryana Petrova v. Bulgaria*, App. no. 57148/08, §§40–45, 21.7.2016.

415 *Regner v. the Czech Republic* [GC], App. no. 35289/11, §§115–119, 125, 152–153 and 161, 19.9.2017 (no violation).

416 *Klausecker v. Germany* (dec.), App. no. 415/07, §76, 6.1.2015.

challenging of a withdrawal of membership from an association. As a disciplinary measure, the applicant had been dismissed from a hunting association after he had filed a police report against one of the members of the association. The Court found a violation of Article 6 because an arbitrary dismissal from an association could also violate Article 11 and, in order to have this issue examined, the applicant needed to have access to a court.[417]

The right of access to a court also concerns criminal matters, which in this context means primarily the right of an accused to have the charges against him examined by a court.[418] The right of access to a court does not, however, give an applicant the right to press charges against third persons[419] or the right to have the State press charges against third parties,[420] because Article 6 only applies to charges brought against an accused. Nevertheless, the right to protection of one's reputation is a right protected by Article 8 and there should be access to a court if this right has been violated. In the case *Arlewin v. Sweden*, the Court held that there should have been the opportunity to bring a defamation action in Sweden even though the television programme in question had been broadcast via satellite through a British company and it was possible to bring action in the United Kingdom. Issues such as the place of residence of the parties, the broadcasting of the programme in Swedish and other practical elements meant that the defamation claim was fundamentally connected to Sweden.[421]

The right of access to a court means that an applicant must have access to a court, both according to the legislation and in practice. It was precisely for this reason that the Court found a violation of Article 6 §1 in the case *Golder v. the United Kingdom*.[422] Although the applicant had a right to bring an action before a court, his access to a court was in practice jeopardised by the fact that he was not allowed to contact his counsel.[423] A partial or temporary obstacle preventing access to a court may also lead to a violation of Article 6.

---

417 *Lovrić v. Croatia*, App. no. 38458/15, §§72–73, 4.4.2017.

418 *Deweer v. Belgium*, App. no. 6903/75, §49, 27.2.1980; and *Kart v. Turkey* [GC], App. no. 8917/05, §67, 3.12.2009.

419 *Rékási v. Hungary* (dec.), App. no. 31506/96, 25.11.1996.

420 *Dubowska and Skup v. Poland* (dec.), App. nos. 33490/95+, 18.4.1997.

421 *Arlewin v. Sweden*, App. no. 22302/10, §§60 and 66–74, 1.3.2016. See also Siofra O'Leary, "Data protection and privacy questions in the digital age", in Michael O'Boyle (Ed.), *Human Rights Challenges in the Digital Age - Judicial Perspectives, in Honour of Lawrence Early*, Council of Europe Publishing, Strasbourg 2020, pp. 93-122, at pp. 101–103.

422 See also *Silver and Others v. the United Kingdom*, App. nos. 5947/72+, §§80–82, 25.3.1983; and *Campbell and Fell v. the United Kingdom*, App. nos. 7819/77+, §107, 28.6.1984.

423 In this case, no relevance was given to the fact that the case in fact concerned more the applicant's right to meet with his counsel than his right of access to a court. The applicant could also have brought an action before a court without an attorney, he could have been in contact with his attorney in other ways than by letter, and by doing so he could even have decided not to bring an action. He could also have contacted his attorney after being released from prison but before the matter became time-barred.

## 4.1.1. RIGHT OF EFFECTIVE ACCESS

### *4.1.1.1. Legal Aid*

As appears from the *Golder* case, access to a court is assumed to be effective. This may require, for example, that there exists a system for applying for legal aid. In the case *Airey v. Ireland*, legal aid was not available in civil matters. The Court took into account the complexity of the separation issue, the need to hear witnesses and the emotional nature of the matter and concluded that the applicant's access to a court could not be regarded as effective, since she would not have been able to present her own case but would have needed legal representation, which she could not afford.[424] Access to a court may thus require that a State takes positive measures, such as the creation of a legal aid scheme, which may have considerable financial consequences for the State.[425]

One cannot, however, conclude from the *Airey* judgment that the right of access to a court in a civil matter always requires the full right to legal aid in the same way as Article 6 §3 (c) requires in criminal matters. Under Article 6 §1 legal aid is required only to the extent that is necessary in order to guarantee effective access to a court.[426] This is clearly the situation in cases where domestic legislation requires compulsory legal representation.[427] In other situations the need for legal aid must be determined on the basis of the facts of the case and, depending on what kind of interest is at stake for the applicant, how complicated the procedural and legislative norms are and whether the applicant is capable of representing him- or herself effectively.[428] No granting of legal aid is required if the applicant's complaints have no chance of success in light of the claimed facts.[429] Nor is legal aid required if the applicant is deemed to have abused the legal aid system[430] or the legal system itself.[431] What is essential is that the

---

424 *Airey v. Ireland*, App. no. 6289/73, §26, 9.10.1979. See also Karen Reid, *A Practitioner's Guide to the European Convention on Human Rights*, Sweet & Maxwell/Thomson Reuters, London 2019, p. 248.

425 Ibid.

426 Ibid.

427 See *Aerts v. Belgium*, App. no. 25357/94, §60, 30.7.1998; and *Staroszczyk v. Poland*, App. no. 59519/00, §§130–139, 22.3.2007. See also Arman Zrvandyan, *Casebook on European Fair Trial Standards in Administrative Justice*, Council of Europe Publishing, Strasbourg 2016, pp. 69–70.

428 *McVicar v. the United Kingdom*, App. no. 46311/99, §§48 and 51, 7.5.2002; *Steel and Morris v. the United Kingdom*, App. no. 68416/01, §61, 15.2.2005; and *P., C. and S. v. the United Kingdom*, App. no. 56547/00, §100, 16.7.2002. See also Karen Reid, *A Practitioner's Guide to the European Convention on Human Rights*, Sweet & Maxwell/Thomson Reuters, London 2019, pp. 248–249.

429 *Gnahoré v. France*, App. no. 40031/98, §§41–42, 19.9.2000; *Del Sol v. France*, App. no. 46800/99, §§23–27, 26.2.2002; and *Stewart-Brady v. the United Kingdom* (dec.), App. nos. 27436/95+, 2.7.1997.

430 *Sujeeun v. the United Kingdom* (dec.), App. no. 27788/95, 18.1.1996.

431 *W. v. the Federal Republic of Germany* (dec.), App. no. 11564/85, 4.12.1985, which concerned divorce proceedings in a situation in which the marriage had originally been contracted in order to obtain a residence permit.

domestic courts handle requests for legal aid with diligence and give reasons for refusing legal aid.[432]

In those cases in which the right of effective access to a court requires granting of legal aid, Article 6 §1 allows the State the freedom to choose the means to achieve this aim. Creating a system of legal aid is only one option. In some cases it might be sufficient to offer legal aid *ex gratia*,[433] or to simplify the proceedings in order to eliminate the need for legal representation.[434] For example, in the case *A. v. the United Kingdom*, free legal representation for two hours was sufficient when thereafter the applicant had the opportunity to hire an attorney.[435] It might also be sufficient to limit the legal aid only to those parts of the proceedings where the applicant's claims have a reasonable prospect of success.[436] If the applicant has, according to domestic law, the right to a lawyer, the State is under an obligation to appoint an attorney who also factually represents the applicant in the case.[437]

In criminal matters, access to legal aid is given more relevance than in civil matters as a result of Article 6 §3 (c). For example, in the case *Salduz v. Turkey*, which concerned a young person, the lack of legal representation from the beginning of the pretrial investigation rendered the whole proceedings unfair, because the applicant's account, which he had given during the pretrial investigation without the presence of his counsel, was used as decisive evidence against him.[438] In any event, the legal aid system established by the legislature must offer individuals substantial guarantees to protect them from arbitrariness.[439]

#### *4.1.1.2. Court Fees*

The obligation to pay court fees is not, as such, contrary to Article 6 of the Convention and does not form an impediment to access to a court. Such a

---

432 *Tabor v. Poland*, App. no. 12825/02, §§45–46, 27.6.2006; and *Saoud v. France*, App. no. 9375/02, §§133–36, 9.10.2007.

433 *Andronicou and Constantinou v. Cyprus*, App. no. 25052/94, §§200–201, 9.10.1997.

434 *Airey v. Ireland*, App. no. 6289/73, §26, 9.10.1979.

435 *A. v. the United Kingdom*, App. no. 35373/97, §98, 17.12.2002. See also John Wadham, Philip Leach, "Cases and comment: selected decisions from the European Court of Human Rights for November and December 2002 – Civil procedure, *A. v. United Kingdom* (Application No. 35373/97)", *European Human Rights Law Review*, Issue 2, 2003, pp. 230–232.

436 *Sinfield and Others v. the United Kingdom* (dec.), App. no. 61332/12, §§41 and 44, 18.2.2014.

437 *Bertuzzi v. France*, App. no. 36378/97, §31, 13.2.2003, in which the applicant had already been appointed three attorneys who had all declined to do anything in the matter. See also Karen Reid, *A Practitioner's Guide to the European Convention on Human Rights*, Sweet & Maxwell/ Thomson Reuters, London 2019, p. 249. See also *Staroszczyk v. Poland*, App. no. 59519/00, §§133–135, 22.3.2007; *Siałkowska v. Poland*, App. no. 8932/05, §§110–116, 22.3.2007; and *Tuziński v. Poland* (dec.), App. no. 40140/98, 30.3.1999.

438 *Salduz v. Turkey* [GC], App. no. 36391/02, §§55, 58 and 60, 27.11.2008.

439 *Gnahoré v. France*, App. no. 40031/98, §41, 19.9.2000; *Essaadi v. France*, App. no. 49384/99, §36, 26.2.2002; *Del Sol v. France*, App. no. 46800/99, §26, 26.2.2002; and *Bakan v. Turkey*, App. no. 50939/99, §§75–76, 12.6.2007.

restriction must, however, be based on law and be proportional in relation to the means used and the aim sought.[440] High court fees in civil proceedings may, however, exceptionally prevent effective access to a court if the persons concerned have no access to legal aid. Also in those cases when applicants pay the court fees from their own pocket, the court fees should be in proper proportion to the circumstances of the case and to the applicant's ability to pay them.[441]

The significance of the obligation to pay court fees vis-à-vis access to a court may be taken into consideration as a precondition to access to a court when a person's inability to pay the fees prevents him from bringing an action,[442] or when it may be significant depending on the outcome of the case.[443] The latter issue was at stake in the case *Stankov v. Bulgaria*, in which the applicant claimed compensation for unfounded detention by indicating a certain amount and the court fees imposed were calculated on the basis of that amount. As the awarded compensation was much lower than the applicant's claim, it meant that 90 per cent of the awarded compensation went on the court fees. As this meant that the applicant had almost entirely lost the compensation awarded by the State, the court fees were considered to unreasonably restrict access to a court, despite the fact that their aim was justified.[444] An unreasonable restriction on the access to a court and a violation of property rights was also found in the case *Cindrić and Bešlić v. Croatia*, in which the applicants, who had lost their case concerning war crimes, were ordered to pay the State's fees – that is, the counterparty's costs and expenses – in full. The Court held that, taking into account the nature of the case, the fact that the counterparty was the State and the applicants' economic situation, this amounted to a disproportionate restriction on the applicants' right of access to court.[445]

The obligation to pay legal costs and the right of access to a court can also arise in a situation in which the person liable to pay is not informed of the exact

---

440 *Stankov v. Bulgaria*, App. no. 68490/01, §§52 and 55, 12.7.2007; *Tolstoy Miloslavsky v. the United Kingdom*, App. no. 18139/91, §61, 13.7.1995; *Apostol v. Georgia*, App. no. 40765/02, §57, 28.11.2006; *Kuczera v. Poland*, App. no. 275/02, §§45–46, 14.9.2010; *Harrison McKee v. Hungary*, App. no. 22840/07, §33, 3.6.2014; and *Tudor-Comert v. Moldova*, App. no. 27888/04, §40, 4.11.2008.

441 *Weissman and Others v. Romania*, App. no. 63945/00, §37, 24.5.2006; *Kreuz v. Poland*, App. no. 28249/95, §66, 19.6.2001; and *Apostol v. Georgia*, App. no. 40765/02, §65, 28.11.2006, in which the Court found that a prepayment for execution violated the right to effective access to a court.

442 *Weissman and Others v. Romania*, App. no. 63945/00, §39, 24.5.2006; *Teltronic-CATV v. Poland*, App. no. 48140/99, §§52–59, 10.1.2006; *Kreuz v. Poland*, App. no. 28249/95, §§62–66, 19.6.2001; and *Hüseyin Özel v. Turkey*, App. no. 2917/05, §§26–30, 10.1.2012. See also Arman Zrvandyan, *Casebook on European Fair Trial Standards in Administrative Justice*, Council of Europe Publishing, Strasbourg 2016, pp. 67–69.

443 *Stankov v. Bulgaria*, App. no. 68490/01, §53, 12.7.2007.

444 *Stankov v. Bulgaria*, App. no. 68490/01, §§51 and 67, 12.7.2007.

445 *Cindrić and Bešlić v. Croatia*, App. no. 72152/13, §§110–111 and 122–123, 6.9.2016.

amount of the payment due when the judgment is rendered or even during the appeal period. In the case *Jensen v. Denmark*, the applicant had been convicted of a violation of intellectual property rights and ordered to pay his lawyer's fees, amounting to 77,000 euros. When the judgment was delivered, he learned about the obligation to pay the lawyer's fees, but the exact amount of this fee was communicated to him only after the period for lodging an appeal had ended. However, the Court found no violation of access to a court since the applicant could have argued, without knowing the exact amount of the legal costs, that the Treasury should contribute, in full or in part.[446]

#### 4.1.1.3. *Discontinuation of the Proceedings*

Article 6 §1 guarantees not only the right to institute proceedings but also the right to obtain a determination of the dispute by a court.[447] The right to effective access to a court may thus be jeopardised when the proceedings have already commenced but they are suspended for an unreasonably long time. For example, in the case *Kutić v. Croatia*, the applicant's proceedings had been postponed while waiting for the enactment of a new law. The Court found that the applicant's right to effective access to a court had been violated when no new legislation had been passed after six years.[448] Similarly, in the case *Ganci v. Italy*, the Court found a violation when a prisoner's appeal concerning his subjection to a highly restricted detention regime was not examined during the time for which the restrictions applied, or even afterwards.[449] The Court also found a violation in a case in which the Albanian Constitutional Court was unable to reach a decision in the applicant's case as a result of a tied vote (the required majority was not achieved) and thereby prevented him from obtaining a final judgment in the matter.[450]

#### 4.1.1.4. *Uncertainty of the Content or Interpretation of Law*

In some cases, effective access to a court has become impossible on the ground that the applicants have not been fully informed of the opportunities

---

446 *Jensen v. Denmark*, App. no. 8693/11, §§39–43, 13.12.2016.

447 *Lupeni Greek Catholic Parish and Others v. Romania* [GC], App. no. 76943/11, §86, 29.11.2016; *Kutić v. Croatia*, App. no. 48778/99, §§25 and 32, 1.3.2002 (staying of proceedings); *Aćimović v. Croatia*, App. no. 61237/00, §41, 9.10.2003; *Beneficio Cappella Paolini v. San Marino*, App. no. 40786/98, §29, 13.7.2004 (denial of justice); and *Marini v. Albania*, App. no. 3738/02, §§118–123, 18.12.2007 (refusal to take a final decision on the applicant's constitutional appeal as a result of a tied vote).

448 *Kutić v. Croatia*, App. no. 48778/99, §32, 1.3.2002.

449 *Ganci v. Italy*, App. no. 41576/98, §31, 30.10.2003.

450 *Marini v. Albania*, App. no. 3738/02, §§119 and 121–122, 18.12.2007. See also *Dubinskaya v. Russia*, App. no. 4856/03, §§42–44, 13.7.2006.

to start proceedings.[451] The Court has often found in these cases a violation of Article 6. For example in the case *F.E. v. France*, the Court found a violation when the applicant, who had contracted HIV as a result of a blood transfusion, had accepted compensation from State funds because he thought, on the basis of legislation that was unclear, that he would still have a further opportunity to bring a claim for additional compensation.[452] In the case *Beneficio Cappella Paolini v. San Marino*, there was a lack of clarity concerning which court should be regarded as competent.[453] By contrast, no violation was found in a case in which it was not clear what appeal documents the applicant was required to submit to the appellate court.[454]

There was also found to be a violation in one case in which the applicants had not been told about the expropriation and therefore had not been able to appeal within the specified time limit.[455] States must guarantee that necessary documents are served to applicants and that they are told about the hearing dates and the time of the pronouncement of the judgments.[456]

### 4.1.2. RESTRICTIONS UPON THE RIGHT OF ACCESS

The right of access to a court is not absolute, and it is possible to restrict it.[457] States' regulations may be different at different times and in different situations, depending on the needs of society and its individuals, as well as the available resources. A State has a certain margin of appreciation as far as access to a court is concerned but the restrictions should not be such that they impair the right of all of its contents.[458] In addition, a restriction must have a legitimate aim and it must be proportional vis-à-vis its purpose.[459]

In its case-law, the Court has allowed restrictions on access to a court in respect of certain groups of people. These groups include prisoners, minors,

---

451 For example, in the case *De Geouffre de la Pradelle v. France*, App. no. 12964/87, §§34–35, 16.12.1992, the Court found that the domestic legal system was not sufficiently clear and uniform as far as access to a court was concerned.

452 *F.E. v. France*, App. no. 38212/97, §40, 30.10.1998. See also *Bellet v. France*, App. no. 23805/94, §37, 4.12.1995.

453 *Beneficio Cappella Paolini v. San Marino*, App. no. 40786/98, §§28–29, 13.7.2004.

454 *Levages Prestations Services v. France*, App. no. 21920/93, §48, 23.10.1996.

455 *Serghides and Christoforou v. Cyprus*, App. no. 44730/98, §70, 5.11.2002.

456 *Sukhorubchenko v. Russia*, App. no. 69315/01, §53, 10.2.1992. See also *Hennings v. Germany*, App. no. 12129/86, §26, 16.12.1992, in which the Court found no violation.

457 *Golder v. the United Kingdom*, App. no. 4451/70, §38, 21.2.1975.

458 *Ashingdane v. the United Kingdom*, App. no. 8225/78, §57, 28.5.1985. See also *Winterwerp v. the Netherlands*, App. no. 6301/73, §75, 24.10.1979.

459 *Ashingdane v. the United Kingdom*, App. no. 8225/78, §57, 28.5.1985; and *Lithgow and Others v. the United Kingdom*, App. nos. 9006/80+, §194, 8.7.1986. As for reasonableness, see also *Mortier v. France*, App. no. 42195/98, §39, 31.7.2001; and *Liakopoulou v. Greece*, App. no. 20627/04, §23, 24.5.2006.

those who have mental illnesses,[460] bankrupt persons,[461] those who have abused the right to appeal[462] and police informants.[463] Nevertheless, the authorities must supervise a person's rights and access to a court, for example, when the legal competences of a mentally ill person are restricted in legal proceedings.[464] One example of this was the case *Marc Brauer v. Germany*, in which the criminally unaccountable applicant, who had been admitted to a psychiatric hospital, did not lodge his appeal within the prescribed time limit when appealing against the decision to admit him. The Court emphasised that, despite correct instructions given to the applicant and the considerations of legal certainty, in such exceptional circumstances flexibility had to be applied to ensure that access to court was not limited in breach of the provisions of the Convention.[465]

The Court has also accepted certain limitations on bringing actions[466] and, in civil matters, certain limitations on the amount of damages[467] if they were reasonable. The Court has also accepted limitations when any appeal could only be made by a lawyer,[468] when an applicant must give a reasonable security for the payment of costs and expenses[469] or when it is possible to impose fines for the abuse of the right to appeal.[470] On the other hand, the right of access to a court was violated when the restrictions on the applicant's access were based on misapplication of law.[471] An acceptable restriction of access to a court in a civil matter can also stem from the fact that there have been attempts to settle the case (friendly settlement) before taking it to court.[472]

---

460 *Golder v. the United Kingdom*, App. no. 4451/70, §39, 21.2.1975. Concerning the mentally ill, it is also accepted that they are obliged to use an attorney in court, see *Stewart-Brady v. the United Kingdom* (dec.), App. nos. 27436/95+, 2.7.1997.

461 *M. v. the United Kingdom* (dec.), App. no. 12040/86, 4.5.1987.

462 *H. v. the United Kingdom* (dec.), App. no. 11559/85, 2.12.1985.

463 *Carnduff v. the United Kingdom* (dec.), App. no. 18905/02, 10.2.2004.

464 *A.N. v. Lithuania*, App. no. 17289/08, §§92–105, 31.5.2016.

465 *Marc Brauer v. Germany*, App. no. 24062/13, §§41–44, 1.9.2016.

466 For example, the minimum length of two years of employment in cases of unreasonable dismissal from work, see *Stedman v. the United Kingdom* (dec.), App. no. 29107/95, 9.4.1997.

467 *Manners and 4 Others v. the United Kingdom* (dec.), App. no. 37650/97, 21.5.1998, which concerned a limitation on the amount of compensation which was based on the Warsaw Convention.

468 *Gillow v. the United Kingdom*, App. no. 9063/80, §69, 24.11.1986.

469 *Tolstoy Miloslavsky v. the United Kingdom*, App. no. 18139/91, §§61–62, 13.7.1995; and *Aït-Mouhoub v. France*, App. no. 22924/93, §57, 28.10.1998. See also *Podbielski and PPU Polpure v. Poland*, App. no. 39199/98, §§69–70, 26.7.2005, which concerned a court fee; and *Weissman and Others v. Romania*, App. no. 63945/00, §42, 24.5.2006, which concerned stamp duty of 323,264 euros.

470 *P. v. France* (dec.), App. no. 10412/83, 14.7.1987; and *Les Travaux du Midi v. France* (dec.), App. no. 12275/86, 2.7.1991.

471 *Peltier v. France*, App. no. 32872/96, §37, 21.5.2002.

472 *Momčilović v. Croatia*, App. no. 11239/11, §§46–57, 26.3.2015.

Access to superior courts has also been restricted in many countries. In the Grand Chamber judgment *Zubac v. Croatia* the Court emphasised the fact that there was no reason to put in doubt the legitimacy and permissibility of any statutory *ratione valoris* restrictions placed on access to the highest courts. In individual cases, however, the restrictions should be proportionate. In this respect, the Court, to varying degrees, took into account certain factors, namely the foreseeability of the restriction, whether it was the applicant or the respondent State who should bear the adverse consequences of the errors made during the proceedings that led to the applicant being denied access to the supreme court, and whether the restrictions in question could be said to involve "excessive formalism".[473]

Article 2 of Protocol No. 7 provides that the right to have one's conviction or sentence reviewed by a higher tribunal may be subject to exceptions in regard to offences of a minor character (minor offence). In the case *Saquetti Iglesias v. Spain* the Court held that an offence resulting in a prison sentence could not be considered a minor offence. As concerned fines, the amounts could vary and the States had a margin of appreciation in that regard. In the case at hand, the fine imposed for a violation of a customs duty had been over 100,000 euros. For the Court, the severity of the sanction and the fact that it had been imposed without taking into account the applicant's personal circumstances meant that the offence in question was not of minor character and the applicant should have been able to have it reviewed by a higher court.[474]

The restrictions on the right of access to a court were also found to be unreasonable when courts closed as a result of a state of emergency and no alternative access to a court was created.[475] One example of an unreasonable restriction was when a partially incompetent person was denied the opportunity to have his legal capacity reviewed by a court.[476] Generally, the procedural rules restricting access to a court should not be interpreted[477] or applied[478] so narrowly that the right to have access to a court is negated.

#### 4.1.2.1. *Time Limits, Statute of Limitations and Errors of Pleading*

Most cases concerning access to a court which the Court has examined have concerned the time limits for lodging an action or an appeal or other procedural

473 *Zubac v. Croatia* [GC], App. no. 40160/12, §§73 and 80–99, 5.4.2018. See also Sofia Galani (Ed.), "Case and comment: selected decisions from the European Court of Human Rights for March and April 2018 – Right of access to Supreme Courts, *Zubac v. Croatia* (Application No. 40160/12)", *European Human Rights Law Review*, Issue 4, 2018, pp. 399–401.

474 *Saquetti Iglesias v. Spain*, App. no. 5051/13, §§36–46 and 61, 30.6.2020.

475 *Khamidov v. Russia*, App. no. 72118/01, §156, 15.11.2007.

476 *Stanev v. Bulgaria* [GC], App. no. 36760/06, §245, 17.1.2012 (violation).

477 *Běleš and Others v. the Czech Republic*, App. no. 47273/99, §51, 12.11.2002.

478 *Pérez de Rada Cavanilles v. Spain*, App. no. 28090/95, §49, 28.10.1998; and *Yagtzilar and Others v. Greece*, App. no. 41727/98, §27, 6.12.2001.

mistakes in lodging a complaint or an appeal.[479] Setting time limits in itself is acceptable if they are reasonable.[480] Because of different practices in different States, the respondent States have in this respect a certain margin of appreciation. However, time limits may become unreasonable: if the time limit for lodging an appeal starts to run from a point when the party did not and could not effectively know the content of the contested court decision; if the time limit is so short and inflexible that the party in practice does not have sufficient time to lodge an appeal; or if the dismissal of an appeal for failure to comply with a time limit is not a foreseeable reaction.[481] However, in the case *Stubbings v. the United Kingdom*, bringing a civil action in a case concerning child abuse within the time limit of six years counting from the time the child turned 18 was found to be reasonable.[482]

On the other hand, in the case *Kurşun v. Turkey*, which concerned the damage caused to the applicant's property by an explosion at an oil refinery, the Court found the domestic decision to dismiss the compensation claims without examining the merits for being lodged out of time problematic. Only a few months before the dismissal of the applicant's claim, another chamber of the Court of Cassation had examined compensation claims brought by other victims of the same explosion and had interpreted the time limit rule in their favour. The Court found it problematic that the Court of Cassation had provided no reasoning as to why it diverged from decisions delivered by another chamber. The decision was also somewhat formalistic, since in reality the applicant could not have obtained sufficient evidence by the expiry of the time limit about the causes of the explosion and those responsible for it as the investigation was difficult and delayed. Declaring the claim inadmissible in these circumstances deprived the applicant of the right of access to a court.[483]

The case *Sanofi Pasteur v. France* concerned the issue from which date the calculation of a limitation period for a civil action should be started. A woman had suffered a number of illnesses, including multiple sclerosis, as a result of a vaccination. She filed a claim for compensation against the applicant company which had developed the vaccine. The applicant company claimed that her action was out of date since the limitation period had begun to run from the launching of the vaccine on the markets. The domestic courts held that the limitation period

479 See, for example, *Miragall Escolano and Others v. Spain*, App. nos. 38366/97+, §36, 25.1.2000; *Tricard v. France*, App. no. 40472/98, §33, 10.7.2001; *Zemanová v. the Czech Republic*, App. no. 6019/03, §21, 13.12.2005; and *Mikulová v. Slovakia*, App. no. 64001/00, §56, 6.12.2005.

480 *Kurşun v. Turkey*, App. no. 22677/10, §103, 30.10.2018.

481 *Jensen v. Denmark*, App. no. 8693/11, §36, 13.12.2016.

482 *Stubbings and Others v. the United Kingdom*, App. no. 22083/93, §57, 22.10.1996 (no violation). See also *Mizzi v. Malta*, App. no. 26111/02, §89, 12.1.2006 in which the Court found a violation as the time limit for lodging a claim for revoking paternity was six months counting from the birth of the child.

483 *Kurşun v. Turkey*, App. no. 22677/10, §§98–106, 30.10.2018.

would begin to run only when the victim's disease was stabilised. As the course of her disease was still progressing and was not stabilised, the prescription period for a compensation claim had not expired. In its appeal, the applicant company requested that a preliminary ruling from the CJEU should be obtained but its request was dismissed by the domestic courts. The applicant company then lodged an application with the Court, claiming that the outcome meant that an action for a progressive disease would not be subject to any limitation period and that it therefore violated the principle of legal certainty. The Court held that the interests to be balanced were the victim's right of access to a court and the applicant company's interest in legal certainty, and that in difficult weighing situations the State had a wide discretion. French law afforded the victim full compensation for personal injury, which could only be assessed after her health condition was fully established. In view of the importance of the protection of personal integrity under Articles 3 and 8, the Court could not call into question the premise of national law to afford the injured party better protection than the person causing the damage. This outcome also provided an opportunity to take into account the needs of those suffering from progressive diseases such as multiple sclerosis. There was thus no violation of Article 6.[484]

A time limit which an applicant cannot be reasonably expected to follow violates his right of access to a court.[485] By contrast, clear and avoidable mistakes resulting in failure to meet the time limit do not do so.[486] If the failure to respect time limits is caused by a counsel's mistake, such a mistake is not in principle repairable. Normally the State is not responsible for the mistakes committed by a privately chosen counsel or a counsel appointed by the State as legal aid.[487] However, in some exceptional circumstances in which the counsel's negligence is apparent and it has been communicated to a court, it can justify the court's examination of an action or application lodged out of time in order to secure the right of access to a court.[488]

Sometimes a material error or deficiency in the letter of complaint or appeal can also prevent its examination and therefore prevent access to a court. In addition, an overly formalistic application of law may prevent access to a court. In the case *Miessen v. Belgium*, the applicant had not in his reply to the

---

484 *Sanofi Pasteur v. France*, App. no. 25137/16, §§50–61, 13.2.2020 (no violation). See also Mollie Cornell, "Reasons for preliminary references – *Sanofi Pasteur v. France* (Application No. 25137/16)", *European Human Rights Law Review*, Issue 3, 2020, pp. 308–311.

485 *Neshev v. Bulgaria*, App. no. 40897/98, §38, 28.10.2004; *Tsironis v. Greece*, App. no. 44584/98, §27, 6.12.2001; and *Aepi S.A. v. Greece*, App. no. 48679/99, §28, 11.4.2002. See also *Cañete de Goñi v. Spain*, App. no. 55782/00, §41, 15.10.2002 (no violation).

486 *Edificaciones March Gallego S.A. v. Spain*, App. no. 28028/95, §35, 19.2.1998 (no violation) in which the mistake concerned the applicant's name and competence to appeal.

487 *Kamasinski v. Austria*, App. no. 9783/82, §65, 19.12.1989; *Artico v. Italy*, App. no. 6694/74, §36, 13.5.1980; *Rutkowski v. Poland* (dec.), App. no. 45995/99, 19.10.2000; and *Cuscani v. the United Kingdom*, App. no. 32771/96, §39, 24.9.2002.

488 *Muscat v. Malta*, App. no. 24297/10, §§53–58, 6.9.2011 (violation).

counterparty's appeal replied to his arguments but had only repeated the content of his own appeal. Nevertheless, since his arguments were clearly apparent in his reply, the Court held that the strict application of the law restricted in a disproportionate way the applicant's ability to have his appeal examined on its merits.[489]

Sometimes a technical mistake may prevent access to a court. In such cases, it becomes relevant with whom responsibility for the mistake lies. This was the case, for example, in *Tence v. Slovenia*, in which the court's fax machine was out of order and did not print out the applicant's letter of appeal, which had been sent within the required time limit. The Court found a violation on the ground that access to a court had been prevented.[490] It is also a court's responsibility to make sure that the defendant is actually summonsed to court and is informed about the time and place of the proceedings, including the proceedings before appeal courts.[491]

In other cases examined by the Court, mistakes have concerned factual or written errors committed by the plaintiffs or appellants.[492] Spelling mistakes committed by the State must not turn to the applicant's disadvantage.[493]

#### *4.1.2.2. Reasons Related to an Applicant's Personal Circumstances and the Requirement of Flexibility*

In cases involving actions lodged by vulnerable people in matters concerning their person, specific requirements are put on the flexibility of a court. For example, in proceedings concerning the limitation of the legal capacity of a mentally ill person, the authorities must see that the person's right of an access to a court is respected.[494] In the Grand Chamber case *Stanev v. Bulgaria*, a limitation on access to a court was found to be disproportionate when a person partially deprived of legal capacity was unable to bring an action directly in a court on the issue of the possible restoration of his legal capacity.[495] This was also the case in *Marc Brauer v. Germany*, in which the applicant, who had been admitted to a psychiatric hospital, was not able to appeal against the decision on his admission to involuntary care within the prescribed time limit. The Court emphasised that, despite the correct instructions to appeal and the requirements of legal certainty,

---

489 *Miessen v. Belgium*, App. no. 31517/12, §§66–74, 18.10.2016.

490 *Tence v. Slovenia*, App. no. 37242/14, §§34–38, 31.5.2016.

491 *Gankin and Others v. Russia*, App. nos. 2430/06+, §39, 31.5.2016.

492 See, for example, *Kadlec and Others v. the Czech Republic*, App. no. 49478/99, §§27–28, 25.5.2004; and *Saez Maeso v. Spain*, App. no. 77837/01, §27, 9.11.2004.

493 *Platakou v. Greece*, App. no. 38460/97, §39, 11.1.2001.

494 *A.N. v. Lithuania*, App. no. 17289/08, §§92–105, 31.5.2016.

495 *Stanev v. Bulgaria* [GC], App. no. 36760/06, §245, 17.1.2012 (violation). See also Oliver Lewis, "*Stanev v. Bulgaria*: on the pathway to freedom", *Human Rights Brief*, vol. 19, issue 2, winter 2012, pp. 2–7.

in such exceptional cases the courts had, because of the applicant's vulnerability, an obligation to apply flexibility.[496]

In *Nikolyan v. Armenia*, the Court found a violation of Article 6 when the applicant, who had been deprived of legal capacity, was refused access to a court. The applicant's son, who was his guardian, had prevented the courts from reviewing the applicant's application for divorce and the decision depriving him of his legal capacity. Because the father-son relationship was contentious, it was doubtful that the son had acted in the best interests of the applicant father. Moreover, the Court considered that Armenian law, which only recognised either full legal capacity or none at all, was too categorical and left no room for exceptions.[497]

#### *4.1.2.3. Limitations on the Right of Action*

Limitations on the right of access to a court also have occurred when the right of action has been given only to certain interested parties at the expense of others.[498] In *Canea Catholic Church v. Greece* the withdrawal of legal personality, which entailed the withdrawal of the legal competence, was also found to be a violation.[499] On the other hand, for example, in *Klass and v. Germany* the inability to challenge the legality of telephone tapping as long as interception was ongoing (because the subject was not informed) was justified for securing the functioning of the legal system. The applicant had several remedies available to him after the telephone tapping had been terminated.[500]

#### *4.1.2.4. Retroactive Laws*

New retroactive substantive laws enacted by a State with the aim of limiting the chances of success for applicants' pending cases violate the right of access to a court, unless they can be regarded as reasonable on the basis of compelling public-interest motives.[501] In the case-law relating to civil matters, a new

---

496 *Marc Brauer v. Germany*, App. no. 24062/13, §§41–44, 1.9.2016.

497 *Nikolyan v. Armenia*, App. no. 74438/14, §§95–103, 3.10.2019.

498 See, for example, *The Holy Monasteries v. Greece*, App. nos. 13092/87+, §83, 9.12.1994; *Lithgow and Others v. the United Kingdom*, App. nos. 9006/80+, §197, 8.7.1986 (no violation); *Philis v. Greece (No. 1)*, App. nos. 12750/87+, §65, 27.8.1991; and *Związek Nauczycielstwa Polskiego v. Poland*, App. no. 42049/98, §41, 21.9.2004.

499 *Canea Catholic Church v. Greece*, App. no. 25528/94, §41, 16.12.1997. See also Karen Reid, *A Practitioner's Guide to the European Convention on Human Rights*, Sweet & Maxwell/ Thomson Reuters, London 2019, pp. 139–140.

500 *Klass and Others v. Germany*, App. no. 5029/71, §75, 6.9.1978.

501 *National & Provincial Building Society, Leeds Permanent Building Society and Yorkshire Building Society v. the United Kingdom*, App. nos. 21319/93+, §112, 23.10.1997 (no violation), which concerned retroactive tax legislation which was enacted in order to fill a lacuna in the legislation and which therefore was justified by public interest.

interpretation adopted by domestic courts does not, however, violate Article 6 if the change of interpretation was foreseeable – for example, as a result of incoherent case-law – or if the change was published and in this way fulfils the foreseeability requirement.[502] The Court has, however, examined most of these cases under Article 6 as matters concerning fair trial or rule of law, rather than as restrictions on access to a court.[503] Changes in procedural rules do not violate the right of access to a court as it is generally known that they are immediately applicable to pending cases.[504]

#### 4.1.2.5. *Annulment and Non-Enforcement of Final Judgments*

Sometimes, the annulment of final judgments has also been found to violate the right of access to a court.[505] Normally they are understood to fall within the scope of a fair trial. In contrast, a failure to execute domestic judgments is clearly a matter concerning access to a court under Article 6.[506]

#### 4.1.2.6. *Immunities, Privileges and Territorial Competence*

Procedural impediments which are based on immunities or privileges enjoyed by the counterparty also restrict the right of access to a court. The Court has divided these situations into those in which the applicant has no arguable claim on the basis of domestic law and those in which such a claim exists but where the success of such a claim is defeated by the counterparty's immunity or privilege. Concerning the former, the Court has found that Article 6 is simply not applicable to such situations, as there is no right under domestic law.[507] Article 6 is, however, applicable to the latter situations. The justification of an

502 *Legrand v. France*, App. no. 23228/08, §§37 and 40–42, 26.5.2011. For example, in the *Legrand* case the new interpretation, which also had an effect on the applicant's pending case, was aimed at correcting the incoherence of the case-law that the applicant had been aware of when bringing the action. In the case *Petko Petkov v. Bulgaria*, App. no. 2834/06, §§33–35, 19.2.2013, the highest court's interpretation in the applicant's pending case deviated from the previous line of interpretation and was thus not foreseeable. The domestic court had applied the new interpretation automatically without even giving the applicant an opportunity to challenge it. The Court found a violation of Article 6 §1 in respect of the applicant's right of access to a court.

503 Sometimes the Court refers to both grounds, as for example in *National & Provincial Building Society, Leeds Permanent Building Society and Yorkshire Building Society v. the United Kingdom*, App. nos. 21319/93+, §112, 23.10.1997.

504 *Brualla Gómez de la Torre v. Spain*, App. no. 26737/95, §35, 19.12.1997 (no violation). See also Karen Reid, *A Practitioner's Guide to the European Convention on Human Rights*, Sweet & Maxwell/Thomson Reuters, London 2019, p. 167.

505 See, for example, *Ryabykh v. Russia*, App. no. 52854/99, §57, 24.7.2003. See also, Kirill Koroteev, Sergey Golubok, "Judgment of the Russian Constitutional Court on supervisory review in civil proceedings: denial of justice, denial of Europe", *Human Rights Law Review*, vol. 7, no. 3, 2007, pp. 619–632.

506 See, for example, *Jasiūnienė v. Lithuania*, App. no. 41510/98, §27, 6.3.2003.

507 See, for example, *James and Others v. the United Kingdom*, App. no. 8793/79, §81, 21.2.1986.

immunity or a privilege in such cases depends on whether what are known as the *Ashingdane* criteria are fulfilled; that is, whether the limitation impairs the very essence of the right, whether it has a legitimate aim and whether it is proportionate vis-à-vis its purpose.[508] It is thus relevant to assess whether the limitation is of a material type or rather a procedural limitation.

It is not always easy to judge whether an applicant has no arguable substantive claim under domestic law or whether there is a procedural limitation on access to a court. For example, in the case *Z and Others v. the United Kingdom*, the Court held that Article 6 was not at all applicable,[509] while in the case *Osman v. the United Kingdom* Article 6 applied and access to a court had been disproportionally limited.[510]

The Court applied the *Ashingdane* criteria to immunities and privileges for the first time in the case *Fayed v. the United Kingdom*, in which it found the privilege connected to defamation cases permissible.[511] The same principles have also been applied in cases involving parliamentary or State immunities. In the case *A. v. the United Kingdom*, the Court held that absolute immunity from liability for defamation for MPs for statements made in parliamentary proceedings did not violate Article 6, for the reason, *inter alia*, that it extended only to statements made in Parliament.[512] By contrast, in the case *Cordova v. Italy*, the Court found that the absolute parliamentary immunity of a senator was disproportionate, as the defamatory statement was given outside of Parliament.[513] The Court held in *Kart v. Turkey* that the inability of a member of parliament to waive his immunity

---

508 *Ashingdane v. the United Kingdom*, App. no. 8225/78, §57, 28.5.1985. See also *Winterwerp v. the Netherlands*, App. no. 6301/73, §75, 24.10.1979. See also Karen Reid, *A Practitioner's Guide to the European Convention on Human Rights*, Sweet & Maxwell/Thomson Reuters, London 2019, p. 136.

509 *Z. and Others v. the United Kingdom* [GC], App. no. 29392/95, §100, 10.5.2001. See also Francis G. Jacobs, Robin C.A. White, Clare Owey, *The European Convention on Human Rights*, Oxford University Press, Oxford 2017, pp. 288–289.

510 *Osman v. the United Kingdom*, App. no. 23452/94, §154, 28.10.1998. See also *Markovic and Others v. Italy* [GC], App. no. 1398/03, 14.12.2006; *T.P. and K.M. v. the United Kingdom* [GC], App. no. 28945/95, 10.5.2001; and *D.P. and J.C. v. the United Kingdom*, App. no. 38719/97, 10.10.2002. See also Karen Reid, *A Practitioner's Guide to the European Convention on Human Rights*, Sweet & Maxwell/Thomson Reuters, London 2019, pp. 149–150.

511 *Fayed v. the United Kingdom*, App. no. 17101/90, §83, 21.9.1994; and Dragoljub Popović, *European Human Rights Law - A Manual: An Introduction to the Strasbourg Court and its Jurisprudence*, Eleven International Publishing, The Hague 2013, p. 190. See also *Taylor v. the United Kingdom* (dec.), App. no. 49589/99, 10.6.2003; and *Mond v. the United Kingdom* (dec.), App. no. 49606/99, 10.6.2003.

512 *A. v. the United Kingdom*, App. no. 35373/97, §87, 17.12.2002. See also John Wadham, Philip Leach, "Cases and comment: selected decisions from the European Court of Human Rights for November and December 2002 - Civil procedure, *A. v. United Kingdom* (Application No. 35373/97)", *European Human Rights Law Review*, Issue 2, 2003, pp. 230–232. See also *Young v. Ireland* (dec.), App. no. 25646/94, 17.1.1996; and *C.G.I.L. and Cofferati v. Italy (No. 2)*, App. no. 2/08, §44, 6.4.2010.

513 *Cordova v. Italy (No. 2)*, App. no. 45649/99, §64, 30.1.2003. See also *Cordova v. Italy (No. 1)*, App. no. 40877/98, §63, 30.1.2003; and *De Jorio v. Italy*, App. no. 73936/01, §47, 3.6.2004.

did not infringe his right of access to a court to have the criminal proceedings against him heard because the immunity was a temporary procedural obstacle to the criminal proceedings, being limited to the duration of his term of parliamentary office.[514]

An investigating judge's immunity from criminal prosecution was found to comply with Article 6.[515] Also limitations on the ability of individuals to take legal proceedings to challenge statements and findings made by civil servants and other State officials have been accepted.[516] Naturally also heads of States have been afforded functional immunity in order to protect their freedom of expression and to maintain the separation of powers within the State. However, perpetual and absolute immunity that can never be lifted would constitute a disproportionate restriction on the right of access to a court.[517]

In the Grand Chamber case *Károly Nagy v. Hungary*, the Court agreed that the domestic courts had been right to refuse to deal with a pecuniary claim stemming from the applicant's service as a pastor of the Reformed Church of Hungary. As the applicant's service with the Church was regulated by ecclesiastical law, the provisions of the Labour Code were not applicable in the case. The civil courts did not therefore have jurisdiction in the matter. The Court concluded that the applicant had had no "right" of access which could have been recognised under domestic law and that Article 6 was not therefore applicable.[518]

The norm of international law according to which States have immunity from civil liability in courts of other States has been held to be a proportionate restriction on the right of access to a court, since its legitimate aim is to promote comity and good relations among States.[519] Therefore, State immunity has been

---

See also Leo Zwaak, Yves Haeck, "Human rights news – Council of Europe", *Netherlands Quarterly of Human Rights*, vol. 21, no. 2, 2003, pp. 255–275, at pp. 269–270.

514 *Kart v. Turkey* [GC], App. no. 8917/05, §§92–93, 95 and 111–113, 3.12.2009. See also James Welch (Ed.), "Cases and comment: selected decisions from the European Court of Human Rights for November and December 2009 – Parliamentary immunity, *Kart v. Turkey* (Application No. 8917/05)", *European Human Rights Law Review*, Issue 2, 2010, pp. 221–224.

515 *Ernst and Others v. Belgium*, App. no. 33400/96, §56, 15.7.2003.

516 *Fayed v. the United Kingdom*, App. no. 17101/90, §70, 21.9.1994; and *Jones and Others v. the United Kingdom*, App. nos. 34356/06+, §§213–215, 14.1.2014.

517 *Urechean and Pavlicenco v. Republic of Moldova*, App. nos. 27756/05+, §§47–55, 2.12.2014.

518 *Károly Nagy v. Hungary* [GC], App. no. 56665/09, §§72–78, 14.9.2017. See also Robert Spano, "'Arbitrary or manifestly unreasonable': the arbitrariness exception to the fourth instance doctrine under Article 6 of the European Convention on Human Rights", in Koen Lemmens, Stephan Parmentier, Louise Reyntjens (Eds.), *Human Rights with a Human Touch – Liber Amicorum Paul Lemmens*, Intersentia, Cambridge/Antwerp/Chicago 2019, pp. 523–537, at pp. 526–527; and Stefan Kieber, "The jurisprudence of the European Court of Human Rights in 2017", *European Yearbook on Human Rights 2018*, pp. 229–265, at p. 238.

519 *Fogarty v. the United Kingdom* [GC], App. no. 37112/97, §34, 21.11.2001; *Al-Adsani v. the United Kingdom* [GC], App. no. 35763/97, §54, 21.11.2001; and *Treska v. Albania and Italy* (dec.), App. no. 26937/04, 29.6.2006. See also Jean-Paul Costa, "The European Court of Human Rights and its recent case law", *Texas International Law Journal*, vol. 38, no. 3, 2003, pp. 455–467, at p. 464.

accepted, for example, in respect of a claim concerning employment in a foreign diplomatic mission[520] and a tort claim for personal injury by a foreign soldier.[521] State immunity also extends to the property of a foreign State and to execution of a judgment against such property.[522] A foreign State may waive its right to immunity before the courts of another State by giving clear and unequivocal consent.[523] Immunity from civil proceedings for international organisations, in accordance with international law, may also be permissible.[524]

In its most recent case-law, the Court has limited State immunity in civil matters. Therefore, for example, State immunity in the context of labour disputes and access to a court has been limited to situations in which there exists a special reason for the immunity, such as a link to State security or if the case concerns a diplomat, a State agent or a citizen of the country. For all other labour disputes, access to a court must be guaranteed. Such a situation was at stake, for example, in the case *Naku v. Lithuania and Sweden*, in which the Court held that the dismissal of the applicant, who worked as a locally hired cultural attaché in the Swedish Embassy in Lithuania, was to be examined in a Lithuanian court.[525]

---

520 *Fogarty v. the United Kingdom* [GC], App. no. 37112/97, §38, 21.11.2001; and *Cudak v. Lithuania* [GC], App. no. 15869/02, §§66–72, 23.3.2010. See also Lucius Caflisch, "International law and the European Court of Human Rights", in *Dialogue between judges*, European Court of Human Rights/Council of Europe, Strasbourg 2007, pp. 23–40, at p. 14; Dragoljub Popović, "Access to Justice in the Recent Grand Chamber Judgments of the European Court of Human Rights", in Sonia Morano-Foadi, Lucy Vickers (Eds.), *Fundamental Rights in the EU – A Matter for Two Courts*, Hart Publishing, Oxford and Portland, Or. 2015, pp. 201–217, at pp. 213–216; and Richard Garnett, "The Strasbourg Court – A Friend to Embassy and Consular Employees", *European Human Rights Law Review*, Issue 6, 2017, pp. 589–595, at pp. 598–591.

521 *McElhinney v. Ireland* [GC], App. no. 31253/96, §40, 21.11.2001 which contained five dissenting opinions. See also *Kalogeropoulou and Others v. Greece and Germany* (dec.), App. no. 59021/00, 12.12.2002. See also Christos L. Rozakis, "The Contribution of the European Court of Human Rights to the Development of the Law on State Immunity", in Lucius Caflisch, Johan Callewaert, Roderick Liddell, Paul Mahoney, Mark Villiger (Eds.), *Liber Amicorum Luzius Wildhaber: Human Rights, Strasbourg Views/Droits de l'Homme, Regards de Strasbourg*, N.P. Engel, Kehl/Strasbourg/Arlington, Va. 2007, pp. 387–402, at pp. 395–399 and 400–402.

522 *Manoilescu and Dobrescu v. Romania and Russia* (dec.), App. no. 60861/00, §81, 3.3.2005.

523 *Ndayegamiye-Mporamazina v. Switzerland*, App. no. 16874/12, §§57 and 59, 5.2.2019.

524 See *Waite and Kennedy v. Germany* [GC], App. no. 26083/94, §73, 18.2.1999; and *Beer and Regan v. Germany* [GC], App. no. 28934/95, §63, 18.2.1999 which both concerned the European Space Agency (ESA). The immunity was not problematic in these cases as the applicants had other, alternatives remedies providing access to a court. See also Jean-Paul Costa, "The European Court of Human Rights and its recent case law", *Texas International Law Journal*, vol. 38, no. 3, 2003, pp. 455–467, at p. 463; and Matti Pellonpää, "The European Court of Human rights and the European Union", in Lucius Caflisch, Johan Callewaert, Roderick Liddell, Paul Mahoney, Mark Villiger (Eds.), *Liber Amicorum Luzius Wildhaber: Human Rights, Strasbourg Views/Droits de L'homme, Regards de Strasbourg*, N.P. Engel, Kehl/Strasbourg/Arlington, Va. 2007, pp. 347–370, at pp.352–353. See also *Stichting Mothers of Srebrenica and Others v. the Netherlands* (dec.), App. no. 65542/12, §139, 11.6.2013 which concerned the granting of immunity to the United Nations (UN) in the national courts.

525 *Naku v. Lithuania and Sweden*, App. no. 26126/07, §§89–91 and 95–96, 8.11.2016; and *Radunović and Others v. Montenegro*, App. nos. 45197/13+, 25.10.2016. See also Richard Garnett, "The Strasbourg Court – A Friend to Embassy and Consular Employees", *European*

In the case *Al-Adsani v. the United Kingdom*, the situation was not very clear. In that case, the applicant had brought a tort claim against the government of Kuwait in the English courts, alleging that Kuwaiti government agents had tortured him, but the defendant State successfully pleaded State immunity. The Court considered such a restriction permissible. Even though the prohibition of torture had already become a peremptory norm (*jus cogens*) of customary public international law, which no longer could bar *criminal* proceedings against an individual for acts of torture, no similar development had taken place in the context of *civil* proceedings. In that respect, a State still retained its absolute immunity from civil suit in respect of torture committed outside its borders.[526]

In the case *Jones and Others v. the United Kingdom*, the Court assessed whether there was a need to change the line of interpretation adopted in the *Al-Adsani* case and whether there had been such developments in public international law which required a reassessment of State immunity. In the *Jones and Others* case, the applicants had brought a tort claim in the English courts against Saudi Arabia, claiming that they had been tortured by Saudi Arabian State agents. Their action was rejected on the basis of State immunity. In conclusion, the Court found that, for the moment, there was no need for a reassessment but that, in light of the developments currently under way in this area of public international law, this was a matter which needed to be kept under review.[527]

The case *Naït-Liman v. Switzerland* concerned an applicant who had been subjected to torture in Tunisia while in detention and who had lodged a compensation action in a Swiss court. The action had been directed against the State of Tunisia and a civil servant who was at the time receiving medical care in a Swiss hospital. The Swiss courts did not examine the action since they considered that it fell outside the scope of their territorial competence. The Grand Chamber accepted the domestic courts' outcome and agreed that the

---

*Human Rights Law Review*, Issue 6, 2017, pp. 589–595, at pp. 591–595. See also *Wallishauser v. Austria*, App. no. 156/04, 17.7.2012 which concerned the service of a summons in proceedings against a foreign State relating to salary arrears; and *Ndayegamiye-Mporamazina v. Switzerland*, App. no. 16874/12, §§49 and 61, 5.2.2019 which concerned a dispute over an employment contract concluded between an embassy/permanent mission and its support staff.

526 *Al-Adsani v. the United Kingdom* [GC], App. no. 35763/97, §66, 21.11.2001. See also Karen Reid, *A Practitioner's Guide to the European Convention on Human Rights*, Sweet & Maxwell/Thomson Reuters, London 2019, pp. 151–152; and Christos L. Rozakis, "The Contribution of the European Court of Human Rights to the Development of the Law on State Immunity", in Lucius Caflisch, Johan Callewaert, Roderick Liddell, Paul Mahoney, Mark Villiger (Eds.), *Liber Amicorum Luzius Wildhaber: Human Rights, Strasbourg Views/Droits de L'homme, Regards de Strasbourg*, N.P. Engel, Kehl/Strasbourg/Arlington, Va. 2007, pp. 387–402, at pp. 389–395.

527 *Jones and Others v. the United Kingdom*, App. nos. 34356/06+, §§213–215, 14.1.2014. See also Chimène I. Keitner, "*Jones v. United Kingdom*, application nos. 34356/06 & [and] 40528/06: European Court of Human Rights, January 14, 2014", *American Journal of International Law*, vol. 108, no. 2, April 2014, pp. 302–308.

margin of appreciation of domestic courts was wide since the action brought had no connection with Switzerland. The Court nevertheless emphasised that torture victims had a right to compensation and that the States should allow them access to a court and examine compensation claims.[528]

State immunity from execution of judgment is not in itself contrary to Article 6 §1. The Court held in the case *Manoilescu and Dobrescu v. Romania and Russia* that all the international legal instruments governing State immunity set forth the general principle that foreign States enjoyed immunity from execution in the territory of the forum State.[529]

#### *4.1.2.7. Limitations Imposed by International Treaties or Owing to International Tribunal Competences*

A national court's jurisdiction, and thereby also the competences of the Court, may be restricted by the competences of an international tribunal. The Court has also applied the *Ashingdane* criteria in situations where the national courts' jurisdiction is ousted by treaties. For example, in the case *Prince Hans-Adam II of Liechtenstein v. Germany* the applicant had brought a claim in Germany concerning the expropriation by the Czechoslovakian authorities of a painting which was temporarily in Germany for exhibition. The German courts held that, under the Settlement Convention between Germany and the Western Allies, they had no jurisdiction to hear the case, which concerned "German external assets". Applying the *Ashingdane* criteria,[530] the Court unanimously found that the restriction on the German courts' jurisdiction had a legitimate aim and that it was proportionate to that end. The natural and most likely forum for such a claim was where the painting was normally kept and, in fact, such a claim had already earlier been unsuccessfully brought in the Czechoslovakian courts.[531]

On a similar basis, access to a court was restricted in the case *Al-Dulimi and Montana Management Inc. v. Switzerland*, in which an order was based

---

528 *Naït-Liman v. Switzerland* [GC], App. no. 51357/07, §§217–220, 15.3.2018. See also Robert Spano, "'Arbitrary or manifestly unreasonable': the arbitrariness exception to the fourth instance doctrine under Article 6 of the European Convention on Human Rights", in Koen Lemmens, Stephan Parmentier, Louise Reyntjens (Eds.), *Human Rights with a Human Touch - Liber Amicorum Paul Lemmens*, Intersentia, Cambridge/Antwerp/Chicago 2019, pp. 523–537, at pp. 532–533.

529 *Manoilescu and Dobrescu v. Romania and Russia* (dec.), App. no. 60861/00, §73, 3.3.2005. See also *Kalogeropoulou and Others v. Greece and Germany* (dec.), App. no. 59021/00, 12.12.2002.

530 That is, whether a limitation impairs the very essence of the right, whether it has a legitimate aim and whether it is proportionate vis-à-vis its purpose.

531 *Prince Hans-Adam II of Liechtenstein v. Germany* [GC], App. no. 42527/98, §69, 12.7.2001. See also Paul Mahoney, "The European Convention on royal rights: royalty, aristocracy and the European Convention on Human Rights", in Marcelo G. Kohen (Ed.), *Promoting Justice, Human Rights and Conflict Resolution through International Law, Liber Amicorum Lucius Caflisch*, Martinus Nijhoff, Leiden 2007, pp. 339–352, at p. 346.

on the decision by the UN Security Council to freeze assets of those people working for Saddam Hussein and in which a Swiss court refused to examine the reasonableness of the freezing vis-à-vis the applicants. Since the UN decision was based on an international instrument promoting the respect of human rights, and international treaties were to be interpreted in harmony with one another, nothing prevented the Swiss court from examining the matter.[532]

Similarly, in the case *Avotiņš v. Latvia*, a question was raised as to whether a Latvian court could execute a judgment rendered by a Cypriot court in accordance with an EU regulation vis-à-vis a Latvian defendant when the defendant did not know about the action brought against him in Cyprus or its outcome, and he had complained about a violation of Article 6 after the judgment had been executed. In this case, the Grand Chamber developed what is known as the equivalent protection principle (*Bosphorus* protection principle). According to this principle, mutual recognition of judgments requires that two conditions are fulfilled: (1) that there is an absence of any margin of manoeuvre for the domestic court receiving a foreign judgment; and (2) that the full potential of the supervisory mechanism provided for by EU law is deployed. The Court's role in such cases is to make sure that the application of the presumption of equivalent protection does not leave any gap or lead to any situation that would render the protection of the human rights guaranteed by the Convention manifestly deficient. However, if such a gap exists and this situation cannot be remedied by EU law, the EU Member States cannot refrain from examining such a complaint under the Convention on the sole ground that they are applying EU law. The Court found no violation in the case, as the applicant still had the chance to lodge an appeal on the matter in Cyprus.[533]

#### 4.1.2.8. *Restrictions on Access to a Court in Criminal Matters and Convictions in Absentia*

The right of access to a court may be restricted in civil, criminal and administrative law cases. In criminal matters a decision may be taken not to prosecute or to discontinue the proceedings without infringing Article 6.[534] Also, a practice

---

532 *Al-Dulimi and Montana Management Inc. v. Switzerland* [GC], App. no. 5809/08, §§134–155, 21.6.2016. See also Karen Reid, *A Practitioner's Guide to the European Convention on Human Rights*, Sweet & Maxwell/Thomson Reuters, London 2019, p. 154; and Zane Ratniece, Kushtrim Istrefi, "The Limits of the Strasbourg Court's Two-Level Harmonization Approach vis-à-vis SC Resolutions in *Al-Dulimi*", *European Yearbook on Human Rights 2015*, pp. 379–390.

533 *Avotiņš v. Latvia* [GC], App. no. 17502/07, §§101–127, 23.5.2016. See also Giacomo Biagioni, "*Avotiņš v. Latvia*: the uneasy balance between mutual recognition of judgments and protection of fundamental rights", *European Papers*, vol. 1, no. 2, 2016, pp. 579–596.

534 *Deweer v. Belgium*, App. no. 6903/75, §49, 27.2.1980.

in which there is no hearing as to guilt or innocence when an accused pleads guilty at the beginning of his trial is still consistent with Article 6, provided that adequate safeguards exist to prevent any abuse.[535]

It is also permissible to issue a penal order by which a person is convicted and sentenced in respect of a minor criminal offence without any court hearing, provided that the person has sufficient opportunity to request a hearing.[536] However, it might be problematic to convict an accused *in absentia*. Even if such conduct may not as such be regarded as contrary to Article 6 of the Convention, a person convicted *in absentia*, who has not been shown to have waived his right to appear at the trial and to defend himself, is deprived of legal protection in cases in which he cannot obtain another court judgment in the matter.[537]

If a person has a valid excuse for not attending a court hearing, he or she must of course have the chance of a new hearing. For example, illness can be a valid excuse for absence from a hearing. However, in order to be accepted, the illness must expressly prevent the person from attending the hearing.[538] For example, in the case *Koski v. Finland*, the applicant had been summonsed to appear at the hearing in person. When he did not appear, did not present any valid excuse for his absence and when his counsel did not attend the hearing either, the domestic court had a sufficient ground for letting his appeal lapse. The applicant had submitted to the court, through his counsel, medical certificates indicating that he was suffering from gastroenteritis. The medical certificates did not, however, show that the applicant was unable to attend the hearing. Nor was he able to show subsequently that he had had a valid excuse and therefore the proceedings were not reopened. The summons had clearly indicated the consequences of an absence without a valid excuse. As the applicant's attorney was not present either, he could not defend the applicant in his absence. It fell to the discretion of the domestic court to decide whether the excuse indicated in the medical certificate justified the applicant's absence from the court hearing.[539]

In the case *Sejdovic v. Italy*, the applicant disappeared following a murder. Nothing, however, showed that he could have known about the proceedings against him or its timing. The Court held that even if the applicant had been indirectly aware of the commencement of the proceedings, it could not be

535 *X. v. the United Kingdom*, App. no. 5076/71, 23.3.1972. The adequate safeguards existed in this case as the judge was satisfied that the accused had understood the effects of his plea and the accused's confession was recorded.

536 *Hennings v. Germany*, App. no. 12129/86, 16.12.1992. See also *X. v. the Federal Republic of Germany*, App. no. 4260/69, 24.7.1970.

537 *Sejdovic v. Italy* [GC], App. no. 56581/00, §§81–85, 1.3.2006.

538 *Koski v. Finland* (dec.), App. no. 53329/10, §§32–34, 12.12.2013.

539 *Koski v. Finland* (dec.), App. no. 53329/10, §§32–34, 12.12.2013.

assumed that he would have waived his right to be present at the hearing in an unequivocal manner. As he did not have the opportunity to obtain a fresh determination of the merits of the charges against him by a court which had heard him in accordance with his defence rights, the Court found a violation.[540] Likewise in the case *Sanader v. Croatia*, the applicant was tried *in absentia* and convicted for war crimes. He lived abroad and after he learned about his conviction, he requested the Croatian court to reopen the proceedings. The court dismissed his request since he lived abroad and was not available to the Croatian authorities. The Court found a violation since the applicant had not been provided with an opportunity to obtain a fresh determination of the charges against him.[541]

The case *Gestur Jónsson and Ragnar Halldór Hall v. Iceland* concerned the issue of whether the Supreme Court proceedings provided a sufficient remedy for applicants convicted *in absentia* in the first instance court. The applicants were attorneys who had been convicted and fined in the District Court for offending the court and causing unnecessary delay in the case, thereby damaging their clients' and the other defendants' interests. They had not been summonsed to appear before the District Court, nor had they been heard. Before the Court, the Chamber held that the fines imposed amounted to a "criminal offence" and that the criminal limb of Article 6 was applicable. The Supreme Court had organised an oral hearing in which the applicants had had full legal representation. The Supreme Court had had full jurisdiction to examine both questions of law and questions of fact. It had fully reviewed the District Court's findings on the merits and confirmed the latter court's judgment by setting forth its own independent reasoning. In conclusion, the Chamber held that the applicants had been provided with sufficient opportunity to obtain before the Supreme Court a fresh factual and legal determination of their case which was in compliance with the fairness guarantees of Article 6 §1.[542] The Grand Chamber, however, disagreed with the Chamber on the question of the applicability of Article 6, considering that the proceedings at issue did not involve the determination of a "criminal charge" within its autonomous meaning and thus rejected the applicants' complaints under Article 6 as incompatible *ratione materiae* with the provisions of the Convention.[543]

A requirement for a convicted person to surrender to custody pending a decision on appeal when he or she has appealed on points of law was deemed

540 *Sejdovic v. Italy* [GC], App. no. 56581/00, §§86–90 and 105–106, 1.3.2006. See also Valerio Colandrea, "On the power of the European Court of Human Rights to order specific non-monetary measures: some remarks in light of the *Assanidze, Broniowski* and *Sejdovic* cases", *Human Rights Law Review*, vol. 7, no. 2, 2007, pp. 396–411, at pp. 405–411.

541 *Sanader v. Croatia*, App. no. 66408/12, §§89–96, 12.2.2015.

542 *Gestur Jónsson and Ragnar Halldór Hall v. Iceland*, App. nos. 68273/14+, §§59–74, 30.10.2018.

543 *Gestur Jónsson and Ragnar Halldór Hall v. Iceland* [GC], App. nos. 68273/14+, §98, 22.12.2020.

excessive, since, in practice, this prevented the right of access to a court on appeal.[544] However, criminal proceedings which have been held *in absentia* and whose reopening has been subsequently refused may also lead to a violation of Article 5 §1 if the accused has been detained with respect to that crime and the reopening is refused.[545]

### 4.1.3. WAIVER OF THE RIGHT OF ACCESS

A waiver of the right of access to a court is not in principle incompatible with the Convention.[546] A person may thus waive his or her right of access to a court in civil, criminal and administrative law cases. For example, arbitration is a very common and accepted reason for waiving the right to a trial.[547] However, a claim of waiver should be established freely and unequivocally and be attended by minimum safeguards,[548] and it should be subjected to particularly careful review. For example, in the case *Deweer v. Belgium* the waiver was found not to have been an act of the applicant's free will because he was faced with the provisional closure of his shop if he chose to go for trial. Therefore, the Court found a violation of Article 6.[549] Similarly, in the case *Marpa Zeeland B.V. and Metal Welding B.V. v. the Netherlands*, the Court found a violation because the applicant companies had been persuaded by the authorities not to appeal against their conviction.[550]

The case *Mutu and Pechstein v. Switzerland* concerned the examination of a dispute between professional sportspeople and their associations in the Court of Arbitration for Sport (CAS) and the question of whether such proceedings were impartial. The central issue was whether sportspeople had, by taking their disputes to arbitration, voluntarily waived at least some of their fair trial guarantees under Article 6. The rulings of the Court of Arbitration for Sport

---

544 *Omar v. France*, App. no. 24767/94, §40, 29.7.1998; *Poitrimol v. France*, App. no. 14032/88, §38, 23.11.1993; *Guérin v. France*, App. no. 25201/94, §45, 29.7.1998; *Khalfaoui v. France*, App. no. 34791/97, §46, 14.12.1999; and *Papon v. France*, App. no. 54210/00, §100, 25.7.2002. See also *Eliazer v. the Netherlands*, App. no. 38055/97, §35, 16.10.2001 (no violation), in which no such requirement existed.

545 *Stoichkov v. Bulgaria*, App. no. 9808/02, §§56 and 58–59, 24.3.2005; and *Baratta v. Italy*, App. no. 28263/09, §§117–119, 13.10.2015.

546 *Deweer v. Belgium*, App. no. 6903/75, §49, 27.2.1980; and *Pastore v. Italy* (dec.), App. no. 46483/99, 25.5.1999.

547 *Nordström-Janzon and Nordström-Lehtinen v. the Netherlands* (dec.), App. no. 28101/95, 27.11.1996.

548 *Suda v. the Czech Republic*, App. no. 1643/06, §§48–49, 28.10.2010; *Tabbane v. Switzerland* (dec.), App. no. 41069/12, §§26–27 and 30–31, 1.3.2016; and *Eiffage S.A. and Others v. Switzerland* (dec.), App. no. 1742/05, 15.9.2009.

549 *Deweer v. Belgium*, App. no. 6903/75, §49, 27.2.1980.

550 *Marpa Zeeland B.V. and Metal Welding B.V. v. the Netherlands*, App. no. 46300/99, §50, 9.11.2004.

could be appealed against to the Swiss Federal Tribunal. The Court held that the second applicant, who was a professional speed skater, had not had any other option than to accept the jurisdiction of the arbitration court and she could not therefore be regarded as having *voluntarily* waived her Article 6 rights. Nevertheless, her complaint that the arbitration court was not impartial because sportspeople's interests were not as well represented in that court as those of the sports federations was not, because of a lack of evidence, successful. Instead, the absence of an oral hearing led to an Article 6 violation. For the first applicant, a professional footballer, the choice of arbitration had not been obligatory, but his club had voluntarily chosen arbitration. He had been able to challenge the impartiality of one arbitrator and his fair trial rights had thus been guaranteed under Article 6. The Court did not find any lack of impartiality and there was no violation of Article 6.[551]

In another case concerning sportspeople, *Platini v. Switzerland*, the applicant – a former professional footballer who had committed financial irregularities at the head of FIFA (Fédération Internationale de Football Association) – incurred fines and had a four-year prohibition to participate on any football activities under a disciplinary decision rendered by the CAS imposed on him. After an unsuccessful appeal, the applicant lodged an application with the Court, arguing that the domestic decision violated his right to pursue a business. The Court declared the complaint inadmissible, even though it considered that the impugned acts or omissions were attributable to the Swiss State. The Court held that the applicant – who was the captain and coach of the French national team – had voluntarily accepted the CAS's jurisdiction and that he had had, both in the proceedings before the CAS and the Swiss Federal Tribunal, appropriate procedural safeguards.[552]

### 4.1.4. RELATIONSHIP WITH ARTICLE 13

The right of access to a court overlaps with Article 13 of the Convention, which guarantees the right to an effective national remedy in respect of a breach of a Convention right.[553] The overlap exists only insofar as the Convention right is also a civil right within the meaning of Article 6.[554] The right of access to a

551 *Mutu and Pechstein v. Switzerland*, App. nos. 40575/10+, §§94, 98, 113–115, 121–123, 156–157 and 175–188, 2.10.2018. See also Daniel Rietiker, "The European Court of Human Rights and FIFA – Current Issues and Potential Challenges", *European Convention on Human Rights Law Review*, vol. 1, no. 1, 2020, pp. 62–104, at pp. 82–83.

552 *Platini v. Switzerland* (dec.), App. no. 526/18, §§65–70, 5.3.2020. The case was examined under Article 8.

553 *Golder v. the United Kingdom*, App. no. 4451/70, §33, 21.2.1975.

554 *Kudła v. Poland* [GC], App. no. 30210/96, §146, 26.10.2000. See also *Powell and Rayner v. the United Kingdom*, App. no. 9310/81, §36, 21.2.1990.

court under Article 6 provides a stricter guarantee than the right to an effective remedy under Article 13, as it requires, unlike Article 13, a remedy before a court.[555]

## 4.2. RIGHT TO A FAIR TRIAL

**Article 6: Right to a fair trial**

1. *... everyone is entitled to a fair ... hearing ...*

### 4.2.1. BASIC PRINCIPLES

Unlike the other rights guaranteed by Article 6 §1 of the Convention, the right to a fair trial is an open class of rights to which the Court can add other relevant rights which have not been guaranteed elsewhere in Article 6. Under this right, the proceedings can also be assessed as a whole in those cases in which none of the specific rights guaranteed by Article 6 have been separately violated.[556] In general, any shortcomings in the fairness of the proceedings may, under certain conditions, be remedied at a later stage, either at the same level or by a higher court.[557]

In criminal matters, the right to a fair trial must be assessed in the light of the rights guaranteed in Article 6 §2 and 6 §3. Although the rights guaranteed in these paragraphs are included also in Article 6 §1, the latter complements the minimum requirements in those paragraphs.[558] When a certain matter falls within Article 6 §2 and 6 §3, the Court can examine that matter either solely under these paragraphs,[559] together with Article 6 §1,[560] or solely under Article 6 §1. If the Court chooses the latter option and finds a violation, it normally means that the proceedings were not fair in their entirety, including the appeal stages.[561]

555 *De Geouffre de la Pradelle v. France*, App. no. 12964/87, §37, 16.12.1992.

556 *Ankerl v. Switzerland*, App. no. 17748/91, §38, 23.10.1996; *Centro Europa 7 S.r.l. and Di Stefano v. Italy* [GC], App. no. 38433/09, §197, 7.6.2012; and *Regner v. the Czech Republic* [GC], App. no. 35289/11, §161, 19.9.2017.

557 *Helle v. Finland*, App. no. 20772/92, §§46 and 54, 19.12.1997; and *Schuler-Zgraggen v. Switzerland*, App. no. 14518/89, §52, 24.6.1993. Compare and contrast with *Albert and Le Compte v. Belgium*, App. nos. 7299/75+, §36, 10.2.1983; and *Feldbrugge v. the Netherlands*, App. no. 8562/79, §§45–46, 29.5.1986.

558 *Artico v. Italy*, App. no. 6694/74, §32, 13.5.1980.

559 See, for example, *Luedicke, Belkacem and Koç v. Germany*, App. nos. 6210/73+, 28.11.1978.

560 See, for example, *Benham v. the United Kingdom*, App. no. 19380/92, §52, 10.6.1996.

561 *Edwards v. the United Kingdom*, App. no. 13071/87, §§33–34, 16.12.1992. See also *Barberà, Messegué and Jabardo v. Spain*, App. nos. 10590/83+, §89, 6.12.1988, in which the Court found a violation of Article 6 §1 cumulatively on the basis of several factors, of which none constituted a violation in themselves.

Although the right to a fair trial applies equally to civil, administrative law and criminal proceedings, the respondent State normally has more room for manoeuvre in civil and administrative law cases than in criminal matters.[562] Even if some guarantees under Article 6 §3 also apply through Article 6 §1 to civil and administrative law cases, they are not necessarily applied with the same intensity and in exactly same manner to civil and administrative law cases as to criminal matters.[563] The same applies also to the rights which have been guaranteed only in Article 6 §1, such as the right to be present at a hearing. In the case *Moreira Ferreira v. Portugal (No. 2)* the Court confirmed that the rights of persons accused of or charged with a criminal offence require greater protection than the rights of parties to civil proceedings.[564]

Over time, several separate rights embodying different aspects of a fair trial have been added to the scope of Article 6 §1. Among the first were equality of arms and the right to a hearing in one's presence. Some other rights, such as the freedom from self-incrimination, were added later, and some rights are still in their nascent stages. A violation of these separate rights is in itself sufficient to find a violation under Article 6 §1 without there being a need to examine the other aspects of the proceedings.

## 4.2.2. HEARING IN ONE'S PRESENCE

The right to a hearing in one's presence is one of the rights guaranteeing a fair trial.[565] An applicant has a clear interest in being present during proceedings relevant to him or her. The right to be present is implicit in the right to "participate effectively" in the proceedings, in the right to adversarial proceedings[566] and, in criminal matters, in the rights guaranteed under Article 6 §3 (c), (d) and (e).[567] It is difficult to see how an applicant could realise these rights without being present at the hearing. If Article 6 did not explicitly require the organisation

562 *Dombo Beheer B.V. v. the Netherlands*, App. no. 14448/88, §32, 27.10.1993; and *Levages Prestations Services v. France*, App. no. 21920/93, §46, 23.10.1996.

563 *Dombo Beheer B.V. v. the Netherlands*, App. no. 14448/88, §32, 27.10.1993.

564 *Moreira Ferreira v. Portugal (No. 2)* [GC], App. no. 19867/12, §§66–67, 11.7.2017. See also Sofia Galani (Ed.), "Case and comment: selected decisions from the European Court of Human Rights from July and August 2017 – Article 6 and remedial practice, *Moreira Ferreira v. Portugal (No. 2)* (Application No. 19867/12)", *European Human Rights Law Review*, Issue 6, 2017, pp. 615–617; and Robert Spano, "'Arbitrary or manifestly unreasonable': the arbitrariness exception to the fourth instance doctrine under Article 6 of the European Convention on Human Rights", in Koen Lemmens, Stephan Parmentier, Louise Reyntjens (Eds.), *Human Rights with a Human Touch – Liber Amicorum Paul Lemmens*, Intersentia, Cambridge/Antwerp/Chicago 2019, pp. 523–537, at pp. 535–537.

565 *Colozza v. Italy*, App. no. 9024/80, §27, 12.2.1985.

566 *Ziliberberg v. Moldova*, App. no. 61821/00, §40, 1.2.2005.

567 *Sejdovic v. Italy* [GC], App. no. 56581/00, §81, 1.3.2006.

of an oral hearing, the applicant would not necessarily have the right to be present either.

While the accused has a general right to be present in person during the criminal proceedings against him or her,[568] a plaintiff in civil proceedings has such a right only in respect to certain types of actions. The right to be present concerns, for example, matters in which the personal characteristics or the way of life of the parties has direct relevance,[569] or matters which concern assessment of the applicant's behaviour. If domestic law requires an oral hearing to be held, the right to be present should be allowed or the hearing of the accused should be organised in some other way. For example, in Russia, 11 prisoners were systematically refused the right to attend civil proceedings, and their hearings were not organised in any other way. Such a categoric refusal constituted a violation of Article 6.[570]

A hearing also needed to be organised in the case *De Tommaso v. Italy*, in which a preventive measure had been imposed upon the applicant as a result of his being considered dangerous and his association with criminals. The measure involved a night-time curfew and restrictions on leaving the district where he lived, attending public meetings or using mobile phones or radio communication devices.[571] Similarly in *Evers v. Germany*, the applicant's hearing in person at the appeal level was necessary. A restraining order had been imposed on the applicant, since he had abused a mentally handicapped woman who had given birth to a child as a result. The Court considered that the case was about an assessment of the applicant's personal characteristics and noted that the restraining order had a far-reaching impact on his relationship with the victim. Since the issue was not only of a legal and technical nature, the appeal court should have given the applicant an opportunity to be heard in person.[572]

In other cases it is sufficient that the applicant's counsel is present.[573] Nevertheless, deciding on a civil matter *in absentia* without the presence of the

---

568 *Hermi v. Italy* [GC], App. no. 18114/02, §58, 18.10.2006. This may require also that prison personnel ensure an accused can attend the hearing if he or she has been informed about it; see *Goddi v. Italy*, App. no. 8966/80, §29, 9.4.1984.

569 For example, matters relating to custody and contact rights of children fall into this category, and certain trade issues may fall into it as well.

570 *Yevdokimov and Others v. Russia*, App. nos. 27236/05+, §§31 and 50–53, 16.2.2016.

571 *De Tommaso v. Italy* [GC], App. no. 43395/09, §§163–168, 23.2.2017. See also Sofia Galani (Ed.), "Case and comment: selected decisions from the European Court of Human Rights from January and February 2017 – Special supervision measures, *De Tommaso v. Italy* (Application No. 43395/09)", *European Human Rights Law Review*, Issue 3, 2017, pp. 332–335; and Stefan Kieber, "The jurisprudence of the European Court of Human Rights in 2017", *European Yearbook on Human Rights 2018*, pp. 229–265, at p. 237.

572 *Evers v. Germany*, App. no. 17895/14, §§98–99, 28.5.2020.

573 An applicant must show that his or her presence is necessary. See *X. v. Switzerland* (dec.), App. no. 7370/76, 28.2.1977.

parties requires that the same legal guarantees are in place as in the criminal proceedings, namely that the applicant has been correctly summonsed to appear or that domestic law provides for the opportunity for a retrial after the applicant has learned about the proceedings.[574] For example, in the case *Petkov v. Bulgaria*, the Court found a violation when a person was not heard in person during the proceedings in a paternity issue but biological paternity of a child was confirmed without his presence and without any DNA test, and subsequently no retrial was allowed.[575] In addition, it must also be remembered that the right to adversarial proceedings often requires that the parties' right to be present in civil proceedings is more widely recognised.[576]

#### 4.2.2.1. *Waiver of the Right to be Present*

A party to civil or criminal proceedings may waive his or her right to be present in person at the trial if this waiver has been given by his or her own free will. The waiver can be either express or tacit but it must have been established in an unequivocal manner. In addition, it is required that the waiver is attended by minimum safeguards commensurate to its importance, and that it does not run counter to any important public interest.[577]

The Court found in the case *T. v. Italy* that waiving the right to take part in a trial requires that the accused applicant has been informed about the proceedings. Vague and informal knowledge about the proceedings does not suffice, and the accused must be informed in accordance with procedural and substantive requirements capable of guaranteeing the effective exercise of the accused's rights.[578] The Grand Chamber relieved these requirements in the case *Sejdovic v. Italy*. It found that it could not rule out the possibility that certain established facts might provide an unequivocal indication that the accused was aware of the existence of the criminal proceedings against him and of the nature and the cause of the accusation and did not intend to take part in the

574 *Dilipak and Karakaya v. Turkey*, App. nos. 7942/05+, §§80, 84–88 and 93–95, 4.3.2014.

575 *Petkov v. Bulgaria*, App. no. 2641/06, §§57–58 and 63, 15.7.2014. The case was examined under Article 8 and a violation of Article 8 was found on procedural grounds. As the applicant was not reached at his permanent residence for summonsing, the summons was published in the official journal (*State Gazette*). The authorities did not make any further inquiries concerning the applicant's whereabouts. He was appointed *ex officio*, without his knowledge, a trustee who did not try to find him, did not appeal against the judgment nor ensured that a DNA test be ordered.

576 *Feldbrugge v. the Netherlands*, App. no. 8562/79, §44, 29.5.1986.

577 *Sejdovic v. Italy* [GC], App. no. 56581/00, §86, 1.3.2006. This case concerned criminal proceedings, but the same principles also apply to civil proceedings.

578 *T. v. Italy*, App. no. 14104/88, §28, 12.10.1992; and *F.C.B. v. Italy*, App. no. 12151/86, §33, 28.8.1991. Concerning summonsing a mentally ill person, see *Vaudelle v. France*, App. no. 35683/97, §§59–60, 30.1.2001.

trial or wished to escape prosecution. This may be the case, for example, where the accused states publicly or in writing that he does not intend to respond to summonses of which he has been made aware through sources other than the authorities, or succeeds in evading an attempted arrest, or when materials are brought to the attention of the authorities which unequivocally show that he is aware of the proceedings pending against him and of the charges he faces.[579] The fact alone that the accused is absent from his or her address or that his or her whereabouts are unknown is not sufficient, however, to show that he or she knew about the proceedings.

A waiver does not need to be express, but it can also be deduced from the applicant's behaviour; for example, when he or she intentionally decides not to take part in the trial. Simply being absent from the proceedings cannot, however, be regarded as being a waiver.[580] The applicant must have been informed well in advance about the time of the hearing[581] in a language which he or she understands.[582] Particular diligence is required when an accused has not been notified in person of a hearing but has been summonsed via his or her counsel.[583] It is not regarded as a waiver if the applicant does not attend a hearing which is held in a language other than his or her own when he or she has requested to be heard in his own language.[584] Nor is a waiver unequivocal when the applicant has not been able to reasonably foresee the consequences of it.[585]

#### *4.2.2.2. Default Judgments*

Default judgments or judgments *in absentia* – that is, judgments rendered in the absence of the applicant – are possible in two situations. First of all, they are possible if the respondent State has with diligence but in vain tried to summons the applicant to the trial. The reason behind this is that being unable to hold

579 *Sejdovic v. Italy* [GC], App. no. 56581/00, §99, 1.3.2006. See also Valerio Colandrea, "On the power of the European Court of Human Rights to order specific non-monetary measures: some remarks in light of the *Assanidze*, *Broniowski* and *Sejdovic* cases", *Human Rights Law Review*, vol. 7, no. 2, 2007, pp. 396–411, at pp. 405–411.

580 *Godlevskiy v. Russia* (dec.), App. no. 14888/03, 9.12.2004; and *Hermi v. Italy* [GC], App. no. 18114/02, §89, 18.10.2006.

581 *Yakovlev v. Russia*, App. no. 72701/01, §21, 15.3.2005; and *Ziliberberg v. Moldova*, App. no. 61821/00, §39, 1.2.2005.

582 *Brozicek v. Italy*, App. no. 10964/84, §41, 19.12.1989.

583 *Yavuz v. Austria*, App. no. 46549/99, §49, 27.5.2004.

584 *Zana v. Turkey*, App. no. 18954/91, §70, 25.11.1997.

585 For example, in the case *Jones v. the United Kingdom* (dec.), App. no. 30900/02, 9.3.2003, the applicant was aware of the hearing date and intentionally decided not to attend. At the relevant time, it was not, however, clear in the legislation that an absence could lead to a default judgment in the matter, in particular as in many other similar cases the proceedings had been suspended until the applicant was present in person.

a trial by default may paralyse the conduct of criminal proceedings, in that it may lead, for example, to dispersal of the evidence, expiry of the time limit for prosecution, or a miscarriage of justice.[586] If the accused in such situations later hears about the proceedings, he or she must be given an opportunity to have the charges re-examined in relation both to the facts and law.[587] The new trial corrects the possible mistakes caused by the absence of the accused, and an omission to provide such an opportunity means denial of justice.[588] Rehearing can be a fresh trial before the same court or alternatively a hearing by the appeal court if the latter is competent to examine the case also in respect of the facts.[589]

Second, default judgments are possible in situations in which the accused, who is aware of the trial, intentionally decides not to attend in order to prevent the continuation of the proceedings.[590] These situations differ from the waiver situations in that in these cases there is no express or tacit consent for the continuation of the proceedings despite the absence of the accused. Awareness of the hearing normally means that the applicant has been officially informed about the hearing, unless his conduct – for example, absconding – clearly signals the state of his or her awareness.[591]

The situations of intentional non-attendance may concern either the normal absconding of the accused, or other less clear situations, such as occurred, for example, in the case *Medenica v. Switzerland.* The applicant, who was accused in Switzerland, moved during the proceedings to the United States to practise his profession as a doctor specialising in the treatment of certain serious forms of cancer. One of his American patients obtained an American court order preventing him from returning to Switzerland and, for this reason, he was convicted in Switzerland *in absentia.* As the applicant had not provided a valid excuse for his absence and it did not involve a *force majeure* situation, the Swiss courts refused his application for re-examination. The Court did not find the situation problematic as it considered that the applicant himself had for the

---

586 *Colozza v. Italy*, App. no. 9024/80, §29, 12.2.1985. In this case the Court found a violation as the Italian authorities had not made sufficient efforts to locate the applicant and a default judgment was a manifestly disproportionate consequence of the applicant's failure to inform the authorities of a change of address. The State had the burden of proof to show that it had acted diligently. The Court did not expect the applicant to prove that he was not seeking to evade justice or that his absence was due to *force majeure* (§30). See also *T. v. Italy*, App. no. 14104/88, §29, 12.10.1992; and *F.C.B. v. Italy*, App. no. 12151/86, §33, 28.8.1991.

587 *Sejdovic v. Italy* [GC], App. no. 56581/00, §82, 1.3.2006.

588 Ibid. For example, destruction of the case file is not a sufficient reason not to organise a fresh hearing; see *Stoichkov v. Bulgaria*, App. no. 9808/02, §§56–58, 24.3.2005.

589 The applicant must have an opportunity to present new evidence at the appeal stage; see, for example, *Jones v. the United Kingdom* (dec.), App. no. 30900/02, 9.3.2003. The applicant must also have sufficient time to prepare his appeal, see *Sejdovic v. Italy* [GC], App. no. 56581/00, §103, 1.3.2006.

590 *Sejdovic v. Italy* [GC], App. no. 56581/00, §82, 1.3.2006.

591 Ibid, §99.

most part created the situation which prevented him leaving the country.[592] In those situations in which the applicant tries to evade justice, he has no right to require a fresh examination. The same applies also to those situations in which the applicant has waived his right to be present at a hearing.[593]

The significance of the absence of an accused has also been at stake in situations in which the lawfully summonsed accused has failed to appear in court but his or her counsel has been present. These kinds of situations are examined more in detail in Chapter 6, section 6.4.

Problems with summonsing may also naturally appear in civil matters and in particular in those situations in which the address of a defendant residing abroad is not known to the domestic authorities. Nevertheless, the authorities also have in these situations an obligation to actively clarify the defendant's address by using different means. This obligation was apparent for example in the case *Schmidt v. Latvia*, which concerned a wife living in Germany who had, without her knowledge, been granted a divorce in Latvia from her husband living in Latvia upon the initiative of the husband. After being summonsed through summons sent to her previous place of residence in Riga, which was still her husband's place of residence, and the court having received the information that she no longer lived there, the applicant had been summonsed to the divorce proceedings through a notice published in the *Official Gazette*. Although her husband claimed to know nothing about her whereabouts, it turned out that the applicant still lived in Germany in the couple's previous place of residence, the landline there was used for their telephone conversations, the husband still received correspondence at that address, and the couple had children together. The applicant only learned about the divorce when she attended her husband's funeral in Latvia. The Court found a violation of Article 6.[594]

#### *4.2.2.3. Applicant's Disruptive Behaviour in the Courtroom or Partial Absence*

Proceedings which have already been started can be continued without the presence of the applicant if he or she has fallen ill or has done something to disrupt the proceedings in some way. In the case *Ensslin, Baader and Raspe v. the Federal Republic of Germany*, the applicants, who were on hunger strike,

---

592 *Medenica v. Switzerland*, App. no. 20491/92, §59, 14.6.2001.

593 *Sejdovic v. Italy* [GC], App. no. 56581/00, §82, 1.3.2006; and *Einhorn v. France* (dec.), App. no. 71555/01, §33, 16.10.2001. The State must create a mechanism which can help establish whether an applicant has really waived his right or does not otherwise intend to attend the hearing. In the case *Somogyi v. Italy*, App. no. 67972/01, §§71–73, 18.5.2004, the Court found a violation on the ground that the applicant's claim that his signature for the acknowledgment of reception of the summons was forged was not examined.

594 *Schmidt v. Latvia*, App. no. 22493/05, §§89–97, 27.4.2017.

could only attend the hearing for a couple of hours per day. The decision to continue the proceedings despite their absence was not contrary to Article 6, as their counsels were present all the time and they had unlimited opportunities to consult their clients.[595]

Similarly, an accused or other plaintiff or applicant whose behaviour disrupts the proceedings may be removed from the courtroom, at least temporarily. For example, in the case *Marguš v. Croatia* the Court did not find a violation of any fair trial criteria when the applicant was removed from the courtroom while his counsel remained there. The applicant had already been warned twice, in vain, that he was disrupting the order in the courtroom. The counsel stayed in the courtroom to present the applicant's closing arguments and he was thus legally represented throughout the proceedings. In these circumstances the Court held that the applicant had had ample opportunity to develop his defence.[596]

Also, an accused who invokes a non-existent illness in order to prolong the proceedings can be convicted *in absentia*.[597]

#### *4.2.2.4. Presence During an Appeal*

An applicant's right to be present in person at an oral hearing organised by an appellant court is limited. In certain situations, the written proceedings are sufficient in themselves and the question of the right to be present does not even arise. The Court has required that an oral hearing be held at the appeal stage in situations where it has been necessary to hear the applicants as witnesses. This naturally means that an applicant's presence is in such situations required.

In the case *Hokkeling v. the Netherlands*, the Court required that the defendant had a right to be present in person at the hearing of the Court of Appeal when he had specifically requested it and when his counsel had requested the postponement of the hearing in order that the applicant, who was detained in Norway, could be brought to the hearing. Although there were reasons for the timely conclusion of the case, it was justified to require that the applicant be present in person and that he be heard, since his sentence was about to be increased from four years and six months in prison to eight years.[598]

---

595 *Ensslin, Baader and Raspe v. the Federal Republic of Germany* (dec.), App. nos. 7572/76+, 8.7.1978. See also *Ninn-Hansen v. Denmark* (dec.), App. no. 28972/95, 18.5.1999.

596 *Marguš v. Croatia* [GC], App. no. 4455/10, §§90–91, 27.5.2014. See also Michael Hamilton, "Human rights courts as norm-brokers", *Human Rights Law Review*, vol. 18, no. 2, 2018, pp. 205–232. See also *Idalov v. Russia* [GC], App. no. 5826/03, §175, 22.5.2012; and *Ananyev v. Russia*, App. no. 20292/04, §43, 30.7.2009.

597 *X. v. the United Kingdom* (dec.), App. no. 4798/71, 22.3.1972.

598 *Hokkeling v. the Netherlands*, App. no. 30749/12, §§59–63, 14.2.2017.

### 4.2.3. EFFECTIVE PARTICIPATION AND LEGAL SAFEGUARDS CONCERNING YOUNG OFFENDERS

The Court found in the case *Stanford v. the United Kingdom* that Article 6 not only guarantees a right to be present at a court hearing but also a right to follow the proceedings and to participate effectively. This right derives from the adversarial nature of the proceedings as well as from the special guarantees provided for by Article 6 §3 (c), (d) and (e), which also can apply to civil matters.[599] The Court has subsequently held that the use of a video link in the proceedings is not, as such, incompatible with the notion of a fair and public hearing but recourse to this measure must serve a legitimate aim and the arrangements for the giving of evidence must be compatible with the requirements of due process. In particular, it must be ensured that the applicant is able to follow the proceedings and to be heard without technical impediments, and that effective and confidential communication with a lawyer is provided for.[600]

Nor is it incompatible with the Article 6 requirements that an accused is placed, for security reasons, in a secure glass enclosure during the hearing if he is able to communicate freely and confidentially both with his counsel and the court.[601] If no security reasons for placing an accused in an enclosure exist, doing so can even be in violation of Article 3 (inhuman or degrading treatment). For example, in the cases *Harutyunyan v. Armenia* and *Khodorkovskiy v. Russia*, the Court found a violation because the applicants were accused of a non-violent crime and no security risks were shown to exist in relation to the hearing.[602]

A similar situation was also at stake in the case *Mariya Alekhina and Others v. Russia*, which concerned a protest held in a cathedral by the members of the feminist punk band Pussy Riot. During the hearing, the applicants were held in an

---

599 *Stanford v. the United Kingdom*, App. no. 16757/90, §26, 23.2.1994. In this case, the applicant had difficulty hearing and following the proceedings because of a hearing impairment and the acoustics of the courtroom. The Court did not, however, find a violation because the domestic court had not been informed about the applicant's hearing problem and the applicant had been represented by competent counsel who had been able to communicate with him. See also *Murtazaliyeva v. Russia* [GC], App. no. 36658/05, §91, 18.12.2018; *Pullicino v. Malta* (dec.), App. no. 45441/99, 15.6.2000; and *Moiseyev v. Russia*, App. no. 62936/00, §214, 9.10.2008.

600 *Marcello Viola v. Italy*, App. no. 45106/04, §§63–67, 5.10.2006; and *Sakhnovskiy v. Russia* [GC], App. no. 21272/03, §98, 2.11.2010.

601 *Auguste v. France* (dec.), App. no. 11837/85, 13.2.1991; *Svinarenko and Slyadnev v. Russia* [GC], App. nos. 32541/08+, §134, 17.7.2014; and *Yaroslav Belousov v. Russia*, App. nos. 2653/13+, §147, 4.10.2016. Nor did the hand-cuffing of the applicant lead to a violation on this ground, see *Campbell v. the United Kingdom* (dec.), App. no. 12323/86, 13.7.1988.

602 *Ashot Harutyunyan v. Armenia*, App. no. 34334/04, §§125–129, 15.6.2010; and *Khodorkovskiy v. Russia*, App. no. 5829/04, §§124–126, 31.5.2011. In the latter case the Court considered that the proceedings concerned an applicant who was accused of a non-violent crime and no security risks for the hearing were shown to exist. Placing the applicant in a metal cage was considered, together the other security arrangements in the courtroom (such as bringing the applicant to court in handcuffs) as degrading under Article 3 of the Convention.

enclosed dock with glass walls, a tight-fitting door and insufficient ventilation. A desk for their lawyers was installed in front of the dock and the applicants could communicate with them only through a small window which was placed only a metre off the ground. The applicants had to take turns to speak to their lawyers as the window was too small for all three of them to use it simultaneously. There was always high security around the dock, which at times included seven armed police officers and a guard dog. Confidential communication with the defence team was impossible as a police officer always stood nearby monitoring their conversations. Although the Court was mindful of the security issues a criminal court hearing might involve, it emphasised the importance attached to the rights of the defence. It held that any measures restricting the defendant's participation in the proceedings or imposing limitations on his or her relations with lawyers should only be imposed insofar as was necessary and should be proportionate to the risks in a specific case. In the applicants' case, these rights had been restricted in such a manner that the proceedings were no longer fair.[603]

Concerning criminal proceedings against young people in particular, the Court has emphasised that the special requirements of the criminal proceedings must be taken into account. The proceedings must be organised in such a manner that the best interest of the child is taken into account.[604] Particular attention must be paid to the child's age and maturity, as well as to his emotional and intellectual capacity. It must be ensured that the child can, as well as possible, understand the conduct of the proceedings and participate in the trial.[605]

In proceedings concerning young people, the fair trial guarantees are accentuated during the pretrial investigation phase in order to secure the fairness of the subsequent trial. The authorities must, from the moment the first measures are taken, consider the vulnerability and strength of the young person, in particular during police interrogations. The authorities must act, as far as possible, to ensure that the young person himself does not feel forced or suppressed, and that he understands, as well as possible, the nature of the investigation, the importance of the case for him, the significance of any sentence potentially imposed on him, his right to a defence and his right not to incriminate himself.[606] Concerning particularly young and vulnerable groups,

---

603 *Mariya Alekhina and Others v. Russia*, App. no. 38004/12, §§166–173, 17.7.2018. See also Sofia Galani, "Case and comment: selected decisions from the European Court of Human Rights for July and August 2018 – Pussy Riot, *Mariya Alekhina v. Russia* (Application No. 38004/12)", *European Human Rights Law Review*, Issue 6, 2018, pp. 625–628.

604 See Article 3 of the UN Convention on the Rights of the Child; and Directive (EU) 2016/800 of the European Parliament and of the Council of 11 May 2016 on procedural safeguards for children who are suspects or accused persons in criminal proceedings.

605 *V. v. the United Kingdom* [GC], App. no. 24888/94, §86, 16.12.1999; *Panovits v. Cyprus*, App. no. 4268/04, §67, 11.12.2008; and *Adamkiewicz v. Poland*, App. no. 54729/00, §70, 2.3.2010.

606 *Panovits v. Cyprus*, App. no. 4268/04, §67, 11.12.2008; *S.C. v. the United Kingdom*, App. no. 60958/00, §29, 15.6.2004; and *Martin v. Estonia*, App. no. 35985/09, §92, 30.5.2013.

the authorities must make sure that the defence of such a person is taken care of and that a legal counsel is appointed to him as early as the beginning of the pretrial investigation.[607] Similarly, the use of written statements from absent witnesses in cases concerning young people must be subject to a detailed analysis and careful assessment.[608]

The Court found a violation in respect of the organisation of the proceedings, for example, in the case *V. v. the United Kingdom*. The case concerned criminal proceedings against an 11-year-old boy in which he was accused of the murder of a two-year-old child. The hearings lasted three weeks in a full courtroom. Although there had been attempts to take into account the young age of the applicant by, for example, explaining to him the course of the proceedings, showing him the courtroom in advance and shortening the hearing, there were still signs that the applicant was panicked and unable to follow the hearing. For example, the fact that the dock had been raised to enable the applicant to better see what was going on, had the effect of increasing his sense of discomfort during the trial, since he felt exposed to the scrutiny of the press and public. The Court held that the applicant's right to participate effectively in the hearing had not been respected. Although his counsels were sitting close to him, the applicant was not able to consult with them or follow altogether what happened in the courtroom.[609]

The legal safeguards of the pretrial investigation phase when a young person is involved were emphasised in the case *Blokhin v. Russia*. The Court found a violation when a 12-year-old defendant had been interrogated in the pretrial investigation without the presence of his counsel and without providing him with an opportunity to contact his family. In these circumstances and taking into account the applicant's very young age, the interrogations were psychologically traumatic and conducive to violating the applicant's right to remain silent. He should have had a legal counsel present at the interrogations. Moreover, his statements were used against him at the trial. Although the applicant had the opportunity to challenge the evidence at the trial, the absence of a counsel during the pretrial investigation weakened his chances of defending himself at the trial. This rendered the proceedings unfair. In addition, the applicant did not have, as a result of the domestic legislation, the opportunity to cross-examine those witnesses whose testimonies against him had been decisive as evidence. The Court also found a violation of Article 5 (right to liberty and security) as

---

607 *Salduz v. Turkey* [GC], App. no. 36391/02, §§50–55, 27.11.2008; and *Blokhin v. Russia*, App. no. 47152/06, §§158–160, 14.11.2013.

608 *Blokhin v. Russia*, App. no. 47152/06, §§161–163, 14.11.2013.

609 *V. v. the United Kingdom* [GC], App. no. 24888/94, §§86 and 90, 16.12.1999. See also the case concerning the applicant's co-defendant *T. v. the United Kingdom* [GC], App. no. 24724/94, §88, 16.12.1999; and Francis G. Jacobs, Robin C.A. White, Clare Owey, *The European Convention on Human Rights*, Oxford University Press, Oxford 2017, pp. 278 and 296.

the applicant's detention had lacked any educational elements and the medical treatment for his neurological problems had been deficient.[610]

In addition, the sentences imposed on young people can be unreasonable. The sentencing as such falls within the margin of appreciation of the respondent State and the Court accepts different practices in this respect. Nevertheless, clear overly strict sanctions can be incompatible with the Convention and can also violate articles other than Article 6. For example, in the case *Gülcü v. Turkey*, the Court found it disproportionate that a 15-year-old boy was sentenced to almost three years' imprisonment for throwing stones at the police during a demonstration. Although the Contracting States have a wide margin of appreciation when it comes to sentencing, the sanction imposed did not take into account the applicant's young age or the fact that he was using his Article 11 right to assembly.[611]

### 4.2.4. EQUALITY OF ARMS

The right to a fair trial requires the equality of arms of the parties.[612] This principle, which applies to both civil and criminal proceedings,[613] is closely linked to the adversarial principle.[614] It requires that each party to the proceedings is given a reasonable opportunity to present their case under conditions that do not place them at a substantial disadvantage vis-à-vis their opponent.[615] However, perfect similarity is not required and therefore, for example, the level of public legal aid does not need to be the same as the funding of legal representation in the private domain.[616] In leave-to-appeal proceedings the principle is not violated when neither of the parties is represented in person in the proceedings.[617]

The principle of equality of arms embodies an idea that there is a fair balance between the parties.[618] In assessing this, the appearance of the fair

610 *Blokhin v. Russia*, App. no. 47152/06, §§158–177, 14.11.2013. See also Sofia Galani (Ed.), "Case and comment: selected decisions from the European Court of Human Rights from March and April 2016 – Detention of minors, *Blokhin v. Russia* (Application No. 47152/06)", *European Human Rights Law Review*, Issue 4, 2016, pp. 461–465.

611 *Gülcü v. Turkey*, App. no. 17526/10, §§115–117, 19.1.2016 (violation of Article 11).

612 *Neumeister v. Austria*, App. no. 1936/63, §22, 27.6.1968.

613 *Dombo Beheer B.V. v. the Netherlands*, App. no. 14448/88, §33, 27.10.1993; and *Feldbrugge v. the Netherlands*, App. no. 8562/79, §44, 29.5.1986. See also Dragoljub Popović, *European Human Rights Law – A Manual: An Introduction to the Strasbourg Court and its Jurisprudence*, Eleven International Publishing, The Hague 2013, p. 193.

614 *Regner v. the Czech Republic* [GC], App. no. 35289/11, §146, 19.9.2017.

615 *Kress v. France* [GC], App. no. 39594/98, §72, 7.6.2001; and *Regner v. the Czech Republic* [GC], App. no. 35289/11, §146, 19.9.2017.

616 *Steel and Morris v. the United Kingdom*, App. no. 68416/01, §72, 15.2.2005.

617 *Monnell and Morris v. the United Kingdom*, App. nos. 9562/81+, §62, 2.3.1987.

618 *Dombo Beheer B.V. v. the Netherlands*, App. no. 14448/88, §33, 27.10.1993.

administration of justice and the significance of the matter to the applicant are relevant considerations.[619] In criminal matters this principle under Article 6 §1 overlaps with the special rights guaranteed under Article 6 §3, but its scope of application is wider since it applies to all aspects of the proceedings.[620] The applicant is not required to provide evidence that the non-application of the principle would have led to a materially unfair *outcome* of the case; rather a purely procedural inequality suffices for finding a violation.[621]

In criminal matters, the principle of equality of arms requires first of all that the prosecutor and the defence are given the same opportunity and approximately the same time to present their case.[622] Both parties must also be given an opportunity to comment on each other's evidence and submissions.[623] The principle also requires that the norms regulating criminal proceedings are laid down in legislation, as they normally have been enacted for the benefit of the defence and their lack of ambiguity is often to the defence's detriment.[624]

Moreover, an expert appointed by the accused must be treated in the same way as an expert who has connections to the prosecutor.[625] An expert appointed by the court itself must be a neutral one.[626] The domestic courts are free to refuse to call experts or witnesses proposed by the defence.[627] However, in certain circumstances a refusal to allow an alternative expert examination of material evidence may be regarded as a violation of Article 6 §1 as it may be hard to challenge an expert report without the assistance of another expert in the relevant field.[628] In the case *J.M. and Others v. Austria*, the applicants alleged that the hearing at the trial of the court-appointed expert witness, who had also acted as an expert appointed by the public prosecutor at the stage of the preliminary proceedings, put them in a less favourable position vis-à-vis the prosecutor. The Court found no violation in the case since the expert was a university law professor who was not employed by the prosecutor's office, his remuneration was not dependent on the outcome of the case, he was under a strict duty of

619 *A.B. v. Slovakia*, App. no. 41784/98, §55, 4.3.2003.

620 *Ofner and Hopfinger v. Austria* (dec.), App. nos. 524/59+, §46, 23.11.1962; and *Ibrahim and Others v. the United Kingdom* [GC], App. nos. 50541/08+, §251, 13.9.2016.

621 *Bulut v. Austria*, App. no. 17358/90, §49, 22.2.1996. See also Karen Reid, *A Practitioner's Guide to the European Convention on Human Rights*, Sweet & Maxwell/Thomson Reuters, London 2019, p. 193.

622 *Ekbatani v. Sweden*, App. no. 10563/83, §30, 26.5.1988; *Borgers v. Belgium*, App. no. 12005/86, 30.10.1991; and *Zahirović v. Croatia*, App. no. 58590/11, §§44–50, 25.4.2013.

623 *Kuopila v. Finland*, App. no. 27752/95, §38, 27.4.2000.

624 *Coëme and Others v. Belgium*, App. nos. 32492/96+, §102, 22.6.2000.

625 *Bönisch v. Austria*, App. no. 8658/79, §32, 6.5.1985.

626 *Brandstetter v. Austria*, App. nos. 11170/84+, §45, 28.8.1991.

627 *Huseyn and Others v. Azerbaijan*, App. nos. 36085/05+, §196, 26.7.2011; *Khodorkovskiy and Lebedev v. Russia (No. 2)*, App. nos. 51111/07+, §§718 and 721, 14.1.2020; and *Poletan and Azirovik v. "the former Yugoslav Republic of Macedonia"*, App. nos. 26711/07+, §95, 12.5.2016.

628 *Stoimenov v. "the former Yugoslav Republic of Macedonia"*, App. no. 17995/02, §38, 5.4.2007; *Matytsina v. Russia*, App. no. 58428/10, §169, 27.3.2014; and *Khodorkovskiy and Lebedev v. Russia (No. 2)*, App. nos. 51111/07+, §187, 14.1.2020.

objectivity and his appearance before the court had not been shown to be biased either. Nor was his statement decisive evidence in the applicants' conviction. The applicants had also had, as defendants, the right to call experts and to challenge the statement made by the expert in question.[629]

There may also be a violation of the principle of equality of arms if the applicant's counsel, but not the prosecutor, has to wait for several hours before the hearing.[630] Similarly, a violation was found when the applicant, who had been convicted on appeal and had requested to be present before the Supreme Court, had been excluded from a preliminary hearing held *in camera*.[631] A court's refusal to hear any witnesses or examine evidence for the defence but examining the witnesses and evidence for the prosecution may also raise an issue from the perspective of equality of arms.[632] The same is true if the trial court refuses to call defence witnesses to clarify an uncertain situation which constitutes the basis of charges.[633] A prosecutor's failure to submit all the evidence to the defence may violate both the principle of equality of arms as well as the right to adversarial proceedings.[634] The same is also true if the accused is given only restricted access to the case file as a result of public-interest considerations.[635] However, the Court has found it compatible with the principle of equality of arms that a civil party's possibilities to appeal are limited without limiting those of the public prosecutor, since their roles and objectives are clearly different.[636]

In civil matters the principle of equality of arms is violated when one party is allowed to attend the hearing and the other is not.[637] The same is true when the parties do not have the same opportunities to call witnesses,[638]

---

629 *J.M. and Others v. Austria*, App. no. 61503/14, §§120–129, 1.6.2017. See also *Khodorkovskiy and Lebedev v. Russia (No. 2)*, App. nos. 51111/07+, §499, 14.1.2020; *Shulepova v. Russia*, App. no. 34449/03, §62, 11.12.2008; and *Poletan and Azirovik v. "the former Yugoslav Republic of Macedonia"*, App. nos. 26711/07+, §94, 12.5.2016.

630 *Makhfi v. France*, App. no. 59335/00, §41, 19.10.2004.

631 *Zhuk v. Ukraine*, App. no. 45783/05, §35, 21.10.2010. See also *Eftimov v. "the former Yugoslav Republic of Macedonia"*, App. no. 59974/08, §41, 2.7.2015 in which an applicant was not allowed to be present at a hearing before the appeal court while the representative of the prosecution *was* present.

632 *Borisova v. Bulgaria*, App. no. 56891/00, §§47–48, 21.12.2006; and *Topić v. Croatia*, App. no. 51355/10, §48, 10.10.2013.

633 *Kasparov and Others v. Russia*, App. no. 21613/07, §§64–65, 3.10.2013.

634 *Bendenoun v. France*, App. no. 12547/86, 24.2.1994 (no violation); and *Kuopila v. Finland*, App. no. 27752/95, §38, 27.4.2000.

635 *Matyjek v. Poland*, App. no. 38184/03, §63, 24.4.2007; *Moiseyev v. Russia*, App. no. 62936/00, §217, 9.10.2008; and *Beraru v. Romania*, App. no. 40107/04, §70, 18.3.2014.

636 *Berger v. France*, App. no. 48221/99, §38, 3.12.2002. See also *Stankiewicz v. Poland*, App. no. 46917/99, §68, 6.4.2006.

637 *Komanický v. Slovakia*, App. no. 32106/96, §50, 4.7.2002.

638 *Dombo Beheer B.V. v. the Netherlands*, App. no. 14448/88, §33, 27.10.1993. See also *Ankerl v. Switzerland*, App. no. 17748/91, §38, 23.10.1996; and *Wierzbicki v. Poland*, App. no. 24541/94, §45, 18.6.2002, in which the Court found no violation.

or to submit written comments on the other party's submissions.[639] In civil matters the Court has also held that the principle of equality of arms requires that a party to the proceedings has the opportunity to cross-examine witnesses, to have material evidence admitted,[640] and to be informed about the reasoning of an administrative decision.[641] An expert appointed by the court must be neutral,[642] and the parties must be guaranteed the same access to the relevant materials.[643] Unequal time limits for appeal[644] and unequally distributed costs and expenses[645] may lead to a violation of the principle of equality of arms. However, equality of arms does not entail a party's right to have disclosed to him or her, before the hearing, submissions which have not been disclosed to the other parties to the proceedings, to the reporting judge, or the judges of the trial bench.[646] The principle of equality of arms has also been invoked in some civil cases in which the State has enacted legislation retroactively with the intention of intervening in pending cases brought against the State.[647] The Court has in some cases rejected complaints about inequality of arms by using the "significant disadvantage" admissibility criterion.[648]

### 4.2.5. ADVERSARIAL PROCEEDINGS

The right to adversarial proceedings means that a party to civil, administrative law or criminal proceedings has the opportunity to have knowledge of and comment on all evidence adduced or observations filed, with a view to influencing the

639 *Ruiz-Mateos v. Spain*, App. no. 12952/87, §65, 23.6.1993. See also Arman Zrvandyan, *Casebook on European Fair Trial Standards in Administrative Justice*, Council of Europe Publishing, Strasbourg 2016, p. 93.

640 *De Haes and Gijsels v. Belgium*, App. no. 19983/92, §58, 24.2.1997.

641 *Hentrich v. France*, App. no. 13616/88, §56, 22.9.1994.

642 *Sara Lind Eggertsdóttir v. Iceland*, App. no. 31930/04, §53, 5.7.2007; and *Letinčić v. Croatia*, App. no. 7183/11, §51, 3.5.2016.

643 *Schuler-Zgraggen v. Switzerland*, App. no. 14518/89, §52, 24.6.1993 (no violation). See also *Van de Hurk v. the Netherlands*, App. no. 16034/90, §57, 19.4.1994 (no violation); *Yvon v. France*, App. no. 44962/98, §37, 24.4.2003; and *Letinčić v. Croatia*, App. no. 7183/11, §51, 3.5.2016.

644 *Platakou v. Greece*, App. no. 38460/97, §48, 11.1.2001; and *Dacia SRL v. Moldova*, App. no. 3052/04, §76, 18.3.2008.

645 *Stankiewicz v. Poland*, App. no. 46917/99, §69, 6.4.2006.

646 *Kress v. France* [GC], App. no. 39594/98, §73, 7.6.2001. See also Arman Zrvandyan, *Casebook on European Fair Trial Standards in Administrative Justice*, Council of Europe Publishing, Strasbourg 2016, pp. 94–95.

647 *Stran Greek Refineries and Stratis Andreadis v. Greece*, App. no. 13427/87, §50, 9.12.1994; and *OGIS-Institut Stanislas, OGEC Saint-Pie X and Blanche de Castille and Others v. France*, App. nos. 42219/98+, §72, 27.5.2004 (no violation).

648 *Liga Portuguesa de Futebol Profissional v. Portugal* (dec.), App. no. 49639/09, §§36–40, 3.4.2012; *Kılıç and Others v. Turkey* (dec.), App. no. 33162/10, 3.12.2013; *Holub v. the Czech Republic* (dec.), App. no. 24880/05, 14.12.2010; *Colloredo Mannsfeld v. the Czech Republic*, App. nos. 15275/11+, §§33–34, 15.12.2016; and *Cavajda v. the Czech Republic* (dec.), App. no. 17696/07, 29.3.2011.

court's decision.[649] It is the duty of the court to inform the accused or the parties to civil proceedings of the existence of such evidence or documents. It is thus not sufficient that the case materials are only at the disposal of the parties when they come to the court without first having been disclosed to them in advance.[650]

In criminal matters the right to adversarial proceedings is emphasised by special regulation under Article 6 §3 (b) and (d).[651] In criminal matters the right to adversarial proceedings requires, for example, that the prosecutor discloses to the defence all material evidence gathered for and against in the case, irrespective of whether it will be used or not.[652] This obligation is not, however, absolute: the accused may be expected to give specific reasons for his or her request for access to evidence, and the domestic courts are entitled to examine the validity of these reasons.[653] The prosecutor may also decline to disclose evidence if such a refusal is absolutely necessary for the protection of the fundamental rights of others or for the protection of an important public interest.[654] Other acceptable reasons are,

---

649 *Vermeulen v. Belgium*, App. no. 19075/91, §33, 20.2.1996; *Rowe and Davis v. the United Kingdom* [GC], App. no. 28901/95, §60, 16.2.2000; *Werner v. Austria*, App. no. 21835/93, §66, 24.11.1997; *Ruiz-Mateos v. Spain*, App. no. 12952/87, §63, 23.6.1993; *McMichael v. the United Kingdom*, App. no. 16424/90, §80, 24.2.1995; *Lobo Machado v. Portugal*, App. no. 15764/89, §31, 20.2.1996; and *Kress v. France* [GC], App. no. 39594/98, §74, 7.6.2001. See also *Milatová and Others v. the Czech Republic*, App. no. 61811/00, §§63–66, 21.6.2005; and *Gaspari v. Slovenia*, App. no. 21055/03, §53, 21.7.2009 for proceedings before a Constitutional Court.

650 *Göç v. Turkey* [GC], App. no. 36590/97, §57, 11.7.2002; *Kerojärvi v. Finland*, App. no. 17506/90, §41, 19.7.1995; and *H.A.L. v. Finland*, App. no. 38267/97, §45, 27.1.2004.

651 This special regulation applies to civil matters through the principle of equality of arms and the right to adversarial proceedings, guaranteed by Article 6 §1, see *Wierzbicki v. Poland*, App. no. 24541/94, §39, 18.6.2002. See also *Leas v. Estonia*, App. no. 59577/08, §80, 6.3.2012.

652 *Edwards and Lewis v. the United Kingdom* [GC], App. nos. 39647/98+, §46, 27.10.2004. This right has sometimes been considered as a separate fair trial requirement of its own. See also *Rowe and Davis v. the United Kingdom* [GC], App. no. 28901/95, §66, 16.2.2000; *Mirilashvili v. Russia*, App. no. 6293/04, §200, 11.12.2008; *Leas v. Estonia*, App. no. 59577/08, §81, 6.3.2012; and *Matanović v. Croatia*, App. no. 2742/12, §161, 4.4.2017. Concerning the disclosure of electronic data, it is important to ensure that the defence is provided with an opportunity to be involved in the laying-down of the criteria for determining what might be relevant for disclosure. Any refusal to allow the defence to have further searches of such data carried out in principle raises an issue, see *Sigurður Einarsson and Others v. Iceland*, App. no. 39757/15, §§90–91, 4.6.2019; and *Rook v. Germany*, App. no. 1586/15, §§67 and 72, 25.7.2019.

653 *C.G.P. v. the Netherlands*, App. no. 29835/96, Commission decision, 15.1.1997; *Janatuinen v. Finland*, App. no. 28552/05, §45, 8.12.2009; *Leas v. Estonia*, App. no. 59577/08, §80, 6.3.2012; and *Matanović v. Croatia*, App. no. 2742/12, §157, 4.4.2017. In legal systems where the prosecuting authorities are obliged by law to take into consideration both the facts for and against the suspect, a procedure whereby the prosecuting authorities themselves attempt to assess what may or may not be relevant to the case, without any further procedural safeguards for the rights of the defence, cannot comply with the requirements of Article 6 §1: see *Natunen v. Finland*, App. no. 21022/04, §§47–49, 31.3.2009; and *Matanović v. Croatia*, App. no. 2742/12, §§158 and 181–182, 4.4.2017.

654 *Edwards and Lewis v. the United Kingdom* [GC], App. nos. 39647/98+, §46, 27.10.2004; *Van Mechelen and Others v. the Netherlands*, App. nos. 21363/93+, §58, 23.4.1997; and *Paci v. Belgium*, App. no. 45597/09, §85, 17.4.2018.

*inter alia*, national security, confidentiality of police undercover operations or the protection of witnesses.[655] If, for example, the public interest has been invoked in the case, it is not the Court's task to assess whether the refusal to disclose evidence was absolutely necessary but only to make sure that such a decision was made in a manner that gave sufficient guarantees for the protection of the interests of the accused.[656] What kind of role the undisclosed evidence would have had in the case is also relevant.[657] More about the right of access to pretrial investigation materials, see Chapter 6, section 6.3.3.2. below.

Similar issues have also been raised in the context of civil proceedings that concerned employment contracts and security clearances. In the case *Regner v. the Czech Republic*, the national security authority withdrew the applicant's security clearance, which had enabled him to occupy a senior role in the Ministry of Defence. The reason for the withdrawal was not disclosed to him, or to his counsel. The Court held that a refusal to disclose the confidential basis for withdrawal of the security clearance to the applicant or his counsel did not constitute a violation of Article 6. It found that the domestic courts had had the necessary independence and impartiality, and unlimited access to all the classified documents. They could assess the reasons given for not disclosing classified documents and order disclosure of those that they considered did not warrant that classification. The domestic courts had duly exercised the powers of scrutiny available to them and had reasoned their decisions to refuse access to classified documents by the need to keep the intelligence service's working methods secret. There was nothing to suggest that the classification of the documents in question had been carried out arbitrarily or for a purpose other than the legitimate interest indicated as being pursued. The Court nevertheless found it desirable – to the extent compatible with the preservation of confidentiality and proper conduct of the investigations – for the national authorities to have explained, if only summarily, the extent of the review they had carried out and the accusations against the applicant.[658]

The right to adversarial proceedings does not require that the applicant might sustain damage as a result of the violation of this right but that the parties

---

655 *Edwards and Lewis v. the United Kingdom* [GC], App. nos. 39647/98+, §46, 27.10.2004.

656 *Jasper v. the United Kingdom* [GC], App. no. 27052/95, §53, 16.2.2000.

657 See *Jasper v. the United Kingdom* [GC], App. no. 27052/95, §55, 16.2.2000; and *M. v. the Netherlands*, App. no. 2156/10, §69, 25.7.2017 and compare and contrast with the above-mentioned judgment in the case *Edwards and Lewis v. the United Kingdom* [GC], App. nos. 39647/98+, §46, 27.10.2004.

658 *Regner v. the Czech Republic* [GC], App. no. 35289/11, §§146–161, 19.9.2017 (no violation). See also Stefan Kieber, "The jurisprudence of the European Court of Human Rights in 2017", *European Yearbook on Human Rights 2018*, pp. 229–265, at pp. 238–239; and Sofia Galani (Ed.), "Case and comment: selected decisions from the European Court of Human Rights from September and October 2017 – National security and the right to a fair trial, *Regner v. Czech Republic* (Application No. 35289/11)", *European Human Rights Law Review*, Issue 1, 2018, pp. 83–85.

to the proceedings have an opportunity to decide whether and how they want to react to the disclosed documents.[659] The Court has applied this strictly in its case-law, finding that all possible material submitted to a court must be disclosed to the parties for their information.[660] The Court has found many violations of this right in the context of civil,[661] criminal[662] and administrative law[663] proceedings.[664] However, statements made by experts who are members of the composition of a court have not been regarded as the kind of documents that should be disclosed to the parties for information as they have been regarded as falling within the scope of confidential deliberations.[665]

The parties must also be informed about the materials which the court acquires *ex officio* and on which it bases its judgment or decision. The court's duty is to give the parties an opportunity to comment on these issues. The court's judgment or decision may not be based on elements that the parties have not been aware of and that they have not been able to comment on.[666]

---

[659] *Walston v. Norway*, App. no. 37372/97, §58, 3.6.2003.

[660] Although this right is strictly applied, the right to adversarial proceedings is not absolute and its scope may vary depending on the specific features of the case in question, see *Hudáková and Others v. Slovakia*, App. no. 23083/05, §§26–27, 27.4.2010.

[661] *Lomaseita Oy and Others v. Finland*, App. no. 45029/98, 5.7.2005 (additional materials submitted to the Appeal Court). Concerning insurance matters, see *Kerojärvi v. Finland*, App. no. 17506/90, 19.7.1995; *K.S. v. Finland*, App. no. 29346/95, 31.5.2001; *K.P. v. Finland*, App. no. 31764/96, 31.5.2001; *H.A.L. v. Finland*, App. no. 38267/97, §47, 27.1.2004; *Kukkonen v. Finland*, App. no. 57793/00, 7.6.2007 (no violation as the note in question was not intended to influence the outcome of the case); *S.H. v. Finland*, App. no. 28301/03, 29.7.2008; and *Vilén v. Finland*, App. no. 22635/04, 17.2.2009. The two last cases concerned a failure to submit to the applicant certain medical certificates for information. See also Satu Heikkilä, *From Final Judgment to Final Resolution – Effectiveness of the Execution of Judgments of the European Court of Human Rights in Finland*, Wolf Legal Publishers, Tilburg 2019, pp. 409–412.

[662] *Kuopila v. Finland*, App. no. 27752/95, 27.4.2000 (additional pretrial investigation report and the prosecutors' comments on it); *M.S. v. Finland*, App. no. 46601/99, 22.3.2005 (statement of the ex-spouse); and *Ferreira Alves v. Portugal (No. 3)*, App. no. 25053/05, §§36–39, 21.6.2007 (evidence adduced by the public prosecutor).

[663] *Fortum Corporation v. Finland*, App. no. 32559/96, 15.7.2003 (memorandum drafted by the Competition Authority); and *McMichael v. the United Kingdom*, App. no. 16424/90, §80, 24.2.1995 (social services' reports).

[664] There are, however, a few exceptional cases where the non-disclosure had no impact on the case, see *Stepinska v. France*, App. no. 1814/02, §18, 15.6.2004; *Salé v. France*, App. no. 39765/04, §19; 21.3.2006; and *Asnar v. France (No. 2)*, App. no. 12316/04, §26, 18.10.2007.

[665] *Markko v. Finland* (dec.), App. no. 61113/00, 13.12.2005; *K.K. v. Finland* (dec.), App. no. 7779/04, 10.5.2007; and *S.H. v. Finland*, App. no. 28301/03, §29, 29.7.2008. Compare and contrast with *Reinhardt and Slimane-Kaïd v. France*, App. nos. 23043/93+, §§105–106, 31.3.1998 (violation) in which the parties had not received the reporting judge's report before the hearing, whereas the Advocate-General had, and in which they had not had an opportunity to reply to the Advocate-General's submissions.

[666] *Prikyan and Angelova v. Bulgaria*, App. no. 44624/98, §42, 16.2.2006; *Skondrianos v. Greece*, App. nos. 63000/00+, §§29–30, 18.12.2003; *Clinique des Acacias and Others v. France*, App. nos. 65399/01+, §38, 13.10.2005; and *Duraliyski v. Bulgaria*, App. no. 45519/06, §§30–32 and 43–35, 4.3.2014.

Although in some cases the right to adversarial proceedings and the principle of equality of arms both apply to a certain situation, these rights are, however, clearly different: the latter has been correctly applied when the parties to the proceedings have been treated in the same manner, while the former requires access to all relevant materials.[667] See more about the right to adversarial proceedings in the criminal context in Chapter 6, section 6.3. below.

## 4.2.6. RULES ON EVIDENCE

### *4.2.6.1. Basic Principles Concerning Evidence*

Admission and assessment of evidence are normally matters which fall under the competence of domestic courts.[668] The right to a fair trial does not require that domestic courts apply certain specific rules on evidence in civil, criminal or administrative law proceedings but each State is free to regulate this matter in its own manner.[669] Nor does the Convention lay down rules on evidence as such.[670] Article 6 §1 does not explicitly guarantee the right to have witnesses called either; rather the admissibility of witness evidence is in principle a matter of domestic law.[671] Therefore a refusal to order an expert opinion is not, in itself, unfair either but the proceedings must remain, as a whole, fair.[672]

The Court is not a fourth instance court,[673] or an appellate court to which domestic court rulings can be appealed against.[674] Nor is it in a position to reassess properly the evidence which has been admitted orally and received directly by the domestic courts with a view to quashing a domestic judgment

---

667 *Nideröst-Huber v. Switzerland*, App. no. 18990/91, §24, 18.2.1997.

668 *Moreira de Azevedo v. Portugal*, App. no. 11296/84, §§83–84, 23.10.1990; *García Ruiz v. Spain* [GC], App. no. 30544/96, §28, 21.1.1999; *Tiemann v. France and Germany* (dec.), App. nos. 47457/99+, 27.4.2000; *Centro Europa 7 S.r.l. and Di Stefano v. Italy* [GC], App. no. 38433/09, §197, 7.6.2012; *Schenk v. Switzerland*, App. no. 10862/84, §§45–46, 12.7.1988; *Moreira Ferreira v. Portugal (No. 2)* [GC], App. no. 19867/12, §83, 11.7.2017; and *Heglas v. the Czech Republic*, App. no. 5935/02, §84, 1.3.2007.

669 *Hämäläinen v. Finland* (dec.), App. no. 351/02, 26.10.2004, which concerned division of the burden of proof in a civil matter.

670 *Mantovanelli v. France*, App. no. 21497/93, §34, 18.3.1997.

671 *Dombo Beheer B.V. v. the Netherlands*, App. no. 14448/88, §31, 27.10.1993.

672 *H. v. France*, App. no. 10073/82, §§61 and 70, 24.10.1989.

673 *Vetrenko v. Moldova*, App. no. 36552/02, §55, 18.5.2010; *Bochan v. Ukraine (No. 2)* [GC], App. no. 22251/08, §61, 5.2.2015; and *López Ribalda and Others v. Spain* [GC], App. nos. 1874/13+, §§149 and 159–161, 17.10.2019.

674 *García Ruiz v. Spain* [GC], App. no. 30544/96, §28, 21.1.1999; *Centro Europa 7 S.r.l. and Di Stefano v. Italy* [GC], App. no. 38433/09, §197, 7.6.2012; *Avotiņš v. Latvia* [GC], App. no. 17502/07, §99, 23.5.2016; *Lupeni Greek Catholic Parish and Others v. Romania* [GC], App. no. 76943/11, §90, 29.11.2016; and *De Tommaso v. Italy* [GC], App. no. 43395/09, §§170–172, 23.2.2017.

or decision.[675] Instead, it is in the Court's competence to examine whether the proceedings in their entirety – including the questions of evidence – have been fair.[676] It should be noted that the fairness required by Article 6 §1 is not "substantive" fairness but "procedural" fairness.[677]

Issues concerning evidence are particularly highlighted in criminal matters.[678] When making a global assessment, the Court takes into account not only the rights of the accused but also the public interest and the interests of the victims to have charges pursued. If appropriate, the rights of witnesses may also be taken into account.[679] Normally this means that the alleged imbalance or unfairness is examined in the light of the whole proceedings and from the point of view of whether the applicant has been able to participate effectively in the domestic proceedings or whether the rights of the defence have been restricted in a way that influenced the outcome of the trial.[680]

In criminal matters attention is also drawn to the methods of acquiring evidence. Particular emphasis has been given to whether the Article 2 (right to life) or Article 3 (prohibition of torture) rights have been violated when acquiring evidence. In addition, the special requirements concerning criminal proceedings in Articles 6 §2 and 6 §3 of the Convention are closely connected to the general fair trial requirement in Article 6 §1, being some of its aspects. They are normally examined together with the general fair trial requirement under Article 6 §1.[681] The Court can also find a violation due to a lack of fairness in respect of evidence on the basis of Article 6 §1 alone. The special requirements in Article 6 §2 and 6 §3 are examined in more detail in Chapters 5 and 6 below.

This kind of global assessment was under consideration in the case *Barberà, Messegué and Jabardo v. Spain*. In this case the Court found no such specific lack of fairness which would have led by itself to a violation. Nevertheless, the circumstances were considered, as a whole, to have been unfair. The applicants had been convicted in Spain of robbery and murder and sentenced to imprisonment for 36 years. The Court found that the proceedings in question, taken as a whole, did not satisfy the requirements of a fair and public hearing due to the belated

675 *Thomas v. the United Kingdom* (dec.), App. no. 19354/02, 10.5.2005.

676 *Barberà, Messegué and Jabardo v. Spain*, App. nos. 10590/83+, §68, 6.12.1988; *Elsholz v. Germany* [GC], App. no. 25735/94, §66, 13.7.2000; *Devinar v. Slovenia*, App. no. 28621/15, §45, 22.5.2018; and *Blücher v. the Czech Republic*, App. no. 58580/00, §65, 11.1.2005.

677 *Star Cate Epilekta Gevmata and Others v. Greece* (dec.), App. no. 54111/07, 6.7.2010; and *Miroļubovs and Others v. Latvia*, App. no. 798/05, §103, 15.9.2009.

678 For more details, see Chapter 6, section 6.5. below.

679 *Al-Khawaja and Tahery v. the United Kingdom* [GC], App. nos. 26766/05+, §118, 15.12.2011.

680 *Al-Khawaja and Tahery v. the United Kingdom* [GC], App. nos. 26766/05+, §118, 15.12.2011; and *Dombo Beheer B.V. v. the Netherlands*, App. no. 14448/88, §33, 27.10.1993. In the latter case the Court emphasised the principle of equality of arms and the fact that a party to the proceedings must have an opportunity to present his case, including evidence, in such circumstances which do not put him at a substantial disadvantage vis-à-vis his opponent.

681 See, for example, *A.S. v. Finland*, App. no. 40156/07, §75, 28.9.2010.

transfer of the applicants from Barcelona to Madrid, the unexpected change in the court's composition immediately before the hearing was opened, the brevity of the trial and, above all, the fact that very important pieces of evidence were not adequately adduced and discussed at the trial in the applicants' presence and under the watchful eye of the public. The proceedings were therefore not, as a whole, fair.[682]

The question of trial manipulation was at stake in the case *Navalnyy and Ofitserov v. Russia*, in which charges of economic crime were brought against the applicant, a political activist, opposition leader, anti-corruption campaigner and popular blogger. At the time the charges were brought, he was standing as a candidate in the mayoral elections in Moscow. The connection between his political activities on the one hand and the criminal investigation and the pressing of charges on the other hand was apparent, and this should have been clear also to the domestic courts. The criminal investigation was extended, *inter alia*, to the followers of his blog and its timing coincided with the publication of the results of his corruption findings. In the criminal proceedings against the applicant, manipulated evidence was used that included an incriminating statement given by his co-accused in a plea-bargaining process. A deviation from this statement would have meant that, in accordance with the plea-bargaining agreement, the witness would have been deprived of the negotiated reduction of his sentence. In addition, the applicant was, around election time, under house arrest, prohibited from using the internet and restricted in the contact he made with the outside world. The Court found that the domestic courts had failed to examine the applicant's allegations that the reason for the trial was political pressure. It found that the trial had been unfair.[683]

#### *4.2.6.2. Admissibility of Evidence*

The Court has found that Article 6 does not as such contain any rules on the admissibility of evidence. This is a matter falling within the scope of domestic law. It is thus not the Court's task to examine whether certain kinds of evidence are admissible or not. Its task is only to examine globally the fairness of the proceedings – including the admissibility of evidence.[684] In practice, relevance

---

682 *Barberà, Messegué and Jabardo v. Spain*, App. nos. 10590/83+, §89, 6.12.1988. See also Karen Reid, *A Practitioner's Guide to the European Convention on Human Rights*, Sweet & Maxwell/ Thomson Reuters, London 2019, p. 200. Such global assessment under Article 6 §1 was done also in the case *D. v. Finland*, App. no. 30542/04, §39, 7.7.2009 which concerned sexual abuse of a child.

683 *Navalnyy and Ofitserov v. Russia*, App. nos. 46632/13+, §§109 and 116–121, 23.2.2016.

684 *Taxquet v. Belgium* [GC], App. no. 926/05, §84, 16.11.2010; *Schenk v. Switzerland*, App. no. 10862/84, §46, 12.7.1988 (no violation); *Jalloh v. Germany* [GC], App. no. 54810/00, §94, 11.7.2006; *Khan v. the United Kingdom*, App. no. 35394/97, §34, 12.5.2000; *P.G. and J.H. v. the United Kingdom*, App. no. 44787/98, §76, 25.9.2001; and *Allan v. the United Kingdom*, App. no. 48539/99, §42, 5.11.2002.

is given to whether the parties have challenged the admissibility of evidence before the domestic courts.[685] Nonetheless, the domestic courts are ultimately responsible for ensuring that the evidence received in the domestic proceedings and admitted to the case file has been acquired in a manner which complies with the fair trial requirements.[686]

The Court has examined whether evidence was obtained in breach of the defendant's rights, for example, in the following contexts: the use of evidence obtained through an identification parade,[687] an improper taking of samples from a suspect for forensic analysis,[688] exertion of pressure on a co-accused,[689] the use of planted evidence against an accused,[690] unfair use of other incriminating witness testimony and material evidence against an accused,[691] use of self-incriminating statements in the proceedings,[692] and use of expert evidence in the proceedings.[693] Similarly, the Court has examined in other cases whether using information allegedly obtained in violation of Article 8 as evidence rendered a trial, as a whole, unfair within the meaning of Article 6. Such cases have related, for example, to the use of evidence obtained by unlawful secret surveillance,[694] and search and seizure operations.[695]

In its recent case-law, the Court has given more detailed guidance on the use of statements given in pretrial investigations as evidence. The Grand Chamber case *Salduz v. Turkey* concerned the use of the accused's pretrial investigation statement as evidence against him when the accused did not have legal counsel present during his interrogation. In the case *Ibrahim and Others v. the United Kingdom*, the Court examined the use of pretrial investigation statements as evidence when such statements were given by people suspected of terrorist crimes without the presence of their lawyer, and it further developed the interpretation

---

685 *X. v. Belgium* (dec.), App. no. 8876/80, 16.10.1980.

686 For example, the case *Al-Khawaja and Tahery v. the United Kingdom* [GC], App. nos. 26766/05+, §120, 15.12.2011, concerned the right to accept the statements of absent witnesses to the case file and the possibility to base the judgment on such evidence.

687 *Laska and Lika v. Albania*, App. nos. 12315/04+, 20.4.2010.

688 *Horvatić v. Croatia*, App. no. 36044/09, 17.10.2013.

689 *Erkapić v. Croatia*, App. no. 51198/08, 25.4.2013; *Dominka v. Slovakia* (dec.), App. no. 14630/12, 3.4.2018; and *Stephens v. Malta (No. 3)*, App. no. 35989/14, §§64–67, 14.1.2020.

690 *Layijov v. Azerbaijan*, App. no. 22062/07, §64, 10.4.2014; *Sakit Zahidov v. Azerbaijan*, App. no. 51164/07, §§46–49, 12.11.2015; and *Kobiashvili v. Georgia*, App. no. 36416/06, §§56–58, 14.3.2019.

691 *Ilgar Mammadov v. Azerbaijan (No. 2)*, App. no. 919/15, 16.11.2017.

692 *Belugin v. Russia*, App. no. 2991/06, §§68–80, 26.11.2019.

693 *Erduran and Em Export Dış Tic A.Ş. v. Turkey*, App. nos. 25707/05+, §§107–112, 20.11.2018; and *Avagyan v. Armenia*, App. no. 1837/10, §41, 22.11.2018.

694 *Bykov v. Russia* [GC], App. no. 4378/02, §§69–83, 10.3.2009; *Khan v. the United Kingdom*, App. no. 35394/97, §34, 12.5.2000; *Dragojević v. Croatia*, App. no. 68955/11, §§127–135, 15.1.2015; *Niţulescu v. Romania*, App. no. 16184/06, 22.9.2015; and *Dragoş Ioan Rusu v. Romania*, App. no. 22767/08, §§47–50, 31.10.2017.

695 *Khodorkovskiy and Lebedev v. Russia*, App. nos. 11082/06+, §§699–705, 25.7.2013; and *Prade v. Germany*, App. no. 7215/10, 3.3.2016.

in the *Salduz* case towards an overall assessment.[696] The Grand Chamber cases *Al-Khawaja and Tahery v. the United Kingdom* and *Schatschaschwili v. Germany* concerned the possibility of using a pretrial investigation statement given by a witness in a situation in which the accused could not use his right to cross-examine the absent witness. These cases are discussed in more detail in Chapter 6, section 6.5. below.

#### 4.2.6.2.1. Co-Defendant's Statement as Evidence and Plea-Bargaining

The question of whether a co-defendant is heard as a witness and his statement accepted as evidence against the accused is often an important issue in criminal proceedings. There are no obstacles to accepting such statements if the proceedings fulfil the fair trial requirements. Special situations may arise in circumstances in which the co-defendant himself is covered by immunity or prerogatives, or in which he uses his right to remain silent. Even in such situations the Court has found that if the defence knows about the situation and the co-defendant can be questioned during the trial in a manner that allows the accused to challenge any statements by posing questions, there is no lack of fair trial guarantees.[697]

However, admitting the co-defendant's statement as evidence is problematic if the accused cannot cross-examine him by putting any questions to him and the conviction is based decisively on, or on relevant parts of, this statement. Such a problem was at stake in the case *Mild and Virtanen v. Finland*, in which the co-defendants had given their statement in other proceedings and they could no longer be heard in the proceedings against the accused. Despite this, their statements were admitted as evidence and had decisive evidential value in convicting the applicants.[698] When using a co-defendant's statement as decisive evidence it is thus relevant whether the accused has been able, at some stage of the proceedings, to cross-examine the person testifying against him or her and to thereby challenge the evidence presented by that person.

---

696 *Ibrahim and Others v. the United Kingdom* [GC], App. nos. 50541/08+, 13.9.2016. See in particular §§258–259 (the meaning of "compelling reasons"), §§255–257 (clarifications of the *Salduz* test) and §274 (relevant factors for the fairness assessment).

697 *Cornelis v. the Netherlands* (dec.), App. no. 994/03, 25.5.2004; *Peltonen v. Finland* (dec.), App. no. 30409/96, 11.5.1999; and *Firkins v. the United Kingdom* (dec.), App. no. 33235/09, 4.10.2011. See also Dean Spielmann, "Article 6 ECHR in criminal proceedings – recent developments", *Cyprus Human Rights Law Review*, vol. 2, issue 1, 2013, pp. 3–15, at pp. 13–15. The case *Kaste and Mathisen v. Norway*, App. nos. 18885/04+, §§51–52 and 54, 9.11.2006, concerned a situation in which the co-defendant, who was present in the court, used his right to remain silent and refused to say anything. The Court found the situation problematic. As it appeared that the co-defendant's statement given during the pretrial investigation had had a decisive influence on the outcome of the case, the Court found a violation in the case.

698 *Mild and Virtanen v. Finland*, App. nos. 39481/98+, §§45–47, 26.7.2005 (violation).

In certain situations, the use of a co-defendant's statement may raise the issue of respecting the right not to incriminate him- or herself or the presumption of innocence and of the effect of these rights on the co-defendant's witness status. The case *Sievert v. Germany* concerned the police officers' right as witnesses not to incriminate themselves and whether the right to cross-examination could be restricted on that ground. The police officers who had testified in the applicant's case had been present when the applicant – their colleague – had assaulted a detained person who subsequently died from the injuries sustained. The police officers in question were not accused and the right to cross-examination at the trial was restricted in such a manner that the defendant and the defence could not pose any questions to them. The Court did not find a violation even though the witnesses had refused to reply to the defendant's questions. This refusal was based on their right not to incriminate themselves, a right which is also extended to witnesses. The defendant had also had other legal safeguards at his disposal, such as the opportunity to challenge the credibility of the witness statements.[699]

The presumption of innocence was at stake in the case *Karaman v. Germany*, in which, in convicting those previously prosecuted separately, the court made reference to the applicant's participation in the crime, even though the latter was to be prosecuted at a later date. The Court held, however, that the wording of the previous judgment did not violate the applicant's presumption of innocence as his role in the matter was presented in a neutral manner and without prejudging his guilt.[700]

In the case *Navalnyy and Ofitserov v. Russia*, a statement given by the applicants' co-accused was used as evidence against them. His case had been processed in a separate and accelerated plea-bargaining process, which the other accused could not attend. When the co-accused gave testimony in the applicants' case, he had to stick to the statement he had given in the plea-bargaining process or otherwise risk being deprived of the negotiated reduction of his sentence. The Court held that the use of such a witness statement as evidence in that particular case was prone to manipulation and violated the right to a fair trial.[701] However, use of this kind of statement does not in itself suffice to render the proceedings unfair, but rather each proceedings must be examined as a whole.[702]

The immunity from prosecution enjoyed by a witness was also at stake in the case *Adamčo v. Slovakia*, where the defendant was convicted at the appeal stage of a murder on the basis of a witness statement which the witness had altered before the appeal court. The witness's own homicide charges had been

---

699 *Sievert v. Germany*, App. no. 29881/07, §§59–69, 19.10.2012.

700 *Karaman v. Germany*, App. no. 17103/10, §§43–44, 27.2.2014 (no violation).

701 *Navalnyy and Ofitserov v. Russia*, App. nos. 46632/13+, §109, 23.2.2016.

702 *Verhoek v. the Netherlands* (dec.), App. no. 54445/00, 27.1.2004; *Cornelis v. the Netherlands* (dec.), App. no. 994/03, 25.5.2004; and *Habran and Dalem v. Belgium*, App. nos. 43000/11+, §96, 17.1.2017.

suspended and had subsequently been dropped. The Court held that when accepting the witness statement as conclusive evidence against the applicant, the domestic court had failed to consider the witness's motive for changing his statement.[703] By contrast, in the case *Kadagishvili v. Georgia* the Court did not consider that the reliance on the statements of suspects who had concluded plea-bargaining agreements with the prosecution rendered the trial as a whole unfair, since the plea-bargaining procedure had been carried out in accordance with the law and was accompanied by adequate judicial review. Moreover, the witnesses concerned had given statements to the trial court in the applicants' case, and the latter had had ample opportunity to cross-examine them. Nor had any finding of fact in the plea-bargaining procedure been admitted in the applicants' case without full and proper examination at the applicants' trial.[704]

#### 4.2.6.2.2. Indirect Evidence or Hearsay Witnesses

It is not incompatible with the Convention if a conviction is based solely on circumstantial evidence.[705] The Court has also taken a stand in its case-law on the hearsay rule, according to which statements of people who do not testify in court cannot be admitted as evidence, except in some exceptional circumstances. First of all, this rule aims to ensure that the best evidence is presented before the court, which can assess its reliability. Second, the rule ensures that no unnecessary weight is given to evidence which cannot be cross-examined.[706] However, even in those cases in which hearsay evidence is the sole and decisive evidence against a defendant, its admission as evidence will not automatically result in a breach of Article 6 §1. In such situations, particular significance is given to the existence of sufficient counterbalancing factors, including the existence of strong procedural safeguards. It is therefore permissible to base a conviction on such evidence if there is an acceptable reason for the absence from the court of the primary source of information, if the hearsay evidence is sufficiently reliable given its importance in the case, and if that evidence has been subject to a fair and proper assessment.[707]

Other indirect evidence can be submitted, for example, by presenting the defendant's criminal records or informing the court about the criminal

---

703 *Adamčo v. Slovakia*, App. no. 450/14, §§57–71, 12.11.2019.

704 *Kadagishvili v. Georgia*, App. no. 12391/06, §§156–157, 14.5.2020.

705 *Alberti v. Italy* (dec.), App. no. 12013/86, 10.3.1989.

706 *Blastland v. the United Kingdom* (dec.), App. no. 12045/86, 7.5.1987.

707 *Al-Khawaja and Tahery v. the United Kingdom* [GC], App. nos. 26766/05+, §147, 15.12.2011. See also Stuart Wallace, "The Empire Strikes Back – Hearsay Rules in Common Law Legal Systems and the Jurisprudence of the European Court of Human Rights", *European Human Rights Law Review*, Issue 4, 2010, pp. 408–418.

background of the defendant during the proceedings. This has not been held to be incompatible with Article 6 of the Convention.[708]

Hearsay evidence was at stake in the case *SA-Capital Oy v. Finland*, which concerned an administrative sanction imposed by an administrative court. The Supreme Administrative Court had ordered the applicant company to pay a penalty of 500,000 euros since it had participated in a nationwide asphalt cartel. The nationwide cartel had encompassed the entire market for State, local authority and private sector asphalt contracts. The applicant company complained that the administrative law proceedings had not been fair since the Supreme Administrative Court had relied on hearsay evidence from unidentified sources which the applicant company had not been able to examine or have examined. The Court reviewed the matter under the criminal limb of Article 6 §1, finding, however, that it was not a requirement under Article 6 of the Convention that proceedings such as those imposing sanctions for breaches of competition law be conducted according to the classic model of a criminal trial. The fairness of the proceedings was to be assessed as a whole, by taking into account that cases concerning restrictions of competition typically involved complex and often wide-ranging economic matters and related factual issues, which meant that the relevant elements of evidence would also be multifaceted. The applicant company had had the opportunity, in the preparatory meeting held by the Supreme Administrative Court, to weigh up in advance the need for and the availability of additional evidence and it had not requested the hearing of any further witnesses apart from the six persons who had been called to appear before the Supreme Administrative Court. The Supreme Administrative Court's finding that the applicant company had participated in the cartel had been reached on the basis of documentary evidence and the testimony of witnesses who had either been heard before the court itself or before the first instance court. The witnesses had told the courts about their own experiences in relation to the impugned restrictive practices but their testimonies could also have included references to second-hand information received from others. The Court was, however, persuaded that information based on hearsay did not play a decisive role in the Supreme Administrative Court's judgment. Moreover, the applicant company had had an opportunity to exercise rights of defence providing adequate safeguards also in respect of the evidence on the basis of which the domestic court reached its judgment in the case. The proceedings before the Supreme Administrative Court had thus been fair as a whole. There was thus no violation of Article 6 §1.[709]

The Court has given more detailed guidance on these complicated evidential situations in its Grand Chamber cases *Al-Khawaja and Tahery v. the United Kingdom*

---

708 *X. v. Austria* (dec.), App. no. 2676/65, 3.4.1967.

709 *SA-Capital Oy v. Finland*, App. no. 5556/10, §§65–97, 14.2.2019.

and *Schatschaschwili v. Germany.*[710] For more about these cases, as well as on the three-step test, see Chapter 6, section 6.5.5. below.

#### 4.2.6.2.3. Illegally Obtained Evidence

Concerning the admission of illegally obtained evidence, the Court has held that it does not as such violate the fair trial principles, provided there are sufficient procedural guarantees for its use and that the nature of the evidence or its source does not render the whole proceedings unfair.[711] If the only issue at stake concerns a lack of a legal basis for obtaining evidence, such a matter is normally an Article 8 issue – not a violation of Article 6.

For example, in the case *Khan v. the United Kingdom*, listening devices had been installed in the defendant's apartment without any legal basis, and the recordings were used as evidence. As the interference with the applicant's right to respect for private life was not in accordance with the law, the Court found a violation of Article 8 of the Convention. Nevertheless, in its overall assessment the Court did not consider the proceedings unfair and did not find a violation of Article 6 even though the recordings had been used as evidence.[712] A similar situation was at stake in the case *Lee Davies v. Belgium*, which concerned a search conducted without proper authorisation and the use of evidence thereby obtained. The Court held in the case that the use of illegal evidence did not breach Article 6, although the evidence had been obtained in violation of Article 8. In addition, the other procedural guarantees were fulfilled: the applicant had been able to challenge the use of the evidence in adversarial proceedings and this challenge was refused with detailed reasoning. Furthermore, the conviction was based also on other evidence.[713] Similarly, in a case involving an illegally conducted post-mortem examination, the Court ruled that this in itself did not lead to a violation of Article 6 of the Convention.[714]

The case *Prade v. Germany* concerned the use of information obtained in the context of a criminal investigation in another criminal trial (additional information). The police had obtained a search warrant in order to investigate

---

710 *Al-Khawaja and Tahery v. the United Kingdom* [GC], App. nos. 26766/05+, §147, 15.12.2011; and *Schatschaschwili v. Germany* [GC], App. no. 9154/10, §§119–121, 15.12.2015. See also Karen Reid, *A Practitioner's Guide to the European Convention on Human Rights*, Sweet & Maxwell/Thomson Reuters, London 2019, p. 202.

711 This means that the evidence is obtained in a manner which is contrary to Article 3 of the Convention.

712 *Khan v. the United Kingdom*, App. no. 35394/97, §§34–40, 12.5.2000. See also David Harris, Michael O'Boyle, Ed Bates, Carla Buckley, *Law of the European Convention on Human Rights*, 4th edition, Oxford University Press, Oxford 2018, pp. 420–421.

713 *Lee Davies v. Belgium*, App. no. 18704/05, §§40–53, 28.7.2009.

714 *Parris v. Cyprus* (dec.), App. no. 56354/00, 4.7.2002. The norm in question was enacted to ensure respect for the corpse of a deceased person and not respect of the procedural rights of an accused.

copyright piracy, but had found hashish at the applicant's home. A search of the residence would not have been allowed even in respect of the crime under investigation. Although the evidence was obtained illegally, the confiscated hashish could be used as evidence without violating Article 6. The Court found that the domestic courts had weighed the applicants' right to respect for home against the public interest in prosecuting the crime of drugs possession. Moreover, taking into account the safeguards which surrounded the evaluation of the admissibility and reliability of the evidence concerned, the nature and degree of the unlawfulness, and the use made of the material obtained through the impugned search, the Court found that the proceedings, considered as a whole, were not contrary to the fair trial requirements.[715] Consequently, the admission of illegally obtained evidence does not automatically mean that the proceedings run, as a result, contrary to Article 6.

However, the use of illegally obtained evidence may also be relevant under Article 8 of the Convention. In the case *K.S. and M.S. v. Germany*, the applicants' home had been searched on the basis of a warrant issued on the strength of evidence allegedly obtained in breach of domestic and international law. The applicants were suspected of tax evasion following the tax authorities' illegal receipt of information about their assets held in a Liechtenstein bank. The Court put emphasis on several procedural aspects, including the following: the fact that the search warrant had been issued by a judge; that there was nothing in the case file to indicate that the tax authorities had deliberately and systematically breached domestic and international law in order to obtain information relevant to the prosecution of tax crimes; and the fact that the legality of the search could be challenged before the courts. The fact that the search warrant was based on illegal data did not therefore violate Article 8 of the Convention.[716]

The Court found no violation of Article 6 either in the case *Vukota-Bojic v. Switzerland*, in which the admitted evidence consisted of surveillance information obtained from the applicant by an insurance company with a view to assessing her ability to work and to estimating the need for granting insurance benefits. The Court held that the domestic legislation regulating the collection and processing of personal data did not contain sufficient safeguards against abuse. It did not contain any provisions detailing the circumstances in which surveillance measures could be used and what their maximum duration was, or about the possibility of judicial challenge. Nor were there any provisions on the procedures to be followed for storing, accessing, examining, using, communicating or destroying the data collected through secret surveillance measures. This led to the finding of a violation of Article 8. There was not,

---

715 *Prade v. Germany*, App. no. 7215/10, §§34–43, 3.3.2016.

716 *K.S. and M.S. v. Germany*, App. no. 33696/11, §§45–58, 6.10.2016.

however, a violation of Article 6 even though such evidence had been used in the trial, since it was not the sole evidence against the applicant.[717]

#### 4.2.6.2.4. Evidence Obtained by Undercover Operations or by Other Covert Methods of Investigation

Evidence obtained through undercover operations is treated similarly to illegally obtained evidence, meaning that the police's undercover activities are not themselves contrary to the fair trial principles and the admission of evidence thereby obtained does not necessarily lead to a violation of Article 6.[718] The basic principle established in the Court's case-law is that the police may act undercover but may not incite crime.[719] Undercover agents may be either State agents or private parties acting under their instructions and control.[720] The Court has examined the use of undercover activities both from the substantive and procedural point of view of Article 6,[721] and it has used the terms "entrapment", "police incitement" and "*agent provocateur*" interchangeably.

The principles applicable to evidence obtained through undercover operations have been crystallised in the case *Ramanauskas v. Lithuania*, in which the Court created specific tests for both the substantive and the procedural aspects of Article 6. The substantive test measures whether the authorities have been essentially passive in respect of the undercover activities, acting in such a way that they have not exerted any influence on the subject to incite the commission of an offence that would otherwise not have been committed. This means that the reason for the undercover activities has been an objective suspicion of a crime and that the authorities have been passive vis-à-vis the undercover activities.[722] The procedural test measures how the domestic courts have dealt with the undercover allegations, that is, whether the defendant has had an opportunity to defend him- or herself against the evidence obtained through undercover actions and whether these allegations have also been examined when the defendant has admitted the charges. In addition, it is the duty of a public prosecutor to show that no undercover methods have been used, unless the defendant's allegation in this respect is clearly without any basis.[723]

---

717 *Vukota-Bojic v. Switzerland*, App. no. 61838/10, §§91–100, 18.10.2016.

718 *Ramanauskas v. Lithuania* [GC], App. no. 74420/01, §51, 5.2.2008.

719 *Khudobin v. Russia*, App. no. 59696/00, §128, 26.10.2006.

720 If the incitement to commit an offence is done by a private party who is not acting under the instructions or control of the authorities, the case must be examined under the general rules on evidence and not as an issue of entrapment, see *Shannon v. the United Kingdom* (dec.), App. no. 67537/01, 6.4.2004.

721 *Bannikova v. Russia*, App. no. 18757/06, §67, 4.11.2010.

722 *Ramanauskas v. Lithuania* [GC], App. no. 74420/01, §§49–61, 5.2.2008.

723 *Ramanauskas v. Lithuania* [GC], App. no. 74420/01, §§49–61, 5.2.2008; and *Matanović v. Croatia*, App. no. 2742/12, §§121–130, 4.4.2017. See also David Harris, Michael O'Boyle, Ed Bates, Carla Buckley, *Law of the European Convention on Human Rights*, 4th edition, Oxford

Under the substantive aspect, the Court has examined whether the undercover activities remained within acceptable limits and whether the crime would also have been committed without these activities.[724] As to the procedural aspect, the Court has given significance to issues such as whether allegations about undercover activities were examined properly in the proceedings and whether the applicant was given the opportunity to defend himself.[725]

In undercover cases it must thus first be examined whether the authorities have been passive in the case or whether they have acted as "*agents provocateurs*". In deciding whether the investigation was "essentially passive", the Court examines, in particular, whether there were objective suspicions that the applicant had been involved in criminal activity or was predisposed to commit a criminal offence.[726] A previous criminal record is not by itself indicative of a predisposition to commit a criminal offence.[727] However, the applicant's familiarity with the modalities of the offence and his failure to withdraw from the agreed course of action despite a number of opportunities to do so or to report the offence to the authorities, have been considered by the Court to be indicative of pre-existing criminal activity or intent.[728]

A member of the security forces or a private individual may have also been pressured into committing the offence in question, for example, when he or she is contacted in the absence of any objective suspicions that he or she has been involved in criminal activity or is predisposed to commit a criminal offence;[729] by reiterating the offer despite the applicant's initial refusal;[730] by raising the price beyond average;[731] and by appealing to the applicant's compassion for a drug-addicted would-be purchaser by mentioning withdrawal symptoms.[732] Also the manner in which the undercover police operation was launched and carried out is relevant in assessing whether the applicant was subjected to entrapment.

---

University Press, Oxford 2018, pp. 428–429; and James Welch (Ed.): "Cases and comment: selected decisions from the European Court of Human Rights for January and February 2008 – Entrapment, *Ramanauskas v. Lithuania* (Application No. 74420/01)", *European Human Rights Law Review*, Issue 3, 2008, pp. 410–413.

724 *Teixeira de Castro v. Portugal*, App. no. 25829/94, §38, 9.6.1998; and *Ramanauskas v. Lithuania* [GC], App. no. 74420/01, §55, 5.2.2008.

725 See, *inter alia*, *Edwards and Lewis v. the United Kingdom*, App. nos. 39647/98+, §51, 22.7.2003.

726 *Bannikova v. Russia*, App. no. 18757/06, §38, 4.11.2010.

727 *Constantin and Stoian v. Romania*, App. nos. 23782/06+, §55, 29.9.2009.

728 *Virgil Dan Vasile v. Romania*, App. no. 35517/11, §53, 15.5.2018; *Gorgievski v. "the former Yugoslav Republic of Macedonia"*, App. no. 18002/02, §53, 16.7.2009; and *Matanović v. Croatia*, App. no. 2742/12, §§142–143, 4.4.2017.

729 *Burak Hun v. Turkey*, App. no. 17570/04, §44, 15.12.2009; and *Sepil v. Turkey*, App. no. 17711/07, §34, 12.11.2013.

730 *Ramanauskas v. Lithuania* [GC], App. no. 74420/01, §67, 5.2.2008. Compare and contrast with *Ramanauskas v. Lithuania (No. 2)*, App. no. 55146/14, §68, 20.2.2018 (no violation) where the applicant himself had asked to be contacted.

731 *Malininas v. Lithuania*, App. no. 10071/04, §37, 1.7.2008.

732 *Vanyan v. Russia*, App. no. 53203/99, §§11 and 49, 15.12.2005.

The absence of clear and foreseeable procedures for authorising, implementing and supervising the investigative measure in question tips the balance in favour of finding that the acts in question constitute entrapment.[733]

The examination of the authorities' level of activeness requires, however, that the case file contains the necessary information in this respect. The Court then examines how the domestic courts have examined the defendant's allegations that the police incited them to commit the crime.[734]

As to the fairness of engaging in undercover activities, the Court has paid attention to the following issues: whether the authorities have given reasoned grounds to suspect that a person has committed illegal acts;[735] at what stage in the committing of a crime have the undercover activities been engaged;[736] and whether the undercover activities have been passive.[737] If the undercover activities have been used to incite the commission of an offence (police incitement), the public interest does not justify the admission of evidence obtained in such a manner. In this scenario, the police activities would have not been limited solely to investigating criminal acts but they would have tried to influence the defendant and to incite him to commit an offence which he otherwise would not have done. The limits of accepted undercover activities are crossed if the offence has been committed as a result of police activities or the activities of a person under police orders, and if there is nothing to show that the offence would have been committed without such intervention. Such intervention renders the proceedings unfair.[738] If the State agents can be deemed to have "joined" or "infiltrated" the criminal activity rather than to have initiated it, their action remains within the bounds of undercover work.[739]

Undercover activities often have a close connection to anonymous witnesses and to the defendant's right to question all witnesses against him. This question

733 *Teixeira de Castro v. Portugal*, App. no. 25829/94, §38, 9.6.1998 (undercover agents' intervention was not a part of an official anti-drug-trafficking operation supervised by a judge); *Ramanauskas v. Lithuania* [GC], App. no. 74420/01, §64, 5.2.2008 (no indication of what reasons or personal motives had led the undercover agent to approach the applicant on his own initiative without bringing the matter to the attention of his superiors); and *Tchokhonelidze v. Georgia*, App. no. 31536/07, §51, 28.6.2018 (no formal authorisation and supervision of the undercover operation).

734 *Pătraşcu v. Romania*, App. no. 7600/09, §§31–35 and 36–41, 14.2.2017.

735 *Teixeira de Castro v. Portugal*, App. no. 25829/94, §38, 9.6.1998. See also Francis G. Jacobs, Robin C.A. White, Clare Owey, *The European Convention on Human Rights*, Oxford University Press, Oxford 2017, pp. 310–311.

736 *Vlachos v. Greece*, App. no. 20643/06, §26, 18.9.2008.

737 *Malininas v. Lithuania*, App. no. 10071/04, §37, 1.7.2008; and *Ramanauskas v. Lithuania* [GC], App. no. 74420/01, §67, 5.2.2008.

738 *Ramanauskas v. Lithuania* [GC], App. no. 74420/01, §§49–61, 5.2.2008; *Pyrgiotakis v. Greece*, App. no. 15100/06, §20, 21.2.2008; *Tsyuz v. Ukraine* (dec.), App. no. 1844/02, 25.3.2008; *V. v. Finland*, App. no. 40412/98, §§70–72, 24.4.2007; and *Furcht v. Germany*, App. no. 54648/09, §§49–53, 23.10.2014.

739 *Milinienė v. Lithuania*, App. no. 74355/01, §§37–38, 24.6.2008; *Sequeira v. Portugal* (dec.), App. no. 73557/01, 6.5.2003; and *Eurofinacom v. France* (dec.), App. no. 58753/00, 7.9.2004.

is examined in more detail below under Article 6 §3 (d) of the Convention in the light of the special regulations for criminal cases.[740]

Basing a conviction on evidence acquired in undercover operations requires that there are sufficient and adequate safeguards against abuse, such as clear procedures for acquiring permission for undercover operations and for supervising them. If the accused raises a complaint about incitement, the court must examine the complaint carefully and give sufficient reasons for its findings.[741] Such complaints must be examined with particular care in situations where there is no sufficient legal framework for the police activities or when there are no proper legal safeguards.[742] For example, the case *Furcht v. Germany* concerned an applicant who had no prior criminal background, nor was he suspected of any crime, but he knew several people suspected of drug trafficking. Two undercover police officers established contact with these suspects through the applicant and managed to convince him to arrange drug purchases with the suspects. The Court held that the police officers had clearly abandoned a passive attitude and caused the applicant to commit the offences. The mitigation of the applicant's sentence was not sufficient to redress the breach of Article 6 §1 of the Convention.[743]

Similarly, the Court found a violation in the case *Pătraşcu v. Romania*. An undercover police officer had called the applicant many times and asked for drugs, and the applicant had promised to procure them via another person. It was not clear why the police had decided to resort to undercover methods. The domestic courts had not investigated the applicant's allegation that the police knew about the applicant's involvement in drug trafficking and had therefore decided to engage in undercover activities, since in the cross-examination the applicant was not allowed to ask questions on this issue. Nor was his allegation that the undercover agent had contacted the applicant before the undercover operation examined. No relevance had been given to the fact that the applicant had no prior criminal record and that no drugs were found in his possession; nor was it investigated whether he received any profit from the concluded deals. The Court thus found that the allegations of police entrapment and incitement had not been examined in an adequate manner.[744]

---

740 See Chapter 6, section 6.5.5.4. below.

741 *Lagutin and Others v. Russia*, App. nos. 6228/09+, §119, 24.4.2014; *Sandu v. the Republic of Moldova*, App. no. 16463/08, §38, 11.2.2014; and *Tchokhonelidze v. Georgia*, App. no. 31536/07, §52, 28.6.2018.

742 *Ramanauskas v. Lithuania* [GC], App. no. 74420/01, §§49–61, 5.2.2008. The Court found a violation in this case as permission to conduct undercover operations had been applied for only after the operation had already started. There were also clear signs that there had been incitement by the police and the domestic courts had not adequately examined such allegations. See also *V. v. Finland*, App. no. 40412/98, §§76–77, 24.4.2007.

743 *Furcht v. Germany*, App. no. 54648/09, §§50–52, 54–59, 49–53 and 69–70, 23.10.2014.

744 *Pătraşcu v. Romania*, App. no. 7600/09, §§43–53, 14.2.2017.

A violation was found also in the case *Tchokhonelidze v. Georgia*, in which Ms K had reported to the police that the applicant, who was a Deputy Governor, had requested a bribe from her in return for a promise to assist her in obtaining the requisite construction permit for a petrol station. The police used Ms K as an undercover agent and she covertly filmed her meeting with the applicant who renewed his request for bribes, saying that the requested money was to cover any official expenses for the building permit. The applicant claimed throughout the proceedings that he had been deliberately entrapped and denied his guilt. The Court emphasised that in situations in which private persons were used as collaborators or informants, it was crucial to establish whether the criminal act was already under way at the time when the source began collaboration with the police or whether it was the collaborator who had instigated the crime. It was also crucial to clarify any ulterior motives of such private collaborators. In cases where the lack of file disclosure or the contradiction between the parties' interpretation of events precluded the Court from establishing with a sufficient degree of certainty whether the applicant was subjected to police incitement, the procedural aspect became decisive. In such situations the Court required such a procedure to be adversarial, thorough, comprehensive and conclusive on the issue of entrapment, with the burden of proof on the relevant prosecution authority to demonstrate that there was no incitement. In this case, it appeared that Ms K had been a collaborator in a number of unrelated criminal investigations. However, it was not clear whether she had had an active role in proposing the bribe. The procedural guarantees had not been fulfilled, since the Prosecutor's Office had failed to discharge the requisite burden of proof, and the domestic courts had not provided a single reason in their decisions as to why the allegations ought to be dismissed. The Court found a violation of Article 6.[745]

The case *Akbay and Others v. Germany* concerned indirect incitement in a situation in which the applicant had been aiding and abetting an offence which another person had been incited to commit by the police. The Court applied the test which it had applied in its earlier direct undercover cases with some adaptations, namely: (1) whether it was foreseeable for the police that the person directly incited to commit the offence was likely to contact other persons to participate in the offence, (2) whether that person's activities were also determined by the conduct of the police officers, and (3) whether the persons involved were considered accomplices in the offence by the domestic courts. The Court further confirmed that, in cases of police incitement, it needs to be established

[745] *Tchokhonelidze v. Georgia*, App. no. 31536/07, §§40–53, 28.6.2018. See also Christopher Gray, "Case and comment: selected decisions from the European Court of Human Rights for May and June 2018 – Police entrapment and undercover work, *Tchokhonelidge v. Georgia* (Application No. 31536/07)", *European Human Rights Law Review*, Issue 5, 2018, pp. 529–532.

first whether there has been such incitement or entrapment (substantive test of incitement), and if there has, whether the subsequent use of evidence obtained thereby in the criminal proceedings against the person concerned raises an issue under Article 6 §1 (procedural test of incitement). If the Court's findings under the substantive test are inconclusive owing to a lack of information in the file, the lack of disclosure or contradictions in the parties' interpretations of events, or if the Court finds, on the basis of the substantive test, that an applicant *was* subjected to incitement, it will be necessary to proceed to the procedural test of incitement in order to see whether any evidence obtained by entrapment was excluded. In the case at hand, the police had directly incited the perpetrator and indirectly the applicant to commit the drugs offence of which they were convicted. The offence would not have been committed without the authorities' influence and therefore the domestic courts should have excluded all evidence obtained as a result of the incitement. The mitigation of the applicants' sentences was not sufficient.[746]

Procedural legal safeguards were at stake, for example, in the case *Schenk v. Switzerland*, in which an illegally obtained recording of the applicant's conversation with another person was admitted as evidence even though it incriminated the applicant. However, the trial was not considered to be unfair as the defence had had an opportunity to challenge both the authenticity of the recording and its admission as evidence, as well as to cross-examine the other party to the conversation and the police officer who had recorded the conversation. Moreover, the recording was not the only evidence on which the applicant's conviction was based, although it was decisive.[747] A similar outcome was also reached in the cases *Khan v. the United Kingdom* and *Chalkley v. the United Kingdom*.[748]

A similar situation arose in the Grand Chamber case *Bykov v. Russia*, which concerned police undercover activities being used as evidence in a conspiracy to murder. The applicant was suspected of having given orders to kill his business partner. The engaged "hitman" did not commit a homicide but instead reported the matter to the police. The police had set up the plans for the murder, after which the conversation between the "hitman" and the applicant was secretly recorded and used as evidence. According to the Court, the admission of materials obtained through secret recording did not violate Article 6, although there was no legal basis for such recordings in domestic law and it had been obtained illegally. The applicant was able to challenge the evidence obtained and

746 *Akbay and Others v. Germany*, App. nos. 40495/15+, §§111–142, 15.10.2020 (violation).

747 *Schenk v. Switzerland*, App. no. 10862/84, §§47–48, 12.7.1988 (no violation). See also David Harris, Michael O'Boyle, Ed Bates, Carla Buckley, *Law of the European Convention on Human Rights*, 4th edition, Oxford University Press, Oxford 2018, p. 420.

748 *Khan v. the United Kingdom*, App. no. 35394/97, §§34–40, 12.5.2000 (no violation); and *Chalkley v. the United Kingdom* (dec.), App. no. 63831/00, 26.9.2002.

he was not convicted solely and decisively on the basis of such evidence.[749] By contrast, in the case *Baltiņš v. Latvia* the Court found a violation of Article 6 because even though the applicant's conviction had been based on several other pieces of evidence, the domestic court had not taken any stand in its judgment on the applicant's allegation that, by their undercover actions, the police had incited him to commit the crime.[750]

These principles were also confirmed in the case *Svetina v. Slovenia*, which concerned a murder investigation. The examination of the applicant's mobile phone had been conducted without a court order, in violation of the domestic law, but the evidence thereby obtained had nevertheless been admitted as evidence since that evidence would have inevitably been discovered. The Court held that the admission of such evidence did not violate Article 6 since there were procedural safeguards and the applicant had had an opportunity to challenge the lawfulness of the examination of his mobile telephone and the admission of evidence. Moreover, the data obtained unlawfully from the applicant's mobile telephone had played a role in the initial stage of the proceedings leading to the applicant's arrest but had not been used as evidence in the trial.[751]

In the case *Matanović v. Croatia*, the problem was that the applicant had not had the chance to defend himself against all the evidence in the case. The applicant had had access and the opportunity to comment on the first piece of evidence, which had been used as a basis for the conviction. The second batch of evidence comprised telephone conversations between the applicant and a third person and it was obtained through undercover methods. The applicant also had access to this information, but it was not used as evidence. There was thus no violation in respect of these two batches of evidence. The third batch of evidence was also obtained through undercover methods concerning a third person but there was a connection to the applicant. This information was not used as evidence, nor was it referred to in the judgment, and the prosecutor had blocked the applicant's access to this information. The applicant had no procedural means to challenge this decision before a court. The Court found that the applicant had had no opportunity to invoke these materials for his defence and the domestic courts had not in any way counterbalanced this shortcoming. There was thus a violation of Article 6 in respect of this portion of the evidence.[752]

---

749 *Bykov v. Russia* [GC], App. no. 4378/02, §§98–105, 10.3.2009. See also Andrew L.-T. Choo, *The Privilege against Self-incrimination and Criminal Justice*, Hart Publishing, Oxford and Portland, Or. 2013, p. 98; and Sverre Erik Jebens, "Illegally obtained evidence in criminal cases – an analysis on the basis of three Grand Chamber judgments", in Dean Spielmann, Marialena Tsirli, Panayotis Voyatzis (Eds.), *La Convention Européenne des Droits de L'homme, un Instrument Vivant – Mélanges en L'honneur de Christos L. Rozakis/The European Convention on Human Rights, a Living Instrument – Essays in Honour of Christos L. Rozakis*, Bruylant, Bruxelles 2011, pp. 219–234, at pp. 223–224.

750 *Baltiņš v. Latvia*, App. no. 25282/07, §§64–65, 8.1.2013.

751 *Svetina v. Slovenia*, App. no. 38059/13, §§42–54, 22.5.2018.

752 *Matanović v. Croatia*, App. no. 2742/12, §§160–188, 4.4.2017.

In the case *Grba v. Croatia*, undercover agents were investigating a money counterfeiting crime. On the basis of an order from an investigating judge, the undercover agents bought from the applicant counterfeit euros on several occasions and, subsequently, the applicant was convicted of counterfeiting offences. The Court held that the undercover agents had not limited themselves to investigating ongoing criminal activity in an essentially passive manner but had, instead, exerted an influence to incite the commission of a greater offence than the applicant had already been planning to commit. The extensive use of undercover methods had not been based on valid reasons, such as a need to acquire more evidence of the crime under investigation; rather the police officers in question had by their own actions incited the applicant to commit further offences. It had not been shown that the applicant had sold counterfeit money to people other than the undercover agents. In such circumstances the Court found it unfair to convict the applicant for acts he had committed under incitement. Even though the Court was unable to conclude that there had been a violation under the substantive test of incitement, it nevertheless found a violation of the procedural test of incitement: the domestic courts had failed to effectively examine the applicant's allegation that he had been incited to commit the further crimes. There was thus a violation of Article 6.[753]

Covert methods of criminal investigation can sometimes also be used in contexts other than pretrial investigations conducted by the police. In the case *López Ribalda and Others v. Spain*, the Court found a violation of Article 8 when a shopkeeper had installed, because of recurring thefts, surveillance cameras in his shop in such a manner that some of them were visible but others hidden. The personnel of the shop were not aware of the hidden cameras. The fact that the shopkeeper did not inform the applicants, who were employees of the shop, of the covert camera surveillance was against the national law. The Court held that the applicants' right to respect for private life had been violated because the surveillance could have been organised in a lawful manner by informing the applicants about it. However, in the criminal proceedings against the employees the video recordings could be used as evidence without Article 6 preventing it.[754]

#### 4.2.6.2.5. Forced Confessions and Other Evidence Obtained by Force

In the Court's early case-law concerning forced confessions, reference was often made to the kind of clarification of events obtained in the domestic proceedings. If the domestic authorities had concluded that a confession was obtained without

753 *Grba v. Croatia*, App. no. 47074/12, §§91–126, 23.11.2017.

754 *López Ribalda and Others v. Spain*, App. nos. 1874/13+, §§58–70 and 92–96, 9.1.2018 (no violation of Article 6).

any force or violation of a person's integrity, this clarification was accepted as such.[755] However, more recently the Court has put more emphasis on the allegations concerning forced obtaining of incriminating evidence, in particular in situations in which there are allegations that evidence has been obtained in violation of Article 3, either by torture or by inhuman or degrading treatment.[756]

In the case *Jalloh v. Germany*, the applicant was a street dealer suspected of drug trafficking. Upon arrest by the police, the applicant swallowed a tiny plastic bag which he had in his mouth and which was believed to contain drugs. The applicant was taken to a doctor who then forcibly administered emetics through a tube introduced into his stomach through the nose while he was immobilised by four police officers. The evidence thereby obtained, a minor amount of cocaine, was used against the applicant. The Court found that the evidence had been obtained as a result of acts of violence or brutality considered to be inhuman and degrading treatment within the meaning of Article 3. The evidence was thus obtained by a measure which breached one of the core rights guaranteed by the Convention. Although the applicant had not been tortured, he had been treated in violation of Article 3 and the use of such evidence could render a trial, as a whole, unfair.[757]

The clear rule is that evidence obtained by torture in violation of Article 3 – whether in the form of a confession or real evidence – should never be relied on as incriminating proof of the victim's guilt, irrespective of its probative value.[758] Admission of evidence obtained under torture thus renders a trial as

---

755 *Ferrantelli and Santangelo v. Italy*, App. no. 19874/92, §§49–50, 7.8.1996.

756 *Jalloh v. Germany* [GC], App. no. 54810/00, §§99 and 105, 11.7.2006; and *Harutyunyan v. Armenia*, App. no. 36549/03, §63, 28.6.2007. Compare with *Mehmet Ali Eser v. Turkey*, App. no. 1399/07, §41, 15.10.2019, where no statements obtained by coercion were in fact used in the applicant's conviction.

757 *Jalloh v. Germany* [GC], App. no. 54810/00, §108, 11.7.2006. See also Karen Reid, *A Practitioner's Guide to the European Convention on Human Rights*, Sweet & Maxwell/ Thomson Reuters, London 2019, p. 203; Boštjan M. Zupančič, "An answer to one crucial question of human rights: an epistemological excursus informing *Jalloh v. Germany* and *Gäfgen v. Germany* cases at the European Court of Human Rights", in Miha Pogačnik (Ed.), *Challenges of Contemporary International Law and International Relations – Liber Amicorum in Honour of Ernest Petrič*, The European Faculty of Law, Nova Gorica 2011, pp. 451–463; Sverre Erik Jebens, "Illegally obtained evidence in criminal cases – an analysis on the basis of three Grand Chamber judgments", in Dean Spielmann, Marialena Tsirli, Panayotis Voyatzis (Eds.), *La Convention Européenne des Droits de L'homme, un Instrument Vivant – Mélanges en L'honneur de Christos L. Rozakis/The European Convention on Human Rights, a Living Instrument – Essays in Honour of Christos L. Rozakis*, Bruylant, Bruxelles 2011, pp. 219–234, at pp. 221–223; and Bostjan Zupancic "A sense of justice, the rule of law, and the exclusionary rule", *Regent Journal of Law & Public Policy*, vol. 2, no. 1, Spring 2010, pp. 51–62.

758 *Jalloh v. Germany* [GC], App. no. 54810/00, §105, 11.7.2006. See also *Gäfgen v. Germany* [GC], App. no. 22978/05, §166, 1.6.2010; *Ibrahim and Others v. the United Kingdom* [GC], App. nos. 50541/08+, §254, 13.9.2016; *El Haski v. Belgium*, App. no. 649/08, §85, 25.9.2012; and *Cēsnieks v. Latvia*, App. no. 9278/06, §§67–70, 11.2.2014.

a whole unfair, regardless of the probative value of such evidence. A witness's or co-defendant's statements obtained under torture are thus not admissible as evidence.[759] The use in a trial of evidence obtained by torture would amount to a flagrant denial of justice even where the person from whom the evidence had thus been extracted was a third party.[760] However, in the above-mentioned *Jalloh* case, the question was left open as to whether the use of evidence obtained by an act deemed to be inhuman and degrading treatment under Article 3 automatically renders a trial unfair if the applicants have had no opportunity to have their lawyer present. According to the current case-law of the Court it does. This is irrespective of the fact whether such evidence has been obtained by torture or inhuman and degrading treatment and irrespective of the evidential value given to the evidence in question.[761]

The coercion used to obtain a confession can also be indirect, which may also render the proceedings unfair. In the case *Allan v. the United Kingdom*, the coercion came from a police officer who had been placed in the applicant's cell and who had pushed the applicant to confess the crime. The Court found that the applicant had been subject to such psychological coercion that it affected the voluntariness of his confession.[762]

The case *Ćwik v. Poland* concerned a situation in which a criminal gang had tortured a witness into giving a statement and this testimony had been recorded. Subsequently the police confiscated the recording and used it as evidence in a drug case. The domestic courts admitted the evidence since the police had not coerced the witness and the recording had been legally confiscated. However, the Court held that the same principles applied to coercion effectuated by private persons as to coercion conducted by the authorities. Since the witness had been subjected to ill-treatment prohibited by Article 3, the State had had a positive obligation to protect the witness against ill-treatment by other people. The admission of such evidence rendered the trial unfair.[763]

In the Grand Chamber case *Gäfgen v. Germany*, the Court then went on to find that the admission as evidence of statements obtained as a result of torture

---

759 *Harutyunyan v. Armenia*, App. no. 36549/03, §66, 28.6.2007; and *Kaciu and Kotorri v. Albania*, App. nos. 33192/07+, §§126–130, 25.6.2013.

760 *Othman (Abu Qatada) v. the United Kingdom*, App. no. 8139/09, §§263 and 267, 17.1.2012; *Kaciu and Kotorri v. Albania*, App. nos. 33192/07+, §128, 25.6.2013; and *Kormev v. Bulgaria*, App. no. 39014/12, §§89–90, 5.10.2017.

761 *Gäfgen v. Germany* [GC], App. no. 22978/05, §§165–166, 1.6.2010; *Hacı Özen v. Turkey*, App. no. 46286/99, §§102–104, 12.4.2007; *Göçmen v. Turkey*, App. no. 72000/01, §75, 17.10.2006; and *Söylemez v. Turkey*, App. no. 46661/99, §123, 21.9.2006.

762 *Allan v. the United Kingdom*, App. no. 48539/99, §§46–48, 5.11.2002. See also John Wadham, Philip Leach, "Cases and comment: selected decisions from the European Court of Human Rights for November and December 2002 – Crime and sentencing, *Allan v. United Kingdom* (Application No. 48539/99)", *European Human Rights Law Review*, Issue 2, 2003, pp. 235–237.

763 *Ćwik v. Poland*, App. no. 31454/10, §§70–93, 5.11.2020.

or of other ill-treatment in breach of Article 3, to establish the relevant facts in criminal proceedings, rendered the proceedings as a whole unfair. This finding applied irrespective of the probative value of the statements and irrespective of whether their use was decisive in securing the defendant's conviction. The same applied to real evidence obtained under torture,[764] where the Court also took a stance on the issue of how one was to assess real evidence obtained by an act classified as inhuman and degrading treatment. Most relevant was found to be the role of the impugned evidence in the applicant's conviction. The Court held that despite the inhuman treatment of the applicant at the pretrial stage, the conviction was not based on evidence thereby acquired but on his confession made before the court, which he had given voluntarily and while in the presence of his lawyer. In addition, there was some other, legally obtained, real evidence in the case. The real evidence obtained through inhuman treatment during the pretrial investigation was admitted to the case file, but it was not used to prove guilt, only to test the authenticity of the confession made in court. The causal link between the confession given before the court and the use of "forbidden" real evidence had been broken, and the rights of the defence and the prohibition of self-incrimination had thus been respected. Therefore, the fact that illegally obtained real evidence was not excluded from the case file did not render the proceedings unfair. The Court found no violation of Article 6.[765] For more about forbidden means of obtaining evidence and self-incrimination, see also section 4.2.10. of this chapter, below.

#### *4.2.6.3. Withholding of Evidence*

In criminal cases the public prosecutor must disclose to the defence the materials obtained during the pretrial investigation, whether incriminating or favourable to the accused.[766] The accused's access to these materials secures the equality of arms of the parties. Nevertheless, the right of access to all information is not an absolute one. The confidentiality of certain materials may be justified by a particularly important reason. Such important reasons are, for example, national security, the protection of witnesses from reprisals or the confidentiality of

---

[764] *Gäfgen v. Germany* [GC], App. no. 22978/05, §§166–167, 1.6.2010.

[765] *Gäfgen v. Germany* [GC], App. no. 22978/05, §§172–188, 1.6.2010. The domestic court did not admit as evidence the confession which had been obtained in violation of Article 3. See also Martha Spurrier, "*Gäfgen v. Germany* – Fruit of the poisonous tree", *European Human Rights Law Review*, Issue 5, 2010, pp. 513–519; and David Harris, Michael O'Boyle, Ed Bates, Carla Buckley, *Law of the European Convention on Human Rights*, 4th edition, Oxford University Press, Oxford 2018, p. 421.

[766] *Jespers v. Belgium*, App. no. 8403/78, §§55–58, 14.12.1981; *Edwards and Lewis v. the United Kingdom* [GC], App. nos. 39647/98+, §§34 and 36, 27.10.2004; and *Rowe and Davis v. the United Kingdom* [GC], App. no. 28901/95, §60, 16.2.2000.

police investigation methods.[767] Withholding of evidence is, however, subject to strict limitations and must occur only when necessary. In addition, the inconveniences to the defence must be balanced and the decision to withhold evidence must fulfil certain safeguards protecting the rights of the defence.[768]

The obligation to disclose case materials may also be at stake in situations in which the accused claims to have been entrapped by the authorities and explains that he or she would not have otherwise committed the offence in question. In the case *Edwards and Lewis v. the United Kingdom*, the Court examined an allegation according to which the police had provoked the defendants to commit a crime. The case materials, which could have proved this allegation, were confidential and the defendants had no access to them. Although the order to declare the case materials confidential was given by a judge, the allegation could then not be examined to its full extent before the court. The Court therefore found that the principle of equality of arms and the right to adversarial proceedings had been breached and found a violation of Article 6 §1.[769] For more details, see Chapter 6, section 6.3.3.2. below.

#### *4.2.6.4. Refusal to Admit Evidence*

According to the Court's case-law, it is at the national court's discretion to decide, on the basis of the circumstances of the case, on the necessity to admit witnesses or testimonies in a certain case. The Court does not normally intervene in the use of this discretion unless there are exceptional circumstances.[770] Article 6 §3 (d) contains special regulation for criminal proceedings, providing a right to obtain the attendance of one's own witnesses. This case-law will be examined in more detail under Chapter 6, section 6.5.6. The Court intervenes in the presentation of evidence only when, from the point of view of the general

---

767 *Rowe and Davis v. the United Kingdom* [GC], App. no. 28901/95, §61, 16.2.2000; *Miryana Petrova v. Bulgaria*, App. no. 57148/08, §§39–40, 21.7.2016; and *Regner v. the Czech Republic* [GC], App. no. 35289/11, §§147–149, 19.9.2017.

768 *Rowe and Davis v. the United Kingdom* [GC], App. no. 28901/95, §§51 and 63–67, 16.2.2000; *Jasper v. the United Kingdom* [GC], App. no. 27052/95, §§52–56 and 58, 16.2.2000; *Fitt v. the United Kingdom* [GC], App. no. 29777/96, §§48–50, 16.2.2000; *Natunen v. Finland*, App. no. 21022/04, §48, 31.3.2009; and *Janatuinen v. Finland*, App. no. 28552/05, §§48–50, 8.12.2009.

769 *Edwards and Lewis v. the United Kingdom* [GC], App. nos. 39647/98+, §§46 and 48, 27.10.2004. See also Philip Leach, James Welch (Eds.), "Cases and comment: selected decisions from the European Court of Human Rights for September and October 2004 – Crime and sentencing, *Edwards and Lewis v. United Kingdom* (Application Nos. 39647/98 and 40461/98)", *European Human Rights Law Review*, Issue 1, 2005, pp. 92–95. See also *V. v. Finland*, App. no. 40412/98, §§76–77 and 80, 24.4.2007.

770 *Kok v. the Netherlands* (dec.), App. no. 43149/98, 4.7.2000; and *M. v. Finland* (dec.), App. no. 66599/01, 25.8.2005.

fairness of the proceedings, the proceedings as a whole contain such imbalances that an accused or a party to civil proceedings is prevented from fully exercising his or her rights.[771]

The sufficiency of the admitted evidence was at stake, for example, in the Grand Chamber case *Elsholz v. Germany*, concerning the contact rights of a child. In that case the Court found that the proceedings did not fulfil the fairness requirement, or the requirement of a public oral hearing. No psychological expert opinion about the child had been obtained in the case; nor was there an oral hearing on appeal, even though such factual and legal issues had been put forward in the case which could not have been properly decided on the basis of the written submissions available to the court.[772] In another case, concerning sexual abuse of children, *Accardi v. Italy*, a psychological expert statement or expert testimony on the children's ability to reliably relate the events was not considered necessary because the domestic courts had considered, on relevant and logical grounds, that, taking into account other clarifications, this issue had no relevance.[773] However, in situations in which an expert changes his opinion before the court from that stated in writing on the matter earlier, there may appear a need to also hear other experts before the court.[774]

On the other hand, in situations where new, exculpatory evidence appears after the applicant's conviction, the Convention does not guarantee a right to a new trial.[775] Similarly, in those cases in which the case is reopened, there is no requirement that all evidence is admitted anew.[776]

#### *4.2.6.5. Assessment of Evidence and Interpretation and Application of Domestic Law*

As for the admission of evidence, the Court also does not intervene in the assessment of evidence carried out by the domestic courts unless there are exceptional circumstances.[777] It is not the task of the Court to deal with errors

---

771 *Vaturi v. France*, App. no. 75699/01, §58, 13.4.2006. The applicant could not at any stage of the proceedings examine or have examined any witnesses. Although the case was a complex one due to its economic dimensions and the presence of several companies, the pretrial investigation had been conducted by a simplified procedure, during which the applicant could neither ask for additional investigations to be conducted nor require that he should be allowed to cross-examine witnesses who had testified against him.

772 *Elsholz v. Germany* [GC], App. no. 25735/94, §66, 13.7.2000.

773 *Accardi and Others v. Italy* (dec.), App. no. 30598/02, 20.1.2005.

774 *G.B. v. France*, App. no. 44069/98, §§68–70, 2.10.2001.

775 *K.H.C. v. the United Kingdom* (dec.), App. no. 2749/66, 11.7.1967; and *X. v. Austria* (dec.), App. no. 7761/77, 8.5.1978.

776 *Oyston v. the United Kingdom* (dec.), App. no. 42011/98, 22.1.2002.

777 *Barberà, Messegué and Jabardo v. Spain*, App. nos. 10590/83+, §68, 6.12.1988.

of fact or law allegedly committed by a national court unless and in so far as such errors are manifest and infringe rights and freedoms protected by the Convention.[778] It is extremely rare for the Court to question under Article 6 §1 the national court's assessment on the grounds that its findings might be regarded as arbitrary or manifestly unreasonable.[779] The Court cannot therefore challenge the interpretation and application of domestic law, international law or of EU law,[780] or the establishment of facts by the domestic courts, unless it has been flagrant and manifestly arbitrary.[781] It is primarily for the domestic courts to resolve problems of interpretation of national legislation, not for the Court, whose role is to verify whether the effects of such interpretation are compatible with the Convention.[782]

Therefore, there is, for example, no rule that a statement given in court should have priority if that statement and the statement given during the pretrial investigation are conflicting. However, the reasoning of the domestic courts may give an impression that the basic fair trial principles have not been respected and that, for example, the burden of proof on that point may have shifted to the accused.[783] The Court does not intervene, either, on the issue of how the relevant facts have been proved; in other words, which witnesses or experts have been heard by the court.[784] The Court intervenes in the assessment of evidence only in such exceptional circumstances where it is apparent that the domestic court has drawn arbitrary or clearly unfair conclusions from the materials submitted to it.[785]

---

778 *García Ruiz v. Spain* [GC], App. no. 30544/96, §28, 21.1.1999; and *Perez v. France* [GC], App. no. 47287/99, §82, 12.2.2004.

779 See, for example, *Dulaurans v. France*, App. no. 34553/97, §38, 21.3.2000 (violation of Article 6 §1 because of a "manifest error of judgment"); *Khamidov v. Russia*, App. no. 72118/01, §170, 15.11.2007 (proceedings had been "grossly arbitrary"); *Anđelković v. Serbia*, App. no. 1401/08, §24, 9.4.2013 (there had been a "denial of justice"); and *Bochan v. Ukraine (No. 2)* [GC], App. no. 22251/08, §§63–65, 5.2.2015 (domestic court's reasoning was regarded as being "grossly arbitrary" or as entailing a "denial of justice"). Compare and contrast, for example, with *Société anonyme d'habitations à loyers modérés Terre et Famille v. France* (dec.), App. no. 62033/00, 17.2.2004. See also *Barać and Others v. Montenegro*, App. no. 47974/06, §§32–34, 13.12.2011; and *Laskowska v. Poland*, App. no. 77765/01, §61, 13.3.2007.

780 *Waite and Kennedy v. Germany* [GC], App. no. 26083/94, §54, 18.2.1999; *Markovic and Others v. Italy* [GC], App. no. 1398/03, §§107–108, 14.12.2006; and *Avotiņš v. Latvia* [GC], App. no. 17502/07, §100, 23.5.2016.

781 *García Ruiz v. Spain* [GC], App. no. 30544/96, §§28–29, 21.1.1999.

782 *Perez v. France* [GC], App. no. 47287/99, §82, 12.2.2004; and *Nejdet Şahin and Perihan Şahin v. Turkey* [GC], App. no. 13279/05, §49, 20.10.2011.

783 *Ali v. Romania*, App. no. 20307/02, §§103–104, 9.11.2010.

784 *Accardi and Others v. Italy* (dec.), App. no. 30598/02, 20.1.2005. However, in the case *Elsholz v. Germany* [GC], App. no. 25735/94, §66, 13.7.2000, the Court made an exception.

785 *Waldberg v. Turkey* (dec.), App. no. 22909/93, 6.9.1995; and *Camilleri v. Malta* (dec.), App. no. 51760/99, 16.3.2000.

## 4.2.7. PRESUMPTION OF INNOCENCE IN NON-CRIMINAL MATTERS

In criminal matters the presumption of innocence is guaranteed in Article 6 §2 of the Convention. Presumption of innocence is also one element of the fair trial guarantees under Article 6 §1 of the Convention. In the Court's earlier case-law, however, there was no clear and consistent line of interpretation of the extent of the presumption of innocence in non-criminal cases.[786]

In the Grand Chamber case *Allen v. the United Kingdom*, such a line of interpretation was created by finding that the presumption of innocence had, besides its primary relevance in criminal matters, a secondary relevance in other procedures involving public officials and authorities. Without such protection, the fair trial guarantees of Article 6 §2 could risk becoming theoretical and illusory. To a certain extent, the presumption of innocence may also overlap with the protection afforded by Article 8, in particular with respect to the right to reputation.[787]

### *4.2.7.1. Confiscation Proceedings*

Several times in its case-law, the Court has come across situations in which the effects of the presumption of innocence needed to be assessed vis-à-vis proceedings other than criminal ones. Such a situation is at stake, for example, when an accused's guilt has already been decided in the criminal proceedings and subsequent, separate confiscation proceedings are based on the outcome of such criminal proceedings. This was the case, for example, in *Phillips v. the United Kingdom*, in which the applicant had already been convicted of a drugs offence. When the proceeds of the crime were confiscated, a statutory presumption was applied that any property appearing to have been held by the applicant at any time since his conviction, or during a period of six years prior to the date on which the criminal proceedings were commenced, was received as a payment or reward from drug trafficking. The Court held that Article 6 §2 did not apply to the confiscation proceedings as these proceedings did not concern a new criminal charge. The applicant had already been convicted in the criminal proceedings and the confiscation sanction was a part of the sentencing to which the presumption of innocence did not apply. The Court did not find any problem either in respect of general fairness under Article 6 §1, since the applicant had

---

786 See also Chapter 5, section 5.4.2. below.

787 *Allen v. the United Kingdom* [GC], App. no. 25424/09, §94, 12.7.2013. See also James Welch, "Case and comment: selected decisions from the European Court of Human Rights from July 2013 – Miscarriage of justice, *Allen v. United Kingdom* (Application No. 25424/09)", *European Human Rights Law Review*, Issue 6, 2013, pp. 646–650.

had the opportunity to rebut the statutory presumption as far as the amount of the proceeds of crime was concerned.[788]

In the case *Minhas v. the United Kingdom*, the Court held that Article 6 §1 was applicable to confiscation proceedings but not Article 6 §2, since its applicability ended when a person was found guilty in criminal proceedings. In that case the applicant was one of three perpetrators of a robbery but the only one who had been caught and convicted. The confiscation claim concerning the proceeds of crime in their totality was directed at the applicant since he did not agree to disclose the identities of the other perpetrators. The value of the stolen jewellery in the applicant's possession corresponded to the amount of the proceeds of crime. When the value of the jewellery had been clarified, the burden of proof shifted to the applicant and it was for him to show that the proceeds of crime were smaller than the value of the jewellery. The applicant could not show this as he refused to disclose the real value of the proceeds of crime. The applicant was represented by a lawyer during the confiscation proceedings and he was heard in an oral hearing. The Court found no violation of Article 6 §1.[789]

Similarly, in the case *Young v. the United Kingdom*, the applicant was convicted of having evaded value-added tax in respect of the sale of 15 cars, although his commercial activities in reality concerned a significantly higher number of such sales. After the criminal proceedings, confiscation proceedings followed, in which the applicant had confiscated from him the value of the proceeds of crime in respect of about 200 cars for which he had not paid the value-added tax. The Court noted that the applicant knew that the charges brought against him only represented a part of his extensive criminal activities. Although the charges and the conviction had been limited to the amount admitted by the applicant, he knew that the prosecutor would not settle for that but that the confiscation order concerned *all* proceeds of crime acquired from the criminal activities. The Court found the national court's calculations appropriate and did not find a violation.[790]

On the other hand, the Court found that the confiscation was not proportionate in the case *Džinić v. Croatia*, when, in order to secure the seizure of one million euros as the proceeds from an economic crime, the whole of the applicant's real estate property, worth about nine million euros, was confiscated. The confiscation also lasted a very long time – some two and a half years – during

---

788 *Phillips v. the United Kingdom*, App. no. 41087/98, §§35–36, 39 and 45–47, 5.7.2001. See also Miklos Hollan, "Confiscation of the proceeds from crime and the principle of presumption of innocence", in Kimmo Nuotio (Ed.), *Festschrift in Honour of Raimo Lahti*, University of Helsinki/Faculty of Law, Helsinki 2007, pp. 363–372.

789 *Minhas v. the United Kingdom* (dec.), App. no. 7618/07, 10.11.2009.

790 *Young v. the United Kingdom* (dec.), App. no. 38759/12, §§42–48, 6.5.2014.

which time the applicant's complaints about unjustified confiscation were not examined.[791]

The presumption of innocence may also have, depending on the situation, more direct links to confiscation proceedings. If it has not been possible to target the criminal proceedings of those people who have received proceeds of a crime, the presumption of innocence may relate to subsequent confiscation proceedings. In the Lithuanian case of *Silickiene*, in which the previously commenced criminal proceedings were continued after the accused's suicide, as confiscation proceedings against his death estate, the Court found no violation of the presumption of innocence.[792] On the other hand, the case *Lagardere v. France* concerned a situation in which no criminal proceedings were ever brought against the father during his lifetime but after his death a crime-based civil action was brought against his son, who was his heir. The Court found a violation in the case and thereby extended the scope of application of the presumption of innocence to also cover subsequent civil proceedings.[793]

#### *4.2.7.2. Subsequent Civil or Administrative Law Proceedings*

The presumption of innocence may also have a bearing on other civil matters, such as compensation actions brought after acquittal. But in this respect the Court's case-law is inconsistent. Generally taken, the more widely accepted interpretation is that the reasoning in the civil matter may no longer put into question the dismissal of charges, thereby also extending the presumption of innocence to civil matters. This line of interpretation was confirmed, *inter alia*, in the cases *Minelli v. Switzerland*, *Sekanina v. Austria*, *Rushiti v. Austria*, *Y. v. Norway*, *Hammern v. Norway*, *O. v. Norway*, *Orr v. Norway* and *Ashendon and Jones v. the United Kingdom*.[794]

---

791 *Džinić v. Croatia*, App. no. 38359/13, §§70–79, 17.5.2016.

792 *Silickienė v. Lithuania*, App. no. 20496/02, §§53–54, 10.4.2012 (no violation). The accused who committed suicide was one of several accused people and the criminal proceedings were continued against all others in the organisation. As concerned the accused who had committed suicide, it could not be shown that he had obtained his property from legal sources.

793 *Lagardere v. France*, App. no. 18851/07, §§86–87, 12.4.2012 (violation).

794 *Minelli v. Switzerland*, App. no. 8660/79, §§31–41, 25.3.1983; *Sekanina v. Austria*, App. no. 13126/87, §§22 and 25–31, 25.8.1993; *Rushiti v. Austria*, App. no. 28389/95, §§27–32, 21.3.2000; *Y. v. Norway*, App. no. 56568/00, §§39–47, 11.2.2003; *Hammern v. Norway*, App. no. 30287/96, §§41–49, 11.2.2003; *O. v. Norway*, App. no. 29327/95, §§33–41, 11.2.2003; *Orr v. Norway*, App. no. 31283/04, §§47–55, 15.5.2008; and *Ashendon and Jones v. the United Kingdom*, App. nos. 35730/07+, §§42–55, 13.9.2011. See also Tom Hickman, Faisal Saifee, "Case Analysis – *Hammern v. Norway, O v. Norway, Ringvold v. Norway* and *Y v. Norway*", *European Human Rights Law Review*, Issue 5, 2003, pp. 539–546.

In the case *Bok v. the Netherlands*, the Court reached, however, another conclusion. The compensation claim from the applicant, who had been accused of a crime but later acquitted, was rejected because he bore in the compensation proceedings the burden of proof that there had not been any reason even to suspect him of having committed any crime. The task of the domestic courts was to assess whether he had proved his case. Although the Court found some of the expressions used by the domestic court unfortunate and inappropriate, it considered that the presumption of innocence had not been violated in the civil case.[795] Moreover, the presumption of innocence may also have a bearing on cases concerning child custody or the taking into public care of a child,[796] on disciplinary matters and dismissals,[797] or on cases concerning social benefits.[798]

In the case *Allen v. the United Kingdom*, the Court provided a general framework for situations in which the criminal presumption of innocence has a bearing on other proceedings. The case was not intended to change the fact that civil proceedings which are based on the same facts as the criminal proceedings may lead, irrespective of the outcome of the criminal proceedings, to civil liability, because of the lower burden of proof. Nevertheless, the presumption of innocence must be respected in the civil proceedings.

The Court found, first of all, that the presumption of innocence means that where there has been a criminal charge and criminal proceedings have ended in an acquittal, the person who was the subject of the criminal proceedings is innocent in the eyes of the law and must be treated in a manner consistent with that innocence. Second, whenever the question of the applicability of Article 6 §2 arises in the context of subsequent proceedings, the applicant must demonstrate the existence of a link between the concluded criminal proceedings and the subsequent proceedings. Such a link is likely to be present, for example, when the subsequent proceedings require examination of the outcome of the prior criminal proceedings or where they oblige the court to: (1) analyse the criminal judgment; (2) engage in a review or evaluation of the evidence in the criminal file; (3) assess the applicant's participation in some or all of the events leading to the criminal charge; or (4) comment on the subsisting indications of the applicant's possible guilt. In any event, much will depend on the nature and context of the proceedings in which the impugned decision was adopted. One such criterion is, for example, the language used by the decision maker and in particular the possible expressions relating to guilt, such as "it was clearly probable that the applicant had committed the offences with which he was charged", or that the criminal file contained "enough evidence to establish that a criminal offence had

795 *Bok v. the Netherlands*, App. no. 45482/06, §§43–48, 18.1.2011 (no violation).

796 *O.L. v. Finland* (dec.), App. no. 61110/00, 5.7.2005.

797 *Moullet v. France* (dec.), App. no. 27521/04, 13.9.2007.

798 *Vassilios Stavropoulos v. Greece*, App. no. 35522/04, §§28–32, 27.9.2007.

been committed". However, even the use of some unfortunate language may not be decisive. Therefore, even though the language used by domestic authorities and courts has been criticised, it does not in itself lead to the conclusion that the presumption of innocence has been violated.[799]

In the case *Allen v. the United Kingdom*, the applicant had been convicted of manslaughter for having killed her four-month-old son and sentenced to three years' imprisonment. According to the expert witnesses, the injuries suffered by her son were consistent with shaking or an impact, suggesting "shaken baby syndrome". The applicant served her time. Subsequently she presented new evidence according to which the baby's injuries could have been attributed to a cause other than shaken baby syndrome. The Court of Appeal quashed the conviction because it had been based on insufficient evidence and found that the new evidence might have affected the jury's decision to convict. The applicant claimed compensation for her punishment, but it was rejected as she had not been able to prove her innocence or to demonstrate beyond reasonable doubt that there had been a miscarriage of justice in this case. The Court found that there had been a link between the criminal and the compensation proceedings, but the language used in the latter proceedings did not indicate that there had been a violation of Article 6 §2 of the Convention.[800]

In the case *Farzaliyev v. Azerbaijan*, the applicant, who was neither charged nor aware of the criminal investigation against him until after its discontinuation as statute barred, was ordered to pay compensation for the "crime" in civil proceedings brought by the prosecutor shortly thereafter. The civil claim was lodged on the basis of a procedure requiring the existence of a "criminal charge". The Court found that the applicant had been "substantially affected" by the conduct of the authorities, having regard to the case-specific sequence of interconnected events considered as a whole and the relatively close temporal proximity of the events in question. The civil proceedings were therefore a "direct consequence" of the discontinued criminal investigation and thus fell within the ambit of Article 6 §2.[801]

The case *Güç v. Turkey* concerned disciplinary proceedings brought against the applicant who worked in a primary school. He was accused of the sexual harassment of a nine-year-old girl, but the charges were dismissed. As a result

---

799 *Allen v. the United Kingdom* [GC], App. no. 25424/09, §§103–104 and 125–126, 12.7.2013; *Adams v. the United Kingdom* (dec.), App. no. 70601/11, §41, 5.12.2013; *A.L.F. v. the United Kingdom* (dec.), App. no. 5908/12, §24, 5.12.2013; and *Vella v. Malta*, App. no. 69122/10, §§56–57 and 60, 11.2.2014.

800 *Allen v. the United Kingdom* [GC], App. no. 25424/09, §§119 and 136, 12.7.2013. See also James Welch (Ed.), "Case and comment: selected decisions from the European Court of Human Rights from July 2013 – Miscarriage of justice, *Allen v. United Kingdom* (Application No. 25424/09)", *European Human Rights Law Review*, Issue 6, 2013, pp. 646–650.

801 *Farzaliyev v. Azerbaijan*, App. no. 29620/07, §§51 and 64–69, 28.5.2020.

of the disciplinary proceedings he was dismissed. The Court found that an investigation under the disciplinary proceedings was separate from a pretrial investigation and that the reason for the applicant's dismissal had been his "shameful or unbecoming conduct that was incompatible with the reputation of official functions". The Court did not therefore consider that the disciplinary investigation had overstepped the boundaries of its civil jurisdiction in such a way as to violate the applicant's right to be presumed innocent. Moreover, even the use of some unfortunate language by domestic courts could be tolerated, provided that the circumstances of the case and the nature of the task that was before them allowed it. The Court found that the language used in the disciplinary and administrative proceedings was compatible with the requirements of Article 6 §2.[802]

The case *Kožemiakina v. Lithuania* concerned the applicant's minor son who had been heard in a criminal trial as a witness and who had during that hearing admitted that he had also assaulted the victim. In the subsequent civil proceedings, a compensation action was brought against the applicant and her son by relying on the said witness statement, but, in awarding compensation against them both, the domestic courts did not carry out a fresh assessment of the applicant's son's role, relying on the *res judicata* effect. The Court considered that since in the criminal proceedings the son was not held liable and the applicant had not been able to challenge her civil liability, the civil proceedings had not been fair. The criminal proceedings had no *res judicata* effect in the civil proceedings.[803]

The case *SA-Capital Oy v. Finland* concerned the imposition of a penalty payment on the applicant company since it had participated in a nationwide asphalt cartel. The applicant company complained about the shifting of the burden of proof and claimed that the presumption of innocence had been violated. The Court examined the matter under Article 6 §§1 and 2 but did not accept the applicant company's views. It held that the Competition Authority had adduced extensive evidence of the existence of a cartel, while the applicant company had not been able to refute the credibility or reliability of that evidence, or of the conclusions which the Competition Authority had drawn from it. The Supreme Administrative Court had thus not shifted the burden of proof to the applicant company; nor was there any indication that the standard of proof applied by the Supreme Administrative Court was in any way arbitrary.[804]

---

802 *Güç v. Turkey*, App. no. 15374/11, 23.1.2018. See also Jeremy McBride, "Some recent practice of the European Court of Human Rights to consider when implementing criminal procedure codes", *Synergy Magazine*, no. 64, issue 2, 2018, pp. 8–10, at p. 9.

803 *Kožemiakina v. Lithuania*, App. no. 231/15, §§50–57, 2.10.2018.

804 *SA-Capital Oy v. Finland*, App. no. 5556/10, §§106–110, 14.2.2019.

### 4.2.8. PRESUMPTION OF INNOCENCE IN SEPARATE PROSECUTIONS

The *Allen* principles were followed in the case *Karaman v. Germany*, which concerned a situation where, in the judgment convicting the separately prosecuted co-accused, the prominent role played by the applicant in the criminal venture was described as background information. He was not a party to the proceedings against the co-accused and was deprived of any opportunity to contest allegations related to his participation. The Court held that the statements, although not binding with respect to the applicant, could nevertheless have had a prejudicial effect on the criminal proceedings pending against him. However, the language used and the continuous reference to him as "separately prosecuted" had made it sufficiently clear that any mention of the applicant did not entail a determination of his guilt. The Court concluded that the domestic courts had avoided, as far as possible, giving the impression of having prejudged the applicant's guilt, so that the applicant's right to be presumed innocent was not violated.[805]

### 4.2.9. PRINCIPLE OF IMMEDIACY

In criminal proceedings one important fair trial guarantee is that the accused gets an opportunity to face the witnesses in the presence of the judge who decides the case.[806] Therefore, under normal circumstances, any changes in the composition of the court after the hearing of witnesses should lead to their rehearing. The principle of immediacy also applies to civil proceedings, although more loosely.[807]

Exceptions may be allowed, *inter alia*, when, on the basis of the circumstances of the case, it can be said that the change in the composition had no bearing on the outcome of the case. Such a situation was at stake in the case *P.K. v. Finland*. Although the presiding District Court judge in this case had changed, the three lay judges had remained the same. The credibility of the witness was never questioned, and the transcript drawn up of her testimony was at the disposal of the new judge. The applicant's conviction was not based only on the said witness statement; nor was there anything suggesting that the presiding judge was changed in order to affect the outcome of the case or for any other improper motive.[808]

---

805 *Karaman v. Germany*, App. no. 17103/10, §§143–44 and 69–70, 27.2.2014 (no violation).

806 *P.K. v. Finland* (dec.), App. no. 37442/97, 9.7.2002.

807 *Pitkänen v. Finland*, App. no. 30508/96, §62, 9.3.2004 (no violation).

808 *P.K. v. Finland* (dec.), App. no. 37442/97, 9.7.2002. See also *Graviano v. Italy*, App. no. 10075/02, §§39–40, 10.2.2005 (no violation); and *Škaro v. Croatia*, App. no. 6962/13, §§22–31, 6.12.2016 (no violation).

In contrast, the Court found a violation of Article 6 in the case *Cutean v. Romania* when none of the judges in the initial panel who had heard the applicant and the witnesses at the first level of jurisdiction had stayed on to continue with the examination of the case. The Court noted that the applicant's and the witnesses' statements constituted relevant evidence for his conviction which was not directly heard by the judge who ultimately decided the case, and that the availability of statement transcripts could not compensate for the lack of immediacy in the proceedings.[809] Violation was found also in the case *Cerovšek and Božičnik v. Slovenia* because the reasons for the applicants' conviction and sentence had not been given by the single judge who pronounced the verdicts but by other judges, who had not participated in the trial.[810]

An issue related to the principle of immediacy may also arise when the appeal court overturns the decision of a lower court acquitting an applicant of the criminal charges, without a fresh examination of the evidence, including the hearing of witnesses.[811] Similarly, the principle of immediacy is relevant in case of a change in the composition of the trial court when the case is remitted for retrial before a different judge. In such a situation, the principles of the Court's case-law concerning the right to examine witnesses for the prosecution are of relevance.[812] The immediacy of criminal proceedings with regard to witnesses and cross-examination will be examined more in detail in Chapter 6, section 6.5.

### 4.2.10. FREEDOM FROM SELF-INCRIMINATION AND RIGHT TO REMAIN SILENT

The right to a fair trial also includes a freedom from self-incrimination. The right to remain silent and the right not to incriminate oneself are generally recognised international standards which lie at the heart of the notion of a fair trial under Article 6 §1.[813] They are also closely connected to the presumption of innocence

---

809 *Cutean v. Romania*, App. no. 53150/12, §§60–73, 2.12.2014 (violation). See also *Beraru v. Romania*, App. no. 40107/04, §66, 18.3.2014 (violation).

810 *Cerovšek and Božičnik v. Slovenia*, App. nos. 68939/12+, §§37–48, 7.3.2017. See also *Svanidze v. Georgia*, App. no. 37809/08, §§34–38, 25.7.2019 which concerned the replacement of the trial judge by a substitute judge who did not participate in the examination of evidence.

811 *Hanu v. Romania*, App. no. 10890/04, §40, 4.6.2013; and *Lazu v. the Republic of Moldova*, App. no. 46182/08, §43, 5.7.2016. See also Chapter 4, section 4.3.2.5.2. below.

812 *Famulyak v. Ukraine* (dec.), App. no. 30180/11, §§36–38, 26.3.2019; and *Chernika v. Ukraine*, App. no. 53791/11, §§40–46 and 54, 12.3.2020.

813 *Bykov v. Russia* [GC], App. no. 4378/02, §92, 10.3.2009; *Saunders v. the United Kingdom* [GC], App. no. 19187/91, §68, 17.12.1996; and *Ibrahim and Others v. the United Kingdom* [GC], App. nos. 50541/08+, §§213–227, 13.9.2016. See also the EU Directive 2016/343 on the strengthening of certain aspects of the presumption of innocence and of the right to be present at the trial in criminal proceedings. Pursuant to Article 2, the Directive applies to suspects or accused persons in criminal proceedings. Article 7 enshrines the right to silence and the

protected under Article 6 §2.[814] They are rights that must be read to any suspect or accused who is being arrested, interrogated or heard.[815] For more about the presumption of innocence, see Article 6 §2 in Chapter 5 below.

#### *4.2.10.1. Nature of Freedom from Self-Incrimination*

The purpose of the freedom from self-incrimination is to secure the equality of the proceedings vis-à-vis the prosecutor. The core idea is to protect the suspect's free will against improper compulsion by the authorities.[816] A suspect cannot be forced, against his or her own will, to act as an active source of information or to provide evidence against him- or herself. An accused is thus not obliged to actively contribute to the establishment of his or her own guilt but has a right to remain passive.[817] When interrogated as a suspect in a criminal matter, an accused, as opposed to a complainant or a witness, has no obligation to tell the truth.

The right not to incriminate oneself and to remain silent is distinct from the right to be assisted by a lawyer. A waiver of one of these rights does not entail a waiver of the other. Nevertheless, these rights are complementary since persons in police custody must *a fortiori* be granted the assistance of a lawyer when they have not previously been informed by the authorities of their right to remain silent.[818] It is very important to inform a suspect of the right to remain

---

privilege against self-incrimination. Article 10 requires States to ensure that, in the assessment of statements made by suspects in breach of the right to remain silent or the right not to incriminate oneself, the rights of the defence and the fairness of the proceedings are respected. In the International Covenant on Civil and Political Rights (ICCPR), the minimum rights in criminal proceedings are listed in Article 14 §3, which provides under subparagraph g): "Not to be compelled to testify against himself or to confess guilt."

814 *Saunders v. the United Kingdom* [GC], App. no. 19187/91, §68, 17.12.1996. See also Michael O'Boyle, "Freedom from self-incrimination and the right to silence: a Pandora's box?", in Paul Mahoney, Franz Matscher, Herbert Petzold, Luzius Wildhaber (Eds.), *Protection des Droits de L'homme: la Perspective Européenne, Mélanges à la Mémoire de Rolv Ryssdal/Protecting Human Rights: the European Perspective, Studies in Memory of Rolv Ryssdal*, Carl Heymanns Verlag, Köln/Berlin/Bonn/München 2000, pp. 1021–1038, at pp. 1025–1028.

815 *Ibrahim and Others v. the United Kingdom* [GC], App. nos. 50541/08+, §273, 13.9.2016.

816 *Allan v. the United Kingdom*, App. no. 48539/99, §50, 5.11.2002.

817 *Saunders v. the United Kingdom* [GC], App. no. 19187/91, §68, 17.12.1996. See also Mark Berger, "Self-Incrimination and the European Court of Human Rights: Procedural Issues in the Enforcement of the Right to Silence", *European Human Rights Law Review*, Issue 5, 2007, pp. 514–533, at pp. 523–524; Tim Ward, Piers Gardner, "The Privilege Against Self-Incrimination - In Search of Legal Certainty", *European Human Rights Law Review*, Issue 4, 2003, pp. 388–399, at pp. 391–392; and Johan Callewaert, "The privilege against self-incrimination in European law: an illustration of the impact of the plurality of Courts and legal sources on the protection of fundamental rights in Europe", *ERA-Forum: scripta iuris europaei*, vol. 5, no. 4, December 2004, pp. 488–499, at pp. 493–494.

818 *Brusco v. France*, App. no. 1466/07, §54, 14.10.2010; and *Navone and Others v. Monaco*, App. nos. 62880/11+, §74, 24.10.2013.

silent: even where a person willingly agrees to give a statement to the police after being informed that his words may be used in evidence against him, this cannot be regarded as a fully informed choice if the suspect has not been expressly notified of his right to remain silent and if his decision has been taken without the assistance of counsel.[819]

The right not to incriminate oneself is primarily concerned with respecting the will of an accused person to remain silent.[820] The right to remain silent means that a suspect or an accused does not have to say anything in relation to the accusation and does not have to reply to questions or give observations on the matter. In addition, the right not to incriminate oneself extends to the obligation to present a document or other real evidence. This aspect of the freedom from self-incrimination was at stake in the case *Funke v. France*, in which the applicant was accused of breaching the currency regulations and customs officials required him to present bank statements from foreign banks. When the applicant refused, he was fined and ordered to present the documents in question. According to the Court, all accused within the meaning of Article 6 of the Convention have a right to remain silent and not to contribute to the establishment of their own guilt. The authorities' conduct breached this right and their conduct could not be justified by the special features of the customs regulations. There was thus a violation of Article 6 §1 of the Convention.[821]

The right not to incriminate oneself is not, however, an absolute right.[822] The consequences of remaining silent or the evidential value of the evidence obtained against the will of the accused is always assessed *in casu*. In this assessment, attention is drawn to the circumstances of the case, the nature of the means used to induce the incriminating evidence, the importance of the conclusions in the assessment of evidence and the legal safeguards of the defence.[823] In jury trials, a judge's directions to the jury – stipulating their responsibilities when drawing conclusions from the defendant's silence, even if that be to his or her detriment – is not in itself incompatible with the fair trial requirements. The defendant's silence cannot, however, be used as the sole evidence against the defendant.

---

819 *Stojkovic v. France and Belgium*, App. no. 25303/08, §54, 27.10.2011.

820 *Saunders v. the United Kingdom* [GC], App. no. 19187/91, §69, 17.12.1996; and *Marttinen v. Finland*, App. no. 19235/03, §60, 21.4.2009. See also Tim Ward, Piers Gardner, "The Privilege Against Self-Incrimination – In Search of Legal Certainty", *European Human Rights Law Review*, Issue 4, 2003, pp. 388–399, at pp. 391–392.

821 *Funke v. France*, App. no. 10828/84, §44, 25.2.1993. See also Mark Berger, "Self-Incrimination and the European Court of Human Rights: Procedural Issues in the Enforcement of the Right to Silence", *European Human Rights Law Review*, Issue 5, 2007, pp. 514–533, at pp. 525–526; and *J.B. v. Switzerland*, App. no. 31827/96, §§63–71, 3.5.2001.

822 *Ibrahim and Others v. the United Kingdom* [GC], App. nos. 50541/08+, §269, 13.9.2016; and *John Murray v. the United Kingdom*, App. no. 18731/91, §47, 8.2.1996.

823 *John Murray v. the United Kingdom*, App. no. 18731/91, §46, 8.2.1996; and *Gäfgen v. Germany* [GC], App. no. 22978/05, §163, 1.6.2010.

Conclusions can be drawn in cases in which other evidence requires that the defendant gives an explanation. In any event, the defendant must be warned about the possibility that his or her remaining silent may lead to conclusions being drawn to his or her detriment. Drawing conclusions from the defendant's silence must not, however, render the proceedings as a whole unfair, and the legal safeguards of a fair trial must be guaranteed.[824]

#### *4.2.10.2. Procedure Violating the Freedom from Self-Incrimination*

The right not to incriminate oneself can be breached when two conditions are fulfilled: when coercive measures, or a threat to use them, are used to break the prohibition of self-incrimination; and when this happens in order to clarify a pending criminal suspicion, either in the same proceedings or in other proceedings conducted in parallel with the criminal proceedings.

The right not to incriminate oneself can be breached in many ways and at several different stages of the proceedings: during the pretrial investigation, during other separate proceedings, or during the criminal trial. The right not to incriminate oneself can be breached in three different ways. First, when there is a sanction or a threat of a sanction imposed on the suspect in the same proceedings or in other pending parallel proceedings if the suspect chooses to remain silent or gives wrong information; second, when coercive measures are employed, whether they be in the form of physical violence or psychological pressure, which are deemed to be torture or inhuman treatment under Article 3; and third, when the authorities use subterfuge to elicit information they were unable to obtain during questioning.[825]

Compulsion, then, can take many different forms. However, not all kinds of compulsion fall within the scope of freedom from self-incrimination; only compulsion that is deemed to be illegal and improper does so.[826] Compulsion can be direct or indirect. Even if the compulsion is direct, it does not necessarily lead to the conclusion, based solely on this ground, that it breaches the right not to incriminate oneself.[827] When evaluating the compulsion, four criteria are mainly taken into account: the nature and degree of the compulsion; the existence of any relevant procedural safeguards; the use to which any material

---

824 *John Murray v. the United Kingdom*, App. no. 18731/91, §47, 8.2.1996; *Condron v. the United Kingdom*, App. no. 35718/97, §56, 2.5.2000; *Beckles v. the United Kingdom*, App. no. 44652/98, §§57–59, 8.10.2002; *Tabbakh v. the United Kingdom* (dec.), App. no. 40945/09, §29, 21.2.2012; *O'Donnell v. the United Kingdom*, App. no. 16667/10, §51, 7.4.2015; and *Averill v. the United Kingdom*, App. no. 36408/97, §45, 6.6.2000.

825 *Ibrahim and Others v. the United Kingdom* [GC], App. nos. 50541/08+, §§266–267, 13.9.2016.

826 *John Murray v. the United Kingdom*, App. no. 18731/91, §46, 8.2.1996 (improper compulsion); and *Condron v. the United Kingdom*, App. no. 35718/97, §56, 2.5.2000.

827 *O'Halloran and Francis v. the United Kingdom* [GC], App. nos. 15809/02+, §53, 29.6.2007.

so obtained is put; and the weight of public interest in the investigation and punishment of the offence in question.[828]

4.2.10.2.1. Documents and Samples Obtained by Coercive Measures

In the Court's case-law, a distinction has been made between evidence based on a person's will and evidence which exists independently from the will of a person. The right not to incriminate oneself does not prevent, for example, the obtaining and using in a criminal matter any material which can be obtained from the accused by using coercive measures but the existence of which is not dependent on his or her will (obligation to take active measures). Such materials include documents acquired pursuant to a search warrant, breath, blood, urine, hair or voice samples and bodily tissue for the purpose of DNA testing.[829] The right not to incriminate oneself does not therefore free the accused from the obligation to be subjected to the use of legal coercive measures and the obligation to tolerate them passively. By the same token, the accused cannot be forced to actively contribute to the establishment of his or her own guilt.

4.2.10.2.2. Situations Unconnected to Criminal Proceedings

The right not to incriminate oneself does not in itself prevent the imposition of obligations and threats of sanctions outside any judicial proceedings. For example, the obligation to file a tax declaration with the tax authorities is not self-incrimination even if a sanction is attached to the failure to do so and the person concerned can be fined for having declared no information or wrong information.

This was exemplified by the case of *Allen v. the United Kingdom*, in which the Court found that there was no case pending against the applicant, nor were any proceedings expected. The fact that he had intentionally given wrong information in order to prevent the authorities from finding out about an act which might possibly lead to charges being pressed did not constitute a situation in which the applicant would have the right not to incriminate himself and contribute to the establishment of his guilt. Such obligations to declare are common in

828 *Jalloh v. Germany* [GC], App. no. 54810/00, §§101 and 117, 11.7.2006; *Heaney and McGuinness v. Ireland*, App. no. 34720/97, §§51–55, 21.12.2000; *Allan v. the United Kingdom*, App. no. 48539/99, §44, 5.11.2002; and *Tirado Ortiz and Lozano Martin v. Spain* (dec.), App. no. 43486/98, 15.6.1999.

829 *Saunders v. the United Kingdom* [GC], App. no. 19187/91, §69, 17.12.1996; *Choudhary v. the United Kingdom* (dec.), App. no. 40084/98, 4.5.1999; *J.B. v. Switzerland*, App. no. 31827/96, §68, 3.5.2001; *P.G. and J.H. v. the United Kingdom*, App. no. 44787/98, §80, 25.9.2001; and *Jalloh v. Germany* [GC], App. no. 54810/00, §102, 11.7.2006.

the Contracting States and concern many different kinds of issues.[830] One such obligation is, for example, the obligation to disclose one's identity to the police and the possible consequences for failing to fulfil this obligation.[831]

#### 4.2.10.2.3. Physical Coercion, Torture and Inhuman Treatment

##### *4.2.10.2.3.1. For Obtaining a Confession*

The most brutal way of breaking a person's will is the use of physical coercion and torture to obtain a confession. Any confession or statement obtained in violation of Article 3 and admitted to the case file renders the proceedings unfair, irrespective of the evidential value given to it in that particular case.[832] In the case *Gäfgen v. Germany*, the Court found that the admission of statements obtained as a result of torture as evidence to establish the relevant facts in criminal proceedings rendered the proceedings as a whole unfair, irrespective of the probative value of the statements and irrespective of whether their use was decisive in securing the defendant's conviction.[833] In subsequent case-law, the Court has further clarified this and has found systematically that all statements obtained in violation of Article 3 and admitted to the case file render the proceedings unfair, irrespective of the evidential value of the statement and whether it was decisive or not.[834]

In the case *El Haski v. Belgium*, the Court went even further and held clearly that the use in criminal proceedings of statements obtained as a result

830 *Allen v. the United Kingdom* (dec.), App. no. 76574/01, 10.9.2002. See also Mark Berger, "Self-Incrimination and the European Court of Human Rights: Procedural Issues in the Enforcement of the Right to Silence", *European Human Rights Law Review*, Issue 5, 2007, pp. 514–533, at p. 518.

831 *Vasileva v. Denmark*, App. no. 52792/99, §§34 and 39–40, 25.9.2003. Nor was it contrary to Article 5 to arrest and detain a person in order to secure the fulfilment of a legal obligation. The excessive length of the detention led, however, to a finding of a violation, not the detention as such, nor the fact that the applicant had been ordered to identify herself.

832 *Gäfgen v. Germany* [GC], App. no. 22978/05, §§166–167, 1.6.2010; *Örs and Others v. Turkey*, App. no. 46213/99, §60, 20.6.2006; *Harutyunyan v. Armenia*, App. no. 36549/03, §§63–64, 28.6.2007; *Levința v. Moldova*, App. no. 17332/03, §§101–105, 16.12.2008; *Söylemez v. Turkey*, App. no. 46661/99, §§107 and 122–124, 21.9.2006; and *El Haski v. Belgium*, App. no. 649/08, §99, 25.9.2012.

833 *Gäfgen v. Germany* [GC], App. no. 22978/05, §166, 1.6.2010. See also Martha Spurrier, "*Gäfgen v. Germany* – Fruit of the poisonous tree", *European Human Rights Law Review*, Issue 5, 2010, pp. 513–519; and Boštjan M. Zupančič, "An answer to one crucial question of human rights: an epistemological excursus informing *Jalloh v. Germany* and *Gäfgen v. Germany* cases at the European Court of Human Rights", in Miha Pogačnik (Ed.), *Challenges of Contemporary International Law and International Relations – Liber Amicorum in Honour of Ernest Petrič*, The European Faculty of Law, Nova Gorica 2011, pp. 451–463.

834 *Tangiyev v. Russia*, App. no. 27610/05, §73, 11.12.2012 (torture); *Zamferesko v. Ukraine*, App. no. 30075/06, §70, 15.11.2012 (threats to kill or assault); *Hajnal v. Serbia*, App. no. 36937/06, §§113–115, 19.6.2012 (physical and mental violence); and *Ryabtsev v. Russia*, App. no. 13642/06, §91, 14.11.2013 (physical and mental violence).

of acts committed in violation of Article 3 – irrespective of the classification of the treatment as torture, or inhuman or degrading treatment – automatically rendered the proceedings as a whole unfair, in breach of Article 6. These principles applied not only where the victim of the treatment contrary to Article 3 was the actual defendant but also where third parties were concerned.[835] The Court referred in this case to the case *Othman (Abu Qatada) v. the United Kingdom*, in which it held that the use in a trial of evidence obtained by torture would amount to a flagrant denial of justice, even where the person from whom the evidence had been thus extracted was a third party.[836] Physical coercion inflicted on a third person thus "poisons" the whole evidence, irrespective of whom it is used against.

The same principle was confirmed in the case *Al Nashiri v. Poland*, which concerned interrogations conducted by CIA agents in a secret prison situated on Polish soil, where the methods of interrogation included torture. The use of evidence obtained by such interrogations in proceedings against a defendant would lead to a flagrant denial of justice. The Court held Poland liable since it had co-operated with the CIA agents by allowing secret transportation of the prisoners, the secret prisons and the methods of interrogation used.[837] The same applicant had also been subjected to similar treatment in Romania.[838]

---

835 *El Haski v. Belgium*, App. no. 649/08, §85, 25.9.2012. See also James Welch (Ed.), "Case and comment: selected decisions from the European Court of Human Rights from September and October 2012 – Torture, *El Haski v. Belgium* (Application No. 649/08)", *European Human Rights Law Review*, Issue 1, 2013, pp. 89–92.

836 *Othman (Abu Qatada) v. the United Kingdom*, App. no. 8139/09, §§263 and 267, 17.1.2012. See also Anand Doobay, "The right to a fair trial in light of the recent ECtHR and CJEU case-law", *ERA forum*, vol.14, issue 2, September 2013, pp. 251–262, at pp. 252–253; Christopher Michaelsen, "The renaissance of non-refoulement? The Othman (Abu Qatada) decision of the European Court of Human Rights", *International and Comparative Law Quarterly*, vol. 61, pt. 3, July 2012, pp. 750–765, at pp. 750–752; and Joe Middleton, "Taking rights seriously in expulsion cases – a case study", *European Human Rights Law Review*, Issue 5, 2013, pp. 520–531.

837 *Al Nashiri v. Poland*, App. no. 28761/11, §§557–562, 24.7.2014. See also Dagmara Rajska, Krisztina Huszti-Orban, *Human Rights Obligations of States in the Context of Counter-terrorism Operations: A Commentary in the Light of Al Nashiri v. Poland and Husayn (Abu Zubaydah) v. Poland*, Aracne, Ariccia 2015; John Wadham: "Rendition, detention and torture in Europe – territorial responsibility and the right to truth: *Husayan (Abu Zubaydah) v. Poland* (app. no. 7511/13) and *Al Nashiri v. Poland* (app. no. 28761/11), Chamber judgments of July 24, 2014 (former fourth section)", *European Human Rights Law Review*, Issue 5, 2014, pp. 519–526; Lori Ann Wanlin, "Responsibility for secret detention and extraordinary rendition: the Strasbourg Court holds Poland to account", *Cyprus Human Rights Law Review*, vol. 3, issue 2, 2014, pp. 185–200; and Michael O'Boyle, "Proof in rendition cases before the European Court of Human Rights", *Revista do Instituto Brasileiro de Direitos Humanos*, App. no. 17/18, 2018, pp. 183–191, at pp. 186–188.

838 *Al Nashiri v. Romania*, App. no. 33234/12, §§721–722, 31.5.2018. See also Alice Venn, "Case and comment: selected decisions from the European Court of Human Rights for May and June 2018 – Extraordinary rendition and secret detention, *Al Nashiri v. Romania* (Application No. 33234/12)", *European Human Rights Law Review*, Issue 5, 2018, pp. 519–523.

### 4.2.10.2.3.2. Real Evidence

In the case *Jalloh v. Germany* the Court developed the scope of the right not to incriminate oneself in the context of Article 3 relating to real evidence. The case concerned the defendant's right not to contribute to the establishment of evidence against him in respect of evidence which was in his body. The applicant, who was suspected of a narcotics offence, had been forced to undergo a treatment during which he was administered emetics through a tube introduced into his stomach through the nose while he was held down and immobilised by four police officers. The Court found that the applicant had been subjected, for the purposes of obtaining evidence, to inhuman and degrading treatment contrary to the substantive provisions of Article 3. The degree of force used against the applicant differed significantly from the degree of compulsion normally required to obtain evidence the existence of which was independent of the will of the suspect, such as breath, blood, urine and voice samples and bodily tissue for the purpose of DNA testing. As the degree of force used in the case differed significantly from the degree of compulsion normally required to obtain the above type of evidence, the applicant's right not to contribute to the establishment of his own guilt applied to the situation. The drugs obtained following the administration of the emetics had been the decisive evidence in the applicant's conviction for drug trafficking. As the case concerned small-scale street drug dealing, the public interest in securing the applicant's conviction did not justify recourse to such a grave interference with the applicant's physical and mental integrity. The proceedings were thus rendered, as a whole, unfair.[839]

The outcome reached by the Court in the *Jalloh* case came about as a result of the particular circumstances of that case. The Court, though, still left open the question of whether the use of real evidence obtained by an act classified as inhuman and degrading treatment, but falling short of torture, always renders a trial unfair, that is, irrespective of, in particular, the weight attached to the evidence, its probative value and the opportunities for the defendant to challenge its admission and use at trial.[840]

---

839 *Jalloh v. Germany* [GC], App. no. 54810/00, §§100–123, 11.7.2006. See also Boštjan M. Zupančič, "An answer to one crucial question of human rights: an epistemological excursus informing *Jalloh v. Germany* and *Gäfgen v. Germany* cases at the European Court of Human Rights", in Miha Pogačnik (Ed.), *Challenges of Contemporary International Law and International Relations – Liber Amicorum in Honour of Ernest Petrič*, The European Faculty of Law, Nova Gorica 2011, pp. 451–463; and Sverre Erik Jebens, "Illegally obtained evidence in criminal cases – an analysis on the basis of three Grand Chamber judgments", in Dean Spielmann, Marialena Tsirli, Panayotis Voyatzis (Eds.), *La Convention Européenne des Droits de L'homme, un Instrument Vivant – Mélanges en L'honneur de Christos L. Rozakis/The European Convention on Human Rights, a Living Instrument – Essays in Honour of Christos L. Rozakis*, Bruylant, Bruxelles 2011, pp. 219–234, at pp. 221–223.

840 *Gäfgen v. Germany* [GC], App. no. 22978/05, §167, 1.6.2010.

In the case *Gäfgen v. Germany*, the Court was called upon to examine this question. It first confirmed that the same rule applying to confessions obtained by torture also applied to real evidence obtained thereby. The use of real evidence obtained by torture therefore rendered the proceedings unfair.[841] The Court further found that in situations falling short of torture the crucial issue was the importance of the evidence for the conviction. If the evidence was decisive in obtaining the conviction, it rendered the trial unfair. However, if there was no causal link to the conviction, the situation was different. In the circumstances of the *Gäfgen* case, the Court found that, irrespective of the inhuman treatment inflicted on the applicant in violation of Article 3 during the pretrial investigation of the case, his conviction had not been based on this evidence but on a voluntary confession made at the trial in the presence of his counsel. In addition, there was other, legally obtained, real evidence in the case. The real evidence obtained by means of inhuman treatment and admitted to the case file had not been used to establish the applicant's guilt but only to test the authenticity of the confession made before the court. The causal link between the confession made before the court and the real evidence obtained in violation of Article 3 was therefore not established. The applicant's rights of defence, as well as his right not to incriminate himself, had been respected in the case, and the fact that the real evidence obtained by inhuman means had not been excluded from the case file did not render the proceedings unfair.[842]

In the case *El Haski v. Belgium*, the Court clarified the *Gäfgen* judgment by finding that the use of any real evidence obtained as a direct result of acts of torture and admitted to the case file rendered the trial unfair. The admission of evidence obtained as a result of an act deemed inhuman treatment in breach of Article 3, but falling short of torture, would only breach Article 6, however, if it was shown that the breach of Article 3 had a bearing on the outcome of the proceedings against the defendant, that is, had an impact on his or her conviction or sentence.[843]

---

[841] *Gäfgen v. Germany* [GC], App. no. 22978/05, §§166–167, 1.6.2010. See also Martha Spurrier, "*Gäfgen v. Germany* – Fruit of the poisonous tree", *European Human Rights Law Review*, Issue 5, 2010, pp. 513–519; Sverre Erik Jebens, "Illegally obtained evidence in criminal cases – an analysis on the basis of three Grand Chamber judgments", in Dean Spielmann, Marialena Tsirli, Panayotis Voyatzis (Eds.), *La Convention Européenne des Droits de L'homme, un Instrument Vivant – Mélanges en L'honneur de Christos L. Rozakis/The European Convention on Human Rights, a Living Instrument – Essays in Honour of Christos L. Rozakis*, Bruylant, Bruxelles 2011, pp. 219–234, at pp. 224–225; and David Harris, Michael O'Boyle, Ed Bates, Carla Buckley, *Law of the European Convention on Human Rights*, 4th edition, Oxford University Press, Oxford 2018, p. 421.

[842] *Gäfgen v. Germany* [GC], App. no. 22978/05, §§172–188, 1.6.2010. The domestic court excluded from the case file the confession obtained in violation of Article 3 of the Convention.

[843] *El Haski v. Belgium*, App. no. 649/08, §85, 25.9.2012. See also James Welch (Ed.), "Case and comment: selected decisions from the European Court of Human Rights from September and October 2012 – Torture, *El Haski v. Belgium* (Application No. 649/08)", *European Human Rights Law Review*, Issue 1, 2013, pp. 89–92.

In short, the Court's case-law provides that the use of all evidence obtained by torture is forbidden, while the use of real evidence obtained by acts classified as inhuman and degrading treatment but falling short of torture under Article 3 is forbidden only if it has a causal link to the conviction. For more information, see also section 4.2.6.2.5. of this chapter, above.

#### 4.2.10.2.4. Indirect Situations

The right not to incriminate oneself is not only at stake when a suspect is directly forced to give statements or evidence detrimental to him or her. This right can also be violated by indirect means when a suspect is forced to confess through intermediaries.

In the case *Allan v. the United Kingdom*, the defendant confessed to a murder to a police "informant", who had been placed in the same cell with him with instructions to make him talk. In the police interrogations the defendant had refused to say anything. The cellmate had persuaded the defendant to confess, and this evidence was decisive for the defendant's conviction. Although no direct compulsion was used in the situation, the applicant had been subjected to psychological pressure which had had an impact on the voluntariness of his confession. The confession made to the cellmate was regarded as an involuntary confession and it violated the applicant's right not to incriminate himself. It was also relevant that the confession had been made in a situation to which the normal legal safeguards concerning interrogations did not apply. However, the police's recording of the applicant's conversations in the cell was not contrary to the right not to incriminate oneself. Such conduct was not illegal; nor had the applicant been forced or brought under false pretences to give those statements which had been recorded.[844]

### *4.2.10.3. Two Typical Situations Concerning Freedom from Self-Incrimination*

The right not to incriminate oneself can be violated in two different kinds of situations. First, when compulsion is used to establish a person's guilt in pending or anticipated proceedings. This refers to a situation in which evidence and/or information is obtained in relation to an offence for which a person has already been charged,[845] or when the pretrial investigation or a trial is pending.

---

844 *Allan v. the United Kingdom*, App. no. 48539/99, §§46, 48 and 51–52, 5.11.2002. See also John Wadham, Philip Leach, "Cases and comment: selected decisions from the European Court of Human Rights for November and December 2002 – Crime and sentencing, *Allan v. United Kingdom* (Application No. 48539/99)", *European Human Rights Law Review*, Issue 2, 2003, pp. 235–237.

845 Within the meaning of the Convention.

Second, there are situations in which the evidence and/or information obtained by compulsion is used in the context of subsequent charges[846] and in which there is a clear temporal and material connection between the obtaining of the information in question and the subsequent charges.

#### 4.2.10.3.1. Pending and Anticipated Trials

Often compulsion is used against a defendant in order to obtain evidence against him or her for pending proceedings. The threat of a sanction or the imposition of a sanction for remaining silent or refusing to disclose information detrimental to oneself violates the right not to incriminate oneself, irrespective of whether the person is later charged or convicted of the crime.[847]

This was the case in *Shannon v. the United Kingdom*, in which the applicant was suspected of a bookkeeping offence and fraud, and the pretrial investigation was pending. Subsequently, the applicant was summonsed to an interrogation about the benefits received from these crimes, but he refused to attend it. The applicant was fined for this refusal. The potential charges against him then lapsed as they had become statute-barred. The Court, however, held that the right not to contribute to the establishment of one's guilt did not require that any evidence obtained by compulsion was actually used. This right could have been invoked even though the charges were dismissed or were never even pressed. The use of compulsion could have been justified, had there not been a criminal suspicion towards the applicant. But there was a criminal suspicion and therefore there was a danger that the information obtained during any interrogations about the crime benefits could have been used in a criminal matter. Nor were there any procedural legal safeguards because the authorities examining the benefits of the crimes had a right to disclose the information obtained to the police. Although no charges were pressed against the applicant, the Court held that the right not to incriminate oneself had been violated because the applicant's refusal to attend an interrogation and submit information which could have been used against him had been justified.[848]

---

846 *Weh v. Austria*, App. no. 38544/97, §§42–43, 8.4.2004.

847 *Heaney and McGuinness v. Ireland*, App. no. 34720/97, §§41, 46 and 55, 21.12.2000; and *Shannon v. the United Kingdom*, App. no. 6563/03, §§34–35, 4.10.2005. See also Stanley H. Naismith, "Witnesses and the right to remain silent", in Josep Casadevall, Egbert Myjer, Michael O'Boyle (Eds.), *Freedom of Expression – Essays in Honour of Nicolas Bratza*, Wolf Legal Publishers, Oisterwijk 2012, pp. 245–256.

848 *Shannon v. the United Kingdom*, App. no. 6563/03, §§33–41, 4.10.2005. See also Mark Berger, "Self-Incrimination and the European Court of Human Rights: Procedural Issues in the Enforcement of the Right to Silence", *European Human Rights Law Review*, Issue 5, 2007, pp. 514–533, at pp. 522–523.

#### 4.2.10.3.2. Subsequent Criminal Charges

The right not to incriminate oneself can also be violated in situations falling outside the context of pending criminal proceedings if such evidence is used in a subsequent criminal prosecution.[849] Such a violation of the right not to incriminate oneself in subsequent proceedings may be at stake, for example, if administrative law proceedings and criminal proceedings have a close connection to each other and they are pending at the same time, or if the administrative law proceedings precede the criminal ones and in the administrative law proceedings compulsion is used in order to obtain information which can be used against the defendant in subsequent criminal proceedings.

This was the situation in the case *Marttinen v. Finland*. A pretrial investigation into debtor's fraud was pending against the applicant when an enforcement inquiry was carried out in which the applicant should have declared his assets in order to enable the bailiff to seize those assets to secure payment of his debts. The applicant refused, since the enforcement inquiry concerned the same facts as the pending pretrial investigation, for which he had the right to remain silent. Nevertheless, he was ordered to provide this information on pain of an administrative fine and this obligation was upheld by the domestic courts. The applicant could have been accused of debtor's fraud, had it become apparent during the enforcement inquiry that he had assets which had not been declared in previous enforcement inquiries or bankruptcies. The domestic law did not contain any legal safeguards vis-à-vis the use of information obtained in enforcement inquiries because, although the bailiff was bound by professional secrecy, the creditors applying for enforcement were not, according to the legislation applicable at the time, prohibited from using any information received for their personal benefit in the pending criminal proceedings. The applicant therefore had the choice to either provide the information requested or face the imposition of an administrative fine. As a pretrial investigation was pending against the applicant and both the enforcement procedure and the pretrial investigation concerned the same facts, the Court found that the "degree of compulsion" imposed on the applicant with a view to compelling him to provide information in the enforcement inquiry destroyed the very essence of his privilege against self-incrimination and his right to remain silent. The effective functioning of the enforcement procedure could not justify such a marked departure from one of the basic principles of a fair procedure. Article 6 §1 of the Convention had thus been violated.[850]

---

849 *Weh v. Austria*, App. no. 38544/97, §§42–43, 8.4.2004.

850 *Marttinen v. Finland*, App. no. 19235/03, §§72–76, 21.4.2009. See also Andrew L.-T. Choo, *The Privilege against Self-incrimination and Criminal Justice*, Hart Publishing, Oxford and Portland, Or. 2013, p. 28.

The privilege against self-incrimination can be applied if a person is already the subject of a pending criminal investigation. It does not therefore prevent, for example, the taxation authorities from requesting correct tax declarations from tax subjects on pain of a penalty. In the case *Allen v. the United Kingdom*, the applicant had breached his duty to correctly declare his income and was subsequently prosecuted. But the privilege against self-incrimination was not violated since his case was not an example of forced self-incrimination for an offence that he had previously committed, but it was the offence itself.[851]

Similarly, in the case *Eklund v. Finland*, the applicant had been convicted of giving false information to an enforcement inquiry in 2004. The right not to incriminate oneself was not applicable since the sanction imposed was a direct consequence of the false information given, without which the obligation to give a declaration would have been used for clarifying any other pending or expected criminal matters. According to the applicant, he could not have given correct information to the 2004 enforcement inquiry because he had given false information to an earlier enforcement inquiry in 1997 and would therefore have contributed to the filing of criminal charges against him had he given correct information in 2004. The Court held that the right not to incriminate oneself was not applicable even in that respect, since no criminal charges were brought against the applicant or even expected after the 1997 enforcement inquiry. This complaint was thus hypothetical. The right not to incriminate oneself thus presupposed that there was already a pending criminal case, or that such a case was anticipated.[852]

In another Finnish case, *Elomaa v. Finland*, the Court did not find a violation as there was no connection between the two proceedings. The applicant had been convicted of debtor's fraud after disclosing wrong information about his assets to an enforcement inquiry. Before the enforcement inquiry took place, a police report had been made on suspicion of money laundering which concerned the concealment of the applicant's assets. The applicant claimed that he had been forced, by giving a full account of his assets to the enforcement inquiry, to admit his guilt in respect of the pending suspicion of money laundering. But this was not the case, since the pretrial investigation into money laundering could not have concerned the applicant, who was suspected of the principal offence. In Finland, money laundering was punishable at the time only as a receiving offence, and the applicant could not have been convicted of it. The enforcement inquiry did not therefore have any connection to the money laundering suspicion.[853]

---

851 *Allen v. the United Kingdom* (dec.), App. no. 76574/01, 10.9.2002.

852 *Eklund v. Finland* (dec.), App. no. 56936/13, §§46–52, 8.12.2015.

853 *Elomaa v. Finland* (dec.), App. no. 37670/04, 16.3.2010.

#### 4.2.10.3.3. Situations Concerning Speeding Controls

Cases concerning speed controls, such as *Weh v. Austria*, do not fall into either of the categories mentioned above; nor do they concern the right not to incriminate oneself. In the *Weh* case, the applicant had been sanctioned for not giving adequate information about the person who had driven the car which was in his possession and had exceeded the speed limit. The applicant had indicated that the driver was a person who subsequently could not be identified. The case did not initially concern the use of incriminating information obtained through compulsion in the context of pending or anticipated proceedings, as no charges had been pressed against the applicant at any stage. Secondly, nor were there any subsequent proceedings since the suspicion was directed at unknown offenders. There was nothing to show that the applicant was "substantially affected" so as to consider him "charged" with the offence of speeding; it was merely in his capacity as the registered car owner that he was required to give information. The case did thus not raise an issue with regard to the applicant's right to remain silent and the privilege against self-incrimination.[854]

This matter was also examined in another case, *O'Halloran and Francis v. the United Kingdom*, in which both applicants had been asked to identify to the police, on pain of sanction, the drivers of their respective cars in a situation where a traffic camera had caught the cars exceeding the speed limit. One of the applicants admitted having driven the car and he was convicted of speeding. The other applicant invoked his right to remain silent and he was convicted of failing to disclose the identity of the driver. In both cases direct compulsion was used against applicants by threatening them with fines if they failed to provide the required information. This obligation was based on the Road Traffic Act 1988, which imposed a specific duty on the registered keeper of a vehicle to give information about the driver of the vehicle in certain circumstances. Those who chose to keep and drive motor cars could be taken to have accepted certain responsibilities and obligations as a part of the regulatory regime relating to motor vehicles. The fact that a person had to provide a certain piece of information did not as such constitute self-incrimination. No criminal proceedings were pending against the applicants; nor had any excessive means been used in the investigation of the cases, and the sanction was reasonable. Also, the procedural safeguards were in place, as no offence could be committed if the keeper of a vehicle could show that he did not know and could not with

---

854 *Weh v. Austria*, App. no. 38544/97, §§51–57, 8.4.2004. See also Mark Berger, "Self-Incrimination and the European Court of Human Rights: Procedural Issues in the Enforcement of the Right to Silence", *European Human Rights Law Review*, Issue 5, 2007, pp. 514–533, at p. 528; and Mark Berger, "Compelled self-reporting and the principle against compelled self-incrimination - some comparative perspectives", *European Human Rights Law Review*, Issue 1, 2006, pp. 25–38, at pp. 26–28.

reasonable diligence have known who the driver of the vehicle was. Having regard to all the circumstances of the case, including the special nature of the regulatory regime in issue and the limited nature of the information sought, the Court considered that the essence of the applicants' right to remain silent and their privilege against self-incrimination had not been breached.[855] These cases are comparable to that mentioned earlier concerning the obligation to give a tax declaration (*Allen v. the United Kingdom*), as in neither case was there any criminal suspicion against the applicants. The applicants were only expected, as car owners, to provide certain information required by the law.

#### *4.2.10.4. Freedom from Self-Incrimination and Legal Safeguards of a Trial*

A problem in the freedom from self-incrimination context can ultimately be caused by the fact that there are no sufficient legal safeguards in the trial vis-à-vis this right. For example, a judge in a jury trial may not give the jurors adequate information about the significance of this right when they are assessing the evidence in a case in front of them.[856] The significance of the legal safeguards was examined by the Court in particular in the case *John Murray v. the United Kingdom*, in which the Court distinguished two different principles when examining an accused's decision to remain silent throughout criminal proceedings and whether that silence should have implications when the trial court seeks to evaluate the evidence against him. On the one hand, it found that the right not to incriminate oneself does not prevent the accused's silence from being considered – in situations which clearly call for an explanation from him – when assessing the persuasiveness of the evidence adduced by the prosecution. On the other hand, a conviction should never be solely or mainly based on the accused's silence or on a refusal to answer questions or to give evidence himself.[857] In the case in question, the defendant could have used his right to remain silent, which was not sanctioned as such. It was relevant that the prosecutor had fulfilled the burden of proof and provided strong evidence

---

855 *O'Halloran and Francis v. the United Kingdom* [GC], App. nos. 15809/02+, §§57–63, 29.6.2007. See also Mark Berger, "Self-Incrimination and the European Court of Human Rights: Procedural Issues in the Enforcement of the Right to Silence", *European Human Rights Law Review*, Issue 5, 2007, pp. 514–533, at pp. 518–519; and John Jackson, "Re-conceptualizing the right of silence as an effective fair trial standard", *International and Comparative Law Quarterly*, vol. 58, pt. 4, October 2009, pp. 835–861, at pp. 850–854.

856 *Condron v. the United Kingdom*, App. no. 35718/97, §66, 2.5.2000; and *Beckles v. the United Kingdom*, App. no. 44652/98, §§64–65, 8.10.2002.

857 *John Murray v. the United Kingdom*, App. no. 18731/91, §47, 8.2.1996. See also Michael O'Boyle, "Freedom from self-incrimination and the right to silence: a Pandora's box?", in Paul Mahoney, Franz Matscher, Herbert Petzold, Luzius Wildhaber (Eds.), *Protection des Droits de L'homme: La Perspective Européenne, Mélanges à la Mémoire de Rolv Ryssdal/Protecting Human Rights: The European Perspective, Studies in Memory of Rolv Ryssdal*, Carl Heymanns Verlag, Köln/Berlin/Bonn/München 2000, pp. 1021–1038, at pp. 1034–1036.

in support of the charges. This evidence clearly required some explanations or comments on the part of the accused. In this respect, it was understandable that conclusions had been drawn from the accused's continued refusal to say anything. The burden of proof had not, however, been shifted to the accused as the prosecutor had presented strong evidence for the crime itself.[858]

In a similar case, *Averill v. the United Kingdom*, the defendant was convicted on the basis of strong technical evidence. In addition, the Court gave significance to the fact that the defendant had not commented on the forensic evidence during the pretrial interrogation, although common sense would expect that such explanations were called for. The Court emphasised also that the extent to which adverse inferences could be drawn from an accused's failure to respond to police questioning had to be necessarily limited. While it no doubt might be expected in most cases that innocent people would be willing to co-operate with the police in explaining that they were not involved in any suspected crime, there may be reasons why in a specific case an innocent person would not be prepared to do so.[859] In the case *O'Donnell v. the United Kingdom*, the silence of a mentally handicapped person could be taken into account in the assessment of the case since the prosecutor had presented very strong evidence of the applicant's guilt and the judge had clearly referred, in his instructions to the jury, to the ability of a mentally handicapped person to reply to questions and to give clarifications to circumstances of the case.[860]

#### 4.2.10.5. Freedom from Self-Incrimination and its Effect on Other Defendants

It is interesting to consider what kind of implications the use of evidence obtained in violation of a person's right not to incriminate himself has on other defendants in the criminal proceedings. Above, in section 4.2.10.2.3., it was seen that if interrogation methods contrary to Article 3 have been used in the case, witness testimonies obtained thereby cannot be used to the detriment of third parties.[861]

---

858 *John Murray v. the United Kingdom*, App. no. 18731/91, §§48, 51, 54 and 56–57, 8.2.1996. See also Stanley H. Naismith, "Self-incrimination: the case law of the European Court of Human Rights", *Human Rights & UK Practice*, vol. 2, issue 4, 2001, pp. 3–14, at pp. 6–7; and John Jackson, "Re-conceptualizing the right of silence as an effective fair trial standard", *International and Comparative Law Quarterly*, vol. 58, pt. 4, October 2009, pp. 835–861. For more about the legal safeguards of the proceedings, see *Gäfgen v. Germany* [GC], App. no. 22978/05, §164, 1.6.2010.

859 *Averill v. the United Kingdom*, App. no. 36408/97, §§44–52, 6.6.2000. See also Stanley H. Naismith, "Self-incrimination: the case law of the European Court of Human Rights", *Human Rights & UK Practice*, vol. 2, issue 4, 2001, pp. 3–14, at pp. 6–7.

860 *O'Donnell v. the United Kingdom*, App. no. 16667/10, §§56–58, 7.4.2015.

861 *El Haski v. Belgium*, App. no. 649/08, §85, 25.9.2012. See also *Othman (Abu Qatada) v. the United Kingdom*, App. no. 8139/09, §§263 and 267, 17.1.2012; and *Kaciu and Kotorri v. Albania*, App. nos. 33192/07+, §§128–130, 25.6.2013.

This issue was raised under Article 7 of the Convention in the case *Huhtamäki v. Finland*, in which the applicant had been convicted of concealing the assets of the other defendant, whose own charges had been dismissed on the basis of his right not to incriminate himself. The Court found acceptable the Finnish Supreme Court's interpretation that the right not to incriminate oneself only covered the accused. Nevertheless, in that case the applicant could be convicted of concealing assets even though the person accused of the principal offence was acquitted. It was thus sufficient that there was a conviction of the principal offence *in abstracto*.[862]

It was not the question of freedom from self-incrimination that was at stake in the case *Navalnyy and Ofitserov v. Russia*, but rather the effects of testimonies given by other defendants in plea-bargaining proceedings which were then used against other defendants. When a co-defendant was a witness in the trial of the other co-defendants, he or she needed to stick to the story given in the plea-bargaining proceedings, on pain of losing the mitigation of sentence. The use of this kind of testimony given by a co-defendant as evidence was prone to manipulation and therefore violated the requirements of a fair trial.[863]

### 4.2.11. PLEA BARGAINING

Many countries have introduced plea bargaining in their legal systems and thereby the possibility to mitigate punishments in order to accelerate and simplify criminal proceedings. Often this means that a defendant waives many of his or her procedural rights in the plea-bargaining process. In order to be effective within the meaning of the Convention, a waiver must be unambiguous, it must contain some minimum legal safeguards vis-à-vis its significance, and it cannot be detrimental to any important issue of public interest.[864]

The case *Natsvlishvili and Togonidze v. Georgia* was the first case in which the Court explored fully the compatibility of plea-bargaining arrangements with the notion of a fair trial within the meaning of Article 6 of the Convention. In that case, an agreement was reached between the defence and the prosecution according to which the prosecutor undertook, in return for the applicant's willingness to "reach an agreement", to request the trial court to convict the applicant without an examination of the merits of the case and to seek a reduced sentence in the form of a fine. The trial court approved the agreement, found

862 *Huhtamäki v. Finland*, App. no. 54468/09, §§48–52, 6.3.2012 (no violation).

863 *Navalnyy and Ofitserov v. Russia*, App. nos. 46632/13+, §109, 23.2.2016.

864 *Navalnyy and Ofitserov v. Russia*, App. nos. 46632/13+, §100, 23.2.2016; *Scoppola v. Italy (No. 2)* [GC], App. no. 10249/03, §135, 17.9.2009; and *Natsvlishvili and Togonidze v. Georgia*, App. no. 9043/05, §§90–91, 29.4.2014.

the applicant guilty and sentenced him to the payment of a fine. The decision could not be appealed. The applicant alleged that the plea-bargaining procedure had been an abuse of process and unfair. He accepted that the bargain he had concluded with the prosecution had entailed a waiver of certain procedural rights but contended that the waiver had not been accompanied by effective safeguards.

The Court noted at the outset that plea bargaining between the prosecution and defence was a common feature of some European criminal justice systems. Initiatives aimed at securing a reduction in sentence or a modification of charges in return for a guilty plea or co-operation with the investigating authorities were not incompatible with Article 6 as such.[865]

The important matter was to determine whether or not the procedure was accompanied by safeguards in order to prevent abuse. The Court addressed that question with reference to the circumstances in the applicant's case. It found in that case that: (1) the bargain was voluntarily entered into by the applicant in full awareness of the relevant circumstances and the consequences of so doing – in fact, the applicant himself had proposed the conclusion of an agreement; (2) the applicant was at all stages represented by lawyers, including at the time of the plea-bargaining negotiations with the prosecution; (3) the applicant confirmed on several occasions before the prosecutor and the judge overseeing the validity of the agreement that he had understood its terms and the legal consequences which it entailed for him; (4) the precise terms of the agreement, which was signed by the applicant and included a summary of the negotiations leading to it, were submitted to the trial judge for consideration at a public hearing; and (5) the trial judge was not bound to approve the agreement. It would have been open to the judge to reject the agreement if he or she was satisfied that either the terms of the agreement or the accompanying procedure were tainted by unfairness. The Court thus concluded that the applicant's acceptance of the plea bargain had undoubtedly been a conscious and voluntary decision. The decision could not be said to have resulted from any duress or false promises made by the prosecution. On the contrary, it was accompanied by sufficient safeguards against possible abuse of process.[866]

---

865 *Natsvlishvili and Togonidze v. Georgia*, App. no. 9043/05, §90, 29.4.2014. See also *Deweer v. Belgium*, App. no. 6903/75, §51, 27.2.1980; *Slavcho Kostov v. Bulgaria*, App. no. 28674/03, §17, 27.11.2008; and *Ruciński v. Poland*, App. no. 33198/04, §12, 20.2.2007.

866 *Natsvlishvili and Togonidze v. Georgia*, App. no. 9043/05, §§92–98, 29.4.2014. See also Sopho Japaridze, "Plea bargaining in Georgia – does the Georgian model of plea bargaining comply with the requirements of the European Convention on Human Rights?", *EHRAC Bulletin*, Issue 22, winter 2014, pp. 7–8; and Christos Mylonopoulos, "Bargain practices and the fundamental values of the ECHR", in Ulrich Sieber, Valsamis Mitsilegas, Christos Mylonopoulos, Emmanouil Billis, Nandor Knust (Eds.), *Alternative Systems of Crime Control – National, Transnational, and International Dimensions*, Max-Planck-Institut/ Duncker & Humblot, Berlin/Freiburg im Breisgau 2018, pp. 89–105, at pp. 92–94.

## 4.2.12. LEGAL REPRESENTATION IN NON-CRIMINAL CASES

Although Article 6 §3 (c) guarantees in criminal matters a right to legal representation and to legal aid, a similar right does not exist for other cases. However, Article 6 §1 guarantees some limited protection in non-criminal cases. This protection materialises rather as a right of access to a court than as a right to a fair trial. In some cases the Court has, however, referred to both rights.[867]

Legal aid in civil proceedings can be organised in several different ways and it can also be restricted. The means include the simplifying of the judicial proceedings and the limitation of the right to legal aid on the basis of the importance and difficulty of the case or the complexity of the law. The granting of legal aid can also be limited depending on the person's ability to defend him- or herself or on the basis of the chances of success of the case.[868] These rights are therefore not violated if the applicant can defend himself in person, if the refusal of the legal aid is not arbitrary but rather takes into account the chances of success of the case, and if the judge supervises the proper course of the proceedings and its fairness.[869]

## 4.2.13. RETROACTIVE LEGISLATION

Retroactive legislation enacted in light of pending compensation proceedings against the State violates both the rule of law as well as the fair trial requirements, unless there are compelling grounds of general interest involved.[870] Compelling grounds of general interest have been recognised as including, *inter alia*, the public interest in clarifying tax laws and securing the levying of taxes,[871] the need to harmonise the level of social security benefits,[872] the need to realise

867 *Airey v. Ireland*, App. no. 6289/73, §26, 9.10.1979. For example, in the case *Webb v. the United Kingdom* (dec.), App. no. 9353/81, 11.5.1983 the Court referred to both and examined thereafter, on the basis of overall assessment, whether the fair trial criteria had been fulfilled.

868 *Airey v. Ireland*, App. no. 6289/73 §26, 9.10.1979; *Steel and Morris v. the United Kingdom*, App. no. 68416/01, §60, 15.2.2005; and *Sinfield and Others v. the United Kingdom* (dec.), App. no. 61332/12, §§41 and 44, 18.2.2014. See also Dragoljub Popović, *European Human Rights Law – A Manual: An Introduction to the Strasbourg Court and its Jurisprudence*, Eleven International Publishing, The Hague 2013, pp. 189–190.

869 *Webb v. the United Kingdom* (dec.), App. no. 9353/81, 11.5.1983.

870 *Zielinski and Pradal and Gonzalez and Others v. France* [GC], App. nos. 24846/94+, §57, 28.10.1999. See also Karen Reid, *A Practitioner's Guide to the European Convention on Human Rights*, Sweet & Maxwell/Thomson Reuters, London 2019, p. 272.

871 *National & Provincial Building Society, Leeds Permanent Building Society and Yorkshire Building Society v. the United Kingdom*, App. nos. 21319/93+, §112, 23.10.1997 (no violation).

872 *OGIS-Institut Stanislas, OGEC Saint-Pie X and Blanche de Castille and Others v. France*, App. nos. 42219/98+, §71, 27.5.2004 (no violation).

regional development or planning,[873] and the promotion of the reunification of Germany.[874]

Although the main essence is the prohibition of retroactive legislation, Article 6 does not prohibit all retroactive interference in civil cases to which the State is a party. However, the stage at which the retroactive legislation enters into force is relevant.[875] In a case against the United Kingdom concerning taxation, the applicant companies knew, when bringing domestic action against the State, that there were lacunae in the legislation and that these lacunae were soon to be filled by new legislation. The retroactive legislation was not directly aimed at the pending cases or the companies in question. The Court found that the applicant companies' intention had been to profit from the loopholes in the legislation and to frustrate the efforts made by the State, which had proceeded to enact new retroactive legislation in order to fill these gaps. There was thus no violation of Article 6 §1.[876]

On the other hand, in the case *Stran Greek Refineries v. Greece*, the intervention in pending proceedings was of a more serious nature. The civil action between the applicant companies and the State had already been pending for nine years, and the proceedings had not yet even reached the stage of hearing of the parties when the retroactive legislation entered into force. The applicant companies had already obtained an enforceable arbitration award against the State. The Court found that the State intervention by the means of retroactive legislation had been calculated to ensure a favourable outcome of proceedings to which it was a party and to defeat the applicant companies' chance of winning their case. There had therefore been a violation of Article 6 §1.[877]

In both cases the Court examined the issue at stake both from the equality of arms angle as well as from the access to a court point of view.[878] In both cases, the State itself was a party to the impugned proceedings, but retroactive legislation may also render the proceedings unfair in other situations.

---

873 *Gorraiz Lizarraga and Others v. Spain*, App. no. 62543/00, §70, 27.4.2004 (no violation). See also Arman Zrvandyan, *Casebook on European Fair Trial Standards in Administrative Justice*, Council of Europe Publishing, Strasbourg 2016, pp. 96–98.

874 *Forrer-Niedenthal v. Germany*, App. no. 47316/99, §64, 20.2.2003 (no violation).

875 *Organisation nationale des syndicats d'infirmiers libéraux (ONSIL) v. France* (dec.), App. no. 39971/98, 29.8.2000 (before the start of proceedings); *Azzopardi and Others v. Malta* (dec.), App. nos. 16467/17+, §44, 12.3.2019 (pending the proceedings); and *Preda and Dardari v. Italy* (dec.), App. nos. 28160/95+, 23.2.1999 (once they have ended).

876 *National & Provincial Building Society, Leeds Permanent Building Society and Yorkshire Building Society v. the United Kingdom*, App. nos. 21319/93+, §§109–110, 23.10.1997. See also and Karen Reid, *A Practitioner's Guide to the European Convention on Human Rights*, Sweet & Maxwell/Thomson Reuters, London 2019, p. 273.

877 *Stran Greek Refineries and Stratis Andreadis v. Greece*, App. no. 13427/87, §§44–50, 9.12.1994. See also Arman Zrvandyan, *Casebook on European Fair Trial Standards in Administrative Justice*, Council of Europe Publishing, Strasbourg 2016, pp. 89–91.

878 See also *Scordino v. Italy (No. 1)* [GC], App. no. 36813/97, §§126–133, 29.3.2006 which concerned compensation paid for expropriation; *Papageorgiou v. Greece*, App. no. 24628/94,

Retroactive legislation was also at stake in the case *Koivusaari and Others v. Finland*, which concerned certain civil claims in respect of a shipwreck and the retroactive amendment of the Antiquities Act (Act no. 295/1963) during the civil proceedings. The Court, however, found that the retroactive amendment of the Antiquities Act had entered into force at an early stage of the civil proceedings and it had not had any bearing on the applicants' position. There were no indications that, because of the amendment, it would have been more difficult for the applicants to win their case.[879]

## 4.2.14. ADEQUATE REASONING

The right to a fair trial requires that the courts give reasons for their judgments and decisions delivered in civil, criminal or administrative law proceedings.[880] The domestic courts have a wide margin of appreciation as to how they formulate their judgments and decisions. However, the domestic judgments and decisions must express, with sufficient clarity, those grounds on which the outcome is based so that the applicant can, on the basis of that information, use his or her right of appeal.[881] In criminal matters this right overlaps with the rights guaranteed in Article 6 §3 (b). Adequate reasoning also gives the applicant the possibility to verify that his arguments have been examined, and, for the wider audience, an opportunity to publicly evaluate the application of the law.[882]

Article 6 §1 of the Convention requires that court decisions and judgments are adequately reasoned, but it cannot be interpreted as requiring that detailed replies are given to all the applicant's arguments.[883] The obligation to reason decisions and judgments may vary according to the nature of the decision or judgment at stake,[884] but in all cases it must be clear from the decision that the

22.10.1997; *Anagnostopoulos and Others v. Greece*, App. no. 39374/98, §§20–21, 7.11.2000; and *Azienda Agricola Silverfunghi S.a.s. and Others v. Italy*, App. nos. 48357/07+, §§76 and 88–89, 24.6.2014.

879 *Koivusaari and Others v. Finland* (dec.), App. no. 20690/06, 23.2.2010.

880 *H. v. Belgium*, App. no. 8950/80, §53, 30.11.1987; *Magnin v. France* (dec.), App. no. 26219/08, §29, 10.5.2012; *Moreira Ferreira v. Portugal (No. 2)* [GC], App. no. 19867/12, §84, 11.7.2017; and *Papon v. France* (dec.), App. no. 344/04, 11.10.2005.

881 *Hadjianastassiou v. Greece*, App. no. 12945/87, §33, 16.12.1992; and *Hirvisaari v. Finland*, App. no. 49684/99, §30, 27.9.2001.

882 *Tatishvili v. Russia*, App. no. 1509/02, §58, 22.2.2007. See also Arman Zrvandyan, *Casebook on European Fair Trial Standards in Administrative Justice*, Council of Europe Publishing, Strasbourg 2016, pp. 117–118.

883 *Van de Hurk v. the Netherlands*, App. no. 16034/90, §61, 19.4.1994; *Fomin v. Moldova*, App. no. 36755/06, §24, 11.10.2011; *García Ruiz v. Spain* [GC], App. no. 30544/96, §26, 21.1.1999; *Jahnke and Lenoble v. France* (dec.), App. no. 40490/98, 29.8.2000; and *Perez v. France* [GC], App. no. 47287/99, §81, 12.2.2004.

884 *Ruiz Torija v. Spain*, App. no. 18390/91, §29, 9.12.1994; *Karakasis v. Greece*, App. no. 38194/97, §27, 17.10.2000; and *Hiro Balani v. Spain*, App. no. 18064/91, §28, 9.12.1994.

essential issues of the case have been addressed and that a specific and explicit reply has been given to the arguments which are decisive for the outcome of the case.[885] In jury proceedings in which the jury does not give reasons for its decision on guilt, the questions put by the judge to the jury must be such that they enable the applicant to understand the grounds of this decision.[886] Although domestic courts have a certain margin of appreciation in choosing the arguments and the supporting evidence, they must in any event justify their conclusions by reasoning them adequately.[887] Normally the court must take a stance on the applicant's main arguments.[888] Nor is it compatible with Article 6 §1 that reasoning is used in a judgment or decision which is not accepted by law.[889]

If a particular allegation has a significant relevance to the outcome of the case, the Court may require that a domestic court specifically addresses this issue. Sometimes it may suffice that an allegation is indirectly rejected if the context is clear.[890] If, for example, negligence is relevant to the case, the obligation to give adequate reasons may not be fulfilled if it is only stated in the judgment that a party has acted negligently without explaining why the court found this to be so in the particular case.[891]

In the case *Ajdarić v. Croatia*, the decision to sentence the applicant to 42 years in prison was not sufficiently reasoned, because the domestic court had either not sufficiently addressed or not addressed at all the obvious discrepancies in the witness statements or the credibility of the main witness, who had suffered from psychiatric problems.[892]

---

885 *Boldea v. Romania*, App. no. 19997/02, §30, 15.2.2007; *Lobzhanidze and Peradze v. Georgia*, App. nos. 21447/11+, §66, 27.2.2020; *Moreira Ferreira v. Portugal (No. 2)* [GC], App. no. 19867/12, §84, 11.7.2017; and *S.C. IMH Suceava S.R.L. v. Romania*, App. no. 24935/04, §40, 29.10.2013 which concerned contradictions in the assessment of evidence. See also *Nechiporuk and Yonkalo v. Ukraine*, App. no. 42310/04, §280, 21.4.2011 (violation); *Rostomashvili v. Georgia*, App. no. 13185/07, §59, 8.11.2018 (violation); and *Zhang v. Ukraine*, App. no. 6970/15, §73, 13.11.2018 (violation).

886 *Taxquet v. Belgium* [GC], App. no. 926/05, §§97–98, 16.11.2010 (violation); *Saric v. Denmark* (dec.), App. no. 31913/96, 2.2.1999; *Legillon v. France*, App. no. 53406/10, §53, 10.1.2013; *Lhermitte v. Belgium* [GC], App. no. 34238/09, §68, 29.11.2016; *R. v. Belgium*, App. no. 15957/90, Commission decision, 30.3.1992; *Zarouali v. Belgium*, App. no. 20664/92, Commission decision, 29.6.1994; *Planka v. Austria*, App. no. 25852/94, Commission decision, 15.5.1996; *Goktepe v. Belgium*, App. no. 50372/99, §28, 2.6.2005; and *Papon v. France* (dec.), App. no. 344/04, 11.10.2005.

887 *Suominen v. Finland*, App. no. 37801/97, §36, 1.7.2003.

888 *Buzescu v. Romania*, App. no. 61302/00, §67, 24.5.2005; and *Pronina v. Ukraine*, App. no. 63566/00, §25, 18.7.2006.

889 *De Moor v. Belgium*, App. no. 16997/90, §55, 23.6.1994.

890 *Ruiz Torija v. Spain*, App. no. 18390/91, §30, 9.12.1994; *Hiro Balani v. Spain*, App. no. 18064/91, §28, 9.12.1994; and *Elo v. Finland* (dec.), App. no. 30742/02, 20.1.2004. See also Karen Reid, *A Practitioner's Guide to the European Convention on Human Rights*, Sweet & Maxwell/Thomson Reuters, London 2019, p. 323.

891 *Georgiadis v. Greece*, App. no. 21522/93, §43, 29.5.1997.

892 *Ajdarić v. Croatia*, App. no. 20883/09, §51, 13.12.2011 (violation).

It is also relevant that the reasons for the judgment are given by the same judge who presided over the oral hearing and who received the evidence. In the case *Cerovšek and Božičnik v. Slovenia*, the presiding judge retired after pronouncing the judgment but without having drafted the written judgment. Subsequently, other judges, who had not participated in the hearing, confirmed the judgment without organising a new oral hearing. The Court held that there was a violation of Article 6 and recommended that the best way of providing *restitutio in integrum* to the applicant was to reopen the case.[893]

In jury trials the jury itself does not reason its decisions on guilt, but the legal safeguards are provided through the questions posed by the judge to the jury that should sufficiently clarify the legally acceptable grounds for guilt or innocence. On the other hand, the accused should have the opportunity to appeal against the judgment. In the Grand Chamber case *Taxquet v. Belgium*, the Court emphasised that the indictment, together with the questions put by the judge to the jury and the issues discussed during the oral hearing, could have formed sufficient reasoning for the judgment. However, where there are several defendants, the questions posed to the jury must clearly concern each of the defendants separately and their specific guilt and implication in the crime. In the *Taxquet* case, which concerned several defendants, the questions had not been defendant-specific enough and therefore the reasoning was considered to be insufficient.[894]

In another Grand Chamber case, *Lhermitte v. Belgium*, the Court found the reasoning of the trial court sufficient. The case concerned a situation in which the accused was held by the jury – but against expert opinion – criminally responsible for the murder of her five children, and she was sentenced to a life sentence. The Court considered that the question of the applicant's criminal responsibility had been at the centre of the criminal investigation and the trial, and that this issue had therefore been thoroughly examined by the court in the presence of the applicant and her counsel. The relevant reasons for the conviction were also spelled out in the judgment. The expert witnesses had also stated in their statements that their opinion was not equivalent to scientific truth. Although the jury did not give any detailed reasons for why it held the applicant criminally responsible, this had not prevented the applicant from receiving sufficient reasoning for the jury's decision.[895]

---

893 *Cerovšek and Božičnik v. Slovenia*, App. nos. 68939/12+, §§40–45, 7.3.2017. See also Stefan Kieber, "The jurisprudence of the European Court of Human Rights in 2017", *European Yearbook on Human Rights 2018*, pp. 229–265, at p. 241.

894 *Taxquet v. Belgium* [GC], App. no. 926/05, §§96–98, 16.11.2010 (violation). See also Francis G. Jacobs, Robin C.A. White, Clare Owey, *The European Convention on Human Rights*, Oxford University Press, Oxford 2017, pp. 294–295; and Anand Doobay, "The right to a fair trial in light of the recent ECtHR and CJEU case-law", *ERA forum*, vol. 14, issue 2, September 2013, pp. 251–262, at pp. 256–257.

895 *Lhermitte v. Belgium* [GC], App. no. 34238/09, §§76–84, 29.11.2016. See also Sofia Galani (Ed.), "Case and comment: selected decisions from the European Court of Human

Similarly, in the case *Ramda v. France*, the principles created in the *Taxquet* case were applied. In that case a lay jury was replaced by a jury made up of professional judges in order to protect the lay judges from any revenge on the part of the applicant, who had been convicted of terrorism. The jury of professional judges did not give any detailed grounds for its decision to convict the applicant of terrorism and to sentence him to life. Nevertheless, the Court found that the several detailed questions put to the applicant during the trial and the answers received had provided sufficient reasons upon which to base his conviction. There was thus no violation of Article 6.[896]

Generally speaking, the Court has stated that a lower court must give such reasons as to enable the parties to make effective use of any existing right of appeal.[897] The obligation to give adequate reasoning concerns both the first instance courts as well as the appellate courts, but normally the latter are not obliged to give as thorough reasoning as the former. The Court has found in its case-law that it is sufficient that a higher instance court refers in its reasoning to the reasoning of the lower court or tribunal.[898] In such cases it is important that the higher court shows, in one way or another, that it has examined the matter and that it has reached the same conclusion as the lower court. It is also required that the lower-court's judgment or decision is attached to the higher court's decision or judgment.[899] In other situations Article 6 §1 also allows for clearly manifestly ill-founded actions or appeals to be rejected in a summary procedure with a short reasoning.[900]

When the matter concerns a refusal of leave to appeal, the courts have no obligation to give detailed reasons or, in some cases, are able to give no reasons

---

Rights from November and December 2016 – Lack of reasons in jury trials, *Lhermitte v. Belgium* (Application No. 34238/09)", *European Human Rights Law Review*, Issue 2, 2017, pp. 210–211.

896 *Ramda v. France*, App. no. 78477/11, §§59–71, 19.12.2017. See also Sofia Galani (Ed.), "Case and comment: selected decisions from the European Court of Human Rights from November and December 2017 – Fair trials and the principle of *ne bis in idem* in criminal proceedings, *Ramda v. France* (Application No. 78477/11)", *European Human Rights Law Review*, Issue 2, 2018, pp. 185–187.

897 *Hadjianastassiou v. Greece*, App. no. 12945/87, §33, 16.12.1992; *Sanchez Cardenas v. Norway*, App. no. 12148/03, §49, 4.10.2007; and *Hirvisaari v. Finland*, App. no. 49684/99, §31, 27.9.2001.

898 *García Ruiz v. Spain* [GC], App. no. 30544/96, §26, 21.1.1999; *Stepanyan v. Armenia*, App. no. 45081/04, §35, 27.10.2009; *Hirvisaari v. Finland*, App. no. 49684/99, §30, 27.9.2001; and *Elo v. Finland* (dec.), App. no. 30742/02, 20.1.2004.

899 *Helle v. Finland*, App. no. 20772/92, §60, 19.12.1997 (no violation); and *Lindner and Hammermayer v. Romania*, App. no. 35671/97, §§32–33, 3.12.2002.

900 *X. v. the Federal Republic of Germany*, App. no. 8769/79, 16.7.1981. See also *Baydar v. the Netherlands*, App. no. 55385/14, §§45–53, 24.4.2018; *Talmane v. Latvia*, App. no. 47938/07, §29, 13.10.2016; and *Dhahbi v. Italy*, App. no. 17120/09, §31, 8.4.2014 concerning the reasoning of decisions by the domestic superior courts refusing to refer a question to the Court of Justice of the European Union (CJEU) for a preliminary ruling.

at all.[901] However, in situations in which the second instance court is tasked with the role of filtering unmeritorious appeals and its competence covers both matters of fact and law in civil cases, the Court has expected that the domestic court will not only repeat the provision applied but also provide some more concrete reasons for refusing an appeal. In the case *Hansen v. Norway*, the appellate court only stated that the appeal did not have any chance of success. Such reasoning did not give the applicant the opportunity to effectively estimate his chances of appealing his case further to the Supreme Court.[902]

In the Court's case-law, the Court has sometimes found a violation as a result of a lack of adequate reasoning. For example in the case *Hirvisaari v. Finland*, which concerned the lowering of the amount of State disability pension, the Court did not consider the short reasoning to be incompatible with Article 6 §1 as such, but held that it did not appear with sufficient clarity from the decision why the amount of the pension was lowered.[903] There was a similar situation in the case *H.A.L. v. Finland*, which concerned the granting of certain daily sickness allowances.[904] The case *Suominen v. Finland* concerned civil proceedings in which the court had given no reasons in its judgment for why it had not accepted certain evidence. According to the Court, this fact made it difficult for the applicant to appeal against that judgment.[905]

### 4.2.15. REQUESTS FOR A PRELIMINARY RULING

The Convention does not guarantee as such applicants a right to have the domestic courts request a preliminary ruling from the Court of Justice of the European Union (CJEU)[906] but in some exceptional circumstances an arbitrary refusal to do so may lead to a finding of a violation under Article 6 of the Convention.[907]

---

901 *Sawoniuk v. the United Kingdom* (dec.), App. no. 63716/00, 29.5.2001; *Nerva v. the United Kingdom* (dec.), App. no. 42295/98, 11.7.2000; *Webb v. the United Kingdom* (dec.), App. no. 33186/96, 2.7.1997; *Burg and Others v. France* (dec.), App. no. 34763/02, 28.1.2003; *Gorou v. Greece (No. 2)* [GC], App. no. 12686/03, §41, 20.3.2009; *Kukkonen v. Finland (No. 2)*, App. no. 47628/06, §24, 13.1.2009; and *Bufferne v. France* (dec.), App. no. 54367/00, 26.2.2002.

902 *Hansen v. Norway*, App. no. 15319/09, §§82–83, 2.10.2014. See also James Welch (Ed.), "Case and comment: selected decisions from the European Court of Human Rights from September and October 2014 – Appeals, *Hansen v. Norway* (Application No. 15319/09)", *European Human Rights Law Review*, Issue 1, 2015, pp. 98–101.

903 *Hirvisaari v. Finland*, App. no. 49684/99, §31, 27.9.2001. See also Arman Zrvandyan, *Casebook on European Fair Trial Standards in Administrative Justice*, Council of Europe Publishing, Strasbourg 2016, pp. 116–117.

904 *H.A.L. v. Finland*, App. no. 38267/97, §50, 27.1.2004.

905 *Suominen v. Finland*, App. no. 37801/97, §38, 1.7.2003.

906 *Coëme and Others v. Belgium*, App. nos. 32492/96+, §114, 22.6.2000; *Dotta v. Italy* (dec.), App. no. 38399/97, 7.9.1999; and *Herma v. Germany* (dec.), App. no. 54193/07, 8.12.2009.

907 *Ullens de Schooten and Rezabek v. Belgium*, App. nos. 3989/07+, §§57–67, 20.9.2011; and *Canela Santiago v. Spain* (dec.), App. no. 60350/00, 4.10.2001.

In many cases the Court has found a violation because of the failure by the domestic courts to sufficiently reason their decisions for not requesting a preliminary ruling.[908] A violation was found, for example, in the case *Dhahbi v. Italy*, since the Court of Cassation did not take any stance on the applicant's request to refer the matter to the CJEU for a preliminary ruling. There was no indication in the court's reasoning as to why the request was rejected, nor was there any reference to the CJEU's case-law to explore whether the request was unnecessary.[909] The lack of reasons for rejecting a request for a preliminary ruling was also at stake in the case *Schipani and Others v. Italy*.[910]

In the case *Baydar v. the Netherlands* the Court, however, relaxed the quite strict duty to give reasons adopted in the above-mentioned cases and accepted that summary reasoning sufficed when the case was examined and decided in summary proceedings, such as refusing leave to appeal. The Court held that domestic courts could dismiss a complaint by mere reference to the relevant legal provisions governing such complaints if the matter raised no fundamentally important legal issue and had no prospect of success. The CJEU had ruled that the domestic courts were not obliged to refer a question about the interpretation of EU law raised before them if the question was not relevant, that is, if the answer to that question, whatever it might be, could not have any effect on the outcome of the particular case. In such situations the summary reasoning contained in such a judgment implied an acknowledgment that a referral to the CJEU could not lead to a different outcome in the case. Where it was clear from the circumstances of the case that the decision was not arbitrary or otherwise manifestly unreasonable, no issue of principle arose under Article 6 §1 of the Convention.[911]

In the case *Somorjai v. Hungary* the Court held that the decision to reject the applicant's request for a preliminary ruling had not been arbitrary, since the domestic court had held that the applicant had not lodged the request in the appropriate phase of the proceedings and no arguments had been offered to show that the Hungarian legislation was incompatible with EU law.[912] Similarly in *Harisch v. Germany*, the Court found no violation even though the domestic court had not made any request for a preliminary ruling, since, in its view, the case was not unclear in the light of EU law. The Court reiterated that the Convention

908 *Somorjai v. Hungary*, App. no. 60934/13, §60, 28.8.2018; and *John v. Germany* (dec.), App. no. 15073/03, 13.2.2007.

909 *Dhahbi v. Italy*, App. no. 17120/09, §§32–34, 8.4.2014. See also Morten Broberg, "National courts of last instance failing to make a preliminary reference: the (possible) consequences flowing therefrom", *European Public Law*, vol. 22, issue 2, June 2016, pp. 243–256.

910 *Schipani and Others v. Italy*, App. no. 38369/09, §§69–73, 21.7.2015.

911 *Baydar v. the Netherlands*, App. no. 55385/14, §§39–52, 24.4.2018. See also *Stichting Mothers of Srebrenica and Others v. the Netherlands* (dec.), App. no. 65542/12, §§173–174, 11.6.2013; and *Astikos Kai Paratheristikos Oikodomikos Synetairismos Axiomatikon and Karagiorgos v. Greece* (dec.), App. nos. 29382/16+, §§46–47, 9.5.2017.

912 *Somorjai v. Hungary*, App. no. 60934/13, §60, 28.8.2018.

did not guarantee a right per se to obtain a request for a preliminary ruling from the CJEU, but rather an arbitrary refusal to do so could constitute a violation of Article 6. In that case there was no arbitrary refusal at stake, since the domestic court had found in adversarial proceedings that the case was clear and this had been clarified for the applicant. On the basis of the comprehensive arguments put forward by the Court of Appeal, the Supreme Court had been able to dismiss both the appeal and the request for a preliminary ruling by refusing him leave to appeal, without any need to further justify the refusal of his request.[913] However, in *Sanofi Pasteur v. France*, the Court concluded by contrast that the appeal court could not, without substantiating and referring to any of the criteria enumerated in the CJEU's *CILFIT* case, reject the request for a preliminary ruling.[914]

## 4.2.16. PRINCIPLE OF LEGAL CERTAINTY

The principle of legal certainty is one of the characteristics of a fair trial,[915] and one of the elements of the rule of law.[916] Legal certainty guarantees a certain stability as well as foreseeability of the authorities' and the courts' actions and conclusions, and it is therefore likely to contribute to the public's confidence in the legal system and the judiciary.[917] Legal certainty can manifest itself either as the finality and stability of a judgment which has acquired legal force, protecting thus against duplication of criminal proceedings,[918] or, on the other hand, as an issue of the coherency of the case-law.

### *4.2.16.1. Supervisory Review Proceedings*

Fair trial requirements require that final judgments are, according to the principle of legal certainty, not called into question. However, in many of the ex-Soviet bloc countries, what are known as supervisory review proceedings are

913 *Harisch v. Germany*, App. no. 50053/16, §§33–43, 11.4.2019. See also Ricardo Buendia, "Reasoned judgments – *Harisch v. Germany* (Application No. 50053/16)", *European Human Rights Law Review*, Issue 4, 2019, pp. 437–439.

914 *Sanofi Pasteur v. France*, App. no. 25137/16, §§68–81, 13.2.2020; and *S.r.l. CILFIT and Lanificio di Gavardo S.p.A. v. Ministry of Health*, ECLI:EU:C:1982:335. See also Mollie Cornell, "Reasons for preliminary references – *Sanofi Pasteur v. France* (Application No. 25137/16)", *European Human Rights Law Review*, Issue 3, 2020, pp. 308–311.

915 *Beian v. Romania (No. 1)*, App. no. 30658/05, §39, 6.12.2007; and *Iordan Iordanov and Others v. Bulgaria*, App. no. 23530/02, §47, 2.6.2009.

916 *Brumărescu v. Romania* [GC], App. no. 28342/95, §61, 28.10.1999; *Nejdet Şahin and Perihan Şahin v. Turkey* [GC], App. no. 13279/05, §§49–58 and 61, 20.10.2011; and *Lupeni Greek Catholic Parish and Others v. Romania* [GC], App. no. 76943/11, §116, 29.11.2016.

917 *Păduraru v. Romania*, App. no. 63252/00, §98, 1.12.2005; and *Vinčić and Others v. Serbia*, App. no. 44698/06, §56, 1.12.2009.

918 *Bratyakin v. Russia* (dec.), App. no. 72776/01, 9.3.2006.

very common. It is very typical that in these legal systems the prosecutors,[919] or others in leading positions who were not party to the initial proceedings, including judges,[920] may request annulment of a final judgment from the highest courts without any time limit, on the grounds that a court has exceeded its competences. For example, in the case *Brumărescu v. Romania*, a prosecutor had initiated new proceedings which completely frustrated the final judgment rendered in the initial proceedings and which had already been executed. The Court found that the new procedure violated the principle of legal certainty and was thus contrary to the fair trial requirements.[921] This principle also applies to the executive, in addition to the judiciary.[922]

The principle of legal certainty does not, however, create an obstacle to the development of jurisprudence.[923] On the other hand, if the case-law is not dynamic and evolutive, it can prevent reforms and other necessary improvements.[924]

Annulment of a final judgment does not, however, always lead to a violation. In many European legal systems final judgments can in certain exceptional circumstances be revoked and annulled on certain conditions. In those situations, it is normally expected that an interference with legal certainty is necessary because of circumstances of a substantial and compelling character, which normally means the correction of judicial mistakes and miscarriages of justice. Moreover, criminal cases must be assessed in the light of Article 4 §2 of Protocol No. 7 to the Convention, which expressly permits a State to reopen a case due to the emergence of new facts, or where a fundamental defect is detected in the previous proceedings, which could affect the outcome of the case. Nevertheless, compliance with Article 4 of Protocol No. 7 is not in itself sufficient to establish compliance with the requirements of a fair trial under Article 6.[925] An extraordinary review cannot be treated as an appeal in disguise, since the mere possibility of two differing views on the subject is not a ground for re-examination.[926]

---

919 *Roşca v. Moldova*, App. no. 6267/02, §26, 22.3.2005.

920 *Tregubenko v. Ukraine*, App. no. 61333/00, §36, 2.11.2004, which concerned a vice-president of the Supreme Court; *Driza v. Albania*, App. no. 33771/02, §66, 13.11.2007, which concerned the president of the Supreme Court; and *Ryabykh v. Russia*, App. no. 52854/99, §54, 24.7.2003, which concerned a president of a regional court.

921 *Brumărescu v. Romania* [GC], App. no. 28342/95, §62, 28.10.1999. See also Jean-Paul Costa, "The European Court of Human Rights and its recent case law", *Texas International Law Journal*, vol. 38, no. 3, 2003, pp. 455–467, at p. 463.

922 *Tregubenko v. Ukraine*, App. no. 61333/00, §36, 2.11.2004.

923 *Unédic v. France*, App. no. 20153/04, §74, 18.12.2008; and *Lupeni Greek Catholic Parish and Others v. Romania* [GC], App. no. 76943/11, §116, 29.11.2016.

924 *Nejdet Şahin and Perihan Şahin v. Turkey* [GC], App. no. 13279/05, §58, 20.10.2011; *Albu and Others v. Romania*, App. nos. 34796/09+, §34, 10.5.2012; and *Atanasovski v. "the former Yugoslav Republic of Macedonia"*, App. no. 36815/03, §38, 14.1.2010.

925 *Nikitin v. Russia*, App. no. 50178/99, §56, 20.7.2004 (no violation).

926 *Pravednaya v. Russia*, App. no. 69529/01, §25, 18.11.2004; *Nikitin v. Russia*, App. no. 50178/99, §59, 20.7.2004 (no violation); *Bratyakin v. Russia* (dec.), App. no. 72776/01, 9.3.2006;

Although the *Brumărescu* case was examined by the Court as a matter of fair trial, similar situations can also be examined as a question of the right of access to a court. In its later cases, the Court has examined supervisory proceedings under fair trial requirements[927] or under access to a court,[928] or under both.[929]

### *4.2.16.2. Coherency of Case-Law*

The principle of legal certainty is also at stake in situations where either the rulings of the highest court[930] or the case-law of the domestic courts[931] in general is not coherent. If the case-law is not coherent, it should be harmonised with a coherent interpretation.[932] In the cases of conflicting domestic case-law, the Court clarifies: whether there are profound and persistent divergences in the case-law; whether the domestic legislation contains mechanisms allowing the elimination of these incoherencies; whether these mechanisms have been applied; and, if so, what kind of effects they have produced.[933]

In its case-law, the Court has emphasised the States' obligation to ensure that there are mechanisms guaranteeing the coherency of the domestic case-law and has stressed their obligation to organise their judiciaries in such a way that they do so.[934] The Court found a violation, for example, in the case *Sine Tsaggarakis A.E.E. v. Greece*, in which the various sections of a lower court had adopted divergent judgments on the same legal issue concerning building permits. Following a Supreme Court ruling, one section of the court had still continued its practice, although it differed from that of the Supreme Court.[935]

---

*Ryabykh v. Russia*, App. no. 52854/99, §52, 24.7.2003; *Roşca v. Moldova*, App. no. 6267/02, §§24–25, 22.3.2005; *Sutyazhnik v. Russia*, App. no. 8269/02, §35, 23.7.2009; and *Vardanyan and Nanushyan v. Armenia*, App. no. 8001/07, §70, 27.10.2016.

927 *Roşca v. Moldova*, App. no. 6267/02, §26, 22.3.2005.

928 *Tregubenko v. Ukraine*, App. no. 61333/00, §36, 2.11.2004; and *Poltorachenko v. Ukraine*, App. no. 77317/01, §34, 18.1.2005.

929 *Ryabykh v. Russia*, App. no. 52854/99, §54, 24.7.2003; and *Pravednaya v. Russia*, App. no. 69529/01, §25, 18.11.2004.

930 *Pérez Arias v. Spain*, App. no. 32978/03, §25, 28.6.2007; *Ştefan and Ştef v. Romania*, App. nos. 24428/03+, §§33–36, 27.1.2009; *Iordan Iordanov and Others v. Bulgaria*, App. no. 23530/02, §§48–49, 2.6.2009; and *Schwarzkopf and Taussik v. the Czech Republic* (dec.), App. no. 42162/02, 2.12.2008.

931 *Tudor Tudor v. Romania*, App. no. 21911/03, 24.3.2009; and *Ştefănică and Others v. Romania*, App. no. 38155/02, 2.11.2010.

932 *Beian v. Romania (No. 1)*, App. no. 30658/05, §§37–39, 6.12.2007; and *Nejdet Şahin and Perihan Şahin v. Turkey* [GC], App. no. 13279/05, §80, 20.10.2011.

933 *Iordan Iordanov and Others v. Bulgaria*, App. no. 23530/02, §§49–50, 2.6.2009; *Nejdet Şahin and Perihan Şahin v. Turkey* [GC], App. no. 13279/05, §53, 20.10.2011; and *Borg v. Malta*, App. no. 37537/13, §108, 12.1.2016.

934 *Schwarzkopf and Taussik v. the Czech Republic* (dec.), App. no. 42162/02, 2.12.2008; *Vrioni and Others v. Albania*, App. no. 2141/03, §58, 24.3.2009; *Mullai and Others v. Albania*, App. no. 9074/07, §86, 23.3.2010; and *Brezovec v. Croatia*, App. no. 13488/07, §66, 29.3.2011.

935 *Sine Tsaggarakis A.E.E. v. Greece*, App. no. 17257/13, §§48–60, 23.5.2019 (violation).

However, evolution of jurisprudence is not contrary to the principle of legal certainty.[936] Stagnation of jurisprudence in the name of legal certainty could pose an obstacle to dynamic and evolutive development of law and prevent necessary reforms.[937] Nor is it contrary to the principle of legal certainty if different competent apex courts come, within their areas of competence and on reasonable grounds, to different conclusions on the same legal issues and concerning the interpretation of the same law.[938] There is a problem from the point of view of legal certainty if the case-law within one domestic court of last instance is inconsistent and this is reflected downwards to the lower courts and causes inconsistency of case-law. The explicit task of the highest court is to resolve these kinds of case-law conflicts.[939]

An issue of legal certainty may also arise in case of a legislative intervention in the pending criminal proceedings.[940] In this respect, see also section 4.2.13. above.

## 4.2.17. PREJUDICIAL PUBLICITY

The fairness of a trial can be adversely affected if a virulent press campaign influencing the public opinion has been taking place and, subsequently, the jurors are called upon to decide the guilt of an accused.[941] Such a virulent press campaign may have an impact both on the impartiality of the court under Article 6 §1 as well as the presumption of innocence enshrined in Article 6 §2.[942] If there is a hostile press campaign surrounding a trial, what is decisive is not the subjective apprehensions of the suspect concerning the absence of prejudice

936 *Borg v. Malta*, App. no. 37537/13, §107, 12.1.2016.

937 *Atanasovski v. "the former Yugoslav Republic of Macedonia"*, App. no. 36815/03, §38, 14.1.2010.

938 *Nejdet Şahin and Perihan Şahin v. Turkey* [GC], App. no. 13279/05, §§85–87, 20.10.2011. Giving two disputes different treatment cannot be considered to give rise to conflicting case-law when this is justified by a difference in the factual situations at issue, see *Hayati Çelebi and Others v. Turkey*, App. no. 582/05, §52, 24.1.2017; *Santos Pinto v. Portugal*, App. no. 39005/04, §41, 20.5.2008; and *Ferreira Santos Pardal v. Portugal*, App. no. 30123/10, §42, 30.7.2015.

939 *Lupeni Greek Catholic Parish and Others v. Romania* [GC], App. no. 76943/11, §§123 and 134, 29.11.2016; and *Nejdet Şahin and Perihan Şahin v. Turkey* [GC], App. no. 13279/05, §58, 20.10.2011.

940 See, for example, *Chim and Przywieczerski v. Poland*, App. nos. 36661/07+, §§199–207, 12.4.2018 in which the Court relied on its case-law under Article 7 of the Convention and found no violation of Article 6 §1 with respect to legislative amendments extending the duration of the limitation periods to the case against the applicant. See also Jeremy McBride, "Some recent practice of the European Court of Human Rights to consider when implementing criminal procedure codes", *Synergy Magazine*, no. 64, issue 2, 2018, pp. 8–10, at p. 10.

941 *Akay v. Turkey* (dec.), App. no. 34501/97, 19.2.2002; *Craxi v. Italy (No. 1)*, App. no. 34896/97, §98, 5.12.2002; and *Beggs v. the United Kingdom* (dec.), App. no. 15499/10, §123, 16.10.2012.

942 *Ninn-Hansen v. Denmark* (dec.), App. no. 28972/95, 18.5.1999; and *Anguelov v. Bulgaria* (dec.), App. no. 45963/99, 14.12.2004. See also section 4.5.3.7. of this chapter and Chapter 5, section 5.4. below.

required of the trial courts but whether, in the particular circumstances of the case, his or her fears can be held to be objectively justified.[943]

When assessing the impact of such a campaign on the fairness of the trial, the Court has identified the following factors as relevant in its case-law: the time elapsed between the press campaign and the commencement of the trial, and in particular the determination of the trial court's composition; whether the impugned publications were attributable to, or informed by, the authorities; and whether the publications in fact influenced the judges or the jury and thus prejudiced the outcome of the proceedings.[944] Moreover, if the trial is by jury, the content of any directions given to the jury is also a relevant consideration.[945] National courts which are entirely composed of professional judges generally possess, unlike members of a jury, appropriate experience and training enabling them to resist any outside influence.[946]

## 4.3. RIGHT TO A PUBLIC HEARING AND PUBLIC ANNOUNCEMENT OF JUDGMENT

**Article 6: Right to a fair trial**

1. *... everyone is entitled to a ... public hearing ... Judgment shall be pronounced publicly but the press and public may be excluded from all or part of the trial in the interests of morals, public order or national security in a democratic society, where the interests of juveniles or the protection of the private life of the parties so require, or to the extent strictly necessary in the opinion of the court in special circumstances where publicity would prejudice the interests of justice.*

The principle of the public nature of court proceedings entails two aspects, namely the holding of public hearings and the public delivery of judgments.[947]

### 4.3.1. PUBLIC HEARING

Article 6 §1 of the Convention guarantees everyone a right to a public hearing. This right has two dimensions. First, it guarantees that a trial is public, and,

---

943 *Włoch v. Poland* (dec.), App. no. 27785/95, 30.3.2000; *Daktaras v. Lithuania* (dec.), App. no. 42095/98, 11.1.2000; *Priebke v. Italy* (dec.), App. no. 48799/99, 5.4.2001; *Butkevičius v. Lithuania* (dec.), App. no. 48297/99, 28.11.2000; *G.C.P. v. Romania*, App. no. 20899/03, §46, 20.12.2011; and *Mustafa (Abu Hamza) v. the United Kingdom* (dec.), App. no. 31411/07, §§37–40, 18.1.2011.

944 *Beggs v. the United Kingdom* (dec.), App. no. 15499/10, §124, 16.10.2012; *Abdulla Ali v. the United Kingdom*, App. no. 30971/12, §§87–91, 30.6.2015; and *Paulikas v. Lithuania*, App. no. 57435/09, §59, 24.1.2017.

945 *Beggs v. the United Kingdom* (dec.), App. no. 15499/10, §124, 16.10.2012.

946 *Craxi v. Italy (No. 1)*, App. no. 34896/97, §104, 5.12.2002; and *Mircea v. Romania*, App. no. 41250/02, §75, 29.3.2007.

947 *Sutter v. Switzerland*, App. no. 8209/78, §27, 22.2.1984; and *Tierce v. San Marino*, App. no. 69700/01, §93, 17.6.2003.

second, that it is not only a written procedure but that there is also an oral hearing. The aim of the publicity is to prevent secret trials and to promote, through transparency, fair trials and confidence in the judiciary.[948] Therefore the participation of the media and press is of the utmost importance.[949] The right to a public hearing concerns civil, criminal and administrative law hearings. It also applies to obligatory arbitration[950] but not to voluntary arbitration in which the parties have themselves decided to seek recourse via an out-of-court procedure.[951]

Arbitration was at stake in the case *Mutu and Pechstein v. Switzerland*, which concerned the examination of a dispute between a professional speed skater and her association in the Court of Arbitration for Sport (CAS). The central issue was whether she had, by taking her dispute to arbitration, voluntarily waived at least some of the fair trial guarantees under Article 6. The Court held that the applicant had had no other option than to accept the jurisdiction of the arbitration court and she could not therefore be regarded as having voluntarily waived her Article 6 rights. Nevertheless, her complaint that the arbitration court was not impartial because sportspeople's interests were not as well represented in that court as those of the sports federations was unsuccessful for lack of evidence. Instead, the lack of an oral hearing led to an Article 6 violation.[952]

#### *4.3.1.1. Public Hearing Requirement*

Trials must be open to the public, both according to the law and in practice. The publicity requirement in Article 6 §1 is fulfilled only if the public is aware of the date and place of the hearing and they have easy access to this place. The latter requirement is often fulfilled when the hearing is held in a normal courtroom

---

948 *Malhous v. the Czech Republic* [GC], App. no. 33071/96, §55, 12.7.2001. In the case *Barberà, Messegué and Jabardo v. Spain*, App. nos. 10590/83+, §89, 6.12.1988, the Court found a violation of Article 6 §1, *inter alia*, on the ground that very important pieces of evidence were not adequately adduced and discussed at the trial in the applicants' presence and under the watchful eye of the public. See also *Diennet v. France*, App. no. 18160/91, §33, 26.9.1995; *Martinie v. France* [GC], App. no. 58675/00, §39, 12.4.2006; *Gautrin and Others v. France*, App. nos. 21257/93+, §42, 20.5.1998; *Hurter v. Switzerland*, App. no. 53146/99, §26, 15.12.2005; and *Lorenzetti v. Italy*, App. no. 32075/09, §30, 10.4.2012.

949 *Axen v. the Federal Republic of Germany*, App. no. 8273/78, Report of the Commission, §77, 14.12.1981.

950 *Bramelid and Malmström v. Sweden*, App. nos. 8588/79+, Report of the Commission, §30, 12.12.1983; and *Scarth v. the United Kingdom*, App. no. 33745/96, Report of the Commission, §34, 21.10.1998.

951 *Bramelid and Malmström v. Sweden*, App. nos. 8588/79+, Report of the Commission, §30, 12.12.1983.

952 *Mutu and Pechstein v. Switzerland*, App. nos. 40575/10+, §§94, 98, 113–115, 121–123, 156–157 and 175–188, 2.10.2018. See also Daniel Rietiker, "The European Court of Human Rights and FIFA – Current Issues and Potential Challenges", *European Convention on Human Rights Law Review*, vol. 1, no. 1, 2020, pp. 62–104, at pp. 82–83.

where seats have been reserved for spectators.[953] In the case *Riepan v. Austria*, the Court found that a hearing was not public when it was held in a prison, even though the public had been informed about its date and location. The problem was that the participation of the public had not been made easy because of a failure to provide adequate directions to the prison, and because the hearing was held in a small room early in the morning.[954]

The right to a public hearing has been particularly problematic when it concerns administrative and disciplinary courts, or other courts which are not general courts. The lack of publicity about such courts may, however, be corrected if there is a possibility to appeal against decisions to a court of full competence where the proceedings are public.[955] This type of solution is not, however, sufficient for the general courts. The lack of a public hearing cannot be corrected in any other way than by organising a new, complete oral hearing at the appeal stage.[956]

#### *4.3.1.2. Exceptions to a Public Hearing*

Although a public hearing is normally required, exceptions can be made on one or several grounds enumerated in Article 6 §1. According to that paragraph, the press and public may be excluded from all or part of a trial in the interests of morals, public order or national security in a democratic society,[957] where the interests of juveniles or the protection of the private life of the parties so require,[958] or to the extent strictly necessary in the opinion of the court in special circumstances where publicity would prejudice the interests of justice.[959] The list is exhaustive: a non-public hearing is incompatible with Article 6 §1 unless

---

953 *Riepan v. Austria*, App. no. 35115/97, §29, 14.11.2000; and *Hummatov v. Azerbaijan*, App. nos. 9852/03+, §144, 29.11.2007.

954 *Riepan v. Austria*, App. no. 35115/97, §30, 14.11.2000. See also Maciej Szpunar, "Right to a public hearing according to Art. 6 ECHR and Art. 47 of the Charter of Fundamental Rights of the EU: constitutional perspectives", in Burkhard Hess, Ana Koprivica Harvey (Eds.), *Open Justice – The Role of Courts in a Democratic Society*, Nomos, Baden-Baden 2019, pp. 47–58, at pp. 52–53.

955 *Riepan v. Austria*, App. no. 35115/97, §39, 14.11.2000; *Le Compte, Van Leuven and De Meyere v. Belgium*, App. nos. 6878/75+, §60, 23.6.1981; and *Albert and Le Compte v. Belgium*, App. nos. 7299/75+, §37, 10.2.1983. In the case *Stallinger and Kuso v. Austria*, App. nos. 14696/89+, §51, 23.4.1997 the Court referred to a possibility that in exceptional circumstances it may be justified to dispense with an oral hearing.

956 *Riepan v. Austria*, App. no. 35115/97, §39, 14.11.2000. With a new, complete oral hearing is meant the hearing of witnesses in the same manner as if the court were an first instance court, see *Göç v. Turkey* [GC], App. no. 36590/97, §48, 11.7.2002.

957 See also *Zagorodnikov v. Russia*, App. no. 66941/01, §26, 7.6.2007; and *B. and P. v. the United Kingdom*, App. nos. 36337/97+, §39, 24.4.2001.

958 See also *Moser v. Austria*, App. no. 12643/02, §97, 21.9.2006; *Diennet v. France*, App. no. 18160/91, §34, 26.9.1995; and *Hurter v. Switzerland*, App. no. 53146/99, §§30–32, 15.12.2005.

959 See also *B. and P. v. the United Kingdom*, App. nos. 36337/97+, §38, 24.4.2001; and *Osinger v. Austria*, App. no. 54645/00, §52, 24.3.2005.

the reasons for the lack of public access are based on the above-mentioned grounds.[960]

Although there does not exist in Article 6 §1 a similar proportionality requirement in respect of the exceptions as there is in Articles 8, 9, 10 and 11, a similar balancing act also needs to be performed under Article 6 §1. This kind of proportionality test was used, *inter alia*, in the case *Campbell and Fell v. the United Kingdom*, which concerned prison disciplinary proceedings that had been held *in camera* in the prison area in order to guarantee public order and safety. The Court did not find a violation in that case. It considered that a publicity requirement in the context of the disciplinary proceedings would have placed a disproportionate burden on the State authorities because it would have required either allowing the public access to the prison area or, alternatively, the transfer of the prisoners to the court.[961]

The Court has not, however, borrowed from Articles 8, 9, 10 and 11 the concept of national margin of appreciation to be used in respect of exceptions to the publicity principle, but has instead made its own assessment of the necessity for the exception to apply, without in any way indicating that the respondent State has its own certain discretion.[962] The wording of Article 6 §1 is not clear in this respect, since, on the one hand, the reference to "fairness" would seem to encourage an interpretation of the possibility of national margin of appreciation broadly, while, on the other hand, it also contains a reference to "strictly necessary", which would seem to require as strict an interpretation as possible. However, in its case-law the Court has held that holding proceedings, whether wholly or partly, *in camera* must be strictly required by the circumstances of the case.[963]

The Court has accepted that a whole group of cases can be excluded from the scope of the publicity requirement if it thinks that one or several exceptions apply to them. For example, in the case *B. and P. v. the United Kingdom*, the Court held that in cases concerning children a presumption of non-publicity of the proceedings could be allowed.[964] If there are such grounds to apply one or more exceptions, the authorities are not obliged, but have the right, to order hearings

---

960 For example, in the case *Osinger v. Austria*, App. no. 54645/00, §52, 24.3.2005, the Court found a violation of Article 6 §1 when no public hearing was held in a case concerning transfer of land ownership, and the exclusion of the public was not justified by the need to protect the private life of the parties.

961 *Campbell and Fell v. the United Kingdom*, App. nos. 7819/77+, §87, 28.6.1984.

962 See, however, the concurring opinion of Judge Morenilla in the case *Nortier v. the Netherlands*, App. no. 13924/88, 24.8.1993; and the opinion of Lord Reed in the case *V. v. the United Kingdom* [GC], App. no. 24888/94, 16.12.1999, both of which cases concerned juveniles.

963 *Welke and Białek v. Poland*, App. no. 15924/05, §74, 1.3.2011; and *Martinie v. France* [GC], App. no. 58675/00, §40, 12.4.2006.

964 *B. and P. v. the United Kingdom*, App. nos. 36337/97+, §39, 24.4.2001.

to be held *in camera* if they consider that such a restriction is warranted.[965] In practice, the Court has applied the test of strict necessity whatever there has been a justification advanced for the lack of publicity.[966] When deciding to hold a hearing *in camera*, the domestic courts are required to provide sufficient reasoning for their decision demonstrating that closure is strictly necessary within the meaning of Article 6 §1.[967]

#### 4.3.1.2.1. Interests of Juveniles

A hearing can be held *in camera*, for example, when the proceedings concern the placement of children with either of their parents in matters of divorce or separation. Such was the case, for example, in *B. and P. v. the United Kingdom*.[968] However, if the case concerns the taking into care of a child by State authorities, then the proceedings must be public.[969] This is explained by the fact that when a State's interests are involved in the proceedings, there must be greater accountability to the public than in situations which only concern internal affairs of a family, that is, an issue between private individuals.

#### 4.3.1.2.2. Protection of Private Life

Protection of private life is one of the exceptions allowed under the publicity requirement. The parties to the proceedings and the witnesses must be able to speak freely about even very private matters without the fear that there will be public interest in or comment on their case. Therefore, divorce proceedings and medical disciplinary proceedings,[970] for example, can take place *in camera* in order to protect the private lives of the parties.

When the parties to the proceedings prefer that the proceedings are held *in camera* rather than publicly, the question arises as to whether the holding of a public hearing may violate either the fair trial requirements under Article 6 §1 or the protection of private life under Article 8. Although, as a principle, such proceedings do take place *in camera*, a public hearing may also be allowed in such cases since the public nature of the proceedings may be justified under Article 8 §2.[971]

---

965 *Toeva v. Bulgaria* (dec.), App. no. 53329/99, 9.5.2006.

966 *Yam v. the United Kingdom*, App. no. 31295/11, §54, 16.1.2020; and *Mraović v. Croatia*, App. no. 30373/13, §45, 14.5.2020.

967 *Chaushev and Others v. Russia*, App. nos. 37037/03+, §24, 25.10.2016; and *Mraović v. Croatia*, App. no. 30373/13, §45, 14.5.2020.

968 *B. and P. v. the United Kingdom*, App. nos. 36337/97+, §38, 24.4.2001.

969 *Moser v. Austria*, App. no. 12643/02, §97, 21.9.2006.

970 *Guenoun v. France* (dec.), App. no. 13562/88, 2.7.1990; and *Imberechts v. Belgium* (dec.), App. no. 15561/89, 25.2.1991, which concerned the protection of the private life of a patient.

971 In the case *B. and P. v. the United Kingdom*, App. nos. 36337/97+, 24.4.2001, the wife had no need to invoke Article 8 as the domestic courts had rejected her husband's request for a public hearing.

In criminal proceedings the fair trial aspects may also support holding the hearing *in camera* in order to protect the safety or private lives of the parties and witnesses, or in order to guarantee the free flow of information and opinions.[972] The non-public nature of pretrial investigations is acceptable for the protection of the privacy of the interrogated persons and for securing the effectiveness of the investigation.[973] It is also acceptable, on several grounds even, to hold a hearing *in camera* in cases concerning accusations of sexual abuse of a child.

In the case *Mraović v. Croatia* the applicant was accused of rape of a basketball star. The trial was conducted *in camera* although the applicant was opposed to it. The Court held that, when deciding on the public character of the proceedings, the protection of the private life of a victim of a sexual offence under Article 8 of the Convention needed to be balanced against the rights of the defence under Article 6. The Court stressed the need to protect the victim of the crime from secondary victimisation and to encourage victims of sexual offences to report humiliating crimes committed against them. The criminal justice system should operate in such a way that it did not increase the suffering of victims and discourage them from participating in criminal proceedings, while ensuring the rights of the accused, including the public character of the proceedings. Although the victim in this case had given press interviews on the matter, this did not remove the State's positive obligation to protect her private life. When giving interviews, the victim had controlled the information she wanted to share. In the trial, however, and especially in the cross-examination, this would not have been possible and extremely intimate aspects of her private life would have been dealt with without control. The Court also referred to EU law and the Istanbul Convention. In these circumstances, the Court concluded that the non-public nature of the trial did not violate the applicant's right to a public hearing.[974]

#### 4.3.1.2.3. Public Order and Security Concerns

Holding a hearing *in camera* on the basis of public order interests was at stake in the case *Campbell and Fell v. the United Kingdom* which concerned prison disciplinary proceedings against convicted prisoners.[975] By contrast, in the case *Riepan v. Austria*, such an exception was not relevant because the hearing in the prison was not strictly *in camera* – it was the lack of publicity as a result of the public having no *de facto* chance to participate in the proceedings because

---

972 *B. and P. v. the United Kingdom*, App. nos. 36337/97+, §37, 24.4.2001.

973 *Ernst and Others v. Belgium*, App. no. 33400/96, §67, 15.7.2003 (no violation).

974 *Mraović v. Croatia*, App. no. 30373/13, §§46–59, 14.5.2020 (no violation). The case was referred to the Grand Chamber which decided to strike it out since the applicant had died during the proceedings, see *Mraovic v. Croatia* [GC], App. no. 30373/13, 9.4.2021.

975 *Campbell and Fell v. the United Kingdom*, App. nos. 7819/77+, §87, 28.6.1984.

of the location.[976] The Court has interpreted the public order concept in this respect widely, extending it from the risk of common, general disorder[977] to include the need to uphold prison security.

Although security problems are a common feature of many criminal proceedings, cases in which security concerns alone justify excluding the public from a trial are nevertheless rare.[978] All security measures should be narrowly tailored and comply with the principle of necessity. Moreover, the judicial authorities should consider all possible alternatives to ensure safety and security in the courtroom and give preference to a less strict measure over a stricter one when it can achieve the same purpose.[979]

#### 4.3.1.2.4. National Security

A hearing can also be held *in camera*, without contravening Article 6, in cases concerning national security. This is clear, as these cases normally involve State secrets. Nevertheless, the mere presence of classified information in the case file does not automatically imply a need to close a trial to the public, without first balancing openness with national-security concerns. Before excluding the public from criminal proceedings, domestic courts must balance whether such a closure is necessary to protect a compelling governmental interest, and must limit secrecy to the extent necessary to preserve such an interest.[980]

It should be noted that the Court is not well-equipped to challenge the national authorities' judgment that national security considerations arise in a case. However, even where national security is at stake, measures affecting fundamental human rights must be subject to some form of adversarial proceedings before an independent body competent to review the reasons for the decision. In cases where the Court does not have sight of the national security material on which decisions restricting human rights are based, it can only scrutinise the national decision-making process to ensure that it incorporated adequate safeguards. It is also relevant whether public interest considerations were balanced with the need for openness, whether all evidence was disclosed to the defence and whether the proceedings as a whole were fair.[981]

---

976 *Riepan v. Austria*, App. no. 35115/97, §34, 14.11.2000. Another reason may have been that this case concerned normal criminal proceedings while the case *Campbell and Fell* concerned prison disciplinary proceedings.

977 *Le Compte, Van Leuven and De Meyere v. Belgium*, App. nos. 6878/75+, §59, 23.6.1981. This wider meaning is concordant with the French term "ordre public" and may also mean general disorder in the courtroom.

978 *Riepan v. Austria*, App. no. 35115/97, §34, 14.11.2000.

979 *Krestovskiy v. Russia*, App. no. 14040/03, §29, 28.10.2010.

980 *Belashev v. Russia*, App. no. 28617/03, §83, 4.12.2008; and *Welke and Białek v. Poland*, App. no. 15924/05, §77, 1.3.2011.

981 *Yam v. the United Kingdom*, App. no. 31295/11, §§55–57, 16.1.2020.

## 4.3.2. ORAL HEARING

An oral hearing is one of the manifestations of a public hearing and therefore forms one of the most important principles under Article 6 §1.[982] Article 6 §1 guarantees a right to an oral hearing,[983] unless there are exceptional circumstances that justify dispensing with such a hearing.[984] The mere presence of classified information in the case file does not automatically imply a need to close a trial to the public.[985] In criminal matters the right to an oral hearing becomes apparent from the requirements of Article 6 §3 (c), (d) and (e).[986] The right to an oral hearing applies both to public hearings and to those hearings held *in camera* to which the exceptions in Article 6 §1 apply.[987] An applicant's incarceration cannot in itself justify not giving him or her an oral hearing before a court, and the prisoner must have the opportunity to ask to be present at the hearing.[988] The lack of an oral hearing may or may not be sufficiently remedied at a later stage in the proceedings.[989]

### *4.3.2.1. Waiver of an Oral Hearing*

The obligation to organise an oral hearing is not absolute,[990] and an applicant can validly waive his right to an oral hearing. The waiver must be clear and given of the applicant's own free will.[991] In addition, matters concerning important issues of public interest do not require the holding of an oral hearing.[992]

---

[982] *Döry v. Sweden*, App. no. 28394/95, §37, 12.11.2002; *Jussila v. Finland* [GC], App. no. 73053/01, §40, 23.11.2006; and *Göç v. Turkey* [GC], App. no. 36590/97, §46, 11.7.2002.

[983] *Fredin v. Sweden (No. 2)*, App. no. 18928/91, §§21–22, 23.2.1994; *Allan Jacobsson v. Sweden (No. 2)*, App. no. 16970/90, §46, 19.2.1998; *Göç v. Turkey* [GC], App. no. 36590/97, §47, 11.7.2002; and *Selmani and Others v. "the former Yugoslav Republic of Macedonia"*, App. no. 67259/14, §§37–39, 9.2.2017.

[984] *Hesse-Anger and Anger v. Germany* (dec.), App. no. 45835/99, 17.5.2001; *De Tommaso v. Italy* [GC], App. no. 43395/09, §§163–67, 23.2.2017; *Lorenzetti v. Italy*, App. no. 32075/09, §30, 10.4.2012; and *Mirovni Inštitut v. Slovenia*, App. no. 32303/13, §36, 13.3.2018.

[985] *Nikolova and Vandova v. Bulgaria*, App. no. 20688/04, §§74–77, 17.12.2013.

[986] *Demebukov v. Bulgaria*, App. no. 68020/01, §44, 28.2.2008.

[987] The Court's case-law does not always make a very clear distinction between a public hearing and an oral hearing. See, for example, *Ekbatani v. Sweden*, App. no. 10563/83, 26.5.1988.

[988] *Igranov and Others v. Russia*, App. nos. 42399/13+, §§34–35, 20.3.2018; *Yevdokimov and Others v. Russia*, App. nos. 27236/05+, §§33–47, 16.2.2016; and *Altay v. Turkey (No. 2)*, App. no. 11236/09, §77, 9.4.2019.

[989] *Le Compte, Van Leuven and De Meyere v. Belgium*, App. nos. 6878/75+, §§60–61, 23.6.1981; *Diennet v. France*, App. no. 18160/91, §34, 26.9.1995; and *Malhous v. the Czech Republic* [GC], App. no. 33071/96, §62, 12.7.2001.

[990] *Jussila v. Finland* [GC], App. no. 73053/01, §41, 23.11.2006.

[991] *Le Compte, Van Leuven and De Meyere v. Belgium*, App. nos. 6878/75+, §59, 23.6.1981; and *Albert and Le Compte v. Belgium*, App. nos. 7299/75+, §35, 10.2.1983.

[992] *Håkansson and Sturesson v. Sweden*, App. no. 11855/85, §66, 21.2.1990; *Schuler-Zgraggen v. Switzerland*, App. no. 14518/89, §58, 24.6.1993; and *Pauger v. Austria*, App. no. 16717/90, §58, 28.5.1997. See also Karen Reid, *A Practitioner's Guide to the European Convention on Human Rights*, Sweet & Maxwell/Thomson Reuters, London 2019, pp. 312 and 315.

The waiver can concern both the right to an oral hearing as well as the access of the public to the hearing.[993] The waiver can also be implicit or tacit, on the condition that it is clear from the circumstances of the case that a waiver has taken place.[994] The Court has accepted the existence of an unequivocal tacit waiver when, for example, the applicants have not requested the holding of an oral hearing in proceedings which normally are written,[995] or when they seek to evade the trial.[996] Nevertheless, any waiver of guarantees under Article 6 must satisfy the test of a "knowing and intelligent" waiver, as established in the Court's case-law.[997]

On the other hand, a failure to request the holding of an oral hearing in a situation in which the court is deprived of the full competence in the matter cannot be regarded as a waiver.[998] Nor has the failure to request an oral hearing in disciplinary proceedings which are normally held *in camera* and where the chance of having such a request accepted are very small, been regarded as a waiver.[999] A waiver has more often been regarded as having taken place in professional disciplinary matters and civil matters than in criminal matters, where the threshold for accepting a waiver is probably higher.

#### *4.3.2.2. Development of the Court's Case-Law*

In the Court's earlier case-law it was emphasised that an oral hearing was to be held in the first instance, especially if it is the only instance, unless there were particular reasons that justified exceptions to this rule.[1000] In its subsequent case-law the Court has specified that the situations in which an oral hearing can be dispensed with must be assessed on the basis of the nature of the case pending before the domestic court, for example where the proceedings concern

---

993 *Håkansson and Sturesson v. Sweden*, App. no. 11855/85, §66, 21.2.1990; and *Pauger v. Austria*, App. no. 16717/90, §58, 28.5.1997.

994 *Le Compte, Van Leuven and De Meyere v. Belgium*, App. nos. 6878/75+, §59, 23.6.1981; and *Hermi v. Italy* [GC], App. no. 18114/02, §98, 18.10.2006.

995 *Håkansson and Sturesson v. Sweden*, App. no. 11855/85, §67, 21.2.1990; *Schuler-Zgraggen v. Switzerland*, App. no. 14518/89, §58, 24.6.1993; and *Zumtobel v. Austria*, App. no. 12235/86, §34, 21.9.1993. See also Arman Zrvandyan, *Casebook on European Fair Trial Standards in Administrative Justice*, Council of Europe Publishing, Strasbourg 2016, pp. 77–79.

996 *Lena Atanasova v. Bulgaria*, App. no. 52009/07, §52, 26.1.2017; and *Chong Coronado v. Andorra*, App. no. 37368/15, §§42–45, 23.7.2020.

997 *Sejdovic v. Italy* [GC], App. no. 56581/00, §§86–87, 1.3.2006.

998 *Göç v. Turkey* [GC], App. no. 36590/97, §48, 11.7.2002. See also Eva Brems, "Conflicting human rights: an exploration in the context of the right to fair trial in the European Convention for the Protection of Human Rights and Fundamental Freedoms", *Human Rights Quarterly*, vol. 27, no. 1, 2005, pp. 294–326, at pp. 307–309.

999 *H. v. Belgium*, App. no. 8950/80, §54, 30.11.1987.

1000 *Håkansson and Sturesson v. Sweden*, App. no. 11855/85, §64, 21.2.1990; *Fredin v. Sweden (No. 2)*, App. no. 18928/91, §§21–22, 23.2.1994; and *Allan Jacobsson v. Sweden (No. 2)*, App. no. 16970/90, §46, 19.2.1998.

exclusively legal or highly technical questions,[1001] rather than on the basis of the frequency of occurrence of such situations.[1002] The reference to particular reasons does not therefore mean that the Court will allow dispensing with an oral hearing only in rare cases.[1003] However, the Article 6 fair trial guarantees must always have a primary role in the assessment.[1004]

#### 4.3.2.3. *Civil and Administrative Law Cases*

Although applicants may not waive their right to an oral hearing, it is not obligatory to organise an oral hearing in all civil and administrative law matters. Dispensing with an oral hearing is acceptable, for example, when the matter in question is very technical. One example may be cases concerning social security benefits based on medical evidence.[1005] For example, in the case *Elo v. Finland*, the Court found that an oral hearing could be dispensed with before the Accident Board and the Insurance Court as the dispute concerned the correct interpretation of written medical certificates and the interpretations given by expert doctors were pointing in the same direction.[1006]

An oral hearing can also be dispensed with when the case only concerns simple juridical questions.[1007] The Court has held that the domestic authorities may naturally take into account the elements of procedural economy and effectiveness of the proceedings.[1008] However, in these cases the applicant must also have the opportunity to request an oral hearing if there are special circumstances in the case, although this request can be rejected after an adequate assessment.[1009] In addition, particular attention has been paid to

---

1001 *Koottummel v. Austria*, App. no. 49616/06, §19, 10.12.2009. However, even where the subject matter of the case concerns an issue of a technical nature, which could normally be decided without an oral hearing, the circumstances of the case may still warrant the holding of an oral hearing, see *Özmurat İnşaat Elektrik Nakliyat Temizlik San. ve Tic. Ltd. Şti. v. Turkey*, App. no. 48657/06, §37, 28.11.2017.

1002 *Miller v. Sweden*, App. no. 55853/00, §29, 8.2.2005; and *Mirovni Inštitut v. Slovenia*, App. no. 32303/13, §37, 13.3.2018.

1003 *Miller v. Sweden*, App. no. 55853/00, §29, 8.2.2005.

1004 *Pélissier and Sassi v. France* [GC], App. no. 25444/94, §52, 25.3.1999; and *Sejdovic v. Italy* [GC], App. no. 56581/00, §90, 1.3.2006.

1005 *Schuler-Zgraggen v. Switzerland*, App. no. 14518/89, §58, 24.6.1993. In the case *Miller v. Sweden*, App. no. 55853/00, §34, 8.2.2005 the matter was not, however, considered to be technical. See also *Martinie v. France* [GC], App. no. 58675/00, §44, 12.4.2006 which concerned a court of auditing; and *Hofbauer v. Austria* (dec.), App. no. 68087/01, 2.9.2004 which concerned fire safety of a door. See also Arman Zrvandyan, *Casebook on European Fair Trial Standards in Administrative Justice*, Council of Europe Publishing, Strasbourg 2016, pp. 78–83.

1006 *Elo v. Finland*, App. no. 30742/02, §§38–39, 26.9.2006 (no violation).

1007 *Allan Jacobsson v. Sweden (No. 2)*, App. no. 16970/90, §48, 19.2.1998; *Valová, Slezák and Slezák v. Slovakia*, App. no. 44925/98, §65, 1.6.2004; and *Varela Assalino v. Portugal* (dec.), App. no. 64336/01, 25.4.2002.

1008 *Schuler-Zgraggen v. Switzerland*, App. no. 14518/89, §58, 24.6.1993.

1009 *Martinie v. France* [GC], App. no. 58675/00, §42, 12.4.2006.

whether the parties can comment on the matter, and on the observations of the other party in writing.[1010] An oral hearing needed to be organised when, for example, a Constitutional Court examined, as the first instance court, a case which concerned the removal of accredited journalists from the press section of Parliament when the parliamentarians caused disturbance in Parliament.[1011]

In civil and administrative law matters there have been, however, situations in which the Court has found the holding of an oral hearing to be necessary. One such group of cases is that concerning the taking into public care of children and the related contact rights. The Court found in the case *L. v. Finland*, for example, that it was not possible, because of the nature of the case and the interests of the applicants, to decide a case concerning taking a child into public care solely on the basis of a written case file, but that a competent domestic authority should have organised an oral hearing in the matter.[1012] Similarly, in the case *C. v. Finland*, which concerned contact rights, the Court considered the lack of an oral hearing as one of the elements leading in the end to the finding of a violation under Article 8.[1013]

Also, insufficient reasoning for the refusal to hold an oral hearing may lead to a violation. In the case *Pönkä v. Estonia*, the Court held that the domestic court's decision to examine a crime-based compensation claim solely in written proceedings was not sufficiently reasoned, since the court had not given any separate reasoning for its refusal not to hold an oral hearing even though the applicant had requested the holding of one for the admission of evidence. The domestic court had only cited the relevant statutory provision. It could have heard the applicant, who was detained in Finland, by using modern communication tools, for example.[1014]

### *4.3.2.4. Criminal Matters*

#### 4.3.2.4.1. Matters Concerning the Core Areas of Criminal Law

An oral hearing is particularly important in criminal matters, especially if no proper right of appeal exists.[1015] Normally in criminal matters the first instance

[1010] *Vilho Eskelinen and Others v. Finland* [GC], App. no. 63235/00, §74, 19.4.2007.

[1011] *Selmani and Others v. "the former Yugoslav Republic of Macedonia"*, App. no. 67259/14, §§39–41, 9.2.2017.

[1012] *L. v. Finland*, App. no. 25651/94, §132, 27.4.2000.

[1013] *C. v. Finland*, App. no. 18249/02, §§58–59, 9.5.2006.

[1014] *Pönkä v. Estonia*, App. no. 64160/11, §§35–39, 8.11.2016.

[1015] *Göç v. Turkey* [GC], App. no. 36590/97, §47, 11.7.2002. See also Eva Brems, "Conflicting human rights: an exploration in the context of the right to fair trial in the European Convention for the Protection of Human Rights and Fundamental Freedoms", *Human Rights Quarterly*, vol. 27, no. 1, 2005, pp. 294–326, at pp. 307–309.

court must fully meet the Article 6 requirements.[1016] On the basis of the special regulation in Article 6 §3, an applicant automatically has the right to have his case "heard" and, *inter alia*, to give evidence in his own defence, hear the evidence against him and examine and cross-examine the witnesses.[1017] Moreover, the right to be present at the hearing allows the accused also to verify the accuracy of his or her defence and to compare it with the statements of victims and witnesses.[1018] Domestic courts must exercise due diligence in securing the presence of the accused by properly summoning him or her,[1019] and they must take measures to discourage his unjustified absence from the hearing.[1020] An applicant should be notified of a court hearing in such a way as to not only have knowledge of the date, time and place of the hearing, but also to have enough time to prepare his or her case and to attend the court hearing.[1021]

Holding a hearing in an accused's absence is not in itself contrary to Article 6.[1022] However, when domestic law permits a trial to be held notwithstanding the absence of a person "charged with a criminal offence" that person should, once he becomes aware of the proceedings, be able to obtain, from a court which has heard him, a fresh determination of the merits of the charge.[1023]

#### 4.3.2.4.2. Other Criminal Matters

The Court found in the context of the case *Jussila v. Finland* that although the right to an oral hearing in criminal matters was particularly important, it was not out of the question in some situations to have it dispensed with.[1024] There are clearly "criminal charges" of differing weight, as there are cases which do not carry any significant degree of stigma. In addition, the autonomous interpretation of the notion of a "criminal charge" by applying the *Engel* criteria has led to a gradual broadening of the criminal head to include cases not strictly belonging to the

---

1016 *Findlay v. the United Kingdom*, App. no. 22107/93, §79, 25.2.1997; *Jussila v. Finland* [GC], App. no. 73053/01, §40, 23.11.2006; *Tierce v. San Marino*, App. no. 69700/01, §94, 17.6.2003; and *Igor Pascari v. the Republic of Moldova*, App. no. 25555/10, §27, 30.8.2016.

1017 *Jussila v. Finland* [GC], App. no. 73053/01, §40, 23.11.2006; *Hermi v. Italy* [GC], App. no. 18114/02, §§58–59, 18.10.2006; *Sejdovic v. Italy* [GC], App. no. 56581/00, §§81 and 84, 1.3.2006; and *Arps v. Croatia*, App. no. 23444/12, §28, 25.10.2016.

1018 *Medenica v. Switzerland*, App. no. 20491/92, §54, 14.6.2001.

1019 *Colozza v. Italy*, App. no. 9024/80, §32, 12.2.1985; and *M.T.B. v. Turkey*, App. no. 47081/06, §§49–53, 12.6.2018.

1020 *Medenica v. Switzerland*, App. no. 20491/92, §54, 14.6.2001.

1021 *Vyacheslav Korchagin v. Russia*, App. no. 12307/16, §65, 28.8.2018.

1022 *Colozza v. Italy*, App. no. 9024/80, §29, 12.2.1985. See also section 4.2.2.2. above.

1023 *Sanader v. Croatia*, App. no. 66408/12, §§77–78, 12.2.2015.

1024 *Jussila v. Finland* [GC], App. no. 73053/01, §43, 23.11.2006. See also Paul Mahoney, "Flogging a dead horse: the appropriate human rights policy for judicial treatment of competition fines", in David Edward, Jackelyn Maclennan, Assimakis Komninos (Eds.), *Ian S. Forrester – A Scot without Borders, Liber Amicorum*, vol. 1, Concurrences Review, New York 2015, pp. 225–240, at pp. 234–235.

traditional core categories of criminal law. Through jurisprudence, the criminal limb of Article 6 applies to, for example, administrative law penalties,[1025] prison disciplinary proceedings,[1026] customs law,[1027] competition law,[1028] tax surcharges,[1029] and penalties imposed by a court with jurisdiction in financial matters.[1030]

The Court held in the *Jussila* case that tax surcharges could not be included in the "hard core" of criminal law and that, consequently, the Article 6 criminal-head guarantees would not necessarily apply to their full extent. In that case the domestic courts could have dispensed with the obligation to hold an oral hearing.[1031] On the other hand, in the cases *Hannu Lehtinen v. Finland*[1032] and *Kallio v. Finland*,[1033] which also concerned tax surcharges, the Court found a violation of Article 6 §1 due to the fact that the Administrative Court had not held an oral hearing. The Court found that these cases differed from the *Jussila* case in that although they concerned the assessment of the correctness of the taxation proceedings, which fell beyond the scope of Article 6, in those cases the facts were unclear and the reliability of the evidence provided by the applicants and witnesses was brought into question. The Court found that in this kind of situation the assessment of evidence required that the parties were heard in person and therefore there should have been an oral hearing.

#### 4.3.2.5. *Oral Hearing at the Appeal Stage*

Unless there are exceptional circumstances that justify dispensing with an oral hearing, the right to a public hearing under Article 6 §1 implies a right to an oral hearing at least at one level of the national jurisdiction.[1034] If the first instance court has held an oral hearing, the obligation to hold one at appeal stage is thus less stringent. The lack of an oral hearing at appeal stage can be justified, first of all, by the special nature of the proceedings in question.[1035] For example, proceedings relating to leave to appeal[1036] and proceedings which only concern

1025 *Öztürk v. Germany*, App. no. 8544/79, §55, 21.2.1984.
1026 *Campbell and Fell v. the United Kingdom*, App. nos. 7819/77+, §73, 28.6.1984.
1027 *Salabiaku v. France* (dec.), App. no. 10519/83, 16.4.1986.
1028 *Société Stenuit v. France* (dec.), App. no. 11598/85, 11.7.1989.
1029 *Jussila v. Finland* [GC], App. no. 73053/01, §38, 23.11.2006.
1030 *Guisset v. France* (dec.), App. no. 33933/96, 9.3.1998.
1031 *Jussila v. Finland* [GC], App. no. 73053/01, §43, 23.11.2006.
1032 *Hannu Lehtinen v. Finland*, App. no. 32993/02, §48, 22.7.2008.
1033 *Kallio v. Finland*, App. no. 40199/02, §50, 22.7.2008.
1034 *Fischer v. Austria*, App. no. 16922/90, §44, 26.4.1995; and *Salomonsson v. Sweden*, App. no. 38978/97, §36, 12.11.2002.
1035 *Hermi v. Italy* [GC], App. no. 18114/02, §60, 18.10.2006.
1036 *Monnell and Morris v. the United Kingdom*, App. nos. 9562/81+, 2.3.1987; and *Miller v. Sweden*, App. no. 55853/00, §30, 8.2.2005.

questions of law[1037] can be conducted without holding an oral hearing. Secondly, less strict requirements also apply to situations in which the right to an oral hearing has been waived in the first instance and has only been requested for the first time on appeal. In the interests of the proper administration of justice, it is normally more expedient that a hearing is held at a first instance court rather than only before an appellate court.[1038] However, if the appellate courts assess the case in a different manner to the first instance court, the need to hold an oral hearing becomes more important.

#### 4.3.2.5.1. Need to Organise an Oral Hearing on Appeal

If an appellate court is competent to examine both legal issues and facts, the necessity to organise an oral hearing depends on whether the fair trial guarantees require one to be held.[1039] In this respect the Court has regard to the nature of the domestic appeal system, the scope of the domestic court's powers and the manner in which the applicant's interests are actually presented and protected before that court,[1040] particularly in the light of the issues to be decided by it, and their importance for the appellant.[1041] Whether the matter raises questions of fact and law which cannot adequately be resolved on the basis of the written material is also relevant.[1042]

Normally an applicant has had a particular interest in attending the hearing on appeal personally, alongside his or her counsel,[1043] and often this interest has been the need to test the evidence. For example, in the case *Ekbatani v. Sweden*, the applicant's guilt could not be validly assessed without hearing the victim of the crime in person, as the facts of the case were not clear and the case concerned reliability of the assessment of evidence.[1044] Similarly in two Finnish cases,

---

1037 *Axen v. the Federal Republic of Germany*, App. no. 8273/78, §28, 8.12.1983.

1038 *Döry v. Sweden*, App. no. 28394/95, §40, 12.11.2002; and *Fexler v. Sweden*, App. no. 36801/06, §59, 13.10.2011.

1039 *Ekbatani v. Sweden*, App. no. 10563/83, §32, 26.5.1988; *Elsholz v. Germany* [GC], App. no. 25735/94, §66, 13.7.2000; *Belziuk v. Poland*, App. no. 23103/93, §38, 25.3.1998; and *Fejde v. Sweden*, App. no. 12631/87, §31, 29.10.1991.

1040 *Ekbatani v. Sweden*, App. no. 10563/83, §28, 26.5.1988; *Helmers v. Sweden*, App. no. 11826/85, §36, 29.10.1991; and *Hermi v. Italy* [GC], App. no. 18114/02, §62, 18.10.2006.

1041 *Kremzow v. Austria*, App. no. 12350/86, §59, 21.9.1993; *Kamasinski v. Austria*, App. no. 9783/82, §106, 19.12.1989; *Ekbatani v. Sweden*, App. no. 10563/83, §§27–28, 26.5.1988; *Seliwiak v. Poland*, App. no. 3818/04, §54, 21.7.2009; and *Sibgatullin v. Russia*, App. no. 32165/02, §36, 23.4.2009.

1042 *Elsholz v. Germany* [GC], App. no. 25735/94, §66, 13.7.2000.

1043 In this respect the right to an oral hearing overlaps with the right to be present and the right to participate effectively in the proceedings.

1044 *Ekbatani v. Sweden*, App. no. 10563/83, §32, 26.5.1988. See also Karen Reid, *A Practitioner's Guide to the European Convention on Human Rights*, Sweet & Maxwell/Thomson Reuters, London 2019, pp. 166 and 314. See also *Kamasinski v. Austria*, App. no. 9783/82, §§107–108, 19.12.1989 (no violation, Article 6 was examined in conjunction with Article 14); *Botten v. Norway*, App. no. 16206/90, §52, 19.2.1996; and *Belziuk v. Poland*, App. no. 23103/93, §38, 25.3.1998.

*Muttilainen v. Finland*[1045] and *R.H. v. Finland*,[1046] the Court found a violation of Article 6 §1 on the basis of a lack of an oral hearing before the Court of Appeal. In both cases the accused denied his guilt and contested on appeal the reliability of the assessment of evidence. Although an oral hearing had already been held in the District Court, the Court found that an oral hearing was necessary also on appeal, because in such situations the assessment of evidence required the hearing of the parties in person.

In contrast, in the case *Jan-Åke Andersson v. Sweden*, no oral hearing was needed, as the case concerned a minor traffic misdemeanour which could be decided on the basis of the written materials.[1047] No oral hearing on appeal was required either in the case *Nömman v. Finland*, since the public prosecutor had already presented alternative charges before the first instance court and had only requested punishment to that effect before the appellate court. The Court found that the fact that the applicant had not requested an oral hearing to be held before the appeal court meant that he had waived his right to it, knowing that the court might decide the case in accordance with the public prosecutor's request.[1048]

The particular importance of the matter to the applicant may also be a reason to organise an oral hearing. For example, the case *Helmers v. Sweden* concerned a defamation matter which was important in terms of the applicant's career and professional reputation.[1049]

#### 4.3.2.5.2. Judgment Changed to the Accused's Detriment

It is also normally necessary to organise an oral hearing when the appellate court changes the lower court's judgment to the detriment of the accused, especially in a criminal case.[1050] This was the case, for example, in *Laaksonen v. Finland*, in which the charges against the applicant had been dismissed in the District Court but

---

1045 *Muttilainen v. Finland*, App. no. 18358/02, §26, 22.5.2007.

1046 *R.H. v. Finland*, App. no. 34165/05, §34, 2.6.2009. In this case no oral hearing was organised as the Court of Appeal had filtered out the case.

1047 *Jan-Åke Andersson v. Sweden*, App. no. 11274/84, §29, 29.10.1991.

1048 *Nömman v. Finland* (dec.), App. no. 28145/10, §§27–29, 8.10.2013.

1049 *Helmers v. Sweden*, App. no. 11826/85, §38, 29.10.1991; and *Ramos Nunes de Carvalho e Sá v. Portugal* [GC], App. nos. 55391/13+, §§208–211, 6.11.2018 (disciplinary sanction against a judge). See also *Kremzow v. Austria*, App. no. 12350/86, §68, 21.9.1993 (the applicant was accused of a serious crime and risked being sentenced to a heavy punishment); *Constantinescu v. Romania*, App. no. 28871/95, §59, 27.6.2000 (the appeal stage was the first instance and the applicant did not have an opportunity to defend himself in person); and *Sigurþór Arnarsson v. Iceland*, App. no. 44671/98, §36, 15.7.2003 (the applicant who had been acquitted in the first instance had been convicted by the appeal court).

1050 *Dondarini v. San Marino*, App. no. 50545/99, §27, 6.7.2004; *Popovici v. Moldova*, App. nos. 289/04+, §68, 27.11.2007; *Lacadena Calero v. Spain*, App. no. 23002/07, §38, 2.11.2011; *Zahirović v. Croatia*, App. no. 58590/11, §57, 25.4.2013; and *Hokkeling v. the Netherlands*, App. no. 30749/12, §58, 14.2.2017.

he was convicted in the Court of Appeal.[1051] A similar situation occurred in the case *Suuripää v. Finland*, in which the applicant was acquitted by the Court of Appeal, acting as the first instance court, but convicted by the Supreme Court without an oral hearing held by the latter.[1052] In both cases the Court found a violation of Article 6 §1. In the latter case the Court took into account, as one of the elements, the fact that the outcome of the proceedings had been of significant importance for the applicant's career and reputation.[1053]

Similarly, in the case *Lazu v. Moldova*, the Court found a violation. In that case the appellate court had changed the first instance court's judgment dismissing the charges and had instead convicted the applicant without holding an oral hearing. The applicant was convicted on the basis of written witness statements even though the first instance court's dismissal of charges had specifically been based on the unreliability of these witness statements.[1054] There was a similar situation in the case *Lorefice v. Italy*, in which the appeal court convicted the applicant, without hearing the key witnesses in person, on the basis of the same evidence that in the first instance court had led to the applicant's acquittal. The assessment of the reliability of the witness testimonies was based solely on the transcriptions made by the first instance court and the appeal court assessed this reliability differently to the first instance court.[1055] A similar situation was also at stake in the case *Júlíus Þór Sigurþórsson v. Iceland*, in which the Supreme Court had changed the assessment of the evidence made by the District Court without hearing the witness orally. In addition, after the District Court had acquitted the applicant, the Supreme Court had convicted him and sentenced him to a suspended prison sentence without giving him an opportunity to comment on the matter.[1056]

However, the Court found no violation in the case *Keskinen and Veljekset Keskinen Oy v. Finland*, even though the lower court's judgment was changed to the applicants' detriment on appeal without the holding of an oral hearing. In that case the Court of Appeal was only asked to examine whether the applicants' conduct could be considered to be an excusable mistake due to the lack of clarity of the law. There was thus no question of assessment of evidence or guilt, as in the above-mentioned cases; rather the only question to be decided concerned the interpretation of law.[1057]

---

1051 *Laaksonen v. Finland*, App. no. 70216/01, §32, 12.4.2007. See also *Botten v. Norway*, App. no. 16206/90, §53, 19.2.1996; *Dănilă v. Romania*, App. no. 53897/00, §41, 8.3.2007; and *Gómez Olmeda v. Spain*, App. no. 61112/12, §32, 29.3.2016.

1052 *Suuripää v. Finland*, App. no. 43151/02, §47, 12.1.2010.

1053 *Suuripää v. Finland*, App. no. 43151/02, §45, 12.1.2010.

1054 *Lazu v. the Republic of Moldova*, App. no. 46182/08, §§31–44, 5.7.2016.

1055 *Lorefice v. Italy*, App. no. 63446/13, §§36–47, 29.6.2017.

1056 *Júlíus Þór Sigurþórsson v. Iceland*, App. no. 38797/17, §§30–44, 16.7.2019.

1057 *Keskinen and Veljekset Keskinen Oy v. Finland*, App. no. 34721/09, §§39–44, 5.6.2012. See also *Bazo González v. Spain*, App. no. 30643/04, 16.12.2008 (no violation). Compare and contrast with *Igual Coll v. Spain*, App. no. 37496/04, §36, 10.3.2009 where the Court considered that

Nor was any violation found in the case *Kashlev v. Estonia*, in which the charges had been dismissed by the first instance court. On appeal the applicant had waived his right to appear in person in court but he was represented by a counsel. The appeal court reassessed the evidence on the basis of the case file accumulated before the first instance court and convicted the applicant as charged. For the Court it was decisive that the applicant had validly waived his right to be present in the appeal court and that the defence had had the opportunity to put questions to witnesses before the first instance court. The judgment was also reasoned in detail and the applicant had still had the chance to challenge the fairness of the proceedings before the Supreme Court.[1058]

#### 4.3.2.5.3. Participation by Video Conference

In some cases, the presence of the defendant in an appeal court hearing can be organised, for security reasons, through a video conference. In such situations it must, however, be guaranteed that the video link is of sufficient technical quality and that the defendant has the ability to be in confidential contact with his or her counsel. If the holding of a video conference impairs the defence's ability to operate effectively, other means must be considered. The case *Marcello Viola v. Italy*, in which the applicant was heard on appeal through a video link, concerned serious mafia crimes and for this reason the applicant's transfer from prison would have constituted a security risk. Because he was given the chance to communicate with his counsel through a protected telephone line and the video link functioned technically very well, there were no problems with accepting his presence through a video link-up.[1059]

---

the appeal court had not simply given a different legal interpretation or applied the law differently to facts already established at first instance, but had in fact carried out a fresh evaluation of facts beyond purely legal considerations. See also *Spînu v. Romania*, App. no. 32030/02, §§55–59, 29.4.2008; *Andreescu v. Romania*, App. no. 19452/02, §§65–70, 8.6.2010; and *Almenara Alvarez v. Spain*, App. no. 16096/08, 25.10.2011. Similarly, in *Marcos Barrios v. Spain*, App. no. 17122/07, §§40–41, 21.9.2010 the Court held that the appeal court had expressed itself on a question of fact, namely the credibility of a witness, thus modifying the facts established at first instance and taking a fresh position on facts which were decisive for the determination of the applicant's guilt. See also *García Hernández v. Spain*, App. no. 15256/07, §§33–34, 16.11.2010. In *Suuripää v. Finland*, App. no. 43151/02, §44, 12.1.2010 the Court noted that the facts and the legal interpretation can be intertwined to an extent that it is difficult to separate the two from each other.

1058 *Kashlev v. Estonia*, App. no. 22574/08, §51, 26.4.2016. See also *Hernández Royo v. Spain*, App. no. 16033/12, §39, 20.9.2016; and *Bivolaru v. Romania (No. 2)*, App. no. 66580/12, §§138–146, 2.10.2018.

1059 *Marcello Viola v. Italy*, App. no. 45106/04, §§67–77, 5.10.2006 (no violation). See also Evert-Jan van der Vlis, "Videoconferencing in criminal proceedings", in Sabine Braun, Judith L. Taylor (Eds.), *Videoconference and remote interpreting in criminal proceedings*, University of Surrey, Guildford 2011, pp. 11–25, at pp. 22–23.

In the case *Sakhnovskiy v. Russia*, video conference was used to overcome the problems caused by long distance and to provide the applicant with an opportunity to be present at his appeal against conviction. However, the problem was the applicant's ability to communicate with his counsel: the applicant, who has been convicted of murder, had had the opportunity to negotiate with his counsel for only 15 minutes, just before the start of the hearing. Taking into account the severity and complexity of the case, the Court held that the applicant had not had sufficient time to discuss with his counsel. It was also doubtful whether the video link provided by the State had provided sufficient privacy for the applicant. On the other hand, transporting the applicant 3,000 kilometres from Novosibirsk to Moscow would have taken a long time and would have been expensive. However, nothing had prevented the authorities from organising, for example, telephone contact between the applicant and his counsel long before the hearing, or from appointing him another counsel in Novosibirsk who could have visited the applicant in prison and been present with him at the court's session. In any case, the hearing could have been postponed *ex officio* in order to give the applicant enough time to negotiate with his counsel. The Court therefore held that the arrangements made by the domestic authorities had been insufficient and had not secured effective legal assistance for the applicant.[1060]

As noted above, there must be an oral hearing on appeal if an appellate court reassesses the evidence and convicts the defendant after the charges have been dismissed before the first instance court. Moreover, an oral hearing must in such cases be organised *ex officio*, irrespective of whether the defendant has requested it or not. In the case *Gómez Olmeda v. Spain*, the first instance court had dismissed the charges against the applicant. On appeal, the case, including the facts, was reassessed and the appeal court convicted the applicant. For its assessment, the appeal court used the videotaped first instance court hearing but it did not organise an oral hearing or request that the applicant attend in person. The Court held that when the reassessment covered both facts and law, and when the appeal court reached a different outcome to that of the first instance court, an oral hearing together with the applicant's personal attendance should have been arranged *ex officio*, even though the applicant had not requested it after the dismissal of charges by the lower court.[1061]

### 4.3.3. REQUIREMENT FOR PUBLIC PRONOUNCEMENT OF A JUDGMENT

In contrast with the right to a public hearing, the right to public pronouncement of a judgment contains no exceptions. The Court has, however, applied the

[1060] *Sakhnovskiy v. Russia* [GC], App. no. 21272/03, §§102–107, 2.11.2010.
[1061] *Gómez Olmeda v. Spain*, App. no. 61112/12, §§30–40, 29.3.2016.

concept of "public pronouncement of judgment" with a certain flexibility.[1062] Although Article 6 would seem to require a public pronouncement of the whole judgment in an oral hearing,[1063] the Court has not agreed to this but has created some exceptions and limitations. As a general rule, it has held that the form and extent of publication of a judgment must be assessed in the light of the special features of the proceedings in question and by reference to the object pursued by Article 6 §1 in this context, namely to ensure scrutiny of the judiciary by the public with a view to safeguarding the right to a fair trial. In making this assessment, account must be taken of the entirety of the proceedings.[1064]

It should be noted that the right to a public hearing and the right to public pronouncement of a judgment are two separate rights under Article 6. The fact that one of these rights is not violated does not in itself mean that the other right cannot be breached. It also means that public pronouncement of the sentence is incapable of remedying the unjustified holding of hearings *in camera*.[1065]

#### *4.3.3.1. How Much of a Judgment Must be Pronounced?*

The Court has not required that a whole judgment be publicly pronounced at all levels of jurisdiction. For example, in the case *Lamanna v. Austria*, the Court did not find a violation of Article 6 in a situation in which the appeal court had publicly pronounced the whole of its own judgment but had only included in it a resumé of the first instance judgment, which had not been published before. In addition, the judgment was only publicly pronounced six years after its delivery – because of a Supreme Court order – owing to the applicant's application before the Court being declared admissible.[1066] In another case, the Court held that, in a criminal matter, it was sufficient that the judgment was read in public stating the offence committed, the accused's guilt, the presence of special circumstances, if any, and the sentence imposed, even if the full reasons for the judgment were filed later.[1067]

On the other hand, it was not sufficient in a civil matter to pronounce only the operative part of the judgment without mentioning anything about

---

1062 *Lamanna v. Austria*, App. no. 28923/95, §31, 10.7.2001; *Moser v. Austria*, App. no. 12643/02, §101, 21.9.2006; *Sutter v. Switzerland*, App. no. 8209/78, §33, 22.2.1984; and *Campbell and Fell v. the United Kingdom*, App. nos. 7819/77+, §91, 28.6.1984.

1063 *Pretto and Others v. Italy*, App. no. 7984/77, §25, 8.12.1983.

1064 *Welke and Białek v. Poland*, App. no. 15924/05, §83, 1.3.2011.

1065 *Artemov v. Russia*, App. no. 14945/03, §109, 3.4.2014.

1066 *Lamanna v. Austria*, App. no. 28923/95, §§33–34, 10.7.2001 (no violation).

1067 *Crociani and Others v. Italy* (dec.), App. nos. 8603/79+, 18.12.1980. See also *Welke and Białek v. Poland*, App. no. 15924/05, §83, 1.3.2011 in which limiting the public pronouncement to the operative part of the judgments in proceedings held *in camera* did not contravene Article 6.

the reasoning.[1068] Nor was it justified in a case concerning national security to completely conceal from the public the entirety of a judicial decision.[1069]

#### 4.3.3.2. *Manner of Pronouncing*

In many Council of Europe Member States, the public pronouncement is done in such a way that judgments are made available for the public at the court's registry. In the case *Pretto v. Italy*, the Court found that the form of publicity to be given to a "judgment" under the domestic law of the respondent State had to be assessed in each case in the light of the special features of the proceedings in question and by reference to the object and purpose of Article 6 §1.[1070] Therefore, Article 6 §1 had not been violated in that case, although the judgment of the cassation court in a civil matter had never been pronounced publicly in a court hearing but only made available to the public at the court's registry. It was also relevant that the cassation court had the competence to review only questions of law and that it had held an oral hearing in the case.[1071] The Court also reached the same outcome in the case *Axen v. Germany*, which concerned criminal proceedings.[1072]

Both cases mentioned above concerned judgments rendered by the highest courts of the country, but the Court has also applied these principles to the pronouncement of judgments of lower courts. In the case *Werner v. Austria*, the first and second instance judgments had not been publicly pronounced but they had been served on the applicant. Other parties could pick up a copy from the court's registry if they could claim to have a justified interest in the matter. The Court found a violation, as neither one of the judgments was publicly pronounced; nor was their publicity guaranteed in other ways.[1073] It seems that the Court would not have found a violation of Article 6 §1 had the judgment been distributed freely to all interested parties at the court's registry.

#### 4.3.3.3. *Exception in Cases Involving Child Custody and Contact Rights*

The Court has in its case-law held that decisions concerning children and their custody and contact rights do not need to be pronounced to the public, but it is sufficient that the pronouncement is restricted to the parties involved.

---

1068 *Ryakib Biryukov v. Russia*, App. no. 14810/02, §45, 17.1.2008. See also Arman Zrvandyan, *Casebook on European Fair Trial Standards in Administrative Justice*, Council of Europe Publishing, Strasbourg 2016, pp. 118–119.

1069 *Raza v. Bulgaria*, App. no. 31465/08, §53, 11.2.2010; and *Fazliyski v. Bulgaria*, App. no. 40908/05, §§67–68, 16.4.2013.

1070 *Pretto and Others v. Italy*, App. no. 7984/77, §26, 8.12.1983.

1071 *Pretto and Others v. Italy*, App. no. 7984/77, §§26–27, 8.12.1983 (no violation).

1072 *Axen v. the Federal Republic of Germany*, App. no. 8273/78, §§31–32, 8.12.1983 (no violation).

1073 *Werner v. Austria*, App. no. 21835/93, §60, 24.11.1997. Compare to the case *Sutter v. Switzerland*, App. no. 8209/78, §34, 22.2.1984 (no violation), which concerned a similar type of situation but in which the judgment was published later in an official case-law report.

In the case *B. and P. v. the United Kingdom*, it was sufficient that anybody who had an interest in the matter could consult or obtain a copy of the judgment from the court's registry. The fact that judgments in cases of special interest were routinely published enabled the public to study the manner in which the courts generally approached such cases and the principles applied in deciding them.[1074] However, it is only natural that if the case has been examined *in camera*, the judgment should not be made public.

#### 4.3.3.4. *Exceptions in Cases Involving Security Reasons*

The Court has also accepted exceptions to public pronouncement for security reasons. In the case *Campbell and Fell v. the United Kingdom*, the Court accepted that a decision rendered in prison disciplinary proceedings did not have to be pronounced in the presence of the media or public on account of prison safety reasons. However, the Court found a violation on the ground that no alternative arrangements had been made for pronouncing the decision later.[1075] In some national security cases, such as those relating to terrorist activities, the Court has accepted a practice that only those parts of the judicial decisions are classified whose disclosure would compromise national security or the safety of others.[1076]

#### 4.3.3.5. *Waiver of the Right*

In its case-law the Court has not taken a stance on the question of whether an applicant can waive his right to the public pronouncement of a judgment.

## 4.4. REASONABLE LENGTH OF THE PROCEEDINGS

**Article 6: Right to a fair trial**

1. *... everyone is entitled to a ... hearing within a reasonable time ...*

According to Article 6 §1 of the Convention, everyone is entitled to a hearing within a reasonable time. The States are required to organise their judicial systems in such a way that their courts are able to guarantee everyone's right to a final decision within a reasonable time.[1077] The aim of the provision is to protect the

1074 *B. and P. v. the United Kingdom*, App. nos. 36337/97+, §47, 24.4.2001 (no violation).

1075 *Campbell and Fell v. the United Kingdom*, App. nos. 7819/77+, §92, 28.6.1984.

1076 *Raza v. Bulgaria*, App. no. 31465/08, §53, 11.2.2010; and *Fazliyski v. Bulgaria*, App. no. 40908/05, §69, 16.4.2013. See also Arman Zrvandyan, *Casebook on European Fair Trial Standards in Administrative Justice*, Council of Europe Publishing, Strasbourg 2016, pp. 119–120.

1077 *Zimmermann and Steiner v. Switzerland*, App. no. 8737/79, §29, 13.7.1983; *Comingersoll S.A. v. Portugal* [GC], App. no. 35382/97, §24, 6.4.2000; *Lupeni Greek Catholic Parish and Others v. Romania* [GC], App. no. 76943/11, §142, 29.11.2016; *Abdoella v. the Netherlands*, App. no. 12728/87, §24, 25.11.1992; and *Dobbertin v. France*, App. no. 13089/87, §44, 25.2.1993.

parties from proceedings of unreasonable length, as lengthy proceedings may put in danger the effectiveness and reliability of the application of the law.[1078] In criminal matters, the aim is to also avoid having the accused wait for a long time, uncertain about his or her fate.[1079]

The obligation to terminate the proceedings within a reasonable time applies to civil, criminal and administrative law proceedings. The reasonableness is assessed in the light of the circumstances of each case and there are no absolute time limits. The whole of the proceedings must be taken into account.[1080] While individual delays may not in themselves give rise to any issue, they may, when viewed together and cumulatively, result in a reasonable time being exceeded.[1081] On the other hand, a delay during a particular phase of the proceedings may be permissible, provided that the total duration of the proceedings is not excessive.[1082] Long periods during which the proceedings are stagnating without any valid reason are not acceptable.[1083] When assessing the reasonableness, three criteria are considered: (1) the complexity of the matter; (2) the conduct of the applicant and of the authorities; and (3) the importance of the matter to the applicant.[1084]

### 4.4.1. MEANS TO SEEK REDRESS FOR LENGTH OF PROCEEDINGS

In the case *Kudła v. Poland*, the Court ordered States to create an effective domestic remedy in order to prevent and compensate for excessively long

---

1078 *H. v. France*, App. no. 10073/82, §58, 24.10.1989; *Katte Klitsche de la Grange v. Italy*, App. no. 12539/86, §61, 27.10.1994; and *Scordino v. Italy (No. 1)* [GC], App. no. 36813/97, §224, 29.3.2006. See also Arman: Zrvandyan, *Casebook on European Fair Trial Standards in Administrative Justice*, Council of Europe Publishing, Strasbourg 2016, pp. 111–113.

1079 *Wemhoff v. Germany*, App. no. 2122/64, §18, 27.6.1968; and *Kart v. Turkey* [GC], App. no. 8917/05, §68, 3.12.2009.

1080 *König v. Germany*, App. no. 6232/73, §98, 28.6.1978; and *Boddaert v. Belgium*, App. no. 12919/87, §36, 12.10.1992. See also Arman Zrvandyan, *Casebook on European Fair Trial Standards in Administrative Justice*, Council of Europe Publishing, Strasbourg 2016, pp. 108–109.

1081 *Deumeland v. Germany*, App. no. 9384/81, §90, 29.5.1986; *Dobbertin v. France*, App. no. 13089/87, §44, 25.2.1993; and *Satakunnan Markkinapörssi Oy and Satamedia Oy v. Finland* [GC], App. no. 931/13, §§210–11, 27.6.2017.

1082 *Pretto and Others v. Italy*, App. no. 7984/77, §37, 8.12.1983.

1083 *Beaumartin v. France*, App. no. 15287/89, §33, 24.11.1994.

1084 *Comingersoll S.A. v. Portugal* [GC], App. no. 35382/97, §19, 6.4.2000; *Frydlender v. France* [GC], App. no. 30979/96, §43, 27.6.2000; *Sürmeli v. Germany* [GC], App. no. 75529/01, §128, 8.6.2006; *Nicolae Virgiliu Tănase v. Romania* [GC], App. no. 41720/13, §209, 25.6.2019; and *Lupeni Greek Catholic Parish and Others v. Romania* [GC], App. no. 76943/11, §143, 29.11.2016. See also Dragoljub Popović, *European Human Rights Law – A Manual: An Introduction to the Strasbourg Court and its Jurisprudence*, Eleven International Publishing, The Hague 2013, p. 199.

proceedings.[1085] The means to seek redress for lengthy proceedings and to provide an applicant with an effective remedy under Article 13 of the Convention are thus either preventive and concern the acceleration of the pending proceedings, or compensatory and concern the paying of compensation *ex post facto* for the excessive length. In many legal systems, both means coexist.[1086] In criminal cases also a mitigation of the sentence can be a means for compensating for any delays.

#### 4.4.1.1. *Acceleration of the Proceedings*

Acceleration of the pending proceedings was one issue in the case *Kuppinger v. Germany*, concerning the custody and visiting rights of a child, where the delays in the domestic proceedings made the applicant's rights under Article 8 illusory. The Court held that an order to accelerate the proceedings without any sanctions for failure to do so was not sufficient with a view to providing an effective remedy under Article 13 of the Convention.[1087] Acceleration of the proceedings can also be necessary in the context of other articles.[1088]

In some exceptional cases it may even be necessary to conclude overly long proceedings and to require that a ruling be rendered within a certain time limit. If this does not happen, it can constitute a violation of Article 13 of the Convention, unless the applicant is compensated for the excessive length. The Court has not considered the conclusion of the proceedings as the sole or even preferable option, since it may cause other fair trial problems. Normally the respondent States have the option to either prevent a prolonging of the proceedings by accelerating them or to compensate *ex post facto* for such delays.

#### 4.4.1.2. *Compensation for Lengthy Proceedings*

Compensation of excessively long proceedings is often a very effective way of providing a remedy. If there is a procedure to obtain compensation for excessively lengthy proceedings at the national level, the Court requires that such a domestic

1085 *Kudła v. Poland* [GC], App. no. 30210/96, §§157–160, 26.10.2000. The obligation was based on Article 13 of the Convention. See also Christoph Grabenwarter, "The right to effective remedy against excessive duration of proceedings", in Jürgen Bröhmer (Ed.), *The Protection of Human Rights at the Beginning of the 21st Century – Colloquium in Honour of Professor Dr. Dr. Dr. h.c. mult. Georg Ress on the Occasion of his 75th Birthday*, Nomos, Baden-Baden 2012, pp. 123–133.

1086 *Sürmeli v. Germany* [GC], App. no. 75529/01, §§99–100, 8.6.2006.

1087 *Kuppinger v. Germany*, App. no. 62198/11, §§140–141 and 145, 15.1.2015.

1088 For example, the case *McCaughey v. the United Kingdom*, App. no. 43098/09, §§144–145, 16.7.2013, concerned a complaint lodged under Article 2: the domestic investigation into several cases of homicide in Northern Ireland had not been swift, and in fact had lasted for more than 20 years. The Court requested that the proceedings were accelerated and that the Committee of Ministers supervise the execution of its order under Article 46 of the Convention.

remedy is used. For instance, for Finland, the Court found in the case *Ahlskog v. Finland* that the Compensation Act provided an effective remedy by means of compensation for excessive length in pending civil and criminal cases.[1089] Therefore, a follow-up case, *S.V. v. Finland*, was declared inadmissible as the applicant had failed to exhaust the domestic remedies by claiming compensation before a domestic court.[1090]

#### *4.4.1.3. Mitigation of Sentence*

Mitigation of a sentence can also be used as a means to remedy excessive length of the proceedings. For example, in the case *Jussi Uoti v. Finland*, the applicant's prison sentence was reduced by half as a result of the excessive length of the proceedings.[1091] In another case, the waiving of "day fines" imposed upon the applicant by way of mitigation of sentence was regarded as sufficient compensation for the extensive delay.[1092]

Compensation for excessive length by mitigating a sentence does require that the domestic judgment or decision clearly indicates what would have been the sentence had it not been mitigated because of the excessive length of proceedings.[1093] If the amount of compensation is not clearly stated in the domestic judgment or decision, the Court cannot assess whether the compensation is sufficient or not.

### 4.4.2. VICTIM STATUS AND EXHAUSTION OF DOMESTIC REMEDIES

The fact that charges have been dismissed against an applicant or that he has won his civil or administrative law case does not prevent him from being a victim in respect of the duration of the proceedings. Nor is it required that the domestic proceedings have already ended. The Court can examine a complaint about delay even if the domestic proceedings are still pending, if the length of the domestic proceedings is already such that it can no longer be regarded as reasonable.[1094]

An applicant cannot, however, claim to be a victim of excessive length of the proceedings if the domestic authorities have acknowledged the violation, either expressly or in substance, and then afforded him redress for the breach

[1089] *Ahlskog v. Finland* (dec.), App. no. 5238/07, 9.11.2010.
[1090] *S.V. v. Finland* (dec.), App. no. 66399/09, 24.1.2012.
[1091] *Jussi Uoti v. Finland* (dec.), App. no. 43180/04, 9.12.2008.
[1092] *Rautonen v. Finland* (dec.), App. no. 2613/09, 15.5.2012.
[1093] *Jussi Uoti v. Finland* (dec.), App. no. 43180/04, 9.12.2008; and *Danker v. Finland* (dec.), App. no. 39543/04, 9.12.2008.
[1094] *Sorvisto v. Finland*, App. no. 19348/04, §72, 13.1.2009.

of the Convention. This requires that the domestic courts acknowledge in a sufficiently clear manner the failure to observe the "reasonable time" requirement, and that they have afforded redress in an express and measurable manner.[1095]

An applicant is required to use effective domestic remedies and to seek compensation in the domestic system if the domestic legislation allows for it. Sometimes it may also be sufficient that there is a well-established domestic practice to award compensation for excessive delay. For example, in Finland, at a time when there was no provision in the legislation for compensation for the excessive length of a pretrial investigation, the well-established case-law to the effect that compensation could be claimed was considered to afford an effective remedy.[1096] The Court will not examine an application if the effective domestic remedies have not been exhausted.

### 4.4.3. PERIOD TO BE CONSIDERED

When assessing the excessive length of the proceedings, the period to be taken into account normally starts in civil matters from the bringing of the action.[1097] If a civil law compensation claim has been presented during the pretrial investigation of a criminal matter, the period starts running from that point in time even if the proceedings started later.[1098] Also, for example, in administrative law proceedings when an applicant must first seek rectification before being able to lodge a proper appeal, the period to be taken into account starts from the filing of the rectification request.[1099]

In criminal proceedings, the period to be taken into account may start (depending on the circumstances) when the applicant is interrogated for the first time,[1100] when a pretrial investigation has been initiated,[1101] when an interim

---

1095 *Eckle v. Germany*, App. no. 8130/78, §66, 15.7.1982. See also Dinah Shelton, "Subsidiarity and human rights law", *Human Rights Law Journal* (HRLJ), vol. 27, no. 1–4, 28 April 2006, pp. 4–11, at p. 8.

1096 *Åkerlund v. Finland* (dec.), App. no. 20998/13, §29, 27.1.2015. This case-law was subsequently incorporated into the Act on Compensation for Excessive Duration of Judicial Proceedings (Finland).

1097 *Poiss v. Austria*, App. no. 9816/82, §50, 23.4.1987; *Bock v. Germany*, App. no. 11118/84, §35, 29.3.1989; and *Petikon Oy and Parviainen v. Finland*, App. no. 26189/06, §27, 27.1.2009.

1098 *Nousiainen v. Finland*, App. no. 45952/08, §20, 23.2.2010.

1099 *König v. Germany*, App. no. 6232/73, §98, 28.6.1978; *X. v. France*, App. no. 18020/91, §31, 31.3.1992; *Schouten and Meldrum v. the Netherlands*, App. nos. 19005/91+, §62, 9.12.1994; *Kress v. France* [GC], App. no. 39594/98, §90, 7.6.2001; *Golder v. the United Kingdom*, App. no. 4451/70, §32, 21.2.1975; *Erkner and Hofauer v. Austria*, App. no. 9616/81, §64, 23.4.1987; *Vilho Eskelinen and Others v. Finland* [GC], App. no. 63235/00, §§65–66, 19.4.2007; and *Kalēja v. Latvia*, App. no. 22059/08, §40, 5.10.2017.

1100 *Eloranta v. Finland*, App. no. 4799/03, §27, 9.12.2008.

1101 *Ringeisen v. Austria*, App. no. 2614/65, §110, 16.7.1971; and *Šubinski v. Slovenia*, App. no. 19611/04, §§65–68, 18.1.2007.

measure is imposed upon him,[1102] when he is arrested or detained,[1103] when he is subject to a search of his domicile or some other search,[1104] when he has given a statement on the matter,[1105] or when he has been charged.[1106] The relevant moment is thus when the applicant became aware of the charge or when he or she was substantially affected by the measures taken in the context of the criminal investigation or proceedings.[1107]

If the case does not proceed further than the pretrial investigation phase because no charges are pressed as a result of a statute of limitations or some other reason, the period to be taken into account runs from the first time the suspect was interrogated until the point he was informed about the conclusion of the investigation.[1108] The period does not start running if the applicant is not aware of the above-mentioned measures imposed on him.[1109] If new charges or new counts are later introduced against the applicant, the period starts to run from the time the charges were brought.[1110] In taxation matters in which tax surcharges have been imposed and which therefore fall under the criminal limb of Article 6, the period to be taken into account starts from the time when the applicant was requested to comment on the tax inspection report, if that report mentions the tax surcharges.[1111]

In civil, criminal and administrative law matters, the period to be considered in assessing the length of the proceedings ends when the highest instance court gives a final judgment or decision.[1112] Often this date is the date of a supreme court decision or equivalent, marking the end of the ordinary appeal proceedings.[1113] Proceedings before a constitutional court are taken into consideration if its decision is capable of affecting the outcome of the dispute before the ordinary courts,[1114] but proceedings for a preliminary ruling from the Court of Justice of

---

1102 *T.K. and S.E. v. Finland*, App. no. 38581/97, §§8 and 25, 31.5.2005.

1103 *Wemhoff v. Germany*, App. no. 2122/64, §19, 27.6.1968; *Suuripää v. Finland*, App. no. 43151/02, §52, 12.1.2010; and *T.K. and S.E. v. Finland*, App. no. 38581/97, §§8 and 25, 31.5.2005.

1104 *Lehtonen v. Finland*, App. no. 11704/03, §18, 13.6.2006.

1105 *Jokitaipale and Others v. Finland*, App. no. 43349/05, §29, 6.4.2010.

1106 *Neumeister v. Austria*, App. no. 1936/63, §18, 27.6.1968.

1107 *Mamič v. Slovenia (No. 2)*, App. no. 75778/01, §§23–24, 27.7.2006; and *Liblik and Others v. Estonia*, App. nos. 173/15+, §94, 28.5.2019.

1108 *Vuori v. Finland* (dec.), App. no. 23263/08, 19.5.2009 (friendly settlement between the parties).

1109 *Guisset v. France*, App. no. 33933/96, §80, 26.9.2000; and *Etcheveste and Bidart v. France*, App. nos. 44797/98+, §§78–80, 21.3.2002.

1110 *Jesso v. Austria*, App. no. 9315/81, §56, 7.5.1986.

1111 *Kesko Oyj v. Finland* (dec.), App. no. 65611/09, §21, 25.9.2012.

1112 *König v. Germany*, App. no. 6232/73, §98, 28.6.1978; *Delcourt v. Belgium*, App. no. 2689/65, §§25–26, 17.1.1970; *V. v. the United Kingdom* [GC], App. no. 24888/94, §109, 16.12.1999; and *Neumeister v. Austria*, App. no. 1936/63, §19, 27.6.1968.

1113 *König v. Germany*, App. no. 6232/73, §98, 28.6.1978; *Poiss v. Austria*, App. no. 9816/82, §50, 23.4.1987; and *Robins v. the United Kingdom*, App. no. 22410/93, §§28–29, 23.9.1997.

1114 *Deumeland v. Germany*, App. no. 9384/81, §77, 29.5.1986; *Pammel v. Germany*, App. no. 17820/91, §§51–57, 1.7.1997; and *Süßmann v. Germany*, App. no. 20024/92, §39, 16.9.1996.

the European Union (CJEU) are not taken into consideration in the assessment of the length of time attributable to the domestic authorities.[1115] The end date is not necessarily the date when the applicant actually receives the final judgment or decision.[1116]

It should also be noted that the execution of a judgment, given by any court, is to be considered an integral part of the proceedings for the purposes of calculating the relevant period.[1117] Time does not thus stop running until the right asserted in the proceedings actually becomes effective.[1118] On the other hand, decisions to discontinue criminal proceedings, even with the possibility of resuming them at a later stage, mean that the subsequent period is not taken into consideration when calculating the length of the criminal proceedings. If a decision to discontinue criminal enquiries is made, the person ceases to be affected and is no longer suffering from any uncertainty.[1119] The person ceases to be so affected only from the moment that such a decision is communicated to the person concerned.[1120]

If a Contracting Party has acceded to the Convention during the domestic proceedings, only the time after its accession will be considered.[1121] On the other hand, the time before the accession may become relevant when assessing the reasonableness of the length.[1122] Normally, the duration relating to the use of extraordinary remedies is also excluded from the period to be counted, as Article 6 does not apply to extraordinary remedies. However, the Court has, in some exceptional cases, taken such time into consideration, especially when the matter has concerned a new set of proceedings that have started as a result of the reopening.[1123] In the assessment of the duration of proceedings, the Court also always considers at how many levels of jurisdiction the case has been examined and how many times.

---

1115 *Pafitis and Others v. Greece*, App. no. 20323/92, §95, 26.2.1998; and *Satakunnan Markkinapörssi Oy and Satamedia Oy v. Finland* [GC], App. no. 931/13, §208, 27.6.2017.

1116 See, for example, *Timo Landgren v. Finland*, App. no. 17889/07, §18, 10.11.2009; and *Vilho Eskelinen and Others v. Finland* [GC], App. no. 63235/00, §66, 19.4.2007. This is due to the fact that in some countries the final judgments and decisions are not served on applicants, meaning that it is not possible for the Court to verify when exactly they have in fact learned about the final judgment or decision. See *Suzi v. Finland* (dec.), App. no. 66697/10, 10.1.2012.

1117 *Martins Moreira v. Portugal*, App. no. 11371/85, §44, 26.10.1988; *Silva Pontes v. Portugal*, App. no. 14940/89, §33, 23.3.1994; *Di Pede v. Italy*, App. no. 15797/89, §24, 26.9.1996; and *Assanidze v. Georgia* [GC], App. no. 71503/01, §§181–183, 8.4.2004.

1118 *Estima Jorge v. Portugal*, App. no. 24550/94, §§36–38, 21.4.1998.

1119 *Nakhmanovich v. Russia*, App. no. 55669/00, §89, 2.3.2006.

1120 *Borzhonov v. Russia*, App. no. 18274/04, §38, 22.1.2009; and *Niedermeier v. Germany* (dec.), App. no. 37972/05, 3.2.2009.

1121 *Foti and Others v. Italy*, App. nos. 7604/76+, §53, 10.12.1982.

1122 *Foti and Others v. Italy*, App. nos. 7604/76+, §§62–63, 10.12.1982.

1123 For example, in the case *Toive Lehtinen v. Finland*, App. no. 43160/98, §38, 22.5.2007, the period considered included the time taken for the reopening and for the new proceedings thereafter.

Several separate proceedings may be so closely connected with each other that they are considered one set of proceedings for the purposes of assessing length. For example, in the case *Kukkola v. Finland*, the proceedings pertaining to the "activity prohibition", the expropriation and the compensation could be considered to be one set of proceedings for the purposes of Article 6 §1.[1124] On the other hand, if the applicant has already received compensation for the excessive length of the proceedings from the Court earlier and he complains again about the total length of the proceedings, the period to be taken into account only contains that part of the length for which the applicant has not yet been compensated.[1125]

### 4.4.4. COMPLEXITY OF THE MATTER

The complexity of a matter is a fact which may justifiably explain the excessive length of the proceedings. Several elements can contribute to the complexity of the case, such as the legal difficulties,[1126] lack of clarity of the facts or the domestic law,[1127] the large number of charges, accused and/or witnesses,[1128] the need to obtain expert statements[1129] or to use financial or accounting expertise,[1130] the international connections of the case,[1131] the scarcity of precedents at national level, or the need to seek a ruling from the CJEU on questions relating to the interpretation of European Union law.[1132] In addition, a large amount of written

1124 *Kukkola v. Finland*, App. no. 26890/95, §41, 15.11.2005. See also *Ekholm v. Finland*, App. no. 68050/01, §62, 24.7.2007.

1125 See, for example, *Kossila v. Finland* (dec.), App. no. 14161/03, 3.7.2007; and *Kossila v. Finland* (dec.), App. no. 37531/05, 6.1.2009.

1126 *Neumeister v. Austria*, App. no. 1936/63, 27.6.1968; *Tričković v. Slovenia*, App. no. 39914/98, §50, 12.6.2001; and *Aho v. Finland*, App. no. 2511/02, §49, 16.10.2007. In the case *Türkiye İş Bankasi v. Finland*, App. no. 30013/96, §31, 18.6.2002, the difficulty lay in the fact that the Finnish courts had to apply Turkish legislation to the case.

1127 *Triggiani v. Italy*, App. no. 13509/88, §17, 19.2.1991; *Horsti v. Finland*, App. no. 39509/08, §40, 10.11.2009; and *Lupeni Greek Catholic Parish and Others v. Romania* [GC], App. no. 76943/11, §150, 29.11.2016.

1128 *Angelucci v. Italy*, App. no. 12666/87, §15, 19.2.1991; *H. v. the United Kingdom*, App. no. 9580/81, §72, 8.7.1987; and *Mattila v. Finland*, App. no. 77138/01, §15, 23.5.2006.

1129 *Väänänen v. Finland*, App. no. 10736/03, §28, 20.2.2007; and *Nicolae Virgiliu Tănase v. Romania* [GC], App. no. 41720/13, §210, 25.6.2019.

1130 *C.P. and Others v. France*, App. no. 36009/97, §30, 1.8.2000.

1131 *Manzoni v. Italy*, App. no. 11804/85, §18, 19.2.1991; *Neumeister v. Austria*, App. no. 1936/63, §20, 27.6.1968; and *Knaster v. Finland*, App. no. 7790/05, §30, 22.9.2009.

1132 *Satakunnan Markkinapörssi Oy and Satamedia Oy v. Finland* [GC], App. no. 931/13, §212, 27.6.2017. See also Sofia Galani (Ed.), "Case and comment: selected decisions from the European Court of Human Rights from May and June 2017 – No journalistic protection for publication of personal taxation data, *Satakunnan Markkinapörssi Oy and Satamedia Oy v. Finland* (Application No. 73607/13)", *European Human Rights Law Review*, Issue 5, 2017, pp. 511–514.

materials[1133] or difficulties in execution[1134] may render a case complex. The economic importance of the case does not as such render it complex; only the facts of the case, the procedural issues and the legal questions have relevance.[1135]

The complexity of a case may allow some prolongation of the proceedings but it cannot be used to justify it indefinitely.[1136] In a complex case, a length of 6 to 8 years could still be within the allowed limits, but 16 or 25 years would not be.[1137]

## 4.4.5. APPLICANT'S CONDUCT

The respondent State is not responsible for the length of the proceedings if this delay is due to the applicant. For example, an applicant who is hiding from justice or is otherwise passive in the proceedings cannot complain about the length of the proceedings if the proceedings are delayed for this reason.[1138] For example, in the case *Ahlskog v. Finland*, the delays caused by the applicant's repetitive biased complaints and his requests for postponement were not attributable to the State.[1139] Nor was the State culpable when the applicants in another case constantly brought new actions and complaints over the course of two years.[1140] Frequent or repeated changes of counsel may also have the same effect.[1141]

However, it cannot be held against the applicant if he has used all possible remedies available to him under the domestic legislation,[1142] or if the delays

1133 *Humen v. Poland* [GC], App. no. 26614/95, §63, 15.10.1999; *Uoti v. Finland*, App. no. 61222/00, §39, 9.1.2007; *T.K. and S.E. v. Finland*, App. no. 38581/97, §29, 31.5.2005; and *Hagert v. Finland*, App. no. 14724/02, §29, 17.1.2006.

1134 *Nuutinen v. Finland*, App. no. 32842/96, §111, 27.6.2000.

1135 *Pélissier and Sassi v. France* [GC], App. no. 25444/94, §71, 25.3.1999; *Katte Klitsche de la Grange v. Italy*, App. no. 12539/86, §55, 27.10.1994; and *Papachelas v. Greece* [GC], App. no. 31423/96, §39, 25.3.1999. See also Karen Reid, *A Practitioner's Guide to the European Convention on Human Rights*, Sweet & Maxwell/Thomson Reuters, London 2019, p. 282.

1136 *Tierce v. San Marino*, App. no. 69700/01, §31, 17.6.2003; *Adiletta and Others v. Italy*, App. nos. 13978/88+, §17, 19.2.1991; and *Rutkowski and Others v. Poland*, App. no. 72287/10, §137, 7.7.2015.

1137 *Boddaert v. Belgium*, App. no. 12919/87, 12.10.1992; *C.P. and Others v. France*, App. no. 36009/97, 1.8.2000; *Katte Klitsche de la Grange v. Italy*, App. no. 12539/86, §62, 27.10.1994; *Ferrantelli and Santangelo v. Italy*, App. no. 19874/92, 7.8.1996; and *Cipolletta v. Italy*, App. no. 38259/09, §44, 11.1.2018.

1138 *Erdoğan v. Turkey* (dec.), App. no. 14723/89, 9.7.1992; and *Vayiç v. Turkey*, App. no. 18078/02, §44, 20.6.2006.

1139 *Ahlskog v. Finland* (dec.), App. no. 8118/07, 6.10.2009. However, the Court found a violation in respect of the other party to the proceedings, as the delays could not be regarded as being attributable to him; see *Rafael Ahlskog v. Finland*, App. no. 23667/06, §§22 and 24, 13.11.2008.

1140 *Andria Oy and Karanko v. Finland*, App. no. 61557/00, §27, 17.7.2007 (no violation). See also *Pereira da Silva v. Portugal*, App. no. 77050/11, §§76–79, 22.3.2016.

1141 *König v. Germany*, App. no. 6232/73, §103, 28.6.1978.

1142 *Eckle v. Germany*, App. no. 8130/78, §82, 15.7.1982; *C.P. and Others v. France*, App. no. 36009/97, §31, 1.8.2000; and *Erkner and Hofauer v. Austria*, App. no. 9616/81, §68, 23.4.1987. See also the case *Timo Landgren v. Finland*, App. no. 17889/07, §24, 10.11.2009, in which the

are linked to his medical condition.[1143] Nor, in criminal matters, has the accused an obligation to actively contribute to the authorities' activities which may lead to his conviction. Still, his conduct may be considered an objective factor not necessarily attributable to the respondent State.[1144] For example in the case *Eckle v. Germany*, although the applicants delayed the proceedings by filing new actions and complaints, the Court still held that the main reason for the excessive length of proceedings was the authorities' conduct.[1145] In the case *Barfuss v. the Czech Republic*, the Court considered that the applicant had changed tactics by bringing in new facts that he had not mentioned during the pretrial investigation.[1146] In the case *Debbasch v. France*, the Court found that the applicant's excessively long letters of appeal had significantly contributed to the total length of the proceedings.[1147] In the case *Humen v. Poland*, the applicant's failure to submit himself to a tomography examination of the brain – which was necessary to properly determine what injuries had been sustained by him for which he claimed compensation – and his inaccurate account of certain facts were held against him.[1148]

It is normally held for the applicant's benefit when the applicant asks for the acceleration of the proceedings. However, such a request may not be necessary if it is known that it is bound to fail and would thus have no relevance in the matter.[1149] Small delays are not normally relevant, unless they can be regarded as having significant relevance to the overall length of the proceedings.[1150]

Although the parties to civil proceedings are normally equally responsible for the progress of the proceedings, this does not exempt the domestic courts from their obligation under Article 6 to conclude the proceedings within a reasonable time.[1151] The applicant's obligations are to simply fulfil the procedural

---

additional pretrial investigation requested by the applicant did not prolong the length of the pretrial investigation as it was still pending. It could not be held against the applicant that he had made full use of the various procedures available to pursue his defence.

1143 *Nicolae Virgiliu Tănase v. Romania* [GC], App. no. 41720/13, §211, 25.6.2019.

1144 *Poiss v. Austria*, App. no. 9816/82, §57, 23.4.1987; *Wiesinger v. Austria*, App. no. 11796/85, §57, 30.10.1991; and *Humen v. Poland* [GC], App. no. 26614/95, §66, 15.10.1999.

1145 *Eckle v. Germany*, App. no. 8130/78, §82, 15.7.1982. See also Dinah Shelton, "Subsidiarity and human rights law", *Human Rights Law Journal* (HRLJ), vol. 27, no. 1–4, 28 April 2006, pp. 4–11, at p. 8.

1146 *Barfuss v. the Czech Republic*, App. no. 35848/97, §74, 31.7.2000.

1147 *Debbasch v. France*, App. no. 49392/99, §41, 3.12.2002.

1148 *Humen v. Poland* [GC], App. no. 26614/95, §66, 15.10.1999.

1149 See *Ceteroni v. Italy*, App. no. 22461/93, §24, 15.11.1996, in which the domestic judge had granted all requested postponements and in which the Court held that the applicant's requests for acceleration would not have had any relevance since they were bound to fail; and the case *Pedersen and Baadsgaard v. Denmark* [GC], App. no. 49017/99, §49, 17.12.2004, in which the fact that the applicants had not opposed the postponement was interpreted as meaning they had contributed to a certain extent to the excessive length of the proceedings.

1150 *Kudła v. Poland* [GC], App. no. 30210/96, §130, 26.10.2000.

1151 *Unión Alimentaria Sanders S.A. v. Spain*, App. no. 11681/85, §35, 7.7.1989; and *Mincheva v. Bulgaria*, App. no. 21558/03, §68, 2.9.2010.

obligations imposed on him, to refrain from using any delaying tactics and to rely on all means provided by domestic law for shortening the length of the proceedings.[1152] The State is not responsible in *civil* matters for a delay caused by the applicant's lawyer. Although the counsel may have been appointed or ordered by the State, he or she does not act on the State's behalf but on his or her client's behalf.[1153] Nor is the respondent State responsible for delays caused by a defendant in a civil matter.[1154]

## 4.4.6. CONDUCT OF THE AUTHORITIES

The respondent State is responsible for the delays caused by its judicial or administrative authorities.[1155] Only delays attributable to the State may justify a finding of failure to comply with the "reasonable time" requirement.[1156] In criminal matters the Court has found a violation, for example, when the pretrial investigation has been delayed,[1157] when there have been difficulties in summonsing,[1158] when there have been delays in appointing a judge[1159] or delays caused by experts,[1160] or when the service of the judgments has been slow.[1161] In civil and administrative law matters, excessive length may be caused

---

1152 *Unión Alimentaria Sanders S.A. v. Spain*, App. no. 11681/85, §35, 7.7.1989; *I.A. v. France*, App. no. 28213/95, §121, 23.9.1998; and *Sociedade de Construções Martins & Vieira, Lda. and Others v. Portugal*, App. nos. 56637/10+, §48, 30.10.2014. See also the case *Lammi v. Finland*, App. no. 53835/00, §33, 15.11.2005 (no violation), in which the Court found that the applicant had, through his conduct, delayed the proceedings considerably by requesting several postponements, applying several times to reopen the case and by lodging unfounded, biased claims. In addition, he no longer resided at the official address he had given for contacting him. A lack of promptness by the parties in filing their submissions may also contribute decisively to the slowing-down of the proceedings, see *Vernillo v. France*, App. no. 11889/85, §34, 20.2.1991.

1153 *H. v. France*, App. no. 10073/82, §55, 24.10.1989. By contrast, in *criminal* matters, the respondent State has an obligation under Article 6 §3 (c) to offer effective legal assistance.

1154 *Bock v. Germany*, App. no. 11118/84, §41, 29.3.1989.

1155 *Martins Moreira v. Portugal*, App. no. 11371/85, §60, 26.10.1988.

1156 *Buchholz v. Germany*, App. no. 7759/77, §49, 6.5.1981; *Papageorgiou v. Greece*, App. no. 24628/94, §40, 22.10.1997; and *Humen v. Poland* [GC], App. no. 26614/95, §66, 15.10.1999.

1157 *Eckle v. Germany*, App. no. 8130/78, §84, 15.7.1982.

1158 See, for example, *Petroff v. Finland*, App. no. 31021/06, §23, 3.11.2009 (summonsing of the accused); and *Nieminen v. Finland*, App. no. 16385/07, §§25–26, 3.11.2009 (summonsing of a witness).

1159 *Georgiadis v. Cyprus*, App. no. 50516/99, §46, 14.5.2002.

1160 *Rawa v. Poland*, App. no. 38804/97, §51, 14.1.2003. See also *T. and Others v. Finland*, App. no. 27744/95, §65, 13.12.2005, in which the obtaining of an expert statement delayed the case concerning a child, which should have been dealt with with due diligence.

1161 *Eckle v. Germany*, App. no. 8130/78, §84, 15.7.1982. See also Dinah Shelton, "Subsidiarity and human rights law", *Human Rights Law Journal* (HRLJ), vol. 27, no. 1–4, 28 April 2006, pp. 4–11, at p. 8.

by delays in performance of procedural acts of a purely routine character[1162] or by the organising of an oral hearing,[1163] by delays in admission of evidence by the State,[1164] by an adjournment of the proceedings pending the outcome of other proceedings,[1165] or by deficiencies in the co-ordination between the authorities.[1166]

Although a domestic legal system is mainly based on the parties' own procedural initiative, the domestic courts are still under a duty to ensure that the proceedings run with sufficient speed.[1167] They thus bear the responsibility for the non-attendance of the relevant participants – such as witnesses, co-accused, and representatives – as a result of which the proceedings have to be postponed.[1168] On the other hand, domestic courts cannot be faulted for a substantial delay in the proceeding caused by an applicant's state of health.[1169] In extreme cases, the passivity of the domestic courts puts the credibility of the whole legal system at stake.[1170]

States are under an obligation to organise their legal systems and to give resources to them in such a way that the domestic courts are able to examine cases within a reasonable time.[1171] The State cannot rely on administrative difficulties or case backlogs as an excuse for excessive delay,[1172] since they have an obligation to organise their legal systems in such a manner that the domestic courts are able to fulfil their obligations under the Convention.[1173] For example, repeated changes of judges cannot absolve the State from its obligations regarding the reasonable-time requirement.[1174] Temporary case backlogs in the courts are not relevant if this issue is being quickly tackled.[1175] If the backlog situation is more

1162 *Guincho v. Portugal*, App. no. 8990/80, §36, 10.7.1984.

1163 *König v. Germany*, App. no. 6232/73, §104, 28.6.1978.

1164 *H. v. the United Kingdom*, App. no. 9580/81, §81, 8.7.1987.

1165 *König v. Germany*, App. no. 6232/73, §110, 28.6.1978.

1166 *Wiesinger v. Austria*, App. no. 11796/85, §62, 30.10.1991.

1167 *Pafitis and Others v. Greece*, App. no. 20323/92, §93, 26.2.1998; *Tierce v. San Marino*, App. no. 69700/01, §31, 17.6.2003; *Capuano v. Italy*, App. no. 9381/81, §§30–31, 25.6.1987; *Versini v. France*, App. no. 40096/98, §29, 10.7.2001; and *Sürmeli v. Germany* [GC], App. no. 75529/01, §129, 8.6.2006.

1168 *Tychko v. Russia*, App. no. 56097/07, §68, 11.6.2015.

1169 *Yaikov v. Russia*, App. no. 39317/05, §76, 18.6.2015.

1170 See, for example, *Berlin v. Luxembourg*, App. no. 44978/98, §59, 15.7.2003, in which the contentious divorce proceedings lasted for 17 years.

1171 *Zimmermann and Steiner v. Switzerland*, App. no. 8737/79, §29, 13.7.1983.

1172 *Probstmeier v. Germany*, App. no. 20950/92, §64, 1.7.1997; *Vocaturo v. Italy*, App. no. 11891/85, §17, 24.5.1991; *Cappello v. Italy*, App. no. 12783/87, §17, 27.2.1992; *Unión Alimentaria Sanders S.A. v. Spain*, App. no. 11681/85, §40, 7.7.1989; *Milasi v. Italy*, App. no. 10527/83, §18, 25.6.1987; *Baggetta v. Italy*, App. no. 10256/83, §23, 25.6.1987; and *Eckle v. Germany*, App. no. 8130/78, §92, 15.7.1982.

1173 *Pélissier and Sassi v. France* [GC], App. no. 25444/94, §74, 25.3.1999.

1174 *Lechner and Hess v. Austria*, App. no. 9316/81, §58, 23.4.1987.

1175 *Buchholz v. Germany*, App. no. 7759/77, §61, 6.5.1981, in which the recession had created a case backlog in the labour courts. The Court did not find a violation in the case as the domestic authorities were aware of their responsibility and had taken measures in that respect.

long-term or requires structural reorganisation, or if temporary measures – such as, for example, prioritisation of certain cases – no longer have sufficient effect, the Member State must take effective measures in order to resolve the problem. For example, in the case *Zimmermann and Steiner v. Switzerland*, the Court held that the number of backlogged cases had grown progressively worse, and therefore the problem could no longer be regarded as temporary but rather as structural, which required more drastic measures from the authorities. As the case in issue had remained stationary for more than three and a half years, the Court found a violation in respect of the excessive length of the proceedings.[1176]

Domestic courts are under an obligation to examine cases carefully.[1177] Therefore, certain weight may be given to courts' decisions, for example, to admit evidence or to join or postpone cases pending the outcome of an important precedent case.[1178] Things that are not in the control of the authorities cannot be attributed to them if they have done everything within their powers to accelerate the proceedings.[1179] The Court has, for example, declined to take into account the time taken for requesting a preliminary ruling from the Court of Justice of the European Union. Although such a request may sometimes take a long time, taking into account that time would adversely affect the EU preliminary ruling system and work against the aim it is pursuing.[1180] Similarly, for example in the case *Väänänen v. Finland*, in which the District Court phase lasted for about seven years, the delay of about three years was not wholly attributable to the State, as for part of this time the case had been adjourned for obtaining witness statements from abroad.[1181]

One important element is also whether the government can provide an acceptable explanation for the delay.[1182] For example, in the case *Jaanti v. Finland*, the Court held that the government had not given an acceptable explanation as to why the Court of Appeal phase of the case lasted for more than two and a half years, i.e. more than a year longer than the District Court phase.[1183] Sometimes the Court has not found a violation despite an excessive length if there has been constant progress in the domestic proceedings.[1184] Similarly, even lengthy passivity by the authorities may be acceptable, provided that the total length of the proceedings is still within reasonable bounds.[1185]

---

1176 *Zimmermann and Steiner v. Switzerland*, App. no. 8737/79, §§31–32, 13.7.1983. See also *Guincho v. Portugal*, App. no. 8990/80, §40, 10.7.1984.

1177 *Von Maltzan and Others v. Germany* (dec.) [GC], App. nos. 71916/01+, §132, 2.3.2005.

1178 *Boddaert v. Belgium*, App. no. 12919/87, §39, 12.10.1992.

1179 *Włoch v. Poland*, App. no. 27785/95, §§149–150, 19.10.2000.

1180 *Pafitis and Others v. Greece*, App. no. 20323/92, §95, 26.2.1998.

1181 *Väänänen v. Finland*, App. no. 10736/03, §29, 20.2.2007.

1182 *Barfuss v. the Czech Republic*, App. no. 35848/97, §83, 31.7.2000.

1183 *Jaanti v. Finland*, App. no. 39105/05, §18, 24.2.2009. See also *Lappalainen v. Finland*, App. no. 22175/06, §18, 3.11.2009; and *Timo Landgren v. Finland*, App. no. 17889/07, §26, 10.11.2009.

1184 *Humen v. Poland* [GC], App. no. 26614/95, §69, 15.10.1999.

1185 *Nuutinen v. Finland*, App. no. 32842/96, §110, 27.6.2000.

## 4.4.7. IMPORTANCE OF THE MATTER TO THE APPLICANT

When assessing the reasonableness of the delays, the importance of the matter to the applicant must also be taken into account. In certain situations, the lapse in time has relevance to the merits of the case. In these cases, it can be expected that the authorities act with particular rapidity or that they exercise what is known as due or special diligence. These types of cases can include, for example, those concerning the taking into public care, the custody of and the contact rights of children,[1186] and cases concerning the civic status of the applicants.[1187] Due diligence is also required in cases concerning subsistence, that is, in cases concerning employment,[1188] salary, social security benefits[1189] or pensions.[1190] Cases relating to an applicant's health,[1191] advanced age,[1192] reputation,[1193] the right to education,[1194] or complaints relating to alleged violence by police officers also require due diligence.[1195]

It is normally expected that criminal proceedings are conducted more swiftly than civil or administrative law proceedings.[1196] Particular urgency is required in cases that are being re-examined.[1197] Also, cases in which the accused is detained must be examined urgently.[1198] This is due to the fact that in such

1186 *Hokkanen v. Finland*, App. no. 19823/92, §72, 23.9.1994; *Ignaccolo-Zenide v. Romania*, App. no. 31679/96, §102, 25.1.2000; *Niederböster v. Germany*, App. no. 39547/98, §39, 27.2.2003; *Tsikakis v. Germany*, App. no. 1521/06, §§64 and 68, 10.2.2011; *Paulsen-Medalen and Svensson v. Sweden*, App. no. 16817/90, §39, 19.2.1998; and *Laino v. Italy* [GC], App. no. 33158/96, §22, 18.2.1999.

1187 *Sylvester v. Austria (No. 2)*, App. no. 54640/00, §32, 3.2.2005; *Bock v. Germany*, App. no. 11118/84, §49, 29.3.1989; *Laino v. Italy* [GC], App. no. 33158/96, §18, 18.2.1999; and *Mikulić v. Croatia*, App. no. 53176/99, §44, 7.2.2002.

1188 *Buchholz v. Germany*, App. no. 7759/77, §52, 6.5.1981; *Launikari v. Finland*, App. no. 34120/96, §36, 5.10.2000; and *Eastaway v. the United Kingdom*, App. no. 74976/01, §52, 20.7.2004; *Vocaturo v. Italy*, App. no. 11891/85, §17, 24.5.1991; *Ruotolo v. Italy*, App. no. 12460/86, §17, 27.2.1992; and *Frydlender v. France* [GC], App. no. 30979/96, §45, 27.6.2000.

1189 In the case *Rangdell v. Finland*, App. no. 23172/08, §33, 19.1.2010, the Court did not require particular swiftness as the applicant's livelihood had been secured through a disability pension.

1190 *Nibbio v. Italy*, App. no. 12854/87, §18, 26.2.1992; *Borgese v. Italy*, App. no. 12870/87, §18, 26.2.1992; *Mocié v. France*, App. no. 46096/99, §22, 8.4.2003 (disability pension); and *Kukkonen v. Finland (No. 2)*, App. no. 47628/06, §32, 13.1.2009 (disability pension).

1191 *Bock v. Germany*, App. no. 11118/84, §38, 29.3.1989; *X. v. France*, App. no. 18020/91, §47, 31.3.1992; *A. and Others v. Denmark*, App. no. 20826/92, §78, 8.2.1996; *Pailot v. France*, App. no. 32217/96, §68, 22.4.1998; and *Gheorghe v. Romania*, App. no. 19215/04, §50, 15.3.2007.

1192 *Codarcea v. Romania*, App. no. 31675/04, §89, 2.6.2009.

1193 *Pieniążek v. Poland*, App. no. 62179/00, §28, 28.9.2004.

1194 *Oršuš and Others v. Croatia* [GC], App. no. 15766/03, §109, 16.3.2010.

1195 *Caloc v. France*, App. no. 33951/96, §120, 20.7.2000.

1196 *Baggetta v. Italy*, App. no. 10256/83, §24, 25.6.1987.

1197 *Henworth v. the United Kingdom*, App. no. 515/02, §29, 2.11.2004.

1198 *Abdoella v. the Netherlands*, App. no. 12728/87, §24, 25.11.1992; and *Starokadomskiy v. Russia (No. 2)*, App. no. 42239/02, §§70–71, 31.7.2008.

cases the requirements of Article 5 §3 (right to be brought promptly before a judge and right to a trial within a reasonable time) also apply to the applicant, requiring especial speed. The applicability of Article 5 ends, however, on the conviction of the accused. If the applicant is still detained after the conviction, the Article 6 §1 requirements protect him against the excessive length of the proceedings.[1199] The fact that the applicant is a public figure and that the case has attracted significant media attention does not, in itself, warrant a ruling that the case merits priority treatment.[1200]

### 4.4.8. REASONABLENESS OF THE LENGTH OF THE PROCEEDINGS

The reasonableness of the length of the proceedings is not a matter for the domestic courts to decide upon within their margin of appreciation; rather the Court makes its own assessment of it by using the criteria enumerated above in sections 4.4.4. to 4.4.7.[1201] This assessment is also dependent on the number of levels of jurisdiction at which the matter has been examined. If the overall length is within reasonable bounds, the Court does not normally find a violation even if at certain stages of the proceedings there have been delays or passivity.[1202] Normally, it is expected that there is a good reason and explanation for the delays.[1203] On the other hand, if the overall length is longer than the time the Court considers reasonable, the overall length would indicate that there has been a violation of Article 6 §1.[1204]

## 4.5. INDEPENDENT AND IMPARTIAL TRIBUNAL ESTABLISHED BY LAW

**Article 6: Right to a fair trial**

1. *... everyone is entitled to a ... hearing ... by an independent and impartial tribunal established by law.*

The right to a fair trial requires that the matter is examined by an independent and impartial tribunal established by law. This requirement applies to criminal and to civil and administrative law proceedings. The requirements of independence and impartiality are often closely connected. A court or tribunal

---

1199 *B. v. Austria*, App. no. 11968/86, 28.3.1990.
1200 *Liblik and Others v. Estonia*, App. nos. 173/15+, §103, 28.5.2019.
1201 *Casciaroli v. Italy*, App. no. 11973/86, §18, 27.2.1992, in which the Court disagreed with the respondent State as to the complexity of the case.
1202 See, for example, *Pretto and Others v. Italy*, App. no. 7984/77, §37, 8.12.1983.
1203 *Nousiainen v. Finland*, App. no. 45952/08, §27, 23.2.2010.
1204 *Comingersoll S.A. v. Portugal* [GC], App. no. 35382/97, §23, 6.4.2000.

that is not independent is unlikely to be impartial either. For this reason, the Court often examines both requirements at the same time and uses the same reasoning.[1205]

### 4.5.1. DEFINITION OF A TRIBUNAL

A tribunal is a body which is competent to give legally binding rulings.[1206] It is not sufficient that it is only competent to give recommendations or advice.[1207] Rulings of a tribunal cannot be changed by any non-judicial body.[1208] An authority which is not classified as one of the courts of a State may nonetheless, for the purposes of Article 6 §1, come within the concept of a "tribunal" in the substantive sense of the term.[1209] A tribunal may also be set up to deal with specific issues outside the ordinary court system, provided that it has both substantive and procedural guarantees in place.[1210]

Although a court or a tribunal normally consists of professional judges, this is not an absolute requirement.[1211] In many national legal systems, the composition of a court also includes lay members. In many countries lay judges are chosen by political bodies, as was the case in *Haarde v. Iceland*.[1212] Civil servants can be members of administrative courts,[1213] and personnel of armed forces, members of disciplinary[1214] or criminal[1215] courts. Also, the fact that the interests of both

---

1205 See, for example, *Cooper v. the United Kingdom* [GC], App. no. 48843/99, §104, 16.12.2003; *Ramos Nunes de Carvalho e Sá v. Portugal* [GC], App. nos. 55391/13+, §§150 and 152, 6.11.2018; and *Findlay v. the United Kingdom*, App. no. 22107/93, §73, 25.2.1997.

1206 *Van de Hurk v. the Netherlands*, App. no. 16034/90, §45, 19.4.1994.

1207 *Benthem v. the Netherlands*, App. no. 8848/80, §§40 and 43, 23.10.1985.

1208 *Cooper v. the United Kingdom* [GC], App. no. 48843/99, §106, 16.12.2003; and *Van de Hurk v. the Netherlands*, App. no. 16034/90, §45, 19.4.1994.

1209 *Sramek v. Austria*, App. no. 8790/79, §36, 22.10.1984 (regional real-property transactions authority); and *Mutu and Pechstein v. Switzerland*, App. nos. 40575/10+, §139, 2.10.2018 (the Court of Arbitration for Sport). See also Karen Reid, *A Practitioner's Guide to the European Convention on Human Rights*, Sweet & Maxwell/Thomson Reuters, London 2019, p. 214.

1210 *Rolf Gustafson v. Sweden*, App. no. 23196/94, §45, 1.7.1997 (criminal damage compensation board); *Argyrou and Others v. Greece*, App. no. 10468/04, §27, 15.1.2009 (forestry disputes resolution committee); and *Lithgow and Others v. the United Kingdom*, App. nos. 9006/80+, §201, 8.7.1986 (arbitration tribunal).

1211 The fact that the members of a body are required to have a law degree is normally a strong indication that a court or a tribunal is independent. See *Le Compte, Van Leuven and De Meyere v. Belgium*, App. nos. 6878/75+, §57, 23.6.1981.

1212 *Haarde v. Iceland*, App. no. 66847/12, §§104–105, 23.11.2017.

1213 *Ettl and Others v. Austria*, App. no. 9273/81, §38, 23.4.1987.

1214 *Engel and Others v. the Netherlands*, App. nos. 5100/71+, §89, 8.6.1976.

1215 *Cooper v. the United Kingdom* [GC], App. no. 48843/99, §110, 16.12.2003. However, in *Mikhno v. Ukraine*, App. no. 32514/12, §§162–165, 1.9.2016, the Court noted a tendency in international human rights law to urge States to act with caution in using military courts

employers and of employees may be represented in the composition of a court cannot be considered to be contrary to Article 6 §1.[1216]

The fact that a body also has other, for example, administrative or legislative functions does not prevent it from being considered a court or a tribunal when it exercises its judicial functions.[1217] It is, however, to be noted that if a body has no judicial function, it cannot be considered a court or tribunal and, consequently, Article 6 is not applicable to the proceedings conducted before such a body. Decisions of such administrative authorities should be subject to subsequent control by a judicial body that has full jurisdiction.[1218] For example, conferring the responsibility for prosecution and punishment of minor "criminal" offences on administrative authorities is not inconsistent with the Convention, provided that the person concerned is enabled to take any decision made against him before a tribunal that does offer the guarantees of Article 6.[1219]

For the purposes of Article 6 §1 of the Convention, a tribunal having full jurisdiction means that it must have jurisdiction to examine all questions of fact and law relevant to the dispute before it, that is, to provide sufficient review and not to abandon any of the elements of its judicial function.[1220] It must also have the power to quash the impugned decision and to either take a fresh decision itself or remit the case for rehearing by the same or a different body.[1221]

---

and, in particular, to exclude from their jurisdiction the determination of charges concerning serious human rights violations, such as extrajudicial executions, enforced disappearances and torture. In the Court's view, an accident at a military airshow causing very serious but unintentional damage did not qualify as such.

1216 *Siglfirðingur ehf v. Iceland* (dec.), App. no. 34142/96, 7.9.1999; and *Stojakovic v. Austria*, App. no. 30003/02, §48, 9.11.2006. In the case *Le Compte, Van Leuven and De Meyere v. Belgium*, App. nos. 6878/75+, §57, 23.6.1981, there was no problem when the composition of a disciplinary board was partly composed of lawyers and partly of medical doctors. However, in this respect there may arise suspicions about the objective independence and impartiality of the court. See *Sramek v. Austria*, App. no. 8790/79, §38, 22.10.1984.

1217 *Campbell and Fell v. the United Kingdom*, App. nos. 7819/77+, §§33 and 81, 28.6.1984; *H. v. Belgium*, App. no. 8950/80, §50, 30.11.1987; and *Demicoli v. Malta*, App. no. 13057/87, §§40–41, 27.8.1991.

1218 *Ortenberg v. Austria*, App. no. 12884/87, §31, 25.11.1994.

1219 *Öztürk v. Germany* [GC], App. no. 22479/93, §56, 28.9.1999; *A. Menarini Diagnostics S.R.L. v. Italy*, App. no. 43509/08, 27.9.2011; and *Flisar v. Slovenia*, App. no. 3127/09, §33, 29.9.2011.

1220 *Ramos Nunes de Carvalho e Sá v. Portugal* [GC], App. nos. 55391/13+, §§176–177, 6.11.2018; *Sigma Radio Television Ltd v. Cyprus*, App. nos. 32181/04+, §152, 21.7.2011; *Terra Woningen B.V. v. the Netherlands*, App. no. 20641/92, §52, 17.12.1996; and *Chevrol v. France*, App. no. 49636/99, §63, 13.2.2003.

1221 *Kingsley v. the United Kingdom* [GC], App. no. 35605/97, §§32 and 34, 28.5.2002; *Ramos Nunes de Carvalho e Sá v. Portugal* [GC], App. nos. 55391/13+, §184, 6.11.2018; *Schmautzer v. Austria*, App. no. 15523/89, §36, 23.10.1995; *Gradinger v. Austria*, App. no. 15963/90, §44, 23.10.1995; and *Grande Stevens and Others v. Italy*, App. nos. 18640/10+, §139, 4.3.2014. See also Chapter 2, section 2.5. above.

## 4.5.2. INDEPENDENT TRIBUNAL

An independent tribunal is defined as a court or tribunal that is independent from the executive powers[1222] and from the parties to the proceedings.[1223] Independence also means independence from the legislative powers, that is, from the national parliament.[1224] A minister of a government is not free from executive powers and therefore a decision taken by a minister does not fulfil the requirements of Article 6.[1225]

When assessing the independence of a court or a tribunal, the Court takes into account the manner of appointing of its members and the duration of their term, the existence of legal guarantees against outside influence and whether the body in question appears to be independent of the other bodies.[1226]

### *4.5.2.1. Manner of Appointment and Duration of Term*

It is acceptable from the Article 6 point of view that members of a court are appointed by the executive powers, provided that the appointees are free from influence or pressure when carrying out their adjudicatory role.[1227] In practice this is also very common.[1228] Appointments by a parliament are also acceptable.[1229] In *Pabla Ky v. Finland*, the fact that one of the expert members of the Court of Appeal, comprising mainly professional judges, was also a member of Parliament did not *per se* breach the right to an independent and impartial tribunal.[1230] On the other hand, it may be problematic if a substitute judge is

---

1222 *Sovtransavto Holding v. Ukraine*, App. no. 48553/99, §80, 25.7.2002; and *Mosteanu and Others v. Romania*, App. no. 33176/96, §42, 26.11.2002.

1223 *Ringeisen v. Austria*, App. no. 2614/65, §95, 16.7.1971; *Sramek v. Austria*, App. no. 8790/79, §42, 22.10.1984; and *Ninn-Hansen v. Denmark* (dec.), App. no. 28972/95, 18.5.1999. See also Arman Zrvandyan, *Casebook on European Fair Trial Standards in Administrative Justice*, Council of Europe Publishing, Strasbourg 2016, pp. 44–46.

1224 *Crociani and Others v. Italy*, App. nos. 8603/79+, 18.12.1980.

1225 *Benthem v. the Netherlands*, App. no. 8848/80, §43, 23.10.1985.

1226 *Campbell and Fell v. the United Kingdom*, App. nos. 7819/77+, §78, 28.6.1984.

1227 *Flux v. Moldova (No. 2)*, App. no. 31001/03, §27, 3.7.2007; *Majorana v. Italy* (dec.), App. no. 75117/01, 26.5.2005 concerning the appointment of judges of the Council of Administrative Law; and *Zolotas v. Greece*, App. no. 38240/02, §24, 2.6.2005, which concerned the appointment of the President of the Court of Cassation.

1228 *Campbell and Fell v. the United Kingdom*, App. nos. 7819/77+, §79, 28.6.1984; *Belilos v. Switzerland*, App. no. 10328/83, §66, 29.4.1988; *Asadov and Others v. Azerbaijan* (dec.), App. no. 138/03, 12.1.2006; and *Haarde v. Iceland*, App. no. 66847/12, §§105–107, 23.11.2017. See also Arman Zrvandyan, *Casebook on European Fair Trial Standards in Administrative Justice*, Council of Europe Publishing, Strasbourg 2016, pp. 33–34.

1229 *Filippini v. San Marino* (dec.), App. no. 10526/02, 26.8.2003; and *Ninn-Hansen v. Denmark* (dec.), App. no. 28972/95, 18.5.1999; and *Sacilor Lormines v. France*, App. no. 65411/01, §67, 9.11.2006.

1230 *Pabla Ky v. Finland*, App. no. 47221/99, §§31–35, 22.6.2004.

appointed or ordered by the judiciary to sit in a certain case only.[1231] In order to be successful, any allegation about a judge's lack of independence requires that it is shown that the appointment procedure was, as a whole, unsatisfactory or that the creation of an ad hoc tribunal was motivated by reasons relating to the outcome of the case.[1232]

A good guarantee of a court's independence is usually the fact that the members of the court have been appointed for a sufficiently long term and that they are irremovable during their term of office.[1233] There is, however, no rule for what might be considered as a minimum term. For example, a term of six years has been seen as sufficiently long to guarantee the independence of the court.[1234] Even shorter terms have been accepted if they have related to administrative or disciplinary courts.[1235] As far as ordinary courts are concerned, an appointment for life or for a fixed term is allowed, but a renewable term of four years has been deemed questionable.[1236]

The independence of a court was at stake in the case *Ali Riza and Others v. Turkey*, in which a dispute over a professional footballer was dealt with in a compulsory sports arbitration procedure, the outcome of which could not be appealed against. The members of the arbitral tribunal were mainly lawyers specialising in sports law who were also former managers of football clubs. There were no ethical rules applying to their activities; they did not take an oath or give assurances before taking on their duties; their time in office had not been defined; and they did not need to signal their partiality. They had been nominated by the board of football clubs which also paid their remuneration. The Court considered that the arbitral tribunal was organisationally dependent on the board and that the board had a strong influence over the arbitral tribunal. Since players did not have the same kind of representation in court as football clubs did, this tipped the balance in contractual disputes to the benefit of the clubs.

---

1231 *Barberà, Messegué and Jabardo v. Spain*, App. nos. 10590/83+, §§53–59, 6.12.1988.

1232 In the case *Zand v. Austria*, App. no. 7360/76, 12.6.1979, the Court found that a domestic court was independent even though its members had been appointed by an administrative body which also could dismiss them. In contrast, in the case *Crociani and Others v. Italy*, App. nos. 8603/79+, 18.12.1980, the judges were chosen by lot only after the charges had been brought against the applicants and it was suspected that political aspects were connected to their appointment. The applicants' allegation was not, however, successful.

1233 The absence of a formal recognition of irremovability in the law does not in itself imply lack of independence, provided that it is recognised in fact and that other necessary guarantees are present, see *Sacilor Lormines v. France*, App. no. 65411/01, §67, 9.11.2006; and *Luka v. Romania*, App. no. 34197/02, §44, 21.7.2009.

1234 *Le Compte, Van Leuven and De Meyere v. Belgium*, App. nos. 6878/75+, §57, 23.6.1981.

1235 In the case *Campbell and Fell v. the United Kingdom*, App. nos. 7819/77+, §80, 28.6.1984, the Court accepted a term of three years' service for members of a disciplinary tribunal as its members were not paid and it might have been difficult to find candidates for any longer period.

1236 *Incal v. Turkey*, App. no. 22678/93, §68, 9.6.1998.

The applicant had therefore had a reasonable suspicion of the independence and impartiality of the arbitral tribunal.[1237]

The Court does not normally interfere with the domestic interpretation on whether a court or tribunal has been established by law, unless such interpretation is in flagrant violation of domestic law. This test requires that the violation of domestic law is fundamental and forms an integral part of the establishment and functioning of the judicial system. The violation must therefore be of a flagrant nature and demonstrate that a breach of the domestic rules on the appointment of judges was deliberate or, at a minimum, constituted a manifest disregard of the applicable national law.

Such an issue came up in the case *Guðmundur Andri Ástráðsson v. Iceland*. The applicant's criminal appeal was rejected by the Court of Appeal, a new judicial institution which had become operational in 2018 and which had fifteen judges. The applicant complained to the Supreme Court that one of the judges on the bench had been appointed to the Court of Appeal in breach of the appointment procedures specified in the applicable legislation. He contended that the Minister of Justice had removed four candidates from the list of the fifteen best qualified proposed by the Evaluation Committee to sit on the new Court of Appeal and, not acting in conformity with the proper procedure, replaced them by four others further down the list including the impugned judge. Moreover, the Parliament, contrary to the relevant rules, had approved the amended list *en bloc* without voting on each candidate separately. The Icelandic Supreme Court acknowledged that the appointment of the judge in question had been irregular, but such irregularity could not, in its view, be considered to have nullified the appointment. The Supreme Court therefore found that the applicant had received a fair trial and refused to quash the conviction and remit the case for a new hearing.

Before the Court, the Chamber disagreed and found that the process amounted to a flagrant breach of the applicable rules at the material time. The executive branch had exercised undue discretion, not envisaged by the legislation in force, on the choice of four judges to the new Court of Appeal, including the judge in question, coupled with Parliament failing to adhere to the legislative scheme previously enacted to secure an adequate balance between the executive and legislative branches in the appointment process. Furthermore, the Minister of Justice had acted, as found by the Supreme Court, in manifest disregard of the applicable rules in deciding to replace four of the fifteen candidates, considered to be the most qualified by the Committee, with other four applicants, assessed as less qualified, including the judge in question. The Chamber held that the process was therefore detrimental to the confidence that the judiciary in a democratic society had to inspire in the public and contravened the very essence of the principle

[1237] *Ali Riza and Others v. Turkey*, App. nos. 30226/10+, §§201–223, 28.1.2020.

that a tribunal must be established by law, one of the fundamental principles of the rule of law. It emphasised that a contrary finding on the facts of the case would be tantamount to holding that the fundamental guarantees provided for by Article 6 §1 of the Convention would be devoid of meaningful protection.[1238]

The Grand Chamber confirmed the Chamber's judgment in its judgment in December 2020. It developed a three-step test to assess whether there had been a breach of the right to be tried by a "tribunal established by law". First of all, there must, in principle, be a manifest breach of domestic law in the sense that it must be objectively and genuinely identifiable. However, the absence of such a breach does not rule out the possibility of a violation, since a procedure that is seemingly in compliance with the rules may nevertheless produce results that are incompatible with the object and purpose of Article 6 §1. Secondly, only those breaches that relate to the fundamental rules of the procedure for appointing judges are likely to result in a violation: for example, the appointment of a person as judge who did not fulfil the relevant eligibility criteria or breaches that may otherwise undermine the purpose and effect of the "established by law" requirement. Accordingly, breaches of a purely technical nature fall below the relevant threshold. Thirdly, the review by domestic courts of the legal consequences of a breach of a domestic rule on judicial appointments must be carried out on the basis of the relevant Convention standards. In particular, a fair and proportionate balance had to be struck to determine whether there was a pressing need, of a substantial and compelling character, justifying the departure from the principles of legal certainty and irremovability of judges, in the particular circumstances of a case. Applied to the present case, the Grand Chamber found that all three criteria were satisfied, leading thus to the finding of a violation. However, it held that the finding of a violation in the present case could not, as such, be taken to impose on the respondent State an obligation to reopen all similar cases that had since become *res judicata*.[1239]

#### *4.5.2.2. Guarantees against Outside Pressure (Dismissal of a Judge)*

The guarantees against outside pressure require that, either by law or in practice, the members of a court are protected from dismissal during their term of office. A judge's right to remain in office during his or her term is an additional element relating to the independence of the courts.[1240]

---

[1238] *Guðmundur Andri Ástráðsson v. Iceland*, App. no. 26374/18, §§100–123, 12.3.2019 (violation).

[1239] *Guðmundur Andri Ástráðsson v. Iceland* [GC], App. no. 26374/18, §§243–252 and 254–290, 1.12.2020 (violation).

[1240] *Parlov-Tkalčić v. Croatia*, App. no. 24810/06, §86, 22.12.2009; *Daktaras v. Lithuania*, App. no. 42095/98, §36, 10.10.2000; and *Moiseyev v. Russia*, App. no. 62936/00, §184, 9.10.2008. See also Anand Doobay, "The right to a fair trial in light of the recent ECtHR and CJEU case-law", *ERA forum*, vol.14, issue 2, September 2013, pp. 251–262, at pp. 253–254.

However, a system in which judges can be dismissed also seems to be compatible with Article 6.[1241] The Court has not required that the right to remain in office be formally recognised in law but deemed it sufficient for this right to be recognised in fact.[1242] This right is not breached when a member of a court is transferred to other duties either.[1243] Any dismissal of a judge needs to be based on reasons that cannot jeopardise the impartiality of the court, and the procedure must follow the principles of the rule of law.[1244]

In the case *Baka v. Hungary*, the Court held that the fact that the applicant – who was the President of the Supreme Court – was prevented from challenging before a court the shortening of his term in office, because the law did not provide for such a challenge, meant that there was a restriction on access to a court in violation of Article 6. The dismissal and the restriction of access to a court were based on a new law that had repealed the earlier law, which had originally provided for such access. The new law did not fulfil the criteria laid down in the *Vilho Eskelinen* case; nor was it in accordance with the rule of law, since it was not intended for general application but instead was directed against the applicant, who had criticised some legislative projects. This impaired the very essence of his right of access to a court and thus constituted a violation of Article 6.[1245]

In the case *Paluda v. Slovakia*, the Court held that it is nowadays more and more important that, in the proceedings leading to the dismissal of a judge, procedural fairness is respected. In this case, a Supreme Court judge had been suspended from his office, as a disciplinary sanction, by a decision of a body headed by the Supreme Court President. The reason for the disciplinary action had been the applicant's criticism of the President. The applicant had not been heard during these proceedings; nor had he had any opportunity to challenge the decision before a court or some other impartial body.[1246]

In the case *Oleksandr Volkov v. Ukraine*, the Court held that the dismissal of a Supreme Court judge and the president of a military court, following a proposal from a parliamentary administrative body (High Council of Justice),

---

1241 In the case *Engel and Others v. the Netherlands*, App. nos. 5100/71+, 8.6.1976, the Court seems to have considered that the independence of the military members who were removable was not in fact an issue. In contrast, in the case *Brudnicka and Others v. Poland*, App. no. 54723/00, §41, 3.3.2005, this issue seemed to have relevance to the fact that the Court found a violation of Article 6.

1242 *Campbell and Fell v. the United Kingdom*, App. nos. 7819/77+, §80, 28.6.1984; and *Eccles and Others v. Ireland* (dec.), App. no. 12839/87, 9.12.1988.

1243 *Sutter v. Switzerland* (dec.), App. no. 8209/78, 1.3.1979.

1244 *Mitrinovski v. "the former Yugoslav Republic of Macedonia"*, App. no. 6899/12, §46, 30.4.2015.

1245 *Baka v. Hungary* [GC], App. no. 20261/12, §§112–122, 23.6.2016. See also Linos-Alexandre Sicilianos, "The Subjective Right of Judges to Independence – Some Reflexions on the Interpretation of Article 6, Para. 1 of the ECHR", in Paulo Pinto de Albuquerque, Krzysztof Wojtyczek (Eds.), *Judicial Power in a Globalized World – Liber Amicorum Vincent de Gaetano*, Springer, Cham 2019, pp. 547–557, at pp. 550–551 and 555.

1246 *Paluda v. Slovakia*, App. no. 33392/12, §§45–55, 23.5.2017.

did not fulfil the criteria of independent and impartial tribunals when, in the composition of the body, the judges were in the minority and were subjected to the disciplinary powers of that very body, and the other members of the composition included, *inter alia*, a representative of the prosecutor. Moreover, when the final decision was made in Parliament, the procedure contained several significant shortcomings, such as allowing MPs present to vote on behalf of absent members. The Court found a violation of Article 6 of the Convention.[1247] In the *Ivanovski* case concerning lustration proceedings, the proceedings to dismiss the President of the Constitutional Court were not impartial since the Prime Minister had, in a public statement, been applying pressure to the court to reach a certain conclusion.[1248]

Another guarantee against outside pressure is that members of a court are not subject to instructions from the executive in their judicial functions.[1249] The executive may still give general guidelines relating to the functioning of the courts if these guidelines are not, in practice, essentially orders to the courts to decide certain matters in certain ways.[1250] For example, the authority given to the executive to grant an amnesty or a pardon must not be used in such a manner as to undermine the judicial function. Also, the confidentiality of deliberations is conducive to preventing outside pressure.[1251] Internal judicial independence also requires that judges be free from directives or pressures from fellow judges or from those who have administrative responsibilities in the court, such as the president of the court or the president of a division in the court.[1252]

#### 4.5.2.3. *Appearance of Independence*

A court or tribunal must also appear to be independent.[1253] What is at stake is the confidence which the courts in a democratic society must inspire in the public

1247 *Oleksandr Volkov v. Ukraine*, App. no. 21722/11, §§114–130, 9.1.2013. See also Kevin Aquilina, "The Independence of the Judiciary in Strasbourg Judicial Disciplinary Case Law – Judges as Applicants and National Judicial Councils as Factotums of Respondent States", in Paulo Pinto de Albuquerque, Krzysztof Wojtyczek (Eds.), *Judicial Power in a Globalized World – Liber Amicorum Vincent de Gaetano*, Springer, Cham 2019, pp. 1–32; Lize R Glas, "European Convention on Human Rights", *Netherlands Quarterly of Human Rights*, vol. 31, no. 2, June 2013, pp. 210–216, at pp. 211–212; and Arman Zrvandyan, *Casebook on European Fair Trial Standards in Administrative Justice*, Council of Europe Publishing, Strasbourg 2016, pp. 55–57.

1248 *Ivanovski v. "the former Yugoslav Republic of Macedonia"*, App. no. 29908/11, §§147–150, 21.1.2016.

1249 In the case *Sramek v. Austria*, App. no. 8790/79, §38, 22.10.1984, this requirement was formally recognised in law, whereas in the case *Campbell and Fell v. the United Kingdom*, App. nos. 7819/77+, §79, 28.6.1984, it was considered sufficient that such practice was recognised in fact.

1250 *Campbell and Fell v. the United Kingdom*, App. nos. 7819/77+, §79, 28.6.1984; and *Sovtransavto Holding v. Ukraine*, App. no. 48553/99, §80, 25.7.2002.

1251 *Sutter v. Switzerland* (dec.), App. no. 8209/78, 1.3.1979.

1252 *Agrokompleks v. Ukraine*, App. no. 23465/03, §137, 25.7.2013; and *Parlov-Tkalčić v. Croatia*, App. no. 24810/06, §86, 22.12.2009.

1253 *Sramek v. Austria*, App. no. 8790/79, §42, 22.10.1984.

and above all, as far as criminal proceedings are concerned, in the accused.[1254] Normally there is a reason to suspect that a court is not independent if there is an objective justification for this suspicion. The Court has held that, for example, a lack of structural independence has given rise to a legitimate doubt about the independence of a court.[1255] On the other hand, no problem arises when the Court is of the view that an "objective observer" would see no cause for concern in the circumstances of the case at hand.[1256]

In the case *Urban v. Poland*, the Court found that a trainee judge acting as a judge did not fulfil the requirement for an independent court. Trainee judges were appointed and/or dismissed by the Minister of Justice and a dismissal could take place at any time during the period of training. It was also relevant that the Polish Constitutional Court had already held that the requirement for the independence of a court had not been fulfilled in respect of trainee judges.[1257] Similarly, the Court has found problems with military judges sitting in ordinary criminal courts, as they can be subject to armed forces disciplinary proceedings.[1258] It is even more problematic when civilians are prosecuted for criminal offences before military courts, except in very exceptional circumstances.[1259] Article 6 requirements were also not seen to have been fulfilled in a situation in which a police officer was a member of a jury, especially as an ex-colleague of his was a witness in the case.[1260]

### 4.5.3. IMPARTIAL TRIBUNAL

Impartiality means that a court or tribunal is not prejudiced or biased.[1261] To satisfy this requirement, the court must comply both with a subjective test and an objective test.[1262] The subjective test identifies whether a particular

---

1254 *Şahiner v. Turkey*, App. no. 29279/95, §44, 25.9.2001.

1255 *Findlay v. the United Kingdom*, App. no. 22107/93, §72, 25.2.1997; and *Whitfield and Others v. the United Kingdom*, App. nos. 46387/99+, §45, 12.4.2005.

1256 *Clarke v. the United Kingdom* (dec.), App. no. 23695/02, 25.8.2005.

1257 *Henryk Urban and Ryszard Urban v. Poland*, App. no. 23614/08, §§46–54, 30.11.2010. See also Karen Reid, *A Practitioner's Guide to the European Convention on Human Rights*, Sweet & Maxwell/Thomson Reuters, London 2019, p. 215.

1258 *Incal v. Turkey*, App. no. 22678/93, §72, 9.6.1998. In the case *Öcalan v. Turkey* [GC], App. no. 46221/99, §118, 12.5.2005 it was not even sufficient that a military member of the court was replaced by a civilian judge during the proceedings.

1259 *Ergin v. Turkey (No. 6)*, App. no. 47533/99, §54, 4.5.2006; and *Martin v. the United Kingdom*, App. no. 40426/98, §§44–45, 24.10.2006.

1260 *Hanif and Khan v. the United Kingdom*, App. nos. 52999/08+, §§148–150, 20.12.2011. See also Dean Spielmann, "Article 6 ECHR in criminal proceedings – recent developments", *Cyprus Human Rights Law Review*, vol. 2, issue 1, 2013, pp. 3–15, at pp. 9–10.

1261 *Wettstein v. Switzerland*, App. no. 33958/96, §43, 21.12.2000; *Micallef v. Malta* [GC], App. no. 17056/06, §93, 15.10.2009; and *Nicholas v. Cyprus*, App. no. 63246/10, §49, 9.1.2018.

1262 *Kyprianou v. Cyprus* [GC], App. no. 73797/01, §118, 15.12.2005; *Piersack v. Belgium*, App. no. 8692/79, §30, 1.10.1982; *Grieves v. the United Kingdom* [GC], App. no. 57067/00, §69, 16.12.2003; and *Morice v. France* [GC], App. no. 29369/10, §73, 23.4.2015.

judge in a given case has a personal bias or partiality, whereas the objective test aims to ascertain that sufficient legal safeguards are available to exclude any legitimate doubt about bias or partiality.[1263] There is no watertight division between subjective and objective impartiality since the conduct of a judge may concurrently fall within both of them.[1264] In some cases it may also be difficult to procure evidence with which to rebut the presumption of the judge's subjective impartiality, and objective impartiality may then provide a further guarantee.[1265] In the vast majority of cases raising impartiality issues, the Court has focused on the objective test.[1266]

In the case *Kyprianou v. Cyprus*, the Court distinguished between situations involving functional partiality and personal partiality. The former concerns situations where a judge's personal conduct is not in question but where, for instance, the same person exercises different functions within the judicial process.[1267] It could also mean that the judge has hierarchical or other links with another participant in the proceedings,[1268] which objectively justify misgivings as to the impartiality of the tribunal. This would then fail to meet the Convention's standard under the objective test. Personal partiality concerns the matter of personal character and derives from the conduct of the judges in a given case. In terms of the objective test, a judge's conduct may be sufficient to raise legitimate and objectively justified concerns, but it may also be of such a nature as to raise an issue under the subjective test and even disclose personal bias. In this context, therefore, whether a case is dealt with under one test or the other, or both, will depend on the particular facts of the contested conduct.[1269]

The Court's case-law concerning the impartiality of a court applies to professional and lay judges, jurors, as well as other officials performing judicial

---

1263 *Piersack v. Belgium*, App. no. 8692/79, §30, 1.10.1982. See also Péter Paczolay, "The Notion of Judicial Independence – Impartiality and Effectiveness of Judges", in Paulo Pinto de Albuquerque, Krzysztof Wojtyczek (Eds.), *Judicial Power in a Globalized World – Liber Amicorum Vincent de Gaetano*, Springer, Cham 2019, pp. 331–343, at p. 340.

1264 *Ramos Nunes de Carvalho e Sá v. Portugal* [GC], App. nos. 55391/13+, §145, 6.11.2018.

1265 *Micallef v. Malta* [GC], App. no. 17056/06, §§95 and 101, 15.10.2009.

1266 *Ramos Nunes de Carvalho e Sá v. Portugal* [GC], App. nos. 55391/13+, §146, 6.11.2018.

1267 *Piersack v. Belgium*, App. no. 8692/79, 1.10.1982.

1268 See, for example, *Grieves v. the United Kingdom* [GC], App. no. 57067/00, 16.12.2003; and *Miller and Others v. the United Kingdom*, App. nos. 45825/99+, 26.10.2004.

1269 *Kyprianou v. Cyprus* [GC], App. no. 73797/01, §121, 15.12.2005. See also David Harris, Michael O'Boyle, Ed Bates, Carla Buckley, *Law of the European Convention on Human Rights*, 4th edition, Oxford University Press, Oxford 2018, pp. 454–455; Giovanni Bonello, "More common law than common sense – how the European Court of Human Rights saves the United Kingdom from itself", *Human Rights Law Journal* (HRLJ), vol. 34, no. 7–12, 31 December 2014, pp. 239–245, at pp. 241–242; and Roderick Liddell, "Reflections on certain aspects of the *Kyprianou* judgment", in Lucius Caflisch, Johan Callewaert, Roderick Liddell, Paul Mahoney, Mark Villiger (Eds.), *Liber Amicorum Luzius Wildhaber: Human Rights, Strasbourg Views/Droits de L'homme, Regards de Strasbourg*, N.P. Engel, Kehl/Strasbourg/ Arlington, Va. 2007, pp. 247–262.

functions, such as lay assessors and registrars or legal secretaries.[1270] It does not apply to the representatives of the prosecution who are only parties to the proceedings.[1271]

#### *4.5.3.1. Subjective Test*

The question in the subjective test is whether it can be shown by the facts that a member of the court has acted with personal bias against the applicant.[1272] There is a presumption that a judge is impartial until there is proof to the contrary.[1273] Such proof could be, for example, that a judge has displayed hostility or ill will or has arranged to have a case assigned to himself for personal reasons.[1274] However, the mere fact that the judge might have adopted procedural decisions unfavourable to the defence is not indicative of a lack of impartiality.[1275]

A breach of the subjective test is normally difficult to establish.[1276] Such a violation was, however, found in the case *Werner v. Poland*, in which the insolvency judge had had a preconceived idea about the applicant's matter since she had herself brought it to the court. The Court found that the judge had demonstrated a personal conviction in the matter.[1277] In contrast, the fact that a judge did not withdraw from dealing with a civil action on appeal following his earlier participation in another related set of civil proceedings did not constitute the required proof to rebut the presumption.[1278]

#### *4.5.3.2. Objective Test*

The objective test requires that the administration of justice must also appear to be impartial.[1279] In this regard impressions are important.[1280] However, the

---

1270 *Bellizzi v. Malta*, App. no. 46575/09, §51, 21.6.2011; and *Holm v. Sweden*, App. no. 14191/88, §30, 25.11.1993.

1271 *Kontalexis v. Greece*, App. no. 59000/08, §57, 31.5.2011; *Haarde v. Iceland*, App. no. 66847/12, §94, 23.11.2017; and *Thiam v. France*, App. no. 80018/12, §71, 18.10.2018.

1272 *Hauschildt v. Denmark*, App. no. 10486/83, §47, 24.5.1989.

1273 *Kyprianou v. Cyprus* [GC], App. no. 73797/01, §119, 15.12.2005; *Hauschildt v. Denmark*, App. no. 10486/83, §47, 24.5.1989; *Le Compte, Van Leuven and De Meyere v. Belgium*, App. nos. 6878/75+, §58, 23.6.1981; and *Micallef v. Malta* [GC], App. no. 17056/06, §94, 15.10.2009.

1274 *De Cubber v. Belgium*, App. no. 9186/80, §25, 26.10.1984.

1275 *Khodorkovskiy and Lebedev v. Russia (No. 2)*, App. nos. 51111/07+, §430, 14.1.2020.

1276 *Kyprianou v. Cyprus* [GC], App. no. 73797/01, §119, 15.12.2005; and *Buscemi v. Italy*, App. no. 29569/95, §§67–68, 16.9.1999.

1277 *Werner v. Poland*, App. no. 26760/95, §41, 15.11.2001.

1278 *Golubović v. Croatia*, App. no. 43947/10, §52, 27.11.2012.

1279 *Morice v. France* [GC], App. no. 29369/10, §§73–78, 23.4.2015; and *Sramek v. Austria*, App. no. 8790/79, §42, 22.10.1984. See also *Harabin v. Slovakia*, App. no. 58688/11, §131, 20.11.2012.

1280 *Micallef v. Malta* [GC], App. no. 17056/06, §98, 15.10.2009; *Harabin v. Slovakia*, App. no. 58688/11, §131, 20.11.2012; and *Deli v. the Rebublic of Moldova*, App. no. 42010/06, §36, 22.10.2019.

objective and subjective tests are not necessarily clearly separable from each other. In some cases, where it may be difficult to procure evidence to rebut the presumption of the judge's subjective impartiality, the requirement of objective impartiality provides a further important guarantee.[1281] Courts in a democratic society must inspire confidence in the public and, above all, as far as criminal proceedings are concerned, in the accused.[1282] This implies that the standpoint of the applicant is important but not decisive.[1283] What is decisive is whether this fear can be regarded as objectively justified.[1284]

Any judge in respect of whom there is a legitimate reason to fear a lack of impartiality must withdraw.[1285] It is the responsibility of the individual judge to identify any impediments to his or her own participation and either to withdraw or, when faced with a situation in which it is arguable that he or she should be disqualified, although not unequivocally excluded from acting by law, to bring the matter to the attention of the parties in order to allow them to challenge the participation of the judge.[1286] Issues of objective impartiality may arise also when the judge is part of an enlarged bench.[1287]

The Court has noted that, in order to remove all reasonable doubts as to the impartiality of a judge or a court and to constitute an attempt to ensure impartiality, the existence of national rules regulating the withdrawal of judges is a relevant factor.[1288] Such rules not only ensure the absence of actual bias but they are also directed at removing any appearance of partiality thereby promoting the public's confidence in courts.[1289]

A violation of the objective test was at stake, for example, in the case *McGonnell v. the United Kingdom*, in which the deciding judge had been directly

---

1281 *Oleksandr Volkov v. Ukraine*, App. no. 21722/11, §105, 9.1.2013; *Kyprianou v. Cyprus* [GC], App. no. 73797/01, §119, 15.12.2005; and *Morice v. France* [GC], App. no. 29369/10, §75, 23.4.2015.

1282 *Fey v. Austria*, App. no. 14396/88, §30, 24.2.1993.

1283 *Morel v. France*, App. no. 34130/96, §§45–50, 6.6.2000; *Pescador Valero v. Spain*, App. no. 62435/00, §23, 17.6.2003 (concerning a judge); and *Luka v. Romania*, App. no. 34197/02, §40, 21.7.2009 (concerning a body sitting as a bench).

1284 *Hauschildt v. Denmark*, App. no. 10486/83, §48, 24.5.1989; *Wettstein v. Switzerland*, App. no. 33958/96, §44, 21.12.2000; *Pabla Ky v. Finland*, App. no. 47221/99, §30, 22.6.2004; *Ferrantelli and Santangelo v. Italy*, App. no. 19874/92, §58, 7.8.1996; *Padovani v. Italy*, App. no. 13396/87, §27, 26.2.1993; and *Micallef v. Malta* [GC], App. no. 17056/06, §96, 15.10.2009.

1285 *Hauschildt v. Denmark*, App. no. 10486/83, §48, 24.5.1989; *Castillo Algar v. Spain*, App. no. 28194/95, §45; 28.10.1998; *Morice v. France* [GC], App. no. 29369/10, §78, 23.4.2015; and *Škrlj v. Croatia*, App. no. 32953/13, §43, 11.7.2019.

1286 *Sigríður Elín Sigfúsdóttir v. Iceland*, App. no. 41382/17, §35, 25.2.2020.

1287 *Morice v. France* [GC], App. no. 29369/10, §89, 23.4.2015; *Otegi Mondragon v. Spain*, App. no. 2034/07, §67, 15.3.2011; *Škrlj v. Croatia*, App. no. 32953/13, §46, 11.7.2019; and *Sigríður Elín Sigfúsdóttir v. Iceland*, App. no. 41382/17, §57, 25.2.2020.

1288 *Micallef v. Malta* [GC], App. no. 17056/06, §§99–100, 15.10.2009.

1289 *Mežnarić v. Croatia*, App. no. 71615/01, §27, 15.7.2005; *Harabin v. Slovakia*, App. no. 58688/11, §132, 20.11.2012; and *A.K. v. Liechtenstein*, App. no. 38191/12, §§82–83, 9.7.2015.

involved in the adoption of the law being applied in the applicant's case.[1290] The Court has also found a violation when the executive intervenes in the judicial process with the intent of influencing the outcome of the case. For example, in the case *Sovtransavto Holding v. Ukraine*, the intervention by the President of the Republic into the pending case established a legitimate reason to fear a lack of independence and impartiality from the court.[1291] In another case there was a servient relationship between the domestic court and the executive.[1292] On the other hand, in the case *Mosteanu and Others v. Romania*, the objective test was not violated by the fact that the Romanian President gave a statement about the execution of cases which were no longer pending when the statement was not directly connected to any pending cases.[1293]

In the case *Harabin v. Slovakia*, the Constitutional Court had not accepted complaints about the alleged partiality of the judges when examining *in plenum* a disciplinary matter initiated against the applicant who was the President of the Supreme Court. The Constitutional Court had reasoned its decision, *inter alia*, by the need to maintain quorum. The Court noted that two of the judges had already been excluded for lack of impartiality in earlier cases involving the applicant. Therefore, the Constitutional Court needed to have strong reasons to reject the applicant's allegations of partiality in this case. Since the reasons invoked by the Constitutional Court were not sufficient to justify the participation of these two judges, the Court found that the applicant's right to a hearing by an impartial tribunal had not been respected.[1294]

---

1290 *McGonnell v. the United Kingdom*, App. no. 28488/95, §55, 8.2.2000. See also Jean-Paul Costa, "The European Court of Human Rights and its recent case law", *Texas International Law Journal*, vol. 38, no. 3, 2003, pp. 455–467, at pp. 463–464; and Giovanni Bonello, "More common law than common sense – how the European Court of Human Rights saves the United Kingdom from itself", *Human Rights Law Journal* (HRLJ), vol. 34, no. 7–12, 31 December 2014, pp. 239–245, at pp. 244–245. However, the mere fact that an expert member of the Court of Appeal was also an MP did not create a legitimate reason to fear a lack of impartiality from the Court of Appeal, see *Pabla Ky v. Finland*, App. no. 47221/99, §34, 22.6.2004.

1291 *Sovtransavto Holding v. Ukraine*, App. no. 48553/99, §80, 25.7.2002. See also Kirill Koroteev, Sergey Golubok, "Judgment of the Russian Constitutional Court on supervisory review in civil proceedings: denial of justice, denial of Europe", *Human Rights Law Review*, vol. 7, no. 3, 2007, pp. 619–632, at p. 621; and Dean Spielmann, "The European Convention on Human Rights – the European Court of Human Rights", in Dawn Oliver, Jörg Fedtke (Eds.), *Human Rights and the Private Sphere – A Comparative Study*, Routledge-Cavendish, London/New York 2007, pp. 427–464, at p. 440.

1292 *Cosmos Maritime Trading and Shipping Agency v. Ukraine*, App. no. 53427/09, 27.6.2019. See also Christopher Gray, "Objective impartiality test – *Cosmos Maritime Trading and Shipping Agency v. Ukraine* (Application No. 53427/09)", *European Human Rights Law Review*, Issue 5, 2019, pp. 569–572.

1293 *Mosteanu and Others v. Romania*, App. no. 33176/96, §42, 26.11.2002.

1294 *Harabin v. Slovakia*, App. no. 58688/11, §§134–143, 20.11.2012.

### *4.5.3.3. Judges Acting in Different Roles*

The objective test is often used in situations in which a judge has acted in different roles and participated in the earlier phases of proceedings.[1295] A judge's earlier participation in a case does not as such create a lack of impartiality; what is relevant is the extent to which he or she has participated earlier.[1296] The fact that the judge has detailed knowledge of the case file and has taken pretrial decisions does not normally entail any prejudice on his part that would prevent his being regarded as impartial when the decision on the merits is taken. Nor does a preliminary analysis of the available information mean that the final analysis has been prejudged.[1297] If judges are sitting as a bench, the fact that some of the judges have previously adopted a particular position is not sufficient in itself to conclude that the bench as a whole is not impartial.[1298]

The Court has often found that in some cases a legitimate reason to fear partiality may be created. For example, in the case *De Cubber v. Belgium*, which concerned a judge who had previously acted as an investigating judge in the matter, the Court held that the impartiality of the judge was capable of appearing to the applicant as being open to doubt.[1299] On the other hand, in situations in which a judge acts independently from pretrial investigation or prosecution, such doubt does not exist.[1300]

In the case *Alony Kate v. Spain*, the Court held that decisions a judge makes concerning pretrial detention do not as such create a legitimate reason for an objective fear of lack of impartiality. However, if in the reasoning of the decision to detain, a judge takes a stance on the possible outcome of the case, such doubt is created. In the case in question, the composition of the bench deciding on the detention issue had used in its reasoning expressions on the basis of which

---

1295 See, for example, *Nordborg v. Sweden*, App. no. 13635/88, 4.4.1990, which concerned an emergency taking into public care of a child; and *Jensen v. Denmark* (dec.), App. no. 14063/88, 7.1.1991, in which the judge had recommended the applicant drop the case.

1296 *Fey v. Austria*, App. no. 14396/88, §30, 24.2.1993.

1297 *Morel v. France*, App. no. 34130/96, §45, 6.6.2000.

1298 *Fazlı Aslaner v. Turkey*, App. no. 36073/04, §§36–43, 4.3.2014; and *Rustavi 2 Broadcasting Company Ltd and Others v. Georgia*, App. no. 16812/17, §363, 18.7.2019.

1299 *De Cubber v. Belgium*, App. no. 9186/80, §30, 26.10.1984. See also Pieter van Dijk, "Article 6 §1 of the Convention and the concept of 'objective impartiality'", in Paul Mahoney, Franz Matscher, Herbert Petzold, Luzius Wildhaber (Eds.), *Protection des Droits de L'homme: La Perspective Européenne, Mélanges à la Mémoire de Rolv Ryssdal/Protecting Human Rights: The European Perspective, Studies in Memory of Rolv Ryssdal*, Carl Heymanns Verlag, Köln/Berlin/Bonn/München 2000, pp. 1495–1510, at pp. 1503–1504.

1300 *Sainte-Marie v. France*, App. no. 12981/87, §34, 16.12.1992, in which two judges had in the earlier phase of the case rejected the applicant's request to be released on bail. However, in the case *Hauschildt v. Denmark*, App. no. 10486/83, §48, 24.5.1989, the fact that the judge had earlier participated in the case by deciding on the applicant's pretrial detention created a legitimate reason to fear a lack of his impartiality as, according to domestic law, a judge had to be, when making such a decision, already convinced that there is "a very high degree of clarity" as to the question of guilt of the detained person.

the applicant had a legitimate reason to objectively fear a lack of impartiality. The court had stated that, in its opinion, the circumstantial evidence was sufficient to show that a crime had been committed and that the applicant was guilty of committing it. When one of the judges, who was part of the composition of the court deciding on detention, had also been subsequently part of the composition deciding the criminal matter on its merits, the applicant had had a legitimate reason to fear that the judge had been prejudiced about his guilt. Article 6 §1 of the Convention had thus been violated.[1301]

Issues of impartiality may also be at stake in situations that concern the dismissal of a judge, in particular if the same judge is both initiating the dismissal procedure and taking part in decision making in a lower court when a higher court has no overall competence in the matter. In the case *Denisov v. Ukraine*, the president of an administrative court was dismissed from the president's post while still continuing as a judge of that court. The initiative for his dismissal had been taken by a council of judges. One of these judges was also part of the composition that decided to dismiss the applicant. Although there was a problem of objective impartiality, the higher court had no competence to examine the case in its entirety and to correct the mistake committed by the lower court.[1302]

The objective impartiality of a judge was also at stake in the case *Deli v. Moldova*, where a judge had convicted a counsel and sentenced him to a fine for contempt of court in the court hearing which the judge was presiding over, meaning that the judge had acted both as the prosecutor and the judge in that case. In such a situation, the confusion of the different roles was prone to cast a reasonable doubt on the impartiality of the judge.[1303]

A judge's impartiality is not brought into question simply by the fact that they have previously during their career acted as a public prosecutor without having any connection to the matter at stake.[1304] In many countries, it is common that legally trained persons take up several different kinds of duties within the judicial system during their career.[1305] However, there was a problem in the case *Hanif and Khan v. the United Kingdom*, in which one of the jury members was

---

1301 *Alony Kate v. Spain*, App. no. 5612/08, §§49–58, 17.1.2012.

1302 *Denisov v. Ukraine* [GC], App. no. 76639/11, §§71–82, 25.9.2018. See also Kevin Aquilina, "The Independence of the Judiciary in Strasbourg Judicial Disciplinary Case Law – Judges as Applicants and National Judicial Councils as Factotums of Respondent States", in Paulo Pinto de Albuquerque, Krzysztof Wojtyczek (Eds.), *Judicial Power in a Globalized World – Liber Amicorum Vincent de Gaetano*, Springer, Cham 2019, pp. 1–32.

1303 *Deli v. the Republic of Moldova*, App. no. 42010/06, §§43–45, 22.10.2019. See also Mushfik Khan, "Case and comment: selected decisions from the European Court of Human Rights for September and October 2019 – Biased judge, *Deli v. The Republic of Moldova* (Application No. 42010/06)", *European Human Rights Law Review*, Issue 1, 2020, pp. 105–107. See also *Kyprianou v. Cyprus* [GC], App. no. 73797/01, §§126–128, 15.12.2005; and *Słomka v. Poland*, App. no. 68924/12, §§44–51, 6.12.2018.

1304 *Paunović v. Serbia*, App. no. 54574/07, §§38–43, 3.12.2019.

1305 *K. v. Denmark* (dec.), App. no. 19524/92, 5.5.1993.

a police officer who had been in close professional contact with the officer who was heard as a witness in the case.[1306] The Court has also held that a time-lapse of nearly two years since the earlier involvement in the same proceedings was not in itself a sufficient safeguard against partiality.[1307]

A legitimate reason to fear lack of impartiality may also arise in a situation in which a judge has previously acted as the counsel for the counterparty. This was the case, for example, in *Wettstein v. Switzerland*, in which a part-time judge in the applicant's civil case was at the same time the counsel for the applicant's counterparty in another civil matter. Although the facts of the civil proceedings were not connected to each other, the applicant could legitimately fear that the judge could still see him as his counterparty.[1308] But there was no such legitimate reason to fear created when a judge had been the counsel for a bank which had been the applicant's counterparty five years earlier.[1309] On similar grounds, a judge was held to be unbiased in the case *Puolitaival and Pirttiaho v. Finland*, although the judge had been the counsel for the applicant's counterparty five years earlier in another civil matter.[1310] Nor was any legitimate reason to fear partiality created when an expert member of the court was at the same time an MP, when he had not used any legislative or executive powers in the pending matter and had not been an advisor in the matter.[1311]

A legitimate suspicion of impartiality may arise, however, if a judge has in the legislative phase influenced legislation by giving his or her opinion on it or subsequently done so when interpreting the law in question. In the above-mentioned case of *McGonnell v. the United Kingdom*, the Court found a violation on the basis of the objective test when the judge had been directly involved in the legislative procedure concerning an act which had been the subject of interpretation in the applicant's case.[1312] In the case *Procola v. Luxembourg*, the Court held that the applicant had not had an impartial trial

---

1306 *Hanif and Khan v. the United Kingdom*, App. nos. 52999/08+, §148, 20.12.2011. See also Anand Doobay, "The right to a fair trial in light of the recent ECtHR and CJEU case-law", *ERA forum*, vol.14, issue 2, September 2013, pp. 251–262, at pp. 254–255; and Dean Spielmann, "Article 6 ECHR in criminal proceedings – recent developments", *Cyprus Human Rights Law Review*, vol. 2, issue 1, 2013, pp. 3–15, at pp. 9–10.

1307 *Dāvidsons and Savins v. Latvia*, App. nos. 17574/07+, §57, 7.1.2016.

1308 *Wettstein v. Switzerland*, App. no. 33958/96, §47, 21.12.2000. See also David Harris, Michael O'Boyle, Ed Bates, Carla Buckley, *Law of the European Convention on Human Rights*, 4th edition, Oxford University Press, Oxford 2018, p. 455. See also *Švarc and Kavnik v. Slovenia*, App. no. 75617/01, §44, 8.2.2007; and *Puolitaival and Pirttiaho v. Finland*, App. no. 54857/00, §§46–54, 23.11.2004, in which the Court did not find a violation.

1309 *Walston v. Norway* (dec.), App. no. 37372/97, 11.12.2001.

1310 *Puolitaival and Pirttiaho v. Finland*, App. no. 54857/00, §§49–54, 23.11.2004.

1311 *Pabla Ky v. Finland*, App. no. 47221/99, §34, 22.6.2004 (no violation).

1312 *McGonnell v. the United Kingdom*, App. no. 28488/95, §55, 8.2.2000. See also Jean–Paul Costa, "The European Court of Human Rights and its recent case law", *Texas International Law Journal*, vol. 38, no. 3, 2003, pp. 455–467, at pp. 463–464; and Giovanni Bonello, "More common law than common sense – how the European Court of Human Rights saves

when four out of five Supreme Court (Conseil d'Etat) judges sitting on the bench had been members of the advisory panel of the court which had taken a stance on the government's bill and its legality (whether the provision could be applied retrospectively). The Court found that, from the applicant's point of view, there was a reason to suspect that the members of the court felt tied to their earlier statement, which meant that the court was not impartial.[1313]

In the case *Kleyn and Others v. the Netherlands*, the impartiality of the judges became relevant in a situation in which the Constitution required an advisory opinion to be submitted on a bill before it could be adopted by Parliament. The body responsible for delivering such an opinion was composed of judges who then subsequently decided in administrative courts on administrative disputes concerning that law. The Court held that application in proceedings of a law on which the judge had previously given a statement during the legislative phase may give rise to a suspicion of a lack of impartiality. The Court noted that the Convention did not require any specific form of how legislative and judicial powers were separated from one another in the domestic legal system. In the *Kleyn and Others* case, more stress was put on the scope of the concrete dispute and, consequently, the Court held that the statement and the administrative dispute did not concern the same case or the same decision. Therefore, the applicants did not have any objective grounds for their suspicion about the court's lack of impartiality.[1314] Similarly, in the case *Pabla Ky v. Finland*, the sole fact that an expert member of the Court of Appeal was also an MP did not create by itself, as an abstract allegation, any legitimate reason to doubt the Court of Appeal's impartiality, since there was no question of "the same case" or "the same decision".[1315]

#### 4.5.3.4. *Judges Participating at More than One Stage or in Parallel*

According to the Court, there does not exist any general rule that requires that a case referred back to a lower court must be examined by a completely

the United Kingdom from itself", *Human Rights Law Journal* (HRLJ), vol. 34, no. 7–12, 31 December 2014, pp. 239–245, at pp. 244–245. However, the fact alone that an expert member of the Court of Appeal was also an MP did not create a legitimate reason to fear lack of impartiality, see *Pabla Ky v. Finland*, App. no. 47221/99, §34, 22.6.2004.

1313 *Procola v. Luxembourg*, App. no. 14570/89, §§41–46, 28.9.1995. See also Karen Reid, *A Practitioner's Guide to the European Convention on Human Rights*, Sweet & Maxwell/Thomson Reuters, London 2019, p. 226.

1314 *Kleyn and Others v. the Netherlands* [GC], App. nos. 39343/98+, §§125–141, 193–195 and 200–202, 6.5.2003. See also Karen Reid, *A Practitioner's Guide to the European Convention on Human Rights*, Sweet & Maxwell/Thomson Reuters, London 2019, p. 226. Moreover, in the case *Sacilor Lormines v. France*, App. no. 65411/01, 9.11.2006, the Court held that the outcome in the case was not based in any part on material which the applicant would not have had access to; that is, material which related to the dialogue between the administrative department of Conseil d'Etat and a ministry concerning the bill.

1315 *Pabla Ky v. Finland*, App. no. 47221/99, §34, 22.6.2004.

new composition.[1316] For example, in the case *Diennet v. France*, in which the case had been referred back to a lower court because of a procedural mistake, there was no legitimate reason to fear a lack of impartiality of the court when three members of its seven-judge composition remained the same.[1317] Nor was there a problem when the same composition of the Supreme Court which had decided to refer the case back to a lower court for procedural reasons eventually decided the matter after a new appeal.[1318] On the other hand, it is clear that the same judge should not be examining the same case in two different stages of appeal,[1319] in particular if they need to assess their own previous decision.[1320]

There was no lack of impartiality when the applicant's case was re-examined by a court which had earlier convicted him *in absentia*. According to the Court, there was no problem since the judges were aware of the fact that they had convicted the applicant the first time on the basis of limited evidence that was non-binding, and that a re-assessment of the case would be based on more extensive and adversarial evidence.[1321] Nor is there any *prima facie* incompatibility with the requirements of impartiality if the same judge is involved, first, in a decision on the merits of a case and, subsequently, in proceedings in which the admissibility (rather than the substance) of an appeal against that decision is examined.[1322]

A judge may also attend the same applicant's parallel civil and criminal proceedings without any legitimate reason for the applicant to fear a lack of impartiality on this ground alone.[1323] There was thus no problem, for example, in the case *Lie and Berntsen v. Norway*, in which the judge had first been a member of the bench in the criminal case and thereafter had participated in the connected compensation proceedings.[1324] Nor were the principles of objective or subjective impartiality violated in the case *Mitrinovski v. "the former Yugoslav Republic of Macedonia"*, when the dismissal of a judge had involved another

1316 *Ringeisen v. Austria*, App. no. 2614/65, §97, 16.7.1971.

1317 *Diennet v. France*, App. no. 18160/91, §38, 26.9.1995. See also Karen Reid, *A Practitioner's Guide to the European Convention on Human Rights*, Sweet & Maxwell/Thomson Reuters, London 2019, p. 227.

1318 *Teslya v. Ukraine*, App. no. 52095/11, §§40–47, 8.10.2020.

1319 *Oberschlick v. Austria (No. 1)*, App. no. 11662/85, §49, 23.5.1991; and *Indra v. Slovakia*, App. no. 46845/99, §53, 1.2.2005.

1320 *De Haan v. the Netherlands*, App. no. 22839/93, §51, 26.8.1997; and *San Leonard Band Club v. Malta*, App. no. 77562/01, §§64–65, 29.7.2004. See also *Driza v. Albania*, App. no. 33771/02, §§78–83, 13.11.2007; and *Pereira da Silva v. Portugal*, App. no. 77050/11, §§59–60, 22.3.2016.

1321 *Thomann v. Switzerland*, App. no. 17602/91, §35, 10.6.1996.

1322 *Warsicka v. Poland*, App. no. 2065/03, §§38–47, 16.1.2007.

1323 *Gillow v. the United Kingdom*, App. no. 9063/80, §73, 24.11.1986; *Kalogeropoulou and Others v. Greece and Germany* (dec.), App. no. 59021/00, 12.12.2002; and *Lindon, Otchakovsky-Laurens and July v. France* [GC], App. nos. 21279/02+, §§78–79, 22.10.2007.

1324 *Lie and Berntsen v. Norway* (dec.), App. no. 25130/94, 16.12.1999.

judge who first had been a member of the Supreme Court composition that had found there had been professional misconduct by the applicant case and who then had been, *ex officio*, a member of the body which decided on that judge's dismissal.[1325]

On the other hand, in a situation in which a case is referred back to a lower-level court for re-examination because of a problem of partiality, the referral concerns the judgment in its entirety. Therefore, the re-examination also covers those charges that have been dismissed in earlier, biased proceedings. This means that the prohibition of *reformatio in peius* does not apply to such cases.[1326]

#### *4.5.3.5. Judge's Family Ties and Personal Relationships*

Objective partiality may also be caused by the existence of a personal relationship between any of the parties. However, the fact that judges know each other as colleagues or even share the same offices is not in itself sufficient to conclude that any concerns as to their impartiality are objectively justified.[1327] Nor does the fact that a member of a tribunal has some personal knowledge of one of the witnesses in a case necessarily mean that he or she will be prejudiced in favour of that person's testimony.[1328] In a very small country, the fact that a legal professional may perform two functions on a part-time basis, for example as a judge and a practising lawyer, is not *per se* problematic either.[1329] In contrast, in the case *Kristiansen v. Norway*, there was deemed to be bias because a member of the jury was the foster mother of the victim's classmate and the victim had once visited her home for a children's birthday party.[1330]

Objective partiality was also at stake in the case *Mitrov v. "the former Yugoslav Republic of Macedonia"*, in which the applicant was accused of causing a car accident. In the car accident, the 18-year-old daughter of a judge, who was the

---

1325 *Mitrinovski v. "the former Yugoslav Republic of Macedonia"*, App. no. 6899/12, §§40–46, 30.4.2015.

1326 *Kuokkanen and Johannesdahl v. Finland* (dec.), App. no. 38147/12, §§26–28, 25.6.2015. In this case, the Court accepted the Finnish Supreme Court's decision and held that such a referral back to a lower court complied with the fair trial criteria.

1327 *Steck-Risch and Others v. Liechtenstein*, App. no. 63151/00, §48, 19.5.2005.

1328 *Pullar v. the United Kingdom*, App. no. 22399/93, §38, 10.6.1996 (presence in the jury of an employee of one of the two key prosecution witnesses); and *Hanif and Khan v. the United Kingdom*, App. nos. 52999/08+, §141, 20.12.2011 (presence of a police officer in the jury). Compare and contrast with *Peter Armstrong v. the United Kingdom*, App. no. 65282/09, §§39–45, 9.12.2014.

1329 *Steck-Risch and Others v. Liechtenstein*, App. no. 63151/00, §39, 19.5.2005; and *Bellizzi v. Malta*, App. no. 46575/09, §57, 21.6.2011. Compare with *Micallef v. Malta* [GC], App. no. 17056/06, §102, 15.10.2009.

1330 *Kristiansen v. Norway*, App. no. 1176/10, §§52–61, 17.12.2015. See also Sofia Galani (Ed.), "Case and comment: selected decisions from the European Court of Human Rights from November and December 2015 – Impartiality of jurors, *Kristiansen v. Norway* (Application No. 1176/10)", *European Human Rights Law Review*, Issue 2, 2016, pp. 205–207.

president of the criminal section of the trial court, was killed and the applicant's case was examined by her fellow judge, a colleague. The fact that there were close personal relations between the judges at the trial court, that the president of the criminal section and her family held a form of victim status and that the case concerned a family tragedy rendered all the judges of that court partial in the applicant's case. As domestic law did not provide for the possibility to transfer the case to another court, the Court found that the applicant's fear of the partiality of the domestic court had been objectively justified.[1331]

In the case *Pastörs v. Germany*, although the two judges dealing with the applicant's case at the first and third level of jurisdiction were married, the Court found no violation of Article 6 §1, since the applicant's complaint of bias had been submitted to the subsequent control of a judicial body with sufficient Article 6 guarantees. The Court also noted that the applicant had not given any concrete arguments why a professional judge – being married to another professional judge – should be biased when deciding on the same case at a different level of jurisdiction which did not, moreover, entail direct review of their spouse's decision.[1332]

Close family ties can also exist between a judge and the representatives of either of the parties. The Court has found in its case-law that objectively justified doubts as to the impartiality of the trial court presiding judge were found to exist when her husband was the head of the team of investigators dealing with the applicants' case.[1333] On the other hand, when a judge has blood ties with an employee of a law firm representing a party in any given proceedings, this does not in and of itself disqualify the judge.[1334] An automatic disqualification on the basis of such ties is not necessarily required. It is, however, a situation or affiliation that could give rise to misgivings about the judge's impartiality. Whether such misgivings are objectively justified would very much depend on the circumstances of the specific case, and a number of factors should be taken into account in this regard. These include, *inter alia*, whether the judge's relative has been involved in the case in question, the position of the judge's relative in the firm, the size of the firm, its internal organisational structure, the financial importance of the case for the law firm, and any possible financial interest or potential benefit (and the extent thereof) on the part of the relative.[1335] Given the importance of appearances, however, when a situation arises that could give rise

1331 *Mitrov v. "the former Yugoslav Republic of Macedonia"*, App. no. 45959/09, §§53–56, 2.6.2016.

1332 *Pastörs v. Germany*, App. no. 55225/14, §§58–70, 3.10.2019.

1333 *Dorozhko and Pozharskiy v. Estonia*, App. nos. 14659/04+, §§56–58, 24.4.2008.

1334 *Ramljak v. Croatia*, App. no. 5856/13, §29, 27.6.2017. In this case, the judge's son was employed as a trainee in the law firm representing the applicant's opponent in the civil proceedings.

1335 *Nicholas v. Cyprus*, App. no. 63246/10, §62, 9.1.2018. In this case the judge's son was married to the daughter of the counsel who represented the defendant company and the young couple worked in the law firm of which the counsel was a managing partner.

to a suggestion or appearance of bias, that situation should be disclosed at the outset of the proceedings and an assessment should be made, taking into account the various factors involved in order to determine whether disqualification is actually necessary in the case. This is an important procedural safeguard which is necessary in order to provide adequate guarantees in respect of both objective and subjective impartiality.[1336]

#### 4.5.3.6. *Special Courts*

The Court has held that, particularly in very technical matters, there may be good reasons for opting for an adjudicatory body other than a court of the classic kind integrated within the standard judicial machinery of the country.[1337] A purely professional connection between the applicant and a member of the court is not normally sufficient to create a legitimate fear of a lack of impartiality of the latter, although it can be expected that a conflict of interest is possible in such a situation. For example, in the case *Le Compte, Van Leuven and De Meyere v. Belgium*, the fact that the Medical Appeals Council was composed of equal numbers of medical practitioners and members of the judiciary did not create any legitimate fear of a lack of impartiality because one of its legal members always acted as chairman and had a casting vote, and the method of election of the medical members could not as such be enough to bear out a charge of bias.[1338] On the other hand, in the case *Langborger v. Sweden*, the Court found that the two lay assessors of the Housing and Tenancy Court had a common interest in the matter before them that was contrary to that of the applicant, since the assessors had close links with two associations that had nominated them and these associations had a continued interest in the matter in question.[1339]

As concerns military courts, the determination by military courts of criminal charges against military service personnel is not in principle incompatible with the provisions of Article 6.[1340] However, an applicant's doubts about the tribunal's independence and impartiality can be objectively justified where all the members of the court martial are subordinate in rank to the convening officer and fall within his chain of command.[1341] Similarly, when a military court has in its composition a military officer, in the service of the army and thus subject to

---

[1336] *Nicholas v. Cyprus*, App. no. 63246/10, §64, 9.1.2018.

[1337] *British-American Tobacco Company Ltd v. the Netherlands*, App. no. 19589/92, §77, 20.11.1995, which concerned a patent right.

[1338] *Le Compte, Van Leuven and De Meyere v. Belgium*, App. nos. 6878/75+, §58, 23.6.1981.

[1339] *Langborger v. Sweden*, App. no. 11179/84, §35, 22.6.1989. See also *Le Compte, Van Leuven and De Meyere v. Belgium*, App. nos. 6878/75+, §58, 23.6.1981; and *Gautrin and Others v. France*, App. nos. 21257/93+, §59, 20.5.1998.

[1340] *Cooper v. the United Kingdom* [GC], App. no. 48843/99, §110, 16.12.2003.

[1341] *Findlay v. the United Kingdom*, App. no. 22107/93, §76, 25.2.1997; and *Miller and Others v. the United Kingdom*, App. nos. 45825/99+, §§30–31, 26.10.2004.

military discipline, who is appointed by his or her hierarchical superior and does not enjoy the same constitutional safeguards provided to judges, it cannot be considered that such a court is independent and impartial within the meaning of Article 6 of the Convention.[1342] The trial of civilians by a court composed in part of members of the armed forces can give rise to a legitimate fear of partiality.[1343] The determination of criminal charges against civilians in military courts can be held to be compatible with Article 6 only in very exceptional circumstances.[1344]

#### 4.5.3.7. *Statements in Public*

A legitimate reason to fear a lack of impartiality of a judge may also be created when the judge gives a statement about the matter in public.[1345] However, in *Previti v. Italy* no violation of Article 6 was found since the statements to the press were made by a number of members of the national legal service and no pronouncement as to the applicant's guilt was made. Moreover, the court hearing in the applicant's case had been made up entirely of professional judges whose experience and training enabled them to rise above external influence.[1346] Nor was there a lack of impartiality when a juror had made comments about the case in a newspaper interview after sentencing.[1347] In contrast, in *Kristiansen v. Norway* the presence on the jury of a juror who knew the victim and commented on her character in circumstances which could be perceived as a comment or reaction to her oral evidence led to a violation under Article 6 §1.[1348]

In the case *Buscemi v. Italy*, the president of the court in which the applicant's case was pending gave a statement to the press in a manner which could be regarded as showing his partiality in the matter.[1349] In the case *Olujić v. Croatia*, the Court held that even appearances could have relevance when assessing objective impartiality. In that case it was held inappropriate that the judge had participated in the examination of the case (disciplinary proceedings against the applicant, another judge) even though he had in an interview stated that he viewed the applicant and his statements about his own lack of independence

---

1342 *Gürkan v. Turkey*, App. no. 1154/04, §§13–20, 29.3.2011.

1343 *Incal v. Turkey*, App. no. 22678/93, §72, 9.6.1998; and *Iprahim Ülger v. Turkey*, App. no. 57250/00, §26, 29.7.2004.

1344 *Martin v. the United Kingdom*, App. no. 40426/98, §44, 24.10.2006; and *Mustafa v. Bulgaria*, App. no. 1230/17, §§28–37, 28.11.2019.

1345 *Lavents v. Latvia*, App. no. 58442/00, §§118–119, 28.11.2002; and *Buscemi v. Italy*, App. no. 29569/95, §67, 16.9.1999.

1346 *Previti v. Italy* (dec.), App. no. 45291/06, §253, 8.12.2009.

1347 *Bodet v. Belgium* (dec.), App. no. 78480/13, §§24–38, 5.1.2017; and *Haarde v. Iceland*, App. no. 66847/12, §105, 23.11.2017.

1348 *Kristiansen v. Norway*, App. no. 1176/10, §§56–61, 17.12.2015. See also Sofia Galani (Ed.), "Case and comment: selected decisions from the European Court of Human Rights from November and December 2015 – Impartiality of jurors, *Kristiansen v. Norway* (Application No. 1176/10)", *European Human Rights Law Review*, Issue 2, 2016, pp. 205–207.

1349 *Buscemi v. Italy*, App. no. 29569/95, §68, 16.9.1999.

as comical. In addition, he had described the applicant as a person lacking experience and knowledge, and as "a foreign body" in the Croatian judiciary. The Court considered that the expressions used by the judge clearly showed his bias against the applicant and that his further participation in the proceedings after the publication of the interview was incompatible with the requirement of impartiality under Article 6 §1 of the Convention.[1350]

The impartiality of a judge was also in question in the case *Morice v. France*, in which the judge had expressed his support for and trust in his colleague who was subject to a disciplinary sanction. The applicant had acted as a counsel in the case that had led to a disciplinary sanction. Nine years later, the judge who had expressed his support was a member of the Supreme Court (Cour de Cassation) bench in the criminal case against the applicant in which he was convicted and sentenced to a disciplinary sanction for having criticised a judge. The doubt about the lack of impartiality was based on the fact that the deciding judge had previously given support to his colleague. The Court found that the applicant's fear about the partiality of the court was reasoned since there was a conflict between the counsel and the judge subject to a disciplinary sanction, and the earlier support of the judge on the bench to his colleague was an objective ground to suspect that the court was not impartial.[1351]

Impartiality can also be at stake in a situation in which media and high-ranking authorities and politicians have expressed their opinion on a matter pending before a court. The case *Čivinskaitė v. Lithuania* concerned disciplinary proceedings against the applicant for allegedly improperly carrying out her duties as a senior prosecutor in a high-profile criminal case involving sexual abuse of a minor. After an inquiry, the Prosecutor-General found many deficiencies in the criminal investigation and lowered the applicant's rank as a prosecutor. A parliamentary commission also conducted an inquiry and came to the same conclusion. In addition, the President of the Republic demanded in a press release that the prosecutors involved be held personally accountable. The disciplinary sanction was confirmed by the administrative courts. The Court held that the fair trial guarantees had not been violated in the disciplinary proceedings. A criminal suspicion of a person holding a high-ranking position in society necessarily led to media attention and reactions. The statements by the President or the parliamentary commission did not put in question the impartiality and independence of the administrative law proceedings, since the matter was decided by professional judges at two levels of jurisdiction.[1352]

---

1350 *Olujić v. Croatia*, App. no. 22330/05, §§58–68, 5.2.2009. See also Kevin Aquilina, "The Independence of the Judiciary in Strasbourg Judicial Disciplinary Case Law – Judges as Applicants and National Judicial Councils as Factotums of Respondent States", in Paulo Pinto de Albuquerque, Krzysztof Wojtyczek (Eds.), *Judicial Power in a Globalized World – Liber Amicorum Vincent de Gaetano*, Springer, Cham 2019, pp. 1–32.

1351 *Morice v. France* [GC], App. no. 29369/10, §§79–92, 23.4.2015.

1352 *Čivinskaitė v. Lithuania*, App. no. 21218/12, §§113–145, 15.9.2020.

### 4.5.3.8. *Judges with their Own Interest in Matters*

The objective test is violated when a judge has a personal interest in a case.[1353] A pecuniary interest in a case renders a judge biased.[1354] However, Article 6 was found not to have been violated in one case where such an interest had been made known to the applicant who then refused the available opportunity to object to it.[1355]

A financial interest was the reason for the disqualification in the case *Sigríður Elín Sigfúsdóttir v. Iceland*. A judge, who had suffered an investment loss of 62,860 euros in the 2008 Icelandic banking crisis, was sitting as a judge on a five-member bench in a trial in which the applicant was convicted of fraud. The applicant was convicted of aiding and abetting market manipulation which had had an impact, *inter alia*, on the judge's investment loss. The judge's own loss was regarded as substantial, both in absolute terms and in relation to his wage income, and this fact gave the applicant objective grounds to doubt the impartiality of the judge. Although the bench had consisted of five members, there was a reasonable doubt as to the impartiality of the court, since, due to the secrecy of deliberations, it was not possible to determine the impact of the partial judge on the court's decision. On the other hand, the investment loss of 12,830 euros of another judge on the same bench did not exceed the threshold that would have called his impartiality into question.[1356]

Non-pecuniary interests may also be relevant. For example, in the case *Demicoli v. Malta*, two judges were found to be biased when they had sat in judgment on a newspaper article in which they had been criticised.[1357] The situation was similar in the case *Alenka Pečnik v. Slovenia*, in which a fine was imposed on the applicant by a judge who had felt offended by her statements, which he had described as "offensive and invented".[1358] On the other hand, in the case *Timperi v. Finland*, a lay member of the District Court was not found to have violated the objective test simply because he was an employee of the complainant. This was apparently because the employer was a city municipal authority employing over a thousand people and the lay judge had only served as a temporary teacher for the city for a short time.[1359]

---

1353 *Langborger v. Sweden*, App. no. 11179/84, §35, 22.6.1989; and *Gautrin and Others v. France*, App. nos. 21257/93+, §59, 20.5.1998.

1354 *Pétur Thór Sigurðsson v. Iceland*, App. no. 39731/98, §45, 10.4.2003.

1355 *D. v. Ireland* (dec.), App. no. 11489/85, 3.12.1986.

1356 *Sigríður Elín Sigfúsdóttir v. Iceland*, App. no. 41382/17, §§54–57, 25.2.2020.

1357 *Demicoli v. Malta*, App. no. 13057/87, §41, 27.8.1991. See also Giovanni Bonello, "More common law than common sense – how the European Court of Human Rights saves the United Kingdom from itself", *Human Rights Law Journal* (HRLJ), vol. 34, no. 7–12, 31 December 2014, pp. 239–245, at pp. 240–241.

1358 *Alenka Pečnik v. Slovenia*, App. no. 44901/05, §§41–44, 27.9.2012.

1359 *Timperi v. Finland* (dec.), App. no. 60963/00, 23.3.2004.

A judge's family relationships may also have effect on his or her impartiality. However, in a situation where the applicants, who were accused of a financial offence, had been informed of the fact that the Supreme Court judge's spouse had been a member of the Board of the Financial Supervisory Authority and the applicants had expressly stated that they had no objections to the impartiality of the judge, the Court found no violation. In contrast, the Court did find a violation vis-à-vis the same judge's son who had worked at the legal department of the bank in question since the applicants had neither been informed nor been given an opportunity to comment on the impartiality of the judge in that respect. Although the bank was not a party to the criminal proceedings, the son had had no contact with the case at issue, and he had already taken over other duties at the time of the proceedings, he had nevertheless been involved, *inter alia*, in the preparation of the bank's civil actions and could be regarded as a representative of the opposing party.[1360]

The fact that a judge is a Freemason does not as such create a legitimate reason to fear a lack of impartiality in a matter in which some of the parties or witnesses are also Freemasons.[1361] The situation may be different if the judge has personal information about these Freemasons or their lodge.[1362] On the other hand, a legitimate reason to fear a lack of impartiality was created when a judge was a professor at a university that was party to proceedings,[1363] and in another case when a judge had threatened some applicant teachers with reprisals after his son had been expelled from school.[1364] But no legitimate fear of partiality was created when a judge had been seen talking with an applicant's wife immediately after a hearing in a divorce case. Nor is the fact of having previously belonged to a political party enough to cast doubt on the impartiality of a judge, in particular when there is no indication that the judge's membership of the political party had any connection or link with the substance of the case.[1365]

### 4.5.4. WAIVER OF THE RIGHT TO AN INDEPENDENT AND IMPARTIAL TRIBUNAL

According to the Court's case-law, it is not clear whether an applicant can waive a right to an independent and impartial tribunal. In any event, if such a waiver is possible, it must be limited, unambiguous and fulfil certain minimum

1360 *Sigurður Einarsson and Others v. Iceland*, App. no. 39757/15, §§45–49 and 60–62, 4.6.2019.
1361 *Kiiskinen and Kovalainen v. Finland* (dec.), App. no. 26323/95, 1.6.1999.
1362 *Salaman v. the United Kingdom* (dec.), App. no. 43505/98, 15.6.2000.
1363 *Pescador Valero v. Spain*, App. no. 62435/00, §27, 17.6.2003.
1364 *Tocono and Profesorii Prometeişti v. Moldova*, App. no. 32263/03, §§31–32, 26.6.2007.
1365 *Otegi Mondragon and Others v. Spain* (dec.), App. nos. 4184/15+, §§25–29, 3.11.2015.

requirements.[1366] If the applicant does not invoke the lack of independence or impartiality in the domestic proceedings, it can in certain situations be interpreted as a tacit waiver, but in others not.[1367]

On the other hand, if a case has been referred back to a lower-level court for a new examination as a result of a lack of impartiality of the court, the referral applies to the ruling as a whole. This means that any retrial will also concern those charges that were already dismissed in the earlier, partial examination. The prohibition of *reformatio in peius* does not therefore apply to a case which has been referred back.[1368]

### 4.5.5. ISSUE CORRECTED ON APPEAL

Problems relating to the lack of independence or impartiality may also be corrected if the proceedings before an appeal court have fulfilled the requirements flowing from the Convention.[1369] This is possible in civil and administrative cases when an appeal court not only considers the complaint but is also fully competent to reassess the correctness of the lower court's decision in respect of the facts and law, to quash it and refer it back to the lower court for a new examination, or to decide it itself.[1370] On the other hand, in criminal matters the right to an independent and impartial tribunal must be guaranteed in the first-instance court.[1371] In these situations, the corrective measure is to refer the case back to that level of jurisdiction in which the procedural mistake took place.

---

1366 The case *Pfeifer and Plankl v. Austria*, App. no. 10802/84, §§38–39, 25.2.1992, concerned a waiver which had been made without an attorney, whereas in the case *Öcalan v. Turkey*, App. no. 46221/99, §116, 12.3.2003, the waiver was not unambiguous. In the case *Oberschlick v. Austria (No. 1)*, App. no. 11662/85, §51, 23.5.1991, it was not shown that the applicant had waived the right to an impartial tribunal. See also Karen Reid, *A Practitioner's Guide to the European Convention on Human Rights*, Sweet & Maxwell/Thomson Reuters, London 2019, p. 229.

1367 See, for example, *McGonnell v. the United Kingdom*, App. no. 28488/95, §45, 8.2.2000, in which the failure to contest the issue was not regarded as a tacit waiver; and *Bulut v. Austria*, App. no. 17358/90, §34, 22.2.1996, in which the passivity was interpreted as a tacit waiver.

1368 *Kuokkanen and Johannesdahl v. Finland* (dec.), App. no. 38147/12, §§26–28, 25.6.2015. In this case, the Court approved the Supreme Court's ruling, finding that the domestic practice in respect of the referring back fulfilled the fair trial requirements.

1369 *De Cubber v. Belgium*, App. no. 9186/80, §33, 26.10.1984; *De Haan v. the Netherlands*, App. no. 22839/93, §§52–55, 26.8.1997; *Helle v. Finland*, App. no. 20772/92, §46, 19.12.1997; *Crompton v. the United Kingdom*, App. no. 42509/05, §79, 27.10.2009; and *Denisov v. Ukraine* [GC], App. no. 76639/11, §§65, 67 and 72, 25.9.2018.

1370 *De Haan v. the Netherlands*, App. no. 22839/93, §§53–54, 26.8.1997; and *Ranson v. the United Kingdom* (dec.), App. no. 14180/03, 2.9.2003.

1371 *Findlay v. the United Kingdom*, App. no. 22107/93, §79, 25.2.1997. See also Giovanni Bonello, "More common law than common sense – how the European Court of Human Rights saves the United Kingdom from itself", *Human Rights Law Journal* (HRLJ), vol. 34, no. 7–12, 31 December 2014, pp. 239–245, at pp. 243–244.

In the case *Słomka v. Poland* the Court held that the mistake committed by the lower court could not be corrected by an impartial higher court. The applicant had been convicted of contempt of court and sentenced to 14 days' imprisonment by the same judges in front of whom the applicant had jumped behind the judges' table and shouted: "This is a mockery of justice". He was not given an opportunity to present his own arguments vis-à-vis his disciplinary sanction. Although the appellate court was impartial and the applicant was given an opportunity to present his arguments, it could not correct the problem of impartiality in the lower court since the 14-day penalty was entirely executed before his interlocutory appeal against it was examined by the appellate court.[1372]

### 4.5.6. ESTABLISHED BY LAW

Article 6 §1 of the Convention requires that a court or tribunal must always be established by law.[1373] This means that there must be a legal basis for the very existence of a tribunal and that the tribunal complies with the particular rules that govern it, including its composition.[1374] The purpose of this provision is to guarantee that none of the courts or tribunals in a democratic society is dependent on the executive and that their functioning is regulated by Parliamentary Acts.[1375] This does not mean that every detail of the judicial system should be regulated by law. If the legislation defines the big basic structures of the organisation and competences of the courts, certain details may be left to the executive through the delegated legislative powers.[1376] Article 6 §1 does not prevent the establishment of special courts either, if they are established by law.[1377]

As it is in the first place for the national courts themselves to interpret the provisions of domestic law, the Court may not question their interpretation

1372 *Słomka v. Poland*, App. no. 68924/12, §§44–52, 6.12.2018.

1373 *Lavents v. Latvia*, App. no. 58442/00, §81, 28.11.2002; *Biagioli v. San Marino* (dec.), App. no. 64735/14, §71, 13.9.2016; *Jorgic v. Germany*, App. no. 74613/01, §64, 12.7.2007; and *Richert v. Poland*, App. no. 54809/07, §41, 25.10.2011.

1374 *Sokurenko and Strygun v. Ukraine*, App. nos. 29458/04+, §24, 20.7.2006; *Buscarini v. San Marino* (dec.), App. no. 24645/94, 18.2.1999; *Lavents v. Latvia*, App. no. 58442/00, §114, 28.11.2002; *Pandjikidze and Others v. Georgia*, App. no. 30323/02, §104, 27.10.2009; *Gorgiladze v. Georgia*, App. no. 4313/04, §68, 20.10.2009; *Posokhov v. Russia*, App. no. 63486/00, §39, 4.3.2003; *Fatullayev v. Azerbaijan*, App. no. 40984/07, §144, 22.4.2010; and *Kontalexis v. Greece*, App. no. 59000/08, §42, 31.5.2011.

1375 *Richert v. Poland*, App. no. 54809/07, §42, 25.10.2011; and *Coëme and Others v. Belgium*, App. nos. 32492/96+, §98, 22.6.2000.

1376 *Zand v. Austria*, App. no. 7360/76, Report of the Commission, §69, 12.10.1978.

1377 *X. and Y. v. Ireland* (dec.), App. no. 8299/78, 10.10.1980.

on the competence of a tribunal, unless there has been a flagrant violation of domestic law.[1378] The Court's task is therefore limited to examining whether reasonable grounds existed for the authorities to establish jurisdiction.[1379]

In the case *Coëme and Others v. Belgium*, the Court found that the requirement of a tribunal established by law was violated when the Cour de cassation, which was not competent to examine any other charges except those pressed against ministers, had convicted, together with some ministers, some people who were not ministers.[1380] Similarly in *Aviakompaniya A.T.I., ZAT v. Ukraine*, the Supreme Court, instead of acting within its jurisdiction as provided for by domestic law (by quashing a decision and remitting the case for further consideration or declaring the proceedings void), had decided the case on the merits in place of the competent body. Accordingly, there was a violation since that court was not deemed to be a "tribunal established by law".[1381] Similarly, in *Pandjikidze and Others v. Georgia* there was a violation since a court composed of lay judges had continued to decide cases in accordance with established tradition, although the law on lay judges had been repealed and no new law had been enacted.[1382] On the other hand, the Court has held that Turkish courts and tribunals in Northern Cyprus had been established by law, even though their establishment was based on laws which were enacted by a State which had not been internationally recognised.[1383]

The requirement of a tribunal established by law also covers situations in which a court or tribunal does not function in accordance with the norms regulating its functioning. The Court found a violation, for example, in a situation in which the internal rules on the appointment of judges had not been followed.[1384] The Court also held in the case *Oleksandr Volkov v. Ukraine* that the practice of tacitly renewing judges' terms of office for an indefinite period after their statutory term of office had expired and pending

---

1378 *Coëme and Others v. Belgium*, App. nos. 32492/96+, §98, 22.6.2000; and *Lavents v. Latvia*, App. no. 58442/00, §114, 28.11.2002.

1379 *Jorgic v. Germany*, App. no. 74613/01, §65, 12.7.2007.

1380 *Coëme and Others v. Belgium*, App. nos. 32492/96+, §108, 22.6.2000. See also Dragoljub Popović, *European Human Rights Law – A Manual: An Introduction to the Strasbourg Court and its Jurisprudence*, Eleven International Publishing, The Hague 2013, p. 194.

1381 *Aviakompaniya A.T.I., ZAT v. Ukraine*, App. no. 1006/07, §44, 5.10.2017.

1382 *Pandjikidze and Others v. Georgia*, App. no. 30323/02, §§108–111, 27.10.2009.

1383 *Cyprus v. Turkey* [GC], App. no. 25781/94, §237, 10.5.2001.

1384 *Posokhov v. Russia*, App. no. 63486/00, §43, 4.3.2003; and *Fedotova v. Russia*, App. no. 73225/01, §43, 13.4.2006, both cases where the lay judge of the court should have been selected by drawing lots. In the case *Lavents v. Latvia*, App. no. 58442/00, §115, 28.11.2002, the problem was that the composition had included two lay judges who, according to Latvian law, should not have participated in the same matter again.

their reappointment was contrary to the principle of a "tribunal established by law" since such a renewal of an appointment could not be based solely on internal practice.[1385] A replacement of a judge must also be devoid of any arbitrariness.[1386]

---

1385 *Oleksandr Volkov v. Ukraine*, App. no. 21722/11, §§151 and 154–156, 9.1.2013. See also Kevin Aquilina, "The Independence of the Judiciary in Strasbourg Judicial Disciplinary Case Law – Judges as Applicants and National Judicial Councils as Factotums of Respondent States", in Paulo Pinto de Albuquerque, Krzysztof Wojtyczek (Eds.), *Judicial Power in a Globalized World – Liber Amicorum Vincent de Gaetano*, Springer, Cham 2019, pp. 1–32; Lize R. Glas, "European Convention on Human Rights", *Netherlands Quarterly of Human Rights*, vol. 31, no. 2, June 2013, pp. 210–216, at pp. 211–212; Gianni Buquicchio, "*Volkov vs. Ukraine* and the Venice Commission's approach to structural independence of the judiciary", in G.G. Harutyunyan (Ed.), *New Millenium Constitutionalism: Paradigms of Reality and Challenges*, NJHAR, Yerevan 2013, pp. 323–340; and Arman Zrvandyan, *Casebook on European Fair Trial Standards in Administrative Justice*, Council of Europe Publishing, Strasbourg 2016, pp. 55–57.

1386 *Pasquini v. San Marino*, App. no. 50956/16, §112, 2.5.2019; and *Biagioli v. San Marino* (dec.), App. no. 64735/14, §§77–78 and 80, 13.9.2016 which concerned a small jurisdiction and a court with a limited number of judges. See also Ricardo Buendia, "Right to a fair trial – *Pasquini v. San Marino* (Application No. 50956/16)", *European Human Rights Law Review*, Issue 5, 2019, pp. 567–569.

# CHAPTER 5
# PRESUMPTION OF INNOCENCE IN ARTICLE 6 §2

**Article 6: Right to a fair trial**

2. *Everyone charged with a criminal offence shall be presumed innocent until proved guilty according to law.*

## 5.1. BASIC PRINCIPLES ON PRESUMPTION OF INNOCENCE

Article 6 §2 of the Convention requires that a person charged with a criminal offence shall be presumed innocent until proved guilty according to law. The presumption of innocence is a basic criminal presumption, the purpose of which is to secure the fairness of the subsequent trial.[1387] If the trial ends in conviction, the presumption of innocence is overturned. If the guilt cannot be proved, official suspicion can no longer be held against that person.

The requirement of presumption of innocence is an independent requirement relating to criminal proceedings, among the other Article 6 fair trial requirements. The presumption of innocence may be violated even if the other Article 6 fair trial guarantees are fulfilled. On the other hand, the presumption of innocence is part of the general fairness requirements. This becomes apparent from the fact that an Article 6 §2 violation is often found together with a lack of the Article 6 §1 legal guarantees.[1388]

---

1387 *Allenet de Ribemont v. France*, App. no. 15175/99, §35, 10.2.1995. See also Karen Reid, *A Practitioner's Guide to the European Convention on Human Rights*, Sweet & Maxwell/ Thomson Reuters, London 2019, p. 304; Eva Brems, "Conflicting human rights: an exploration in the context of the right to fair trial in the European Convention for the Protection of Human Rights and Fundamental Freedoms", *Human Rights Quarterly*, vol. 27, no. 1, 2005, pp. 294–326, at pp. 312–313; and Sverre Erik Jebens, "The Scope of the Presumption of Innocence in Article 6 §2 of the Convention – Especially on its Reputation-Related Aspect", in Lucius Caflisch, Johan Callewaert, Roderick Liddell, Paul Mahoney, Mark Villiger (Eds.), *Liber Amicorum Luzius Wildhaber: Human Rights, Strasbourg Views/Droits de L'homme, Regards de Strasbourg*, N.P. Engel, Kehl/Strasbourg/Arlington, Va. 2007, pp. 207–227, at pp. 211–213.

1388 In many cases in which the Court has already found a violation of Article 6 §1 of the Convention, it may find that it is no longer necessary to examine separately the alleged

The basic elements of the presumption of innocence are the following requirements of the criminal proceedings: (1) the members of a court should not have a preconceived idea that the accused has committed the offence he or she is charged with; (2) the burden of proof is on the prosecution; (3) any doubt should benefit the accused; (4) it is for the prosecution to inform the accused of the case that will be made against him; and (5) the accused has the right to prepare and present his defence accordingly.[1389]

## 5.2. DIMENSIONS OF PRESUMPTION OF INNOCENCE

### 5.2.1. PERSONAL DIMENSION

Article 6 §2 of the Convention protects persons who are subject to the widely and autonomously interpreted concept of "a criminal charge". The point of departure is the national concept of a criminal charge, but this concept also refers to other proceedings factually leading to punishment or sanctions.[1390] Pretrial investigation is a part of the concept of a criminal charge, and therefore the presumption of innocence also protects the accused during the pretrial investigation. Article 6 §2 thus governs criminal proceedings in their entirety, irrespective of the outcome of the prosecution, and not solely the examination of the merits of the charge.[1391] Therefore, the presumption of innocence applies even to the reasons given in a judgment acquitting the accused in its operative provisions, from which the reasoning cannot be dissociated. It may be breached if the reasoning reflects an opinion that the accused is in fact guilty.[1392]

---

Article 6 §2 violation. See, for example, *Funke v. France*, App. no. 10828/24, §45, 25.2.1993; and *Heaney and McGuinness v. Ireland*, App. no. 34720/97, §§40 and 59, 21.12.2000. The connection to Article 6 §1 may also appear in situations in which there are crime-based claims directed against the defendant but to which Article 6 §2 does not apply. For example, in the case *Phillips v. the United Kingdom*, App. no. 41087/98, §39, 5.7.2001, Article 6 §2 did not apply to the proceedings concerning confiscation of the proceeds of a crime but Article 6 §1 and the concept of a criminal charge did. The confiscation order was regarded as analogous to the criminal proceedings and Article 6 §1 applied. The Court did not, however, find a violation of Article 6 §1, as the legal presumption, which was based on the facts of the case, was in all respects reasonable.

1389 *Barberà, Messegué and Jabardo v. Spain*, App. nos. 10590/83+, §77, 6.12.1988.

1390 See, for example, *Deweer v. Belgium*, App. no. 6903/75, §§42, 44 and 46, 27.2.1980; *Eckle v. Germany*, App. no. 8130/78, §73, 15.7.1982; *Foti and Others v. Italy*, App. nos. 7604/76+, §52, 10.12.1982; *Engel and Others v. the Netherlands*, App. nos. 5100/71+, §82, 8.6.1976; *König v. Germany*, App. no. 6232/73, §89, 28.6.1978; *Adolf v. Austria*, App. no. 8269/78, §30, 26.3.1982; and *T., A., J. and S. v. Finland* (dec.), App. no. 27744/95, 9.9.2003.

1391 *Poncelet v. Belgium*, App. no. 44418/07, §50, 30.3.2010; *Minelli v. Switzerland*, App. no. 8660/79, §30, 25.3.1983; and *Garycki v. Poland*, App. no. 14348/02, §68, 6.2.2007.

1392 *Cleve v. Germany*, App. no. 48144/09, §41, 15.1.2015.

The presumption of innocence cannot, however, apply to those who are detained for other reasons, such as for the execution of an expulsion[1393] or extradition order.[1394] The presumption of innocence also does not apply to persons who are suspected of a crime but who are factually not yet or no longer in the position of an accused, within the autonomous meaning given to the concept of a criminal charge by the Convention.[1395]

However, if a statement given by an individual during the pretrial investigation is referred to when establishing the guilt of others, even in the context of other proceedings, this may mean a violation of that individual's presumption of innocence. In cases in which it is necessary to sever proceedings from one another, it is possible to refer to a statement of a person who is subject to subsequent proceedings provided the reasoning of the judgment clearly indicates that the court does not consider the person's guilt as established.[1396]

### 5.2.2. MATERIAL DIMENSION

Even if the pretrial investigation falls within the scope of the criminal charge, different crime-solving methods and the fact that a person is subject to those measures, due to a suspicion of guilt or the need to prevent crime, do not violate the presumption of innocence. Therefore, for example, alcohol breath-testing, the taking of blood, saliva and urine samples,[1397] other medical examinations, fingerprinting, the taking of DNA samples, the bodily inspection of a person or participation in identity parades do not, as investigative measures, violate the presumption of innocence.[1398]

---

1393 *X. v. Netherlands* (dec.), App. no. 1983/63, 13.12.1965.

1394 *X. v. Austria* (dec.), App. no. 1918/63, 18.12.1963.

1395 *Adolf v. Austria*, App. no. 8269/78, §30, 26.3.1982; and *Mikolajova v. Slovakia*, App. no. 4479/03, §§42–43, 18.1.2011. In the latter case the criminal report could not have led to the pressing of charges as the applicant's husband did not consent to the pursuit of criminal proceedings against her. Nor was the applicant questioned, summonsed or in any other way notified by the police or any other domestic authority. See also *Gogitidze and Others v. Georgia*, App. no. 36862/05, §§125–126, 12.5.2015; *Larrañaga Arando and Others v. Spain* (dec.), App. nos. 73911/16+, §§45–46, 25.6.2019; and *Khodorkovskiy and Lebedev v. Russia (No. 2)*, App. nos. 51111/07+, §543, 14.1.2020.

1396 *Karaman v. Germany*, App. no. 17103/10, §§43–44 and 64–71, 27.2.2014.

1397 *Tirado Ortiz and Lozano Martin v. Spain* (dec.), App. no. 43486/98, 15.6.1999.

1398 See, for example, *X. v. the Netherlands* (dec.), App. no. 8239/78, 4.12.1978; and *Schmidt v. Germany* (dec.), App. no. 32352/02, 5.1.2006. However, when acquiring evidence by using methods which interfere with the applicant's physical or mental integrity, the existence of alternative means must be examined, and it must be considered whether the use of the investigative measures could cause harm to the applicant's health. The methods used must not, in any event, trespass the threshold of Article 3. See, for example, *Nevmerzhitsky v. Ukraine*, App. no. 54825/00, §§94–97, 5.4.2005; *Schmid v. Germany* (dec.), App. no. 32352/02, 5.1.2006; *Peters v. the Netherlands* (dec.), App. no. 21132/93, 6.4.1994; *Saunders v. the United Kingdom* [GC], App. no. 19187/91, §69, 17.12.1996; *Choudhary v. the United Kingdom* (dec.),

Nor do certain limitations during the pretrial detention – such as possible dressing orders, restrictions on correspondence or the prison conditions – mean a violation of the presumption of innocence. Normal, lawful investigative measures directed at a person do not therefore lead as such to the violation of the presumption of innocence. On the other hand, the fact that a suspected person is convicted of not having submitted the required material may invoke both the presumption of innocence as well as the right not to self-incriminate.[1399]

### 5.2.3. DURATION OF PRESUMPTION OF INNOCENCE

As a main rule, the presumption of innocence lasts until the point that there is a final ruling in the case.[1400] Therefore, it is applicable at the appeal stage until a final judgment or decision is being rendered. Once applicable, the presumption of innocence does not cease to apply solely because the first-instance proceedings resulted in the defendant's conviction when the proceedings are continuing on appeal.[1401] The presumption of innocence does not, however, apply to situations in which there is only a question about sentencing, if the person has already been found guilty and convicted of a crime.[1402] If an accused has properly been proved guilty, Article 6 §2 can have no application in relation to allegations made about the accused's character and conduct as part of the sentencing process, unless such accusations are of such a nature and degree as to amount to the bringing of a new "charge" within the autonomous Convention meaning.[1403]

Despite the fact that the presumption of innocence applies only to pending proceedings, it may also have implications further than the terminated proceedings, provided that the terminated proceedings and the new proceedings are clearly connected.[1404] The presumption of innocence therefore covers situations in which the assessment of guilt and the examination of the criminal

App. no. 40084/98, 4.5.1999; *J.B. v. Switzerland*, App. no. 31827/96, §68, 3.5.2001; *P.G. and J.H. v. the United Kingdom*, App. no. 44787/98, §80, 25.9.2001; and *Jalloh v. Germany* [GC], App. no. 54810/00, §§ 70, 102, 116–117 and 122, 11.7.2006.

1399 *Funke v. France*, App. no. 10828/24, §§44–45, 25.2.1993; and *Heaney and McGuinness v. Ireland*, App. no. 34720/97, §40, 21.12.2000. More about the right not to self-incriminate above in Chapter 4, section 4.2.10.

1400 *Nölkenbockhoff v. the Federal Republic of Germany*, App. no. 10300/83, §43, 9.10.1985.

1401 *Konstas v. Greece*, App. no. 53466/07, §36, 24.5.2011.

1402 *Engel and Others v. the Netherlands*, App. nos. 5100/71+, §90, 8.6.1976; and *Phillips v. the United Kingdom*, App. no. 41087/98, §§35–36, 5.7.2001.

1403 *Bikas v. Germany*, App. no. 76607/13, §57, 25.1.2018; *Böhmer v. Germany*, App. no. 37568/97, §55, 3.10.2002; *Geerings v. the Netherlands*, App. no. 30810/03, §43, 1.3.2007; and *Phillips v. the United Kingdom*, App. no. 30810/03, §35, 5.7.2001.

1404 *Yassar Hussain v. the United Kingdom*, App. no. 8866/04, §19, 7.6.2006; *Sekanina v. Austria*, App. no. 13126/87, §22, 25.8.1993; *Böhmer v. Germany*, App. no. 37568/97, §67, 3.10.2002; *Diamantides v. Greece (No. 2)*, App. no. 71563/01, §35, 19.5.2005; and *Eshonkulov v. Russia*, App. no. 68900/13, §§74–75, 15.1.2015.

charge continue in one way or another. This could be, for example, when discontinued proceedings are continued,[1405] or when the damages and/or costs and expenses based on discontinued proceedings are being decided.[1406] The presumption of innocence also applies to situations where circumstances presented in proceedings involving the sentencing of a convicted person give rise to the pressing of new charges.[1407]

The temporal dimension of the presumption of innocence also extends beyond the criminal proceedings in situations where, in a civil matter for example, a judge is deciding on damages and/or the costs and expenses of the criminal matter,[1408] or some other public authority states after an acquittal that the acquitted person was nevertheless guilty. This was confirmed in the cases *Minelli v. Switzerland*, *Sekanina v. Austria*, *Rushiti v. Austria*, *Y. v. Norway*, *Hammern v. Norway*, *O. v. Norway*, *Orr v. Norway* and *Ashendon and Jones v. the United Kingdom*.[1409] The presumption of innocence does not, however, apply to an application by which a convicted person seeks the reopening of his or her case.[1410]

## 5.3. CONTENT OF PRESUMPTION OF INNOCENCE

### 5.3.1. PRESUMPTION OF INNOCENCE AND BURDEN OF PROOF BY THE PROSECUTION

One of the essential elements of the presumption of innocence is the prosecutor's duty to bear the burden of proof, that is, the obligation that the

1405 *Adolf v. Austria*, App. no. 8269/78, §§19–40, 26.3.1982.

1406 *Minelli v. Switzerland*, App. no. 8660/79, §§30, 32 and 40, 25.3.1983. See also Reid, Karen: A practitioner's guide to the European Convention on Human Rights, Sweet & Maxwell/Thomson Reuters, London 2019, p. 300.

1407 *Engel and Others v. the Netherlands*, App. nos. 5100/71+, §90, 8.6.1976; *Phillips v. the United Kingdom*, App. no. 41087/98, §35, 5.7.2001; *Böhmer v. Germany*, App. no. 37568/97, §55, 3.10.2002; and *V. v. Finland*, App. no. 40412/98, §88, 24.4.2007.

1408 *Yassar Hussain v. the United Kingdom*, App. no. 8866/04, §22, 7.6.2006; *Sekanina v. Austria*, App. no. 13126/87, §30, 25.8.1993; and *Lamanna v. Austria*, App. no. 28923/95, §40, 10.7.2001.

1409 *Minelli v. Switzerland*, App. no. 8660/79, §§31–41, 25.3.1983; *Sekanina v. Austria*, App. no. 13126/87, §§22 and 25–31, 25.8.1993; *Rushiti v. Austria*, App. no. 28389/95, §§27–32, 21.3.2000; *Y. v. Norway*, App. no. 56568/00, §§39–47, 11.2.2003; *Hammern v. Norway*, App. no. 30287/96, §§41–49, 11.2.2003; *O. v. Norway*, App. no. 29327/95, §§33–41, 11.2.2003; *Orr v. Norway*, App. no. 31283/04, §§47–55, 15.5.2008; and *Ashendon and Jones v. the United Kingdom*, App. nos. 35730/07+, §§42–55, 13.9.2011. See also Tom Hickman, Faisal Saifee, "Case Analysis – *Hammern v. Norway*, *O v. Norway*, *Ringvold v. Norway* and *Y v. Norway*", *European Human Rights Law Review*, Issue 5, 2003, pp. 539–546; and Sverre Erik Jebens, "The limits of the presumption of innocence – Some clarifications in the Court's recent case-law", in *Liber Amicorum Dean Spielmann – Mélanges en L'honneur de/Essays in Honour of Dean Spielmann*, Wolf Legal Publishers, Oisterwijk 2015, pp. 255–262.

1410 *X. v. the Federal Republic of Germany* (dec.), App. no. 914/60, 16.12.1961.

accused does not have to prove his or her innocence. However, the defence may be required to provide an explanation after the prosecution has made a prima facie case against an accused.[1411] Therefore, for example, the drawing of adverse inferences from a statement by an accused which is found to be untrue does not raise an issue under Article 6 §2.[1412]

For example, in the case *John Murray v. the United Kingdom*,[1413] the defendant refused to reply to the question about his presence at the crime scene and this failure to reply was given relevance when assessing the evidence. The Court held that the other evidence presented by the public prosecutor had been strong. In this respect, it was understandable that the domestic court had made assumptions about the continuous failure of the accused to explain his presence at the crime scene. In this case, the burden of proof remained with the prosecutor, who had presented strong evidence, and it had not been shifted to the defendant. The presumption of innocence was not therefore violated.[1414]

By contrast, in the case *Telfner v. Austria*, the burden of proof was shifted when the applicant was found guilty, as the driver of a vehicle, of a traffic accident, even though there was no direct evidence against the driver. The evidence was based on the fact that the applicant was the principal user of the car and that he was not at home at the time of the accident. The applicant had refused to reply to any questions concerning the driving of the car. According to domestic law, these circumstances required that the applicant show he had not driven the car. The case differed from the *John Murray* case in that there was no other evidence against the applicant. The Court found that the domestic courts had shifted the burden of proof to the applicant and that Article 6 §2 had been violated in this case.[1415]

Reversed burden of proof may also be in question in confiscation proceedings where the proceeds of crime are confiscated from the defendant.[1416]

---

1411 *Telfner v. Austria*, App. no. 33501/96, §18, 20.3.2001; and *Poletan and Azirovik v. "the former Yugoslav Republic of Macedonia"*, App. nos. 26711/07+, §§63–67, 12.5.2016.

1412 *Kok v. the Netherlands* (dec.), App. no. 43149/98, 4.7.2000.

1413 *John Murray v. the United Kingdom*, App. no. 18731/91, §§45–54, 8.2.1996. See also John Jackson, "Re-conceptualizing the right of silence as an effective fair trial standard", *International and Comparative Law Quarterly*, vol. 58, pt. 4, October 2009, pp. 835–861; and Michael O'Boyle, "Freedom from self-incrimination and the right to silence: a Pandora's box?", in Paul Mahoney, Franz Matscher, Herbert Petzold, Luzius Wildhaber (Eds.), *Protection des Droits de L'homme: La Perspective Européenne, Mélanges à la Mémoire de Rolv Ryssdal/ Protecting Human Rights: The European Perspective, Studies in Memory of Rolv Ryssdal*, Carl Heymanns Verlag, Köln/Berlin/Bonn/München 2000, pp. 1021–1038, at pp. 1034–1036.

1414 See, for example, *Narinen v. Finland* (dec.), App. no. 13102/03, 13.12.2005.

1415 *Telfner v. Austria*, App. no. 33501/96, §§17–20, 20.3.2001; *Heaney and McGuinness v. Ireland*, App. no. 34720/97, 21.12.2000; and *Natunen v. Finland*, App. no. 21022/04, §54, 31.3.2009. See also Francis G. Jacobs, Robin C.A. White, Clare Owey, *The European Convention on Human Rights*, Oxford University Press, Oxford 2017, p. 314.

1416 These cases have most often been examined under Article 6 §1 when the confiscation is ordered in a separate set of proceedings after the principal criminal issue has already become

In these situations, it is important that the prosecution bears a clear burden of proof of the crime itself as well as of the fact that the defendant has received assets around the time of the crime. Thereafter the burden of proof may shift to the defendant, obliging him or her to provide a valid alternative explanation for the increase in assets. Such shifting of the burden of proof has not been considered to be a violation of the fair trial guarantees or the presumption of innocence.[1417]

A claim about the violation of the presumption of innocence and the reversed burden of proof can also be raised in the sense that, in the pretrial investigation of the case, only evidence against the suspect is collected and all evidence speaking for him or her is ignored. In these situations, the procedural legal safety guarantees become important: it is important to know whether the defendant in the criminal matter is being assisted by counsel, whether he or she has requested during the pretrial investigation that such material should be obtained and whether he or she has had the opportunity during the court proceedings to present evidence in order to defend him- or herself against the evidence admitted by the prosecution.[1418]

The burden of proof cannot be reversed in compensation proceedings following a final decision to discontinue the proceedings.[1419] Exoneration from criminal liability does not preclude the establishment of civil liability to pay compensation arising out of the same facts on the basis of a less strict burden of proof.[1420]

---

final. In this context, a question may arise as to whether there still exists a criminal charge within the meaning of the Convention and whether the presumption of innocence still applies to these proceedings. See *Phillips v. the United Kingdom*, App. no. 41087/98, §§35–36, 5.7.2001. See also Miklos Hollan, "Confiscation of the proceeds from crime and the principle of presumption of innocence", in Kimmo Nuotio (Ed.), *Festschrift in Honour of Raimo Lahti*, University of Helsinki/Faculty of Law, Helsinki 2007, pp. 363–372.

1417 *Phillips v. the United Kingdom*, App. no. 41087/98, §§40–47, 5.7.2001; *Geerings v. the Netherlands*, App. no. 30810/03, §44, 1.3.2007; *Grayson and Barnham v. the United Kingdom*, App. nos. 19955/05+, §§45–49, 23.9.2008; and *Minhas v. the United Kingdom* (dec.), App. no. 7618/07, 10.11.2009.

1418 *Landgren v. Finland* (dec.), App. no. 17889/07, 10.11.2009. The case *Bernard v. France*, App. no. 22885/93, §§37–40, 23.4.1998, concerned the content of psychiatric expert statements which, according to the applicant, inculpated him. The Court found that these measures were taken to investigate whether the applicant suffered from some mental illness that could have been connected to the act he was accused of. The applicant had had the opportunity to contest the statements and to have them declared null and void. In addition, witnesses appointed by the applicant had been heard and his counsel had had an opportunity to comment on the witness testimonies. The Court did not find a violation of the presumption of innocence.

1419 *Capeau v. Belgium*, App. no. 42914/98, §25, 13.1.2005.

1420 *Ringvold v. Norway*, App. no. 34964/97, §38, 11.2.2003; *Y. v. Norway*, App. no. 56568/00, §41, 11.2.2003; and *Lundkvist v. Sweden* (dec.), App. no. 48518/99, 13.11.2003. See also Sverre Erik Jebens, "The Scope of the Presumption of Innocence in Article 6 §2 of the Convention – Especially on its Reputation-Related Aspect", in Lucius Caflisch, Johan Callewaert, Roderick Liddell, Paul Mahoney, Mark Villiger (Eds.), *Liber Amicorum Luzius Wildhaber: Human Rights,*

The Court has also held that the *in dubio pro reo* principle (doubts should benefit the accused) is a specific expression of the presumption of innocence.[1421] Such an issue may arise if the domestic courts' decisions finding an applicant guilty are not sufficiently reasoned,[1422] or if an extreme and unattainable burden of proof is placed on the applicant so that his or her defence does not have even the slightest prospect of success.[1423]

### 5.3.2. PRESUMPTION OF INNOCENCE, LEGAL PRESUMPTIONS AND DIFFERENT REQUIREMENTS FOR BURDEN OF PROOF

Although the burden of proof in criminal matters is on the prosecution, it does not prevent the existence of certain legal presumptions which may in certain circumstances shift the burden of proof to the defendant. According to the Court's case-law, legal presumptions are not incompatible with Article 6 §2 of the Convention, and therefore a person can in certain circumstances be convicted on the basis of such a presumption, despite the fact that no personal intent or knowledge can be shown in the case.[1424] Legal presumptions may not, however, trespass on certain reasonable limits or put the defendant in an unreasonable situation, and he or she must have the chance to defend him- or herself and to have the presumption reversed.[1425] In the case *Salabiaku v. France*, the applicant was convicted of drug trafficking on the basis of a presumption inherent in the customs regulations. He had brought narcotic substances through the customs green line at a French airport, in a box, the contents of which he claimed to have been unaware of. The Court held that the presumption did not violate the presumption of innocence as the applicant had had the chance to rebut default

*Strasbourg Views/Droits de L'homme, Regards de Strasbourg*, N.P. Engel, Kehl/Strasbourg/Arlington, Va. 2007, pp. 207–227, at pp. 217–222.

1421 *Barberà, Messegué and Jabardo v. Spain*, App. nos. 10590/83+, §77, 6.12.1988; and *Tsalkitzis v. Greece (No. 2)*, App. no. 72624/10, §60, 19.10.2017.

1422 *Melich and Beck v. the Czech Republic*, App. no. 35450/04, §§49–55, 24.7.2008; and *Ajdarić v. Croatia*, App. no. 20883/09, §51, 13.12.2011.

1423 *Nemtsov v. Russia*, App. no. 1774/11, §92, 31.7.2014; *Topić v. Croatia*, App. no. 51355/10, §45, 10.10.2013; and *Frumkin v. Russia*, App. no. 74568/12, §166, 5.1.2016.

1424 *Falk v. the Netherlands* (dec.), App. no. 66273/01, 19.10.2004.

1425 *Salabiaku v. France*, App. no. 10519/83, §28, 7.10.1988; *Radio France and Others v. France*, App. no. 53984/00, §24, 30.3.2004 (presumption of criminal liability of a publishing director for defamatory statements made in radio programmes); *Västberga Taxi Aktiebolag and Vulic v. Sweden*, App. no. 36985/97, §113, 23.7.2002 (objective responsibility for tax surcharges); *Klouvi v. France*, App. no. 30754/03, §41, 20.6.2011 (inability to defend a charge of malicious prosecution owing to a statutory presumption that an accusation against a defendant acquitted for lack of evidence was false); *Iasir v. Belgium*, App. no. 21614/12, §30, 26.1.2016 (substantive presumption on participation in an offence by co-accused); and *Zschüschen v. Belgium* (dec.), App. no. 23572/07, §22, 2.5.2017 (money laundering proceedings).

presumption and to show that it had been impossible for him to know about the contents of the box.[1426]

Similarly, in the case *Janosevic v. Sweden*, which concerned tax surcharges, the Court found that it was the State's obligation to set reasonable limits for factual and legal presumptions applicable within the criminal law domain that consider, on the one hand, the importance of the matter, and, on the other hand, the rights of the defence. In that case, importance was given to the economic interests of the State as the taxes formed the main source of revenue for the State. The taxation system would not function properly if it were not possible to punish in some manner those who had given a wrong or deficient declaration of their taxes. Moreover, the great number of tax declarations and the need to secure foreseeable and uniform application of the sanctions required that the sanctions could be imposed according to standardised rules. As the relevant rules on tax surcharges provided certain means of defence based on subjective elements, and as an efficient system of taxation was important to the State's financial interests, the Court considered that the presumptions applicable in Swedish law with regard to tax surcharges were within reasonable limits.[1427]

Different parts of a crime may also require a different burden of proof. In the case *Bikas v. Germany*, the applicant was accused of repeated sexual offences against the same victim. He was accused on 54 different counts, but for 50 of them the charges were dismissed since the exact timing of the offences could not be determined. These incidents were nevertheless taken into account as aggravating elements of the crime. The Court did not find a violation of the presumption of innocence. The Court put emphasis on the procedural fact that the 50 incidents had been investigated and examined until the pronouncement of the verdict and the applicant had had an opportunity to defend himself against these charges. He knew that they could be taken into account and that this was allowed under domestic law. The domestic courts took these 50 incidents into account only in the reasoning of the judgment and they were not included in the operative part. The Court accepted that, in accordance with national law, the standard of proof in respect of these 50 incidents could be different to that of the four crimes the applicant had been convicted of.[1428]

A certain circumstance or position can form a basis for criminal liability. The presumption of innocence was not found to have been violated, for example, in cases which include: the president of a company who was criminally liable,

---

1426 *Salabiaku v. France*, App. no. 10519/83, §§28 and 30, 7.10.1988. See also Sverre Erik Jebens, "The limits of the presumption of innocence – Some clarifications in the Court's recent case-law", in *Liber Amicorum Dean Spielmann – Mélanges en L'honneur de/Essays in Honour of Dean Spielmann*, Wolf Legal Publishers, Oisterwijk 2015, pp. 255–262.

1427 *Janosevic v. Sweden*, App. no. 34619/97, §§96–110, 23.7.2002.

1428 *Bikas v. Germany*, App. no. 76607/13, §§51–61, 25.1.2018. See also Jeremy McBride, "Some recent practice of the European Court of Human Rights to consider when implementing criminal procedure codes", *Synergy Magazine*, no. 64, issue 2, 2018, pp. 8–10, at p. 9.

because of his position, for a crime committed in the company;[1429] a dog owner who was liable, on the basis of the ownership, for the danger presented by the animal;[1430] or a person who was liable for the sexual abuse of a child even though it was not shown that the person knew about the child's age.[1431] Nor was the presumption of innocence violated when an employer was held liable when his employee violated the maximum driving and minimum resting periods,[1432] or when an editor-in-chief of a newspaper was held liable, on the basis of his position, for material published in the newspaper.[1433]

### 5.3.3. PRESUMPTION OF INNOCENCE AND ADMISSION AND ADEQUACY OF EVIDENCE

The presumption of innocence is also connected to the adequacy of evidence and to other questions concerning evidence. Although the Court does not act as a fourth-instance court and does not reassess the evidence admitted and assessed by the domestic courts, the admission of evidence must nevertheless fulfil certain human rights guarantees. Therefore, for example, evidence obtained through the use of torture or otherwise obtained in violation of Article 3 cannot be used as evidence.[1434] It is, however, possible to use the pretrial investigation material accumulated in a criminal trial in proceedings other than criminal proceedings, that is, in civil and administrative law proceedings. In such situations, the applicant must be guaranteed, at least in certain circumstances and in relevant parts, the fair trial guarantees of criminal proceedings.[1435] It is not contrary to the presumption of innocence

---

1429 *Attorney General v. Malta* (dec.), App. no. 16641/90, 10.12.1991.

1430 *Bullock v. the United Kingdom* (dec.), App. no. 29102/95, 6.1.1996.

1431 *G. v. the United Kingdom* (dec.), App. no. 37334/08, 30.8.2011. According to the law, the objective element (*actus reus*) of the sexual abuse of a child was penile penetration, by any person old enough to hold criminal responsibility, of the vagina, anus or mouth of a child aged 12 or under. The subjective element (*mens rea*) was the intention to penetrate. Knowledge of, or recklessness as to, the age of the child or as to the child's unwillingness to take part in the sexual activity were not elements of the offence. The Court accepted that it was not relevant that the applicant believed the child to be over 12 years old.

1432 *Hansen v. Denmark* (dec.), App. no. 28971/95, 16.3.2000.

1433 *Radio France and Others v. France*, App. no. 53984/00, §24, 30.3.2004; and *Pekka Karhuvaara and Kustannusosakeyhtiö Iltalehti v. Finland* (dec.), App. no. 53678/00, 1.6.2004.

1434 See the selected case-law in the case *Gäfgen v. Germany* [GC], App. no. 22978/05, §§162–168 and 187, 1.6.2010. In the Court's case-law, a distinction is made between statements and real evidence which has been obtained in violation of Article 3.

1435 *Vanjak v. Croatia*, App. no. 29889/04, §§45–50, 14.1.2010. The case concerned disciplinary proceedings in which witness statements given in the pretrial investigation had been used as evidence without the applicant having had any chance of a cross-examination. See, however, *Allen v. the United Kingdom* [GC], App. no. 25424/09, §§103–105, 12.7.2013, concerning a situation in which a court refers in its reasoning to earlier, dismissed charges. In such a situation, the subsequent ruling must not in any way "annul" the earlier dismissal of the charges.

to disclose the defendant's criminal record or his or her criminal past before a conviction.[1436]

## 5.3.4. PRESUMPTION OF INNOCENCE AND ORGANISATION OF A TRIAL

The Court has also examined complaints alleging that the organisation and conduct of a trial violates the presumption of innocence. For example, it may be degrading and contrary to the presumption of innocence to place an accused in the courtroom in an isolated glass enclosure, cage or other isolated place for anything other than clearly apparent security reasons.[1437] The same applies if an accused is held handcuffed in the courtroom.[1438] In one case, the presumption of innocence was violated when one defendant had to wear the outfit of a pretrial detainee in the courtroom while the other defendant was allowed to wear his civilian clothes.[1439] However, it was not found to be contrary to the presumption of innocence to arrest a witness for perjury in a courtroom immediately after a witness statement.[1440]

The presumption of innocence is also not violated by the fact that an oral hearing is held before the same composition of the court which has decided on detention[1441] or on whether a suspect should be released on bail.[1442] Nor is the presumption of innocence violated by the fact that a court refuses, in the preparatory hearing, to hear in the main hearing a certain witness named by the defendant.[1443] However, an obligation to pay tax surcharges, even though they have been contested and the issue is still pending, may create a problem in relation to Article 6 §2 unless there is a reasonable solution which provides a proper balance between the interests of the taxpayers and those of the defendant.[1444]

---

1436 *X. v. Austria* (dec.), App. no. 2742/66, 30.5.1967.

1437 *Yaroslav Belousov v. Russia*, App. nos. 2653/13+, §§145–154, 4.10.2016.

1438 *X. v. Austria* (dec.), App. no. 2291/64, 1.6.1967.

1439 *Jiga v. Romania*, App. no. 14352/04, §§102 and 103, 16.3.2010.

1440 *X. and Y. v. the Federal Republic of Germany* (dec.), App. no. 8744/79, 2.3.1983.

1441 *Cuvillers and Da Luz v. France* (dec.), App. no. 55052/00, 16.9.2003.

1442 *X. v. the Federal Republic of Germany* (dec.), App. no. 2646/65, 30.3.1966.

1443 *Jussi Uoti v. Finland*, App. no. 20388/02, §§39–40, 23.1.2003.

1444 *Janosevic v. Sweden*, App. no. 34619/97, §106, 23.7.2002; and *Paulow v. Finland* (dec.), App. no. 53434/99, 14.2.2006. In the latter case the taxation authorities had the burden of proving that the applicant had failed to pay the taxes, after which the applicant had a possibility, by presenting arguments, clarifications and different evidence, to defend himself. Nor was it contrary to the presumption of innocence that the tax was due before the final decision was rendered, as the applicant would have been reimbursed the paid amount with interest if the obligation to pay had changed in the final instance.

## 5.4. STATEMENTS GIVEN IN PENDING CASES

### 5.4.1. STATEMENTS GIVEN AT DIFFERENT STAGES OF THE PROCEEDINGS

The presumption of innocence is violated if a court or other influential authority expresses, in its decision or in any other statement, its view on the defendant's guilt when the impugned proceedings are still pending. It is thus contrary to the presumption of innocence if a statement concerning the defendant, given before the final judgment, suggests that the defendant is guilty, even though he or she has yet to be convicted and has not had the opportunity to defend him- or herself.[1445] However, if statements are made by private entities – such as newspapers – an issue does not arise under Article 6 §2 but may arise under Article 8 of the Convention (right to respect for private life).[1446]

Naturally, not all statements concerning a suspicion of crime violate the presumption of innocence, but there is a risk of a violation when the statement is expressly linked to the probability of conviction. It is self-evident that there is no violation when the police or the prosecution gives their opinion about the probability of the next procedural stage, in accordance with the role they play in the case, which is a precondition for taking the case further. The police may therefore act and give statements in accordance with the "reason to suspect" probability, and the prosecution may do the same in accordance with the "probable cause" probability. Nor does the fact that a prosecutor presses charges and presents the prosecution's views about the accused's guilt mean that there is a violation of the presumption of innocence. In this respect, there is a clear difference between a situation in which an authority informs the public about the current procedural state of the case, and when the authorities express

---

1445 *Minelli v. Switzerland*, App. no. 8660/79, §38, 25.3.1983. In this case, the examination of charges lapsed since the crime had become statute-barred. The defendant was nevertheless ordered to pay the costs and expenses of the complainant, with the reasoning that, had the charges not been statute-barred, the applicant would most likely have been convicted. It was relevant in the case that the court took a stance on the applicant's guilt, although this issue was never adjudicated. The situation was similar when the defendant died during the proceedings, when the case was still pending before the appeal court, see *Nölkenbockhoff v. the Federal Republic of Germany*, App. no. 10300/83, §§54–55, 9.10.1985; and *Mirosław Garlicki v. Poland*, App. no. 36921/07, §131, 14.6.2011. See also Sverre Erik Jebens, "The Scope of the Presumption of Innocence in Article 6 §2 of the Convention – Especially on its Reputation-Related Aspect", in Lucius Caflisch, Johan Callewaert, Roderick Liddell, Paul Mahoney, Mark Villiger (Eds.), *Liber Amicorum Luzius Wildhaber: Human Rights, Strasbourg Views/Droits de L'homme, Regards de Strasbourg*, N.P. Engel, Kehl/Strasbourg/Arlington, Va. 2007, pp. 207–227, at p. 210. See also *Nerattini v. Greece*, App. no. 43529/07, §23, 18.12.2008; *Didu v. Romania*, App. no. 34814/02, §41, 14.4.2009; and *Gutsanovi v. Bulgaria*, App. no. 34529/10, §§202–203, 15.10.2013.

1446 *Mityanin and Leonov v. Russia*, App. nos. 11436/06+, §§102 and 105, 7.5.2019.

their view on the defendant's guilt. The former situation is in accordance with Article 6 and does not violate the presumption of innocence, whereas the latter situation does.[1447]

The authorities are allowed – and in some particularly important cases they are even under a duty – to give information about the pretrial investigation or the progress of the trial, provided that the suspect or accused is not stigmatised as guilty.[1448] The authorities may therefore organise press conferences and inform the public about the objective circumstances of the case without taking a stance on the suspect's guilt.[1449] In this respect, it is important how the statements are phrased, namely whether they point to a person's guilt or just to the fact that a person is under suspicion.[1450] The latter kind of statement is also allowed even when there is not yet any final judgment on the person's guilt. Naturally, it is not prohibited to express a suspicion in situations which concern preparatory measures, since a suspicion is a necessary prerequisite for the taking of such measures.[1451] On the other hand, in such a situation a statement about the defendant's guilt does not translate into a violation of the presumption of innocence.[1452] The Court did find a violation, for example, when the court expressed its opinion about the accused's guilt in the proceedings concerning the prolonging of his detention.[1453] In this respect, there is a clear difference as to whether the authorities only give information on the current state of the proceedings or whether they express their opinion on the accused's guilt.[1454]

However, in certain situations a statement concerning a suspicion may also be contrary to the presumption of innocence. Such a situation may arise if a court has expressed a suspicion after the charges have been dismissed.[1455] Nevertheless, the presumption of innocence is not violated if, after the charges have been dismissed, the court expresses its belief that, at the time of the pretrial

---

1447 *Kostadinov v. Bulgaria*, App. no. 37124/10, §§115 and 118, 27.1.2015.

1448 *Arrigo and Vella v. Malta* (dec.), App. no. 6569/04, 10.5.2005; and *Mirosław Garlicki v. Poland*, App. no. 36921/07, §132, 14.6.2011.

1449 *Butkevičius v. Lithuania*, App. no. 48297/99, §§50–52, 26.3.2002; *Lavents v. Latvia*, App. no. 58442/00, §127, 28.11.2002; *Y.B. and Others v. Turkey*, App. nos. 48173/99+, §45, 28.10.2004; and *Shagin v. Ukraine*, App. no. 20437/05, §83, 10.12.2009.

1450 *Fatullayev v. Azerbaijan*, App. no. 40984/07, §159, 22.4.2010; *Allenet de Ribemont v. France*, App. no. 15175/99, §38, 10.2.1995; and *Garycki v. Poland*, App. no. 14348/02, §69, 6.2.2007.

1451 *Nölkenbockhoff v. the Federal Republic of Germany*, App. no. 10300/83, §50, 9.10.1985; and *Gökceli v. Turkey*, App. nos. 27215/95+, §46, 4.3.2003.

1452 *Baars v. the Netherlands*, App. no. 44320/98, §§29–32, 28.10.2003; *Panteleyenko v. Ukraine*, App. no. 11901/02, §§67 and 70, 29.6.2006; and *Mirosław Garlicki v. Poland*, App. no. 36921/07, §132, 14.6.2011.

1453 *Matijasevic v. Serbia*, App. no. 23037/04, §§46–51, 19.9.2006 (violation).

1454 *Kostadinov v. Bulgaria*, App. no. 37124/10, §§115 and 118, 27.1.2015.

1455 *Sekanina v. Austria*, App. no. 13126/87, §§25 and 28–31, 25.8.1993; *Rushiti v. Austria*, App. no. 28389/95, §§31–32, 21.3.2000; and *Paraponiaris v. Greece*, App. no. 42132/06, §32, 25.9.2008.

investigation, charges or pretrial detention, there were grounds for suspicion.[1456] Nor is there any violation if the court makes a statement about the guilt during pending proceedings when examining a request for the termination of the proceedings because of excessive length, and refers to the extensive scope and complexity of the case.[1457]

## 5.4.2. POSITION OF THE PERSON GIVING A STATEMENT

The presumption of innocence is relevant when the domestic authorities give statements about persons suspected of a crime. In such situations, it might be more natural to examine the fairness of the proceedings from the point of view of the impartiality of the courts.[1458]

According to the Court, no representative of the State should say that a person is guilty of an offence before his guilt has been established by a court. The domestic authorities must thus carefully consider their choice of words when giving statements before there is any conviction. What is relevant is the real meaning of the remarks made, not their literal form.[1459]

### *5.4.2.1. Judges, Prosecutors and Police*

The Court has examined the presumption of innocence particularly in situations in which a judge has stated his or her opinion about the defendant's guilt or otherwise acted in violation of that presumption, either during the trial or outside of it. Statements given by judges are subject to more profound examination than those of, for example, the police or the prosecution.[1460] In the case *Pandy v. Belgium*, the Court found that an investigative judge had, in an oral hearing, violated the presumption of innocence when he had compared the applicant to famous serial killers. Not even the fact that the applicant had himself

1456 *Hibbert v. the Netherlands* (dec.), App. no. 38087/97, 26.1.1999.

1457 *Danker v. Finland* (dec.), App. no. 39543/04, 29.5.2007; and *Uoti v. Finland* (dec.), App. no. 43180/04, 29.5.2007.

1458 Such was the situation in the case *Buscemi v. Italy*, App. no. 29569/95, §§67–69, 16.9.1999. A judge had given a statement to the press in the case concerning the taking into public care of children. The Court emphasised that the judiciary had to act very tactfully in order to reinforce the image of unbiased judges. This required that judges did not abuse the press, not even when provoked. In this case, the chief judge had given, before the case was decided, public statements which had insinuated that the upcoming decision would not be in the applicant's favour. This conduct clearly violated the impartiality requirement and therefore the Court found a violation of Article 6 §1 of the Convention.

1459 *Konstas v. Greece*, App. no. 53466/07, §33, 24.5.2011.

1460 *Pandy v. Belgium*, App. no. 13583/02, §43, 21.9.2006.

provoked the exchange by his own statements prevented the Court from finding a violation.[1461] A judge must also carefully choose his or her words outside the courtroom. The presumption of innocence was violated, for example, when a judge stated in a newspaper interview that he was not sure whether he was going to convict the applicant on all or just on some of the counts, and expressed his astonishment over the fact that the applicant had contested the charges.[1462]

The conduct of a lay judge or a member of the jury may also lead to the violation of fair trial principles. In the case *Dallas v. the United Kingdom*, the applicant – who was a member of the jury – had, contrary to the specific directions of the judge, found out on the internet, when the jury had retired to consider the verdict, that the accused had a criminal background and relayed this to other members of the jury. As a result, she was convicted of contempt of court. Her case was examined by the Court as an Article 7 case (no punishment without law) and her conviction was considered to be compatible with it.[1463]

In addition to judges, the police and the prosecution must also be careful to use words in a way that does not violate the presumption of innocence.[1464] The presumption is immediately violated when a statement gives an impression that the person has committed a crime. However, the Court has been less strict in respect of the statements made by the police and the prosecution than in respect of those made by judges. In the case *Daktaras v. Lithuania*, the Court found no violation when the prosecution had stated, when rejecting the applicant's application for the discontinuation of charges, that the defendant was guilty of the offence. The Court separated in this case statements made in the trial context from statements made elsewhere.[1465] Had the statement been given by a judge, the outcome could have been different.[1466]

---

1461 *Pandy v. Belgium*, App. no. 13583/02, §§45–46, 21.9.2006.

1462 *Lavents v. Latvia*, App. no. 58442/00, §127, 28.11.2002.

1463 *Dallas v. the United Kingdom*, App. no. 38395/12, §§74–78, 11.2.2016 (no violation of Article 7). See also Sofia Galani (Ed.), "Case and comment: selected decisions from the European Court of Human Rights from November and December 2015 – Jurors and contempt of court, *Dallas v. United Kingdom* (Application No. 38395/12)", *European Human Rights Law Review* Issue 3, 2016, pp. 317–319.

1464 *Allenet de Ribemont v. France*, App. no. 15175/99, §41, 10.2.1995; *Shagin v. Ukraine*, App. no. 20437/05, §§84–86, 10.12.2009; *Kalliola and Others v. Finland* (dec.), App. no. 36741/97, 6.9.2001; and *Mirosław Garlicki v. Poland*, App. no. 36921/07, §133, 14.6.2011.

1465 *Daktaras v. Lithuania*, App. no. 42095/98, §§42–45, 10.10.2000. See also Danute Jociene, "The European Convention on Human Rights in the Lithuanian legal system: lessons learned and prospects for the future", in Lucius Caflisch, Johan Callewaert, Roderick Liddell, Paul Mahoney, Mark Villiger (Eds.), *Liber Amicorum Luzius Wildhaber: Human Rights, Strasbourg Views/Droits de L'homme, Regards de Strasbourg*, N.P. Engel, Kehl/Strasbourg/Arlington, Va. 2007, pp. 229–245, at pp. 236–237; and Karen Reid, *A Practitioner's Guide to the European Convention on Human Rights*, Sweet & Maxwell/Thomson Reuters, London 2019, p. 305. See also *Khuzhin and Others v. Russia*, App. no. 13470/02, §§94 and 96, 23.10.2008; *Arrigo and Vella v. Malta* (dec.), App. no. 6569/04, 10.5.2005; *Turyev v. Russia*, App. no. 20758/04, §21, 11.10.2016; and *Gutsanovi v. Bulgaria*, App. no. 34529/10, §§195–201, 15.10.2013.

1466 Compare and contrast with *Lavents v. Latvia*, App. no. 58442/00, §§125–127, 28.11.2002.

### 5.4.2.2. *Other State Authorities*

Other State authorities must also respect the presumption of innocence in their statements and consider carefully what they say when giving statements about pending cases. In this context, the possible effect of the public authorities' statement on the court's consideration is relevant. The case *Butkevičius v. Lithuania* concerned a statement by a Parliament spokesman after the arrest of the Minister of Defence, who had received an envelope containing money. According to the spokesman, there was no doubt that the minister was guilty of corruption. According to the Court, this statement by a high-level authority indicated a presumption about the applicant's guilt, which violated the presumption of innocence.[1467]

Statements by ministers and their relevance to the presumption of innocence have also been in question in other cases. In the case *Konstas v. Greece*, three ministers had made statements in Parliament about a criminal matter in which an appeal was pending against the conviction by the first-instance court. The Court considered that the presumption of innocence did not prevent competent authorities from mentioning the conviction or from giving information about it, even though there was not yet a final judgment. Such references should, however, be made with as much discretion and restraint as needed to respect the requirements of the presumption of innocence. The Prime Minister's comments were regarded as being a general reference to the subject matter of the case rather than an attempt to prejudge the Court of Appeal's verdict. On the other hand, the remarks made by the Deputy Minister of Finance, who used the term "crooks", and the Minister of Justice, who declared that the Greek courts had "boldly and resolutely" convicted those involved, gave an impression that they were satisfied with the lower-instance verdict and wanted the Court of Appeal to uphold that judgment.[1468] The Court thus found a violation of the presumption of innocence.

---

[1467] *Butkevičius v. Lithuania*, App. no. 48297/99, §§50–53, 26.3.2002. See also Danute Jociene, "The European Convention on Human Rights in the Lithuanian legal system: lessons learned and prospects for the future", in Lucius Caflisch, Johan Callewaert, Roderick Liddell, Paul Mahoney, Mark Villiger (Eds.), *Liber Amicorum Luzius Wildhaber: Human Rights, Strasbourg Views/Droits de L'homme, Regards de Strasbourg*, N.P. Engel, Kehl/Strasbourg/Arlington, Va. 2007, pp. 229–245, at p. 237. See also *Ismoilov and Others v. Russia*, App. no. 2947/06, §161, 24.4.2008.

[1468] *Konstas v. Greece*, App. no. 53466/07, §§41–45, 24.5.2011. See also Theofania Antoniou, "The Right to the Presumption of Innocence Versus the Right to Freedom of Expression in Parliament – The European Court of Human Rights Judgment in *Konstas v. Greece*", *European Human Rights Law Review*, Issue 3, 2012, pp. 319–326. See also *Mirosław Garlicki v. Poland*, App. no. 36921/07, §117, 14.6.2011. Similar comments were given by the President of the Republic in the case *Peša v. Croatia*, App. no. 40523/08, §149, 8.4.2010; and the Prime Minister or the Minister of the Interior in the case *Gutsanovi v. Bulgaria*, App. no. 34529/10, §§194–198, 15.10.2013.

However, the presumption of innocence was not violated in the case *Rywin v. Poland*, in which an official research report on corruption was published at the time corruption charges against the applicant were being examined. Although the research report mentioned the applicant's role in the corruption scandal, the research results were published in parallel with the criminal case. The Court emphasised the importance of the wording used in the research report, its role from the point of view of public interest and the fact that it was separate from the criminal proceedings. The aim of the research had not been to clarify the guilt of the applicant, nor was any stance taken on that issue in the report.[1469] Nor was there a violation when the statements were made by the chairman of a political party which was legally and financially independent from the State.[1470]

#### 5.4.2.3. *Adverse Press Campaigns*

It may also be problematic from the point of view of the presumption of innocence if the media actively reports on criminal matters and any allegations are made to the effect that such press campaigns against the accused violate his or her presumption of innocence.[1471] It is to be noted that the State is not liable for the acts of the media or for the fact that they have violated the presumption of innocence, provided that the authorities giving the information have formulated their statements appropriately without violating that presumption.[1472] The publication of photographs of suspects does not in itself breach the presumption of innocence,[1473] nor does the taking of photographs by the police raise an issue in this respect.[1474] However, broadcasting of the suspect's images on television may in certain circumstances raise an issue under Article 6 §2.[1475]

In the case *Jiga v. Romania*, the Court found that, in the corruption proceedings against a senior ministerial official, the interest from the media and the public were caused by the applicant's senior position and the nature of the case against him. It was not shown that such an intensive press campaign against the applicant had had an impact on the opinion of the judges deciding the case; nor had the authorities by their own actions and statements contributed to the

1469 *Rywin v. Poland*, App. nos. 6091/06+, §§203–219, 18.2.2016.

1470 *Mulosmani v. Albania*, App. no. 29864/03, §141, 8.10.2013.

1471 *Akay v. Turkey* (dec.), App. no. 34501/97, 19.2.2002; and *Bédat v. Switzerland* [GC], App. no. 56925/08, §51, 29.3.2016.

1472 *Y.B. and Others v. Turkey*, App. nos. 48173/99+, §48, 28.10.2004; and *Shagin v. Ukraine*, App. no. 20437/05, §83, 10.12.2009.

1473 *Y.B. and Others v. Turkey*, App. nos. 48173/99+, §47, 28.10.2004.

1474 *Mergen and Others v. Turkey*, App. nos. 44062/09+, §68, 31.5.2016.

1475 *Rupa v. Romania (No. 1)*, App. no. 58478/00, §232, 16.12.2008. See also Anand Doobay, "The right to a fair trial in light of the recent ECtHR and CJEU case-law", *ERA forum*, vol. 14, issue 2, September 2013, pp. 251–262, at p. 258.

press campaign. Moreover, the experience and training of professional judges should prevent any outside influence from affecting the proceedings.[1476]

A press campaign was the subject of the case *Abdulla Ali v. the United Kingdom*, in which the Court held that the coverage had not deprived the applicant of a chance of a fair trial. In that case, the jury trial and the press campaign had taken place six months apart, and the judge had given the jury clear instructions on the need for impartiality and on their obligation to disregard the press campaign. The outcome of the case also showed that the press campaign had not influenced the jury's reasoning.[1477]

### 5.4.3. EXTENDING THE PRESUMPTION TO OTHER CRIMINAL PROCEEDINGS

Statements given by other co-defendants in other proceedings and the conclusions drawn by a court from them can also have relevance to the defendant's position as an accused. The case *Karaman v. Germany* concerned a situation in which background information on a judgment that had led to the conviction of several other people of aggravated fraud mentioned the name of the applicant and his central participation in using the proceeds from the fraud. He was not a party to those proceedings, nor could he defend himself in the criminal trial against the co-defendants. Since criminal proceedings were also already pending against the applicant, the presumption of innocence had relevance in his situation. The wording used by the court in its judgment, referring to the applicant as being "separately prosecuted", made it clear that the court had not yet determined his guilt. The domestic courts had therefore avoided giving the impression that they were prejudging the applicant's guilt and thereby avoided violating the presumption of his innocence.[1478]

Article 6 §2 also applies where two sets of criminal proceedings are in parallel pending against the applicant. Thus, considering in one set of proceedings concerning a particular offence that an applicant has committed another offence

[1476] In this case, the allegation was declared inadmissible as being manifestly ill-founded. See *Jiga v. Romania*, App. no. 14352/04, §§93–95, 16.3.2010.

[1477] *Abdulla Ali v. the United Kingdom*, App. no. 30971/12, §§95–99, 30.6.2015. See also James Welch (Ed.), "Case and comment: selected decisions from the European Court of Human Rights from May and June 2015 – Fair trial, *Abdulla Ali v. United Kingdom* (Application No. 30971/12)", *European Human Rights Law Review*, Issue 5, 2015, pp. 543–546.

[1478] *Karaman v. Germany*, App. no. 17103/10, §§43–44 and 69–70, 27.2.2014 (no violation). See also *Bauras v. Lithuania*, App. no. 56795/13, §52, 31.10.2017; and *Navalnyy and Ofitserov v. Russia*, App. nos. 46632/13+, §104, 23.2.2016.

which is subject to a trial in a parallel set of proceedings, is contrary to the applicant's right to be presumed innocent with respect to that other offence.[1479]

## 5.4.4. EXTENDING THE PRESUMPTION TO NON-CRIMINAL PROCEEDINGS

While there are many instances that concern the making of statements during the pretrial investigation or during the trial itself, the presumption of innocence may also be applicable in situations that concern parallel or otherwise separate proceedings.

The presumption of innocence is not violated if the court refers in its judgment to a connection between the accused and another person, provided that the court is not called upon to determine the guilt of this second person.[1480] Nor is the presumption of innocence violated by the fact that a civil matter is suspended pending the outcome of a criminal matter.[1481] Separate, civil-based compensation proceedings may, however, be based on the same facts examined within the criminal proceedings, notwithstanding the fact that these non-criminal proceedings may require a lower standard of proof than the criminal proceedings. Similarly, in a separate civil matter, pretrial investigation material can be used, at least to a certain extent, as evidence.[1482] If the preventive effect of dismissed charges also stretches to civil-based compensation proceedings, it would mean a restriction of the complainant's right of access to a court.[1483]

Although there is no presumption of innocence in civil proceedings,[1484] it is in accordance with the presumption of innocence and the fair trial guarantees that the courts respect, in a civil matter, a judgment in which charges have been dismissed. Therefore, if civil proceedings have been initiated against the defendant on the basis of the same facts, or the proceedings are otherwise connected to facts relating to the criminal suspicion, a court cannot in the civil matter "annul" the dismissal of the charges.[1485] This has been confirmed,

---

1479 *Kangers v. Latvia*, App. no. 35726/10, §§60–61, 14.3.2019. See also Christopher Gray, "Presumption of innocence – *Kangers v. Latvia* (Application No. 35726/10)", *European Human Rights Law Review*, Issue 4, 2019, pp. 439–442.

1480 *Gjerde v. Norway* (dec.), App. no. 18672/91, 31.3.1993.

1481 *Farragut v. France* (dec.), App. no. 10103/82, 6.7.1984.

1482 *Vanjak v. Croatia*, App. no. 29889/04, §§41, 45 and 56, 14.1.2010. The case concerned a disciplinary matter in which pretrial investigation material collected during the criminal proceedings was used as evidence.

1483 *Y. v. Norway*, App. no. 56568/00, §41, 11.2.2003; and *Ringvold v. Norway*, App. no. 34964/97, §§41–42, 11.2.2003.

1484 *X. v. the Federal Republic of Germany* (dec.), App. no. 6062/73, 18.12.1974.

1485 *Allen v. the United Kingdom* [GC], App. no. 25424/09, §103, 12.7.2013; *X., Y. and Z. v. Austria* (dec.), App. no. 7950/77, 4.3.1980; *X. v. Austria* (dec.), App. no. 9295/81, 6.10.1982; *Diamantides v. Greece (No. 2)*, App. no. 71563/01, §§35–36 and 51, 19.5.2005; and *Yassar Hussain v. the United Kingdom*, App. no. 8866/04, §22, 7.3.2006.

for example, in the cases *Minelli v. Switzerland*, *Sekanina v. Austria*, *Rushiti v. Austria*, *Y. v. Norway*, *Hammern v. Norway*, *O. v. Norway*, *Orr v. Norway* and *Ashendon and Jones v. the United Kingdom*, as well as in the Grand Chamber judgment in *Allen v. the United Kingdom*.[1486] This may be the case in a situation where a person who has been illegally detained applies for compensation, or in proceedings in which the prosecutor has withdrawn charges or the charges have been dismissed. In such situations it is not contrary to the presumption of innocence to state that the person was at the time of the impugned measure under suspicion.[1487] However, conjectures about the person's guilt are not allowed.[1488]

Although the right to compensation for illegal detention is a right covered by Article 5 §5 of the Convention, the right to have the costs and expenses reimbursed after a dismissal of charges is not a right guaranteed by the Convention, nor does the presumption of innocence create such a right.[1489] But if such a right is included in domestic law, the proceedings or the reasoning of the ruling must not violate the presumption of innocence. In the case *Ashendon and Jones v. the United Kingdom*, the Court held that it was not contrary to the presumption of innocence for a trial judge to refuse to make an order for costs and expenses on the ground that the applicant had brought suspicion on himself and misled the prosecution into believing that the case against him was stronger than it was in reality. The same applied to a situation in which the applicant had brought the prosecution upon himself because he had availed himself of the right to silence. The refusal to make an order did not amount to a penalty for exercising that right.[1490]

There is no clear and consequent answer in the Court's case-law to the question as to how extensively the presumption of innocence covers those proceedings other than criminal proceedings. In the case *Bok v. the Netherlands*,

---

1486 *Minelli v. Switzerland*, App. no. 8660/79, §§31–41, 25.3.1983; *Sekanina v. Austria*, App. no. 13126/87, §§22 and 25–31, 25.8.1993; *Rushiti v. Austria*, App. no. 28389/95, §§27–32, 21.3.2000; *Y. v. Norway*, App. no. 56568/00, §§39–47, 11.2.2003; *Hammern v. Norway*, App. no. 30287/96, §§41–49, 11.2.2003; *O. v. Norway*, App. no. 29327/95, §§33–41, 11.2.2003; *Orr v. Norway*, App. no. 31283/04, §§47–55, 15.5.2008; *Ashendon and Jones v. the United Kingdom*, App. nos. 35730/07+, §§42–55, 13.9.2011; and *Allen v. the United Kingdom* [GC], App. no. 25424/09, §103, 12.7.2013. See also Tom Hickman, Faisal Saifee, "Case Analysis – *Hammern v. Norway, O v. Norway, Ringvold v. Norway* and *Y v. Norway*", *European Human Rights Law Review*, Issue 5, 2003, pp. 539–546.

1487 It can thus be said that, behind the measures taken, there has been a suspicion of a crime. See *Lutz v. the Federal Republic of Germany*, App. no. 9912/82, §§62–64, 25.8.1987; and *Leutscher v. the Netherlands*, App. no. 17314/90, §31, 26.3.1996. Contrast and compare with *Capeau v. Belgium*, App. no. 42914/98, §25, 13.1.2005.

1488 *Sekanina v. Austria*, App. no. 13126/87, §30, 25.8.1993; *Hammern v. Norway*, App. no. 30287/96, §47, 11.2.2003; and *O. v. Norway*, App. no. 29327/95, §41, 11.2.2003.

1489 *Masson and Van Zon v. the Netherlands*, App. nos. 15346/89+, §49, 28.9.1995.

1490 *Ashendon and Jones v. the United Kingdom*, App. nos. 35730/07+, §49, 13.9.2011.

the action for compensation by the applicant who had been accused but later acquitted was rejected in the civil proceedings, as in those proceedings he had borne the burden of proof to show there had been no reason to suspect him of a crime. As he had not proven this, no compensation was awarded. The Court held that it was the task of the domestic courts to assess whether the applicant had fulfilled his burden of proof. The applicant's acquittal in criminal proceedings did not mean that he was discharged from the obligation of having to prove his claim for damages brought in civil proceedings in accordance with the applicable domestic rules. Although the expressions used by the domestic court were unfortunate and, given the confusion those expressions caused, inappropriate, they were not a statement of his guilt but aimed at explaining what the applicant was obliged to prove and why he had failed to do so. The Court thus found that the presumption of innocence had not been violated in the civil proceedings.[1491]

In the above-mentioned Grand Chamber case *Allen v. the United Kingdom*, the Court created a test for situations in which the presumption of innocence has implications for other proceedings. First, where there has been a criminal charge and criminal proceedings have ended in an acquittal, the person subject to the criminal proceedings is innocent in the eyes of the law and must be treated in a manner consistent with that innocence. Second, the applicant must demonstrate the existence of a link between the concluded criminal proceedings and the subsequent proceedings (necessary link). Such a link is likely to be present, for example, when the subsequent proceedings require examination of the outcome of the prior criminal proceedings and, in particular, when they oblige the court to: analyse the criminal judgment; engage in a review or evaluation of the evidence in the criminal file; assess the applicant's participation in some or all of the events leading to the criminal charge; or comment on the subsisting indications of the applicant's possible guilt.[1492]

However, when assessing whether there is a violation of the presumption of innocence in other proceedings, much will ultimately depend on the nature and context of the proceedings in which the impugned decision was adopted. In this respect the language used by the decision maker will be of critical importance when assessing the compatibility of the decision and its reasoning

---

1491 *Bok v. the Netherlands*, App. no. 45482/06, §§43–48, 18.1.2011 (no violation).

1492 *Allen v. the United Kingdom* [GC], App. no. 25424/09, §§103–104 and 125–126, 12.7.2013. See also James Welch (Ed.), "Case and comment: selected decisions from the European Court of Human Rights from July 2013 – Miscarriage of justice, *Allen v. United Kingdom* (Application No. 25424/09)", *European Human Rights Law Review*, Issue 6, 2013, pp. 646–650. See also *Martínez Agirre and Others v. Spain* (dec.), App. nos. 75529/16+, §§46–52, 25.6.2019 in which no link was established between the subsequent compensation proceedings and the earlier criminal investigations.

with Article 6 §2. When regard is had to the nature and context of the particular proceedings, even the use of some unfortunate language may not be decisive.[1493]

In the *Allen* case, the applicant was convicted of a fatal assault on her child on the basis of expert testimony. Subsequently, having already served her prison sentence, she presented new evidence to suggest that the child's injuries may have been caused by other reasons. The domestic court quashed, on the basis of the new evidence, the previous manslaughter conviction, as that evidence, had it been given at the trial, might have reasonably affected the decision of the trial jury to convict. The applicant's compensation claim was, however, rejected, because her innocence had not been proven, nor had it been demonstrated that there had been a miscarriage of justice. The Court found that there had been a link between the two sets of proceedings but the language used in the compensation proceedings did not demonstrate a lack of respect for the presumption of innocence.[1494]

The burden of proof may also become relevant in separate but criminal-based confiscation proceedings. This was the case in *Phillips v. the United Kingdom*. In that case, the applicant had already been convicted of a narcotics offence. In the separate confiscation proceedings concerning the proceeds of crime, a presumption was applied according to which all assets the applicant had at the time of the conviction or acquired in the six years before it were considered to be proceeds from the crime. The Court found that, although the criminal limb of Article 6 was applicable to confiscation orders as such, in this case Article 6 §2 did not apply to the situation as the confiscation proceedings did not constitute any factually new criminal charge but concerned only the proceeds from a crime of which the applicant had already been convicted. The Court found no problem under the Article 6 §1 general fairness guarantees either, as the applicant had had the chance to have overturned the legal presumption about the amount of the assets acquired from crime.[1495]

A confiscation order may also, depending on the domestic legislation and without violating Article 6 §1 of the Convention, extend further than those crimes of which an applicant was convicted in the criminal proceedings. In the

---

1493 *Allen v. the United Kingdom* [GC], App. no. 25424/09, §§103–104 and 125–126, 12.7.2013; *Adams v. the United Kingdom* (dec.), App. no. 70601/11, §41, 5.12.2013; *Lähteenmäki v. Estonia*, App. no. 53172/10, §45, 21.6.2016; *Müller v. Germany*, App. no. 54963/08, §§51–52, 27.3.2014; and *A.L.F. v. the United Kingdom* (dec.), App. no. 5908/12, §24, 5.12.2013.

1494 *Allen v. the United Kingdom* [GC], App. no. 25424/09, §§119 and 136, 12.7.2013. See also Sverre Erik Jebens, "The limits of the presumption of innocence – Some clarifications in the Court's recent case-law", in *Liber Amicorum Dean Spielmann – Mélanges en L'honneur de/ Essays in Honour of Dean Spielmann*, Wolf Legal Publishers, Oisterwijk 2015, pp. 255–262.

1495 *Phillips v. the United Kingdom*, App. no. 41087/98, §§35–36, 39 and 45–47, 5.7.2001. See also Miklos Hollan, "Confiscation of the proceeds from crime and the principle of presumption of innocence", in Kimmo Nuotio (Ed.), *Festschrift in Honour of Raimo Lahti*, University of Helsinki/Faculty of Law, Helsinki 2007, pp. 363–372.

case *Noel Young v. the United Kingdom*, the defendant was convicted of a tax offence, but when he pleaded guilty to it, he also admitted at the same time that his business activities, which had not been taxed, had been more extensive. The Court examined the case under the general fairness provision without taking a stance on the presumption of innocence, and found that the confiscation order could be directed against all of his business activities.[1496]

The presumption of innocence was a central issue in the case *Silickiene v. Lithuania*, in which the already pending criminal proceedings had been continued, after the suicide of one of the accused persons, against his estate in respect of a confiscation claim. The Court found no violation of the presumption of innocence.[1497] Similarly, in the case *Lagardere v. France*, the presumption of innocence was extended to cover subsequent civil proceedings in a situation in which no charges had been brought against the person during his lifetime but in which separate, criminal-based civil proceedings had been initiated against his heirs after his death.[1498]

In the case *Carrefour France v. France*, the criminal liability was transferred to the acquiring applicant company, with which a company accused of distorting competition had merged during the proceedings. The Court held that all the assets and obligations of the merging company which had committed the abuses were transferred to the acquiring company and that the shareholders of the former became shareholders of the latter. The core business of the acquiring company was the same as the activities of the merging company and the acquiring company had benefited from the merging company's operations. The Court considered that merging company, which had been convicted of the irregularities and sentenced to fines and to pay compensation in the amount of 60,000 euros, was not in fact "alien" vis-à-vis the acquiring company and that it was justified to collect the compensation from the acquiring company. Any other solution would have rendered the financial responsibility of companies meaningless. This outcome was also in line with EU competition law.[1499]

A criminal suspicion may be present in judicial administrative proceedings if the outcome of the criminal proceedings is linked to those proceedings and to the reasoning in such a way that Article 6 §2 may be regarded as applicable.[1500] Such proceedings are, for example, proceedings concerning the

---

1496 *Noel Young v. the United Kingdom* (dec.), App. no. 38759/12, §44, 28.5.2014.

1497 *Silickiene v. Lithuania*, App. no. 20496/02, §§53–54, 10.4.2012 (no violation). In this case, the person having committed suicide was one of the accused persons. The criminal proceedings were continued against all the other members of the organisation. Concerning the person having committed suicide, it could not be shown that he had acquired his assets from legal sources.

1498 *Lagardere v. France*, App. no. 18851/07, §§86–87, 12.4.2012 (violation).

1499 *Carrefour France v. France* (dec.), App. no. 37858/14, §§39–54, 24.10.2019.

1500 *Çelik (Bozkurt) v. Turkey*, App. no. 34388/05, §§30–31 and 34–36, 12.4.2011.

taking into public care of a child, or proceedings concerning civil servants.[1501] Also in these situations, the reasoning and the expressions used become relevant. It is also important that the ruling in the civil or administrative law proceedings does not call an acquittal in the criminal proceedings into question.[1502]

## 5.5. CORRECTION OF A VIOLATION

A violation of the presumption of innocence by lower courts may be corrected on appeal.[1503] In situations in which the presumption of innocence has been violated outside of the court proceedings, for example by a statement made by some high official or in a police press conference, the fact that the courts have acted in compliance with the presumption of innocence cannot correct the violation.[1504] Such a violation does not, however, prevent any criminal proceedings from taking place or any criminal liability from being established in a trial by an impartial court.

In the case *Mirosław Garlicki v. Poland*, the Court held that the civil proceedings against the person who had violated the presumption of innocence, and the obligation for him to present his public apologies and to pay compensation, corrected the situation and deprived the applicant of victim status in respect of the violation of the presumption of innocence.[1505] The Court's case-law is not, however, fully clear as to whether civil proceedings are sufficient in this respect, or whether the violation of the presumption of innocence should lead to criminal proceedings against the person violating it.[1506]

---

1501 *O.L. v. Finland* (dec.), App. no. 61110/00, 5.7.2005. In this case, the prosecutor had decided not to press charges against the applicant concerning the sexual abuse of a child. The Court found that the fact that the child had been taken into public care did not create a "criminal charge" against the applicant, nor was the criminal pretrial investigation as such decisive for the outcome of the public care issue. There was no link or dependence between these two issues. The taking into public care was not an immediate consequence of the outcome of the pretrial investigation. The Supreme Administrative Court's decision did not in any way suggest the applicant had committed those acts that he had not been charged with by the prosecutor. A statement to the effect that the possibility of sexual abuse could not be excluded was not incompatible with the prosecutor's decision and did not "annul" it. The Court found that Article 6 §2 of the Convention was not applicable to the matter of the child being taken into public care and that there was no violation of the said article. See also *T., A., J. and S. v. Finland* (dec.), App. no. 27744/95, 9.9.2003; and *Çelik (Bozkurt) v. Turkey*, App. no. 34388/05, §§30–31 and 34–36, 12.4.2011.

1502 See also Chapter 4, section 4.2.7., above.

1503 *Adolf v. Austria*, App. no. 8269/78, §40, 26.3.1982; and *Arrigo and Vella v. Malta* (dec.), App. no. 6569/04, 10.5.2005.

1504 *Shagin v. Ukraine*, App. no. 20437/05, §82, 10.12.2009.

1505 *Mirosław Garlicki v. Poland*, App. no. 36921/07, §§135–139, 14.6.2011.

1506 *Konstas v. Greece*, App. no. 53466/07, §29, 24.5.2011.

## 5.6. PRESUMPTION OF INNOCENCE AND FREEDOM FROM SELF-INCRIMINATION

The presumption of innocence is often closely connected with another central concept of criminal proceedings, namely the freedom from self-incrimination created by the Court's case-law.[1507] There is no specific mention of the freedom from self-incrimination in Article 6 of the Convention, but in the Court's case-law it has been considered one of the most central elements of the fair trial guarantees.[1508] Moreover, this right has been included in many international standards.[1509]

The rights to remain silent and not to incriminate oneself are not absolute rights; rather conclusions can in some circumstances be drawn from the accused's silence.[1510] In jury trials, a judge's instruction to the jury explaining that they may draw conclusions from a defendant's silence, to his or her detriment, is not itself incompatible with fair trial guarantees. The defendant's silence cannot, however, constitute the sole evidence against him or her. Conclusions can be drawn in cases in which, on the basis of other factors, an explanation is clearly required. In any event, the defendant must be warned when questioned of the fact that adverse conclusions can be drawn from his or her silence. However, the drawing of conclusions from the defendant's silence must not render the proceedings unfair as a whole.[1511]

The right to remain silent can be violated in three different ways. First, a breach may occur by threatening a person with a sanction or a risk of a sanction if he or she remains silent. Second, it can be violated by inflicting violence on the person with a view to obtaining a statement or real evidence, often also contrary to Article 3. Third, the right can be violated by dishonest and unethical police interrogation methods intended to break the person's silence.[1512]

The right to remain silent and the right not to incriminate oneself do not, however, extend in criminal proceedings to the use of evidential material that may be obtained from the accused through the use of compulsory powers, but

---

1507 *Staines v. the United Kingdom* (dec.), App. no. 41552/98, 16.5.2000; and *Heaney and McGuinness v. Ireland*, App. no. 34720/97, §40, 21.12.2000.

1508 For more details on freedom from self-incrimination, see Chapter 4, section 4.2.10. above.

1509 *Saunders v. the United Kingdom* [GC], App. no. 19187/91, §68, 17.12.1996. See also *Heaney and McGuinness v. Ireland*, App. no. 34720/97, §40, 21.12.2000; *Jalloh v. Germany* [GC], App. no. 54810/00, §100, 1.7.2006; and *Gäfgen v. Germany* [GC], App. no. 22978/05, §168, 1.6.2010; and, *inter alia*, Article 14 §3 (g) of the International Covenant on Civil and Political Rights.

1510 *Ibrahim and Others v. the United Kingdom* [GC], App. nos. 50541/08+, §269, 13.9.2016.

1511 *John Murray v. the United Kingdom*, App. no. 18731/91, §47, 8.2.1996; *Condron v. the United Kingdom*, App. no. 35718/97, §61, 2.5.2000; *Beckles v. the United Kingdom*, App. no. 44652/98, §§57–59, 8.10.2002; *Tabbakh v. the United Kingdom* (dec.), App. no. 40945/09, §29, 21.2.2012; and *Averill v. the United Kingdom*, App. no. 36408/97, §45, 6.6.2000.

1512 *Ibrahim and Others v. the United Kingdom* [GC], App. nos. 50541/08+, §267, 13.9.2016.

which has an existence independent of the will of the suspect. This could include, *inter alia*, documents acquired pursuant to a warrant, breath, blood and urine samples or bodily tissue for the purpose of DNA testing.[1513] However, if the accused is required to present, for example, an incriminating document, such a matter would fall within the scope of the right not to incriminate oneself.[1514] This right thus extends further than the simple refusal to reply to questions or to give statements, since it also includes the right to refuse to submit any incriminating material to the authorities.[1515]

The rights to remain silent and not to incriminate oneself are not absolute rights because only improper compulsion is forbidden.[1516] Compulsion can take different forms; for example, the use of force to obtain a confession or evidence,[1517] or a requirement for an accused to testify in his own matter.[1518] A threat of a criminal sanction,[1519] or the imposition of a sanction,[1520] in situations in which a person is refusing to submit information, constitutes compulsion and may violate the right not to incriminate oneself, even if the person is not subsequently accused[1521] or convicted[1522] of an offence. Also, any norm which allows negative conclusions to be drawn from the exercise of the right to remain silent must also be regarded as compulsion, as it adds pressure to reply to the questions.[1523]

The use of undercover methods to obtain information may similarly contain an element of compulsion. For example, in the case *Allan v. the United Kingdom*, the applicant confessed to a murder to his cellmate, who was a police informant, after having been first intensively interrogated by the police and thereafter by his "cellmate".[1524]

---

1513 *Saunders v. the United Kingdom* [GC], App. no. 19187/91, §69, 17.12.1996.

1514 *Funke v. France*, App. no. 10828/84, §44, 25.2.1993; and *J.B. v. Switzerland*, App. no. 31827/96, §§63–71, 3.5.2001.

1515 *Jalloh v. Germany* [GC], App. no. 54810/00, §111, 11.7.2006.

1516 *John Murray v. the United Kingdom*, App. no. 18731/91, §46, 8.2.1996.

1517 *Jalloh v. Germany* [GC], App. no. 54810/00, §114, 11.7.2006.

1518 *John Murray v. the United Kingdom*, App. no. 18731/91, §47, 8.2.1996; and *Serves v. France*, App. no. 20225/92, §47, 20.10.1997.

1519 *Saunders v. the United Kingdom* [GC], App. no. 19187/91, §70, 17.12.1996.

1520 *Funke v. France*, App. no. 10828/84, 25.2.1993.

1521 *Idem.*

1522 *Heaney and McGuinness v. Ireland*, App. no. 34720/97, 21.12.2000. See also Tim Ward, Piers Gardner, "The Privilege Against Self-Incrimination – In Search of Legal Certainty", *European Human Rights Law Review*, Issue 4, 2003, pp. 388–399, at pp. 395–397.

1523 *Condron v. the United Kingdom*, App. no. 35718/97, §61, 2.5.2000.

1524 *Allan v. the United Kingdom*, App. no. 48539/99, §§50–53, 5.11.2002. The undercover police informant was regarded as an authority whose "questioning" was comparable to the real police interrogation. See also Karen Reid, *A Practitioner's Guide to the European Convention on Human Rights*, Sweet & Maxwell/Thomson Reuters, London 2019, p. 344; and John Wadham, Philip Leach, "Cases and comment: selected decisions from the European Court of Human Rights for November and December 2002 – Crime and sentencing, *Allan v. United Kingdom* (Application No. 48539/99)", *European Human Rights Law Review*, Issue 2, 2003, pp. 235–237.

Compulsion is improper if it compromises the very essence of the privilege against self-incrimination. In the case *John Murray v. the United Kingdom*, the Court did not find this to be the case since there existed sufficient legal guarantees against it. Adverse inferences could have been drawn from the accused's silence, as he had been warned about such a possibility. It was relevant that the case was otherwise so strong that, despite his silence, the accused could be convicted. Moreover, the judge was competent to assess whether it was appropriate to draw adverse inferences from the applicant's silence and if he did so, it needed to be reasoned. Although it was contrary to the right not to incriminate oneself to base a conviction wholly or in a large part on the accused's silence, it did not prevent the court from taking the silence into account in situations which clearly required an explanation, on the condition that sufficient legal safeguards existed.[1525]

On the other hand, in the case *Funke v. France* the degree of compulsion was considered to be such that the very essence of the right not to incriminate oneself was compromised when the applicant was fined for refusing to submit incriminating bank statements.[1526] The sanction imposed for remaining silent was an important element when assessing whether the very essence of the right not to incriminate oneself was at stake.[1527]

---

1525 *John Murray v. the United Kingdom*, App. no. 18731/91, §§47–57, 8.2.1996. See also Karen Reid, *A Practitioner's Guide to the European Convention on Human Rights*, Sweet & Maxwell/ Thomson Reuters, London 2019, p. 345; John Jackson, "Re-conceptualizing the right of silence as an effective fair trial standard", *International and Comparative Law Quarterly*, vol. 58, pt. 4, October 2009, pp. 835–861; and Michael O'Boyle, "Freedom from self-incrimination and the right to silence: a Pandora's box?", in Paul Mahoney, Franz Matscher, Herbert Petzold, Luzius Wildhaber (Eds.), *Protection des Droits de L'homme: La Perspective Européenne, Mélanges à la Mémoire de Rolv Ryssdal/Protecting Human Rights: The European Perspective, Studies in Memory of Rolv Ryssdal*, Carl Heymanns Verlag, Köln/Berlin/Bonn/München 2000, pp. 1021–1038, at pp. 1034–1036.

1526 *Funke v. France*, App. no. 10828/84, §44, 25.2.1993. See also Mark Berger, "Self-Incrimination and the European Court of Human Rights: Procedural Issues in the Enforcement of the Right to Silence", *European Human Rights Law Review*, Issue 5, 2007, pp. 514–533, at pp. 525–526; Tim Ward, Piers Gardner, "The Privilege Against Self-Incrimination – In Search of Legal Certainty", *European Human Rights Law Review*, Issue 4, 2003, pp. 388–399; S.H. Naismith, "Current topic: Self-incrimination, fairness or freedom?", *European Human Rights Law Review*, no. 3, 1997, pp. 229–236; and Michael O'Boyle, "Freedom from self-incrimination and the right to silence: a Pandora's box?", in Paul Mahoney, Franz Matscher, Herbert Petzold, Luzius Wildhaber, (Eds.), *Protection des Droits de L'homme: La Perspective Européenne, Mélanges à la Mémoire de Rolv Ryssdal/Protecting Human Rights: The European Perspective, Studies in Memory of Rolv Ryssdal*, Carl Heymanns Verlag, Köln/Berlin/Bonn/München 2000, pp. 1021–1038, at pp. 1024–1025.

1527 In the case *Allen v. the United Kingdom* (dec.), App. no. 76574/01, 10.9.2002, the Court found no violation as the case concerned only a minor fine (at the most £300). In the case *Heaney and McGuinness v. Ireland*, App. no. 34720/97, §49, 21.12.2000 (violation), the Court did not see any difference between the cumulative fines imposed in the *Funke* case and the six-month prison sentence imposed in that case, but considered that in both cases the threat of a sanction and its imposition were the same.

In the case *Jalloh v. Germany*, the Court held that, in order to determine whether the applicant's right not to incriminate himself had been violated, regard had to be had to the following factors: the nature and degree of compulsion used to obtain the evidence; the weight of the public interest in the investigation and punishment of the offence in question; the existence of any relevant safeguards in the procedure; and the use to which any material so obtained was put.[1528]

The Court confirmed these criteria in its Grand Chamber judgment in the case *O'Halloran and Francis v. the United Kingdom*.[1529] The case concerned the applicants' duty to identify, at the risk of a criminal sanction, the driver of a vehicle from a photograph taken by a speed camera. The first applicant identified himself in the photograph and was fined for speeding. The second applicant refused to identify the driver and was fined on that ground. The Grand Chamber found that the essence of the applicants' right to remain silent and their privilege against self-incrimination had not been compromised in that case. This was because the use of cars was recognised as having the potential to cause grave injuries and it was therefore subject to a regulatory regime. Moreover, the compulsion applied was of a limited nature, namely only to acquire information "as to the identity of the driver", which was not in itself incriminating. There also existed relevant procedural safeguards and the identity of the driver was not the only element required for a conviction. It was also relevant that everyone who owned or drove motor cars knew that, by doing so, they subjected themselves to a regulatory regime.[1530] Similarly, obliging drivers to submit to a breathalyser or blood test is not contrary to the principle of presumption of innocence.[1531] The right to not to incriminate oneself is examined in more detail above in Chapter 4, section 4.2.10.

---

1528 *Jalloh v. Germany* [GC], App. no. 54810/00, §117, 11.7.2006. See also Boštjan M. Zupančič, "An answer to one crucial question of human rights: an epistemological excursus informing *Jalloh v. Germany* and *Gäfgen v. Germany* cases at the European Court of Human Rights", in Miha Pogačnik (Ed.), *Challenges of Contemporary International Law and International Relations – Liber Amicorum in Honour of Ernest Petrič*, The European Faculty of Law, Nova Gorica 2011, pp. 451–463; and Sverre Erik Jebens, "Illegally obtained evidence in criminal cases – an analysis on the basis of three Grand Chamber judgments", in Dean Spielmann, Marialena Tsirli, Panayotis Voyatzis (Eds.), *La Convention Européenne des Droits de L'homme, un Instrument Vivant – Mélanges en L'honneur de Christos L. Rozakis/The European Convention on Human Rights, a Living Instrument – Essays in Honour of Christos L. Rozakis*, Bruylant, Bruxelles 2011, pp. 219–234, at pp. 221–223.

1529 *O'Halloran and Francis v. the United Kingdom* [GC], App. nos. 15809/02+, §62, 29.6.2007.

1530 *O'Halloran and Francis v. the United Kingdom* [GC], App. nos. 15809/02+, §§57–59, 29.6.2007. See also John Jackson, "Re-conceptualizing the right of silence as an effective fair trial standard", *International and Comparative Law Quarterly*, vol. 58, pt. 4, October 2009, pp. 835–861, at pp. 850–854.

1531 *Tirado Ortiz and Lozano Martin v. Spain* (dec.), App. no. 43486/98, 15.6.1999.

# CHAPTER 6

# ARTICLE 6 §3 AND SPECIAL GUARANTEES IN CRIMINAL PROCEEDINGS

**Article 6: Right to a fair trial**

*3. Everyone charged with a criminal offence has the following minimum rights:*

*(a) to be informed promptly, in a language which he understands and in detail, of the nature and cause of the accusation against him;*
*(b) to have adequate time and facilities for the preparation of his defence;*
*(c) to defend himself in person or through legal assistance of his own choosing or, if he has not sufficient means to pay for legal assistance, to be given it free when the interests of justice so require;*
*(d) to examine or have examined witnesses against him and to obtain the attendance and examination of witnesses on his behalf under the same conditions as witnesses against him;*
*(e) to have the free assistance of an interpreter if he cannot understand or speak the language used in court.*

## 6.1. BASIC PRINCIPLES OF ARTICLE 6 §3

Article 6 §3 of the Convention guarantees certain rights which are necessary in order to prepare and conduct a good defence. The aim of this provision is to give the accused an equal opportunity to defend himself vis-à-vis the prosecution and to guarantee the procedural equality of arms of the parties.[1532] The rights guaranteed by Article 6 §3 of the Convention are minimum rights and nothing prevents the Contracting States from providing a higher level of protection. An accused may also always waive his rights guaranteed under Article 6. The waiver must be made of the accused's own free will, either expressly or implicitly, and it must be unambiguous. In order to be valid, the purpose of the waiver must not remain unclear.[1533]

---

1532 *Al-Khawaja and Tahery v. the United Kingdom*, App. nos. 26766/05+, §34, 20.1.2009.

1533 See, for example, *Sejdovic v. Italy* [GC], App. no. 56581/00, §86, 1.3.2006; *Talat Tunç v. Turkey*, App. no. 32432/96, §59, 27.3.2007; and *Sakhnovskiy v. Russia* [GC], App. no. 21272/03, §90, 2.11.2010.

The requirements of Article 6 §3 are closely connected to the requirements of Article 6 §1 of the Convention. The rights guaranteed in Article 6 §3 comprise elements of the general fair trial requirements under Article 6 §1, representing particular aspects of fairness.[1534] Therefore, any shortcomings under Article 6 §3 often also constitute a violation under Article 6 §1 of the Convention.[1535] On the other hand, even though no violation of Article 6 §3 may be found, the proceedings can still be considered, as a whole, unfair.[1536] Although the rights under Article 6 §3 expressly apply to criminal proceedings, the same principles can be applied *mutatis mutandis* to civil and administrative law proceedings,[1537] although in such cases they are formulated as Article 6 §1 violations.[1538] This shows that the requirements of Article 6 §3 generally represent those practices connected to a fair trial.

The rights guaranteed under Article 6 §3 apply, within the autonomous meaning of the Convention, to anyone charged with a criminal offence. The wording is the same as in Article 6 §2 and the same interpretation practice applies to both paragraphs.[1539] A person is thus charged with a criminal offence from the moment his or her position is affected by pretrial investigation measures, such as interrogation, apprehension, arrest, coercive measures or search of a premises, or by any other measures relating to the criminal investigation.[1540] The guarantees do not apply if there is only a suspicion and no concrete measures have yet been taken against that person. Neither do they apply when an accused is being extradited to another country to be tried there.[1541]

Article 6 §3 cannot be interpreted to mean that all its minimum guarantees should be available to the accused immediately from the moment he or she becomes "charged with a criminal offence". They become relevant when the proceedings have reached the relevant stage. One such right that becomes relevant only in the later stages of the proceedings is the right to cross-examine witnesses. Otherwise, the Article 6 §3 guarantees should, as a rule, exist

1534 *Gäfgen v. Germany* [GC], App. no. 22978/05, §169, 1.6.2010; and *Sakhnovskiy v. Russia* [GC], App. no. 21272/03, §94, 2.11.2010.

1535 *A.S. v. Finland*, App. no. 40156/07, §75, 28.9.2010. As an example of the latter kind of situation, see *Vidal v. Belgium*, App. no. 12351/86, §35, 22.4.1992.

1536 *Barberà, Messegué and Jabardo v. Spain*, App. nos. 10590/83+, §89, 6.12.1988.

1537 *Pitkänen v. Finland*, App. no. 30508/96, §59, 9.3.2004.

1538 *Airey v. Ireland*, App. no. 6289/73, §§79–81, 9.10.1979. The case concerned access to free legal assistance in a family law matter and the fact that its unavailability for such a case meant in practice an obstacle to the right of access to court.

1539 Therefore, the precondition to the applicability of Articles 6 §2 and 6 §3 is that Article 6 §1 is applicable to the case. This became apparent, for example, in the case *Adolf v. Austria*, App. no. 8269/78, §§34–35 and 40, 26.3.1982.

1540 *Simeonovi v. Bulgaria* [GC], App. no. 21989/04, §121, 12.5.2017.

1541 In this respect it must, however, be secured that the Article 3 requirements are fulfilled. See *Soering v. the United Kingdom*, App. no. 14038/88, §80, 7.7.1989.

throughout the proceedings until the end of the appeal stage. However, in the appeal phase their extent is dependent on the content of the appeal as well as the competences of the appeal jurisdictions.[1542]

The fairness of the proceedings is normally estimated by using the fair trial criteria enumerated in Article 6 §1 and 6 §3. However, ultimately the Court makes the fairness assessment on the basis of an overall assessment in which the examination of one single fairness criterion does not necessarily contribute to a finding of unfairness of the proceedings as a whole. In criminal proceedings, the fair trial requirements apply to all proceedings, including those which concern the most serious terrorist crimes. On the other hand, Article 6 should not be applied in such a manner as to put disproportionate difficulties in the way of the police authorities in taking effective measures to protect the right to life and the right to personal security of members of the public. Nevertheless, public-interest concerns cannot justify measures which extinguish the very essence of an applicant's defence rights.[1543]

## 6.2. RIGHT TO BE INFORMED OF ACCUSATIONS

**Article 6: Right to a fair trial**

*3. Everyone charged with a criminal offence has the following minimum rights:*

*(a) to be informed promptly, in a language which he understands and in detail, of the nature and cause of the accusation against him.*

Article 6 §3 (a) guarantees the accused a right to prompt and detailed information about the nature and cause of the accusation against him, and in a language which he understands. The wording of this provision corresponds to that of Article 5 §2, according to which an arrested person shall be informed promptly, in a language which he understands, of the reasons for his arrest and of any charge against him. The aims of these provisions are, however, different. Article 5 of the Convention secures the rights of arrested persons and gives them the right to challenge the ground of the arrest or detention. On the other hand, the purpose of Article 6 §3 (a) is to give an accused information about the charges they need to defend themselves against in the upcoming proceedings. In this respect, the rights guaranteed under Article 6 §3 (a) must be seen primarily

---

1542 *Belziuk v. Poland*, App. no. 23103/93, §§37 and 39–40, 25.3.1998; *Kremzow v. Austria*, App. no. 12350/86, §§57–59, 21.9.1993; *Helmers v. Sweden*, App. no. 11826/85, §§31–32, 29.10.1991; and *Suuripää v. Finland*, App. no. 43151/02, §40, 12.1.2010.

1543 *Ibrahim and Others v. the United Kingdom* [GC], App. nos. 50541/08+, §§250–252, 13.9.2016.

as an element securing the proper use of the right to prepare one's defence under Article 6 §3 (b) of the Convention.[1544]

## 6.2.1. INFORMATION ABOUT THE NATURE AND CAUSES OF ACCUSATIONS

The right to receive information about charges includes the right to receive information both about those material facts on which the charges are based and their legal characterisation.[1545] Also, in those situations in which the content of the charges changes, either in respect of the facts or the legal characterisation, and either before the trial or during it, the accused must be informed well in advance of these changes in order to be able to defend him- or herself against the modified charges.[1546] The right to receive information about charges is violated if the accused is informed about the charges only at the last minute and has no opportunity to reply to them, or if he reads about them only in the judgment.[1547] Shortcomings in communicating the information may, however, be corrected if the accused has the chance, on appeal, to defend him- or herself against the modified or new charges. This requires that a higher court examines the appeal and that it also has the competence to examine the appeal in this respect.[1548]

### *6.2.1.1. Detailed Information*

The wording "in detail" in Article 6 §3 (a) means that the information must be more detailed than the information referred to in Article 5 §2, which is given to an arrested person. In the case *Mattoccia v. Italy*, the Court held that the accused had to be informed about those material facts on which the charges were based. Although the scope of the "detailed" information depends on the particular circumstances of the case, the accused must in any event be given

1544 *Pélissier and Sassi v. France* [GC], App. no. 25444/94, §54, 25.3.1999; and *Dallos v. Hungary*, App. no. 29082/95, §47, 1.3.2001.

1545 *Pélissier and Sassi v. France* [GC], App. no. 25444/94, §51, 25.3.1999; *Kamasinski v. Austria*, App. no. 9783/82, §79, 19.12.1989; *Mattoccia v. Italy*, App. no. 23969/94, §59, 25.7.2000; and *Penev v. Bulgaria*, App. no. 20494/04, §§33 and 42, 7.1.2010.

1546 *Mattoccia v. Italy*, App. no. 23969/94, §61, 25.7.2000. In the case *Backström and Andersson v. Sweden* (dec.), App. no. 67930/01, 5.9.2006, the information about the modified charges came somewhat late. The applicants' counsel, however, replied to it and did not request postponement of the case.

1547 *Pélissier and Sassi v. France* [GC], App. no. 25444/94, §51, 25.3.1999; *Sipavičius v. Lithuania*, App. no. 49093/99, §29, 21.2.2002; and *Sadak and Others v. Turkey*, App. nos. 29900/96+, §§57–58, 17.7.2001.

1548 *Dallos v. Hungary*, App. no. 29082/95, §§47–52, 1.3.2001; and *Sipavičius v. Lithuania*, App. no. 49093/99, §§31–33, 21.2.2002.

sufficient information, as far as necessary, so that he or she fully understands the content of the charges and can properly prepare his or her defence. Similarly, if the charges are modified, the accused must be given proper and full information about the change. In these situations, he or she must also be given sufficient time and facilities to react to the changes as well as to organise the defence on the basis of the new information or allegations.[1549] The information need not necessarily mention the evidence on which the charge is based.[1550]

As to the sufficiency of the facts, the criterion is that a proper defence against them is possible. In most cases, it is possible to identify the constituent elements of the crime, its time and location, the complainant and other detailed information on it, and this information must be communicated to the accused.[1551] However, with some continuous or repetitive offences, it may not be possible to give detailed information about the facts. Such a situation may occur, for example, in cases concerning the sexual abuse of a child which has continued for years, or in drugs cases in which it may not be possible to identify each discrete act precisely.[1552] Normally some specific details of the offence should be ascertainable not only from the indictment but also from other documents prepared by the prosecution in the case and from other file materials.[1553] Factual details of the offence may be clarified and specified during the proceedings.[1554]

#### *6.2.1.2. Modified Charges*

The accused must be duly and fully informed of any changes in the charges, including changes in its "cause", and must be provided with adequate time and facilities to react to them and organise his defence on the basis of any new information or allegation.[1555] When assessing whether charges have been modified and whether there is sufficient information about the facts, the Court

---

1549 *Mattoccia v. Italy*, App. no. 23969/94, §59, 25.7.2000. The case concerned rape charges against a school bus driver, who was accused of having raped a girl with disabilities. The charges did not mention any time or location of the crime, even though this information was known to the prosecutor. See also *Bäckström and Andersson v. Sweden* (dec.), App. no. 67930/01, 5.9.2006.

1550 *X. v. Belgium*, App. no. 7628/76, Commission decision, 9.5.1977.

1551 *Brozicek v. Italy*, App. no. 10964/84, §42, 19.12.1989.

1552 Such a situation was in question, for example, in the case *E.H. v. Finland* (dec.), App. no. 60966/00, 16.3.2004, which concerned sexual crime. The accused claimed that he had been convicted of an offence that he had not been accused of. The Court did not find that the applicant's conviction went further in respect of the facts or the constituent elements than had been indicated in the charges against him.

1553 *Previti v. Italy* (dec.), App. no. 1845/08, §208, 12.2.2013.

1554 *Sampech v. Italy* (dec.), App. no. 55546/09, §110, 19.5.2015; and *Pereira Cruz and Others v. Portugal*, App. nos. 56396/12+, §198, 26.6.2018.

1555 *Mattoccia v. Italy*, App. no. 23969/94, §61, 25.7.2000; *Bäckström and Andersson v. Sweden* (dec.), App. no. 67930/01, 5.9.2006; and *Varela Geis v. Spain*, App. no. 61005/09, §54, 5.3.2013.

uses a pragmatic approach. Changes which are legally insignificant or which are just reformulations by a court do not mean that charges have been modified. A reclassification of the offence is considered to be sufficiently foreseeable to the accused if it concerns an element which is intrinsic to the accusation.[1556] Whether the elements of the reclassified offence were debated in the proceedings is a further relevant consideration.[1557] If the facts are reclassified during the course of the proceedings, the accused must be afforded the possibility of exercising his defence rights in a practical and effective manner, and in good time.[1558]

In the case *Launiala v. Finland*, the Court found that the applicant's ability to defend himself in a case concerning a breach of official duty was not weakened by the fact that the court had referred in its reasoning to certain other norms, which were not mentioned in the charges, in order to give substance to those provisions on which the applicant's conviction had been based. The applicant's conviction was not based on provisions other than those invoked by the prosecutor, nor had the relevant facts or the legal characterisation of these facts changed at any point in the proceedings.[1559] Spelling mistakes or clerical errors in the charges do not lead to a violation either.[1560] On the other hand, if the accused is convicted of an offence other than those mentioned in the charges or raised during the trial, and this comes as a surprise to him or her, there can be a violation of Article 6 §3 (a).[1561]

When it comes to the required legal characterisation of a charge, the Court's case-law has become stricter over the years. In the case *De Salvador Torres v. Spain*, the Court found no violation, even though the applicant was convicted of embezzlement of public funds under aggravating circumstances and the charges failed to mention these aggravated circumstances. This conclusion was based on the fact that the applicant knew that he was in a public position and that this underlying factual element could constitute an aggravating circumstance for the purpose of determining the sentence.[1562] The Court's interpretation became stricter in the Grand Chamber case *Pélissier and Sassi v. France*. In that case, the

---

1556 *De Salvador Torres v. Spain*, App. no. 21525/93, §33, 24.10.1996; *Sadak and Others v. Turkey (No. 1)*, App. nos. 29900/96+, §§52 and 56, 17.7.2001; and *Juha Nuutinen v. Finland*, App. no. 45830/99, §32, 24.4.2007.

1557 *Penev v. Bulgaria*, App. no. 20494/04, §41, 7.1.2010.

1558 *Pélissier and Sassi v. France* [GC], App. no. 25444/94, §62, 25.3.1999; *Block v. Hungary*, App. no. 56282/09, §24, 25.1.2011; *Haxhia v. Albania*, App. no. 29861/03, §§137–138, 8.10.2013; and *Pereira Cruz and Others v. Portugal*, App. nos. 56396/12+, §198, 26.6.2018.

1559 *Launiala v. Finland* (dec.), App. no. 55171/08, 13.9.2011.

1560 *Gea Catalán v. Spain*, App. no. 19160/91, §§27–29, 10.2.1995.

1561 *Kyprianou v. Cyprus*, App. no. 73797/01, §66, 27.1.2004. Subsequently the Grand Chamber gave a judgment in the case, but it did not touch upon this matter. A violation was found in the case *Penev v. Bulgaria*, App. no. 20494/04, §§39–43, 7.1.2010. In that case, the offence mentioned in the charges and examined at the trial had been different from the offence the applicant was finally convicted of.

1562 *De Salvador Torres v. Spain*, App. no. 21525/93, §33, 24.10.1996. The case concerned embezzlement of public funds.

charges were dismissed by the court of first instance. On appeal, the applicants were convicted of aiding and abetting without having been notified of the alternative charges. The Court found that aiding and abetting did not concern the same facts as the original charges and hence a violation of Article 6 §3 had occurred.[1563]

The current stricter line of interpretation was also applied in the cases *Laaksonen v. Finland* and *Juha Nuutinen v. Finland*. In the case *Laaksonen v. Finland*, the prosecutor had brought charges of debtor's dishonesty and the District Court had dismissed them. The applicant was then convicted by the Court of Appeal of aiding and abetting debtor's dishonesty without the prosecutor having modified the charges to cover the aiding and abetting element. The Court held that under the requirements of the fairness of proceedings the applicant should have been given an opportunity to challenge the charges of aiding and abetting in an oral hearing. The proceedings before the Court of Appeal had therefore not been fair and there was a violation of Article 6 of the Convention.[1564] In the case *Juha Nuutinen v. Finland*, the applicant was accused of, *inter alia*, aggravated tax fraud and convicted as charged by the District Court. On appeal, he requested the dismissal of the charges and claimed that, in any event, the case concerned only aiding and abetting tax fraud. The Court of Appeal convicted him of aiding and abetting without examining in the oral hearing whether the applicant's acts could be characterised as aiding and abetting. The Court found that the applicant had been convicted of acts that he had had no opportunity to defend himself against in adversarial proceedings.[1565] In both cases the Court emphasised the significance of dialogue at the trial and the fact that the basis of the conviction and the legal characterisation of the facts needed to be discussed by the parties.

Defects in the notification of the reformulated charge can be cured in the appeal proceedings if the accused has the opportunity to advance before the higher court his defence in respect of the reformulated charge and to contest his conviction in respect of all relevant legal and factual aspects.[1566]

#### *6.2.1.3. Alternative Charges*

Alternative charges either presented before the trial or during it can be accepted, since they do not violate the accused's right to receive information about the

1563 *Pélissier and Sassi v. France* [GC], App. no. 25444/94, §§61–63, 25.3.1999.

1564 *Laaksonen v. Finland*, App. no. 70216/01, §§30–31, 12.4.2007. The case was examined under Article 6 §1 without any reference to the special criminal provisions under Article 6 §3 of the Convention.

1565 *Juha Nuutinen v. Finland*, App. no. 45830/99, §§32–34, 24.4.2007. The case was examined under Article 6 §1 together with Article 6 §3 (a) and (b).

1566 *Dallos v. Hungary*, App. no. 29082/95, §§49–52, 1.3.2001; *Sipavičius v. Lithuania*, App. no. 49093/99, §§30–33, 21.2.2002; *Zhupnik v. Ukraine*, App. no. 20792/05, §§39–43, 9.12.2010; *I.H. and Others v. Austria*, App. no. 42780/98, §§36–38, 20.4.2006; and *Gelenidze v. Georgia*, App. no. 72916/10, §30, 7.11.2019.

nature and cause of the charges. For example, a person who has been found in possession of stolen property can be accused of theft or, alternatively, of concealing property, or a debtor can be accused of a debtor's offence or other offences. This does not go against the fair trial principles and does not weaken a person's ability to defend themselves, provided that the alternative charges are clearly presented during the proceedings and that there is also a real opportunity for the accused to defend himself against the alternative charges so that any conviction on the basis of alternative charges does not come as a surprise.[1567]

### 6.2.1.4. *Manner of Service*

The information about charges must be communicated to the accused in such a manner that he or she actually receives information about it. No specific manner of service is, however, required.[1568] The manner of serving the charges may vary from case to case and in accordance with the circumstances.[1569] Generally the charges must be in written form.[1570] If they are sent by post, normally it is expected that there is an acknowledgment of receipt.[1571] Other means of serving are also acceptable, and even the serving of the charges orally may be sufficient in a specific case.

If a person has been interrogated extensively and in detail about the facts of the case, he or she cannot reasonably claim to be ignorant about those facts which form the basis of the accusations and which have been orally communicated to him or her.[1572] Similarly, if a person has been summonsed to appear in court but has failed to do so, he or she cannot reasonably claim not to have been informed about the grounds of the accusations.[1573] The duty to inform the accused rests entirely on the prosecution and cannot be complied with passively by making

---

1567 *Pélissier and Sassi v. France* [GC], App. no. 25444/94, §56, 25.3.1999; and *Penev v. Bulgaria*, App. no. 20494/04, §41, 7.1.2010.

1568 *Pélissier and Sassi v. France* [GC], App. no. 25444/94, §53, 25.3.1999; *Drassich v. Italy*, App. no. 25575/04, §34, 11.12.2007; *Giosakis v. Greece (No. 3)*, App. no. 5689/08, §29, 3.5.2011; and *Erdoğan v. Turkey* (dec.), App. no. 14723/89, 9.7.1992. In the latter case it was found to be the applicant's own fault that he had not been informed about the charges at the earliest possible opportunity, since he had been beyond the reach of the authorities for fear of being arrested and detained.

1569 The applicant himself was held responsible for failing to take the necessary steps, during his absence, to ensure receipt of his mail and to verify its contents. See *Hennings v. Germany*, App. no. 12129/86, §26, 16.12.1992.

1570 *Kamasinski v. Austria*, App. no. 9783/82, §79, 19.12.1989.

1571 *C. v. Italy*, App. no. 10889/84, Commission decision, 11.5.1988. The applicant claimed that the subpoena and charges had been served in his apartment but that their receipt had been acknowledged by somebody other than him. The Court found that the legal safeguards had in any event worked properly and declared the case inadmissible.

1572 *Kamasinski v. Austria*, App. no. 9783/82, §80, 19.12.1989.

1573 *Campbell and Fell v. the United Kingdom*, App. nos. 7819/77+, §96, 28.6.1984.

information available without bringing it to the attention of the defence.[1574] If the person concerned has mental difficulties, the authorities are required to take additional steps to enable the person to be informed in detail of the nature and cause of the accusations against him.[1575]

### 6.2.2. PROMPT INFORMATION

In respect of the speed of service of charges, the Court's case-law is not very exacting. Generally, the charges must be communicated to the accused within a time frame that allows a defence to be prepared.[1576] The Court has not found a violation in cases in which the service of charges may have taken a long time, provided that the information had been served well before the beginning of the criminal trial.[1577] On the other hand, if a person is not informed for several years about charges against him or her, a violation may be found on this ground.[1578]

### 6.2.3. LANGUAGE OF THE CHARGES

Charges must be in a language which the accused understands. If it is shown or there are reasons to believe that the accused has insufficient knowledge of the language in which the information is given, the authorities must provide him with a translation.[1579] For example, in the case *Brozicek v. Italy*, the applicant was not Italian, nor did he live in Italy. He had informed the court about his poor Italian skills. According to the authorities, the applicant understood Italian. The Court did not, however, give any significance to the fact that the Italian State had ascertained the applicant's language skills, and held that the information about charges should have been translated into a language which the applicant understood.[1580]

---

1574 *Mattoccia v. Italy*, App. no. 23969/94, §65, 25.7.2000; and *Chichlian and Ekindjian v. France*, App. no. 10959/84, Report of the Commission, §71, 16.3.1989.

1575 *Vaudelle v. France*, App. no. 35683/97, §65, 30.1.2001.

1576 *C. v. Italy*, App. no. 10889/84, Commission decision, 11.5.1988, where the notification of charges to the applicant four months before his trial was deemed acceptable. Compare and contrast with *Borisova v. Bulgaria*, App. no. 56891/00, §§43–45, 21.12.2006 (violation) in which the applicant had only a couple of hours to prepare her defence, and without a lawyer.

1577 *Padin Gestoso v. Spain* (dec.), App. no. 39519/98, 8.12.1998.

1578 *Casse v. Luxembourg*, App. no. 40327/02, §§74–75, 27.4.2006.

1579 *Brozicek v. Italy*, App. no. 10964/84, §41, 19.12.1989; and *Tabaï v. France* (dec.), App. no. 73805/01, 17.2.2004.

1580 *Brozicek v. Italy*, App. no. 10964/84, §§41–42, 19.12.1989.

Article 6 §3 (a) does not specify that the relevant information should be given in writing or translated into written form for a foreign defendant. Therefore a defendant not familiar with the language used by the court may be at a practical disadvantage if he is not provided with a written translation of the indictment into a language which he understands.[1581] However, sufficient information on the charges may also be provided through an oral translation of the indictment if this allows the accused to prepare his defence.[1582] In any event, there is no right under this provision for the accused to have a full translation of the court files.[1583] The costs incurred in the interpretation of the accusation must be borne by the State in accordance with Article 6 §3 (e), which guarantees the right to the free assistance of an interpreter.[1584]

## 6.3. RIGHT TO ADEQUATE TIME AND FACILITIES FOR PREPARING A DEFENCE

**Article 6: Right to a fair trial**

*3. Everyone charged with a criminal offence has the following minimum rights:*

...

*(b) to have adequate time and facilities for the preparation of his defence.*

### 6.3.1. CONTENT OF THE RIGHT

Article 6 §3 (b) of the Convention guarantees the accused the right to have adequate time and facilities for the preparation of his or her defence.[1585] Its scope is extensive, covering all kinds of necessary preparations for a defence. In other words, it enables an accused to organise a proper defence that allows all arguments necessary and relevant to the outcome of the proceedings to be presented to the court.[1586] The main elements of the definition of "adequate time and facilities" are: 1) adequate time for preparation; 2) the ability to contact a counsel; and 3) access to documents and, more generally, all case

---

1581 *Kamasinski v. Austria*, App. no. 9783/82, §79, 19.12.1989; and *Hermi v. Italy* [GC], App. no. 18114/02, §68, 18.10.2006.

1582 *Kamasinski v. Austria*, App. no. 9783/82, §81, 19.12.1989; and *Husain v. Italy* (dec.), App. no. 18913/03, 24.2.2005.

1583 *X. v. Austria*, App. no. 2291/64, Commission decision, 1.6.1967.

1584 *Luedicke, Belkacem and Koç v. Germany*, App. nos. 6210/73+, §45, 28.11.1978. See also Karen Reid, *A Practitioner's Guide to the European Convention on Human Rights*, Sweet & Maxwell/Thomson Reuters, London 2019, p. 236.

1585 *Galstyan v. Armenia*, App. no. 26986/03, §84, 15.11.2007.

1586 *Can v. Austria*, App. no. 9300/81, §53, 30.9.1985; *Connolly v. the United Kingdom* (dec.), App. no. 27245/95, 26.6.1996; *Gregačević v. Croatia*, App. no. 58331/09, §51, 10.7.2012; and *Mayzit v. Russia*, App. no. 63378/00, §78, 20.1.2005.

files. The adequate conditions for preparation of a defence relate not only to the time for that preparation but also to the opportunity for the accused to obtain the necessary legal assistance to reply to the charges, and to have access to information about any material collected during the pretrial investigation and the proceedings.[1587] The rights guaranteed to the accused reflect the right to adversarial proceedings and the right to be heard, as well as the fact that the parties to proceedings must have the right to receive and give information and to influence the outcome of the proceedings.

No general rules can be given on the specific requirements, but the adequacy of the time and facilities is always assessed on a case-by-case basis according to the circumstances of the case and from the point of view that the legal safeguards should be practical and real.[1588]

## 6.3.2. ADEQUATE TIME FOR PREPARING A DEFENCE

Adequate time to prepare a defence ensures that a trial does not take place too quickly, and complements the reasonable time requirement in Article 6 §1.[1589] As in other Article 6 criminal limb guarantees, this right also becomes effective when a person is charged or when his or her position is affected by some pretrial investigation measure.[1590]

No general and exact rule can be given as to what is considered to be adequate time but this issue must be assessed in the circumstances of the specific case.[1591] Importance is given to the extent and complexity of the case file,[1592] the stage of the proceedings,[1593] the duration of the trial,[1594] and to whether

1587 *C.G.P. v. the Netherlands*, App. no. 29835/96, Commission decision, 15.1.1997; and *Foucher v. France*, App. no. 22209/93, §§26–38, 18.3.1997.

1588 *Iglin v. Ukraine*, App. no. 39908/05, §65, 12.1.2012; and *Galstyan v. Armenia*, App. no. 26986/03, §84, 15.11.2007.

1589 *Kröcher and Möller v. Switzerland*, App. no. 8463/78, Commission decision, 9.7.1981; *Bonzi v. Switzerland*, App. no. 7854/77, Commission decision, 12.7.1978; *Borisova v. Bulgaria*, App. no. 56891/00, §40, 21.12.2006; *Malofeyeva v. Russia*, no. 36673/04, §115, 30.5.2013; and *Gafgaz Mammadov v. Azerbaijan*, App. no. 60259/11, §§76–82, 15.10.2015.

1590 Such measures can be interrogation, apprehension, arrest, coercive measures, or a search of a domicile.

1591 *Mattick v. Germany* (dec.), App. no. 62116/00, 31.3.2005.

1592 *Albert and Le Compte v. Belgium*, App. nos. 7299/75+, §41, 10.2.1983; and *Gregačević v. Croatia*, App. no. 58331/09, §51, 10.7.2012.

1593 *H.H. v. Austria* (dec.), App. no. 5523/72, 5.10.1974. The Court found that a fixed time limit for lodging an appeal may in some cases be problematic. However, this was not the situation in this case.

1594 *Makhfi v. France*, App. no. 59335/00, §§34–42, 19.10.2004. In this case, as a result of the trial running for a long time, the counsel had to give the closing arguments to the jury at 4.25 in the morning. The Court held that a counsel should not be put in a situation in which he or she has to present closing arguments when excessively tired.

the applicant takes care of his or her own defence or whether he or she has a counsel.[1595] To some extent, attention can also be given to the other workload of the counsel and the chance he or she has to concentrate on the applicant's case.[1596] For the preparation of the defence, it is also relevant that the legal counsel, who is either chosen by the applicant or assigned to him or her, has been chosen well in advance of the start of the proceedings.[1597] If the counsel is changed for a valid reason, the new counsel must also be given an opportunity to familiarise him- or herself with the case.[1598]

A period of two weeks for preparing a defence in a case that contained a case file of 17,000 pages was not considered adequate,[1599] nor were the few hours given to prepare a defence in a case concerning an administrative misdemeanour.[1600] On the other hand, 17 days was considered sufficient for preparing a somewhat complicated case,[1601] likewise five days for a disciplinary case[1602] and 21 days for the defence team to familiarise themselves with a document containing 49 pages.[1603] If the charges are modified on the last day of a long hearing, there might in certain circumstances be problems with regard to adequate preparation time. For example, if the defendant has responded to the initial charges with the help of his or her counsel earlier in the hearing but the counsel is no longer present when the charges are modified, there may very well be a problem concerning an inadequate time for preparing the defence.[1604] At the appeal stage, the time considered adequate for preparing a defence is clearly shorter than before a first-instance court.[1605]

If the accused finds the time for preparing the defence to be insufficient, he or she must react to it in time and request an adjournment of the proceedings,[1606] save in exceptional circumstances or where there is no basis for such a right in domestic law and practice.[1607] In certain circumstances a court may be required

1595 *X. v. Austria* (dec.), App. no. 2370/64, 11.2.1967.

1596 *X. v. Austria* (dec.), App. no. 7909/77, 12.10.1978; and *Twalib v. Greece*, App. no. 24294/94, §40, 9.6.1998.

1597 The State is not, however, responsible if counsel does not carry out his or her duties or if the delays are attributable to the counsel's negligence.

1598 *Goddi v. Italy*, App. no. 8966/80, §§30–31, 9.4.1984.

1599 *Öcalan v. Turkey* [GC], App. no. 46221/99, §147, 12.5.2005.

1600 *Galstyan v. Armenia*, App. no. 26986/03, §§87–88, 15.11.2007.

1601 *X. and Y. v. Austria* (dec.), App. no. 7909/77, 12.10.1978.

1602 *Campbell and Fell v. the United Kingdom*, App. nos. 7819/77+, §98, 28.6.1984.

1603 *Kremzow v. Austria*, App. no. 12350/86, §48, 21.9.1993.

1604 *Sadak and Others v. Turkey*, App. nos. 29900/96+, §§57–58, 17.7.2001.

1605 *H.H. v. Austria* (dec.), App. no. 5523/72, 5.10.1974.

1606 *J.J.M. v. the United Kingdom* (dec.), App. no. 4681/70, 3.10.1972; *Campbell and Fell v. the United Kingdom*, App. nos. 7819/77+, §98, 28.6.1984; *Bäckström and Andersson v. Sweden* (dec.), App. no. 67930/01, 5.9.2006; and *Craxi v. Italy (No. 1)*, App. no. 34896/97, §72, 5.12.2002.

1607 *Goddi v. Italy*, App. no. 8966/80, §31, 9.4.1984; and *Galstyan v. Armenia*, App. no. 26986/03, §85, 15.11.2007.

to adjourn a hearing of its own motion in order to give the defence sufficient time.[1608] If the time to prepare a defence is insufficient in the first-instance proceedings, this shortcoming may be corrected on appeal.[1609]

## 6.3.3. ADEQUATE FACILITIES FOR PREPARING A DEFENCE

The right to adequate facilities for preparing a defence under Article 6 §3 (b) contains two types of rights. First, an accused must have access to assistance from a legal counsel before the proceedings,[1610] and, second, he or she must have access to the pretrial investigation material.[1611] Both rights are special aspects of the fair trial guarantees and are normally examined together with the general fair trial guarantee in Article 6 §1 of the Convention.[1612]

### *6.3.3.1. Access to a Lawyer*

The right to adequate facilities for preparing a defence contains in particular the ability to have access to assistance from a legal counsel during the pretrial investigation before the start of the proceedings.[1613] In this respect, Article 6 §3 (b) overlaps to a certain extent with Article 6 §3 (c), which contains a right to defend oneself through legal assistance. Quite often such cases are examined under Article 6 §3 (c), also in respect of the pretrial investigation, and without a separate reference to Article 6 §3 (b).[1614]

Access to assistance from a legal counsel is particularly important for people in pretrial detention. They are subject to pretrial investigation and awaiting the start of a trial while in detention. According to the Court's case-law, a detainee on remand must have the right to meet with his or her counsel and to conduct confidential negotiations with him or her in such a manner that the prison staff cannot hear their conversations or otherwise intervene in them.[1615]

---

1608 *Sadak and Others v. Turkey*, App. nos. 29900/96+, §57, 17.7.2001; and *Sakhnovskiy v. Russia* [GC], App. no. 21272/03, §§103 and 106, 2.11.2010.

1609 *Twalib v. Greece*, App. no. 24294/94, §42, 9.6.1998.

1610 *Goddi v. Italy*, App. no. 8966/80, §31, 9.4.1984.

1611 *Huseyn and Others v. Azerbaijan*, App. nos. 35485/05+, §175, 26.7.2011; and *OAO Neftyanaya Kompaniya Yukos v. Russia*, App. no. 14902/04, §538, 20.9.2011.

1612 *Rowe and Davis v. the United Kingdom* [GC], App. no. 28901/95, §59, 16.2.2000; *Edwards v. the United Kingdom*, App. no. 13071/87, §§33–34, 16.12.1992; and *Leas v. Estonia*, App. no. 59577/08, §76, 6.3.2012.

1613 *Salduz v. Turkey* [GC], App. no. 36391/02, §50, 27.11.2008; *Sakhnovskiy v. Russia* [GC], App. no. 21272/03, §97, 2.11.2010; and *Castravet v. Moldova*, App. no. 23393/05, §49, 13.3.2007.

1614 See more about Article 6 §3 (c) in section 6.4. below.

1615 *Campbell and Fell v. the United Kingdom*, App. nos. 7819/77+, §113, 28.6.1984; *Öcalan v. Turkey* [GC], App. no. 46221/99, §§131, 134, 137 and 148, 12.5.2005; and *Salduz v. Turkey* [GC], App. no. 36391/02, §52, 27.11.2008.

Restrictions on one's right to meet with a counsel, or to have access to adequate facilities, can only be justified in the most exceptional circumstances and for valid reasons that must be based on some particularly convincing public-interest requirements.[1616] Such case-specific grounds could include the risk of a detainee absconding or the danger a detainee poses.[1617] Any other restrictions on access to assistance from a legal counsel or restrictions on meetings are highly questionable.

In the light of the recent case-law of the Court, it has become more and more important that an accused is guaranteed the chance to obtain legal assistance as early as the pretrial investigation stage. Nowadays, the Court assesses very carefully whether guilt has been admitted by the accused during a pretrial investigation without the presence of a counsel and whether the subsequent conviction has been based on such a confession (even if the accused has later withdrawn it), albeit from the point of view of the overall fairness of the proceedings.[1618] The restrictions on access to a counsel may appear ultimately as a violation of Article 6 §3 (c) of the Convention.[1619]

The right to be in contact with a counsel in order to prepare a defence for a trial concerns both oral and written contact. The confidentiality of the communication with the counsel cannot be jeopardised or restricted by any practical obstacles,[1620] such as using a glass partition between the counsel and the detainee that necessitates raising voices for conversations,[1621] or by the fact that contact with a lawyer is only through a video link.[1622] There is also an excessive barrier to confidential communication with a counsel if the suspect cannot relay to his or her counsel, because of a professional duty of secrecy, some elements needed for the preparation of his or her defence. In the case *M v. the Netherlands*, the fact that the applicant was employed by the General Intelligence and Security Service and thus under the duty of secrecy meant that the risk of being prosecuted for a breach of this duty created a barrier to effective communication with his counsel and thus hindered the preparation

---

1616 *Salduz v. Turkey* [GC], App. no. 36391/02, §52, 27.11.2008.

1617 *Campbell and Fell v. the United Kingdom*, App. nos. 7819/77+, §113, 28.6.1984. In this case the second applicant was not able to meet with his counsel for two months at the beginning of his pretrial detention. See also *Brennan v. the United Kingdom*, App. no. 39846/98, §45, 16.10.2001; and *Kröcher and Mölle v. Switzerland*, App. no. 8463/78, Commission decision, 9.7.1981.

1618 *Ibrahim and Others v. the United Kingdom* [GC], App. nos. 50541/08+, §§249–254 and 257, 13.9.2016; and *A.T. v. Luxembourg*, App. no. 30460/13, §§67–75, 9.4.2015.

1619 See, for example, *Salduz v. Turkey* [GC], App. no. 36391/02, §§58 and 60–62, 27.11.2008; *Dayanan v. Turkey*, App. no. 7377/03, §33, 13.10.2009; and *Płonka v. Poland*, App. no. 20310/02, §§38–39 and 41, 31.3.2009. See further, section 6.4 below.

1620 *Sakhnovskiy v. Russia* [GC], App. no. 21272/03, §102, 2.11.2010.

1621 *Istratii and Others v. Moldova*, App. nos. 8721/05+, §§87–91, 27.3.2007. The Court referred to Article 6 but factually the case was examined under Article 5 §4 of the Convention.

1622 *Sakhnovskiy v. Russia* [GC], App. no. 21272/03, §104, 2.11.2010.

of his defence.[1623] Although restrictions imposed by the authorities on correspondence between a detainee and his or her counsel can be examined under Article 6 §3 (b) as a question of preparation of defence, usually they are examined as an Article 8 complaint (right to respect for correspondence).[1624]

#### *6.3.3.2. Right to Disclosure of Pretrial Investigation Material*

Another right covered by Article 6 §3 (b) on the preparation of a defence is the right of the accused to obtain information about the pretrial investigation material. In particular, the access of the accused to this material guarantees the equality of arms of the parties. The prosecution has at its disposal all means of pretrial investigation in order to collect information – interrogations, searches of premises, other coercive measures and forensic investigation methods – which the defendant does not have. The right to information about the collected material balances this inequality. "Material" can be defined as anything that can be used either against the accused or for his or her benefit. It covers both the material obtained by the authorities during the pretrial investigation and the material which should have been obtained and which could lead to an acquittal or a reduction of a sentence.[1625]

An accused does not have to be given direct access to the case file but it is sufficient that he or she is informed of the material in the file by his representatives.[1626] However, an accused should have the evidence made available to him before the trial and be given an opportunity to comment on it through his lawyer in oral submissions.[1627] When an accused has been allowed to conduct his own defence, denying him access to the case file amounts to an infringement of the rights of the defence.[1628]

However, it may be necessary to conceal material from the suspect in the pretrial investigation phase when he or she is interrogated. In this phase, the suspect nevertheless has the following legal safeguards: the right to remain silent; and the presence of a counsel. The right of access to the material will arise in the later stages of the proceedings when the matter has reached the prosecution phase.[1629]

---

1623 *M. v. the Netherlands*, App. no. 2156/10, §§91–98, 25.7.2017.

1624 *Petrov v. Bulgaria*, App. no. 15197/02, §44, 22.5.2008.

1625 *C.G.P. v. the Netherlands*, App. no. 29835/96, Commission decision, 15.1.1997; and *Jasper v. the United Kingdom* [GC], App. no. 27052/95, §51, 16.2.2000.

1626 *Kremzow v. Austria*, App. no. 12350/86, §52, 21.9.1993.

1627 *Öcalan v. Turkey* [GC], App. no. 46221/99, §140, 12.5.2005. See also Karen Reid, *A Practitioner's Guide to the European Convention on Human Rights*, Sweet & Maxwell/ Thomson Reuters, London 2019, p. 161.

1628 *Foucher v. France*, App. no. 22209/93, §§33–36, 18.3.1997.

1629 *A.T. v. Luxembourg*, App. no. 30460/13, §§79–84, 9.4.2015.

Despite this, the right to obtain information about all the material is not an absolute right, even in the prosecution or trial phase. Withholding of certain material may be necessary for a particularly important reason, such as national security, to protect witnesses from reprisals or the confidentiality of the investigation methods of the police. When deciding on the withholding of certain material, the interests protected must be weighed against the interests of the accused. By default, the rights of the defence weigh heavier. Limitations of these rights are justified only when absolutely necessary and when they do not render the proceedings as a whole unfair. In addition, the fair trial requirements demand that any difficulties caused to the defence by limitations on its rights must be sufficiently counterbalanced by the procedures followed by the judicial authorities.[1630]

Withholding of material was at stake in three Grand Chamber cases which were adopted on the same day. The case *Jasper v. the United Kingdom* concerned the accused's right to obtain information about pretrial investigation material when the prosecutor could not disclose certain material. The case involved an armed robbery, the planning of which the police had learned about, and where officers had observed the perpetrators at the crime scene. Before the start of the trial, the prosecution asked the judge to order that certain material not be disclosed to the accused while allowing that judge to see the material. The judge accepted the prosecutor's request and held that he would have ordered the material to be disclosed had it contained something that could have helped the defence. The Court held that the proceedings had been fair as they contained certain legal safeguards: 1) the decision to withhold was rendered by a judge who knew the content of the material and could weigh the competing interests in its disclosure; 2) the applicant had been kept informed about the matter and he had been allowed to participate in the decision-making procedure as far as it had been possible without disclosing the material; 3) the withheld material did not form a part of the evidence invoked by the prosecution; and 4) the judge continued to assess, throughout the proceedings, whether fair trial guarantees required the disclosure of the material. According to the Court, the domestic court had applied standards which followed, as far as possible, the requirements of adversarial proceedings and of the equality of arms.[1631] The acceptability of such conduct was confirmed in another British case, *Fitt v. the United Kingdom*.[1632]

However, the Court came to a different conclusion in a third case, *Rowe and Davis v. the United Kingdom*. In that case the prosecution had itself

---

1630 *Rowe and Davis v. the United Kingdom* [GC], App. no. 28901/95, §61, 16.2.2000.

1631 *Jasper v. the United Kingdom* [GC], App. no. 27052/95, §§52–56 and 58, 16.2.2000.

1632 *Fitt v. the United Kingdom* [GC], App. no. 29777/96, §§48–50, 16.2.2000. See also Karen Reid, *A Practitioner's Guide to the European Convention on Human Rights*, Sweet & Maxwell/ Thomson Reuters, London 2019, p. 207.

decided, without informing the judge, to withhold part of the material on the grounds of public interest. The procedure in which the prosecution assessed the significance of the withheld information for the defence and weighed it against the public interest did not fulfil the Article 6 requirements. The Court found a violation, as the prosecution had neither presented the material to the judge, nor provided him with an opportunity to decide on the withholding of the material.[1633]

The principles applied in the *Jasper* and *Fitt* cases have subsequently been applied, *inter alia*, in two Finnish cases that led to a violation. These cases concerned pretrial investigation material which was subsequently either destroyed or withheld and which the defendants could not therefore use in their defence. The case *Natunen v. Finland* concerned the destruction of evidence by virtue of the applicable domestic law at the time. The case involved a drugs offence where some of the evidence was procured by telephone tapping. The applicant claimed that he was dealing arms, not drugs, and that the telephone calls which had been admitted as evidence gave a wrong impression of his actions. He had requested access to all tapped telephone calls in order to clear up the matter, but this was no longer possible since all other recordings of the telephone calls had been destroyed. The destruction had been done by virtue of the domestic law at the time which required the destruction of all other recorded calls which related to the ongoing criminal investigation. Therefore, the applicant was in a situation in which he could not prove his account of the facts. By applying the *Jasper* and *Fitt* test, the Court examined whether the domestic proceedings had been, as far as possible, adversary and whether they had contained sufficient safeguards protecting the rights of the accused. The Court found it problematic that the choice of material was left to the discretion of the investigative authorities and the accused did not have any opportunity to participate in this process. Nor was there any judicial control by a judge. The Court therefore found a violation of Articles 6 §1 and 6 §3 (b) of the Convention.[1634] Another similar case is that of *Janatuinen v. Finland*, which also concerned a drugs offence. The Court found in this case that there were no sufficient legal safeguards to protect the interests of the accused and therefore the requirements of adversarial proceedings or equality of arms were not fulfilled.[1635]

---

1633 *Rowe and Davis v. the United Kingdom* [GC], App. no. 28901/95, §§63–67, 16.2.2000.

1634 *Natunen v. Finland*, App. no. 21022/04, §48, 31.3.2009. See also Anand Doobay, "The right to a fair trial in light of the recent ECtHR and CJEU case-law", *ERA forum*, vol.14, issue 2, September 2013, pp. 251–262, at p. 257; Satu Heikkilä, *From Final Judgment to Final Resolution – Effectiveness of the Execution of Judgments of the European Court of Human Rights in Finland*, Wolf Legal Publishers, Tilburg 2019, pp. 372–373; and James Welch (Ed.), "Cases and comment: selected decisions from the European Court of Human Rights for March and April 2009 – Criminal procedure, *Natunen v. Finland* (Application No. 21022/04)", *European Human Rights Law Review*, Issue 4, 2009, pp. 590–593.

1635 *Janatuinen v. Finland*, App. no. 28552/05, §§48–50, 8.12.2009.

Access to pretrial investigation material also requires that the applicant has sufficiently specified his or her request, especially in cases where the pretrial investigation material is very extensive. In the case *Sigurður Einarsson and Others v. Iceland*, the prosecutor had singled out certain material from the massive amount of evidence by using test words but the applicants had not been given an opportunity to participate in the selection of the material; nor had the restrictions on the material been examined by the domestic court. However, the applicants had not used the opportunity provided by law to claim, before a court, access to full material; nor had they specified the evidence they wished to request to obtain, for example by proposing other test words.[1636] Similarly in *Rook v. Germany*, the telephone tapping and electronic material in a corruption case was massive. The evidence on which the charges were based was available to the applicant. Other material was also made available for him on the police premises. The applicant had not identified which material he wished to have access to and he had not used the opportunity to familiarise himself with the available evidence on the police premises, although it had been kept available for about a year. The Court considered that the applicant had had sufficiently wide access to the material in question and adequate time to prepare his defence.[1637]

The need to withhold pretrial investigation material in the public interest may be necessary in situations in which telephone tapping and other secret surveillance methods are used, for example, to prevent terrorism, or when mass surveillance is used to investigate terrorism.[1638] The Court's case-law will most likely become more precise in this respect in the coming years.

In the case *Van Wesenbeeck v. Belgium*, the Court found it justified that confidential information acquired in the context of undercover operations was not disclosed. In this case the Court considered that the confidentiality was necessary in order to protect the identity of the undercover police officers and the nature of the investigation methods. Moreover, the selection of the material submitted to the case file had been done by the public prosecutor but under the supervision of an independent and impartial panel. There was thus no violation.[1639]

The obligation to disclose evidence to the defence may also be at stake in situations where an accused claims to have been "entrapped" by the authorities into committing a crime that would not otherwise have taken place. In the case *Edwards and Lewis v. the United Kingdom*, the Court examined an allegation that the police had provoked the defendants into committing the crime. This

---

1636 *Sigurður Einarsson and Others v. Iceland*, App. no. 39757/15, §§87–93, 4.6.2019.

1637 *Rook v. Germany*, App. no. 1586/15, §§59–75, 25.7.2019 (no violation). See also Jordan Owen, "Access to electronic evidence – *Rook v. Germany* (Application No. 1586/15)", *European Human Rights Law Review*, Issue 6, 2019, pp. 671–675.

1638 *Kennedy v. the United Kingdom*, App. no. 26839/05, §§186–191, 18.5.2010. See also *Big Brother Watch and Others v. the United Kingdom*, App. nos. 58170/13+, §511, 13.9.2018.

1639 *Van Wesenbeeck v. Belgium*, App. no. 67496/10, §§69–84, 23.5.2017 (no violation).

allegation was pertinent because, if entrapment by the authorities could be shown, the charges would have had to be dropped. However, the material which could have proved the entrapment allegation correct had been concealed and the defendants were unable to obtain access to it. Although the decision to withhold this material had been taken by a judge, it had not been possible for the defence to argue the case on entrapment in full before the court. The Court found that the procedure employed to determine the issues of disclosure of evidence and entrapment did not comply with the requirements to provide adversarial proceedings and equality of arms, nor did it incorporate adequate safeguards to protect the interests of the accused. It therefore found a violation of Article 6 §1 of the Convention.[1640]

Withholding of pretrial investigation material and non-disclosure of certain information were also in question in the case *V. v. Finland*, which concerned police enticement to commit a drugs offence and the withholding of information detailing the police's methods. The applicant claimed that he would not have committed the crime without provocation, which involved the police asking someone to make an order by telephone. The person placing the order was at the time in the police custody. This information was, however, withheld from the accused, the prosecution and the court, and subsequently the police refused to disclose any circumstances relating to the telephone call. The Court held that, by withholding important details of the case, the police had deprived the applicant of an opportunity to prove his allegation of entrapment. No public-interest grounds were put forward for withholding the information in question. In addition, the withheld material had been connected to a fact which was particularly important for the applicant. Nor had the domestic court been given sufficient information to assess the importance of the withheld material to the defence. The Court thus found that the proceedings had not been fair.[1641]

In the case *Matanović v. Croatia*, there was no opportunity to challenge all the evidence admitted to the case file. The case concerned an investigation conducted in a corruption case in which some of the material acquired during undercover operations concerning other people was not disclosed to the applicant, even though there was a link to his case. This material had not been used as evidence in the proceedings against other people, nor had it been referred to in any judgment. The public prosecutor had prevented the applicant's access to this information since it contained information about other people's private lives. The problem was that the applicant had no procedural means at his

---

1640 *Edwards and Lewis v. the United Kingdom* [GC], App. nos. 39647/98+, §§46 and 48, 27.10.2004. See also Philip Leach, James Welch (Eds.): "Cases and comment: selected decisions from the European Court of Human Rights for September and October 2004 – Crime and sentencing, *Edwards and Lewis v. United Kingdom* (Application Nos. 39647/98 and 40461/98)", *European Human Rights Law Review*, Issue 1, 2005, pp. 92–95.

1641 *V. v. Finland*, App. no. 40412/98, §§76–77 and 80, 24.4.2007.

disposal to allow the competent courts to assess the relevance of this material to his case. The Court held that the applicant had been unable to use any elements potentially contained in this material for his defence, nor had the domestic court made any balancing exercise between the other people's Article 8 rights and the applicant's right to the disclosure of evidence. There was thus a violation of Article 6 in respect of this set of evidence.[1642]

The case *Furcht v. Germany* concerned the sufficiency of compensation when the applicant had been convicted and sentenced in a situation in which undercover policemen had exceeded the boundaries of passive measures and had actively incited the applicant to commit a drugs offence. The applicant had no prior criminal background, nor was he suspected of the crime, but he knew some of the suspects. The police set up meetings with the suspects through him and forced him to deal in drugs even after he had refused to do so. Even though the domestic courts acknowledged that there had been a violation of the applicant's Article 6 rights, the Court found that the mitigation of his sentence did not compensate sufficiently for this violation.[1643]

Similar issues have also come up in civil proceedings concerning a person's employment and a decision on granting or revoking security clearance to that person but which could not be disclosed to the person himself or to his counsel. In the case *Regner v. the Czech Republic*, the Court held that even if the reasons for revocation of a classified security clearance were not disclosed to the applicant, or to his counsel, there was no violation of Article 6. The domestic courts had been independent and impartial. They had had unlimited access to all the classified documents on which the revocation decision had been based and could have ordered disclosure if they felt classification was not warranted. The domestic courts' jurisdiction had been broader than the items pleaded by the applicant and had extended to all the facts of the case so that they could, for example, compensate for any gaps in the defence due to the lack of disclosure. The courts had had the power to review the merits and quash the revocation decision as arbitrary. Although the Court found that there were sufficient safeguards in place, it nevertheless suggested that the revocation proceedings could have been improved, while respecting the necessary confidentiality: it would have been desirable for the authorities or courts to have explained to the applicant, even summarily, the substance of the accusations which led to the revocation and the extent of the review carried out by them.[1644]

---

1642 *Matanović v. Croatia*, App. no. 2742/12, §§178–188, 4.4.2017.

1643 *Furcht v. Germany*, App. no. 54648/09, §§54–59 and 71, 23.10.2014.

1644 *Regner v. the Czech Republic* [GC], App. no. 35289/11, §§146–161, 19.9.2017. See also Stefan Kieber, The jurisprudence of the European Court of Human Rights in 2017", *European Yearbook on Human Rights 2018*, pp. 229–265, at pp. 238–239; and Sofia Galani (Ed.), "Case and comment: selected decisions from the European Court of Human Rights from September and October 2017 – National security and the right to a fair trial, *Regner v. Czech Republic* (Application No. 35289/11)", *European Human Rights Law Review*, Issue 1, 2018, pp. 83–85.

### 6.3.3.3. *Information about Material Submitted by Other Parties*

For an adequate preparation of a defence, it is not merely sufficient for an accused to have access to the pretrial investigation material; he or she must also be privy to information about all other material submitted to the court by other parties. The principle of adversarial proceedings requires that all material is communicated to the parties, including material submitted to the court by other parties. Normally any allegations of non-communication of such material are examined under the general fairness requirement in Article 6 §1 in criminal cases without examining them separately under Article 6 §3 (b). This obligation to be given access to all material submitted to the court has been violated in many Finnish cases, largely concerning civil and administrative law proceedings.[1645] This problem has been particularly visible in proceedings before the Finnish Insurance Court.[1646]

The Court has interpreted this obligation strictly and has required application of the principle of adversarial proceedings without exception. According to the Court, it is not the task of a domestic court to evaluate whether the other party to the proceedings has a reason to comment on the material submitted by the counterparty. A party will, in any event, submit material to the court with the intention that the material is relevant to the case. The counterparty must therefore have an opportunity to comment on it, irrespective of what relevance the court ultimately gives to the submitted material.

In order to guarantee the parties' right to adversarial proceedings, it is relevant that the counterparty has an opportunity to comment, also at the appeal stage, on material submitted to the court by the other party. In the criminal case *Kuopila v. Finland*, the material at stake was an additional pretrial investigation report which the prosecutor had submitted to the Court of Appeal, but which had not been communicated to the defendant. The case concerned fraud charges relating to the purchase of a painting. At the Court of Appeal stage, the prosecutor requested an additional investigation be conducted into the authenticity of the painting and submitted the additional report to the Court of Appeal, but neither the prosecutor nor the court communicated it to the accused. The Court held that it was not known whether the Court of Appeal had given any relevance to the additional report, but this in fact did not matter. The procedural fairness required that the applicant should have had an opportunity to assess the relevance of the additional report and to comment on it, if necessary.[1647] In the

---

1645 In these cases, Article 6 §3 (b), which concerns only the criminal proceedings, would not naturally apply as such. See *Pitkänen v. Finland*, App. no. 30508/96, §59, 9.3.2004.

1646 See, for example, *Kerojärvi v. Finland*, App. no. 17506/90, 19.7.1995; *K.S. v. Finland*, App. no. 29346/95, 31.5.2001; *K.P. v. Finland*, App. no. 31764/96, 31.5.2001; and *S.H. v. Finland*, App. no. 28301/03, 29.7.2008.

1647 *Kuopila v. Finland*, App. no. 27752/95, §38, 27.4.2000. It is worth noting in this case that the applicant had asked for an additional investigation to be conducted. The Court held that

case *Adamčo v. Slovakia*, the Court found a violation since the appellate court had not submitted to the applicant for information the prosecutor's replies to the applicant's complaints which concerned the merits of the case.[1648]

#### 6.3.3.4. *Information about Material Obtained Ex Officio*

The right to adversarial proceedings also contains a party's right to obtain information and to comment on any material acquired by the court *ex officio* or otherwise.

A shortcoming in the exercise of this right featured in the case *M.S. v. Finland*, in which the applicant was convicted of the sexual abuse of his stepdaughter. The applicant attached to his letter of appeal a letter written by his wife, stating that she supported an acquittal. However, after the written procedure had been closed, she sent a letter to the Court of Appeal in which she withdrew her previous statement. The applicant learned about his wife's letter and her revised opinion only from the Court of Appeal judgment. The Court found that the fair trial guarantees required that the applicant was aware of all the evidence submitted with an intention to influence the court's decision. The letter was directly connected to the question of the credibility of the wife as a witness named by the applicant. As the letter was never communicated to the applicant, the Court found a violation of Article 6 §1 of the Convention.[1649]

Failure to communicate documents to the parties during the first-instance court proceedings may, however, be remedied at the appeal stage if the applicant is then told about that information and he or she is given the opportunity to comment on it.[1650]

## 6.4. RIGHT TO DEFEND ONESELF IN PERSON OR THROUGH LEGAL ASSISTANCE

**Article 6: Right to a fair trial**

*3. Everyone charged with a criminal offence has the following minimum rights:*

...

*(c) to defend himself in person or through legal assistance of his own choosing or, if he has not sufficient means to pay for legal assistance, to be given it free when the interests of justice so require.*

---

the applicant had been denied an opportunity to properly participate in the hearing before the Court of Appeal, as required by the principle of equality of arms. Article 6 had thus been violated.

1648 *Adamčo v. Slovakia*, App. no. 450/14, §§44–46, 12.11.2019 (no violation).

1649 *M.S. v. Finland*, App. no. 46601/99, §36, 22.3.2005.

1650 *Vazvan v. Finland* (dec.), App. no. 61815/13, §32, 26.11.2015.

Article 6 §3 (c) comprises three separate rights: the right to defend oneself through legal assistance of one's own choosing, the right to defend oneself in person, and, subject to certain conditions, the right to be given legal assistance free.[1651]

## 6.4.1. RIGHT TO A LAWYER

The purpose of Article 6 §3 (c) is to ensure that the proceedings against the accused do not take place without an adequate opportunity to defend him- or herself in person or through legal assistance.[1652] Any statutory prohibition on using legal assistance in a pretrial investigation automatically constitutes a violation of Article 6.[1653] This paragraph also guarantees the realisation of the principle of equality of arms, that is, the equal treatment of the accused vis-à-vis the prosecutor.

An accused's legal assistant has a wider role to play in supervising the fairness of the proceedings beyond just defending his or her client. In addition to overseeing the interests of the accused, he or she also functions as a public-interest "watchdog", by generally supervising the fairness of the proceedings.[1654] The right guaranteed by Article 6 §3 (c) partly overlaps with Article 6 §3 (b) but its material content is wider. Article 6 §3 (c) is not limited only to the preparation of a defence but covers the whole proceedings until the examination by the court of final appeal.[1655]

The right to a legal assistant is not absolute, however; nor does Article 6 §3 (c) define the manner in which the defence of an accused should be secured. Therefore, the practical arrangements of organising a defence fall within the margin of appreciation of the States. The Court's task is to ascertain whether the chosen manner secures the fairness of the proceedings and that the Convention rights are practical and effective.[1656]

As with the other special provisions in Article 6 §3 concerning criminal proceedings, Article 6 §3 (c) also applies when a person has been charged,

---

1651 *Pakelli v. Germany*, App. no. 8398/78, §31, 25.4.1983.

1652 *Pakelli v. Germany*, App. no. 8398/78, Report of the Commission, §84, 12.12.1981.

1653 *Salduz v. Turkey* [GC], App. no. 36391/02, §56, 27.11.2008; *Dayanan v. Turkey*, App. no. 7377/03, §§31–33, 13.10.2009; and *Borg v. Malta*, App. no. 37537/13, §60, 12.1.2016.

1654 *Ensslin, Baader and Raspe v. the Federal Republic of Germany* (dec.), App. nos. 7572/76+, 8.7.1978.

1655 *Imbrioscia v. Switzerland*, App. no. 13972/88, §37, 24.11.1993.

1656 *Dvorski v. Croatia* [GC], App. no. 25703/11, §79, 20.10.2015; *Sakhnovskiy v. Russia* [GC], App. no. 21272/03, §95, 2.11.2010; *Ibrahim and Others v. the United Kingdom* [GC], App. nos. 50541/08+, §§250–251, 13.9.2016; *Simeonovi v. Bulgaria* [GC], App. no. 21989/04, §§112–113, 12.5.2017; and *Imbrioscia v. Switzerland*, App. no. 13972/88, §38, 24.11.1993. See, for example, *Subicka v. Poland*, App. no. 29342/06, §§12–21, 40 and 47–48, 14.9.2010, concerning the Polish appeal system to higher courts.

within the autonomous meaning of the Convention. Therefore, Article 6 §3 (c) also applies to the pretrial investigation phase. The right of access to legal assistance during the pretrial investigation phase depends on what effect the lack of assistance in the pretrial investigation phase might have on the subsequent proceedings and their fairness. If the lack of a legal assistant in the pretrial investigation phase is likely to seriously prejudice the fairness of the trial, this right must be guaranteed at that early stage.[1657] The case-law of the Court on the use of legal assistance in criminal matters has been reviewed in the Grand Chamber case *Simeonovi v. Bulgaria*.[1658]

#### 6.4.1.1. *Pretrial Investigation and the Right to a Lawyer*

##### 6.4.1.1.1. From the Beginning of a Pretrial Investigation

In general, the requirement of access to a counsel as early as the pretrial investigation phase has become more strictly applied in the Court's case-law. This requirement has been clarified in many Grand Chamber judgments starting from *Salduz v. Turkey*, in which the Court held that the pretrial investigation was important for the preparation of a criminal case.[1659] In the case *Simeonovi v. Bulgaria*, this criterion was particularised by finding that the right to a lawyer started, within the meaning of the Convention, from the point a criminal charge was made against the applicant, which in that case was from the moment the applicant was arrested on suspicion of murder.[1660] In the case *Ibrahim and Others v. the United Kingdom* the Court reflected upon what kind of compelling reasons could justify temporary restrictions on the applicants' access to legal advice at certain stages of the investigation.[1661] In the most recent Grand Chamber

---

1657 *Salduz v. Turkey* [GC], App. no. 36391/02, §§54–55, 27.11.2008; *Schatschaschwili v. Germany* [GC], App. no. 9154/10, §§159–160, 15.12.2015; *Ibrahim and Others v. the United Kingdom* [GC], App. nos. 50541/08+, §253, 13.9.2016; *Imbrioscia v. Switzerland*, App. no. 13972/88, §36, 24.11.1993; *Öcalan v. Turkey* [GC], App. no. 46221/99, §131, 12.5.2005; *Magee v. the United Kingdom*, App. no. 28135/95, §41, 6.6.2000; and *Płonka v. Poland*, App. no. 20310/02, §§33–34, 31.3.2009. See also David Harris, Michael O'Boyle, Ed Bates, Carla Buckley, *Law of the European Convention on Human Rights*, 4th edition, Oxford University Press, Oxford 2018, pp. 474–475.

1658 *Simeonovi v. Bulgaria* [GC], App. no. 21989/04, §§112–131, 12.5.2017.

1659 *Salduz v. Turkey* [GC], App. no. 36391/02, §§54–55, 27.11.2008. See also Andrew L.-T. Choo, "The privilege against self-incrimination and criminal justice", Hart Publishing, Oxford/ Portland, Or. 2013, pp. 84-89; and Egbert Myjer, "One *Salduz* a year is enough - 20 associative thoughts on judge Rozakis, judicial activism and the *Salduz* judgment", in Dean Spielmann, Marialena Tsirli, Panayotis Voyatzis (Eds.), *La Convention Européenne des Droits de L'homme, un Instrument Vivant - Mélanges en L'honneur de Christos L. Rozakis/ The European Convention on Human Rights, a Living Instrument - Essays in Honour of Christos L. Rozakis*, Bruylant, Bruxelles 2011, pp. 419–430.

1660 *Simeonovi v. Bulgaria* [GC], App. no. 21989/04, §§114 and 121, 12.5.2017.

1661 *Ibrahim and Others v. the United Kingdom* [GC], App. nos. 50541/08+, §§276–279 and 298–300, 13.9.2016.

judgment in the case *Beuze v. Belgium* the Court once more recalled the concrete content of the right of access to a lawyer and emphasised that the right of access to a lawyer started as soon as a person was arrested, whether or not that person was interviewed or participated in any other investigative measure during the relevant period.[1662] Moreover, in *Soytemiz v. Turkey*, the Court stressed that the right to be assisted by a lawyer required not only that the lawyer was permitted to be present, but also that he was allowed to actively assist the suspect during questioning by the prosecuting authorities.[1663]

The evidence gathered during a pretrial investigation defines the boundaries within which the charges are examined during the trial. Therefore, the Convention normally requires that an accused has access to a counsel in the initial phase of the interrogations. The ground for this is the accused's particularly vulnerable position in this initial phase. The position of an accused is worsened by the fact that criminal proceedings have become ever-more complicated, especially in respect of collecting and using evidence. In most cases the vulnerability of an accused may be sufficiently compensated for by legal assistance. The task of a legal assistant is to ensure, *inter alia*, that the accused does not contribute to the establishment of his or her own guilt or to incriminating him- or herself.[1664]

The right to early access to a counsel is one of the most important guarantees of procedural fairness. This is especially true in cases in which a person is accused of severe crimes which can lead to severe punishments. The need to have access to a lawyer in the pretrial investigation phase may thus depend on many circumstances, such as the severity and complexity of the matter,[1665] the age of an accused,[1666] his or her vulnerability[1667] and, in particular, whether the account given during the pretrial investigation has an irreparable effect on the subsequent proceedings.[1668]

---

1662 *Beuze v. Belgium* [GC], App. no. 71409/10, §124, 9.11.2018. See also Stefan Kieber, "The jurisprudence of the European Court of Human Rights in 2018", *European Yearbook on Human Rights 2019*, pp. 189–220, at pp. 201–202; and Goss, Ryan: The undermining of Article 6 ECHR, *European yearbook on human rights 2019*, pp. 295–312.

1663 *Soytemiz v. Turkey*, App. no. 57837/09, §§44–46, 27.11.2018.

1664 *Salduz v. Turkey* [GC], App. no. 36391/02, §§54–55, 27.11.2008; and *Beuze v. Belgium* [GC], App. no. 71409/10, §§125–130, 9.11.2018.

1665 *Quaranta v. Switzerland*, App. no. 12744/87, §§32–34, 24.5.1991. See also Karen Reid, *A practitioner's guide to the European Convention on Human Rights*, Sweet & Maxwell/Thomson Reuters, London 2019, p. 264.

1666 *Salduz v. Turkey* [GC], App. no. 36391/02, §60, 27.11.2008.

1667 *Płonka v. Poland*, App. no. 20310/02, §38, 31.3.2009.

1668 *Öcalan v. Turkey* [GC], App. no. 46221/99, §131, 12.5.2005. The accused's right to a counsel was violated, for example, when the applicant was interrogated for seven days by State security forces, the prosecutor and the investigative judge without being allowed contact with his counsel, and when, during these interrogations, he gave statements detrimental to his interests which were considered to have a decisive and irreparable effect on the subsequent proceedings.

In the Grand Chamber case *Beuze v. Belgium* the Court gave a concrete definition of what the right to a lawyer means in practice. An effective right to a lawyer means, first of all, that suspects must be able to enter into contact with a lawyer from the time when they are taken into custody and be able to consult with their lawyer prior to an interview, or even where there is no interview. The lawyer must be able to confer with his or her client in private and receive confidential instructions. Second, an effective right to a lawyer means that suspects have the right for their lawyer to be physically present during their initial police interviews and whenever they are questioned in the subsequent pretrial proceedings. A refusal or difficulties encountered by a lawyer in seeking access to the criminal case file, or the non-participation of a lawyer in investigative measures such as identity parades or reconstructions, may undermine the fairness of the proceedings. Third, the overall fairness of proceedings must be assessed on a case-by-case basis. In the overall assessment, the following non-exhaustive list of factors, drawn from the Court's case-law – in particular the *Ibrahim and Others* case – are to be taken into account: (1) whether the applicant was particularly vulnerable; (2) the legal framework governing the pretrial proceedings and the admissibility of evidence at trial, and whether it was complied with; (3) whether the applicant had the opportunity to challenge the authenticity of the evidence and oppose its use; (4) the quality of the evidence and whether the circumstances in which it was obtained cast doubt on its reliability or accuracy; (5) where evidence was obtained unlawfully, the unlawfulness in question; (6) in the case of a statement, the nature of the statement and whether it was promptly retracted or modified; (7) the use to which the evidence was put, and in particular whether the evidence formed an integral or significant part of the probative evidence upon which the conviction was based; (8) whether the assessment of guilt was performed by professional judges or lay magistrates, or by lay jurors; (9) the weight of the public interest in the investigation and punishment of the particular offence at issue; and (10) other relevant procedural safeguards afforded by domestic law and practice.[1669]

#### 6.4.1.1.2. Young Suspects

The young age of a person undergoing interrogation and the suspicion of a serious crime are two particular reasons that necessitate the availability of a

[1669] *Beuze v. Belgium* [GC], App. no. 71409/10, §§131–150, 9.11.2018. See also Christopher Gray, "Right to access a lawyer – *Beuze v. Belgium* (Application No. 71409/10)", *European Human Rights Law Review*, Issue 2, 2019, pp. 222–226; Ryan Goss, "The undermining of Article 6 ECHR", *European Yearbook on Human Rights 2019*, pp. 295–312; and Stefan Kieber, "The jurisprudence of the European Court of Human Rights in 2018", *European Yearbook on Human Rights 2019*, pp. 189–220, at pp. 201–202.

counsel. In the *Salduz* case, the applicant was a minor who was interrogated without the presence of a counsel, during which he gave statements that were used against him in court. In the case *Panovits v. Cyprus*, the 17-year-old defendant was interrogated about a murder and forced to confess by five police officers who had placed a gun on the table and had informed the applicant that there was strong evidence against him. Furthermore, the suspect's father was not allowed to attend the interrogation until the applicant had confessed. In such cases, the Court has emphasised the right of a minor to have his guardian and a legal assistant present during the questioning.[1670] Similarly, any other vulnerability of the defendant requires that a counsel is present. In *Płonka v. Poland*, the accused, who had confessed to homicide during the pretrial investigation, was an alcoholic who was heavily intoxicated during the interrogation.[1671]

#### 6.4.1.1.3. Use of Pretrial Statements as Evidence and Right to a Lawyer

As a matter of principle, an accused should in particular have access to legal assistance if the court is to subsequently rely on statements given during the pretrial investigation phase, irrespective of whether they point to the accused's guilt or not. There may also be a need for access to a counsel in cases in which the defendant exercises the right to remain silent during the pretrial investigation. This kind of situation was at stake in the case *John Murray v. the United Kingdom*, in which the defendant was accused of terrorism and was prevented from having access to his counsel during the first 48 hours of detention. During this time, he was interrogated but remained silent. The Court examined closely the issue of whether this had an irreparable effect on the fairness of the proceedings. It found that there was no good cause for the restriction on access to counsel since inferences could be drawn from his silence throughout the interrogation and used against him in the subsequent trial.[1672]

#### 6.4.1.1.4. Non-Interrogation Situations

While the right to assistance from a lawyer concerns in particular the pretrial investigation phase and the subsequent court hearing, the right does not exist

---

1670 *Panovits v. Cyprus*, App. no. 4268/04, §§69 and 73, 11.12.2008.

1671 *Płonka v. Poland*, App. no. 20310/02, §38, 31.3.2009.

1672 *John Murray v. the United Kingdom*, App. no. 18731/91, §§63 and 66, 8.2.1996. See also John Jackson, "Re-conceptualizing the right of silence as an effective fair trial standard", *International and Comparative Law Quarterly*, vol. 58, pt. 4, October 2009, pp. 835–861; and Michael O'Boyle, "Freedom from self-incrimination and the right to silence: a Pandora's box?", in Paul Mahoney, Franz Matscher, Herbert Petzold, Luzius Wildhaber (Eds.), *Protection des Droits de L'homme: La Perspective Européenne, Mélanges à la Mémoire de Rolv Ryssdal/ Protecting Human Rights: The European Perspective, Studies in Memory of Rolv Ryssdal*, Carl Heymanns Verlag, Köln/Berlin/Bonn/München 2000, pp. 1021–1038, at pp. 1034–1036.

in situations such as traffic spot-checks carried out by the police. This became apparent in the case *Aleksandr Zaichenko v. Russia*, in which a police officer stopped the applicant's car and the applicant confessed that some canisters in his car were from his employer's yard. He was subsequently prosecuted for theft and his spontaneous statement to the police was referred to in the case. The Court held that the applicant had not been detained during the spot-check and that his right under Article 6 §3 (c) had not been violated.[1673] However, when a person is being interrogated during a pretrial investigation into traffic offences or drunk driving, the presence of a lawyer may prove necessary if the suspect later withdraws the account and claims that it was given under pressure, and if the interrogations are used as evidence against the suspect.[1674]

In addition to pretrial investigations, Article 6 §3 (c) also applies to court proceedings until the appeal stages. However, the extent of the right is dependent on the special characteristics of the appeal proceedings and the extent of the appeal.[1675] If an appeal court has the competence to examine only questions of law, this has relevance also to the right to defend oneself.[1676] Therefore, for example, the denial of access to a counsel before a first-instance court will not be corrected on appeal if the competence of the appeal court does not cover both the questions of fact and law.[1677] In matters concerning leave to appeal, the interests of justice and fairness do not require a hearing in person, and it is sufficient that the applicants are able to present relevant considerations in the form of written submissions.[1678]

##### 6.4.1.1.5. Informing a Suspect of his Rights and Calling a Lawyer

After the *Ibrahim* and *Simeonovi* cases, the Court found a violation in the Grand Chamber case *Beuze v. Belgium*. The applicant was arrested in France under a European arrest warrant as a suspect for the murder of his former girlfriend and was subsequently surrendered to the Belgian authorities for investigation and trial. He had no access to a lawyer upon his arrest, nor had he access to a lawyer when he was interrogated by the police, investigating judge and the prosecutor. Once the applicant had access to a lawyer, he nevertheless continued to be deprived of the lawyer's presence during the

---

1673 *Aleksandr Zaichenko v. Russia*, App. no. 39660/02, §§48–51, 18.2.2010. See also Dean Spielmann, "Article 6 ECHR in criminal proceedings – recent developments", *Cyprus Human Rights Law Review*, vol. 2, issue 1, 2013, pp. 3–15, at p. 7.

1674 *Sirghi v. Romania*, App. no. 19181/09, §§39–53, 24.5.2016.

1675 *Sakhnovskiy v. Russia* [GC], App. no. 21272/03, 2.11.2010.

1676 *Meftah and Others v. France* [GC], App. nos. 32911/96+, §41, 26.7.2002.

1677 *Quaranta v. Switzerland*, App. no. 12744/87, §37, 24.5.1991.

1678 *Monnell and Morris v. the United Kingdom*, App. nos. 9562/81+, §68, 2.3.1987. See also Karen Reid, *A Practitioner's Guide to the European Convention on Human Rights*, Sweet & Maxwell/ Thomson Reuters, London 2019, pp. 166 and 265.

subsequent interviews, examinations and other investigative acts conducted in the course of the judicial pretrial investigation. During the trial, the applicant was represented by a lawyer. The Court held that the restrictions on the applicant's right to a lawyer were not justified by any compelling reason. Even if the applicant's statements were not directly self-incriminatory and he did not confess, he made significant statements and fully availed himself of his freedom to select or conceal facts.[1679]

The right to legal assistance does not mean that a counsel should necessarily be present during an accused's interrogations. Nor is it the authorities' responsibility to ask a counsel to be present. But if the accused or the counsel so requests, access to interrogations must be allowed. Practical advice concerning at least the most severe crimes is that investigators should make sure that if and when the defendant admits the charges, he or she is assisted by a counsel. This prevents any subsequent allegations about the inappropriateness of the interrogations. In situations in which it is claimed that the police have used inappropriate interrogation means for obtaining a confession, the presence of a legal assistant or the videotaping of the interrogations are the best means of verifying the situation. In some specific cases, the appropriateness of the conditions of the interrogation can also be shown by other means.[1680]

#### *6.4.1.2. Restrictions on the Right to Legal Assistance from a Lawyer*

The right to legal assistance from a lawyer is a fundamental right for securing a fair trial, but it is not an absolute right.[1681] Access to legal assistance has often been denied either when the accused do not have a legal representative present during the interrogations or when they are refused the right to choose a lawyer of their choice. The former situation requires that there are compelling reasons for the absence of a legal representative and the latter requires that relevant and sufficient grounds are given for the restriction on the freedom of choice.[1682]

It is less serious to restrict an accused's right to choose his or her counsel than to deprive him or her completely of the right to legal assistance. However,

---

1679 *Beuze v. Belgium* [GC], App. no. 71409/10, §§154–181, 9.11.2018. See also Christopher Gray, "Right to access a lawyer – *Beuze v. Belgium* (Application No. 71409/10)", *European Human Rights Law Review*, Issue 2, 2019, pp. 222–226; Ryan Goss, "The undermining of Article 6 ECHR", *European Yearbook on Human Rights 2019*, pp. 295–312; and Stefan Kieber, "The jurisprudence of the European Court of Human Rights in 2018", *European Yearbook on Human Rights 2019*, pp. 189–220, at pp. 201–202.

1680 *Brennan v. the United Kingdom*, App. no. 39846/98, §53, 16.10.2001.

1681 *Salduz v. Turkey* [GC], App. no. 36391/02, §55, 27.11.2008; *Ibrahim and Others v. the United Kingdom* [GC], App. nos. 50541/08+, §260, 13.9.2016; and *Dvorski v. Croatia* [GC], App. no. 25703/11, §79, 20.10.2015.

1682 *Dvorski v. Croatia* [GC], App. no. 25703/11, §§79–80, 20.10.2015; and *Ibrahim and Others v. the United Kingdom* [GC], App. nos. 50541/08+, §§258–259, 13.9.2016.

in both situations it is relevant whether self-incriminating statements have been included in the case file or not. As a last resort, the most relevant criterion is the overall fairness of the proceedings; that is, the assessment of what kind of relevance the restriction had to the proceedings as a whole and how the statements given without the presence of a lawyer were used by the courts. In practical terms, this means that there must be an evaluation of what role is to be allocated to statements given without the presence of a lawyer, what kinds of other evidence were admitted in the case and what kinds of options the defence otherwise had in the trial.[1683]

#### 6.4.1.2.1. Limiting the Freedom of Choice of the Accused

Article 6 §3 (c) guarantees an accused the right to legal assistance of his own choosing.[1684] As a general rule, the accused's choice of lawyer should be respected. An accused's trust in his or her counsel is a central element of legal assistance and therefore an accused should be able to choose a counsel that he or she can trust.

An accused's wish can, however, be overridden if it is necessary for the proper conduct of the proceedings and such a decision is based on relevant and sufficient grounds. The first question therefore is whether there are sufficient grounds to override the accused's wishes. If no such grounds exist, the restriction of the free choice requires that the overall fairness of the proceedings is assessed. In this overall assessment, attention is paid to the nature of the proceedings, the professional qualifications of the counsel, the circumstances in which the counsel was appointed and the possibility to challenge this appointment, and to whether the accused's right not to incriminate himself has been respected. It is also of relevance how old the accused is and how his or her statements have been used in the trial. The overall assessment must secure the accused's right to real and practical legal protection.[1685]

An accused may choose relatively freely his or her legal assistant if the accused pays the representation costs from his or her own pocket. Nevertheless, the State may exceptionally refuse to accept a certain legal assistant for relevant

---

1683 *Ibrahim and Others v. the United Kingdom* [GC], App. nos. 50541/08+, §§257 and 262, 13.9.2016; and *Simeonovi v. Bulgaria* [GC], App. no. 21989/04, §§112–113, 12.5.2017.

1684 *Dvorski v. Croatia* [GC], App. no. 25703/11, §77, 20.10.2015; *Campbell and Fell v. the United Kingdom*, App. nos. 7819/77+, §99, 28.6.1984; *Pakelli v. Germany*, App. no. 8398/78, §31, 25.4.1983; *Whitfield and Others v. the United Kingdom*, App. nos. 46387/99+, §48, 12.4.2005; and *Martin v. Estonia*, App. no. 35985/09, §§90–93, 30.5.2013.

1685 *Dvorski v. Croatia* [GC], App. no. 25703/11, §§78–81, 20.10.2015; *Pavlenko v. Russia*, App. no. 42371/02, §98, 1.4.2010; *Meftah and Others v. France* [GC], App. nos. 32911/96+, §§45–47, 26.7.2002; *Zagorodniy v. Ukraine*, App. no. 27004/06, §§52–55, 24.11.2011; *Martin v. Estonia*, App. no. 35985/09, §§90–97, 30.5.2013; and *Vitan v. Romania*, App. no. 42084/02, §§58–64, 25.3.2008.

and sufficient reasons.[1686] Therefore, for example, rules requiring the use of attorneys as legal assistants for the highest courts are permissible.[1687] Similarly, certain rules governing the qualifications and conduct of lawyers are permissible. The wording of Article 6 §3 (c) does not exclude the possibility of allowing the accused to choose to accept assistance from a person who is not a qualified lawyer, if domestic law does not prevent it.[1688]

It can also be expected that a lawyer follows certain professional conduct. A lawyer may therefore be excluded, for example: for a failure to comply with professional ethics;[1689] for refusal to wear robes in court if the use of them is required by the rules; for showing disrespect to the court; because he or she is appearing as a witness, or has a personal interest in the case; or if there is a conflict of interest created by the same representative assisting two different people.[1690] A restriction upon the number of lawyers appointed by the accused is permissible, provided that a proper defence can be afforded with a smaller team of lawyers on an equal footing with the prosecution.[1691]

An accused is therefore relatively free to choose his or her legal assistant. However, if he or she cannot find a lawyer willing to act for him or her, the State is not responsible for it, provided that the difficulty of finding a lawyer is not the result of actions of the State. Practical situations in which the counsel chosen by the accused cannot be appointed are, for example, when the counsel named by the accused cannot be contacted. The accused must then be offered the chance to choose another qualified counsel.[1692]

The freedom of an accused to choose a lawyer requires that the accused has appropriate information about his or her situation. In the case *Dvorski v. Croatia*, the Court found a violation of Article 6 when the detained applicant had himself chosen a counsel from a list presented to him while unaware that his parents had already acquired him a counsel. The counsel chosen by the parents was not allowed to meet with the applicant on the day of interrogations. The applicant subsequently confessed in the presence of another counsel and this confession was used as evidence against him. The Court held that the applicant had not been able decide on his counsel because of the failure by the police to provide him with the proper information. The domestic courts had not remedied the problem by, for example, excluding the incriminating statement from the

1686 *Croissant v. Germany*, App. no. 13611/88, §30, 25.9.1992.
1687 *Meftah and Others v. France* [GC], App. nos. 32911/96+, §47, 26.7.2002.
1688 *Engel and Others v. the Netherlands*, App. nos. 5100/71+, §91, 8.6.1976; and *Morris v. the United Kingdom*, App. no. 38784/97, §§90–92, 26.2.2002.
1689 *Ensslin, Baader and Raspe v. the Federal Republic of Germany* (dec.), App. nos. 7572/76+, 8.7.1989.
1690 *Twalib v. Greece*, App. no. 2494/94, §40, 9.6.1998.
1691 *Ensslin, Baader and Raspe v. the Federal Republic of Germany* (dec.), App. nos. 7572/76+, 8.7.1989.
1692 *Pishchalnikov v. Russia*, App. no. 7025/04, §74, 24.9.2009.

case file, which irrevocably violated the applicant's right to legal assistance and undermined the fairness of the proceedings as a whole.[1693] In the case *Simeonovi v. Bulgaria*, the Court held that the applicant could not be regarded as having waived his right to a lawyer when there was no indication in the case file that he had been informed about his right to have a lawyer.[1694]

#### 6.4.1.2.2. Denial of Any Legal Assistance in the Pretrial Investigation Phase

If a suspect is denied any legal assistance during the pretrial investigation, any denial must be based on specific compelling reasons. Despite the existence of compelling reasons, a denial of legal assistance must not unnecessarily harm the accused's rights. The test applied in these cases is strict, and there will be an irrevocable violation of the rights of the defence if the accused's self-incriminating statement, given without the presence of a lawyer, is used as a basis for a conviction.[1695]

A compelling reason for delaying access to a lawyer and for interrogating the suspect without the presence of a lawyer must be exceptional, temporary and based on individual assessment. It must also have a legal basis in domestic legislation. Such a compelling reason may be, for example, an urgent need to warn other people who are in immediate life-threatening danger.[1696] It is not a compelling reason if the counsel's presence in the interrogations may simply prevent the acquisition of evidence.[1697] However, the question of whether or not there exists a compelling reason is always assessed vis-à-vis the proceedings as a whole. Where compelling reasons are found to have been established, a holistic assessment of the entirety of the proceedings must be conducted to determine whether they were "fair" in accordance with Article 6 §1. Where there are no compelling reasons for restricting access to legal advice, the Court applies a very strict scrutiny in its fairness assessment. The failure of the respondent State

---

1693 *Dvorski v. Croatia* [GC], App. no. 25703/11, §§98, 101 and 106–111, 20.10.2015. See also Anneli Soo, "Divergence of European Union and Strasbourg standards on defence rights in criminal proceedings?: *Ibrahim and the others v. the UK* (13th of September 2016)", *European Journal of Crime, Criminal Law and Criminal Justice*, vol. 25, issue 4, 2017, pp. 327–346, at p. 334.

1694 *Simeonovi v. Bulgaria* [GC], App. no. 21989/04, §§115 and 127–128, 12.5.2017.

1695 *Dvorski v. Croatia* [GC], App. no. 25703/11, §§80–81, 20.10.2015; *John Murray v. the United Kingdom*, App. no. 18731/91, §63, 8.2.1996; and *Salduz v. Turkey* [GC], App. no. 36391/02, §55, 27.11.2008. See also the case *Sakhnovskiy v. Russia* [GC], App. no. 21272/03, §95, 2.11.2010, concerning the effectiveness of legal aid; and *Beuze v. Belgium* [GC], App. no. 71409/10, §§142–143, 9.11.2018.

1696 *Ibrahim and Others v. the United Kingdom* [GC], App. nos. 50541/08+, §§258–259, 13.9.2016.

1697 *John Murray v. the United Kingdom*, App. no. 18731/91, §§64 and 66, 8.2.1996. In this case, the applicant was detained and suspected of terrorism. His right of access to a lawyer during the first 48 hours of police detention was restricted and he was interrogated several times during this period. See also *Salduz v. Turkey* [GC], App. no. 36391/02, §55, 27.11.2008.

to show compelling reasons weighs heavily in the balance when assessing the overall fairness of the trial and may tip the balance in favour of finding a breach of Article 6 §§1 and 3 (c).[1698]

When examining the proceedings as a whole in order to assess the impact of procedural shortcomings at the pretrial stage on the overall fairness of the criminal proceedings, the Court has used the following non-exhaustive list of factors which should, where appropriate, be taken into account: (1) whether the applicant was particularly vulnerable, for example, by reason of his age or mental capacity; (2) whether the legal framework governing the pretrial proceedings and the admissibility of evidence at the trial were complied with; where an exclusionary rule is applied to exclude unfairly obtained evidence, it is particularly unlikely that the proceedings as a whole would be considered unfair; (3) whether the applicant had the opportunity to challenge the authenticity of the evidence and oppose its use; (4) the quality of the evidence and whether the circumstances in which it was obtained cast doubt on its reliability or accuracy, taking into account the degree and nature of any compulsion; (5) where evidence was obtained unlawfully, the unlawfulness in question and, where it stems from a violation of another Convention article, the nature of the violation found; (6) in the case of a statement, the nature of the statement and whether it was promptly retracted or modified; (7) the use to which the evidence was put, and in particular whether the evidence formed an integral or significant part of the probative evidence upon which the conviction was based, and the strength of the other evidence in the case; (8) whether the assessment of guilt was carried out by professional judges or lay jurors, and, in the case of the latter, the content of any jury directions; (9) the weight of the public interest in the investigation of and punishment for the particular offence in question; and (10) other relevant procedural safeguards afforded by domestic law and practice.[1699]

In the case *Brennan v. the United Kingdom*, the Court found it acceptable to restrict the applicant's access to his lawyer during the first 24 hours' detention in order to ensure that the other suspects in the matter could be arrested without being alerted, and especially because the applicant in fact did not give any statements detrimental to himself during that time.[1700] In general, the Court has found no violation in situations in which the accounts given by the accused during the pretrial investigation have not been referred to during the trial.[1701]

---

1698 *Ibrahim and Others v. the United Kingdom* [GC], App. nos. 50541/08+, §§262–265, 13.9.2016.

1699 *Ibrahim and Others v. the United Kingdom* [GC], App. nos. 50541/08+, §274, 13.9.2016; *Simeonovi v. Bulgaria* [GC], App. no. 21989/04, §120, 12.5.2017; and *Beuze v. Belgium* [GC], App. no. 71409/10, §§150, 9.11.2018.

1700 *Brennan v. the United Kingdom*, App. no. 39846/98, §§45–48, 16.10.2001.

1701 *Yurttas v. Turkey*, App. nos. 25143/94+, §77, 27.5.2004.

The Court did not find a violation, either, in the case *Bandaletov v. Ukraine*, in which the applicant confessed to a crime when first interrogated as a witness and reiterated his confession later on when he was interrogated as a suspect. He subsequently repeated his confession in court in the presence of a lawyer.[1702] The fact that a statement remained unchanged was also decisive for the overall assessment of fairness in the case *Blaj v. Romania*. There the Court found no violation in a situation in which the applicant had stated his innocence in the interrogations and had not later changed this statement. In such circumstances the use of the first statements in the trial did not violate the fairness of the proceedings.[1703] However, in the Court's case-law the approach has gradually become stricter as far as pretrial investigation statements given without the presence of a lawyer are concerned, and may even concern such statements given without the presence of a lawyer which are not self-incriminating. If such a statement is used in the trial as comparative material, the Court has in some cases found a violation.[1704]

An exceptional situation in which there were compelling reasons to deny an applicant legal assistance arose in the case *Ibrahim and Others v. the United Kingdom*. Three of the four applicants, who were suspected of terrorism and of detonation of bombs, were interrogated without the presence of a lawyer during the first two hours in "safety interviews", in order to clarify whether there were still unexploded bombs around.[1705] The statements given in these interviews formed a part of the case file. In the subsequent interrogations and in the trial the applicants' lawyer was present. The Court found no violation of Article 6. It found that there had been compelling reasons contained within national legislation to conduct the safety interviews. The necessity of the interviews was assessed individually and verified by a judge, and the authorities had concluded them as soon as it was possible. When assessing the overall fairness of the proceedings, relevance was attached to the legality of the measure, to the fact that a judge had assessed the admission of the evidence and that all applicants had been represented by a counsel, which in itself could have enabled them to dispute their statements and request their exclusion from the case file. There had also been a lot of other evidence (such as scientific evidence about the bomb, how the applicants had procured the material, the evidence gathered in the search of a house, etc.) and the judge had directed the jury appropriately on the assessment of evidence. There was also a very strong public interest in having the matter clarified. In conclusion, the Court found that the proceedings as a whole in respect of the three applicants had been fair.[1706]

---

1702 *Bandaletov v. Ukraine*, App. no. 23180/06, §§60–73, 31.10.2013. When interrogating the applicant as a witness, the police had no doubt about his guilt.

1703 *Blaj v. Romania*, App. no. 36259/04, §§91–99, 8.4.2014.

1704 *A.T. v. Luxembourg*, App. no. 30460/13, §§67–75, 9.4.2015.

1705 *Ibrahim and Others v. the United Kingdom* [GC], App. nos. 50541/08+, §21, 13.9.2016.

1706 *Ibrahim and Others v. the United Kingdom* [GC], App. nos. 50541/08+, §§276–294, 13.9.2016.

The fourth applicant had been initially heard in the pretrial investigation as a witness, in the context of which he had given self-incriminating statements and revealed important details about the guilt of the three other applicants. Because of his self-incriminating statements, his status had not been immediately changed from that of a witness to that of an accused. When he was heard as an accused during the trial, he did not withdraw the statement he had given as a witness. The Court held that there had not been a fair trial. Although there was also other evidence against the fourth applicant, he had not benefited from proper legal safeguards and his trial had thus been unfair.[1707]

In the Grand Chamber case *Simeonovi v. Bulgaria*, the applicant, who was suspected of murder and subsequently convicted and sentenced to life imprisonment, had been without a lawyer for the first three days following his arrest. In a subsequent interrogation he had voluntarily confessed to the murder in the presence of his lawyer and this confession, together with other evidence, was used against him. Since there was no indication in the case file that he had been told about his right to have a lawyer present, he could not be regarded as having waived his right to a lawyer immediately after his arrest. Nor were there any compelling reasons, such as the need to protect another's life and health, justifying denying the applicant access to a lawyer. However, when assessing the case as a whole, the Court held that the proceedings had not been unfair and found no violation since no investigative measures (interrogations, identification parades or biological samples) had been conducted vis-à-vis the applicant during the time he was without a lawyer. Moreover, domestic legislation provided for an exclusion of evidence obtained in a manner incompatible with national law, which in the applicant's case required that legal assistance during questioning was *a sine qua non* for the admissibility in evidence. The matter had also been carefully examined at three levels of jurisdiction.[1708]

In the Grand Chamber case *Beuze v. Belgium*, issued after the *Ibrahim* and *Simeonovi* cases, the Court found a violation of Article 6. The applicant

---

[1707] *Ibrahim and Others v. the United Kingdom* [GC], App. nos. 50541/08+, §§295–311, 13.9.2016. See also Anneli Soo, "Divergence of European Union and Strasbourg standards on defence rights in criminal proceedings?: *Ibrahim and the others v. the UK* (13th of September 2016)", *European Journal of Crime, Criminal Law and Criminal Justice*, vol. 25, issue 4, 2017, pp. 327–346; James Welch (Ed.), "Case and comment: selected decisions from the European Court of Human Rights from December 2014 to February 2015 – Access to lawyer, *Ibrahim v. United Kingdom* (Application Nos. 50541/08, 50571/08, 50573/08 and 40351/09)", *European Human Rights Law Review*, Issue 2, 2015, pp. 219–222; and Ryan Goss, "Out of many, one?: Strasbourg's *Ibrahim* decision on Article 6", *The Modern Law Review*, vol. 80, no. 6, 2017, pp. 1137–1150.

[1708] *Simeonovi v. Bulgaria* [GC], App. no. 21980/04, §§121–144, 12.5.2017 (no violation). See also Sofia Galani (Ed.), "Case and comment: selected decisions from the European Court of Human Rights from May and June 2017 – Access to legal assistance in police custody, *Simeonovi v. Bulgaria* (Application No. 21980/04)", *European Human Rights Law Review*, Issue 5, 2017, pp. 514–517.

was arrested in France under a European arrest warrant as a suspect for the murder of his former girlfriend and was subsequently surrendered to the Belgian authorities for investigation and trial. He had no access to a lawyer upon his arrest, nor did he have access to a lawyer when he was interrogated by the police, the investigating judge and the prosecutor. Once the applicant had access to a lawyer, he continued to be deprived of the lawyer's presence during the subsequent interviews, examinations and other investigative acts conducted in the course of the judicial pretrial investigation. During the trial, the applicant was represented by a lawyer. The Court held that the restrictions on the applicant's right to a lawyer were not justified by any compelling reason. Even if the applicant's statements were not directly self-incriminatory and he did not confess, he still made significant statements and fully availed himself of his freedom to select or conceal facts.[1709]

In the case *Doyle v. Ireland*, the applicant had been able to have only a telephone connection to his counsel during the pretrial investigation. The law in force at the time contained no positive right for a counsel to be present during the interrogation but the suspect had the right to call by telephone his or her counsel when needed. The Court considered that there were no convincing reasons to prohibit a counsel's presence during the interrogation. However, it did not find a violation since there had been other factors in the criminal proceedings compensating for this deficiency, and the trial had thus been fair.[1710]

Restrictions on access to a counsel may also be connected to the fact that a person's procedural status changes. In the case *Kalēja v. Latvia*, the applicant had first been questioned as a witness who did not have the right of access to a counsel and then as a suspect who did have that right. On the basis of an overall assessment, the Court did not find a violation in the case. When the applicant had been questioned as a witness, she had enjoyed the right not to testify against herself. Although the lack of legal assistance could undermine a full use of the right not to incriminate oneself, she could benefit from legal assistance from the point when she was officially charged and became an accused person. In addition, she had also been given ample opportunity to contest the evidence used against her during the pretrial investigation and trial.[1711]

Although statements given during the pretrial investigation may not be referred to in a subsequent trial, the restrictions on access to a counsel have

---

1709 *Beuze v. Belgium* [GC], App. no. 71409/10, §§154–181, 9.11.2018. See also Christopher Gray, "Right to access a lawyer – *Beuze v. Belgium* (Application No. 71409/10)", *European Human Rights Law Review*, Issue 2, 2019, pp. 222–226; Ryan Goss, "The undermining of Article 6 ECHR", *European Yearbook on Human Rights 2019*, pp. 295–312; and Stefan Kieber, "The jurisprudence of the European Court of Human Rights in 2018" in *European Yearbook on Human Rights 2019*, pp. 189–220, at pp. 201–202.

1710 *Doyle v. Ireland*, App. no. 51979/17, §§67–103, 23.5.2019 (no violation).

1711 *Kalēja v. Latvia*, App. no. 22059/08, §§67–69, 5.10.2017 (no violation).

in all cases a certain time limit. In the case *Magee v. the United Kingdom*, the Court held that to deny access to a lawyer for over a year in a situation where the rights of the defence were irretrievably prejudiced was – whatever the justification for such a denial – incompatible with the rights of the accused under Article 6.[1712]

Nor is a systematic restriction on access to counsel in the pretrial investigation phase, when laid down in national legislation, compatible with the Convention. The case *Dayanan v. Turkey* concerned membership of the illegal Hezbollah organisation. The applicant was interrogated but he remained silent. Subsequently he was convicted on the basis of evidence unconnected to his silence. But the Court found a violation because the domestic law did not guarantee a right to legal assistance during detention. Such a systematic restriction in the legislation violated Article 6 of the Convention irrespective of the fact that the applicant had remained silent during the whole detention time.[1713]

#### 6.4.1.3. *Waiver of the Right to a Lawyer*

A defendant can also waive his or her right to a legal counsel. The waiver must be voluntary and the defendant must truly be able to foresee its consequences.[1714] The minimum requirement is that the authorities inform the accused of his or her right to remain silent and of the right to legal assistance.[1715] In the case *Simeonovi v. Bulgaria*, the Court held that the applicant could not be regarded as having waived his right to a lawyer during the first days of his arrest when the case file contained no indication of whether he had even been informed about his right to a counsel.[1716]

If an accused has first waived his or her right to legal assistance but subsequently requests a counsel, the interrogations cannot continue without

---

1712 *Magee v. the United Kingdom*, App. no. 28135/95, §§43–44, 6.6.2000. In this case the applicant was interrogated and examined by a doctor on two occasions during this time. See also James Welch (Ed.), "Case and comment: selected decisions from the European Court of Human Rights from May and June 2015 – Detention, *Magee v. United Kingdom* (Application Nos. 26289/12, 29062/12 and 29891/12)", *European Human Rights Law Review*, Issue 5, 2015, pp. 524–527.

1713 *Dayanan v. Turkey*, App. no. 7377/03, §33, 13.10.2009. See also Stanley H. Naismith, "Witnesses and the right to remain silent", in Josep Casadevall, Egbert Myjer, Michael O'Boyle (Eds.), *Freedom of Expression – Essays in Honour of Nicolas Bratza*, Wolf Legal Publishers, Oisterwijk 2012, pp. 245–256.

1714 *Ibrahim and Others v. the United Kingdom* [GC], App. nos. 50541/08+, §272, 13.9.2016; and *Pishchalnikov v. Russia*, App. no. 7025/04, §77, 24.9.2009.

1715 *Ibrahim and Others v. the United Kingdom* [GC], App. nos. 50541/08+, §272, 13.9.2016; *Rodionov v. Russia*, App. no. 9106/09, §151, 11.12.2018; and *Simeonovi v. Bulgaria* [GC], App. no. 21989/04, §118, 12.5.2017.

1716 *Simeonovi v. Bulgaria* [GC], App. no. 21989/04, §§127–128, 12.5.2017.

the presence of the counsel.[1717] Moreover, if an applicant has been subjected to inhuman and degrading treatment by the police, it cannot be considered that in such circumstances he or she can validly waive the right of access to a lawyer.[1718] It is in the first place the trial court's duty to establish in a convincing manner whether or not an applicant's confessions and waivers of legal assistance were voluntary.[1719]

### 6.4.2. DEFENCE IN PERSON

Article 6 §3 (c) also guarantees a right to defend oneself in person. However, this right is not absolute. The legislation in many States requires that in certain kinds of matters or before certain levels of jurisdiction a person must be represented, in the interests of justice, by a legal counsel.[1720] In the Court's case-law it has been held that the choice between the two possibilities referred to in Article 6 §3 (c) – that is, whether the applicant will defend him- or herself in person or be represented by a lawyer of his or her own choosing, or, in certain circumstances, by one appointed by the court – is a matter for the competent authorities to decide.[1721]

Although Article 6 §3 (c) guarantees the right of the accused to defend himself through legal assistance, a person can always waive his Article 6 rights. A valid waiver must be given of a person's own free will, either expressly or tacitly, and it must be unambiguous.[1722]

If the accused defends himself in person and has deliberately waived his right to be assisted by a lawyer, he is under a duty to show diligence. He cannot therefore subsequently claim a violation of Article 6 for a lack of diligence in defending his case.[1723] In the case *Todor and Hriska Georgievi v. Bulgaria*, the Court held that the applicant, who suffered from an anxiety disorder and who had defended herself in person before the late appointment of her counsel, could

---

1717 *Pishchalnikov v. Russia*, App. no. 7025/04, §§79–80, 24.9.2009; and *Artur Parkhomenko v. Ukraine*, App. no. 40464/05, §81, 16.2.2017.

1718 *Turbylev v. Russia*, App. no. 4722/09, §96, 6.10.2015.

1719 *Türk v. Turkey*, App. no. 22744/07, §§53–54, 5.9.2017; and *Rodionov v. Russia*, App. no. 9106/09, §167, 11.12.2018.

1720 For example, for the Polish system concerning an appeal to the highest courts, see *Subicka v. Poland*, App. no. 29342/06, §§40–47, 14.9.2010; *Subicka v. Poland (No. 2)*, App. nos. 34043/05+, §60, 21.6.2011; and *Smyk v. Poland*, App. no. 8958/04, §§63–64, 28.7.2009. In the first case, the Court found a violation as the counsel did not have adequate time to prepare a defence.

1721 *Correia de Matos v. Portugal* (dec.), App. no. 48188/99, 15.11.2001.

1722 *Sejdovic v. Italy* [GC], App. no. 56581/00, §86, 1.3.2006; *Talat Tunç v. Turkey*, App. no. 32432/96, §59, 27.3.2007; and *Sakhnovskiy v. Russia* [GC], App. no. 21272/03, §90, 2.11.2010.

1723 *Melin v. France*, App. no. 12914/87, §25, 22.6.1993.

not validly complain about any shortcomings in her defence as she had not sought an adjournment of the hearing before the court in order for her newly appointed counsel to be able to acquaint herself better with the case file and prepare her defence more thoroughly. Nor had she tried to appeal against that court's judgment or raise the point before the higher court. It did not appear that the applicant was so severely handicapped as to be unable to adopt any of these courses of action, as her disorder did not prevent her from understanding her actions and controlling her conduct.[1724]

On the other hand, a State may be held responsible if it has inhibited the defendant from freely exercising his right of defence, including the right to defend himself in person. Such a situation was at stake in the case *Brandstetter v. Austria*, in which the applicant was found guilty of criminal defamation committed when defending himself at an earlier trial. He had argued that his right to defend himself in person was restricted by the fact that he was subsequently charged for having used his right. The Court did not find a violation of Article 6 §3 (c) as the applicant did have an opportunity to defend himself in person.[1725]

The Grand Chamber case *Correia de Matos v. Portugal* concerned a lawyer who had been suspended from the Bar Council's roll and was accused of having insulted a judge. He asked to represent himself in the criminal proceedings against him but, under the provisions of Portuguese law, even a lawyer is not entitled to act in criminal proceedings without mandatory representation. The court therefore appointed a defence counsel to him. The Grand Chamber provided a test for examining the compliance of cases of mandatory legal assistance in criminal proceedings with Article 6 §§1 and 3 (c) of the

---

1724 *Todor and Hriska Georgievi v. Bulgaria* (dec.), App. no. 40265/04, §28, 10.5.2012.

1725 *Brandstetter v. Austria*, App. nos. 11170/84+, §§51 and 53, 28.8.1991. The Court held that a mere possibility of an accused being subsequently prosecuted on account of allegations made in his defence cannot be deemed to infringe his rights under Article 6 §3 (c). A legal counsel, when representing himself or his clients, could thus not be beyond criminal liability if he committed a crime while defending. It was left for the domestic authorities to assess whether a crime had been committed or not. In the case *Nikula v. Finland*, the criminal liability of the counsel was examined from the Article 10 point of view. In that case the Court found that it was only in exceptional cases that a restriction of a defence counsel's freedom of expression, when defending a client, could be accepted as necessary in a democratic society. The Court found a violation of Article 10 of the Convention, see *Nikula v. Finland*, App. no. 31611/96, §55, 21.3.2002. The case *Ignatius v. Finland* (dec.), App. no. 41410/02, 17.1.2006, concerned the question of whether the counsel's freedom of expression had been violated when he was convicted and ordered to pay compensation for having made libellous accusations about civil servants in connection with the pending proceedings. According to the Court, an interference with a counsel's freedom of expression in the course of a trial might raise an issue under Article 6 of the Convention with regard to the right of an accused client to receive a fair trial. Equality of arms militated in favour of a free and forceful exchange of arguments between the parties. However, as the applicant's clients in the domestic proceedings were not applicants before the Court, the Convention was not applicable.

Convention. According to the Court, the following principles had to be applied: (1) Article 6 §§1 and 3 (c) did not necessarily give the accused the right to decide himself in what manner his defence should be assured; (2) the decision as to which of the two alternatives mentioned in that provision should be chosen – namely the applicant's right to defend himself in person or to be represented by a lawyer of his own choosing, or in certain circumstances by one appointed by the court – depended, in principle, upon the applicable domestic legislation or rules of court; and (3) Member States enjoyed a margin of appreciation as regards this choice, albeit one which was not unlimited. In the light of these principles, the Court had to examine, first, whether relevant and sufficient grounds were provided for the legislative choice applied in the case at hand. Second, even if relevant and sufficient grounds were provided, it was still necessary to examine, in the context of the overall assessment of the fairness of the criminal proceedings, whether the domestic courts, when applying the impugned rule, also provided relevant and sufficient grounds for their decisions. In the latter case, it would be relevant to assess whether an accused was afforded scope in practice to participate effectively in his or her trial.[1726]

In this case the Court held that mandatory legal representation had been based on extensive domestic legislation which sought to protect the accused. Even a defendant trained in advocacy, like the applicant, could be unable, as a result of being personally affected by the charges, to conduct an effective defence in his or her own case. The legitimacy of such considerations applied even more forcefully where a defendant was suspended from the Bar. Moreover, the accused had had the right to be present at all stages of the proceedings, to make statements or remain silent concerning the substance of the charge and to submit observations, statements and requests, in which he could address questions of law and facts and which, without having to be signed by counsel, were added to the case file. An accused represented by counsel could also revoke any measure carried out on his or her behalf and was the last person who could address the court after oral pleadings had ended. If an accused was not satisfied with the court-appointed defence counsel, he or she could request a change of counsel on a valid ground. In the case at hand, the applicant had chosen not to attend the hearings and had deliberately decided not to avail himself of the possibility of participating effectively in his defence together with his counsel. He did not appear to have challenged the qualifications or quality of the court-appointed lawyer in the proceedings before the domestic courts, nor had he raised any issues of unfairness of the proceedings. There was thus no violation of Article 6.[1727]

---

1726 *Correia de Matos v. Portugal* [GC], App. no. 56402/12, §143, 4.4.2018 (no violation).

1727 *Correia de Matos v. Portugal* [GC], App. no. 56402/12, §§143 and 153–169, 4.4.2018 (no violation). See also Nicolas A.J. Croquet, "The Right to Self-representation Under the European Convention on Human Rights – What Role for the Limitation Analysis?", *European Human Rights Law Review*, Issue 3, 2012, pp. 292–308, at pp. 296–298; Stefan Kieber, "The

### 6.4.3. FREE LEGAL AID

According to Article 6 §3 (c), if an accused does not have sufficient means to pay for legal assistance, he should be given it for free when the interests of justice so require. The right to free legal aid thus requires that two conditions are fulfilled: the accused is not able to pay for the legal assistance he or she is receiving;[1728] and the interests of justice require that free legal aid is granted.[1729]

The Convention does not contain any definition of the "sufficient means to pay for legal assistance". The point of departure is that it is for the accused to show, for example by providing a declaration of means, that he or she does not have such means. In cases in which the accused has been in detention for several years, this fact may in itself demonstrate that he or she does not have sufficient means.[1730] Nor is it incompatible with Article 6 §3 (c) to order the accused to repay to the State, after conviction, the costs and expenses of the legal assistance.[1731] In this respect free legal aid is in a different position to the right under Article 6 §3 (e) to receive the free assistance of an interpreter.

The other condition for free legal aid is that "the interests of justice so require". This criterion is assessed in the light of the circumstances of the case. In this respect, the situation may change during the proceedings if the case subsequently becomes more complicated than anticipated at the beginning.[1732]

In the Court's case-law, several criteria have been created to ensure the fairness of the proceedings. First, the seriousness of the case at hand is important. Serious crimes, for which one can be sentenced to a severe punishment, are self-evidently cases in which fairness requires the granting of free legal aid.[1733] This criterion becomes relevant when, according to domestic practice, a prison sentence is a possibility, even a short sentence.[1734] In contrast, fairness has not

---

jurisprudence of the European Court of Human Rights in 2018", *European Yearbook on Human Rights 2019*, pp. 189–220, at pp. 200–201; and Jeremy McBride, "Some recent practice of the European Court of Human Rights to consider when implementing criminal procedure codes", *Synergy Magazine*, no. 64, issue 2, 2018, pp. 8–10, at p. 10.

1728 *Caresana v. the United Kingdom* (dec.), App. no. 31541/96, 29.8.2000.

1729 *Quaranta v. Switzerland*, App. no. 12744/87, §27, 24.5.1991; and *Granger v. the United Kingdom*, App. no. 11932/86, §46, 28.3.1990.

1730 *Pakelli v. Germany*, App. no. 8398/78, §34, 25.4.1983.

1731 *Croissant v. Germany*, App. no. 13611/88, §§35–36, 25.9.1992; and *Breukhoven v. the Czech Republic*, App. no. 44438/06, §62, 21.7.2011. See also Nicolas A.J. Croquet, "The Right to Self-representation Under the European Convention on Human Rights – What Role for the Limitation Analysis?", *European Human Rights Law Review*, Issue 3, 2012, pp. 292–308, at pp. 298–299.

1732 *Granger v. the United Kingdom*, App. no. 11932/86, §47, 28.3.1990.

1733 See, for example, *Twalib v. Greece*, App. no. 2494/94, §§51–54, 9.6.1998. The case concerned charges on drugs-related offences.

1734 *Benham v. the United Kingdom*, App. no. 19380/92, §60, 10.6.1996; *Quaranta v. Switzerland*, App. no. 12744/87, §30, 24.5.1991; *Shabelnik v. Ukraine*, App. no. 16404/03, §58, 19.2.2009; and *J.N. v. Finland* (dec.), App. no. 26920/10, 31.1.2012. A friendly settlement was concluded between the parties and the case was struck out of the list of cases.

been regarded as an issue requiring free legal assistance in relatively simple cases where the maximum sentence is a fine.[1735] Second, the nature and complexity of the case are relevant. The imposition of considerable fines and the complexity of the factual or legal questions in a case may require that free legal assistance is granted.[1736] The third criterion is the ability and capacity of the applicants to defend themselves in their case. In this respect, it is relevant whether the accused is, for example, a foreigner who does not have sufficient language skills or familiarity with the legal system,[1737] or whether the applicant's mental health prevents him from adequately defending himself.[1738] The fourth fairness criterion concerns the interests of justice. This may be the case, for example, when the legal question at stake is a new one and it has particular relevance for the development of the case-law.[1739]

The right to legal aid is also relevant for the appeal proceedings.[1740] At the appeal stage, it is not relevant whether the applicant's chances of success are uncertain. If the accused has the possibility, within the domestic system, to appeal the case, he or she should have access to free legal assistance, in accordance with the above-mentioned criteria, at the appeal stage too.[1741] The Court takes into account three factors in particular: (1) the breadth of the appellate court's power; (2) the seriousness of the charges against applicants; and (3) the severity of the sentence they face.[1742]

Although it is at the discretion of the authorities to appoint a free legal assistant, the wishes of the accused must be considered.[1743] For relevant and sufficient reasons, these wishes may be overridden if that is necessary in the interests of justice. This was the case in *Lagerblom v. Sweden*, in which the accused, whose mother tongue was Finnish, was accused of assault and road traffic offences and wanted the lawyer chosen for him by the court to be replaced by a Finnish-speaking lawyer. The Court found that the appointed lawyer had already done a lot of work on the case and that the applicant had both sufficient knowledge of Swedish and an interpreter at his disposal in the hearing.[1744]

---

1735 *Gutfreund v. France*, App. no. 45681/99, §39, 12.6.2003.

1736 *Pham Hoang v. France*, App. no. 13191/87, §§40–41, 25.9.1992.

1737 *Twalib v. Greece*, App. no. 2494/94, §50, 9.6.1998.

1738 *Vaudelle v. France*, App. no. 35683/97, §§58–59, 30.1.2001.

1739 *Artico v. Italy*, App. no. 6694/74, §35, 13.5.1980; and *Alimena v. Italy*, App. no. 11910/85, §20, 19.2.1991.

1740 *Shekhov v. Russia*, App. no. 12440/04, §46, 19.6.2014; and *Volkov and Adamskiy v. Russia*, App. nos. 7614/09+, §§56–61, 26.3.2015.

1741 *Boner v. the United Kingdom*, App. no. 18711/91, §§37, 41 and 44, 28.10.1994.

1742 *Mikhaylova v. Russia*, App. no. 46998/08, §80, 19.11.2015.

1743 *Breukhoven v. the Czech Republic*, App. no. 44438/06, §60, 21.7.2011.

1744 *Lagerblom v. Sweden*, App. no. 26891/95, §§54 and 62, 14.1.2003. In the case *Breukhoven v. the Czech Republic*, App. no. 44438/06, §61, 21.7.2011 the accused was not considered to need a counsel familiar with Romanian law as the applicable law was the Czech law.

## 6.4.4. RIGHT TO DEFEND ONESELF THROUGH LEGAL ASSISTANCE

One of the fundamental features of a fair trial in a criminal matter is that the defendant may defend himself at appellate level through counsel even though he may have been summonsed to appear in court in person. The absence of the defendant in criminal proceedings does not therefore justify depriving him of his right to be defended through legal assistance. It does not matter whether there is a valid excuse or not for the absence, or whether, when there is a valid excuse, there is a possibility of a new trial. It is also irrelevant whether the defendant was able to defend himself properly before the lower court.[1745] However, the mere presence of the applicant's lawyer cannot compensate for the absence of the accused before a first instance court.[1746]

The case *Van Geyseghem v. Belgium* concerned an application to set aside a conviction imposed by a default judgment given *in absentia*. In these proceedings the applicant, who was the accused in the criminal case, was represented by a lawyer but did not attend the hearing in person. The domestic court found that the claim to set aside the judgment had not been legally presented. The Court, however, found a violation of Article 6 §3 (c) in respect of the applicant's rights.[1747]

A similar situation was in question in the case *Kari-Pekka Pietiläinen v. Finland*. In that case, the appeal of the accused, who had been summonsed to appear in person before the Court of Appeal, lapsed when he failed to appear before that court although he had been represented by his lawyer. The Court of Appeal held an oral hearing in the case which was to last many days and to which the applicant was summonsed. The applicant failed to appear in person on one day but he was represented by his lawyer. All other days he was present. The Court held that the presence of an accused was of capital importance, both because of his right to a hearing and because of the need to verify the accuracy of his statements. Therefore, the legislature had to be able to discourage unjustified absences. However, it was also of crucial importance for the fairness of the criminal justice system that the accused be adequately defended, both at

1745 *Stroek v. Belgium*, App. nos. 36449/97+, §§23–25, 20.3.2001; and *Goedhart v. Belgium*, App. no. 34989/97, §§26–28, 20.3.2001.

1746 *Zana v. Turkey* [GC], App. no. 18954/91, §72, 25.11.1997.

1747 *Van Geyseghem v. Belgium* [GC], App. no. 26103/95, §§33–45, 21.1.1999. See also Ineta Ziemele, "International courts and ultra vires acts", in Lucius Caflisch, Johan Callewaert, Roderick Liddell, Paul Mahoney, Mark Villiger (Eds.), *Liber Amicorum Luzius Wildhaber: Human rights, Strasbourg Views/Droits de L'homme, Regards de Strasbourg*, N.P. Engel, Kehl/Strasbourg/Arlington, Va. 2007, pp. 537–556, at p. 554. See also *Lala v. the Netherlands*, App. no. 14861/89, §34, 22.9.1994; *Pelladoah v. the Netherlands*, App. no. 16737/90, §40, 22.9.1994; and *Tolmachev v. Estonia*, App. no. 73748/13, §§51–57, 9.7.2015.

first instance and on appeal. The interests of fairness prevailed and consequently the fact that a defendant, in spite of having been properly summonsed and failing to appear on one day, could not – even in the absence of an excuse – be justifiably deprived of his right under Article 6 §3 of the Convention to be defended by a counsel. It was for the court to ensure that a trial was fair and, accordingly, that the counsel who attended the trial for the apparent purpose of defending the accused in his absence was given the opportunity to do so.[1748] This was also the situation in the case *Neziraj v. Germany*, when the attorney of the applicant, who had been absent without a valid excuse, was not given an opportunity to represent his client before an appeal court and the appeal was dismissed without examining the merits because of the absence of the accused.[1749]

However, in a situation in which there is no valid excuse for the defendant's absence in person from the appeal court and the lawyer representing the defendant is *also* absent, the case can lapse. In the case *Koski v. Finland*, the Court held that the fact that the applicant, who had been summonsed to appear in person, had failed to appear while his representative did not appear before the court either, was a sufficient ground for his appeal to lapse. The applicant had submitted to the court, through his lawyer, medical certificates according to which he was suffering from gastroenteritis. The medical certificates did not, however, indicate that the applicant could not have attended the court hearing. The applicant was not able to show, even afterwards, that he had a valid excuse for his absence and therefore his case was not re-examined. The Court found that the summons had clearly indicated the consequences of an absence without a valid excuse. The applicant's counsel did not appear either; had he done so, the case could have been examined to the necessary extent. The wording of the medical certificates was conditional and they did not detail any obstacles preventing the applicant from attending the hearing. The possibility of reopening the proceedings was an important safeguard which the applicant had also used. The Court found that it was within the margin of appreciation of the respondent State to decide in what manner the appeal proceedings were organised and when an excuse was considered as valid.[1750]

---

1748 *Kari-Pekka Pietiläinen v. Finland*, App. no. 13566/06, §§31–35, 22.9.2009. In that case it did not seem that, on the day when the applicant failed to appear, the court had intended to examine any issues for which the applicant's attendance in person was strictly necessary. In addition, the hearing was to last several days and it had not been indicated in the summons that even one day's absence would be regarded as absence from the whole oral hearing. In these circumstances, the discontinuation of the applicant's case despite the fact that his counsel had been present constituted a particularly rigid and heavy sanction for his absence. There was thus a violation of Article 6 §1 taken together with Article 6 §3 (c) of the Convention.

1749 *Neziraj v. Germany*, App. no. 30804/07, §§50–67, 8.11.2012.

1750 *Koski v. Finland* (dec.), App. no. 53329/10, §§32–34, 12.12.2013.

## 6.4.5. PRACTICAL AND EFFECTIVE LEGAL ASSISTANCE

Article 6 §3 (c) guarantees an accused the right to legal assistance which is both practical and effective.[1751] The organisation of legal aid is often expensive for States. The lack of funding or resources in a society are not, however, an acceptable reason to limit access to free legal assistance if the right to legal assistance would, after such a limitation, no longer be effective.

### *6.4.5.1. The State's Responsibility for Legal Assistants' Mistakes*

Although a State is responsible for practical and effective legal assistance, the State cannot be responsible for the mistakes or omissions made by a legal aid lawyer.[1752] Legal aid lawyers are practitioners who are independent and impartial from the State and not representatives of the State. The preparation of the accused's defence and its conduct are matters to be agreed between the defendant and his counsel, irrespective of whether the counsel has been appointed under a legal aid scheme or is privately financed. For example, a legal assistant's omission to appeal against a first-instance court judgment, despite clear instructions to appeal, was not attributable to the State; nor did it form a ground for the applicant to request a hearing of the letter of appeal prepared by him after the expiry of the time limit for appealing.[1753] The competent national authorities are required under Article 6 §3 (c) to intervene only if a failure by a legal aid counsel to provide effective representation is manifest or sufficiently brought to their attention in some other way.[1754]

The State's responsibility to supervise the effectiveness of the defence was an issue in the case *Artico v. Italy*, in which the defendant's counsel, who had been appointed under the legal aid scheme for the appeal proceedings, did not at any stage take any action: the counsel invoked as an excuse his other commitments and health problems. The defendant requested several times that the counsel be changed but without success. Finally, the applicant had to take care of his own defence even though a legal assistant would have been useful to him. The Court found that a State could not be held responsible for every

---

1751 *Sakhnovskiy v. Russia* [GC], App. no. 21272/03, §95, 2.11.2010.

1752 *Kamasinski v. Austria*, App. no. 9783/82, §65, 19.12.1989.

1753 *Kaasik v. Estonia* (dec.), App. no. 8235/10, 24.8.2010. Moreover, the Court held that the applicant, who was a prisoner, had not sought annulment of the judgment and had thereby failed to exhaust all effective domestic remedies provided by domestic legislation in order to have the mistake corrected.

1754 *Kamasinski v. Austria*, App. no. 9783/82, §65, 19.12.1989; *Rutkowski v. Poland* (dec.), App. no. 45995/99, 19.10.2000; *Sannino v. Italy*, App. no. 30961/03, §49, 27.4.2006; *Imbrioscia v. Switzerland*, App. no. 13972/88, §41, 24.11.1993; and *Daud v. Portugal*, App. no. 22600/93, §38, 21.4.1998. This may exceptionally apply also in the context of a privately hired lawyer, see *Güveç v. Turkey*, App. no. 70337/01, §131, 20.1.2009.

shortcoming on the part of a lawyer appointed for legal aid purposes but, in the particular circumstances, it was for the competent authorities to take steps to ensure that the applicant effectively enjoyed the right that they had recognised he was entitled to.[1755]

Similarly, in the case *Sakhnovskiy v. Russia*, the Court found that the applicant, who was accused of a murder, had not validly waived his right to a counsel when he had communicated his dissatisfaction about the conduct of his defence to the court in a manner that could be expected from a lay person. The applicant could not be expected to take procedural steps which normally required some legal knowledge and skills. The applicant's conduct did thus not absolve the authorities from their obligation to take further steps to guarantee the effectiveness of his defence.[1756] Also, in the case *Vamvakas v. Greece*, the State should have guaranteed the effectiveness of the applicant's defence when his counsel failed to appear before the appeal court and the applicant's appeal was consequently rejected with a final decision. According to the Court, the domestic court should have adjourned the examination of the case and clarified the reasons for the counsel's absence before rejecting the appeal.[1757]

The State's obligation to react with positive measures may also become relevant when a counsel appointed to a defendant fails to take some decisive procedural measures. In such situations the counsel should, for the sake of the effectiveness of the defence, be reminded about the failure rather than face an immediate dismissal of the procedural measure in question. For example, in the case *Czekalla v. Portugal*, an appeal could no longer be examined before the domestic courts as a result of a procedural mistake committed by the counsel. The appeal was lodged by a foreigner who did not speak the language and who was completely dependent on his counsel. The circumstances of the case therefore imposed on the relevant court the positive obligation to ensure practical and effective respect for the applicant's right to due process.[1758]

However, not all situations in which a counsel fails to act correctly create a positive obligation for the State to act. For example, in the case *Alvarez Sanchez v. Spain*, no violation of the State's positive obligation was found when the

---

1755 *Artico v. Italy*, App. no. 6694/74, §36, 13.5.1980. See also Dragoljub Popović, *European Human Rights Law – A Manual: An Introduction to the Strasbourg Court and its Jurisprudence*, Eleven International Publishing, The Hague 2013, p. 202.

1756 *Sakhnovskiy v. Russia* [GC], App. no. 21272/03, §91, 2.11.2010.

1757 *Vamvakas v. Greece*, App. no. 2870/11, §§39–43, 9.4.2015.

1758 *Czekalla v. Portugal*, App. no. 38830/97, §§68 and 70–71, 10.10.2002. Domestic legislation required that, at the end of the letter of appeal, the grounds for the appeal be summarily repeated. In this case, the domestic courts found that the grounds of appeal had not been satisfactorily explained as the appeal contained no submissions and did not indicate in what way the legal provisions allegedly breached should have been interpreted and applied. See also Karen Reid, *A Practitioner's Guide to the European Convention on Human Rights*, Sweet & Maxwell/Thomson Reuters, London 2019, pp. 267–268.

counsel had failed to lodge an appeal in time, because the appeal was about the fair trial guarantees and not about the validity of the conviction or the length of the sentence imposed. The applicant was also able to bring an action for damages against that lawyer for professional misconduct.[1759]

The State's positive obligation may become relevant when there has been manifest negligence in taking crucial procedural measures. On the other hand, the State is not liable for defects in a defence, such as a lack of argumentation skills or other professional errors in presenting the accused's defence.[1760] A lack of professional skills in a counsel cannot create State liability, irrespective of whether the counsel was chosen by the applicant or appointed by the State under the free legal aid scheme.

#### 6.4.5.2. *Other Requirements of Effectiveness*

An important part of an effective defence is the private access the accused has to his or her counsel in conditions in which confidentiality can be assured. An accused must be able to meet sufficiently often with his or her counsel in order to adequately prepare his or her defence. An accused must also be able to communicate to the counsel any elements relevant for the defence.[1761] The confidentiality of the communication cannot therefore be restricted, for example, by tapping the telephone conversations between an accused and his lawyer,[1762] by strictly limiting the number and length of lawyers' visits to the accused,[1763] by failing to guarantee the privacy of a video-conference,[1764] by the fact that the prosecuting authorities are supervising interviews,[1765] by surveilling the detainee's contacts with his defence counsel,[1766] by supervising communication between the accused and the lawyer in the courtroom,[1767] or by preventing free communication with a lawyer due to threat of sanction.[1768]

---

1759 *Alvarez Sanchez v. Spain* (dec.), App. no. 50720/99, 23.10.2001.

1760 *Czekalla v. Portugal*, App. no. 38830/97, §60, 10.10.2002; and *Tripodi v. Italy*, App. no. 13743/88, §30, 22.2.1994 (the counsel's failure to request adjournment of the case). See also *Stanford v. the United Kingdom*, App. no. 16759/90, §§27–28, 23.2.1994 (the counsel's failure to inform the court about the accused's hearing problem).

1761 *S. v. Switzerland*, App. nos. 12629/87+, §48, 28.11.1991; and *Brennan v. the United Kingdom*, App. no. 39846/98, §58, 16.10.2001.

1762 *Zagaria v. Italy*, App. no. 58295/00, §36, 27.11.2007. See also Evert-Jan van der Vlis, "Videoconferencing in criminal proceedings", in Sabine Braun, Judith L. Taylor (Eds.), *Videoconference and Remote Interpreting in Criminal Proceedings*, University of Surrey, Guildford 2011, pp. 11–25, at p. 23.

1763 *Öcalan v. Turkey* [GC], App. no. 46221/99, §135, 12.5.2005.

1764 *Sakhnovskiy v. Russia* [GC], App. no. 21272/03, §104, 2.11.2010; and *Gorbunov and Gorbachev v. Russia*, App. nos. 43183/06+, §37, 1.3.2016.

1765 *Rybacki v. Poland*, App. no. 52479/99, §58, 13.1.2009.

1766 *Lanz v. Austria*, App. no. 24430/94, §52, 31.1.2002.

1767 *Khodorkovskiy and Lebedev v. Russia*, App. nos. 11082/06+, §§642–647, 25.7.2013.

1768 *M. v. the Netherlands*, App. no. 2156/10, §92, 25.7.2017.

In this respect also the complexity, extent and seriousness of the case must be taken into account.[1769]

One aspect of the effectiveness of the defence is the accused's right to choose his or her counsel, which requires proper information on the situation. In the case *Dvorski v. Croatia*, the Court found a violation when the detained applicant had himself chosen a legal counsel to assist him in the interrogations from the list given to him by the police. The police, however, failed to inform the applicant that his parents had already chosen a counsel for him. The counsel hired by the parents had come to the police station to meet the applicant but the police did not allow the meeting to take place. The Court held that the applicant was not able to make a decision on choosing his counsel since he was lacking proper information. Because of the acts of the police, the applicant did not have an adequate opportunity to choose his counsel.[1770]

The effectiveness of the legal assistance may also depend on various practical considerations. A State will violate the effectiveness of the defence if it negligently fails to notify the accused's counsel, whose identity is known to it, of the hearing, with the result that the accused is not represented at all.[1771] A problem of effectiveness may also be raised if there are frequent changes of lawyers appointed for the defence. However, in cases where the accused is ordered to reimburse the State for the fees of his counsel or legal aid assistant, this does not render the defence ineffective.[1772]

---

1769 *Öcalan v. Turkey* [GC], App. no. 46221/99, §135, 12.5.2005; and *Sakhnovskiy v. Russia* [GC], App. no. 21272/03, §§102–107, 2.11.2010. In the latter case, the applicant, who was accused of a murder, had been able to communicate with his counsel for 15 minutes before the beginning of the trial. Considering the complexity and seriousness of the case, the Court found that the time allotted for communication was clearly not sufficient. It was also questionable whether communication by video-link operated by the State offered sufficient privacy. The Court considered that the applicant might legitimately have felt ill at ease when he discussed his case with his counsel. On the other hand, transporting the applicant 3,000 kilometres from Novosibirsk to Moscow for a meeting with his lawyer would have been a lengthy and costly operation. It thus had to be examined whether in view of this particular geographic obstacle the respondent State had undertaken measures which sufficiently compensated for the limitations of the applicant's rights. Nothing prevented the authorities, for example, from organising at least a telephone conversation between the applicant and his counsel more in advance of the hearing, or from appointing a lawyer from Novosibirsk who could have visited the applicant in the detention centre and would have been with him during the hearing. Furthermore, it was unclear why the representation of the applicant was not conferred on the lawyer who had already defended him before the first-instance court and prepared the original statement of appeal. In any event, the Supreme Court could have adjourned the hearing on its own motion to give the applicant sufficient time to discuss the case with his counsel. The domestic authorities had not made sufficient arrangements to secure effective legal assistance to the applicant. See also *M. v. the Netherlands*, App. no. 2156/10, §§91–98, 25.7.2017.

1770 *Dvorski v. Croatia* [GC], App. no. 25703/11, §§98, 101 and 106–111, 20.10.2015.

1771 *Goddi v. Italy*, App. no. 8966/80, §30, 9.4.1984. See also Karen Reid, *A Practitioner's Guide to the European Convention on Human Rights*, Sweet & Maxwell/Thomson Reuters, London 2019, p. 266.

1772 *Breukhoven v. the Czech Republic*, App. no. 44438/06, §62, 21.7.2011.

The ability to defend oneself may also be affected by the way in which the trial is organised in the courtroom. In several judgments against Russia, the Court has found a violation of Article 3 of the Convention on the grounds that it considers the use in courtrooms of metal cages, to hold defendants during a trial, to amount to degrading treatment.[1773] In these cases the Court has emphasised that it is within the State's margin of appreciation to decide how the security in the courtrooms is maintained, and it is not as such forbidden to isolate the accused in a glass cubicle in the courtroom. In the case *Yaroslav Belousov v. Russia*, the Court found, however, that enclosing the applicant in a small glass cubicle together with other defendants during the trial prevented his participation in the trial and denied him access to his counsel. Also, at a point during the trial when there were no longer any other defendants in the glass cubicle, the domestic authorities had failed to secure the applicant's participation in the trial in an adequate way. There was thus a violation of Article 6 §§1 and 3.[1774]

## 6.5. RIGHT TO CALL AND CROSS-EXAMINE WITNESSES

**Article 6: Right to a fair trial**

*3. Everyone charged with a criminal offence has the following minimum rights:*

...

*(d) to examine or have examined witnesses against him and to obtain the attendance and examination of witnesses on his behalf under the same conditions as witnesses against him.*

### 6.5.1. ASSESSING OVERALL FAIRNESS OF THE PROCEEDINGS

As in respect of other Article 6 §3 special provisions concerning criminal proceedings, the rights guaranteed by Article 6 §3 (d) are also particular aspects of a fair trial and they are often examined together with the general fairness requirement in Article 6 §1 of the Convention.[1775] The existence of a violation is examined in light of whether the lack of Article 6 §3 safeguards leads to the proceedings not being regarded as, on the whole, fair.[1776]

The role of the Court is guided by the principle that the provision on admissibility of evidence falls to the competences of the domestic legislator, and

1773 *Svinarenko and Slyadnev v. Russia* [GC], App. nos. 32541/08+, §§114–118 and 138, 17.7.2014.

1774 *Yaroslav Belousov v. Russia*, App. nos. 2653/13+, §§145–154, 4.10.2016.

1775 See also Chapter 4, section 4.2.6. above.

1776 *Al-Khawaja and Tahery v. the United Kingdom* [GC], App. nos. 26766/05+, §118, 15.12.2011.

that it is the task of the domestic courts to decide on the admission of evidence and assess it in any given case. It is not for the Court to pronounce whether the evidence and its assessment by the domestic courts were appropriate but only to examine whether the proceedings as a whole, including the taking of evidence, were fair.[1777]

From the fairness point of view, a situation is problematic if: (1) a piece of evidence has been acquired in violation of Article 3 of the Convention; (2) the defendant's statements given in the pretrial investigation phase are used as decisive evidence and those statements were given without the presence of counsel; and (3) the sole and decisive evidence for conviction is evidence which has been admitted without the defendant being given the opportunity to cross-examine the witness in question.

Article 6 §3 (d) concerns the accused's rights in criminal proceedings. Article 6 does not explicitly require that attention be drawn to the interests of witnesses or complainants who are heard as witnesses. The need to protect the witnesses is not, however, excluded from the scope of human rights; they have been secured under Article 2 concerning the right to life and under Article 8 concerning the right to respect for private and family life.[1778] As the Convention protects these interests, it is the duty of the Contracting States to organise, on this ground, their criminal proceedings in such a way that those interests are not unjustifiably imperilled.[1779] However, in the Grand Chamber case *Al-Khawaja and Tahery v. the United Kingdom*, the Court found that the rights of witnesses and other persons participating in the proceedings fell also within the scope of Article 6. The Court held that in the overall assessment of the fairness of proceedings, attention should also be paid, in addition to the rights of the defence, to the interests of the public and victims, to ensure that crime is properly prosecuted. Where necessary, the Court will also look at the rights of witnesses.[1780]

### 6.5.2. CONCEPT OF A WITNESS

The concept of a witness has its own, autonomous meaning under the Convention, which does not necessarily correspond to national definitions.[1781] It is not only limited to people who are heard as witnesses during the trial but also applies to those who have given statements during the pretrial investigation but who

1777 *Doorson v. the Netherlands*, App. no. 20524/92, §67, 26.3.1996.

1778 *Van der Heijden v. the Netherlands* [GC], App. no. 42857/05, §76, 3.4.2012 (no violation).

1779 *Doorson v. the Netherlands*, App. no. 20524/92, §70, 26.3.1996.

1780 *Al-Khawaja and Tahery v. the United Kingdom* [GC], App. nos. 26766/05+, §118, 15.12.2011. See also Anand Doobay, "The right to a fair trial in light of the recent ECtHR and CJEU case-law", *ERA forum*, vol. 14, issue 2, September 2013, pp. 251–262, at pp. 258–260.

1781 *Damir Sibgatullin v. Russia*, App. no. 1413/05, §45, 28.5.2014; and *S.N. v. Sweden*, App. no. 34209/96, §45, 2.7.2002.

are not heard by the court.[1782] Also, complainants and victims who have been heard during the pretrial investigation are witnesses within the meaning of the Convention, irrespective of whether they have been heard in person by the court for witness purposes or not.[1783]

Experts or expert witnesses are also considered to be witnesses, whether they are called by the prosecution or the defence.[1784] An expert appointed by the court is also a witness.[1785] However, expert witnesses may not be fully associated with "eye-witnesses", at least not for all purposes.[1786] A co-accused is also a witness and his depositions made during the pretrial investigation or at the trial constitute evidence. The co-accused are also witnesses when they have given their depositions in a separate trial and these depositions are used as evidence at the accused's trial.[1787] Article 6 §3 (d) may also be applied to documentary evidence, including reports prepared by an arresting officer.[1788]

### 6.5.3. HEARING WITNESSES IN THE PRESENCE OF AN ACCUSED

According to the main rule, before an accused can be convicted, all evidence admitted against him or her must be received in an oral hearing in his or her presence and the accused must have an opportunity to cross-examine the witnesses of the counterparty.

1782 *Kostovski v. the Netherlands*, App. no. 11454/85, §40, 20.11.1989; *Asch v. Austria*, App. no. 12398/86, §25, 26.4.1991; *Mirilashvili v. Russia*, App. no. 6293/04, §§158–159, 11.12.2008; *Kaste and Mathisen v. Norway*, App. nos. 18885/04+, §53, 9.11.2006; *Lucà v. Italy*, App. no. 33354/96, §41, 27.2.2001; and *Vanfuli v. Russia*, App. no. 24885/05, §110, 3.11.2011. See also Eva Brems, "Conflicting human rights: an exploration in the context of the right to fair trial in the European Convention for the Protection of Human Rights and Fundamental Freedoms", *Human Rights Quarterly*, vol. 27, App. no. 1, 2005, pp. 294–326, at pp. 309–311.

1783 *S.N. v. Sweden*, App. no. 34209/96, §45, 2.7.2002; and *Vladimir Romanov v. Russia*, App. no. 41461/02, §97, 24.7.2008.

1784 *Doorson v. the Netherlands*, App. no. 20524/92, §§81–82, 26.3.1996; and *Balsytė-Lideikienė v. Lithuania*, App. no. 72596/01, §§63 and 66, 4.11.2008. In the latter case experts were not regarded as witnesses within the meaning of Article 6 §3 (d) but in practice the same approach was applied to them as to witnesses. See also *Gregačević v. Croatia*, App. no. 58331/09, §67, 10.7.2012; and *Constantinides v. Greece*, App. no. 76438/12, §§37–38, 6.10.2016. Police officers can also be witnesses, see *Ürek and Ürek v. Turkey*, App. no. 74845/12, §50, 30.7.2019.

1785 *Bönisch v. Austria*, App. no. 8658/79, §§29 and 32, 6.5.1985. The case concerned the neutrality of an expert appointed by the court when the expert started to support the prosecution's views, and the accused's position and ability to call his own witnesses.

1786 *Khodorkovskiy and Lebedev v. Russia*, App. nos. 11082/06+, §711, 25.7.2013.

1787 *Mild and Virtanen v. Finland*, App. nos. 39481/98+, §43, 26.7.2005; *Trofimov v. Russia*, App. no. 1111/02, §37, 4.12.2008; and *Oddone and Pecci v. San Marino*, App. nos. 26581/17+, §§94–95, 17.10.2019.

1788 *Mirilashvili v. Russia*, App. no. 6293/04, §§158–159, 11.12.2008; *Chap Ltd v. Armenia*, App. no. 15485/09, §48, 4.5.2017; and *Butkevich v. Russia*, App. no. 5865/07, §§98–99, 13.2.2018.

The accused's right to cross-examine witnesses against him or her, or the right to have his or her own witnesses heard at the trial, is a central rule in criminal proceedings. Although this is an important indicator of the fairness of criminal proceedings, it is not an absolute right, and exceptions can be made to it on reasonable grounds. When exceptions are made on necessity grounds to a central rule guaranteeing the accused's basic rights, the limitations must be consistent with the principle of equality of arms and be such that they do not breach the essential aim of Articles 6 §1 and 6 §3 (d) of the Convention.[1789] In problematic situations in which it is not possible to obtain direct and oral evidence at the trial, certain special arrangements are possible, provided that the inconveniences to the defence caused by their use are compensated for in one way or another.

The rights guaranteed in Article 6 §3 (d) apply to the proceedings before the first-instance court as well as on appeal. Generally they do not apply at the pretrial stage.[1790] Article 6 §3 (d) does not therefore require that the accused be allowed to question witnesses during the pretrial investigation phase, provided that these witnesses can be cross-examined at the trial.[1791] Nor is a refusal to hear a defence witness during the pretrial investigation a violation of Article 6 §3 (d) if the witness may be called at the trial.[1792] On the other hand, the courts have a right to limit the hearing of witnesses at the trial phase only to what is necessary. However, if no possibility to receive evidence is provided during the first-instance proceedings or on appeal, for example, because of the summary nature of the proceedings, there can be a violation.[1793] It should be noted that Article 6 §§1 and 3 (d) of the Convention contain a presumption against the use of hearsay evidence against a defendant in criminal proceedings.[1794]

The use of the defendant's own pretrial account as decisive evidence against him requires the existence of certain legal safeguards. In the case *Salduz v. Turkey*,

1789 *Engel and Others v. the Netherlands*, App. nos. 5100/71+, §91, 8.6.1976; *Al-Khawaja and Tahery v. the United Kingdom* [GC], App. nos. 26766/05+, §118, 15.12.2011; *Hümmer v. Germany*, App. no. 26171/07, §38, 19.7.2012; *Lucà v. Italy*, App. no. 33354/96, §39, 27.2.2001; and *Solakov v. "the former Yugoslav Republic of Macedonia"*, App. no. 47023/99, §57, 31.10.2001. See also Eva Brems, "Conflicting human rights: an exploration in the context of the right to fair trial in the European Convention for the Protection of Human Rights and Fundamental Freedoms", *Human Rights Quarterly*, vol. 27, no. 1, 2005, pp. 294–326, at pp. 309–311.

1790 *Can v. Austria*, App. no. 9300/81, §47, 30.9.1985; and *Adolf v. Austria*, App. no. 8269/78, §64, 26.3.1982.

1791 *X. v. Germany* (dec.), App. no. 8414/78, 4.7.1979.

1792 *Schertenleib v. Switzerland* (dec.), App. no. 8339/78, 12.7.1979. The court has a right to limit the hearing of witnesses only to what is necessary.

1793 *Vaturi v. France*, App. no. 75699/01, §58, 13.4.2006. The refusal to hear witnesses does not, however, render the proceedings unfair in all situations. This was the case, for example, in the case *Panarisi v. Italy*, App. no. 46794/99, §113, 10.4.2007, in which the defendant could not cross-examine his co-defendant. His account did not, however, constitute decisive evidence but merely supported other evidence that had been received according to the adversarial principle.

1794 *Thomas v. the United Kingdom* (dec.), App. no. 19354/02, 10.5.2005.

the Court found that a conviction based on an account given by the accused during the pretrial investigation without the presence of a counsel could violate the overall fairness of the proceedings. The accused's particular vulnerability in the early investigation stage is compensated for by the presence of a counsel in the interrogations, in particular in cases concerning aggravated crime and in situations in which it is known that the conviction will be based on the pretrial investigation report.[1795] This assessment requires, however, that the overall fairness of the proceedings is assessed.[1796]

The right to call and cross-examine witnesses means that there is a right to hear witnesses in the presence of the parties and the deciding judge. If the deciding judge is replaced after a witness has been heard, generally the witness must be recalled.[1797] A failure to apply this rule does not mean, however, that there is a violation in all situations. In the case *P.K. v. Finland*, the witnesses were not reheard after the judge had been replaced. The Court found in that case that the rights of the accused were not violated as he had had an opportunity to challenge the testimonies received at the trial and there was no reason to doubt their credibility in the light of the case file. Moreover, the three lay judges remained the same during the whole proceedings and the new presiding judge was able to become acquainted with the witness statements recorded in the minutes. Nor was the judge replaced with an intent to influence the outcome of the case or for any other arbitrary reason.[1798]

The gravity of the crime in question is not a reason to substantially limit the rights of defence of the accused or to deprive him or her of the possibility of cross-examination. In the case *Breukhoven v. the Czech Republic*, the victims of human trafficking had been heard at the beginning of the investigation without the accused being present, owing to the fact that he had left the country. Subsequently, the victims also left the country. In the criminal proceedings, they were no longer heard in person, nor were their hearings organised in any alternative way, for example, by hearing them in their home country through

---

1795 *Salduz v. Turkey* [GC], App. no. 36391/02, §§54–60, 27.11.2008. See also Tom van de Laar, Regien de Graaf, "Salduz and Miranda – Is the US Supreme Court Pointing the Way?", *European Human Rights Law Review*, Issue 3, 2011, pp. 304–317; Andrew L.-T. Choo, *The Privilege Against Self-incrimination and Criminal Justice*, Hart Publishing, Oxford and Portland, Or. 2013, pp. 84–89; and Egbert Myjer, "One *Salduz* a year is enough – 20 associative thoughts on judge Rozakis, judicial activism and the *Salduz* judgment", in Dean Spielmann, Marialena Tsirli, Panayotis Voyatziz (Eds.), *La Convention Européenne des Droits de L'homme, un Instrument Vivant – Mélanges en L'honneur de Christos L. Rozakis/ The European Convention on Human Rights, a Living Instrument – Essays in Honour of Christos L. Rozakis*, Bruylant, Bruxelles 2011, pp. 419–430.

1796 *Ibrahim and Others v. the United Kingdom* [GC], App. nos. 50541/08+, §257, 13.9.2016.

1797 *Graviano v. Italy*, App. no. 10075/02, §38, 10.2.2005.

1798 *P.K. v. Finland* (dec.), App. no. 37442/97, 9.7.2002. Neither was a violation found in a civil case in which the presiding judge changed during the trial but the previously heard witnesses were not reheard; see *Pitkänen v. Finland*, App. no. 30508/96, §§62–65, 9.3.2004.

the means of international judicial assistance. Although many other testimonies were received in the case, the conviction was exclusively based on the statements given to the police by the victims, whom the accused could not cross-examine at any stage. The Court found a violation of Article 6 §3 (d) in respect of the rights of the accused. The State's obligation to effectively fight human trafficking did not mean that on that pretext the rights of the accused could be violated.[1799] A similar conclusion was reached in the case *Schatschaschwili v. Germany*, which will be discussed in more detail below.[1800]

### 6.5.4. WAIVING THE RIGHT TO CROSS-EXAMINE WITNESSES

The right of the accused to cross-examine witnesses against him or her can be waived either implicitly or tacitly. However, the waiver must be established in an unequivocal manner; it cannot run counter to any important public interests; and, in addition, certain minimum legal safeguards must be connected to its use.[1801] A tacit waiver of Article 6 rights also requires that the accused has been reasonably able to foresee the consequences of his or her actions.[1802]

Waiving the right to cross-examine witnesses was not valid, for example, in the case *A.S. v. Finland*, which concerned the sexual abuse of a child. The defendant had agreed to watch a video of the hearing of the child victim. Merely by consenting to the viewing of the video recording, the applicant could not be understood as having waived of his own free will, either expressly or tacitly, his right to put questions to the child. On the contrary, the applicant had consistently argued that the proceedings were flawed in that he had not been afforded an opportunity to cross-examine the child.[1803] Nor was the waiving of the right valid when the applicant told the court, acting without his counsel and not understanding the consequences of his actions, that the hearing of witnesses in person was not necessary, after explicitly requesting the hearing of witnesses on appeal.[1804] There was no valid waiver of this right, either, in the case *Idalov v. Russia*, in which the defendant had been removed from the courtroom as a result of bad behaviour and the testimonies had been received without his presence. The Court found a violation since the defendant had not been clearly warned about the consequences of his behaviour, nor had it been verified during the receiving of testimonies that the defendant might have agreed to behave properly had he been allowed to return to the courtroom.[1805]

---

1799 *Breukhoven v. the Czech Republic*, App. no. 44438/06, §§54–56, 21.7.2011.
1800 *Schatschaschwili v. Germany* [GC], App. no. 9154/10, §§161–165, 15.12.2015.
1801 See, for example, *Hermi v. Italy* [GC], App. no. 18114/02, §73, 18.10.2006.
1802 *Jones v. the United Kingdom* (dec.), App. no. 30900/02, 9.9.2003.
1803 *A.S. v. Finland*, App. no. 40156/07, §74, 28.9.2010.
1804 *Bonev v. Bulgaria*, App. no. 60018/00, §41, 8.6.2006.
1805 *Idalov v. Russia* [GC], App. no. 5826/03, §§175–178, 22.5.2012.

However, in the child abuse case *B. v. Finland* and in the rape case *Gani v. Spain*, the applicants were considered to have waived their right to cross-examination of the witnesses when they were given an opportunity to cross-examine the witnesses during the pretrial investigation but had declined.[1806] In the case *Poletan and Azirovik v. "the former Yugoslav Republic of Macedonia"*, the Court held that the applicants had waived their right to cross-examination when the witness in question had been examined in a Montenegrin court under oath and the applicants had not raised any objection or sought later in the proceedings to have questions put to these witnesses.[1807]

### 6.5.5. CROSS-EXAMINATION AND PRETRIAL INVESTIGATION STATEMENTS

The accused's right to cross-examine witnesses against him is a central right guaranteed by Article 6 §3 (d). This right is violated if a statement given by a witness called by the prosecution or the complainant is admitted as evidence without this witness being heard at the trial. Therefore, all evidence must in general be received in the adversarial proceedings in a public trial in the presence of the accused.[1808]

However, this ideal situation is not always possible; in practice there may be situations in which other alternatives must be considered. The right to cross-examine is thus not an absolute one, and in certain specific circumstances it may be necessary to make exceptions to this rule.[1809]

In the Court's case-law, Article 6 §3 (d) has often been invoked in two kinds of problematic situations. First, exceptions to the right to cross-examine may have to be made in situations concerning absent witnesses, that is, witnesses whose identity is known to the parties and the court but who are, for some reason, prevented from attending the court hearing. Second, the provision has been invoked in the context of anonymous witnesses when the identity of the witness has been concealed for the purpose of protecting the witness against reprisals or protecting undercover activities. These categories are not, however, mutually exclusive, as a witness can be both absent and anonymous at the same time.[1810]

1806 *B. v. Finland*, App. no. 17122/02, §§44–45, 24.4.2007; and *Gani v. Spain*, App. no. 61800/08, §44, 19.2.2013.

1807 *Poletan and Azirovik v. "the former Yugoslav Republic of Macedonia"*, App. nos. 26711/07+, §87, 12.5.2016.

1808 See, for example, *A.S. v. Finland*, App. no. 40156/07, §53, 28.9.2010; *Tarău v. Romania*, App. no. 3584/02, §74, 24.2.2009; and *Graviano v. Italy*, App. no. 10075/02, §38, 10.2.2005.

1809 *Unterpertinger v. Austria*, App. no. 9120/80, §31, 24.11.1986; and *Saidi v. France*, App. no. 14647/89, §43, 20.9.1993. The latter case concerned drugs-related deaths.

1810 *Al-Khawaja and Tahery v. the United Kingdom*, App. nos. 26766/05+, §35, 20.1.2009; and *Al-Khawaja and Tahery v. the United Kingdom* [GC], App. nos. 26766/05+, §127, 15.12.2011.

In the Court's case-law, exceptional ways to proceed have been examined in situations that have concerned, variously, the protection of witnesses and their families against reprisals,[1811] the protection of the secrecy of the investigation methods of the police,[1812] the protection of victims of sexual crimes from facing their perpetrators,[1813] and also when assessing the existence of a valid excuse of witnesses not present in a court hearing on the basis of the fact that they have fallen ill,[1814] disappeared[1815] are in fear,[1816] or dead.[1817] Different situations call for different approaches. For example, a situation involving a dead witness is different to that of an anonymous witness who can attend a court hearing but who may have a valid reason not to disclose his or her identity. These situations differ further from those in which the witness is a vulnerable child who has been a victim of a sexual crime or is otherwise a known but scared witness.

In the Court's case-law a very strict test has been traditionally applied when assessing the admission of statements from absent witnesses as evidence, at least when such statements have been the sole or decisive evidence leading to a conviction.[1818] If the conviction has been based on statements given in the pretrial investigation from witnesses whom the accused has not been able to cross-examine in the trial, the proceedings have been considered as unfair. In the Grand Chamber case *Al-Khawaja and Tahery v. the United Kingdom*, the Court changed its approach and relaxed its previously strict case-law. In that case, the Court defined a three-step test to be applied when statements from absent witnesses are admitted to the case file and taken into consideration as evidence.[1819] In a subsequent Grand Chamber case, *Schatschaschwili v. Germany*, the test was further elaborated and specified in the light of the problems encountered in practice.[1820]

#### 6.5.5.1. *The Three-Step Test*

The main rule is that in all cases in which special arrangements are needed to protect witnesses, the State must take positive balancing measures in order

1811 *Van Mechelen and Others v. the Netherlands*, App. nos. 21363/93+, §56, 23.4.1997.

1812 *Lüdi v. Switzerland*, App. no. 12433/86, §49, 15.6.1992. In this case, the undercover police officer was not heard. The Court found that the police's methods of investigation could have been protected in other ways than the manner chosen by the domestic courts.

1813 *S.N. v. Sweden*, App. no. 34209/96, §47, 2.7.2002.

1814 *Wester v. Sweden* (dec.), App. no. 31076/96, 14.1.1998.

1815 *Verdam v. the Netherlands* (dec.), App. no. 35253/97, 31.8.1999.

1816 *Al-Khawaja and Tahery v. the United Kingdom* [GC], App. nos. 26766/05+, §§122–125, 15.12.2011.

1817 *Ferrantelli and Santangelo v. Italy*, App. no. 19874/92, §52, 7.8.1996. See also *Al-Khawaja and Tahery v. the United Kingdom* [GC], App. nos. 26766/05+, §121, 15.12.2011 (no violation).

1818 See *Doorson v. the Netherlands*, App. no. 20524/92, §76, 26.3.1996 and the subsequent case-law. See also Karen Reid, *A Practitioner's Guide to the European Convention on Human Rights*, Sweet & Maxwell/Thomson Reuters, London 2019, p. 367.

1819 *Al-Khawaja and Tahery v. the United Kingdom* [GC], App. nos. 26766/05+, §147, 15.12.2011.

1820 *Schatschaschwili v. Germany* [GC], App. no. 9154/10, §§119–121, 15.12.2015.

to guarantee the accused a fair trial. Even in exceptional cases, the fair trial guarantees provided by Article 6 §3 cannot be deprived of all of their content.[1821]

In special situations, when witness statements given in the pretrial investigation are used as evidence, the three-step test which was created in the Grand Chamber case *Al-Khawaja and Tahery v. the United Kingdom* must be followed. The test requires an answer to the following three questions. (1) Is there a good reason for the non-attendance of a witness at the trial? (2) If such a good reason exists, is the evidence of the absent witness the sole or decisive basis for the defendant's conviction? The concept of "sole evidence" means that there is no other evidence against the defendant. If the case file contains corroborative evidence other than the untested evidence, there is no question of sole evidence. The concept of "decisive evidence" must be interpreted strictly to mean only evidence which explicitly has a decisive role in the outcome. The stronger the corroborative evidence, the more likely it will be that the untested evidence is not decisive.[1822] (3) Is there sufficient counterbalancing factors to compensate for the handicaps under which the defence labours? If the untested evidence is sole or decisive, it does not necessarily mean that there is a violation of the fair trial guarantees. In such a situation it becomes relevant whether there are sufficient counterbalancing factors, including strong procedural safeguards, to compensate for the handicaps caused to the defence given the admission of the untested evidence, and to ensure that the trial, judged as a whole, is fair.[1823] Although, according to the main rule, a conviction cannot be based solely or decisively on statements from witnesses whom the defence has not been able to cross-examine at some stage of the proceedings,[1824] this does not, according to the previous case-law, automatically lead to a violation of Article 6. However, relevance is given to whether there are elements capable of balancing the restrictions on the accused's rights of defence and whether the court's assessment of evidence is conducted with care.[1825]

In the Grand Chamber case *Schatschaschwili v. Germany*, the Court further specified the *Al-Khawaja* test by clarifying the relationship between the three steps of the test. In this judgment the Court answered three questions. The

---

1821 *Sadak and Others v. Turkey*, App. nos. 29900/96+, §67, 17.7.2001.

1822 *Al-Khawaja and Tahery v. the United Kingdom* [GC], App. nos. 26766/05+, §131, 15.12.2011. See also Jane Elliott-Kelly, "Case Analysis – *Al-Khawaja and Tahery v. United Kingdom*", *European Human Rights Law Review*, Issue 1, 2012, pp. 81–87.

1823 *Al-Khawaja and Tahery v. the United Kingdom* [GC], App. nos. 26766/05+, §§119 and 147, 15.12.2011.

1824 *Doorson v. the Netherlands*, App. no. 20524/92, §76, 26.3.1996.

1825 *Al-Khawaja and Tahery v. the United Kingdom* [GC], App. nos. 26766/05+, §147, 15.12.2011. See also Jane Elliott-Kelly, "Case Analysis – *Al-Khawaja and Tahery v. United Kingdom*", *European Human Rights Law Review*, Issue 1, 2012, pp. 81–87; and Mike Redmayne, "Hearsay and human rights: *Al-Khawaja* in the Grand Chamber", *Modern Law Review*, vol. 75, no. 5, 2012, pp. 865–878.

first question was that if the reply to the first step (a good reason for the non-attendance) and/or second step (sole or decisive evidence) is negative, is it still necessary to assess the existence of any counterbalancing factors. The Court's reply was that if there is no good reason for the non-attendance of a witness, this fact alone is not decisive vis-à-vis the fairness of the proceedings. The analysis does not stop at step one but continues to the second and third steps. However, in the overall assessment, this fact may carry a lot of weight and may, in a particular case, also render the proceedings unfair.

The second question was that if the reply to the second step (sole or decisive evidence) is negative, is it still necessary to assess the existence of any counterbalancing factors. According to the Court, a court must proceed to the assessment of counterbalancing factors not only in situations in which the untested witness statement is the sole or decisive evidence, but also in situations in which such evidence is not sole or decisive but carries significant weight and, by its admission, may handicap the defence. The need to proceed to the assessment of counterbalancing factors depends therefore on the evidential value of the statement of an absent witness.

The third question was: is the order of the steps decisive? The Court replied that, in principle, all three steps in the *Al-Khawaja* test should be analysed in the correct order from one to three. In special cases it may be necessary to deviate from the normal order if a certain step is particularly decisive from the fairness point of view.

In addition, in the *Schatschaschwili* case the Court gave some clarifications on each of the steps. Concerning the first step on the good reason for the witnesses' absence, the Court emphasised the positive obligation of the authorities to obtain, through police and international legal assistance, the attendance of the witness for cross-examination.[1826] Concerning the second step (sole or decisive evidence), the Court stressed that it must review the domestic courts' evaluation in the light of the meaning it has given to "sole" and "decisive" evidence and ascertain for itself whether the domestic courts' evaluation of the weight of the evidence was unacceptable or arbitrary.[1827]

The Court also gave examples of factors which may counterbalance the defence's situation. Such factors may include: that statements of an absent witness carry less weight; there is detailed reasoning as to why such evidence is considered reliable; there is a video recording of the absent witness's questioning at the investigation stage in order to allow the court, prosecution and defence to observe the witness's demeanour under questioning and to form their own impression of his or her reliability; and the availability at the trial of corroborative

---

1826 *Schatschaschwili v. Germany* [GC], App. no. 9154/10, §§119–121, 15.12.2015.

1827 *Schatschaschwili v. Germany* [GC], App. no. 9154/10, §§123–124, 15.12.2015; and *Poletan and Azirovik v. "the former Yugoslav Republic of Macedonia"*, App. no. 26711/07, §88, 12.5.2016.

evidence supporting the untested witness statement. This corroborative evidence can be forensic evidence and/or strong similarities between the absent witness's description of the alleged offence committed and the description of a comparable offence committed by the same defendant, given by another witness with whom there was no evidence of collusion. Another significant safeguard is the possibility offered to the defence to put its own questions to the witness indirectly, for instance in writing, during the trial or the pretrial investigation phase. If it is foreseen that a witness may not be heard at the trial, the applicant or defence counsel should have an opportunity to question this witness during the investigation stage. A relevant counterbalancing factor is also that the accused is afforded the opportunity to give his own version of the events and to cast doubt on the credibility of the absent witness, pointing out any incoherence or inconsistency with the statements of other witnesses.[1828]

### 6.5.5.2. *Absence, Disappearance, Illness or Death of a Witness, or Absence Owing to Fear*

#### 6.5.5.2.1. Measures Taken to Summons a Witness to a Court

In situations in which witnesses fail to attend the court hearing, it is expected that the court has taken all reasonable measures in order to reach them and to ensure their attendance.[1829] If, despite attempts, these measures are not successful, this fact alone does not call for the discontinuation of the proceedings.[1830]

In the case *Makeyev v. Russia*, the Court held that the State was responsible when the witness could not attend the court hearing due to fact that she had to look after her child, and she was not heard in person despite the fact that her testimony was of decisive importance for the legal characterisation of the offence the applicant was convicted of.[1831] In the case *Mild and Virtanen v. Finland*, the problem was securing the attendance of the previously convicted co-defendants as witnesses before the court when there was no legislative means for summonsing them. According to the Court, they could have been summonsed to the Court

1828 *Schatschaschwili v. Germany* [GC], App. no. 9154/10, §§125–131, 15.12.2015.

1829 *Pello v. Estonia*, App. no. 11423/03, §35, 12.4.2007; *Bonev v. Bulgaria*, App. no. 60018/00, §43, 8.6.2006; *Breukhoven v. the Czech Republic*, App. no. 44438/06, §44, 21.7.2011; *Karpenko v. Russia*, App. no. 5605/04, §62, 13.3.2012; *Damir Sibgatullin v. Russia*, App. no. 1413/05, §51, 28.5.2014; *Tseber v. the Czech Republic*, App. no. 46203/08, §48, 22.11.2012; *Lučić v. Croatia*, App. no. 5699/11, §§79–80, 27.2.2014; and *Mild and Virtanen v. Finland*, App. nos. 39481/98+, §47, 26.7.2005. Measures taken to summons witnesses may also have relevance in respect of the reasonable length of the proceedings, see *Kalle Kangasluoma v. Finland*, App. no. 5635/09, §23, 15.2.2011.

1830 *Artner v. Austria*, App. no. 13161/87, §21, 28.8.1992; *Scheper v. the Netherlands* (dec.), no. 39209/02, 5.4.2005; *Mayali v. France*, App. no. 69116/01, §32, 14.6.2005; and *Haas v. Germany* (dec.), App. no. 73047/01, 17.11.2005.

1831 *Makeyev v. Russia*, App. no. 13769/04, §§41–43, 5.2.2009.

of Appeal hearing to see whether they would have complied with the request. The Court thus found that not all reasonable measures had been taken to secure their attendance at court. Also, the legislation was in this respect deficient, as it did not provide for the summonsing of co-defendants to a court hearing. As the statements given by the co-defendants during the pretrial investigation and at their own trial had been the decisive evidence against the applicants, the Court found a violation.[1832]

In the case *Gossa v. Poland*, the evidence contained a statement given during the pretrial investigation by a person who lived in an unknown place in the United States. The domestic authorities had actively tried to locate the witness though the embassy in order to summons her to appear before the court, but without success. These measures were considered by the Court to be sufficient. In addition, the statement of the witness in question was not the sole or decisive evidence in the case.[1833] Similarly, in the drugs case *Fafrowicz v. Poland*, there was a valid excuse for the witness's absence from the court and his statement could be taken into account without hearing him in person, because he could not be summonsed, despite active attempts, from the United States. The witness's statement was not the sole or decisive evidence in this case, and in any event his statement was in line with the statements given by other witnesses during the pretrial investigation.[1834]

The Court also found the domestic court's efforts to secure the attendance of a witness at the hearing sufficient in the case *Tseber v. the Czech Republic*, when the judge had actively tried, with the help of the police, to secure the attendance of the witness who was abroad by issuing orders for his arrest and by making inquiries to the registration authorities in order to locate him. Only when these measures had proved to be unproductive was the written statement of the witness admitted as evidence. The Court held in the case that the domestic authorities had not breached their positive obligation to use all possible efforts to guarantee for the defence the opportunity to cross-examine the witness, and therefore the written statement of the witness was properly admitted as evidence.[1835]

In the case *Schatschaschwili v. Germany*, in which a violation was found, the authorities summonsed the witnesses residing abroad to appear in court and, when they refused, the authorities asked a foreign court to hear them through international legal assistance. This did not help either, as the witnesses still refused to testify. The Court therefore found that the domestic court had made all reasonable efforts within the existing legal framework to secure the

---

1832 *Mild and Virtanen v. Finland*, App. nos. 39481/98+, §§45–47, 26.7.2005.

1833 *Gossa v. Poland*, App. no. 47986/99, §§58–59 and 63, 9.1.2007.

1834 *Fafrowicz v. Poland*, App. no. 43609/07, §§56 and 58–59, 17.4.2012 (no violation). The other witnesses changed their testimonies during the trial.

1835 *Tseber v. the Czech Republic*, App. no. 46203/08, §§50–52, 22.11.2012.

attendance of those witnesses.[1836] However, since it was already clear in the pretrial investigation phase that the witnesses were going to leave the country, the risk of failing to contact them later on could have been avoided during the pretrial investigation phase, and their hearing could have been organised at that stage.[1837]

#### 6.5.5.2.2. Valid Excuse for a Witness's Absence and Sufficient Safeguards of the Defence

If a witness is absent for some reason, the domestic courts must assess, before admitting a written statement as evidence without hearing the witness in person, whether there is a good reason for the witness's absence. In the case *Al-Khawaja and Tahery v. the United Kingdom*, the Court explicitly required that there needed to be a good reason for the witness's absence.[1838] This requirement was subsequently relaxed in the case *Schatschaschwili v. Germany*, in which the Court held that the absence of a good reason for the non-attendance of a witness could not in itself be conclusive for the unfairness of a trial. The three-step analysis did not have to end there; rather the analysis could in those situations be carried on. However, the lack of a good reason for a witness's absence was a very important factor to be considered when assessing the overall fairness of a trial, and one which could tip the balance in favour of finding a breach of Article 6 §§1 and 3 (d).[1839]

##### 6.5.5.2.2.1. Dead Witness

An admission of a statement given during the pretrial investigation phase may be necessary if the witness has died. In such an event, the State cannot naturally be accused of failing to ensure the attendance of the witness. It is, however, relevant whether a conviction was based on other evidence or whether it was based, to a decisive extent, on a statement whose reliability cannot be tested because, for example, there is no other material supporting it.[1840]

In the case *Al-Khawaja and Tahery v. the United Kingdom*, a doctor was suspected of the indecent assault of two of his female patients during hypnosis. One of the patients had subsequently committed suicide. She had, however,

---

1836 *Schatschaschwili v. Germany* [GC], App. no. 9154/10, §§137–140, 15.12.2015.

1837 *Schatschaschwili v. Germany* [GC], App. no. 9154/10, §§157–160, 15.12.2015.

1838 *Al-Khawaja and Tahery v. the United Kingdom* [GC], App. nos. 26766/05+, §120, 15.12.2011 (partial violation).

1839 *Schatschaschwili v. Germany* [GC], App. no. 9154/10, §113, 15.12.2015; and *Poletan and Azirovik v. "the former Yugoslav Republic of Macedonia"*, App. no. 26711/07, §83, 12.5.2016.

1840 *Mika v. Sweden* (dec.), App. no. 31243/06, 27.1.2009; and *Ferrantelli and Santangelo v. Italy*, App. no. 19874/92, §52, 7.8.1996.

previously told of the assault during the pretrial investigation and confided in some of her friends. Also, the other victim had spoken about the indecent assault inflicted on her and her account tallied with that of the first victim. The domestic courts admitted the statement as evidence and the applicant was convicted of indecent assault. The Court held that the admission of the statement had been appropriate as the witness had subsequently died. The statement had been decisive evidence, and therefore the procedural safeguards relating to the assessment of the reliability of the statement were crucial. The Court found that the reliability of the statement was supported by the fact that the dead witness had also made her complaint to two of her friends promptly after the events in question. These friends had given evidence in person at the trial and their testimonies were consistent with the statement given by the late witness. Most importantly, there were strong similarities between the late witness's description of the alleged assault and that of the other complainant, with whom there was no evidence of any collusion. In addition, it was relevant that the jury had been directed to put less weight on the written statement as the applicant had not been able to cross-examine the witness. In these circumstances, the assessment of evidence had been fair and proper, and there were sufficient counterbalancing factors to conclude that the admission as evidence of the dead witness's statement did not result in a breach of Article 6 §1 read in conjunction with Article 6 §3 (d) of the Convention, even though the applicant was not able to cross-examine the key witness against him.[1841]

A statement from a dead witness was also at issue in the case *Horncastle and Others v. the United Kingdom*, in which the applicants were accused of an assault. Their victim had given the police a written statement but had died before the trial from causes unconnected with the assault. The victim's death justified the inclusion of his written statement in the case file. Although the statement was considered to be decisive evidence for the conviction, there was also other incriminating evidence in the case, including the applicants' admissions that they had been present at the victim's flat that night but were not responsible for the assault. There were also procedural counterbalancing elements in this case which had balanced the defence's inability to cross-examine the source of the evidence.[1842]

---

1841 *Al-Khawaja and Tahery v. the United Kingdom* [GC], App. nos. 26766/05+, §§121 and 153–158, 15.12.2011. See also Jane Elliott-Kelly, "Case Analysis – *Al-Khawaja and Tahery v. United Kingdom*", *European Human Rights Law Review*, Issue 1, 2012, pp. 81–87; and Mike Redmayne, "Hearsay and human rights: *Al-Khawaja* in the Grand Chamber", *Modern Law Review*, vol. 75, no. 5, 2012, pp. 865–878.

1842 *Horncastle and Others v. the United Kingdom*, App. no. 4184/10, §§140–143, 16.12.2014. See also J.R. Spencer, "Squaring up to Strasbourg: Horncastle in the Supreme Court", *Archbold Review*, Issue 1, 2010, pp. 6–9; and James Welch (Ed.), "Case and comment: selected decisions from the European Court of Human Rights from December 2014 to February 2015 – Evidence, *Horncastle v. United Kingdom* (Application No. 4184/10)", *European Human Rights Law Review*, Issue 2, 2015, pp. 216–219.

The case *Dimitrov and Momin v. Bulgaria* also concerned a dead witness. A young woman accused the applicants of having raped her. She had immediately filed a police report and had been questioned but subsequently she withdrew her report since she had been threatened and since she was in poor health following cancer treatment. Before the trial she died and her pretrial investigation statement was accepted as evidence. The untested statement constituted central evidence but not the sole evidence since there was other evidence, such as a medical certificate and the statement given by the police who had received the victim's police report. The Court held that no cross-examination could have been organised during the pretrial investigation since the victim had been in a vulnerable state. The applicants had had sufficient legal safeguards which had compensated for the lack of a cross-examination, and they had had an opportunity to make known their point of views. The case had been examined extremely carefully by the courts and their reasoning had been adequate.[1843]

#### 6.5.5.2.2.2. Witnesses in Fear

The case *Al-Khawaja and Tahery v. the United Kingdom* has also added important guidance to the case-law as far as witnesses in fear are concerned. The Court held that accepting the absence of a witness owing to fear requires that an analysis has been made of the source of the fear and the objectivity of the perception of fear. When a witness's fear is attributable to the defendant or those acting on the defendant's behalf, it is appropriate to allow the evidence of that witness to be introduced at trial without the need for the witness to give live evidence or be examined by the defendant or his representatives, even if such evidence is the sole or decisive evidence against the defendant. To allow the defendant to benefit from the fear he has engendered in a witness would be incompatible with the rights of victims and witnesses. Therefore, a defendant who is deemed threatening to a witness must be taken to have waived his rights to question that witness under Article 6 §3 (d).

However, the situation is different if witnesses have a general fear of testifying without that fear being directly attributable to threats made by the defendant or his agents. In such situations there is in principle no reason to accept the witness's absence from the trial. Any subjective fear of the witness will not suffice. The trial court therefore must determine first whether or not there are objective grounds for that fear, and, second, whether those objective grounds are supported by evidence. In any case, before a witness can be excused from testifying on grounds of fear, the trial court must be satisfied that all available alternatives, such as witness anonymity, testifying behind a screen, the removal of the defendant from the courtroom or use of unilateral voice or video

[1843] *Dimitrov and Momin v. Bulgaria*, App. no. 35132/08, §§51–74, 7.6.2018.

communication, would be inappropriate or impracticable.[1844] Those witnesses who are present can also be protected in such a manner that they are heard in person at the trial while the defendant is not present in the courtroom. The accused's counsel must, however, be able to be present when testimonies are given and be able to present the accused's questions to the witness.[1845]

In the *Tahery* case there were no sufficient grounds to base the conviction solely on a written witness statement. Tahery was convicted of a stabbing during a gang fight. At the crime scene, nobody had seen the stabbing and the victim was unable to identify the perpetrator. Some days later, a person present at the crime scene told the police that the perpetrator had been Tahery. The witness was fearful of appearing at the trial and for this reason his pretrial investigation statement was admitted as evidence. Subsequently, the jury based the conviction on the written statement. The Court held that there had been sufficient grounds for the admission of the statement as evidence. Appropriate enquiries had been made to determine whether there were objective grounds for the witness's fear by hearing both the witness and a police officer. The trial judge had also been satisfied that special measures, such as testifying behind a screen, would not have allayed the witness's fears. Nevertheless, the Court found that no sufficient counterbalancing factors were connected to the assessment of evidence. The untested written statement of the witness was, if not the sole, at least the decisive evidence against the applicant. Even though the testimony may have been coherent and convincing at face value, it contained weaknesses which could not be corroborated by other evidence. The witness had been the only witness who claimed to have seen the stabbing but he had only made his statement implicating the applicant two days after the event. The Court did not consider that a warning given to the jury that it was necessary to approach the evidence given by the absent witness with care, could be a sufficient counterbalance where an untested statement of the only prosecution eyewitness was the only direct evidence against the applicant. Examining the fairness of the proceedings as a whole, the Court therefore concluded that there had not been sufficient counterbalancing factors to compensate for the difficulties caused to the defence which resulted from the admission of the witness's statement. It therefore found that there had been a violation of Article 6 §1 read in conjunction with Article 6 §3 (d) of the Convention.[1846]

---

1844 *Al-Khawaja and Tahery v. the United Kingdom* [GC], App. nos. 26766/05+, §§122–125, 15.12.2011.

1845 *Kurup v. Denmark* (dec.), App. no. 11219/84, 10.7.1985; and *X. v. Denmark* (dec.), App. no. 8395/78, 16.12.1981. See also *Breijer v. the Netherlands* (dec.), App. no. 41596/13, §§32–33, 3.7.2018.

1846 *Al-Khawaja and Tahery v. the United Kingdom* [GC], App. nos. 26766/05+, §§159–165, 15.12.2011 (violation). See also Jane Elliott-Kelly, "Case Analysis – *Al-Khawaja and Tahery v. United Kingdom*", *European Human Rights Law Review*, Issue 1, 2012, pp. 81–87; and Mike

The case *Horncastle and Others v. the United Kingdom* also concerned the hearing of a fearful witness. Two of the applicants had kidnapped a woman in the context of a burglary and had threatened to assault her. She gave a written statement to the police but, owing to her fear, she refused to attend the trial. The Court held that her untested witness statement was not decisive and there was other strong incriminating evidence in the case. Her statement was therefore not the sole or decisive evidence. In these circumstances there was no need to proceed to an examination of the existence of any counterbalancing elements.[1847]

#### 6.5.5.2.2.3. Witnesses Who have Fallen Ill

In order to secure their hearing, active measures should also be taken when witnesses fall ill or are otherwise absent from the trial with a valid reason.[1848] They can be heard with the help of technical means, such as a video link, allowing the reliability of the witness to be assessed. A witness statement can also be recorded as early as in the pretrial investigation phase and an opportunity for cross-examination can be organised in a convenient manner. Also, the use of such statements as decisive evidence requires that the accused can in some way challenge the evidence through cross-examination.[1849]

In the case *Zadumov v. Russia*, a witness was voluntarily hospitalised for treatment for alcohol-induced psychosis. Her pretrial testimony was read out at the trial without the applicant being able to put questions to her. The Court held that there were no good reasons for the witness's absence from the trial hearings and for the reading out of her pretrial statements as evidence because she could have been summonsed to appear at the trial that was still ongoing when she was released from the hospital. Her witness statement had been decisive since she had been the only eye-witness to the crime. Despite the existence in the Russian legal system of robust procedural guarantees securing the right of an accused to examine witnesses testifying against him, the domestic courts had in this case failed to put in place sufficient safeguards capable of compensating for the handicaps caused to the defence.[1850]

---

Redmayne, "Hearsay and human rights: *Al-Khawaja* in the Grand Chamber", *Modern Law Review*, vol. 75, no. 5, 2012, pp. 865–878.

1847 *Horncastle and Others v. the United Kingdom*, App. no. 4184/10, §§144–152, 16.12.2014. See also J.R. Spencer, "Squaring up to Strasbourg: Horncastle in the Supreme Court", *Archbold Review*, Issue 1, 2010, pp. 6–9.

1848 *Bobeş v. Romania*, App. no. 29752/05, §§39–40, 9.7.2013; and *Vronchenko v. Estonia*, App. no. 59632/09, §58, 18.7.2013.

1849 Concerning the hearing of a victim of a sexual crime, see *Bocos-Cuesta v. the Netherlands*, App. no. 54789/00, §§71–72, 10.11.2005 and the cases mentioned below in section 6.5.5.3.

1850 *Zadumov v. Russia*, App. no. 2257/12, §§56, 61 and 65–72, 12.12.2017.

#### 6.5.5.2.2.4. Witnesses Who are Abroad and Unreachable

A witness can also be unable to attend a court hearing as a result of being abroad and therefore unreachable.[1851] In the case *Schatschaschwili v. Germany*, the domestic courts had convicted the applicant of aggravated burglary and extortion. Two Latvian women who worked as prostitutes reported the burglary to the police. These two victims were questioned in the pretrial investigation by the police when they told officers that they intended to return to Latvia. Subsequently, they were summonsed to appear in court but refused to do so, claiming to be too traumatised by the crime. They did not agree to come to Germany, or to be heard in a Latvian court through international legal assistance. Since the respondent State had no means of securing the attendance of these witnesses, their statements were admitted to the case file as evidence. There was also plenty of other evidence, *inter alia*, evidence placing the applicant at the crime scene, his own confession that he had been in the building but for another purpose, the neighbour's testimony about disturbances at the time of the crime, and the testimony of two other Latvian women living in another city that they had been victims of a similar crime committed by the applicant a year earlier.

The Court held that the domestic courts and authorities had made all reasonable efforts within the existing legal framework to secure the attendance of the witnesses and that there was thus a valid excuse for their absence. The two women were the only eye-witnesses to the crime and the role of their statement as evidence was therefore decisive. As to the counterbalancing elements, the Court found that although there were several counterbalancing elements to balance the admission of the untested evidence by the absent witnesses, the investigative authorities knew that the witnesses were residing in Germany only temporarily and that they intended to return to Latvia as soon as possible. In these circumstances, the authorities failed to provide the applicant's counsel with an opportunity to put questions to the witnesses during the pretrial investigation stage. By proceeding in that manner, they took a foreseeable risk, which subsequently materialised, that neither the applicant nor his counsel would be able to question the witnesses at any stage of the proceedings. This omission in relation to decisive evidence rendered the trial as a whole unfair.[1852]

The case *Tseber v. the Czech Republic* also concerned an absent witness residing abroad. The written statement of the victim, who had been assaulted, had been admitted as evidence. This statement was decisive evidence while the other evidence gave only indirect support to it. The victim had been interrogated

1851 *Štefančič v. Slovenia*, App. no. 18027/05, §39, 25.10.2012.
1852 *Schatschaschwili v. Germany* [GC], App. no. 9154/10, §§132–165, 15.12.2015.

during the pretrial investigation in the presence of the investigative judge and he had then identified the applicant as the perpetrator. Subsequently, he left the country and could not be found. The Court found that the presence of the investigative judge was a guarantee that the police conducted the interrogation properly. On the other hand, his presence had no relevance as far as the content and reliability of the witness's statement was concerned, since no challenging arguments had at that stage yet been put forward. The arguments which, *inter alia*, were relevant for the reliability of the witness were that the witness was involved in organised crime, that he had been guilty of making threats and assault, and that he tried take revenge on the applicant. Despite these allegations, the domestic courts did not assess in their reasoning the reliability of the witness in detail but only stated that his statement had been detailed and that the witness had sufficiently identified the applicant. The authorities did not try to acquire other evidence on the issue of reliability. For example, the interrogations were not videotaped, as is done in many countries when there is doubt about a witness appearing at the trial. The Court held that the domestic authorities had not taken necessary procedural measures in order to counterbalance the difficulties caused to the applicant's defence by the witness's absence. As the witness's account had been decisive and there was no strong supporting evidence, the Court held that Articles 6 §1 and 6 §3 (d) had been violated.[1853]

In the case *Paić v. Croatia*, which was delivered after the *Schatschaschwili* judgment, the Court applied the three-step test. The applicant was accused of theft. During the criminal proceedings against him, the female victim, who was of Czech origin, was heard through international legal assistance in the Czech Republic, but neither the applicant nor his representative was given an opportunity to cross-examine her on that occasion. Nor was the victim summonsed to appear at the applicant's trial. Instead, her written statement was read out aloud in the court. The Court held that the victim's written statement was the only and therefore the decisive incriminating evidence against the applicant. The domestic authorities had not even tried to summons the victim. The domestic courts in Croatia had not approached the written statement with care, nor had the applicant had at any point an opportunity to cross-examine the witness. The Court therefore concluded that there were not sufficient counterbalancing factors to compensate for the handicaps faced by the defence as a result of the admission of witness statement. There was thus a violation of Article 6.[1854]

In two other recent cases the outcome was different and the Court did not find a violation. The case *Bátěk and Others v. the Czech Republic* concerned three customs officers who worked at the Slovak border and who were accused of having

1853 *Tseber v. the Czech Republic*, App. no. 46203/08, §§56 and 58–69, 22.11.2012.
1854 *Paić v. Croatia*, App. no. 47082/12, §§49–53, 29.3.2016.

taken bribes from lorry drivers. The charges were based on observations made by a police officer who worked undercover at the customs office. The pretrial investigation was conducted in an accelerated manner in order to interrogate about 20 foreign truck drivers who could probably not be summonsed to the court hearing. They had been interrogated in the presence of a judge but neither the applicants nor their counsels attended these hearings. The truck drivers could not be summonsed to the trial since they could not be reached. Instead, the undercover police officer was heard as a witness in a way that protected his identity; he was placed in another room and only his voice could be heard in the courtroom. The Court found that there had not in fact been any attempts to summons the foreign truck drivers and that there was therefore no good reason for their absence. The use of pretrial investigation statements was therefore deemed unacceptable. Although these statements were not the sole or decisive evidence, they still carried significant weight as evidence. The same was true also for the police officer's statement. The assessment of evidence had, nevertheless, been conducted carefully as a whole and there had also been other evidence against the applicants. The applicants knew the identity of the lorry drivers and could challenge their witness testimonies. It was also relevant that the witnesses had been heard in special proceedings created for dealing with absent witnesses and this hearing had taken place in the presence of a judge. The applicants had also been able to put questions to the police officer and challenge his testimony. In its overall assessment, the Court emphasised the importance of prosecuting perpetrators of corruption crimes and the fact that the proceedings had not been arbitrary. There was thus no violation.[1855]

In the case *Štulíř v. the Czech Republic*, the applicant was accused of coercion in respect of his former partner. In this case, the victim had also been heard during the pretrial investigation in the presence of a judge but without the presence of the applicant. The victim had come from the United Kingdom, where she currently lived, for the hearing but refused to attend the court hearing and her pretrial investigation statement was presented in writing. The applicant was convicted as charged. The Court held that the domestic courts had not even tried to summons the victim, for example, through international legal assistance. Although her statement was not the sole or decisive evidence, it still carried significant weight as evidence. As to the counterbalancing factors, the Court held that the domestic court had assessed the evidence carefully and that there had also been other evidence in the case. The victim had been heard in a procedure especially created for this kind of situation and the applicant could also challenge her statement. No violation was found in this case either.[1856]

---

1855 *Bátěk and Others v. the Czech Republic*, App. no. 54146/09, §§41–63, 12.1.2017 (no violation).
1856 *Štulíř v. the Czech Republic*, App. no. 36705/12, §§57–74, 12.1.2017 (no violation).

#### 6.5.5.2.2.5. Absent Witness Who has been Cross-Examined During Pretrial Investigation

The right of cross-examination of the accused may be arranged in a sufficient manner during the pretrial investigation and the evidence thereby obtained may form a basis for the judgment, even if the witness is absent from the court hearing. The cross-examination conducted during the pretrial investigation phase was found to be sufficient, for example, in the cases *Chmura v. Poland*, *Aigner v. Austria*, *Gani v. Spain* and *Palchik v. Ukraine*. In the first three cases *Chmura*, *Aigner* and *Gani*, the Court also found that the witness in question had had a valid reason for the absence from the court hearing. In contrast, in the case *Palchik v. Ukraine*, there was no such valid reason but the applicant had not even claimed that it would undermine his defence. Moreover, the witness's cross-examination had been video recorded and the recording was viewed at the hearing.[1857]

On the other hand, in situations where the cross-examination of a witness in the pretrial investigation phase is carried out by an investigator who is not independent and impartial; who has the right, at his or her discretion, not to put the accused's questions to the witness; and where the accused is not represented, that questioning cannot replace the hearing of the witness in trial. This was the case, for example, in cases *Melnikov v. Russia*, *Karpenko v. Russia*, *Vanfuli v. Russia* and *Nechto v. Russia*.[1858]

It may also happen that although a witness is present at a court hearing, certain procedural errors or other incidents may prevent his or her being heard. In such cases the *Al-Khawaja and Tahery* criteria apply. For example, the Court found a violation in the case *Ürek and Ürek v. Turkey*, in which the witnesses had been heard in court, in the absence of the accused, on a date other than when they had been summonsed to appear because the witnesses had had a valid reason not to appear on the date they had been summoned.[1859]

#### 6.5.5.2.2.6. Hearing of (Silent) Co-Defendants

Co-defendants are often heard as witnesses as part of a process to establish the guilt of another defendant. In these situations, the same principles apply as to other situations where evidence is given. In the case *Mild and Virtanen v. Finland*,

---

1857 *Chmura v. Poland*, App. no. 18475/05, §§50 and 56–57, 3.4.2012; *Aigner v. Austria*, App. no. 28328/03, §§39 and 41–46, 10.5.2012; *Gani v. Spain*, App. no. 61800/08, §§45 and 48–50, 19.2.2013; and *Palchik v. Ukraine*, App. no. 16980/06, §§50–52, 2.3.2017.

1858 *Melnikov v. Russia*, App. no. 23610/03, §§78–81, 14.1.2010; *Karpenko v. Russia*, App. no. 5605/04, §§67–69, 13.3.2012; *Vanfuli v. Russia*, App. no. 24885/05, §115, 3.11.2011; and *Nechto v. Russia*, App. no. 24893/05, §123, 24.1.2012.

1859 *Ürek and Ürek v. Turkey*, App. no. 74845/12, §49, 30.7.2019.

the Court found a violation when the statements given by the co-accused in another trial were used as written evidence without the co-accused being heard in person at the trial.[1860]

Problematic situations may arise if a co-defendant present at the trial uses his or her right to remain silent and refuses to say anything, in which case the prosecution may admit the co-defendant's written statement as evidence. In the case *Kaste and Mathisen v. Norway*, the problem was that the co-defendant remained silent and that it was impossible to challenge the reliability of his statements. On appeal, the co-defendant had appealed only against the sentence and was present only for that. The Court found that there was a genuine problem because the written statement of the co-defendant had been considered decisive, and it therefore found a violation in the case.[1861]

In the post-*Schatschaschwili* case of *Seton v. the United Kingdom*, the applicant was accused of a murder which, according to him, had been committed by his co-defendant. The co-defendant had refused to comment on the issue in the pretrial investigation and to appear as a witness at the hearing. Since the co-defendant, who was detained, had commented on the murder in a telephone conversation which was recorded by the prison authorities, the phone recordings were presented as evidence at the applicant's trial. This witness was not summonsed to appear in court since there were no realistic chances that his testimony would generate any useful evidence. The Court was not convinced that all possible means had been used to secure the attendance of the witness. However, the fact alone that a witness was absent without a good reason or was not summonsed to the hearing did not render the proceedings unfair. The witness had actually been an available but reluctant witness. Even though this untested evidence was not the sole or decisive basis for the applicant's conviction, it still needed to be determined whether there existed sufficient factors counterbalancing any handicaps that the admission of that evidence might have entailed for the defence. Besides the phone recordings, there had been other overwhelming evidence incriminating the applicant. Because of the existence of this other evidence, which was decisive, and the sufficient counterbalancing factors, the Court held that there was no violation of Article 6 even though the untested phone recordings were used as evidence against the applicant.[1862]

###### 6.5.5.2.2.7. Spouse's Refusal to Testify

It is quite common that a spouse refuses to testify against the other spouse, especially in cases concerning domestic violence. In the case *N.K. v. Germany*

1860 *Mild and Virtanen v. Finland*, App. nos. 39481/98+, §§45–47, 26.7.2005.
1861 *Kaste and Mathisen v. Norway*, App. nos. 18885/04+, §§51–52 and 54, 9.11.2006.
1862 *Seton v. the United Kingdom*, App. no. 55287/10, §§61–70, 31.3.2016.

the applicant's wife had been subjected to domestic violence by the applicant and she had moved to a women's shelter. During the pretrial investigation, she told about the applicant's violence to an investigating judge, but neither the applicant nor his counsel was provided with an opportunity to cross-examine her during the investigative stage of the proceedings. At the trial the wife refused to testify. At the trial the domestic court heard a counsellor from the women's shelter who said that the severely traumatised wife had given a detailed account of the violence and had consistently named the applicant as the perpetrator. The court also heard the wife's son, who said that he had heard the couple scream; the neighbours to whom the wife had run for help; and the police officers on call who had heard the wife's account of the abuse by the applicant. In addition, the court had as evidence a letter which the applicant had forced his wife to write to the wife of her former lover.[1863]

The Court held that the wife had been entitled, according to domestic law, to refuse to give evidence against the applicant because she was married to him. There had thus been a good reason for her not appearing for cross-examination at the trial. The account given by the wife to the investigating judge was thus accepted as evidence since the other evidence in the case supported it. The wife's account carried significant weight in the applicant's conviction. As noted already by the domestic court, the applicant's counsel should have been given an opportunity to cross-examine the wife during the pretrial investigation. Therefore, the investigating authorities carried the risk of the wife's refusal to testify and the unacceptability of the pretrial statements as evidence. Nevertheless, the domestic courts had carefully assessed the credibility of the wife's statement and it was strongly supported by the other evidence. The applicant had had an opportunity to present his version of the incident, which he had also done. The Court held that, when making an overall assessment, the weight of the wife's statement for the applicant's conviction, the domestic court's approach to assessing that statement, the availability and strength of further incriminating evidence and the compensatory procedural measures taken by the domestic court were all capable of compensating for the handicaps under which the defence laboured, and that the proceedings were thus not unfair.[1864]

Another interesting case concerning a spouse's right not to testify was the case *Kryževičius v. Lithuania*, in which the applicant, a company director, had been called as a witness in a case in which his wife, the finance director, was heard as a "special witness", testifying about alleged illegal money transfers made by the company. To such a witness the prosecutor could put questions about his or her own criminal activity. The applicant refused to testify against his wife, relying on a law provision releasing family members from testifying against each

[1863] *N.K. v. Germany*, App. no. 59549/12, §§19–29, 26.7.2018.
[1864] *N.K. v. Germany*, App. no. 59549/12, §§56–62, 26.7.2018 (no violation).

other, and he was fined. The Court examined the matter under the family life aspect of Article 8 and held that the status of a special witness could be equated with that of a suspect and could not provide protection against indictments. Therefore, a family member had the right to refuse to testify in the matter. The imposition of fines on the applicant therefore violated his right to respect for family life under Article 8.[1865]

#### 6.5.5.2.2.8. Changed Composition of the Court and Related Absences

The principle of immediacy requires that an accused can cross-examine witnesses in the presence of the judge who is going to decide the case.[1866] Therefore, in general, when the composition of a court changes, the key witnesses should be heard again. Although this is not an absolute principle, it is nevertheless essential that the judges taking over a case have an appropriate understanding of the arguments put forward and the evidence presented. This can be secured, for example, by providing a transcript of witness testimonies in cases where the reliability of witnesses is not at stake or by rehearing certain witnesses on certain evidence themes.[1867] The Court has found an Article 6 violation in cases such as *Crovšek and Božičnik v. Slovenia*, *Cutean v. Romania* and *Svanidze v. Georgia*, where the composition of the domestic court had changed in its entirety and the witnesses had not been heard again.[1868] On the other hand, no violation was found in the cases *P.K. v. Finland*, *Graviano v. Italy* and *Škaro v. Croatia*, in which evidence was not received again when only part of the composition of the court had changed.[1869]

The case *Chernika v. Ukraine* concerned a drug offence committed by a police officer. Three witnesses had been heard in the pretrial investigation and the applicant had been able to cross-examine them. During the trial, two witnesses did not appear in court and one witness present repeated his statement given during the pretrial investigation. The applicant was convicted and sentenced to a prison sentence of eight years. On appeal, the Court of Appeal referred the case back to the District Court because of the missing witnesses. Meanwhile, the judge had changed. During the retrial, none of the witnesses appeared in court, two of them being seriously ill. The court heard other, indirect witnesses and

1865 *Kryževičius v. Lithuania*, App. no. 67816/14, §§51–55 and 59–70, 11.12.2018 (violation of Article 8). See also *Van der Heijden v. the Netherlands* [GC], App. no. 42857/05, §§62 and 76, 3.4.2012 (no violation); and *Sofri and Others v. Italy* (dec.), App. no. 37235/97, 4.3.2003.

1866 See also Chapter 4, section 4.2.9. above.

1867 *Cutean v. Romania*, App. no. 53150/12, §61, 2.12.2014.

1868 *Cerovšek and Božičnik v. Slovenia*, App. nos. 68939/12+, §§44–48, 7.3.2017 (violation); *Cutean v. Romania*, App. no. 53150/12, §§70–73, 21.4.2009 (violation); and *Svanidze v. Georgia*, App. no. 37809/08, §§35–38, 25.7.2019 (violation).

1869 *P.K. v. Finland* (dec.), App. no. 37442/97, 9.7.2002; *Graviano v. Italy*, App. no. 10075/02, §§39–40, 10.2.2005; and *Škaro v. Croatia*, App. no. 6962/13, §§22–31, 6.12.2016.

the applicant was convicted and sentenced again to the same sentence as before. The Court considered that all three witnesses were decisive. The composition of the District Court had changed in its entirety and the new composition had not reheard the witnesses. The Court considered that, on the one hand, the domestic court had not been sufficiently active in seeking the attendance of one of the witnesses and, on the other hand, no explanation had been given for the absence of the two others from the first hearing. As all three witnesses had been decisive witnesses, weight needed to be given to the counterbalancing factors. Such factors were, for example, the possibility for an applicant to present his or her own version of the case (which the applicant in this case did), other evidence given by other witnesses supporting the charge, and whether or not an applicant had been able to cross-examine the witnesses during the pretrial investigation (which the present applicant had been able to do). However, the fact that an applicant had an opportunity to challenge and rebut the absent witnesses' statements could not, of itself, be regarded as a sufficient counterbalancing factor to compensate for the handicap for the defence created by the witnesses' absence. Also any probative evidence would be of limited evidential value only. The value of the cross-examination at the pretrial investigation stage was naturally undermined by the fact that the applicant had had only limited access to the investigation file but this was not in the Court's view so severe as to render, on its own, the confrontations entirely inadequate as a procedural safeguard. Moreover, despite the above handicaps, another problem was that the judge who had convicted the applicant had had access to the pretrial statements but had not been able to hear the witnesses himself, nor did he have access to video recordings of the witnesses' hearings. Nor was there any valid reason for the absence of one witness from the court. In these circumstances, there were no strong counterbalancing factors involved and therefore, on the basis of the overall assessment, the Court found a violation.[1870]

### 6.5.5.3. *Hearing Witnesses in Sexual Crime Cases*

In the context of sexual crime, the Court has held that the methods that in a "normal" case would not fulfil the requirements of Article 6 §3 (d) concerning the cross-examination of a witness at the trial can be necessary and sufficient in cases concerning sexual crime.

#### 6.5.5.3.1. Sexual Abuse of a Child

Witness-related problems often appear in cases concerning the sexual abuse of a child. When a child is interrogated during the pretrial investigation phase and

---

1870 *Chernika v. Ukraine*, App. no. 53791/11, §§39–78, 12.3.2020 (violation).

this interrogation has been videotaped, if the accused and his or her counsel can either directly or through the investigator put questions to the victim, and if the evidence is carefully assessed, the rights of the defence have adequately been taken care of and the conviction can be based on such untested evidence. If the evidence is decisive, it must be assessed with a particular care.

These central principles applying to cases concerning the sexual abuse of a child were laid down in the case *S.N. v. Sweden*. In that case the Court held that Article 6 §3 (d) was to be interpreted with a certain flexibility and that the particular characteristics of trials concerning sexual crime were to be taken into account. For the victim of a sexual crime, the trial is often an ordeal, especially if he or she has to face the accused unwillingly. These characteristics are even more accentuated in cases concerning children. Attention must also be paid to the victim's right to respect for private life. Therefore, in cases concerning sexual abuse, measures can be taken in order to protect the victim if such measures can be reconciled with the proper and effective exercise of the rights of the accused.[1871] In the *S.N. v. Sweden* case, the statement of a 10-year-old boy was in practice the only evidence upon which the accused was convicted.[1872] The child was not heard at the trial but the video recording made of his first interrogation was viewed by the court. Moreover, the minutes drafted from his second interrogation were read out loud and the tape recording of the interrogation was played at the trial. The counsel for the accused was not present in the interrogations but the second interrogation took place because the counsel had extra questions to put to the victim. The Court found that the accused had had, through his counsel, an adequate opportunity to challenge the witness statement and its reliability.[1873] Moreover, the Court emphasised that in cases in which evidence is acquired in circumstances where the rights of the accused cannot be secured to the extent normally required by the Convention, the assessment of evidence must be done with particular care.[1874]

In many child abuse cases the Court has detected procedural mistakes and has often found a violation in such cases. The problem has often been that defendants have not been given at any stage of the proceedings the chance to put questions to the child either directly or through the investigator. In the case *B. v. Finland*, the Court did not find any violation as the accused was provided with an opportunity to do so but she did not use it. It was thus considered that she had waived her right to cross-examine the child.[1875]

---

1871 *S.N. v. Sweden*, App. no. 34209/96, §§47 and 52, 2.7.2002.

1872 *S.N. v. Sweden*, App. no. 34209/96, §46, 2.7.2002.

1873 *S.N. v. Sweden*, App. no. 34209/96, §§49–52, 2.7.2002.

1874 *S.N. v. Sweden*, App. no. 34209/96, §53, 2.7.2002. The Court held that the standards for a hearing involving a child had been respected, and that the domestic court had carefully considered the weaknesses caused by the untested evidence.

1875 *B. v. Finland*, App. no. 17122/02, §§44–45, 24.4.2007. Similarly, for rape cases, see *Gani v. Spain*, App. no. 61800/08, §44, 19.2.2013.

On the other hand, if the child's account has been the sole or decisive evidence but the accused has not been provided with an opportunity to put questions either during the pretrial investigation or later at the trial, the Court has found a violation. A typical case is that of *W. v. Finland*, which concerned the sexual abuse of children by the next-door neighbour. The interrogations of the children during the pretrial investigation were videotaped and submitted as evidence at the trial. In addition, the court also heard parents and an expert who testified about the reliability of the children's accounts. The defendant was not, however, provided with an opportunity to put questions to the children. The children's accounts were, however, the sole direct evidence on which the conviction was based.[1876]

The situation was similar in the case *A.H. v. Finland*, which concerned child abuse which had taken place in a kindergarten. The child's interrogation was videotaped but the applicant was not provided with any opportunity to put questions to the child. The child's account was the decisive evidence. The Court did not find any obstacles preventing the organisation one way or another of a cross-examination. In these circumstances, the use of untested evidence against the accused violated his right to an extent that the proceedings could no longer be regarded as fair.[1877] The same mistake was also found in the cases *A.L. v. Finland*,[1878] *D. v. Finland*[1879] and *A.S. v. Finland*.[1880]

Similarly, in the case *Vronchenko v. Estonia*, which concerned the rape and sexual abuse of a child by her step-father, the child's interrogation during the pretrial investigation was videotaped. However, no opportunity for cross-examination was organised either during the pretrial investigation or at the trial. The Court found, in the light of the *Al-Khawaja and Tahery* case, that there was an acceptable reason for the absence of the abused child from the trial and that the interrogations recorded during the pretrial investigation formed the decisive evidence on which the conviction was based. However, there were insufficient counterbalancing factors to remedy the limitation of the rights of the defence. The pretrial investigation authorities had, from the beginning, prepared the investigation in such a manner that the child was not to be heard at the trial, but they still failed to organise any cross-examination during the pretrial investigation and to reply to the applicant's requests to that effect. All other witnesses who gave testimonies before the court could only provide indirect evidence. The experts did not analyse the reliability of the child's account and their statements were only written and not tested in person at the trial. Nor did any other evidence, such as DNA evidence and the medical examination of the child, support the charges. There was thus no strong, supporting evidence

---

1876 *W. v. Finland*, App. no. 14151/02, §§46–47, 24.4.2007.

1877 *A.H. v. Finland*, App. no. 46602/99, §§43–44, 10.5.2007.

1878 *A.L. v. Finland*, App. no. 23220/04, §§40–44, 27.1.2009.

1879 *D. v. Finland*, App. no. 30542/04, §51, 7.7.2009.

1880 *A.S. v. Finland*, App. no. 40156/07, §§66 and 68, 28.9.2010.

for the child's account. Although the authorities had acted in the best interests of the child and her account could be assessed on the basis of the video recording, the rights of the defence had not been properly secured. The Court also took into account the seriousness of the charges and the fact that the pretrial investigation authorities should have looked into organising the cross-examination during the pretrial investigation phase. There were thus no sufficient counterbalancing factors to make good the limitation of the rights of the defence.[1881]

#### 6.5.5.3.2. Sexual Abuse of an Adult

The Court has up until now followed a very strict line in cases concerning sexual crime when the sole or decisive evidence has been untested. It is possible that the Grand Chamber judgment in *Al-Khawaja and Tahery v. the United Kingdom*, which was rendered in 2011, may to a certain extent alleviate this strict line of interpretation if there is strong expert or other evidence supporting the written statement and if it is possible to assess the reliability of the statement, for example, on the basis of a video recording.[1882]

Such signs may be detected from the case *Gani v. Spain*, in which the hearing of the victim of a rape and other aggravated assaults had to be interrupted because of her post-traumatic stress reaction before the defence's cross-examination had taken place, and her statement given during the pretrial investigation was subsequently admitted as evidence. In its judgment the Court referred to the opportunity given to the applicant to put questions to the victim during the investigative stage of the proceedings, to the careful and detailed comparison made by the domestic courts concerning the reliability of the victim's and the accused's versions of the facts, and to the medical opinions and reports confirming that the victim's bodily injuries and psychological condition were consistent with her account of the facts. There had therefore been sufficient counterbalancing factors to conclude that the admission as evidence of the victim's statements had not resulted in a breach of Article 6 §1 read in conjunction with Article 6 §3 (d) of the Convention.[1883]

### *6.5.5.4. Anonymous Witnesses*

The Court has also created significant case-law under Article 6 §3 (d) in cases concerning anonymous witnesses.[1884] The situation of an anonymous witness and

---

1881 *Vronchenko v. Estonia*, App. no. 59632/09, §§57–66, 18.7.2013.

1882 *Al-Khawaja and Tahery v. the United Kingdom* [GC], App. nos. 26766/05+, §147, 15.12.2011.

1883 *Gani v. Spain*, App. no. 61800/08, §§48–49, 19.2.2013. See also the case *D.T. v. the Netherlands* (dec.), App. no. 25307/10, §§44–52, 2.4.2013.

1884 *Al-Khawaja and Tahery v. the United* Kingdom [GC], App. nos. 26766/05+, §127, 15.12.2011; *Scholer v. Germany*, App. no. 14212/10, §51, 18.12.2014; *Balta and Demir v. Turkey*,

that of an absent witness do not, as such, differ much from each other. The Court has first of all held that the Convention does not prevent to use of anonymous police reports in criminal investigations. Nor is it necessarily incompatible with the Convention to rely, at the investigation stage, on sources such as anonymous informants.[1885] It cannot always be required that the accused or his or her counsel directly cross-examines a witness; nor is it always necessary to hear a witness publicly at the trial.[1886]

Anonymous witnesses are often used in the context of undercover operations. More information about undercover operations from the point of view of Article 6 §1 and about the material and procedural test created by the Court in its Grand Chamber judgment *Ramanauskas v. Lithuania*[1887] are found in Chapter 4, section 4.2.6.2.4. above.

It is, however, apparent from the Court's case-law that in all situations in which evidence cannot be received according to the "ideal standards", the Court requires that the rights of the defence and those of the witnesses are balanced against each other. When using anonymous witnesses, there is also a markedly strict obligation to explain why such a method is chosen. In such situations, the domestic courts must also assess whether the evidence received from anonymous witnesses was the sole or decisive evidence on which the conviction was based.[1888]

The same rules thus apply to anonymous witnesses as to the receipt of evidence from an absent witness: there must be a good reason for the anonymity,

---

App. no. 48628/12, §§36–41, 23.6.2015; and *Asani v. "the former Yugoslav Republic of Macedonia"*, App. no. 27962/10, §§36–37, 1.2.2018.

1885 *Doorson v. the Netherlands*, App. no. 20524/92, §69, 26.3.1996.

1886 *Doorson v. the Netherlands*, App. no. 20524/92, §73, 26.3.1996. In this case the counsel of the accused was present at the interrogation and could put questions to the witnesses. He was not, however, allowed to know the identity of the witnesses or to formulate such questions which could have disclosed their identity. The questions were asked by the investigative judge who knew the identity of the witnesses. As the evidence given by the witnesses was not decisive, the Court found no violation.

1887 The principles applicable to evidence obtained through undercover operations have been crystallised in the case *Ramanauskas v. Lithuania*, in which the Court created specific tests both for the substantive and procedural aspects of Article 6. The substantive test measures whether the authorities have been essentially passive in respect of the undercover activities in such a way that they have not exerted any influence on the subject as to incite the commission of an offence that would otherwise not have been committed. This means that the reason for the undercover activities has been an objective suspicion of a crime and that the authorities have been passive vis-à-vis the undercover activities. The procedural test measures how the domestic courts have dealt with the undercover allegations, that is, whether the defendant has had an opportunity to defend him- or herself against the evidence obtained through undercover actions and whether these allegations have also been examined when the defendant has admitted the charges. In addition, it is the duty of a public prosecutor to show that no undercover activities have been used where the defendant so alleges, unless the defendant's allegation in this respect is clearly without any basis. See *Ramanauskas v. Lithuania* [GC], App. no. 74420/01, §§49–61, 5.2.2008.

1888 *Al-Khawaja and Tahery v. the United Kingdom* [GC], App. nos. 26766/05+, §128, 15.12.2011.

and even when evidence given by an anonymous witness is the sole or decisive evidence, its admission as evidence does not automatically lead to a violation of Article 6 §1 of the Convention. Particular emphasis in these situations is placed on procedural safeguards which counterbalance the shortcomings of the procedure. In practice this means that the protection of a witness does not go any further than is strictly necessary, and that all possible alternative ways of hearing witnesses are used. In addition, it is expected that the assessment of evidence is thorough and appropriate so that the reliability of the evidence is analysed in detail and a stance is taken on the views expressed by the accused. It is only acceptable to base a conviction solely or decisively on evidence given by an anonymous witness when such evidence can be found to be sufficiently reliable.[1889]

#### 6.5.5.4.1. Valid Reasons for Using Anonymous Witnesses

In all situations, the domestic courts are under a duty to explain why a witness needs to be protected by anonymity. This issue has come up in the Court's case-law, in particular in the context of drugs offences. In the case *Doorson v. the Netherlands*, the domestic court appropriately reasoned the need to protect the witnesses from the threat of reprisals by the drug dealers because one of the witnesses had earlier been assaulted in a similar situation and the other had been threatened.[1890] In the case *Krasniki v. the Czech Republic*, on the other hand, the Court held that although the domestic court had apparently taken into account the fact that drug dealers often threatened and assaulted witnesses and that the witnesses therefore had a reason to fear reprisals, this did not appear in the court's reasoning.[1891]

The need to protect witnesses was reasoned in the case *Sarkizov and Others v. Bulgaria* concerning procuration (or "pimping"), in which the Court held that the threat of reprisals by the procurers was a good reason for protecting the witnesses.[1892] In the case *Ellis and Simms and Martin v. the United Kingdom*, the ground for the anonymity was the witnesses' credible fear that their lives could be in danger owing to the fact that they had been witnesses to a gang war which had resulted in casualties.[1893]

---

[1889] *Al-Khawaja and Tahery v. the United Kingdom* [GC], App. nos. 26766/05+, §§142 and 145–147, 15.12.2011 (partial violation).

[1890] *Doorson v. the Netherlands*, App. no. 20524/92, §71, 26.3.1996. See also Eva Brems, "Conflicting human rights: an exploration in the context of the right to fair trial in the European Convention for the Protection of Human Rights and Fundamental Freedoms", *Human Rights Quarterly*, vol. 27, no. 1, 2005, pp. 294–326, at pp. 316–318.

[1891] *Krasniki v. the Czech Republic*, App. no. 51277/99, §§81–84, 28.2.2006. The Court found a violation as the conviction was to a large extent based on statements by anonymous witnesses.

[1892] *Sarkizov and Others v. Bulgaria*, App. nos. 37981/06+, §56, 17.4.2012.

[1893] *Ellis and Simms and Martin v. the United Kingdom* (dec.), App. nos. 46099/06+, §80, 10.4.2012.

As to the good reason, the Court has paid particular attention to situations in which the anonymous witnesses have been police officers. In the case *Van Mechelen and Others v. the Netherlands*, the Court held that there was a difference between a situation in which witnesses needed protection because they were a victim of a crime or a bystander and, because of a fear of reprisals, needed anonymity, and that in which the witness needing protection was a police officer. Although a police officer also has an undeniable interest in protecting his or her family, a police officer is still part of the State apparatus and the prosecuting authorities. The Court considered that there was no sufficient information in the case to suggest that the witnesses would have been subjected to a threat of reprisals, or that alternative and less drastic means of protection were not possible.[1894]

#### 6.5.5.4.2. Significance of Anonymous Witnesses

The principles concerning the use of anonymous witnesses were established in some of the Court's older case-law. The Court's newer jurisprudence is represented by its rulings given after the above-mentioned case *Al-Khawaja and Tahery v. the United Kingdom.*

A good example of the older type of case is *Kostovski v. the Netherlands*,[1895] in which the police and the investigative judge heard witnesses who, because of fear of reprisals, wanted to remain anonymous and who were thus not heard in person at the trial. The defence was, however, provided with an opportunity to cross-examine the police officers and the investigative judge that had interrogated the witnesses. The Court found, however, a violation of Article 6 §3 (d), as the anonymous statements given to the police and the investigative judge formed decisive evidence from witnesses whom the defence was not able to cross-examine, either during the pretrial investigation or later at the trial.[1896]

---

1894 *Van Mechelen and Others v. the Netherlands*, App. nos. 21363/93+, §§56 and 63, 23.4.1997. See also Eva Brems, "Conflicting human rights: an exploration in the context of the right to fair trial in the European Convention for the Protection of Human Rights and Fundamental Freedoms", *Human Rights Quarterly*, vol. 27, no. 1, 2005, pp. 294–326, at p. 318; and Luzius Wildhaber, "Precedent in the European Court of Human Rights", in Paul Mahoney, Franz Matscher, Herbert Petzold, Luzius Wildhaber (Eds.), *Protection des Droits de L'homme: La Perspective Européenne, Mélanges à la Mémoire de Rolv Ryssdal/Protecting Human Rights: The European Perspective, Studies in Memory of Rolv Ryssdal*, Carl Heymanns Verlag, Köln/Berlin/Bonn/München 2000, pp. 1529–1545, at pp. 1543–1545.

1895 *Kostovski v. the Netherlands*, App. no. 11454/85, §41, 20.11.1989.

1896 *Kostovski v. the Netherlands*, App. no. 11454/85, §§42–44, 20.11.1989. See also Yvonne McDermott, "Absent witnesses and the right to confrontation: the influence of the jurisprudence of the European Court of Human Rights on international criminal law", in Paolo Lobba, Triestino Mariniello (Eds.), *Judicial Dialogue on Human Rights – The Practice of International Criminal Tribunals*, Brill Nijhoff, Leiden/Boston 2018, pp. 225–242, at pp. 228–230.

In a later case, *Doorson v. the Netherlands*, the Court interpreted even more strictly the criterion of decisiveness of the untested evidence as a basis for conviction and extended it to apply also to any evidence based solely or to a decisive extent on statements from witnesses whom the accused had not been able to cross-examine. In addition, the Court found that although the inconveniences caused to the defence would have been counterbalanced appropriately, the decisive evidence could not be based on statements by anonymous witnesses.[1897]

This principle was also spelled out in the case *Van Mechelen and Others v. the Netherlands*, in which anonymous police officers were heard as witnesses via special arrangements in a case concerning attempted murder and robbery. The investigative judge interrogated them in a separate room linked by an audio feed to another room in which the accused and their counsel were present. In this case, the Court paid attention to the fact that the defence could not observe the witnesses' behaviour during the interrogations in order to assess their reliability and, additionally, the identity of the witnesses was not disclosed to the defence. It was not sufficient for the rights of the defence that the investigative judge gave a statement about the reliability of the witnesses and knew their identity. What was also relevant in this case was that the sole and decisive evidence was the anonymous evidence from witnesses whom the defence had no opportunity to cross-examine appropriately.[1898] This line of reasoning has been followed by the Court ever since.[1899]

In situations where the conviction of the accused has not been based to a decisive extent on untested evidence and where the witness in question has not been a key witness,[1900] the counterbalancing has been focused on the question of whether the rights of the defence have been respected. In the case *Doorson v. the Netherlands*, the Court found that if the anonymous testimony was relevant

---

1897 *Doorson v. the Netherlands*, App. no. 20524/92, §76, 26.3.1996. See also Eva Brems, "Conflicting human rights: an exploration in the context of the right to fair trial in the European Convention for the Protection of Human Rights and Fundamental Freedoms", *Human Rights Quarterly*, vol. 27, no. 1, 2005, pp. 294–326, at pp. 316–318.

1898 *Van Mechelen and Others v. the Netherlands*, App. nos. 21363/93+, §§59–64, 23.4.1997. It was also relevant in this case that the sole and decisive evidence was based on anonymous testimonies which the defence was unable to challenge in a proper manner. See also Eva Brems, "Conflicting human rights: an exploration in the context of the right to fair trial in the European Convention for the Protection of Human Rights and Fundamental Freedoms", *Human Rights Quarterly*, vol. 27, no. 1, 2005, pp. 294–326, at p. 318; and Luzius Wildhaber, "Precedent in the European Court of Human Rights", in Paul Mahoney, Franz Matscher, Herbert Petzold, Luzius Wildhaber (Eds.), *Protection des Droits de L'homme: La Perspective Européenne, Mélanges à la Mémoire de Rolv Ryssdal/Protecting Human Rights: The European Perspective, Studies in Memory of Rolv Ryssdal*, Carl Heymanns Verlag, Köln/Berlin/Bonn/München 2000, pp. 1529–1545, at pp. 1543–1545.

1899 *Visser v. the Netherlands*, App. no. 26668/95, §50, 14.2.2002. In this case the conviction was based to a decisive extent on anonymous testimonies. See also *Krasniki v. the Czech Republic*, App. no. 51277/99, §84, 28.2.2006.

1900 *Mirilashvili v. Russia*, App. no. 6293/04, §164, 11.12.2008.

but not decisive vis-à-vis the outcome of the case, the limitation of the rights of the defence was not of the same gravity as when the evidence was decisive. This principle was repeated in the case *Kok v. the Netherlands*,[1901] in which the anonymous testimony was necessary but not decisive. In that case the Court found that the defence was handicapped to a lesser degree than it would have been had the anonymous evidence been decisive to the outcome.[1902]

The newer, clearer analysis has been applied in the Court's case-law following the *Al-Khawaja and Tahery v. the United Kingdom* case. These principles were applied in the case *Ellis and Simms and Martin v. the United Kingdom*, which concerned a gang war which led to casualties. Because of a fear of reprisals, one of the witnesses was given a pseudo-identity during the pretrial investigation and he was heard as an anonymous witness. The prosecution also submitted as evidence some telephone tapping material. The jury, judge, counsels and the prosecutor both saw and heard the anonymous witness. The accused and those in the public gallery could not see the witness but heard his testimony. The Court found first of all that a fear of reprisals was a valid reason to accept the use of anonymous witnesses. The Court examined next whether anonymous testimony was the sole or decisive evidence in the case, finding that it was not the sole but indeed the decisive evidence in the case. Then the Court examined whether the procedural safeguards of the defence were sufficient and deemed that they were, because members of the court and the defence counsels could see the witness and could ask him questions. Moreover, the judge had carefully considered the granting of the anonymity and had taken a careful approach to it, and had given detailed instructions to the jury on how to assess such evidence. In addition, the defence had some necessary information about the anonymous witness so that a cross-examination was possible, and the defence could assess and challenge the reliability of the witness. There were thus sufficient safeguards to prevent the rights of the defence being limited to an extent that would lead to a violation of Articles 6 §1 and 6 §3 (d).[1903]

Almost the same arrangements were in use in the case of *Pesukic v. Switzerland*, which concerned a drug-related homicide. The witness had seen the accused kill a person by shooting him in the neck. As he feared reprisals, his hearing was organised so that he was together with the judge, jury and the prosecutor in one room while the accused, his counsel and the public were in another room. Between the rooms there was an audio link and the voice of the

---

1901 *Kok v. the Netherlands* (dec.), App. no. 43149/98, 4.7.2000.

1902 Similarly, for example, in *Nesterov v. Estonia* (dec.), App. no. 30389/03, 21.10.2005; *Haas v. Germany* (dec.), App. no. 73047/01, 17.11.2005; *Calabro v. Italy and Germany* (dec.), App. no. 59895/00, 21.3.2002; and *Gossa v. Poland*, App. no. 47986/99, §§60–63, 9.1.2007.

1903 *Ellis and Simms and Martin v. the United Kingdom* (dec.), App. nos. 46099/06+, §§80–89, 10.4.2012. The witness's voice, which was transmitted to the defendants and the public, was modified to secure his anonymity.

witness was altered. The counsel for the accused was able to put questions to the witness through the audio link. The Court held first of all that there had been sufficient grounds for granting the victim anonymity because of the nature of the crime in question, the link to drugs and the witness's genuine fear of reprisal. Second, the Court found that the anonymous evidence had been decisive but not the sole evidence against the accused. Also, the legal safeguards counterbalancing the detriment to the rights of the defence had been sufficient, as the witness was heard by the judge, his identity was known to the judge, prosecutor and the police, and a statement had been given about the witness's clean criminal record and his reputation. Moreover, the witness had been heard before the deciding authorities, who could directly assess his credibility. The Court did not consider it necessary for the counsel of the accused to be in the same room as the witness, as this might have jeopardised the witness's safety. The legal safeguards counterbalancing the limitations to the rights of the defence had been sufficient and the Court did not therefore find a violation.[1904]

The use of anonymous police witnesses was also an issue in the case *Van Wesenbeeck v. Belgium*, in which the Court held that undercover activities were a necessary tool in the fight against organised crime, as long as they are only used in exceptional cases. In addition to anonymous testimonies, there was also other evidence in this case and the proceedings contained sufficient procedural safeguards since a specific panel had verified the identity of the anonymous police witnesses as well as the legality of the undercover operation. The applicant thus had the opportunity to challenge the evidence and no violation was found by the Court.[1905]

Sufficient legal safeguards were also in place in the case *Sarkizov and Others v. Bulgaria*, which concerned the protection of the victims of sexual procuration through anonymity. The Court held that the threat of reprisals from the procurers was a good reason for protecting the witnesses. The limited rights of the defence had been sufficiently counterbalanced by the fact that, during the pretrial investigation phase, the hearing of witnesses had been done by the judge. Moreover, after the interrogation of the witnesses, the defendants had been given an opportunity to ask their own questions and to challenge the evidence. They, however, declined to do so, for which reason the Court considered that they had waived their right to a cross-examination. In addition, it was relevant that the conviction was not based solely or decisively on the anonymous testimonies. A lot of other evidence had also been admitted to the domestic court, such as reports on money transfers, information from the border control database, results from the use of special surveillance measures and statements from other witnesses, which the defendants could challenge and on which they could base

---

1904 *Pesukic v. Switzerland*, App. no. 25088/07, §§48–52, 6.12.2012.

1905 *Van Wesenbeeck v. Belgium*, App. no. 67496/10, §§96–112, 23.5.2017 (no violation).

an assessment of the reliability of the anonymous witnesses' testimonies. The domestic court based its conviction on a careful assessment of the evidence and on the fact that other evidence supported the anonymous testimonies. In conclusion, the Court found that the applicants' rights under Article 6 were not unacceptably restricted and that they were able to participate effectively in the proceedings.[1906]

Problems with the interrogation of an anonymous witness were also a feature of the case *Papadakis v. "the former Yugoslav Republic of Macedonia"*, in which undercover activities had been used to reveal drug crimes. An undercover police officer was heard at the trial in the presence of the judge and the prosecutor under a cloak of complete anonymity, meaning that the defendant or his counsel were able to assess the reliability of the witness through visual or oral contact, or through putting direct questions to the witness. Domestic legislation, however, allowed for several alternative means for arranging hearings, such as the use of an audio link. There was a need for cross-examination as the statement of the undercover police officer had been used to undermine the other testimonies. His statement was thus not the sole evidence but it was decisive. The lack of direct cross-examination was not sufficiently compensated for by the statement of the president of the court about the reliability of the witness's statement. The Court found that the protection of the witness had gone too far and that there were no sufficient counterbalancing measures to compensate for the limitations on the defence, nor were there sufficient procedural safeguards.[1907]

## 6.5.6. RIGHT TO CALL AND HEAR WITNESSES

Article 6 §3 (d) also contains the right to obtain the attendance and examination of witnesses on one's behalf as well as the right to present one's own evidence. However, such a right can also be waived. A waiver must be established in an unequivocal manner and be attended by minimum safeguards commensurate with its importance. Although a waiver does not need to be express and can also be tacit, it needs to be done of one's own free will and it must be shown that applicant could reasonably have foreseen what the consequences of his or her

---

1906 *Sarkizov and Others v. Bulgaria*, App. nos. 37981/06+, §§56–59, 17.4.2012. After the judge had interrogated the witnesses, their written statements were given to the defendants and their counsels for their questions. The defendants gave a written statement that they did not have any questions to put to the witnesses. Later, an attempt was made to summons the witnesses, who had left the country, but they could not be reached and therefore their written statements were read out at the trial. The applicants requested that the witnesses be heard in person at the trial but the domestic court did not find that necessary.

1907 *Papadakis v. "the former Yugoslav Republic of Macedonia"*, App. no. 50254/07, §§88–95, 26.2.2013.

conduct would be. Moreover, a waiver must not run counter to any important public interest.[1908]

For example, in the case *Murtazaliyeva v. Russia*, the Court considered that the applicant had waived her right to examine a witness in person since her two counsels had agreed to the reading out of the witness statement at trial and did not request the hearing of the witness in person, or invoke this matter on appeal. The applicant thus had, by agreeing to the reading out of the witness's pretrial statement and by not insisting on her request that he be heard in court, waived her right to examine that particular witness.[1909]

#### *6.5.6.1. Restrictions on Hearing Witnesses*

##### 6.5.6.1.1. General Principles

The right to call witnesses is not unlimited. According to the main rule, it is first and foremost within the margin of appreciation of domestic courts to limit the admissible evidence in a case.[1910] The domestic courts can decide, in accordance with the circumstances of the case, how many witnesses are heard and whether it is necessary to admit evidence. The Court intervenes in the use of this margin of appreciation only very exceptionally.[1911] This "hands-off" principle has its basis, *inter alia*, in the wording of Article 6 §3 (d), which speaks of "witnesses on one's behalf" – not, for example, "witnesses called by the accused". This point of departure is compatible also with the principle that the Court is not a fourth-instance court that functions as an appeal court for the rulings of the domestic courts.

Previously the principles for restricting the calling of witnesses had been laid down in the Grand Chamber case *Perna v. Italy* in 2003. In that case the Court presented the following two-stage test: (1) whether the applicant substantiated his or her request to call a particular witness by referring to the relevance of that individual's testimony for "the establishment of the truth"; and (2) whether the domestic court's refusal to call that witness undermined the overall fairness of the proceedings.[1912]

---

1908 *Murtazaliyeva v. Russia* [GC], App. no. 36658/05, §§117–118, 18.12.2018.

1909 *Murtazaliyeva v. Russia* [GC], App. no. 36658/05, §§121–127, 18.12.2018. See also Jordan Owen, "Questioning of witnesses – *Murtazaliyeva v. Russia* (Application No. 36658/05)", *European Human Rights Law Review*, Issue 2, 2019, pp. 217–221; and Stefan Kieber, "The jurisprudence of the European Court of Human Rights in 2018", *European Yearbook on Human Rights 2019*, pp. 189–220, at pp. 202–203.

1910 *Vidal v. Belgium*, App. no. 12351/86, §33, 28.10.1992; and *Perna v. Italy* [GC], App. no. 48898/99, §29, 6.5.2003. See also Karen Reid, *A Practitioner's Guide to the European Convention on Human Rights*, Sweet & Maxwell/Thomson Reuters, London 2019, pp. 366–367.

1911 *Kok v. the Netherlands* (dec.), App. no. 43149/98, 4.7.2000.

1912 *Perna v. Italy* [GC], App. no. 48898/99, §§29 and 32, 6.5.2003. See also Philip Leach (Ed.), "Cases and comment: selected decisions from the European Court of Human Rights for May

These principles and the subsequent case-law were further clarified in the recent Grand Chamber judgment in the case *Murtazaliyeva v. Russia* in 2018. In that case the Court adopted the following three-step test to test the fairness of restrictions on calling witnesses: (1) whether the request to examine a witness was sufficiently reasoned and relevant to the subject matter of the accusation; (2) whether the domestic courts had considered the relevance of that testimony and provided sufficient reasons for their decision not to examine a witness at trial; and (3) whether the domestic courts' decision not to examine a witness undermined the overall fairness of the proceedings. The first step is to examine what relevance the calling of a particular witness is capable of bringing to the outcome of a trial, also taking into account other witnesses who can reasonably be expected to strengthen the position of the defence. According to the second step, the stronger and weightier the arguments advanced by the defence, the closer must be the scrutiny and the more convincing must be the reasoning of the domestic courts if they refuse the defence's request to examine a witness. The third step relates to the conclusions under the first two steps of the test, but it cannot be excluded that in certain, exceptional cases considerations of fairness might warrant the opposite conclusion.[1913]

These principles have been followed in many of the Court's cases. The case *Laukkanen v. Finland* concerned aggravated theft and a complaint that certain named witnesses had not been heard by the District Court or the Court of Appeal. The Court considered that the judgment had been based on very extensive circumstantial evidence. There was no indication as to why the conclusions of the domestic courts might have been arbitrary. The applicant had been represented by counsel during the whole proceedings and it had not even been claimed at the time that he had not had an opportunity to put the necessary questions to the witnesses heard by the District Court. The application was declared inadmissible for being manifestly ill-founded.[1914]

No violation was found either in the case *Kari Uoti v. Finland*, in which the written evidence submitted by the prosecutor contained documents drafted by a witness. The domestic court's judgment was based, *inter alia*, on this material. The Court of Appeal rejected the request to orally hear this witness as unnecessary, since there was no lack of clarity about the identity of the witness or the content

and June 2003 – Media law, *Perna v. Italy* (Application No. 48898/99)", *European Human Rights Law Review*, Issue 5, 2003, pp. 561–564; and Leo Zwaak, Yves Haeck, "Human rights news – Council of Europe", *Netherlands Quarterly of Human Rights*, vol. 21, no. 3, 2003, pp. 510–525, at pp. 514–515.

1913 *Murtazaliyeva v. Russia* [GC], App. no. 36658/05, §§150–168, 18.12.2018. See also Jordan Owen, "Questioning of witnesses – *Murtazaliyeva v. Russia* (Application No. 36658/05)", *European Human Rights Law Review*, Issue 2, 2019, pp. 217–221; and Stefan Kieber, "The jurisprudence of the European Court of Human Rights in 2018", *European Yearbook on Human Rights 2019*, pp. 189–220, at pp. 202–203.

1914 *Laukkanen v. Finland* (dec.), App. no. 48910/99, 21.5.2002.

of the documents. The Court considered that the procedural inconvenience caused by the fact that the witness was not heard was lessened by the fact that the applicant had had an opportunity to comment on the written evidence and to challenge it before two levels of jurisdiction. Nor was the conviction based solely on these documents.[1915]

The Court also found the domestic court's ruling appropriate in the case *B. v. Finland*, which concerned the applicant's conviction for the sexual abuse of two children. The conviction was based on the video-recorded statements of the children and on other evidence. While the case was pending before the Court of Appeal, one of the children visited the accused in prison and withdrew his earlier accusations. Subsequently the counsel for the accused asked the Court of Appeal to hear the child in an oral hearing or in an additional investigation. The Court of Appeal rejected these requests, considering that the child had not changed his earlier account of his own free will. Moreover, the hearing would have been particularly stressful for him. The Court accepted this outcome and held that the Court of Appeal had assessed the significance of the withdrawal. Its reasoning was sufficient and the rights of the defence had not been violated by the fact that the child had not been reheard.[1916]

In the above-mentioned case *Murtazaliyeva v. Russia*, the Court applied the new three-step test in a case concerning terrorism. The applicant, who was of Chechen origin, was accused of planning a terrorist crime. Her two counsels wanted to call two police officers, who had participated in the applicant's arrest, as witnesses in order to show that they had placed explosives in her bag and had framed her as a suspect. At the trial the other police witnesses called by the prosecution had specifically said that the bag had been in the applicant's possession when she was being searched. The Court held that the applicant had, under the first step, failed to concretely elaborate on how the testimony of the two police officers could reasonably be expected to strengthen the case for the defence. Moreover, the defence had remained generally passive during the cross-examination of these witnesses and the reasoning of the domestic courts had been sufficient. Nor had the overall fairness of the proceedings been undermined since there was a considerable body of evidence against the applicant which she had been able to effectively challenge with the help of her counsels.[1917]

A refusal to hear a witness may, however, in certain circumstances constitute a violation of the Convention. This was the case in *Vidal v. Belgium*, in which the domestic appellate court refused, without giving any reasons, to

1915 *Kari Uoti v. Finland*, App. no. 21422/02, §35, 23.10.2007.

1916 *B. v. Finland*, App. no. 17122/02, §§44–49, 24.4.2007.

1917 *Murtazaliyeva v. Russia* [GC], App. no. 36658/05, §§169–177, 18.12.2018. See also Jordan Owen, "Questioning of witnesses – *Murtazaliyeva v. Russia* (Application No. 36658/05)", *European Human Rights Law Review*, Issue 2, 2019, pp. 217–221; and Stefan Kieber, "The jurisprudence of the European Court of Human Rights in 2018", *European Yearbook on Human Rights 2019*, pp. 189–220, at pp. 202–203.

hear witnesses called by the accused in a referred case, and, without any new received evidence, changed the earlier suspended prison sentence of three years to an unconditional sentence of four years.[1918] Similarly, in the case *Lazu v. Moldova*, the appellate court had changed the first-instance court's dismissal of charges and convicted the applicant on the basis of written witness statements without hearing witnesses, even though the first-instance court had dismissed the charges on the basis of a lack of credibility of the witnesses.[1919] In the case *Frumkin v. Russia*, the applicant had been arrested in the context of a demonstration. He claimed that his right to a fair trial had been violated as the court did not admit as evidence a video recording of his arrest, nor had it agreed to summons the arresting police officers as witnesses. The Court accepted the applicant's complaints as relevant and found a violation of Article 6.[1920] The Court has also found a violation in a Finnish civil case in which the witnesses called by a party had not been heard.[1921]

The State is not responsible for a defence lawyer's failure to call witnesses.[1922] On the other hand, if the defence has summonsed the witnesses to appear correctly, the court must take measures to secure their attendance.[1923] If the reason for the witness's non-appearance is not in the hands of the court, naturally no liability under Article 6 §3 (d) is created.[1924]

#### 6.5.6.1.2. Expert Witnesses

Many situations limiting the appearance of witnesses have concerned expert witnesses, where an expert, who has given a written statement, is not heard in person at an oral hearing. In the case *Eskelinen and Others v. Finland*, the criminal conviction was partly based on a legal expert opinion the source of which was not, despite a request to appear, heard in person at the trial. The Court allowed this conduct since the opinion was based on case file material that was accessible to the parties and the court, and it did not have any decisive relevance to the conclusions of the court.[1925]

---

1918 *Vidal v. Belgium*, App. no. 12351/86, §§34–35, 22.4.1992.

1919 *Lazu v. the Republic of Moldova*, App. no. 46182/08, §§31–44, 5.7.2016.

1920 *Frumkin v. Russia*, App. no. 74568/12, §§159–168, 5.1.2016. See also Anne-Katrin Speck, "Strasbourg in 2016 – figures and case law trends: the European Court of Human Rights' annual report 2016", *EHRAC Bulletin*, Issue 27, summer 2017, pp. 8–9.

1921 *Tamminen v. Finland*, App. no. 40847/98, §§38–41, 5.6.2004. The domestic court refused to hear a witness the applicant had called only in the oral hearing. The Court found that the request could not be considered as a new, last-minute request as the applicant had already earlier tried to call witnesses. The refusal to accept the witness in the circumstances of the case was not compatible with the Convention and the Court therefore found a violation.

1922 *W.W. v. the United Kingdom* (dec.), App. no. 18123/91, 14.10.1992.

1923 *Sadak and Others v. Turkey*, App. nos. 29900/96+, §67, 17.7.2001.

1924 Similarly, in the case of a witness falling ill, see *Ubah Mortes v. Andorra* (dec.), App. no. 46253/99, 4.5.2000.

1925 *Eskelinen and Others v. Finland*, App. no. 43803/98, §34, 8.8.2006.

In the case *Constantinides v. Greece*, the applicant was convicted of fraud on the strength of, *inter alia*, the evidence of a handwriting expert commissioned by the prosecutor. The expert, although summonsed, failed to appear and testify at the trial. The expert's report had been included in the file and was read out during the trial. The applicant's own expert attended the trial and provided written and oral evidence contradicting the findings of the prosecution's expert. Applying the three-step test, the Court did not find a violation of Article 6. It held that the domestic courts had not made all reasonable efforts to secure the attendance of the initial expert. However, although the expert report was considered by the domestic courts to be of significant evidential value, it was not the sole or decisive basis for the applicant's conviction but served to corroborate witness and documentary evidence adduced at the trial as proof of the applicant's guilt. Moreover, there were sufficient safeguards in place to compensate for the applicant's inability to question the expert directly, in particular the active participation at the trial of the applicant's own expert witness. It was also relevant that the report of the absent expert did not concern matters which the latter had seen or heard about in relation to the charges against the applicant. The report was technical in nature and its author was an independent expert who had been commissioned by the judicial authorities at the investigation stage to help clarify certain issues in the file. The applicant's own expert had had every opportunity at the trial to cast doubt on the findings.[1926]

### *6.5.6.2. A Witness's Refusal to Testify*

The right to call and hear witnesses also contains the right of the witness not to testify. Generally, the Court recognises that there are two competing public interests at stake as far as compelling witnesses to appear is concerned. The first is the public interest in the prosecution of serious crime. The second is the public interest in the protection of family life from State interference and the right of close relatives not to testify against their own family members.[1927]

A witness has a normal civic duty to testify in a criminal matter.[1928] Exceptions to this obligation are the right of the accused not to incriminate himself,[1929] the right of journalists not to disclose their sources[1930] and the right of a close relative not to testify against a family member. Normally, domestic legislation

---

1926 *Constantinides v. Greece*, App. no. 76438/12, §§37–52, 6.10.2016.

1927 *Van der Heijden v. the Netherlands* [GC], App. no. 42857/05, §62, 3.4.2012.

1928 *Voskuil v. the Netherlands*, App. no. 64752/01, §86, 22.11.2007.

1929 *Jalloh v. Germany* [GC], App. no. 54810/00, §97, 11.7.2006; *Gäfgen v. Germany* [GC], App. no. 22978/05, §168, 1.6.2010; *Vidgen v. the Netherlands*, App. no. 29353/06, §42, 10.7.2012; *Sievert v. Germany*, App. no. 29881/07, §§59–61, 19.7.2012; and *Cabral v. the Netherlands*, App. no. 37617/10, §34, 28.8.2018.

1930 *Goodwin v. the United Kingdom*, App. no. 17488/90, §45, 27.3.1996; and *Sanoma Uitgevers B.V. v. the Netherlands* [GC], App. no. 38224/03, §§59–63, 14.9.2010.

grants an exemption from the duty to give evidence based on family life, and often it is limited to close relatives, that is, spouses, former spouses, registered partners and former registered partners of suspects. The Court has accepted that States are entitled to set boundaries on the scope of testimonial privilege and to draw the line at marriage or registered partnerships. The legislature is thus entitled to confer a special status on marriage or registration and not to confer it on other *de facto* types of cohabitation.[1931]

A common situation is that a spouse refuses to testify against the other spouse, especially in cases concerning domestic violence. For example, in the case *N.K. v. Germany*, the applicant's wife had been beaten by him and she had given her statement to the investigating judge. She then refused to testify against the applicant at the trial. The Court held that the wife had been entitled, according to domestic law, to refuse to give evidence against the applicant because she was married to him. There had thus been a good reason for her not appearing for cross-examination at the trial.[1932]

#### *6.5.6.3. Right to Present One's Own Evidence*

As mentioned above, it is within the margin of appreciation of the domestic courts to limit the admissible evidence in the case. The Court may, however, find a violation on the ground that the refusal to admit certain evidence by the domestic courts is not sufficiently reasoned. This was the case in *Suominen v. Finland.*[1933] The case concerned civil proceedings in which the applicant was not able to submit certain documents to the Court of Appeal as evidence. The Court held that, although the domestic court had a certain margin of appreciation when limiting the complaints and evidence in the case, they had an obligation to reason their decision. The lack of reasons led to the finding of a violation under Article 6 §1 of the Convention.

## 6.6. RIGHT TO A FREE INTERPRETER

**Article 6: Right to a fair trial**

*3. Everyone charged with a criminal offence has the following minimum rights:*

...

*(e) to have the free assistance of an interpreter if he cannot understand or speak the language used in court.*

---

[1931] *Van der Heijden v. the Netherlands* [GC], App. no. 42857/05, §§69 and 76, 3.4.2012 (no violation). The case was examined under Article 8.

[1932] *N.K. v. Germany*, App. no. 59549/12, §§56–62, 26.7.2018. See also section 6.5.5.2.2.7. above, where this case has been explained in more detail.

[1933] *Suominen v. Finland*, App. no. 37801/97, §38, 1.7.2003.

As in the context of other rights guaranteed by Article 6 §3, the right to a free interpreter starts when a person is, within the meaning of the Convention, criminally charged. It is therefore not applicable, for example, to situations in which the police, prior to the pretrial investigation, informally question the suspect. On the other hand, the provision applies from the moment the pretrial investigation starts and applies to all subsequent phases of the proceedings up until the appeal instances.[1934] One can waive one's right to a free interpreter,[1935] but any waiver must be the decision of the accused, not of his or her counsel.[1936]

The assistance of an interpreter should be provided during the investigating stage unless it is demonstrated in the light of the particular circumstances of each case that there are compelling reasons to restrict this right.[1937] In the case *Baytar v. Turkey*, the applicant did not understand Turkish. Subsequently her answers during the police interview were used against her in the trial. The Court held that, without the assistance of an interpreter (and a lawyer) at the police station, she was unable to appreciate the consequences of her declining the assistance of a lawyer.[1938]

## 6.6.1. EXTENT OF THE RIGHT

The right to a free interpreter applies both to oral statements and to written material. These issues guarantee the fairness of the proceedings.[1939] Article 6 §3 (e) does not, however, require that during the trial every word is interpreted or that all documents are translated. The wording of Article 6 §3 (e) does not directly require the translation of the documents as it speaks only about the right to have the assistance of an interpreter.[1940] Basically this means the right to have the oral assistance of an interpreter.[1941] A criterion for the sufficiency of the requirements is that the accused understands sufficiently in order to respond

1934 *Kamasinski v. Austria*, App. no. 9783/82, §§76–77, 19.12.1989. See also David Harris, Michael O'Boyle, Ed Bates, Carla Buckley, *Law of the European Convention on Human Rights*, 4th edition, Oxford University Press, Oxford 2018, pp. 487–488.

1935 *Kamasinski v. Austria*, App. no. 9783/82, §§24 and 80, 19.12.1989.

1936 *Cuscani v. the United Kingdom*, App. no. 32771/96, §38, 24.9.2002; and *Sardinas Albo v. Italy* (dec.), App. no. 56271/00, 8.1.2004.

1937 *Diallo v. Sweden* (dec.), App. no. 13205/07, §25, 5.1.2010.

1938 *Baytar v. Turkey*, App. no. 45440/04, §§53–59, 14.10.2014 (violation).

1939 *Kamasinski v. Austria*, App. no. 9783/82, §74, 19.12.1989; and *Hermi v. Italy* [GC], App. no. 18114/02, §69, 18.10.2006. See also Dragoljub Popović, *European Human Rights Law – A Manual: An Introduction to the Strasbourg Court and its Jurisprudence*, Eleven International Publishing, The Hague 2013, pp. 204–205.

1940 This provision does not, for example, contain an absolute right to have a court's ruling translated, see *Kamasinski v. Austria*, App. no. 9783/82, §85, 19.12.1989.

1941 *Vizgirda v. Slovenia*, App. no. 59868/08, §78, 28.8.2018. See also Stefan Kieber, "The jurisprudence of the European Court of Human Rights in 2018", *European Yearbook on Human Rights 2019*, pp. 189–220, at pp. 203–204.

properly to the charges and to present to the court his or her own version of the facts and thereby influence the outcome of the proceedings.[1942] It is therefore not necessary to translate word for word, for example, the charges or the oral statements at the trial if the oral information about the content of the charges or the oral statements makes it possible to respond to the charges. It can also be acceptable that an interpreter makes a summary of the oral statements.[1943]

Article 6 §3 (e) does not cover the relations between the accused and his counsel but only applies to the relations between the accused and the judge.[1944] However, an applicant's inability to communicate with his or her lawyer due to linguistic limitations may give rise to an issue under Article 6 §3 (c) of the Convention.[1945] In situations in which the accused is assisted at the trial by his or her counsel, it is normally not sufficient that the counsel speaks and understands the language of the court if the accused does not. Participation in the hearing requires that the accused understands what happens at the trial and what issues are at the stake.

In the case *Vizgirda v. Slovenia* the Court clarified the need for an interpreter and the criterion "cannot understand" by noting that every defendant had the right to the free assistance of an interpreter and that it was the obligation of the competent authorities to appoint an interpreter to the accused. The domestic courts also had an obligation to verify the defendant's interpretation needs and that he or she understood the language of the trial. Also, in a situation in which a "third language" was used by the interpreter – namely a language which was not the trial language or the mother tongue of the accused – the domestic courts had to specifically make sure that the accused truly understood that language. Having basic knowledge in such a language did not necessarily mean that the defendant had a sufficient command in order to defend him- or herself in a trial. A number of open-ended questions might be sufficient to establish the defendant's language needs. Moreover, an accused had to be notified of the right to interpretation in a language he or she understood. In the case at stake, the Lithuanian defendant had been appointed a Russian-speaking interpreter, Russian being a language he understood to a certain extent. The problem was, however, that of knowing whether his command of Russian was sufficient for fair trial purposes. The domestic courts assumed that it was, without making a specific verification of his skills. The Court disagreed and found a violation.[1946]

1942 *Hermi v. Italy* [GC], App. no. 18114/02, §70, 18.10.2006; *Husain v. Italy* (dec.), App. no. 18913/03, 24.2.2005; and *Güngör v. Germany* (dec.), App. no. 31540/96, 17.5.2001.

1943 *Kamasinski v. Austria*, App. no. 9783/82, §§74, 81 and 83, 19.12.1989; and *Hermi v. Italy* [GC], App. no. 18114/02, §70, 18.10.2006.

1944 *X. v. Austria*, App. no. 6185/73, Commission decision, 29.5.1975.

1945 *Lagerblom v. Sweden*, App. no. 26891/95, §§61–64, 14.1.2003; and *Pugžlys v. Poland*, App. no. 446/10, §§85–92, 14.6.2016.

1946 *Vizgirda v. Slovenia*, App. no. 59868/08, §§80–87 and 91–103, 28.8.2018. See also Stefan Kieber, "The jurisprudence of the European Court of Human Rights in 2018", *European Yearbook on Human Rights 2019*, pp. 189–220, at pp. 203–204.

It is important that an accused can draw the counsel's attention to any issues during the trial which are relevant for his or her defence.[1947] The accused's right to an interpreter for communication with the counsel depends on how the counsel has been appointed for him. In cases of free legal aid, the State is responsible for appointing a person that can communicate with the accused in a language which the latter understands, or that there is an interpreter present.[1948] On the other hand, in situations in which the accused chooses his or her own counsel, it is for the accused to make sure that he or she can communicate with the counsel.

It is to a certain extent not clear whether the State has a duty to inform the accused about his or her right to an interpreter. In any event, in situations in which an interpreter may be necessary, the judge must verify with the accused that he or she understands the language used by the court to the necessary extent.[1949] A lack of language skills must not prevent the accused from participating properly in proceedings against him.[1950]

The right to a free interpreter applies only to the language used by the court. Therefore, an accused who understands the language of the court cannot claim the services of an interpreter in order to defend himself in some other language, not even in the language of a minority to which he himself belongs.[1951]

In order for the right under Article 6 §3 (e) to be practical and effective, the interpreter must be qualified for the task. The authorities must be convinced about the skills of the interpreter to fulfil the task when he or she is appointed. Moreover, it is the task of the domestic courts to supervise during the proceedings to ensure that the interpreter is properly doing their job.[1952] The Convention

---

1947 *Kamasinski v. Austria*, App. no. 9783/82, §74, 19.12.1989; and *Cuscani v. the United Kingdom*, App. no. 32771/96, §38, 24.9.2002.

1948 In the case *Lagerblom v. Sweden*, App. no. 26891/95, §62, 14.1.2003 the request was rejected on the ground that the accused could speak and sufficiently understand Swedish. He had also been organised an interpretation before two levels of justice.

1949 *Cuscani v. the United Kingdom*, App. no. 32771/96, §39, 24.9.2002; *Hermi v. Italy* [GC], App. no. 18114/02, §72, 18.10.2006; and *Katritsch v. France*, App. no. 22575/08, §44, 4.11.2010.

1950 *Cuscani v. the United Kingdom*, App. no. 32771/96, §§38–39, 24.9.2002 (violation). The case concerned serious crimes and the accused's difficulties in communicating with the counsel had been brought to the attention of the court. However, the court did not decide on the matter, and the defendant's brother was entrusted with helping the defendant with interpretation. The Court held that the onus had been on the judge to reassure himself that the absence of an interpreter at the hearing would not prejudice the applicant's full involvement in a matter of crucial importance for him. See also Evert-Jan van der Vlis, "Videoconferencing in criminal proceedings", in Sabine Braun, Judith L. Taylor (Eds.), *Videoconference and Remote Interpreting in Criminal Proceedings*, University of Surrey, Guildford 2011, pp. 11–25, at pp. 24–25.

1951 *Lagerblom v. Sweden*, App. no. 26891/95, §62, 14.1.2003; and *K. v. France* (dec.), App. no. 10210/82, 7.12.1983, in which the applicant had been born in France and had received his education there. There was thus no doubt about his ability to understand French.

1952 *Kamasinski v. Austria*, App. no. 9783/82, §74, 19.12.1989; *Hermi v. Italy* [GC], App. no. 18114/02, §70, 18.10.2006; *Protopapa v. Turkey*, App. no. 16084/90, §80, 24.2.2009; and *Knox v. Italy*, App. no. 76577/13, §§182–187, 24.1.2019.

does not require that the interpreter be independent or impartial; nor is the right to an interpreter made null and void by the fact that he or she has connections to the police or that it is the police that appoint the interpreter. Nevertheless, the services of the interpreter must provide the accused with effective assistance to conduct his defence and the interpreter's conduct must not be of a nature that impinges on the fairness of the proceedings.[1953]

## 6.6.2. SERVICE FOR FREE

The right to free assistance from an interpreter does not depend on the wealth of the accused or his ability to pay but solely on whether he understands or speaks the language of the court or not. The services provided by an interpreter are thus part of the basic services provided by the State in the context of criminal proceedings. The fact that this service is free of charge means that the accused cannot be ordered to pay the interpreter's fee, even if he is found guilty and sentenced.[1954] In all situations, the costs and expenses of the interpreter are borne by the State. Were it otherwise, the risk of having to pay the costs of an interpreter could lead to a situation in which an accused is forced to give up one of his fair trial guarantees purely on financial grounds.[1955] However, in a situation where the accused fails to appear at court without a valid reason, he or she can be ordered to pay the fees of the interpreter.[1956]

---

1953 *Ucak v. the United Kingdom* (dec.), App. no. 44234/98, 24.1.2002.

1954 *Luedicke, Belkacem and Koç v. Germany*, App. nos. 6210/73+, §§40, 42 and 49–50, 28.11.1978; *Işyar v. Bulgaria*, App. no. 391/03, §45, 20.11.2008; and *Öztürk v. Germany*, App. no. 8544/79, §58, 21.2.1984.

1955 *Luedicke, Belkacem and Koç v. Germany*, App. nos. 6210/73+, §42, 28.11.1978.

1956 *Fedele v. Germany* (dec.), App. no. 11311/84, 9.12.1987.

# BIBLIOGRAPHY

## MONOGRAPHS

Choo, Andrew L.-T.: *The Privilege Against Self-incrimination and Criminal Justice*, Hart Publishing, Oxford and Portland, Or. 2013

Harris, David – O'Boyle, Michael – Bates, Ed – Buckley, Carla: *Law of the European Convention on Human Rights*, 4th edition, Oxford University Press, Oxford 2018

Heikkilä, Satu: *From Final Judgment to Final Resolution – Effectiveness of the Execution of Judgments of the European Court of Human Rights in Finland*, Wolf Legal Publishers, Tilburg 2019

Jacobs, Francis G. – White, Robin C.A. – Owey, Clare: *The European Convention on Human Rights*, Oxford University Press, Oxford 2017

Popović, Dragoljub: *European Human Rights Law – A Manual: An Introduction to the Strasbourg Court and its Jurisprudence*, Eleven International Publishing, The Hague 2013

Rajska, Dagmara – Huszti-Orban, Krisztina: *Human Rights Obligations of States in the Context of Counter-terrorism Operations: A Commentary in the Light of Al Nashiri v. Poland and Husayn (Abu Zubaydah) v. Poland*, Aracne, Ariccia 2015

Reid, Karen: *A Practitioner's Guide to the European Convention on Human Rights*, Sweet & Maxwell/Thomson Reuters, London 2019

Vilaça, José Luís Da Cruz: *EU Law and Integration – Twenty Years of Judicial Application of EU Law*, Hart Publishing, Oxford and Portland, Or. 2014

Zrvandyan, Arman: *Casebook on European Fair Trial Standards in Administrative Justice*, Council of Europe Publishing, Strasbourg 2016

## ARTICLES AND BOOK CHAPTERS

Antoniou, Theofania: "The Right to the Presumption of Innocence Versus the Right to Freedom of Expression in Parliament – The European Court of Human Rights Judgment in *Konstas v. Greece*", *European Human Rights Law Review*, Issue 3, 2012, pp. 319–326

Aquilina, Kevin: "The Independence of the Judiciary in Strasbourg Judicial Disciplinary Case Law – Judges as Applicants and National Judicial Councils as Factotums of Respondent States", in Pinto de Albuquerque, Paulo – Wojtyczek, Krzysztof (Eds.): *Judicial Power in a Globalized World – Liber Amicorum Vincent de Gaetano*, Springer, Cham 2019, pp. 1–32

Aubry, Eléonore: "Disciplinary proceedings – *Ramos Nunes de Carvalho E SÁ v. Portugal* (Application Nos. 57728/13, 55391/13)", *European Human Rights Law Review*, Issue 2, 2019, pp. 221–224

Berger, Mark: "Compelled self-reporting and the principle against compelled self-incrimination – some comparative perspectives", *European Human Rights Law Review*, Issue 1, 2006, pp. 25–38

Berger, Mark: "Self-Incrimination and the European Court of Human Rights: Procedural Issues in the Enforcement of the Right to Silence", *European Human Rights Law Review*, Issue 5, 2007, pp. 514–533

Biagioni, Giacomo: "*Avotiņš v. Latvia*: the uneasy balance between mutual recognition of judgments and protection of fundamental rights", *European Papers*, vol. 1, no. 2, 2016, pp. 579–596

Bonello, Giovanni: "More common law than common sense – how the European Court of Human Rights saves the United Kingdom from itself", *Human Rights Law Journal* (HRLJ), vol. 34, nos. 7–12, 31 December 2014, pp. 239–245

Brems, Eva: "Conflicting human rights: an exploration in the context of the right to fair trial in the European Convention for the Protection of Human Rights and Fundamental Freedoms", *Human Rights Quarterly*, vol. 27, no. 1, 2005, pp. 294–326

Broberg, Morten: "National courts of last instance failing to make a preliminary reference: the (possible) consequences flowing therefrom", *European Public Law*, vol. 22, issue 2, June 2016, pp. 243–256

Buendia, Ricardo: "Reasoned judgments – *Harisch v. Germany* (Application No. 50053/16)", *European Human Rights Law Review*, Issue 4, 2019, pp. 437–439

Buendia, Ricardo: "Right to a fair trial – *Pasquini v. San Marino* (Application No. 50956/16)", *European Human Rights Law Review*, Issue 5, 2019, pp. 567–569

Buquicchio, Gianni: "*Volkov vs. Ukraine* and the Venice Commission's approach to structural independence of the judiciary", in Harutyunyan, G.G. (Ed.): *New Millenium Constitutionalism: Paradigms of Reality and Challenges*, NJHAR, Yerevan 2013, pp. 323–340

Caflisch, Lucius: "International law and the European Court of Human Rights", in *Dialogue between judges*, European Court of Human Rights/Council of Europe, Strasbourg 2007, pp. 23–40

Callewaert, Johan: "The privilege against self-incrimination in European law: an illustration of the impact of the plurality of Courts and legal sources on the protection of fundamental rights in Europe", *ERA-Forum: scripta iuris europaei*, vol. 5, no. 4, December 2004, pp. 488–499

Colandrea, Valerio: "On the power of the European Court of Human Rights to order specific non-monetary measures: some remarks in light of the *Assanidze*, *Broniowski* and *Sejdovic* cases", *Human Rights Law Review*, vol. 7, no. 2, 2007, pp. 396–411

Cornell, Mollie: "Reasons for preliminary references – *Sanofi Pasteur v. France* (Application No. 25137/16)", *European Human Rights Law Review*, Issue 3, 2020, pp. 308–311

Costa, Jean-Paul: "The European Court of Human Rights and its recent case law", *Texas International Law Journal*, vol. 38, no. 3, 2003, pp. 455–467

Croquet, Nicolas A.J.: "The Right to Self-representation Under the European Convention on Human Rights – What Role for the Limitation Analysis?", *European Human Rights Law Review*, Issue 3, 2012, pp. 292–308

Doobay, Anand: "The right to a fair trial in light of the recent ECtHR and CJEU case-law", *ERA forum*, vol. 14, issue 2, September 2013, pp. 251–262

Đurkin, Klara: "Abuse of whistle-blowers – *Magnitskiy v. Russia* (Application Nos. 32631/09 and 53799/12)", *European Human Rights Law Review*, Issue 6, 2019, pp. 669–671

Elliott-Kelly, Jane: "Case Analysis – *Al-Khawaja and Tahery v. United Kingdom*", *European Human Rights Law Review*, Issue 1, 2012, pp. 81–87

Forrester, Ian S.: "Due process in competition cases: is *Menarini* the last word?", in *Liber Amicorum Dean Spielmann – Mélanges en l'honneur de/Essays in honour of Dean Spielmann*, Wolf Legal Publishers, Oisterwijk 2015, pp. 187–198

Frowein, Jochen A.: "The transformation of constitutional law through the European Convention on Human Rights", in *Dialogue between judges*, European Court of Human Rights/Council of Europe, Strasbourg 2007, pp. 71–90

Galani, Sofia: "Case and comment: selected decisions from the European Court of Human Rights for July and August 2018 – Pussy Riot, *Mariya Alekhina v. Russia* (Application No. 38004/12)", *European Human Rights Law Review*, Issue 6, 2018, pp. 625–628

Galani, Sofia (Ed.): "Case and comment: selected decisions from the European Court of Human Rights from November and December 2015 – Impartiality of jurors, *Kristiansen v. Norway* (Application No. 1176/10)", *European Human Rights Law Review*, Issue 2, 2016, pp. 205–207

Galani, Sofia (Ed.): "Case and comment: selected decisions from the European Court of Human Rights from November and December 2015 – Jurors and contempt of court, *Dallas v. United Kingdom* (Application No. 38395/12)", *European Human Rights Law Review*, Issue 3, 2016, pp. 317–319

Galani, Sofia (Ed.): "Case and comment: selected decisions from the European Court of Human Rights from March and April 2016 – Detention of minors, *Blokhin v. Russia* (Application No. 47152/06)", *European Human Rights Law Review*, Issue 4, 2016, pp. 461–465

Galani, Sofia (Ed.): "Case and comment: selected decisions from the European Court of Human Rights from July and August 2016 – State's unilateral declarations, *Jeronovičs v. Latvia* (Application No. 44898/10)", *European Human Rights Law Review*, Issue 6, 2016, pp. 687–690

Galani, Sofia (Ed.): "Case and comment: selected decisions from the European Court of Human Rights from November and December 2016 – Access to a court and religious minorities, *Lupeni Greek Catholic Parish v. Romania* (Application No. 76943/11)", *European Human Rights Law Review*, Issue 2, 2017, pp. 204–206

Galani, Sofia (Ed.): "Case and comment: selected decisions from the European Court of Human Rights from November and December 2016 – Lack of reasons in jury trials, *Lhermitte v. Belgium* (Application No. 34238/09)", *European Human Rights Law Review*, Issue 2, 2017, pp. 210–211

Galani, Sofia (Ed.): "Case and comment: selected decisions from the European Court of Human Rights from January and February 2017 – Special supervision measures, *De Tommaso v. Italy* (Application No. 43395/09)", *European Human Rights Law Review*, Issue 3, 2017, pp. 332–335

Galani, Sofia (Ed.): "Case and comment: selected decisions from the European Court of Human Rights from May and June 2017 – Access to legal assistance in police custody, *Simeonovi v. Bulgaria* (Application No. 21980/04)", *European Human Rights Law Review*, Issue 5, 2017, pp. 514–517

Galani, Sofia (Ed.): "Case and comment: selected decisions from the European Court of Human Rights from May and June 2017 – No journalistic protection for publication of personal taxation data, *Satakunnan Markkinapörssi Oy and Satamedia Oy v. Finland* (Application No. 73607/13)", *European Human Rights Law Review*, Issue 5, 2017, pp. 511–514

Galani, Sofia (Ed.): "Case and comment: selected decisions from the European Court of Human Rights from July and August 2017 – Article 6 and remedial practice, *Moreira Ferreira v. Portugal (No. 2)* (Application No. 19867/12)", *European Human Rights Law Review*, Issue 6, 2017, pp. 615–617

Galani, Sofia (Ed.): "Case and comment: selected decisions from the European Court of Human Rights from September and October 2017 – National security and the right to a fair trial, *Regner v. Czech Republic* (Application No. 35289/11)", *European Human Rights Law Review*, Issue 1, 2018, pp. 83–85

Galani, Sofia (Ed.): "Case and comment: selected decisions from the European Court of Human Rights from November and December 2017 – Fair trials and the principle of *ne bis in idem* in criminal proceedings, *Ramda v. France* (Application No. 78477/11)", *European Human Rights Law Review*, Issue 2, 2018, pp. 185–187

Galani, Sofia (Ed.): "Case and comment: selected decisions from the European Court of Human Rights for March and April 2018 – Right of access to Supreme Courts, *Zubac v. Croatia* (Application No. 40160/12)", *European Human Rights Law Review*, Issue 4, 2018, pp. 399–401

Garnett, Richard: "The Strasbourg Court – A Friend to Embassy and Consular Employees", *European Human Rights Law Review*, Issue 6, 2017, pp. 589–595

Glas, Lize R.: "European Convention on Human Rights", *Netherlands Quarterly of Human Rights*, vol. 31, no. 2, June 2013, pp. 210–216

Goss, Ryan: "Out of many, one?: Strasbourg's *Ibrahim* decision on Article 6", *The Modern Law Review*, vol. 80, no. 6, 2017, pp. 1137–1150

Goss, Ryan: "The undermining of Article 6 ECHR", *European yearbook on human rights*, vol. 2019, pp. 295–312

Grabenwarter, Christoph: "The right to effective remedy against excessive duration of proceedings", in Bröhmer, Jürgen (Ed.): *The Protection of Human Rights at the Beginning of the 21st Century – Colloquium in Honour of Professor Dr. Dr. Dr. h.c. mult. Georg Ress on the Occasion of his 75th Birthday*, Nomos, Baden-Baden 2012, pp. 123–133

Gray, Christopher: "Case and comment: selected decisions from the European Court of Human Rights for May and June 2018 – Police entrapment and undercover work, *Tchokhonelidge v. Georgia* (Application No. 31536/07)", *European Human Rights Law Review*, Issue 5, 2018, pp. 529–532

Gray, Christopher: "Objective impartiality test – *Cosmos Maritime Trading and Shipping Agency v. Ukraine* (Application No. 53427/09)", *European Human Rights Law Review*, Issue 5, 2019, pp. 569–572

Gray, Christopher: "Presumption of innocence – *Kangers v. Latvia* (Application No. 35726/10)", *European Human Rights Law Review*, Issue 4, 2019, pp. 439–442

Gray, Christopher: "Right to access a lawyer – *Beuze v. Belgium* (Application No. 71409/10)", *European Human Rights Law Review*, Issue 2, 2019, pp. 222–226

Hamilton, Michael: "Human rights courts as norm-brokers", *Human Rights Law Review*, vol. 18, no. 2, 2018, pp. 205–232

Hickman, Tom – Saifee, Faisal: "Case Analysis – *Hammern v. Norway, O v. Norway, Ringvold v. Norway* and *Y v. Norway*", *European Human Rights Law Review*, Issue 5, 2003, pp. 539–546

Hollan, Miklos: "Confiscation of the proceeds from crime and the principle of presumption of innocence", in Nuotio, Kimmo (Ed.): *Festschrift in Honour of Raimo Lahti*, University of Helsinki/Faculty of Law, Helsinki 2007, pp. 363–372

Jackson, John: "Re-conceptualizing the right of silence as an effective fair trial standard", *International and Comparative Law Quarterly*, vol. 58, pt. 4, October 2009, pp. 835–861

Japaridze, Sopho: "Plea bargaining in Georgia – does the Georgian model of plea bargaining comply with the requirements of the European Convention on Human Rights?", *EHRAC Bulletin*, Issue 22, winter 2014, pp. 7–8

Jebens, Sverre Erik: "Illegally obtained evidence in criminal cases – an analysis on the basis of three Grand Chamber judgments", in Spielmann, Dean – Tsirli, Marialena – Voyatzis, Panayotis (Eds.): *La Convention Européenne des Droits de L'homme, un Instrument Vivant – Mélanges en L'honneur de Christos L. Rozakis/The European Convention on Human Rights, a Living Instrument – Essays in Honour of Christos L. Rozakis*, Bruylant, Bruxelles 2011, pp. 219–234

Jebens, Sverre Erik: "The limits of the presumption of innocence – Some clarifications in the Court's recent case-law", in *Liber Amicorum Dean Spielmann – Mélanges en L'honneur de/Essays in Honour of Dean Spielmann*, Wolf Legal Publishers, Oisterwijk 2015, pp. 255–262

Jebens, Sverre Erik: "The Scope of the Presumption of Innocence in Article 6 §2 of the Convention – Especially on its Reputation-Related Aspect", in Caflisch, Lucius – Callewaert, Johan – Liddell, Roderick – Mahoney, Paul – Villiger, Mark (Eds.): *Liber Amicorum Luzius Wildhaber: Human Rights, Strasbourg Views/Droits de L'homme, Regards de Strasbourg*, N.P. Engel, Kehl/Strasbourg/Arlington, Va. 2007, pp. 207–227

Jociene, Danute: "The European Convention on Human Rights in the Lithuanian legal system: lessons learned and prospects for the future", in Caflisch, Lucius – Callewaert, Johan – Liddell, Roderick – Mahoney, Paul – Villiger, Mark (Eds.): *Liber Amicorum Luzius Wildhaber: Human Rights, Strasbourg Views/Droits de L'homme, Regards de Strasbourg*, N.P. Engel, Kehl/Strasbourg/Arlington, Va. 2007, pp. 229–245

Kártyás, Gábor: "The labour lawyer's reading of the Baka case", *Hungarian Yearbook of International Law and European Law*, 2014, pp. 131–138

Keitner, Chimène I.: "*Jones v. United Kingdom*, application nos. 34356/06 & [and] 40528/06: European Court of Human Rights, January 14, 2014", *American journal of international law*, vol. 108, no. 2, April 2014, pp. 302–308

Khan, Mushfik: "Case and comment: selected decisions from the European Court of Human Rights for September and October 2019 – Biased judge, *Deli v. The Republic of Moldova* (Application No. 42010/06)", *European Human Rights Law Review*, Issue 1, 2020, pp. 105–107

Kieber, Stefan: "The jurisprudence of the European Court of Human Rights in 2017", *European Yearbook on Human Rights*, vol. 2018, pp. 229–265

Kieber, Stefan: "The jurisprudence of the European Court of Human Rights in 2018", *European Yearbook on Human Rights*, vol. 2019, pp. 189–220

Koroteev, Kirill – Golubok, Sergey: "Judgment of the Russian Constitutional Court on supervisory review in civil proceedings: denial of justice, denial of Europe", *Human Rights Law Review*, vol. 7, no. 3, 2007, pp. 619–632

Leach, Philip (Ed.): "Cases and comment: selected decisions from the European Court of Human Rights for May and June 2003 – Media law, *Perna v. Italy* (Application No. 48898/99)", *European Human Rights Law Review*, Issue 5, 2003, pp. 561–564

Leach, Philip – Welch, James (Eds.): "Cases and comment: selected decisions from the European Court of Human Rights for September and October 2004 – Crime and sentencing, *Edwards and Lewis v. United Kingdom* (Application Nos. 39647/98 and 40461/98)", *European Human Rights Law Review*, Issue 1, 2005, pp. 92–95

Leigh, Ian: "Bias, necessity and the Convention", *Public Law*, Autumn 2002, pp. 407–414

Lewis, Oliver: "*Stanev v. Bulgaria*: on the pathway to freedom", *Human Rights Brief*, vol. 19, issue 2, winter 2012, pp. 2–7

Liddell, Roderick: "Reflections on certain aspects of the *Kyprianou* judgment", in Caflisch, Lucius – Callewaert, Johan – Liddell, Roderick – Mahoney, Paul – Villiger, Mark (Eds.): *Liber Amicorum Luzius Wildhaber: Human Rights, Strasbourg Views/Droits de L'homme, Regards de Strasbourg*, N.P. Engel, Kehl/Strasbourg/Arlington, Va. 2007, pp. 247–262

Loucaides, Loukis: "Environmental protection through the jurisprudence of the European Convention on Human Rights", *British Yearbook of International Law*, vol. 75, 2004, pp. 249–267

Mahoney, Paul: "Flogging a dead horse: the appropriate human rights policy for judicial treatment of competition fines", in Edward, David – Maclennan, Jackelyn – Komninos, Assimakis (Eds.): *Ian S. Forrester – A Scot Without Borders, Liber Amicorum*, vol. 1, Concurrences Review, New York 2015, pp. 225–240

Mahoney, Paul: "The European Convention on royal rights: royalty, aristocracy and the European Convention on Human Rights", in Kohen, Marcelo G. (Ed.): *Promoting Justice, Human Rights and Conflict Resolution Through International Law, Liber Amicorum Lucius Caflisch*, Martinus Nijhoff, Leiden 2007, pp. 339–352

McBride, Jeremy: "Some recent practice of the European Court of Human Rights to consider when implementing criminal procedure codes", *Synergy Magazine*, no. 64, issue 2, 2018, pp. 8–10

McDermott, Yvonne: "Absent witnesses and the right to confrontation: the influence of the jurisprudence of the European Court of Human Rights on international criminal law", in Lobba, Paolo – Mariniello, Triestino (Eds.): *Judicial Dialogue on Human Rights – The Practice of International Criminal Tribunals*, Brill Nijhoff, Leiden/Boston 2018, pp. 225–242

Michaelsen, Christopher: "The renaissance of non-refoulement? The Othman (Abu Qatada) decision of the European Court of Human Rights", *International and Comparative Law Quarterly*, vol. 61, pt. 3, July 2012, pp. 750–765

Middleton, Joe: "Taking rights seriously in expulsion cases – a case study", *European Human Rights Law Review*, Issue 5, 2013, pp. 520–531

Myjer, Egbert: "One *Salduz* a year is enough – 20 associative thoughts on judge Rozakis, judicial activism and the *Salduz* judgment", in Spielmann, Dean – Tsirli, Marialena – Voyatzis, Panayotis (Eds.): *La Convention Européenne des Droits de L'homme, un Instrument Vivant – Mélanges en L'honneur de Christos L. Rozakis/The European Convention on Human Rights, a Living Instrument – Essays in Honour of Christos L. Rozakis*, Bruylant, Bruxelles 2011, pp. 419–430

Mylonopoulos, Christos: "Bargain practices and the fundamental values of the ECHR", in Sieber, Ulrich – Mitsilegas, Valsamis – Mylonopoulos, Christos – Billis, Emmanouil – Knust, Nandor (Eds.): *Alternative Systems of Crime Control – National, Transnational, and International Dimensions*, Max-Planck-Institut/Duncker & Humblot, Berlin/Freiburg im Breisgau 2018, pp. 89–105

Naismith, Stanley H.: "Current topic: Self-incrimination, fairness or freedom?", *European Human Rights Law Review*, no. 3, 1997, pp. 229–236

Naismith, Stanley H.: "Self-incrimination: the case law of the European Court of Human Rights", *Human Rights & UK Practice*, vol. 2, issue 4, 2001, pp. 3–14

Naismith, Stanley H.: "Witnesses and the right to remain silent", in Casadevall, Josep – Myjer, Egbert – O'Boyle, Michael (Eds.): *Freedom of Expression – Essays in honour of Nicolas Bratza*, Wolf Legal Publishers, Oisterwijk 2012, pp. 245–256

O'Boyle, Michael: "Freedom from self-incrimination and the right to silence: a Pandora's box?", in Mahoney, Paul – Matscher, Franz – Petzold, Herbert – Wildhaber, Luzius (Eds.): *Protection des droits de L'homme: La Perspective Européenne, Mélanges à la Mémoire de Rolv Ryssdal/Protecting Human Rights: The European Perspective, Studies in Memory of Rolv Ryssdal*, Carl Heymanns Verlag, Köln/Berlin/Bonn/München 2000, pp. 1021–1038

O'Boyle, Michael: "Proof in rendition cases before the European Court of Human Rights", *Revista do Instituto Brasileiro de Direitos Humanos*, nos. 17/18, 2018, pp. 183–191

O'Leary, Síofra: "Data protection and privacy questions in the digital age", in O'Boyle, Michael (Ed.): *Human rights challenges in the digital age – judicial perspectives, in honour of Lawrence Early*, Council of Europe Publishing, Strasbourg 2020, pp. 93–122

Owen, Jordan: "Access to electronic evidence – *Rook v. Germany* (Application No. 1586/15)", *European Human Rights Law Review*, Issue 6, 2019, pp. 671–675

Owen, Jordan: "Questioning of witnesses – *Murtazaliyeva v. Russia* (Application No. 36658/05)", *European Human Rights Law Review*, Issue 2, 2019, pp. 217–221

Parmar, Sejal: "*Vilho Eskelinen v. Finland*: The Further Extension of ECHR Article 6 to Disputes Concerning Civil Servants", *European Human Rights Law Review*, Issue 4, 2007, pp. 441–449

Paczolay, Péter: "The Notion of Judicial Independence – Impartiality and Effectiveness of Judges", in Pinto de Albuquerque, Paulo – Wojtyczek, Krzysztof (Eds.): *Judicial Power in a Globalized World – Liber Amicorum Vincent de Gaetano*, Springer, Cham 2019, pp. 331–343

Pastor Vilanova, Pere: "Third parties involved in international litigation proceedings: what are the challenges for the ECHR?", in Pinto de Albuquerque, Paulo – Wojtyczek, Krzysztof (Eds.): *Judicial Power in a Globalized World – Liber Amicorum Vincent de Gaetano*, Springer, Cham 2019, pp. 377–393

Pellonpää, Matti: "The European Court of Human rights and the European Union", in Caflisch, Lucius – Callewaert, Johan – Liddell, Roderick – Mahoney, Paul – Villiger, Mark (Eds.): *Liber Amicorum Luzius Wildhaber: human rights, Strasbourg views/Droits de l'homme, regards de Strasbourg*, N.P. Engel, Kehl/Strasbourg/Arlington, Va. 2007, pp. 347–370

Popović, Dragoljub: "Access to Justice in the Recent Grand Chamber Judgments of the European Court of Human Rights", in Morano-Foadi, Sonia – Vickers, Lucy (Eds.): *Fundamental Rights in the EU – A Matter for Two Courts*, Hart Publishing, Oxford and Portland, Or. 2015, pp. 201–217

Ratniece, Zane – Istrefi, Kushtrim: "The Limits of the Strasbourg Court's Two-Level Harmonization Approach vis-à-vis SC Resolutions in *Al-Dulimi*", *European Yearbook on Human Rights 2015*, pp. 379–390

Redmayne, Mike: "Hearsay and human rights: *Al-Khawaja* in the Grand Chamber", *Modern law review*, vol. 75, no. 5, 2012, pp. 865–878

Rietiker, Daniel: "The European Court of Human Rights and FIFA – Current Issues and Potential Challenges", *European Convention on Human Rights Law Review*, vol. 1, no. 1, 2020, pp. 62–104

Rozakis, Christos L.: "The Contribution of the European Court of Human Rights to the Development of the Law on State Immunity", in Caflisch, Lucius – Callewaert, Johan – Liddell, Roderick – Mahoney, Paul – Villiger, Mark (Eds.): *Liber Amicorum Luzius Wildhaber: Human Rights, Strasbourg Views/Droits de l'Homme, Regards de Strasbourg*, N.P. Engel, Kehl/Strasbourg/Arlington, Va. 2007, pp. 387–402

Shelton, Dinah: "Subsidiarity and human rights law", *Human Rights Law Journal* (HRLJ), vol. 27, no. 1–4, 28 April 2006, pp. 4–11

Sicilianos, Linos-Alexander: "The Subjective Right of Judges to Independence – Some Reflexions on the Interpretation of Article 6, Para. 1 of the ECHR", in Pinto de Albuquerque, Paulo – Wojtyczek, Krzysztof (Eds.): *Judicial Power in a Globalized World – Liber Amicorum Vincent de Gaetano*, Springer, Cham 2019, pp. 547–557

Soo, Anneli: "Divergence of European Union and Strasbourg standards on defence rights in criminal proceedings?: *Ibrahim and the others v. the UK* (13th of September 2016)", *European Journal of Crime, Criminal Law and Criminal Justice*, vol. 25, issue 4, 2017, pp. 327–346

Spano, Robert: "'Arbitrary or manifestly unreasonable': the arbitrariness exception to the fourth instance doctrine under Article 6 of the European Convention on Human Rights", in Lemmens, Koen – Parmentier, Stephan – Reyntjens, Louise (Eds.): *Human Rights with a Human Touch – Liber Amicorum Paul Lemmens*, Intersentia, Cambridge/Antwerp/Chicago 2019, pp. 523–537

Speck, Anne-Katrin: "Strasbourg in 2016 – figures and case law trends: the European Court of Human Rights' annual report 2016", *EHRAC Bulletin*, Issue 27, summer 2017, pp. 8–9

Spencer, J.R.: "Squaring up to Strasbourg: Horncastle in the Supreme Court", *Archbold Review*, Issue 1, 2010, pp. 6–9

Spielmann, Dean: "Article 6 ECHR in criminal proceedings – recent developments", *Cyprus Human Rights Law Review*, vol. 2, issue 1, 2013, pp. 3–15

Spielmann, Dean: "The European Convention on Human Rights – the European Court of Human Rights", in Oliver, Dawn – Fedtke, Jörg (Eds.): *Human rights and the private sphere – a comparative study*, Routledge-Cavendish, London/New York 2007, pp. 427–464

Spurrier, Martha: "*Gäfgen v. Germany* – Fruit of the poisonous tree", *European Human Rights Law Review*, Issue 5, 2010, pp. 513–519

Susi, Mart: "The Baka case: the unbearable price of individual justice", *Hungarian Yearbook of International Law and European Law*, 2014, pp. 121–130

Szemesi, Sandor: "Introductory note to *Baka v. Hungary* (Eur. Ct. H.R.): [June 23, 2016]", *International Legal Materials*, vol. 56, no. 2, 2017, pp. 273–274

Szpunar, Maciej: "Right to a public hearing according to Art. 6 ECHR and Art. 47 of the Charter of Fundamental Rights of the EU: constitutional perspectives", in Hess, Burkhard – Koprivica Harvey, Ana (Eds.): *Open Justice – The Role of Courts in a Democratic Society*, Nomos, Baden-Baden 2019, pp. 47–58

van de Laar, Tom – de Graaf, Regien: "*Salduz* and *Miranda* – Is the US Supreme Court Pointing the Way?", *European Human Rights Law Review*, Issue 3, 2011, pp. 304–317

van der Vlis, Evert-Jan: "Videoconferencing in criminal proceedings", in Braun, Sabine – Taylor, J.L. (Eds.): *Videoconference and remote interpreting in criminal proceedings*, University of Surrey, Guildford 2011, pp. 11–25

van Dijk, Pieter: "Article 6 §1 of the Convention and the concept of 'objective impartiality'", in Mahoney, Paul – Matscher, Franz – Petzold, Herbert – Wildhaber, Luzius (Eds.): *Protection des Droits de L'homme: La Perspective Européenne, Mélanges à la Mémoire de Rolv Ryssdal/Protecting Human Rights: The European Perspective, Studies in Memory of Rolv Ryssdal*, Carl Heymanns Verlag, Köln/Berlin/Bonn/München 2000, pp. 1495–1510

van Dijk, P.: "The Benthem case and its aftermath in the Netherlands", *Netherlands International Law Review*, vol. 34, no. 1, 1987, pp. 5–24
Venn, Alice: "Case and comment: selected decisions from the European Court of Human Rights for May and June 2018 – Extraordinary rendition and secret detention, *Al Nashiri v. Romania* (Application No. 33234/12)", *European Human Rights Law Review*, Issue 5, 2018, pp. 519–523
Wadham, John: "Rendition, detention and torture in Europe – territorial responsibility and the right to truth: *Husayan (Abu Zubaydah) v. Poland* (app. no. 7511/13) and *Al Nashiri v. Poland* (app. no. 28761/11), Chamber judgments of July 24, 2014 (former fourth section)", *European Human Rights Law Review*, Issue 5, 2014, pp. 519–526
Wadham, John – Leach, Philip: "Cases and comment: selected decisions from the European Court of Human Rights for November and December 2002 – Civil procedure, *A. v. United Kingdom* (Application No. 35373/97)", *European Human Rights Law Review*, Issue 2, 2003, pp. 230–232
Wadham, John – Leach, Philip: "Cases and comment: selected decisions from the European Court of Human Rights for November and December 2002 – Crime and sentencing, *Allan v. United Kingdom* (Application No. 48539/99)", *European Human Rights Law Review*, Issue 2, 2003, pp. 235–237
Wallace, Stuart: "The Empire Strikes Back – Hearsay Rules in Common Law Legal Systems and the Jurisprudence of the European Court of Human Rights", *European Human Rights Law Review*, Issue 4, 2010, pp. 408–418
Wanlin, Lori Ann: "Responsibility for secret detention and extraordinary rendition: the Strasbourg Court holds Poland to account", *Cyprus Human Rights Law Review*, vol. 3, issue 2, 2014, pp. 185–200
Ward, Tim – Gardner, Piers: "The Privilege Against Self-Incrimination – In Search of Legal Certainty", *European Human Rights Law Review*, Issue 4, 2003, pp. 388–399
Welch, James (Ed.): "Cases and comment: selected decisions from the European Court of Human Rights for January and February 2008 – Entrapment, *Ramanauskas v. Lithuania* (Application No. 74420/01)", *European Human Rights Law Review*, Issue 3, 2008, pp. 410–413
Welch, James (Ed.): "Cases and comment: selected decisions from the European Court of Human Rights for March and April 2009 – Criminal procedure, *Natunen v. Finland* (Application No. 21022/04)", *European Human Rights Law Review*, Issue 4, 2009, pp. 590–593
Welch, James (Ed.): "Cases and comment: selected decisions from the European Court of Human Rights for November and December 2009 – Parliamentary immunity, *Kart v. Turkey* (Application No. 8917/05)", *European Human Rights Law Review*, Issue 2, 2010, pp. 221–224
Welch, James (Ed.): "Case and comment: selected decisions from the European Court of Human Rights from September and October 2012 – Torture, *El Haski v. Belgium* (Application No. 649/08)", *European Human Rights Law Review*, Issue 1, 2013, pp. 89–92
Welch, James (Ed.): "Case and comment: selected decisions from the European Court of Human Rights from July 2013 – Miscarriage of justice, *Allen v. United Kingdom* (Application No. 25424/09)", *European Human Rights Law Review*, Issue 6, 2013, pp. 646–650
Welch, James (Ed.): "Case and comment: selected decisions from the European Court of Human Rights from September and October 2014 – Appeals, *Hansen v. Norway*

(Application No. 15319/09)", *European Human Rights Law Review*, Issue 1, 2015, pp. 98–101

Welch, James (Ed.): "Case and comment: selected decisions from the European Court of Human Rights from December 2014 to February 2015 – Evidence, *Horncastle v. United Kingdom* (Application No. 4184/10)", *European Human Rights Law Review*, Issue 2, 2015, pp. 216–219

Welch, James (Ed.): "Case and comment: selected decisions from the European Court of Human Rights from December 2014 to February 2015 – Access to lawyer, *Ibrahim v. United Kingdom* (Application Nos. 50541/08, 50571/08, 50573/08 and 40351/09)", *European Human Rights Law Review*, Issue 2, 2015, pp. 219–222

Welch, James (Ed.): "Case and comment: selected decisions from the European Court of Human Rights from May and June 2015 – Detention, *Magee v. United Kingdom* (Application Nos. 26289/12, 29062/12 and 29891/12)", *European Human Rights Law Review*, Issue 5, 2015, pp. 524–527

Welch, James (Ed.): "Case and comment: selected decisions from the European Court of Human Rights from May and June 2015 – Fair trial, *Abdulla Ali v. United Kingdom* (Application No. 30971/12)", *European Human Rights Law Review*, Issue 5, 2015, pp. 543–546

Wildhaber, Luzius: "Precedent in the European Court of Human Rights", in Mahoney, Paul – Matscher, Franz – Petzold, Herbert – Wildhaber, Luzius (Eds.): *Protection des Droits de L'homme: La Perspective Européenne, Mélanges à la Mémoire de Rolv Ryssdal/ Protecting Human Rights: The European Perspective, Studies in Memory of Rolv Ryssdal*, Carl Heymanns Verlag, Köln/Berlin/Bonn/München 2000, pp. 1529–1545

Ziemele, Ineta: "International courts and ultra vires acts", in Caflisch, Lucius – Callewaert, Johan – Liddell, Roderick – Mahoney, Paul – Villiger, Mark (Eds.): *Liber Amicorum Luzius Wildhaber: Human Rights, Strasbourg Views/Droits de L'homme, Regards de Strasbourg*, N.P. Engel, Kehl/Strasbourg/Arlington, Va. 2007, pp. 537–556

Zwaak, Leo – Haeck, Yves: "Human rights news – Council of Europe", *Netherlands Quarterly of Human Rights*, vol. 21, no. 2, 2003, pp. 255–275

Zwaak, Leo – Haeck, Yves: "Human rights news – Council of Europe", *Netherlands Quarterly of Human Rights*, vol. 21, no. 3, 2003, pp. 510–525

Zupančič, Boštjan M.: "An answer to one crucial question of human rights: an epistemological excursus informing *Jalloh v. Germany* and *Gäfgen v. Germany* cases at the European Court of Human Rights", in Pogačnik, Miha (Ed.): *Challenges of Contemporary International Law and International Relations – Liber Amicorum in Honour of Ernest Petrič*, The European Faculty of Law, Nova Gorica 2011, pp. 451–463

Zupancic, Bostjan: "A sense of justice, the rule of law, and the exclusionary rule", *Regent Journal of Law & Public Policy*, vol. 2, no. 1, Spring 2010, pp. 51–62

# INDEX

# ABOUT THE AUTHORS

Päivi Hirvelä is a Supreme Court Justice and former Judge of the European Court of Human Rights with regard to Finland (2007–2015). Before the Judge's post in Strasbourg, she was a State prosecutor in the Office of the Prosecutor-General, a district court judge and a researcher in the University of Helsinki. She is a Doctor of Laws and holds the title of a docent in the field of human rights at the Universities of Helsinki, Turku and Lapland. She is a substitute member of the Venice Commission and is lecturing in the field of criminal procedure and human rights.

Satu Heikkilä has worked in the European Court of Human Rights since 2007, dealing with cases brought against Finland and Sweden. She has acted as a non-judicial rapporteur for Finland since 2010, and for Sweden since 2017. Since 2018, she is also one of the quality checkers in the Court's Rule 39 team. Before coming to the Court, she worked at the Council of Europe's Department for the Execution of Judgments of the European Court of Human Rights, and in Finland in the Supreme Administrative Court, the Market Court as well as in the Ministry for Foreign Affairs. She is a Doctor of Laws from both the Universities of Helsinki and Strasbourg and is currently also lecturing at the latter.

Lightning Source UK Ltd.
Milton Keynes UK
UKHW031905200721
387492UK00005B/185

9 781839 700941